Mandatory Reporting Laws and the Identification of Severe Child Abuse and Neglect

Child Maltreatment

Contemporary Issues in Research and Policy

Series Editors

Jill E. Korbin, Ph.D.
Professor of Anthropology
Associate Dean, College of Arts and Sciences
Director, Schubert Center for Child Studies
Crawford Hall, 7th Floor
10900 Euclid Avenue
Cleveland, OH 44106-7068, USA
jill.korbin@case.edu

Richard D. Krugman, MD
Professor of Pediatrics and Dean
University of Colorado School of Medicine
Room C-1003 Bldg 500
Anschutz Medical Campus
13001 E. 17th Place
Aurora, CO 80045, USA
richard.krugman@ucdenver.edu

This series provides a high-quality, cutting edge, and comprehensive source offering the current best knowledge on child maltreatment from multidisciplinary and multicultural perspectives. It consists of a core handbook that is followed by two or three edited volumes of original contributions per year. The core handbook will present a comprehensive view of the field. Each chapter will summarize current knowledge and suggest future directions in a specific area. It will also highlight controversial and contested issues in that area, thus moving the field forward. The handbook will be updated every five years. The edited volumes will focus on critical issues in the field from basic biology and neuroscience to practice and policy. Both the handbook and edited volumes will involve creative thinking about moving the field forward and will not be a recitation of past research. Both will also take multidisciplinary, multicultural and mixed methods approaches.

More information about this series at http://www.springer.com/series/8863

Ben Mathews • Donald C. Bross
Editors

Mandatory Reporting Laws and the Identification of Severe Child Abuse and Neglect

Springer

Editors
Ben Mathews
Australian Centre for Health Law Research
Faculty of Law, Queensland University
of Technology
Brisbane, QLD, Australia

Donald C. Bross
Program in Pediatric Law, Policy and Ethics
Kempe Center for the Prevention and
Treatment of Child Abuse and Neglect
Aurora, CO, USA

Department of Pediatrics, School
of Medicine
University of Colorado Denver
Aurora, CO, USA

ISSN 2211-9701 ISSN 2211-971X (electronic)
Child Maltreatment
ISBN 978-94-024-0074-8 ISBN 978-94-017-9685-9 (eBook)
DOI 10.1007/978-94-017-9685-9

Springer Dordrecht Heidelberg New York London

Softcover reprint of the hardcover 1st edition 2015

Printed on acid-free paper

Springer Science+Business Media B.V. Dordrecht is part of Springer Science+Business Media (www.springer.com)

Contents

Author Bios

Krisann M. Alvarez, Ph.D. is a clinical supervisor with Early Childhood Mental Health Services, a program of the State of Nevada's Division of Child and Family Services. She oversees family therapy and case management services provided to underserved families of young children, many of whom have involvement with the child welfare system. Her major area of research is in child maltreatment reporting. She is also interested in developmentally appropriate diagnosis and intervention with young children as well as the impact of attachment concerns on mental health and early development.

Dr. Leah Bromfield is Associate Professor and Deputy Director of the Australian Centre for Child Protection at the University of South Australia and Professorial Fellow to the Royal Commission into Institutional Responses to Child Sexual Abuse. Previously she was a Senior Research Fellow at the Australian Institute of Family Studies and managed the National Child Protection Clearinghouse. She is a well-regarded research expert in issues affecting child protection systems, chronic maltreatment and cumulative harm, and research to practice. She has worked closely with government on establishing and implementing child welfare reforms.

Donald C. Bross is Professor of Pediatrics and Associate Director for Pediatric Law, Policy and Ethics at the Kempe Center for the Prevention and Treatment of Child Abuse and Neglect, Department of Pediatrics, University of Colorado School of Medicine. A graduate of Dartmouth College he received an NIMH Traineeship in Medical Sociology at the University of Wisconsin, Madison, earning M.S. and Ph.D. degrees in Sociology. A graduate of the University of Colorado School of Law, having clerked for the Office of the University Counsel, he was appointed to the faculty of the University of Colorado School of Medicine in 1976. As part of his work, Bross incorporated and served as lawyer for the International Society for the Prevention of Child Abuse and Neglect (ISPCAN) for 8 years, and incorporated the National Association of Counsel for Children (NACC), for which he served as its first President and later as its pro bono Executive Director until 1990. He currently serves on the Kempe Child Protection Team and COMIRB (reviewing human subject research involving children). He teaches medical students, pediatric residents and fellows, child psychiatry residents, and law interns. In 2013, he became Co-Editor in Chief of *Child Abuse & Neglect: The International Journal.*

Dr. Helen Buckley is an Associate Professor in the School of Social Work and Social Policy, Trinity College Dublin. Her research interests are in child protection policy and practice. She is chair of the National Review Panel, an independent body that examines serious incidents including the deaths of children in care and known to the child protection system. She has published a number of books and papers on child protection and recently completed a research study on the development of effective recommendations from child abuse inquiries.

Dr. Roni Buckley is currently working as a researcher in the Office of the Attorney General, based in Dublin. She completed her Ph.D. in Child Protection Mandatory Reporting in 2013 in the School of Social Work and Social Policy, Trinity College Dublin. She undertook her undergraduate degree in Law and European Studies in the University of Limerick and a Master's degree in Criminal Justice at University College Cork. Roni also worked as a legal researcher for the Dublin Commission of Investigation on both the Dublin and Cloyne reports from 2007 to 2010.

Katherine Casillas has been involved for over 15 years in applied clinical and programmatic research on the assessment, etiology and treatment of dysfunctional family interactions. Since February 2009, she has been a research project manager for the Child Protection Research Center at the American Humane Association, which has included organizational assessment of a state child welfare system and leading the analyses of a UNICEF report on child discipline in low- and middle-income countries. Dr. Casillas previously worked at the Family Translational Research Group at SUNY at Stony Brook University. While there, she secured a National Institutes of Health (NIH) Diversity Supplement Grant, which extended her new work on parental behavioral styles.

Theodore P. Cross is Research Full Professor in the Children and Family Research Center at the School of Social of the University of Illinois at Urbana-Champaign. He has conducted research on the investigative and service response to child maltreatment for 25 years. He has published over 100 articles, monographs and reports on such topics as the investigation and prosecution of child abuse, children's advocacy centers, delivery of children's mental health services, and well-being of child maltreatment victims. He taught advanced statistics for 15 years.

Jonathan Davidov, Ph.D. is a researcher at The Center for the Study of Society (located in the University of Haifa), having just completed an appointment as a Haruv post-doctoral research fellow at the Kempe Center for the Prevention and Treatment of Child Abuse and Neglect, University of Colorado. His research interests include child abuse and neglect, children at risk, and the impact of extreme situations on identity and self-perception.

Professor Sibnath Deb, (Ph.D., D.Sc.) is Head of the Department of Applied Psychology, Pondicherry University and Adjunct Professor, School of Public Health and Social Work, Faculty of Health, Queensland University of Technology, Brisbane, Australia. He has 25 years of teaching and research experience. His current areas of research interest include child safety/protection, students' mental health, adolescent reproductive health, HIV/AIDS and applied social psychology. Professor Deb has completed more than 50 large-scale qualitative and quantitative studies (funded by national and international funding agencies), and has published more than 120 research papers in addition to writing 8 books and editing 4. He has received three international and three national awards for his contributions in the field of child safety and applied psychology. Professor Deb is a member of the editorial board of the *Journal of Interpersonal Violence* and from 2004 to 2008 was a Council Member of the International Society for Prevention of Child Abuse and Neglect (ISPCAN).

Bridget V. Dever, Ph.D is an Assistant Professor of School Psychology at Lehigh University, where she specializes in statistics and research methodology in the Department of Education and Human Services. Dr Dever graduated from the University of Michigan in 2009 from the Combined Program in Education and Psychology (CPEP). After receiving her Ph.D., she was an Institute of Educational Sciences (IES) Postdoctoral Fellow as part of the Georgia Measurement and Assessment Training (GMAT) program. Prior to joining the faculty at Lehigh, Dr Dever was an Assistant Professor of Research, Measurement, and Statistics at Georgia State University. Her research interests include motivation among at-risk students, the assessment of behavioral and emotional risk, and promoting educational resilience.

Jaap E. Doek is an Emeritus Law Professor (family and juvenile law) of the VU University of Amsterdam. He was one of the founding members of the International Society for the Prevention of Child Abuse and Neglect (ISPCAN). He was a member of the UN Committee on the Rights of the Child (1999–2007) and the chairperson of that Committee (2001–2007). He is a member of the Board of Trustees of the African Child Policy Forum (ACPF), the legal senior advisor of the international NGO End Child Prostitution, Child Pornography and Trafficking of Children for Sexual Purposes (ECPAT), and a consultant for different country offices of UNICEF.

Brad Donohue Professor, Department of Psychology, is Director of Family Research and Services, University of Nevada, Las Vegas, which is chiefly focused on the development, evaluation and dissemination of family-supported interventions to assist in goal achievement. He is one of the developers of family behavior therapy (FBT), an evidence-based treatment listed in various national clearinghouses. His specific interests include the development and adoption of evidence-based treatments (primarily FBT), psychometric development of clinical measures to assist in understanding and measuring treatment outcomes, and improving the functioning of mental health clinics through effective supervision and quality assurance. He enjoys treatment development in severely troubled populations (e.g., substance abuse, child maltreatment, family violence, conduct disorders), and concurrent improvement of mental health and sport performance in athletes.

Heather Douglas is a Professor and Director of Research at the Law School, The University of Queensland. Heather's research focuses on the way the law impacts on and constructs women. She has written on domestic violence, child protection and criminal justice issues. Her most recent book, with Mark Finnane, was *Indigenous Crime and Settler Law: White Sovereignty After Empire* (Palgrave Macmillan, 2012). She is currently the lead researcher on the Australian Feminist Judgments Project.

Dr. Brett Drake has been a professor at the George Warren Brown School of Social Work at Washington University in St. Louis since 1991, having received his Ph.D. in Social Welfare from the University of California at Los Angeles. He has been interested in early child welfare system response. His work spans epidemiology, practice and policy. In particular, Dr Drake has focused on issues of racial disproportionality, substantiation and mandated reporting. He has authored over 50 peer-reviewed publications, books and book chapters. He has taught at the Master's and Doctoral levels, mainly in the area of research methodology. Prior to his academic career, Dr Drake worked as a child protective services investigator in San Diego, California.

Zvi Eisikovits, Ph.D. is a Professor of Social Welfare and Criminology at the University of Haifa. He is former Dean of the faculty of Welfare and Health at the University of Haifa and presently Head of School of Criminology and Director of the Center for the Study of Society. Professor Eisikovits is co-PI with Professor Rachel Lev of a nationwide study of child abuse and neglect funded by Traiana High Tech CO. Professor Eisikovits is a nationally and internationally known expert in interpersonal violence and in the use of qualitative methods in studying woman abuse. He serves as a member of editorial boards in several journals on woman abuse and qualitative research and recipient of large grants from prestigious sources such as the HF Guggenheim Foundation, Minerva Foundation, DIP and Israel Science Foundation.

Emalee Flaherty, M.D. is the Head of the Division of Child Abuse Pediatrics at Ann and Robert H Lurie Children's Hospital of Chicago and Professor of Pediatrics at Northwestern University Feinberg School of Medicine. Dr Flaherty received her medical degree from the Indiana University School of Medicine and completed her residency at the University of Illinois Hospital in Chicago. Dr Flaherty is serving her second term on the American Academy of Pediatrics Committee on Child Abuse and Neglect (COCAN). Formerly, she was elected to the Executive Committee of the AAP Section on Child Abuse and Neglect (SOCAN). She serves as Member-at-Large for the Ray E Helfer Society. She was named *Outstanding Professional, 2009* by the American Professional Society on the Abuse of Children (APSAC).

John D. Fluke is an Associate Director at the Kempe Center for the Prevention of Treatment of Child Abuse and Neglect in the Department of Pediatrics, University of Colorado School of Medicine. He has over 32 years of experience in social service delivery system research in the area of Child Welfare and Mental Health Services for children. John is an internationally renowned researcher specializing in assessing and analyzing decision making in human services delivery systems. He is also active in the area of national child maltreatment data collection systems and analysis. He is also known for his work in the areas of child maltreatment prevalence, child welfare administrative data analysis, workload and costing, and performance and outcome measurement for children and family services. John is also co-chair of the Working Group on Child Maltreatment Data Collection for ISPCAN.

Jennifer Fraser is an Associate Professor of Nursing at Sydney Nursing School, The University of Sydney. She has experience and research interest in the area of recognizing and responding to child abuse and neglect and has experience with evaluating staff training programs. Her work builds on the combined research efforts of identification, assessment, and reporting child abuse and neglect, and analysis of the application of staff training programs for health professional staff with mandatory reporting obligations. She uses a combination of experimental, cross-sectional and longitudinal studies to develop research instruments and to measure knowledge, beliefs and attitudes towards reporting. Her efforts have impacted clinical, research and social practice.

Tamara Fuller, Ph.D. is Director of the Children and Family Research Center and Research Associate Professor at the School of Social Work at the University of Illinois at Urbana-Champaign. A clinical psychologist by training, Dr Fuller is the Principal Investigator of the statewide experimental evaluation of Differential Response in Illinois and the Title IV-E Waiver Demonstration Evaluation in Wisconsin. Over the past 15 years, she has evaluated the effectiveness of numerous child welfare programs, including Differential Response, the Child Endangerment Risk Assessment Protocol, Child Death Review Teams, and post-reunification and adoption services. Within this program of research, there has been emphasis on examining predictors of maltreatment and maltreatment recurrence, and more recently family engagement in child welfare services.

Jacqueline J. Glover is a Professor in the Departments of Pediatrics and Preventive Medicine and Biometrics at the University of Colorado. She is also a Professor in the Center for Bioethics and Humanities, where she directs the Center's Clinical Ethics Program and the Interdisciplinary Education Program. Professor Glover is a member of the Colorado Multiple Institutional Review Board, Panel C, which reviews proposed human subject research involving children. She is a widely published researcher, with current research emphases on pediatric ethics, clinical ethics, professionalism education and evaluation, interdisciplinary ethics education, and rural bioethics.

Edward Goldson is a Professor of Pediatrics at the University of Colorado. He has specialties in development and behaviour, psychiatry and behavioral sciences, and Down syndrome. His clinical focus at the Children's Hospital, Colorado, is general pediatrics and child development, with an emphasis on care of the high risk infant and the chronically ill child, follow-up of premature and sick infants, behavior and medical management of children with the fragile X syndrome, clinical aspects of autism, and child abuse.

Betsy Goulet, M.A. has been an adjunct instructor for UIS since 1992, and has been working in the field of child sexual abuse since 1986. She was the founding director of the Sangamon County Child Advocacy Center from 1989 to 1995 and organized the Illinois Chapter of Children's Advocacy Centers, serving as that organization's first president. From 1995 until June of 2002, Betsy was the Children's Policy Advisor to the Illinois Attorney General. She was also a Membership Consultant for the National Children's Alliance in Washington D.C., conducting national accreditation site reviews and providing training for multidisciplinary team members and children's advocacy center staff. She continues to train nationally and recently developed a new advanced victim advocacy curriculum for the National Children's Advocacy Center. Betsy is a doctoral candidate in the DPA program at UIS.

Jesse J. Helton is an Assistant Research Professor at the University of Illinois at Urbana-Champaign School of Social Work and a research specialist at the Children and Family Research Center. His research focus is on the well-being of children who have been maltreated.

Melissa Jonson-Reid, Ph.D. is Professor of Social Work at the Brown School at Washington University and Director of the Brown Center for Violence and Injury Prevention funded by the Centers for Disease Control and Prevention. Prior to entering academia, Dr Jonson-Reid administered school-based programming for youth in foster care and other high risk populations as well as worked as a counselor with a domestic violence agency. Dr Jonson-Reid's research includes cross-sector children's services epidemiology, understanding the longer term impact of child maltreatment, and prevention of child maltreatment through innovations to existing agency programs. She teaches in the public health and social work master's programs and social work PhD program. She is the author and co-author of over 75 peer-reviewed publications and book chapters/books.

Lisa M. Justis is Social Work Coordinator and Instructor in Pediatrics in the Kempe Child Protection Team Faculty at The Kempe Foundation for the Prevention and Treatment of Child Abuse and Neglect in Denver, Colorado. The Child Protection Team provides comprehensive medical evaluations in a weekly outpatient clinic and through inpatient and emergency department consultations at Children's Hospital Colorado.

Maureen C. Kenny, Ph.D. is a Professor in Counselor Education program in the College of Education at Florida International University, in Miami, Florida. Dr Kenny has published extensively in the area of child abuse, particularly sexual abuse prevention and education as well as professionals' compliance with child abuse reporting. She was the director of an externally funded project, *Kids Learning about Safety*, a primary prevention program geared toward Latino families in Miami Dade. Dr Kenny is a licensed psychologist in Florida, a National Board Certified Counselor and a Fellow of the American Psychological Association.

John E. Kesner is an Associate Professor in the Department of Early Childhood Education in the College of Education at Georgia State University. He earned his doctorate in Family Relations and Human Development from The Ohio State. Dr Kesner has researched and conducted family violence research throughout his career. After receiving his Ph.D., he joined the faculty at Georgia State University as an Assistant Professor of Early Childhood Education. After his promotion to Associate Professor in 2002, Dr Kesner continued his research and publishing in the areas of family issues. Most notably, his research includes child maltreatment and mandated reporting of maltreatment.

Rachel Lev-Wiesel, Ph.D. is a Professor and Head of the Graduate School of Creative Art Therapies and the Emili Sagol Research Center for CAT at the University of Haifa. Her main research domains are child abuse, trauma and post-traumatic growth, and analysis of drawings for diagnostic and therapeutic purposes.

Bob Lonne is the Head of the Social Work and Human Services disciplinary group at QUT. Bob has a distinguished career in direct practice and has held managerial positions in the mental health, statutory child protection and juvenile justice fields in both Queensland and Western Australia. Bob is particularly active in the issues that affect social work and the human services sector at the international, national and local levels, with a particular focus on workforce issues and planning and reforming child protection. In 2010 he published a report, funded by the Australian Learning and Teaching Council, focusing on the social work and human services workforce and curriculum, which highlighted a range of issues including ageing, rapid growth and diversification, and the relevance of general social and behavioural science courses for direct practice roles in this sector. Bob was the National President of the Australian Association of Social Workers from 2005 to 2011.

Emily Lux is a third year doctoral student at the University of Illinois at Urbana-Champaign. She received her BA and MSW at the University of Illinois at Urbana-Champaign. Emily has experience providing clinical services to child welfare-involved youth in residential treatment and alternative education settings, therapeutic activity to the elderly, and case management and direct support to developmentally delayed adults. Her research interests concern the effects of trauma on child testimony in child-welfare involved youth.

Ben Mathews is an Associate Professor in the School of Law at Queensland University of Technology in Brisbane, Australia and Co-Director of the Children's Health Program in QUT's *Australian Centre for Health Law Research*. He conducts research in law and child maltreatment, mandatory reporting, civil claims for child abuse, medico-legal issues, children's rights, and female genital mutilation. He has conducted large multidisciplinary studies of mandatory reporting law, theory and practice and has over 60 publications. He has conducted the two largest empirical studies of mandatory reporting in Australia. The *Teachers Reporting Child Sexual Abuse* Study (2010) led to reform of legislation, policy, and professional training. In 2014, he completed a project for Australia's Royal Commission into Institutional Responses to Child Sexual Abuse: *A history of mandatory reporting of child sexual abuse in Australia: A legislative history*. Currently, he is leading a national study for Australia's Commonwealth Government exploring State and Territory mandatory reporting systems, analysing 10 year datasets of child protection reports.

Patrick Parkinson is a Professor of Law at the University of Sydney, Australia, and President of the International Society of Family Law. He served from 2004 to 2007 as Chairperson of the Family Law Council, an advisory body to the federal Attorney-General, and also chaired a review of the Child Support Scheme in 2004–2005 which led to the enactment of major changes to the child support system. Professor Parkinson has been a member of the NSW Child Protection Council, and was Chairperson of a major review of the NSW state law concerning child protection which led to the enactment of the Children and Young Persons (Care and Protection) Act 1998. He also works with churches on child protection issues. His books include *Tradition and Change in Australian Law* (5th ed, 2013), *Australian Family Law in Context* (5th ed, 2012), *Family Law and the Indissolubility of Parenthood* (2011), *The Voice of a Child in Family Law Disputes* (with Judy Cashmore, 2008), *Child Sexual Abuse and the Churches* (2nd ed, 2003) and *Principles of Equity* (editor, 2nd ed., 2003).

Edward P. Richards is Clarence W. Edwards Professor of Law, and the Director, Program in Law, Science and Public Health, at the LSU Law Center at Louisiana State University. He has researched and published for over 30 years in various aspects of medical law, public health law, and a range of issues at the intersection of law, health and public policy. In recent years, he has conducted extensive research in national security law. He has been a consultant to the Centers for Disease Control and Prevention and other federal agencies, and has authored over 140 articles and five books.

Desmond K. Runyan is the Jack and Viki Thompson Professor of Pediatrics at the University of Colorado, and Executive Director of the Kempe Center for the Prevention and Treatment of Child Abuse and Neglect. He has researched child abuse for over 32 years while maintaining a clinical practice evaluating possible child abuse victims and as a general pediatrics attending. He co-founded a comprehensive child abuse center and has been appointed to the initial new sub-board of child abuse pediatrics at the American Board of Pediatrics. In 1989 he designed and secured funding for LONGSCAN: the longest multi-site prospective study of the consequences of child abuse. LONGSCAN, now over 20 years old, is a prospective study of 1,354 children in five states who either were reported for maltreatment or who were judged to be at very high risk of maltreatment. He has worked with International Clinical Epidemiology Network medical school faculty in Egypt, India, the Philippines, Brazil, and Chile to increase child abuse knowledge among medical schools internationally. He has also worked with WHO and UNICEF to study child abuse epidemiology.

Kimberly N. Schubert is a Clinical Doctoral Student at the University of Nevada Las Vegas. She is also a performance coach and the Quality Assurance Coordinator for The Optimum Performance Program in Sports, which is a subprogram within Family Research and Services. Her major area of research is in substance abuse and juvenile delinquency. She is also interested in creating, evolving, implementing, and examining the effectiveness of various evidence-based treatments, specifically those with a behavioral focus. Her long term goals are to work in academia as a university professor while also obtaining clinical licensure and working with adolescent clients. She plans to continue to conduct research on substance use, and abuse, using evidence-based treatments.

Debbie Scott is a Research Fellow at the Australian Institute of Family Studies (AIFS). She has a nursing background, a Master of Public Health and a Doctor of Health Science. Debbie has a history of work in the injury prevention field, particularly as it applies to childhood injury. Her experience in injury surveillance has led to an interest in child maltreatment. Debbie's research interests include the use of data to inform child maltreatment prevention and early intervention programs and policy development, child and family wellbeing and the impact of child maltreatment on the wellbeing of children and young people.

Leonie Segal is Professor of Health Economics and Foundation Chair of the Health Economics and Social Policy Group at the University of South Australia. Professor Segal conducts high quality rigorous research and builds research capacity in health economics and social policy to achieve evidence-informed public policy and practice. Her research interests are broadly concerned with allocative efficiency, ensuring the community's resources are spent wisely to maximise societal health and well-being. The broad focus is to determine the optimal mix of health and human services, and to analyse the drivers or incentives that can facilitate evidenced-based resource shifts, to achieve changes that improve health and well-being. She leads a highly innovative program of research around the role of the family in health, the nature, causes and consequences of child maltreatment, and evaluation of options for disrupting intergenerational cycles of disadvantage.

Laura Sigad, Ph.D. is a researcher at the Center for the Study of Society and Lecturer at the School of Criminology, University of Haifa. Her research interests include insider's perspectives on child abuse and neglect, cultural contexts and child abuse, and transnational migration and the family.

Dr. Tamara Walsh is an Associate Professor in the School of Law at the University of Queensland in Brisbane, Australia. She has degrees in both law and social work. She lectures in human rights law and constitutional law. Tamara's research interests lie in the broad field of social welfare law. Her work, to date, has included examinations of homelessness, child protection interventions, social security fraud and social exclusion. She draws on empirical research, as well as citizenship theory and human rights discourse in her work. Her research has been widely published, both in Australia and internationally.

Donald Woodhouse, JD, MPA is research administrator at Antioch University New England. He has worked with the Colorado Department of Health and the El Paso County Department of Health in the Sexually Transmitted Disease and HIV control programs, and was research coordinator and a lead investigator for CDC AIDS Project 90, a prospective 5-year multi-city study of the role of social networks in HIV transmission. He also served as legal advisor to the El Paso County Department of Health STD and HIV control programs and Confidential HIV Test Site, focusing on legal and ethical issues associated with testing and partner notification, and helping formulate and apply "health hold" regulations. A founding member of the Lock Haven (PA) Hospital Ethics Committee, he has studied and written about the ethical issues associated with research among vulnerable populations.

Introduction

Mandatory reporting of child abuse and neglect is the law in a large number of nations, but not in the majority of all nations worldwide. Nations with the most experience of mandatory reporting of child abuse and neglect have the capacity to describe relatively detailed trends in its epidemiology and progress in various kinds of responses and prevention efforts. At the same time, countries that do not require reporting tend to have less information on the extent of child maltreatment within their borders, and less information on how well child abuse and neglect are addressed, treated and prevented through a variety of social and legal responses.

Mandatory reporting laws have existed across the USA since the 1960s and are a well-known phenomenon in that country, although even there they remain contested theoretically, and continue to present multiple legal, clinical and practical questions. Even more significantly for the purpose of this book, which has been designed for an international audience, issues surrounding mandatory reporting laws continue to be highly relevant worldwide. Countries continue to enact the laws, in jurisdictions as diverse as Saudi Arabia and India, and with legislation forthcoming in Ireland in 2015. Other nations such as the United Kingdom are currently in heated debates about whether the laws are a good strategy, with law reform efforts underway. Other jurisdictions continue to amend and refine their longstanding mandatory reporting laws, including many US states, and states and territories in Australia. Nations that have not adopted mandatory reporting laws often cite criticisms of them as a justification for not doing so, but those jurisdictions that have adopted the laws as part of their strategy to identify and respond to serious child maltreatment have concluded that the advantages outweigh any anticipated costs. Debates will no doubt continue in many jurisdictions around the world about the benefits and disadvantages of enacting the laws, the various forms in which they may be judiciously employed, and if adopted how to optimize their benefits while minimizing any disadvantages.

Many perspectives can be used to understand mandatory reporting of child maltreatment: philosophical, human rights, empirical research, and disciplinary frameworks for theoretical evaluation and clinical practice (pediatrics, public health, social work, psychology/psychiatry, child development, and law) are among the vantage points available. All of these are represented in this book. Given the continuing debates and developments worldwide regarding mandatory reporting laws and related aspects of child protection generally, we hope to provide in one reference work for the international field a substantial and up-to-date coverage of some of the best current work on important features of mandatory reporting law, theory, policy and practice.

The chapters contained in this book provide many views and illustrate a wide variety of opinions, experiences and insights. The authors include clinicians, academics, researchers, and individuals having more than one of these backgrounds. Contributors were chosen for their intellectual honesty, credibility, and ability to contribute in a meaningful way to analyzing the theoretical, policy and practical issues of mandatory child abuse reporting. The Editors believe that one can argue about the laws from any or all of these frameworks referred to above, but to the extent possible we should develop better empirical studies for determining when and under what circumstances mandatory reporting achieves the goals of keeping the problem of child maltreatment visible in an effective manner and permits and encourages effective responses. Wekerle's recent article illustrates the importance of this approach with her review of research relating to how the effects on children of a report can depend on the way in which the information is gathered from the child before the report is made.[1]

Chapters 1, 2, 3, 4, 5, and 6 focus on historical and legal developments, and empirical data on reporting. In Chap. 1 Ben Mathews outlines the origins and provenance of the first mandatory reporting laws, discusses the nature and parameters of the laws, describes major developments in the laws over time, and identifies some of their major effects on reporting and case identification. In Chap. 2, Desmond K. Runyan treats the epidemiology of child maltreatment as a scientific and public health issue, and reviews and compares various methods employed to date to enumerate the incidence and prevalence of child physical abuse, corporal punishment and parental behaviors that have been shown to create substantial risks for harm. In Chap. 3, Brett Drake and Melissa Jonson-Reid provide a "case statement" to the effect that, notwithstanding "conventional wisdom," many of the criticisms of the working and results of child protection systems in parts of Europe, North America and Australia either disregard or defy data, making the criticisms questionable at best. They argue that only through research at least equivalent to the various empirical studies which they offer – to challenge what they describe as many prevalent "myths" of contemporary child protection services – can real improvements be made. They add that elements of the system that are only claimed to be detrimental

[1]Wekerle, C. (2013) Resilience in the context of child maltreatment: Connections to the practice of mandatory reporting. *Child Abuse & Neglect* 37, 93–101: "Reporting is an intervention that requires substantial inter-professional investment in research to guide best practices, with methodological expectations of any clinical intervention. Child abuse reporting is consistent with a clinician's other duties to report (i.e., suicidality, homicidality), practice-based skills (e.g. delivering 'bad' news, giving assessment feedback), and the pervasive professional principle of best interests of the child. Resilience requires the presence of resources and, mandated reporting, is one such resource to the maltreated child." (93). See also Chap. 18 in this book which also promotes training as a means of improving reporting practices.

should not be abandoned absent good research data to support alternatives. Drake and Jonson-Reid report data that empirically refutes claims of a detrimental cost-benefit result from mandatory child abuse reporting. One of their interesting findings is that the percentage of the child protection budget expended on investigations "is most likely below 10 % and possibly below 5 %".

In Chap. 4, John E. Kesner and Bridget V. Dever analyze NCANDS data, revealing in the process the extent to which mandatory reporting provides important markers for the overall problem. In Chap. 5, Donald C. Bross examines the existence of mandatory reporting of child abuse and neglect during a period of worldwide debate over the degree to which privacy is being eroded. His analysis of privacy protections provides recognition that the value of privacy normally means restrictions on the availability of information, which can, at the same time, deny information that is necessary to hold responsible those individuals and institutions behaving in ways that are harmful and also unjust, unethical or even illegal. Complete privacy would create a world in which it would be very difficult to hold individuals or corporate bodies accountable for behaviors that can cause injury of every kind, no matter how devastating the harm that results. In Chap. 6, Edward P. Richards examines the history of mandatory reporting laws in public health. This framework is important if the original context of mandatory reporting of child abuse that began in 1963 is to be accurately appreciated.[2] Given that Richard D. Krugman, Chairman of the first US Advisory Board on Child Abuse, has proposed for many years that child abuse should be characterized as a health and public health issuc, which does not justify a primarily accusatory approach to child abuse or neglect, this early chapter on public health separates reporting of health conditions from the canard that child abuse reporting is inherently accusatory in nature.

Chapters 7, 8, 9, and 10 explore mandatory reporting from a variety of theoretical approaches. Chapter 7, by Ben Mathews, presents human rights, human justice, and Western philosophical traditions as powerful sources of theoretical support for the right of children who are severely abused or neglected to be made known to society at large. Jacqueline J. Glover and Lisa M. Justis present, in Chap. 8, a balanced, nuanced, and yet practical exploration of the ethical considerations informing hospital practitioners in a society which mandates child abuse reporting. Donald Woodhouse presents a practical law and public health ethics view of child abuse

---

[2] The first mandatory child abuse reporting laws were enacted in the USA beginning in 1963, largely through the efforts of C. Henry Kempe, M.D. and his colleagues. As a virologist as well as a pediatrician, Dr. Kempe was familiar with communicable dangers in the form of bacteria and viruses. Reporting of these dangerous and reportable conditions was essential before there were antibiotics and reporting of these conditions remains important today for knowing the extent, trends, and needed investments for responding to infections inducing illness and death. Child abuse reporting was a natural response, as part of a scientific management model, once the Battered-Child Syndrome had been identified. The original article touched on a possible mechanism for a disorder of empathy that was behaviorally transmitted physical abuse of children reappearing in their own behavior as parents. Now we know that child abuse also is associated with the transmission of many risks for poor physical health, poor behavioral health, and criminal involvement, both as victim and perpetrator.

reporting in Chap. 9, as an activity completely consistent with classic public health law tradition. In Chap. 10, Leonie Segal addresses economic issues related to the community response to child maltreatment, providing, for most child protection professionals of every background, a unique, important, yet rarely employed set of concepts and tools for analyzing child protection systems. The view offered by Segal is complex in detail and implication, with mandatory reporting treated as only one of a great many factors that must be considered in designing and maintaining an "economical" approach to reducing child maltreatment.

Chapters 11, 12, 13, and 14 continue to combine theoretical and practical perspectives. Pediatrician Edward Goldson agrees that the current approach to child neglect needs work, but he suggests in Chap. 11 that the effort will be better invested in improving the response through funding services, improving interventions, and investing in better understanding than simply doing away with a measure, reporting, that he finds helpful in his daily practice of advocating for children and parents. Bob Lonne's argument in Chap. 12 against the reporting of child neglect provides much to consider regarding the scope and merits of mandatory reporting for this type of maltreatment. In Chap. 13, Helen Buckley and Roni Buckley consider the context of Ireland, and the forthcoming introduction of mandatory reporting laws in the wake of revelations of institutional child sexual abuse. They present an argument from the perspective of those who will become mandated reporters, express reservations about whether mandatory reporting will produce better outcomes for children, and argue that professional capacity to comply with the duty must be enhanced and response systems must be equipped to respond to reports in an appropriate and prompt manner. Patrick Parkinson explores issues and different options for the mandatory reporting of child sexual abuse in religious institutional settings in Chap. 14, an interesting contribution which has much relevance internationally.

Chapters 15, 16, 17, 18, and 19 expand on the theme noted by some previous chapters relating to the experience of reporters of child maltreatment. These chapters examine some of the obstacles and solutions for making the reporting of child maltreatment a refined and helpful professional activity. In Chap. 15, Emalee Flaherty reports on the research she and others have conducted on reporting of child abuse and neglect by physicians, revealing factors that encourage or discourage reporting. Maureen C. Kenny discusses the critical issue of training for reporters in Chap. 16, including the current state of play and proposing a case for necessary progress. In another very extensive exploration of the importance of training for reporters, in Chap. 17 Brad Donohue, Krisann M. Alvarez, and Kimberly N. Schubert describe the results of committing substantial efforts and resources into helping reporters know when to report as well as how to report possible child abuse and neglect. Their chapter provides results of evaluations to the effect that training will increase the chances that child maltreatment reports will be made accurately and justifiably, as well as specific examples of the type of training that can be provided. Chapter 18 sees Debbie Scott and Jennifer Fraser combine the perspectives of understanding the role of health professionals as reporters and the types of support that can help them fulfill their duties more appropriately. In Chap. 19, Zvi Eisikovits, Jonathan Davidov, Laura Sigad and Rachel Lev-Wiesel delve deeply into the psychological environment and processes in which reporters can be immersed, with implications for whether reporting should be a legal duty.

The next to last section includes chapters which ask: What occurs after a report? Theodore P. Cross, Betsy Goulet, Jesse J. Helton, Emily Lux, and Tamara Fuller report research on the outcomes of reporting child maltreatment in Chap. 20, and in Chap. 21 John D. Fluke and Katherine Casillas present the case for better research and understanding of the way in which caseworkers and their employing systems arrive at decisions based on a report. In Chap. 22, Leah Bromfield analyzes efforts in different states and territories of Australia to reduce mandatory referrals of child maltreatment by increasing preventive services. This form of a public health approach depends in part on a "differential response" (DR) to notifications regarding children's well being, so that needed and available services need not be delayed until child abuse or neglect is confirmed. Heather Douglas and Tamara Walsh present in Chap. 23 a discussion of mandatory reporting of child abuse using the analogy of domestic violence reporting. They present available reports of perceptions of domestic violence victims and conclude that if mandatory reporting is not to discourage mothers from self-identifying domestic violence and abuse of their children there must be services available that will help the mothers and children as a result of the report.

The final two chapters, Chap. 24 by Jaap E. Doek and Chap. 25 by Sibnath Deb, broaden the discussion of child abuse reporting to problems of children's well being and protection that have received increasing international attention in recent years. Doek's chapter considers the range of problems that include child labor, sex trafficking and child pornography, including pornography communicated over the internet, that in general are not addressed by child abuse reporting despite international condemnation. Sibnath Deb focuses expressly on sexual abuse and child trafficking for sexual purposes. Using his parent society of India as an example, Deb describes the current state of a problem that occurs in every country to a greater or lesser extent. His concluding position is clear: "Introducing mandatory reporting of child sexual abuse and trafficking will not cost much especially compared with the benefits which can flow. This should be introduced in the existing system and with other strategies it will help to bring positive changes in society."

As Editors, we might owe a statement of our position to our readers, even if our position might be self-evident. If not, perhaps we can be permitted to say what it is or at least to take an Editorial privilege to do so. In this way it will be easier to recognize that there are chapters where we agree, do not agree, or agree partially with our fellow authors. Between the two of us there remains continuing discussion of several issues, including, for example, which kinds of severe neglect should be reportable. In reality, we agree to some extent with all of our colleagues. Above all, however, we believe that without careful research and a robust evidence base, assumptions can be made about the consequences of mandatory reporting that are not or might not be supportable. We should move past simplistic arguments about the possible faults with reporting. For sound changes to occur in mandatory reporting there must be careful research. In other words, various arguments about mandatory reporting should be given more or less credence depending on the extent to which they are supported by valid research.

There has been a tendency of critics of modern child protection to ascribe many of the problems of contemporary child welfare, especially in a handful of primarily English speaking societies, to the inherent wrongfulness of reporting. The argument might be unconsciously linked to the historical association of any "investigation" being a bad model in general. However infectious disease prevention and management, environmental regulation, and zoning compliance investigations are viewed generally as non-criminal in nature. Each of these forms of notification can involve private aspects of personal lives, and in the example of contact tracing for sexually transmissible infections, the information involves activities as private or "intimate" as child abuse in families. All of these activities have a primarily ameliorative purpose. To write or speak as if the training and other cultural aspects of ameliorative investigations do not matter makes it more difficult to separate the response to severe abuse and neglect between criminal, versus unacceptable but not criminal conditions and behaviors that must be addressed, from conditions for which only voluntary interventions are justified. Reporting alone is reporting. What is done with reports can be data collection for epidemiological purposes, evaluation for clinical needs, "investigation" by a child protection agency, or criminal proceedings if a wrong great enough is done. To make reporting a "false dichotomy" of good and bad disserves a more nuanced and thorough consideration of all of the factors that will have to be addressed for a humane and effective approach to child protection. Moving away from false dichotomies encourages examination of variations in mandatory reporting, so that, for example, the Dutch system of confidential notifications to physicians of possible child maltreatment might satisfy at least some of the needs for child protection in that culture without broader duties of reporting for a greater range of professions, although this would still need to be supported by a sound evidence base. What is necessary for a large, extremely diverse nation such as the USA might not be necessary for more homogenous or smaller nations with greater cohesion, consistency and social agreement on how to address health or social issues.

Do costs of an "investigatory system" divert resources to an intolerable degree from other programs? Without research to support it, the claim may assume legitimacy; but to explore the claim properly requires a rigorous evidence base and analysis. Too often in child protection, great swings in policy have occurred based on laudable goals that can become slogans, such as child protection, family preservation, and permanency planning, unless the new policies are implemented through research supported initiatives. As noted above, analysis in the USA concludes that under 10 % of current child protection service budgets are used to support investigations. Abolishing human services of any kind based only on their negative attributes, or the assumption that resources will remain available or fund better services if the particular service is abolished, has proven not to be true in every instance. It can be argued that persons with mental illness who were freed from institutions during the latter part of the twentieth century are better off than before, but reform has not relieved the considerable number of individuals who only shifted their "institutionalized address" to prisons and jails. Others have lived short and sometime mean lives on the streets. Autonomy is a cherished value in liberal societies but there are always policy tradeoffs.

Many reports of child maltreatment are not founded. This statistic has been used by some as an argument that the reporting policy is inherently flawed. However, others have rejected this. The reality that many children reported but not "founded" as maltreated are reported again suggests that reporting per se might not be the real problem. Repeated reports might be at least as much an indication of inadequate methods for diagnosis, prognosis and triage, and a confirmation that at least something is quite wrong in the life of the child reported, rather than a defect of reporting itself. In fact, the later occurrence of additional reports suggests that the "case finding" of the reporting system, even though generating many more reports than are founded, is actually identifying a large problem that continues to be underfunded and will continue to prevail, waiting for more effective demonstrations of the potential for community development and other alternative approaches to child safety to be proven. The attention brought to the problem of maltreatment through mandatory reporting has resulted in only some 3–5 % of the children born in any given year ever entering the records of child protection agencies.[3]

It is not clear why complementary reforms and approaches cannot take place with the mandatory reporting system still in place. This is the approach taken by Differential Response pilots. Mandatory reporting has not blocked the most scientifically established primary prevention program in the USA: The Nurse Family Partnership[4] is now found in about 15 % of America's roughly 3,400 counties, and was and is implemented on an entirely voluntary basis. However, the research that first established its power as a child abuse preventive was conducted in the State of New York using official records of child abuse reports. The results of the program extend at least 15 years, a rather exceptional result for a program based in part on behavioral interventions.

Making reporting of severe child abuse mandatory does not mean that child maltreatment will always be reported, and certainly does not mean that child abuse and neglect will always be founded, managed or treated appropriately. However, there is evidence that mandatory reporting produces substantial positive effects for children and communities. Identification of child abuse as a formal societal and legal obligation serves as an essential means of asserting that a society is willing to be informed of child abuse and to take steps to respond to it. In countries in which mandatory reporting is implemented, it is harder to ignore not only the reality of child maltreatment but also the success or lack of success in responding to it. In the most successful "democratic societies of law," legal duties, voluntary services, public and private engagement, and change supported from below, above and across society, are mixed together to achieve maximal results. Maltreated children deserve laws which create direct, enforceable responsibilities for addressing severe abuse and neglect.

[3] Merkonnen, R., Noonan, K., & Rubin, D. (2009). Achieving better health care outcomes for children in foster care. *Pediatric Clinics of North America, 56*(2), 405–415, 406.

[4] Donelan-McCall, N., Eckenrode, J., & Olds, D. L. (2009) Home visiting for the prevention of child maltreatment: Lessons learned during the past twenty years. *Pediatric Clinics of North America, 56*(2), 389–404.

Part I
Historical and Current Context of Mandatory Reporting Laws

Chapter 1
Mandatory Reporting Laws: Their Origin, Nature, and Development over Time

Ben Mathews

Introduction

Most children have relatively happy childhoods in loving and capable families, but some do not. Throughout human history, a significant proportion of children have endured severe maltreatment from their parents and caregivers. Due to the innate vulnerability of infants and children, the extreme power asymmetry of the parent/child relationship, and the private setting of severe maltreatment, these infants and children are uniquely marginalised and oppressed. Their experience of severe maltreatment is hidden in the family sphere, where parents' activities are guarded by a heavy ideological curtain. Broken bones and beatings, rape and sexual assaults, severe emotional deprivation, and profound and even life-threatening neglect: all have traditionally remained silenced and protected from view. Even when another person became aware of such a situation, they would usually avert their gaze, such was children's lack of status relative to their parents'; and given the severity of the conduct, the person might reasonably wonder what they could possibly do anyway.

Until relatively recently, there have been no systematic sociolegal measures or systems anywhere in the world to enable intervention by protective agencies to stop the continuance of maltreatment and enable provision to the child of health rehabilitation and safe environment. In what has been described as a 'tectonic shift' (Runyan 2014), the social response to child suffering changed in the early 1960s in the USA, moving beyond earlier measures such as those in English Poor Laws and societies for the protection of children. The key advance was to create a measure to open the curtain shading the private family sphere and shed light on instances of serious child

B. Mathews (✉)
Australian Centre for Health Law Research, Faculty of Law,
Queensland University of Technology, GPO Box 2434, 4001 Brisbane, QLD, Australia
e-mail: b.mathews@qut.edu.au

B. Mathews, D.C. Bross (eds.), *Mandatory Reporting Laws and the Identification of Severe Child Abuse and Neglect*, Child Maltreatment 4,
DOI 10.1007/978-94-017-9685-9_1

maltreatment. Laws were enacted across the USA which required designated persons to report serious child physical abuse to authorities; those authorities would receive the reports and determine the appropriate course of action.

As other forms of serious maltreatment became recognised and understood, these 'mandatory reporting laws' were extended to encompass those types of maltreatment as well. The laws have since been adopted by many countries, in different forms (Mathews and Kenny 2008; Daro 2006). They are a heterogeneous, organic, flexible mechanism enabling social intervention where otherwise such intervention is severely compromised or impossible. Their primary function is to comprise but one aspect of a multifaceted child welfare apparatus by identifying cases of serious maltreatment which would not otherwise come to light; their essential role is therefore primarily tertiary and is not a purely preventative one. As noted later in this chapter, the evidence indicates that on this basis they have greatly assisted in case identification and remain superior to alternative approaches. As well as the laws imposing a direct obligation on selected individuals to act, as a strategy endorsed by parliament as representatives of the community, they embody a declaration about what is and is not acceptable conduct and about what interests it values society must and will protect. In this sense they are also an instrument to influence positive development in attitudes, behaviours, and societal culture (Mathews and Bross 2014).

Dozens of countries have now enacted mandatory reporting laws in various forms. However, in many countries, such measures still do not exist. Others like England are currently considering them; others like Saudi Arabia have recently introduced them (Al Eissa and Almuneef 2010); and others like Ireland are introducing them. Even where they exist, debates continue about their use and effects, both for general and for specific types and extents of maltreatment (Besharov 1985; Drake and Jonson-Reid 2007; Mathews and Bross 2008; Melton 2005; Wald 2014a, b). This chapter outlines the origins and provenance of the first mandatory reporting laws, discusses their nature, describes major developments over time, and identifies some major effects and their consequences.

Origins and Provenance: The First Mandatory Reporting Laws

The impetus behind the first mandatory reporting law about any kind of child abuse or neglect was the work of the Colorado paediatrician C. Henry Kempe and his medical colleagues (1962) in identifying cases of severe child physical abuse and conceptualising this as 'the battered-child syndrome'. Kempe et al. were seeing numerous cases of severe intentional physical injury to children in their hospitals; an example was given of 1 day's intake including four infants suffering parent-inflicted battering, two of whom died, another of whom died 4 weeks later, and with the fourth recovering. Kempe et al. acknowledged that this battering of children by their caregivers occurred on a spectrum of less severe cases to extremely severe cases. However, their emphasis was on severe injury, especially cases involving bone fractures (whether of the skull, arms, or legs) and/or subdural hematoma.

Because of their understanding and empathy toward the child's situation – notably, it is the child who is the primary subject of concern, not the parents – they had been disturbed by doctors encountering these cases and not taking appropriate action to prevent avoidable harm to the child. Children who were known or should have been known to have been victims of severe physical injury were being ignored and returned to the offending parents and would continue to suffer and in some cases would die.

Kempe et al. (1962, p. 17) defined the battered-child syndrome as

> A term used by us to characterize a clinical condition in young children who have received serious physical abuse, generally from a parent or foster parent…It is a significant cause of childhood disability and death. Unfortunately, it is frequently not recognized or, if diagnosed, is inadequately handled by the physician because of hesitation to bring the case to the attention of the proper authorities…The battered-child syndrome may occur at any age, but, in general, the affected children are younger than 3 years.

Their conclusion was that appropriate management by doctors involved making (1962, p. 23)

> the correct diagnosis so that he can institute proper therapy and make certain that a similar event will not occur again. He should report possible wilful trauma to the police department or any special children's protective services that operate in his community. The report that he makes should be restricted to the objective findings which can be verified and, where possible, should be supported by photographs and roentgenograms.

Kempe had identified and publicised not only the situation of severe intentional injury being inflicted on parents but also the widespread reluctance and/or seeming inability of many doctors to recognise it and deal with it appropriately by reporting it to authorities (Bross and Mathews 2014). Their position was that such serious instances of maltreatment must no longer be tolerated, and a mechanism had to be devised to circumvent individuals' reluctance and/or inability to act and to enable outside intervention to assist the child. Doctors' repeated failure to act on clear cases of violent assault to infants embodied the phenomenon of 'gaze aversion'; they looked away when they encountered a situation which caused them discomfort or psychological confusion. This gaze aversion was not limited to doctors, and it continues today, although in cultures where people are more informed about and sensitised to child abuse and its consequences and more supportive of children's rights, it is arguably less likely to persist.

Kempe et al.'s research was accompanied by intensive lobbying for legislative reform. As a result, the first mandatory reporting laws were enacted in every state of the USA (except Hawaii) between 1963 and 1967 (Besharov 1985; Kalichman 1999; Nelson 1984; Paulsen et al. 1966; Paulsen 1967). In accordance with the scope of Kempe's work at this time, these laws were initially limited to requiring medical professionals to report suspected serious *physical* injury inflicted by a child's parent or caregiver. The fundamental premise was that doctors regularly encounter children by virtue of their profession, and because of this are well placed to identify cases of severe maltreatment, and by reporting it enable intervention by welfare agencies to interrupt the abuse and facilitate health rehabilitation and other services for the child and family.

The Nature of a Mandatory Reporting Law: What It Is, and What It Is Not

Before proceeding to explain how the laws have developed over time, it is important to make some observations about the nature of a mandatory reporting law. First, they are different from a specific duty in a criminal statute requiring all persons to disclose a serious indictable offence which they know or believe to have been committed. These provisions do exist in some jurisdictions. In Australia, the New South Wales *Crimes Act* s 316 is one example, and Victoria has just introduced a similar provision which in fact has as its sole object of concern the disclosure of child sexual abuse (*Crimes Amendment (Protection of Children) Bill 2014* clause 4). However, these are not 'mandatory reporting laws' in the true sense of the term; one reason for this is that these provisions are a more limited ad hoc approach to crime detection, whereas mandatory reporting laws are a more systematic approach to child welfare accompanied by a range of structural mechanisms to support them, such as expert reporter training[1] and child protection response systems to assist children and families.

Different Approaches to Reporting Laws: A Spectrum of Choice

Second, as will be shown below, because mandatory reporting laws are made by each specific jurisdiction according to its preferred design and function within its sociopolitical system, they have a similar schematic approach but have different dimensions and application. There is a spectrum of different approaches from which a jurisdiction can choose: the laws can be very broad or very narrow. They can apply to a broad or a narrow range of reporter groups. They can apply to a broad or a narrow range of types of maltreatment; they do not always apply to every *form* of abuse and neglect; and, importantly, they do not apply to every *instance* where abuse or neglect occurs. Rather, they are usually limited to cases where the reporter knows or suspects it is a case of serious or significant harm that has already been caused by the abuse or neglect or where the harm may not yet have appeared but is likely to eventuate from the abuse or neglect suspected to have occurred.[2] The laws do not

[1] See the chapters by Kenny (Chap. 16) and by Donohue et al. (Chap. 17) in this volume.

[2] The primary subject matter of the reporting provisions is 'abuse' either explicit or as a natural and coexisting consequence of being the *cause* of the significant or serious 'injury' or 'harm' specified. The two are inextricably linked, and the coexisting causal relationship and link are often acknowledged directly in the provisions by the use of the term 'caused by'. There are some instances where a type of abuse must be reported without any mention of harm – most often, for sexual abuse (e.g. in Australia, ACT, NT, SA, Tas, WA) and for physical injury by abuse (ACT). In five statutes the first concept used is 'abuse', with proceeding words or provisions relating to the abuse causing harm and the extent of this harm required to activate the reporting duty (ACT, Qld, SA, Tas, WA). In four statutes the first concept used is 'harm', with proceeding words or provisions identifying or recognising that this 'harm' is *caused by* various kinds of abuse and neglect (NSW, NT, Qld, Vic).

require reports of trivial incidents or of less than ideal parenting. In addition, the reporting laws are primarily an exercise in reporting known and suspected *existing* cases of abuse or neglect and serious harm; they are not an exercise in pure prediction of future events. They do not require people to report any situation in which they perceive any kind of 'risk' to a child.

An example of the text from a reporting law is indicative.[3] The mandatory reporting legislation in two states of Australia (South Australia and Tasmania) is identical in this respect, identifying 'abuse or neglect' as (author's emphasis)[4]:

1. Sexual abuse or
2. Physical or emotional injury or other abuse or neglect, *to the extent that*
   (a) The injured, abused, or neglected person has suffered, or is likely to suffer, physical or psychological *harm detrimental to the person's wellbeing.*
   (b) The injured, abused, or neglected person's *physical or psychological development is in jeopardy.*

In sum, together with the other parts of the reporting law and as clarified in formal reporter training and accompanying documentation, a mandated reporter in these two jurisdictions would be required to report any suspected case of child sexual abuse; the other types must only be reported if the abuse or harm is present to the specified extent of significance.

In federated jurisdictions such as the USA, Canada, and Australia, each state, territory, and province will create its own legislation. This can produce considerable variation across jurisdictions within the same country (Mathews and Kenny 2008). Other national jurisdictions will also naturally be able to fashion their reporting law according to their preference. Consequently, there are major differences in the laws made by different jurisdictions both across and within countries concerning who has to report, what types of maltreatment must be reported, and other dimensions of the duty. Below I outline the common schematic approach to the legislative schemes, with notes showing how they can differ across jurisdiction (and within the same jurisdiction over time) (Mathews and Kenny 2008) (Table 1.1).

It should also be noted that the laws also enable *non-mandated* persons to report suspected cases, and in fact, the data shows that mandated reporters make only around 50–60 % of all reports. These explanations are important because one of the asserted problems caused by mandatory reporting – that 'it produces too many unwarranted reports' – is based on an incorrect assumption about their nature, a failure to distinguish between different patterns of reporting by different reporter groups and for different types of maltreatment, and a misunderstanding about the nature of substantiation (Drake 1996; Drake and Jonson-Reid 2007; Kohl et al.

---

[3] As anyone who has taken the time to access and read a piece of legislation will know, mandatory reporting provisions, like many other types of legal provisions, are long and complex, may involve numerous different numbered provisions scattered through different parts of a statute (and sometimes several different statutes), and on top of this are subject to the rules of statutory construction (both legislative and common law) which apply to all legislation. A 'mandatory reporting law' is therefore not a simple creature which can be easily located, read, and understood.

[4] Children's Protection Act 1993 (SA) s 6; Children, Young Persons and Their Families Act 1997 (Tas) s 3.

Table 1.1 Dimensions of the schematic approach common to all mandatory reporting laws, with notes on their usual features and typical differences

Dimension of the reporting law	Usual features and typical differences
Defines *which persons* must make reports	Usually restricted to members of key professions who deal regularly with children in the course of their work, such as police, teachers, nurses and doctors; but sometimes applied to all citizens[a]
Defines what *state of mind* a reporter must have before the reporting duty is activated	Usually the possession of 'reasonable grounds to suspect' or 'reasonable grounds to believe'; certainty is not necessary, but it requires something more than an inkling
Defines the *types of abuse and neglect* that must be reported	Varies widely across jurisdictions: some only require reports of sexual abuse; some only of physical and sexual abuse; many require reports of physical, sexual, and emotional abuse and neglect; some require reports of these four types *and* exposure to family violence and more
Defines the *extent of harm/abuse or neglect* which requires a report	The 'significant harm' aspect is defined using a range of terms and is used in most but not all jurisdictions. Often, the significant harm aspect is not applied to sexual abuse. Some jurisdictions do not clearly specify the degree of 'harm'; unless complemented in reporter training, this may produce more reports (but this may fit with the more preventative intention of these jurisdictions)
Defines whether the duty applies only to past or present abuse/harm or also to future abuse/harm which has not occurred yet but which is thought likely to occur	All laws apply to the former (the classical Kempe scenario of tertiary response). Some laws include the latter also: this is clearly a more preventative aspiration, and a good example of this is the duty to report suspected likely future sexual abuse – which can be seen in situations of grooming of a child for sexual abuse
Defines *other familial circumstances which must be present* to require a report	Some jurisdictions (e.g. several in Canada, Victoria in Australia) limit the reporting duty by only requiring a report if the reporter believes the child's parents 'have not protected, or are unlikely to protect the child' from the harm
Defines *penalties* for failure to report	These vary widely but are meant to encourage reporting rather than police it; prosecutions are extremely rare, but high penalties may produce hypersensitive reporting. The New South Wales legislation removed its penalty in 2010
Provides a reporter with *confidentiality* regarding their identity	An important protection for reporters
Provides a reporter with *immunity from suit*	Also a critical protection for reporters, as shown by the experience of jurisdictions without legislation (Mathews et al. 2009)[b]
States *when* the report must be made	Usually immediately

(continued)

Table 1.1 (continued)

Dimension of the reporting law	Usual features and typical differences
States to whom the report must be made	Usually to the government agency responsible for child protection; but now, often, reports of lesser situations of need rather than harm can be reported to differential response agencies
States what details a report should contain	Usually all relevant information about the child, the injuries, the circumstances, the statements, the child's family situation, and the contact details

[a]It is not uncommon for clergy to be mandated reporters; in the USA, 27 jurisdictions include clergy as mandated reporters (Children's Bureau, *Clergy as Mandated Reporters of Child Abuse and Neglect*, Child Welfare Information Gateway, Washington, 2012)
[b]A barrier to reporting can arise in jurisdictions without mandatory reporting legislation's protective shields for reporters. A soft policy-based duty to report provides no direct protections. In England and Wales, paediatricians have reported anxiety about parental complaints and fear of disciplinary action if reports are made and not substantiated. Cases of complaints against paediatricians appear to have impacted on others' willingness to report and to take on leadership roles in child protection. The government and the House of Lords have confirmed that paediatricians' first legal duty is to the care of the child so that reports should be made (Department for Children, Schools and Families and Department of Health 2007; JD v East Berkshire Community Health NHS Trust & Ors, 2005), but anxiety within the profession remains

2009). It is true that instances of 'undesirable' reporting have sometimes occurred, but in these instances, arguably the major factors have been poor planning and drafting and a failure of public administration by governments in not properly preparing reporters to comply with their duty and in inadequate resourcing of response systems (Mathews 2012). Later in this chapter, I will indicate a clear example of flawed public administration which appeared to produce undesired effects but which does not detract from the principle animating the reporting law.

Developments over Time: Extensions and Contractions of Mandatory Reporting Laws and Adoption by Many Countries in Various Forms

In the USA, the scope of states' initial legislation was restricted to require medical practitioners to report *serious* intentional physical injury,[5] with the laws being heavily informed in this respect by draft legislation recommended by the Children's Bureau, the American Medical Association, and the Council of State Governments (Paulsen 1967). Only a few states included a requirement to report serious injury caused by neglect. The general ambit of these laws soon expanded in three ways. Importantly, and unlike many other countries, these expansions were strongly influ-

[5] A few States chose not to incorporate the 'serious' injury qualification (Paulsen 1967).

enced by the effect of the passage in 1974 of the Federal Child Abuse Prevention and Treatment Act (CAPTA), which allocated funds to states based on the parameters of their laws. In essence, state laws were obliged to make their reporting laws have certain parameters to qualify for receipt of federal economic support for child welfare. One key provision in this regard in the first version of CAPTA was the definition of 'child abuse and neglect' as (author's emphasis)[6]

> The physical or mental injury, sexual abuse, negligent treatment, or maltreatment of a child under the age of eighteen by a person who is responsible for the child's welfare under circumstances which indicate the child's *health or welfare is harmed or threatened* thereby.

The three major expansions were as follows. First, state laws were gradually amended to require members of additional professional groups beyond medical practitioners to report suspected cases of abuse; some states would require all citizens to make reports. For example, in 1974, all laws required medical practitioners to report, but only nine required police officers to report; by 1986, many more states had added other professions to their lists of mandated reporters (Fraser 1986; Zellman and Fair 2002).

Second, the types of reportable abuse were expanded to include not only physical abuse but sexual abuse, emotional or psychological abuse, and neglect (Zellman and Fair 2002). Third, as seen in the definition above, the extent of harm to have been caused or suspected to be likely to activate the reporting duty was required by CAPTA to be unqualified by expressions such as 'serious' or 'significant' harm; most states abandoned such qualifications, and this would broaden the scope of the reporting duty (Kalichman 1999; Mathews and Kenny 2008).

It can be noted that these extensions were in part influenced by growing recognition of the nature and consequences of other forms of child maltreatment. After Kempe's initial primary concern with severe physical abuse, different maltreatment types were recognised: *sexual abuse*, emotional or psychological abuse, and neglect. For example, research in the late 1970s and early 1980s brought incest and other classes of child sexual abuse to greater prominence (Giarretto 1977; Kempe 1978; Summit and Kryso 1978; Finkelhor 1979).

CAPTA would periodically be amended and reauthorised and was completely rewritten in 1988 (P.L. 100–294). At this point, the definition in s 14(4) still retained the essential features established in 1974, although it had broadened the concept of sexual abuse.[7] By 1986, most states had mandated teachers, nurses, social workers, and mental health professionals as reporters (Fraser 1986).

However, a significant change was made in 1996 (P.L. 104–235), when the definition of 'child abuse and neglect' was modified by s 110(3) inserting a qualification of 'serious' harm. The definition then read (author's emphasis):

---

[6] The Child Abuse Prevention and Treatment Act 1974 (CAPTA, P.L. 93–247) s 3. The relevant provisions of the US Code are 42 U.S.C. 5101 et seq; 42 U.S.C 5116 et seq.

[7] The term 'child abuse and neglect' was defined as meaning 'the physical or mental injury, sexual abuse or exploitation, negligent treatment, or maltreatment of a child by a person who is responsible for the child's welfare, under circumstances which indicate that the child's health or welfare is harmed or threatened thereby'.

the term 'child abuse and neglect' means, at a minimum, any recent act or failure to act on the part of a parent or caretaker, which results in death, *serious* physical or emotional harm, sexual abuse or exploitation, or an act or failure to act which presents an imminent risk of *serious* harm.

The most recent revision of CAPTA in 2010 retains this definition of 'child abuse and neglect' (42 U.S.C. s 5106 g(2)).[8] The emphasis is clearly on, at a minimum, acts of abuse and neglect which have caused significant harm. This insertion of the 'serious harm' qualification effectively contracts the required scope of state legislation. However, state legislatures may still choose to adopt a broader definition, and some states have done so (Mathews and Kenny 2008). Where such qualifications regarding significant harm are not present, a jurisdiction has chosen to have a higher emphasis on prevention of more serious maltreatment by intervening at an earlier point in the process of maltreatment, as well as interrupting serious harm or abuse. Such an approach often uses both child protection systems' investigative function and a differential response approach which focuses on a different post-report response pathway.

A more explicit focus on significant harm is found in most US state laws and in most of the legislation across Australia. Moreover, some jurisdictions add a further qualification to the reporting duty, also restricting it to cases where not only is the significant harm qualification present but, in addition, the child does not have a parent able to protect them from the harm. Examples of this approach can be found in several provinces of Canada and in Victoria in Australia (Mathews and Kenny 2008).

Mandatory Reporting Evolving to Include Differential Response Approaches

Mandatory reporting legislation continues to evolve and adapt in virtually all jurisdictions which have adopted it. One of the most significant recent changes can be seen in many jurisdictions which are attempting to balance, on the one hand, the need for government child protection agencies to receive reports of significant harm and employ a traditional investigative response from child protective services teams to determine whether maltreatment has occurred and what response is most appropriate and, on the other hand, to ease the burden on child protection departments by diverting reports to welfare agencies of clearly less serious situations in which either there is no maltreatment at all, but simply need based on poverty, or which involve only minor harm or maltreatment which does not require more formal systemic responses. This latter focus on 'differential response' is seen by most as a generally positive development and is becoming more widespread both in the USA and

[8] The Child Abuse and Prevention and Treatment Act as amended by P.L. 111–320, the CAPTA Reauthorization Act of 2010 (42 U.S.C. 5101).

Australia,[9] although its contours and implementation are not uniform (Fluke et al. 2013; Conley and Berrick 2010; American Humane Association 2008). In general, it aims to provide an additional mechanism to respond more efficiently and justifiably to reported cases of a different type of situation which have a different type of needed response. The focus is on provision of services to the child's caregivers and the child. In principle, a nuanced approach to response is essential: an otherwise happy and healthy 8 year old who sometimes does not have appropriate clothing or food due solely to his single mother's poverty requires a far different response to a 3-week-old neonate whose drug-addicted parents beat him severely, and will not engage with support.

Arguably, if implemented soundly, differential response is as essential a part of a public health approach as are the reporting laws. However, it has been observed that such systems must be shown to be successful (and not only by measures of parental satisfaction), should not compromise the child's safety, should be backed by a capacity to compel parental compliance where necessary (noting that parental engagement is voluntary), and must not be used by politicians to withdraw net funding from the child protection and child welfare endeavour (Bartholet 2012; Bartholet and Heimpel 2013; Heimpel and Bartholet 2014).

The process of development and evolution of the laws, including the incorporation of differential response mechanisms, and the adoption of different approaches across the spectrum of choice can be illustrated by a concise chronological overview of developments in Australia from the 1960s to date.

---

[9] In Australia, examples include Victoria's *Child and Family Information, Referral and Support Teams* (ChildFIRST) system, which enables individuals who have a significant concern about a child's wellbeing to refer their concern to ChildFIRST for help, rather than reporting to the department responsible for child protection (*Children, Youth and Families Act 2005* (Vic) s 31). This provision complements the mandatory reporting provisions, where reports of specified cases of a child being 'in need of protection' must be made to the secretary of the department (*Children, Youth and Families Act 2005* (Vic) s 184). Children and families who are referred to ChildFIRST are assessed and may be offered home-based family support or referred to other health and welfare services (*Children, Youth and Families Act 2005* (Vic) s 33). ChildFIRST must forward reports to child protection services if the community-based child and family service considers that the situation may involve more significant harm or risk of harm, that is, that the child may be 'in need of protection' (*Children, Youth and Families Act 2005* (Vic) s 33(2)). Equally, reports made to child protective services may be redirected to ChildFIRST if deemed not to require a child protection response (*Children, Youth and Families Act 2005* (Vic) ss 187, 30). The ChildFIRST model was adopted in Tasmania under the name 'Gateways'. Tasmania also amended its mandatory reporting laws to facilitate a preventative approach. Mandatory reporters could report their concerns about the care of a child to a 'community-based intake service', and this would fulfil their reporting duty (*Children, Young Persons and Their Families Act 1997* Part 5B). In New South Wales, s 27A of the *Children and Young Persons (Care and Protection) Act 1998* (NSW) enabled mandated reporters to make reports to 'Child Wellbeing Units' which were established in the four major state government departmental groups (health, education, police, and family and community services). These units provide support and advice to mandated reporters on whether a situation warrants a mandated report and on local services which might be of assistance. The units' focus is on ascertaining what the family needs to minimise or overcome their situation and on facilitating the most appropriate assistance.

An Example of Developments and Differences: An Australian Overview

Soon after Kempe's work, some early Australian research also made similar observations about the physical abuse of children (Birrell and Birrell 1966; Wurfel and Maxwell 1965). This research helped to inform the development of the first mandatory reporting laws in Australia, including the first enactment in South Australia in 1969. The first Australian mandatory reporting laws in the late 1960s and early 1970s focused primarily on physical abuse and, to an extent, severe neglect. Like their American counterparts, usually these first laws were limited to requiring medical practitioners to report.

Subsequently, all eight Australian states and territories have introduced, and incrementally expanded, mandatory reporting requirements. Legal historical analysis by Mathews (2014) revealed the disjointed process of introduction of mandatory reporting laws in time, place, and subject matter in Australia. Table 1.2 shows the national chronology.

A Dynamic, Flexible Instrument of Social Policy

The example of Australia also shows how the laws are a dynamic, organic measure which is adaptable to change. As with all legislation, mandatory reporting legislation are instruments of sociolegal policy which are able to be refined and developed – whether by expansion, contraction, or refinement – to accommodate new knowledge, policy imperatives, and systems changes. The developments in the laws

Table 1.2 Chronology of introduction in Australian states and territories of first mandatory reporting laws and their focus

Date of first mandatory reporting provision	Jurisdiction	Focus of original reporting duty
27 November 1969	South Australia	Neglect and ill-treatment by parents and caregivers
22 October 1975	Tasmania	Physical abuse and neglect
1 July 1977	New South Wales	Physical abuse and neglect
14 June 1980	Queensland	Physical abuse and neglect
20 April 1984	Northern Territory	All forms of child abuse and neglect, where the child does not have a parent who can protect the child from the abuse
4 November 1993	Victoria	Children in need of care and protection as a result of harm from physical injury or sexual abuse and lack of a parent who can protect the child from that harm
1 June 1997	Australian Capital Territory	Physical abuse and sexual abuse
1 January 2009	Western Australia	Sexual abuse

and in differential response systems in the last decade or so provide a clear example of this. The refinements made in each Australian state and territory in the last decade alone show how governments can choose to modify this important instrument, either enlarging, contracting, or otherwise modifying its technical scope (parameters of the law) and practical implementation (e.g. mandated reporter training and systems approaches). Research is important in this respect as it can identify differential reporting practices between jurisdictions with different legal frameworks, between reporter groups, and between different types of maltreatment and can help to identify areas of more or less effective reporting practice and areas of systemic need. National research in Australia is currently being undertaken in this regard.[10] Research into reporting systems is an essential aspect of the monitoring component of a public health approach.

This point is important because it demonstrates how, when research and monitoring reveal problems with the law, appropriate changes can be devised and implemented. Creation of a legal framework does not bind policy and strategy forever. It also means that when a problem is identified, we can carefully consider principles and evidence and figure out how best to respond to it. This reasoned approach guards against unnecessary 'all or nothing' overreactions and extreme exhortations to abandon the entire policy; such exhortations are extremely rare but have been made (Melton 2005) and later strongly criticised (Drake and Jonson-Reid 2007; Mathews and Bross 2008).

Legislative analysis of each Australian jurisdiction reveals many changes in the decade 2003–2012, of which the following are the most substantial developments (Mathews 2014) (Table 1.3).

International Overview

Many countries now have mandatory reporting laws. The three early adopters were the USA, Canada, and Australia. Mathews and Kenny (2008) found that mandatory reporting legislation of some kind had been enacted in every jurisdiction in the USA, every jurisdiction in Canada, and all but one in Australia. The outlying Australian jurisdiction has since passed a mandatory reporting law, limited to sexual abuse (Mathews et al. 2009).

Beyond these nations, others with legislative mandatory reporting duties include Denmark, Norway, Sweden, France, Hungary, Israel, and Brazil (Mathews and Kenny 2008; Daro 2006). The adoption of the laws continues: one nation to recently introduce them is Saudi Arabia, where the laws have been judged to produce a positive effect on case identification (Al Eissa and Almuneef 2010). Ireland recently introduced into Parliament the Children First Bill 2014. A recent survey of 62 nations involved 33 developed nations, and 29 developing nations found, overall, that some form of mandatory reporting existed in 81.8 % of the 33 developed nations

[10] By Mathews, Bromfield, and colleagues.

Table 1.3 Chronology of notable legislative developments and refinements in Australian state and territory mandatory reporting laws, 2003–2012

Jurisdiction	Notable legislative developments and refinements
Australian Capital Territory	1 August 2006: clarification that no need to report if reporter believes someone else already has
New South Wales	30 March 2007: new duty to report prenatally where birth mothers subject of prenatal report do not engage with services
	24 January 2010
	Clearer requirement of significant harm to activate reporting duty
	Duty to report failure to attend school
	Removal of penalty for not reporting
	Reports by mandated reporters enabled to be made to differential response agencies
Northern Territory	8 December 2008: 'maltreatment' definition replaced by 'harm', which is defined to include all forms of abuse and neglect *as well as* exposure to physical violence, with 'harm' requiring suffering of 'significant detrimental effect' on physical, psychological, or emotional wellbeing or development
Queensland	31 August 2005: new duty for nurses to report all sexual abuse and to report physical abuse, emotional abuse, and neglect where it has caused or is likely to cause significant harm
	9 July 2012: new duty for school staff to report all suspected child sexual abuse
South Australia	31 December 2006: penalty for not reporting increased from $2,500 to $10,000
	New reporter groups added: ministers of religion and employees and volunteers in religious, spiritual, sporting, and recreational organisations
Tasmania	30 March 2005: new duty to report exposure of child to family violence where child's 'safety, psychological wellbeing, or interests are affected or likely to be affected by family violence' – family violence defined very broadly
	1 August 2009
	Reports by mandated reporters can be made to a differential response agency
	New duty to report prenatally where thereporters suspect that the child after birth will suffer abuse or neglect, will be killed, or will require medical treatment as a result of the mother's behaviour or the behaviour of a person with whom the mother resides or is likely to reside
Victoria	No substantial changes for mandated reporters, but differential response emphasised from 23 April 2007 and non-mandated reports can be made to these agencies
Western Australia	1 January 2009: reporting duty introduced for child sexual abuse, for doctors, nurses, teachers, police, and midwives

and 78.6 % of the 29 developing nations (Daro 2006). By region, some form of mandatory reporting was present in 90 % of the nations in the Americas, 86.4 % of the nations in Europe, 77.8 % of the nations in Africa, and 72.2 % of the nations in Asia.

Usually, legislative mandatory reporting duties are placed in child protection legislation. However, another approach to mandatory reporting is to enshrine the duty in the criminal law. For example, France has a mandatory reporting duty enshrined in its Penal Code,[11] as does Israel.[12] Other nations, such as Sweden, enshrine the mandatory reporting duty in social services legislation.[13]

Major Effects of Mandatory Reporting Laws and Consequences of These Effects

Mandatory reporting laws have indisputably resulted in the identification of many more cases of severe child maltreatment than would otherwise have been revealed (Besharov 2005; Zellman and Fair 2002). After introduction of the laws and their associated mechanisms – reporter training and dedicated child protection systems – reports of known and suspected maltreatment increased substantially, compared with the situation before the reporting laws. Many of these reports resulted in identification of severely abused and neglected children. Besharov (1985, p. 545) declared 'there is no dispute that the great bulk of reports now received … would not have been made but for the passage of mandatory reporting laws and the media campaigns that accompanied them'. Besharov (1990, 2005, p. 287) estimated that due to increased reporting and investigation and treatment services, annual child deaths in the USA have fallen from 3,000 to 5,000 to about 1,100 (they now number around 1,500 annually).

Overall Positive Effect

In addition to the effect on fatalities, if one considers the situation both historically and from the perspective of the maltreated child, the overall effect on child protection and child welfare must be viewed as remarkably positive. This ongoing impact for so many thousands of children over many years, compared with the position without mandatory reporting, can be judged on numerous bases.

First, the laws do result in more reports, at least initially, and substantial proportions of these result in substantiated cases and other outcomes which assist the child. In 1963, in the USA, only around 150,000 reports were made to welfare agencies, and this quadrupled by 1976 (Besharov 1990) and continued to increase, especially until the 1990s. In New South Wales, Australia, after the introduction of a reporting law for sexual abuse, the number of reports (and of substantiated reports) by the same reporter group tripled over a 3-month period (Lamond 1989). This has been found in other Australian jurisdictions for child sexual abuse reporting (Mathews 2014). Hence, reporting and case identification by the same specified

[11] Penal Code art 434.

[12] Penal Law s 368D.

[13] Social Services Act Ch 14 s 1.

reporter group within a jurisdiction will change after introduction of the reporting law.

Second, it is known that the same professional reporter group (e.g. doctors or teachers) in a jurisdiction within a country which has a reporting law will make more reports and identify more cases than the same reporter group in another jurisdiction without a reporting law (Mathews et al. 2010; Mathews 2014; Victorian Law Reform Commission 1988). Hence, even taking population difference into account, the presence of a reporting law (and associated mechanisms, e.g. reporter training) influences case identification by a specified reporter group.

Third, the known presence of a reporting law can influence what would otherwise be a reluctance to report. Studies have found that when asked if their decision not to report a suspected case would be changed if they knew at the time they were under a legal duty to report, a substantial number of initial non-reporters would change their mind and make a report (Webberley 1985; Shamley et al. 1984).

A comment is warranted regarding the substantial decline in child physical abuse and sexual abuse which has been traced in the USA since the early 1990s. These declines were declared in 2012 as being 'as well established as crime trends can be in contemporary social science' (Finkelhor and Jones 2012, p. 3). They were identified after analysis of seven different sources of data extending beyond official substantiated reports to include different kinds of national and state community incidence studies and self-report surveys (Finkelhor and Jones 2012). If accurate, these declines are a significant advance in child welfare. It has been postulated that several factors may have influenced this decline, including increased social agents of intervention, pharmacological treatments for depression and anxiety, incarceration of sexual offenders, economic upturns, and the flow-on effect of abortion law leading to fewer unwanted children being born (Finkelhor and Jones 2006; Finkelhor 2008). The precise reasons for these declines remain unclear, but it seems plausible that mandatory reporting and its placement within the rubric of the social agents of intervention may be a contributing factor.

Reports Do Not Always Increase, and Trends Are Not Constant Across Maltreatment Types or Reporter Groups

This overall trend of increasing reports has been seen in both the USA and Australia, although before continuing, it should be noted that this trend does not continue forever, nor is it constant for each type of maltreatment. For example, rates of all reports in the USA have been little changed from 1999 to 2012 (US DHHS 2001, 2006, 2007, 2014). It must also be recognised that non-mandated reporters make roughly 45 % of all reports. Initial increases after introduction or expansion of the laws are more notable: in the USA, the rate of reports per 1,000 children increased from 10.1 in 1976 to 45.0 in 1992 (Zellman and Fair 2002). Yet, large proportions of reports – around 40 % – are screened out and therefore result in barely any systems burden. Substantial multiple numbers of reports are made about the same child.

The numbers of reports and the number of children involved in them can also decline. In Australia, in the 3 years 2008/2009 to 2011/2012, the number of total notifications has declined from 339,454 to 252,962, and the number of children involved in these notifications has declined from 207,462 to 173,502 (Australian Institute of Health and Welfare 2013). Shifts in report patterns can be influenced by changes in legal frameworks and the introduction of differential response pathways. Reporting patterns differ markedly for different reporter groups and different maltreatment types. Neglect and emotional abuse are far more frequently reported than physical and sexual abuse. Mathews (2012) showed how the overwhelming systems burden in New South Wales in the middle of the last decade in Australia was due to the reporting of one kind of maltreatment (domestic violence) by one reporter group (police). This means that care must be taken not to make simplified generalisations about the effect of a mandatory reporting law.

Substantiated and Unsubstantiated Reports

Care must also be taken in drawing conclusions about the effects of mandatory reporting based on 'substantiated reports'. The number of substantiated cases found as a result of reports is sometimes used as a proxy for measuring how many reports by a group of reporters are 'effective' or 'justified' and by extension whether mandatory reporting is good policy. This is a mistaken assumption because, as has been shown by Drake (1996) and Kohl et al. (2009), while there may be some variance between the cases the subject of the two kinds of outcome, there is little difference in the need for assistance and services between children in substantiated and unsubstantiated cases. As well, there are numerous reasons for a finding of 'unsubstantiated' in a case where there is nevertheless maltreatment and/or harm: the report may have been a duplicate report made about the same child; it may have been referred directly to differential response; it may have involved maltreatment but insufficient evidence of harm; it may have involved evidence of harm but insufficient evidence of maltreatment; and there may have been insufficient resources to investigate. In fact, many 'unsubstantiated' reports are actually just as (if not more) useful because they allow service provision and prevent a milder situation escalating. Numerically, more than twice the number of children in unsubstantiated reports receive services in the USA than do children in substantiated reports (Drake and Jonson-Reid 2007; US DHHS 2014).

Responses to Arguments Against the Laws

Partly based on the unsubstantiated report premise, some have criticised the use of mandatory reporting laws. It has been claimed that the laws produce a surge in reports and that the burden to the system (and to parents) of receiving and especially investigating these outweighs the benefit (Ainsworth and Hansen 2006; Melton 2005). Yet, as well as not acknowledging the 'substantiation' fallacy outlined above, this argument does not recognise many features of the context: that close to half of all reports are made by non-mandated reporters, that a large proportion are multiple reports about the same children, that many reports are screened out and are not investigated, hence resulting in very little burden, and that in any event the substantiation rate of investigated cases is significantly higher (Mathews 2012). Others have also rebutted this claim (Drake and Jonson-Reid 2007; Dalziel and Segal 2007; Finkelhor 2005). Moreover, by far the bulk of the economic cost involved in child protection is absorbed by foster care and residential care, accounting for at least half of the entire systemic cost. In contrast, Drake and Jonson-Reid's chapter in this volume concludes that the cost of investigations is extremely low.

These and other arguments have been considered recently by five major government child protection inquiries in Australia when contemplating the merits and parameters of mandatory reporting. In Australia, five recent inquiries have occurred in New South Wales (Wood 1997), South Australia (Layton 2003), New South Wales again (Wood 2008), Victoria (Cummins et al. 2012), and Queensland (Carmody 2013).

These inquiries have consistently supported mandatory reporting laws as a necessary component of social policy to identify and respond to child abuse and neglect.

In 2012, the Victorian Inquiry recommended extending the mandated reporter groups (Cummins et al. 2012, p. 349 Recommendation 44). In 2013, the Queensland Inquiry recommended harmonisation and refinement of fragmented and inconsistent mandatory reporting laws, improving reporter education and increasing a differential response approach, but did not recommend abolishing them (Carmody 2013).

Even in New South Wales, where there had been an example of poor legislative drafting and administration leading to isolated subsets of unintended reporting – namely, reports by police of nearly any encounter with domestic violence (Mathews 2012) – the Wood Inquiry (2008) rejected isolated claims that mandated reporting produced a general flood of reports.[14] Instead, it concluded that 'the requirement to report should remain', for several reasons including:

- About 40 % of all reports in NSW were made around this time by non-mandated reporters.
- Child protection system workers generally supported mandatory reporting while endorsing amendments to how it operated.
- On a closer inspection of the data, there was in fact no 'evidence of a flood of reports with a reduction in outcomes, at least by reference to investigations and substantiations'.

[14] The Wood Inquiry (2008) noted that the child protection system in New South Wales was under strain, but rejected the 'limited, and primarily academic support expressed to the Inquiry for abolition of the mandatory reporting based on the alleged result that MR caused it to be 'flooded with reports, the response to which used up scarce resources and diverted attention from those families whose children were in need of the State's intervention'.

- Rather, a very large proportion of reports involved *the same small group of children*, and many reports were multiple reports about the same child or the same incident.
- Multiple reporting had increased.
- The reporting of less serious circumstances had increased.
- A *decrease* had occurred in the number of children subject to reports.
- Mandatory reporting is not the cause of undue increased reporting as reports increase in jurisdictions without mandatory reporting.
- Substantiation rates had almost doubled in 3 years.
- Reports receiving SAS 2 (the highest level of investigation) had more than doubled since 2004/2005.

Wood (2008) concluded that rather than abolishing the reporting laws, the system needed greater effectiveness in reporting and more appropriate treatment of cases, including by a differential response pathway. In addition, amendments to the mandatory reporting provisions should be made to promote reports only being made about the kinds of case the system aimed to receive, namely, cases of *significant* abuse or harm (Wood 2008, pp. xiii, 195–197).

This is not to say there are no issues with mandatory reporting and no areas where it may be improved. There are well-known issues with reporter training, many of which are dealt with in this volume. Research needs to identify what educational measures are most effective in preparing reporters for their role. Child protection systems need to interact effectively with reporters, providing feedback on reports and their outcomes. There are also areas of undesirable reporting practice; poverty per se should not be reported, and low levels of neglect and lawful corporal punishment that is clearly disciplinary in intention and not producing clear injuries should not be reported. Better reporter training and public education are essential. Refinement of reporting laws is well-worth implementation, if necessary, if carefully constructed, and if supported by principle and data. Investigation and differential response pathways are likely both needed but require ongoing monitoring to ensure principled and efficient operation. Marginalised groups such as the homeless, and refugees, should be dealt with particularly sensitively if they are the subject of a report. Child protection systems should be better resourced, so they can fulfil their remit. Some have claimed that neglect is not a justifiable province for mandatory reporting, yet neglect is the most frequent cause of child fatality of all forms of maltreatment and is particularly dangerous for neonates (babies in the first month of life) and infants, and there are numerous cases of clearly criminal parental neglect in which the parents' culpability is clear and is far different to minor poverty-related neglect.

Reporting of suspected serious child abuse and neglect is not an exact science and cannot be expected to be. The success of a complex policy in a sensitive domain of human conduct must not be gauged against an unreasonable expectation. Legal and social policy responses cannot be judged only to succeed if they always or even predominantly achieve their direct goal. Rather, the success of such measures should be judged holistically: overall, has the measure produced good results and created a better culture, and does it appear to be the best strategy currently available? Other emergency systems, such as hospital emergency department visits, emergency telephone calls to police, fire and ambulance departments, and police arrests, are subject to apparently substantial inefficiencies, yet nobody would seriously suggest they should be abandoned.[15] Instead, they are seen correctly as essential public services regarding which ongoing efforts should be made to educate people to use them correctly and to enhance triage methods within those systems (Finkelhor 1990, 2005).

Conclusion

Mandatory reporting laws can be designed to take one of many forms to suit the goals of the particular society. Societies considering their implementation can choose to adopt a more narrowly framed approach, especially if resources are extremely scarce. Whether couched broadly or narrowly, they should be a part of a system of responses to child protection and family welfare concerns. The different components of this system are necessary owing to the differences between types of maltreatment recognising that within the spectrum of circumstances, different responses are appropriate. A case of severe battering of a 6-month-old infant, or of sexual abuse of a 3 year old, requires different responses than a case of mild neglect of a 14-year-old arising only from conditions of poverty in an otherwise healthy and well-functioning family. Different responses cater to the needs of children, families, communities, and child protection systems. There is nothing to be gained from the inappropriate use of mandatory reporting laws for cases which are not their primary object; an ambulance should not be used for a minor health complaint. It is important to avoid overburdening child protection systems wherever possible. Yet, equally, it is inappropriate to expect many cases of serious maltreatment inflicted by parents and caregivers and of sexual abuse inflicted by anyone on a child, to come to the attention of welfare agencies without the assistance of members of the community. Nor is it realistic to imagine that this need will not continue regardless of future necessary efforts in prevention and community building.

---

[15] Australian Bureau of Statistics, Patient Experiences in Australia: Summary of findings, 4,839.0, found that in the 12-month period 2012–2013 2.5 million visits to emergency departments were made by people aged 15 and over (71 % visited once, 23 % 2–3 times, 5.8 % 4 or more times): 13.6 % of the national population. Self-report data showed that only 49.6 % considered their condition serious or life-threatening, 25.5 % said they went simply because the time of day or week suited them, and 22.6 % admitted they could have been treated by a general practitioner. In Australia, over 12 million calls to the 000 emergency phone line are made per year; only around 44 % are genuine emergencies (M. Russel, 'Abuse of 000 calls risk to lives – police' 10 February 2008, Sun-Herald). Data are similar in the UK and USA. In the UK, 31 million calls are made annually, and half do not involve requests for help: British Telecom Press Release '999 celebrates its 75th birthday', 29 June 2012. In the USA, there are 240 million calls per year (National Emergency Number Association).

In noting the growing modern emphasis on prevention efforts, Mikton et al. (2013, p. 1238) observed that 'only a small proportion of victims of child maltreatment ever come to the attention of child protection services – e.g. 5–10 % in the West, 0.3 % in Hong Kong, and none in the many countries where such services do not exist'. The evidence of far superior case finding in jurisdictions which have introduced mandatory reporting indicates it is a powerful and life-changing tertiary response for many thousands of children every year and their families. Compared with approaches which do not include a form of mandatory reporting, it appears that jurisdictions with it are better at identifying case of severe maltreatment.

As but one part of a public health system for child maltreatment, the laws fulfil a necessary tertiary role in helping sentinel reporters outside the child's family bring cases to attention when they have already occurred. In some cases they also have a valuable secondary preventative role by identifying cases before the maltreatment occurs. More systematic secondary intervention is also an essential component of a balanced and coherent child protection system. It is known that certain characteristics at a child's birth are significant predictors of future child protective service contact (Putnam-Hornstein and Needell 2011) and that some factors strongly predict repeated reports after early encounters with the system (Proctor et al. 2012). As well as primary prevention at the population level, if societies are to take child abuse and neglect seriously, investment in both secondary and tertiary dimensions is required to promote the welfare of children and their families and the community.

References

Ainsworth, F., & Hansen, P. (2006). Five tumultuous years in Australian child protection: Little progress. *Child and Family Social Work, 11*, 33–41.

Al Eissa, M., & Almuneef, M. (2010). Child abuse and neglect in Saudi Arabia: Journey of recognition to implementation of national prevention strategies. *Child Abuse & Neglect, 34*(1), 28–33.

American Humane Association. (2008). Protecting children exploring differential response: One pathway toward reforming child welfare. 23(1&2).

Australian Institute of Health and Welfare. (2013). *Child protection Australia 2011–12*. Canberra: AIHW.

Bartholet, E. (2012). Creating a child-friendly child welfare system: Effective early intervention to prevent maltreatment and protect victimized children. *Buffalo Law Review, 60*, 1315–1365.

Bartholet, E., & Heimpel, D. (2013, December 24). Saving children from our child welfare system. *The Boston Globe*. http://www.bostonglobe.com/opinion/2013/12/24/saving-children-from-our-child-welfare-system/euxaDvobzhfhY7zpm1CYmO/story.html. Accessed 1 June 2014.

Besharov, D. (1985). "Doing something" about child abuse: The need to narrow the grounds for state intervention. *Harvard Journal of Law and Public Policy, 8*(3), 539.

Besharov, D. (1990). *Recognizing child abuse*. New York: Free Press.

Besharov, D. (2005). Overreporting and underreporting child abuse and neglect are twin problems. In D. Loseke, R. Gelles, & M. Cavanaugh (Eds.), *Current controversies on family violence* (p. 285). Thousand Oaks: Sage.

Birrell, R., & Birrell, J. (1966). The "Maltreatment Syndrome" in children. *Medical Journal of Australia, 2*, 1184.

Bross, D., & Mathews, B. (2014). The battered child syndrome: Changes in the law and child advocacy. In R. Krugman & J. Korbin (Eds.), *C. Henry Kempe: A 50 year legacy to the field of child abuse and neglect* (pp. 39–50). Dordrecht: Springer Scientific.
Children's Bureau. (2012). *Clergy as mandated reporters of child abuse and neglect*. Washington, DC: Child Welfare Information Gateway.
Conley, A., & Berrick, J. (2010). Community-based child abuse prevention: Outcomes associated with a differential response program in California. *Child Maltreatment, 15*, 282.
Cummins, P., Scott, D., & Scales, B. (2012). *Report of the protecting Victoria's vulnerable children inquiry*. Melbourne: State of Victoria Department of Premier and Cabinet.
Dalziel, K., & Segal, L. (2007). Analysis and interpretation of child protection data: A comment on Ainsworth and Hansen. *Child and Family Social Work, 12*, 434–435.
Daro, D. (Ed.). (2006). *World perspectives on child abuse* (7th ed.). Chicago: International Society for the Prevention of Child Abuse and Neglect.
Department for Children, Schools and Families and Department of Health. (2007). *Joint statement on the duties of doctors and other health professionals in investigations of child abuse*. http://www.everychildmatters.gov.uk/resources-and-practice/IG00251/. Accessed 1 July 2014.
Drake, B. (1996). Unraveling "unsubstantiated". *Child Maltreatment, 1*(3), 261–271.
Drake, B., & Jonson-Reid, M. (2007). A response to Melton based on the best available data. *Child Abuse & Neglect, 31*, 343–360.
Finkelhor, D. (1979). *Sexually victimized children*. New York: Free Press.
Finkelhor, D. (1990). Is child abuse overreported? *Public Welfare, 48*(1), 22.
Finkelhor, D. (2005). The main problem is underreporting child abuse and neglect. In D. Loseke, R. Gelles, & M. Cavanaugh (Eds.), *Current controversies on family violence* (p. 299). Thousand Oaks: Sage.
Finkelhor, D. (2008). *Childhood victimization*. Oxford: Oxford University Press.
Finkelhor, D., & Jones, L. (2006). Why have child maltreatment and child victimization declined? *Journal of Social Issues, 62*, 685–716.
Finkelhor, D., & Jones, L. (2012). *Have sexual abuse and physical abuse declined since the 1990s?* Durham: Crimes Against Children Research Center.
Fluke, J., Merkel-Holguin, L., & Schene, P. (2013). Thinking differentially: A response to issues in differential response. *Research on Social Work Practice, 23*(5), 545–549.
Fraser, B. (1986). A glance at the past, a gaze at the present, a glimpse at the future: A critical analysis of the development of child abuse reporting statutes. *Journal of Juvenile Law, 10*, 641–686.
Giarretto, H. (1977). Humanistic treatment of father-daughter incest. *Child Abuse and Neglect, 1*, 411–426.
Heimpel, D., & Bartholet, E. (2014, January 24). DCF shift puts children's safety at risk. *The Hartford Courant*. http://articles.courant.com/2014-01-24/news/hc-op-dheimpel-connecticut-dcf-children-safety-at--20140124_1_dcf-response-children. Accessed 1 June 2014.
Kalichman, S. (1999). *Mandated reporting of suspected child abuse: Ethics, law and policy*. Washington, DC: American Psychological Association.
Kempe, C. H. (1978). Sexual abuse, another hidden pediatric problem: The 1977 C. Anderson Aldrich lecture. *Pediatrics, 62*(3), 382–389.
Kempe, C. H., Silverman, F., Steele, B., Droegemueller, W., & Silver, H. (1962). The battered-child syndrome. *Journal of the American Medical Association, 181*, 17–24.
Kohl, P., Jonson-Reid, M., & Drake, B. (2009). Time to leave substantiation behind: Findings from a national probability study. *Child Maltreatment, 14*(1), 17.
Lamond, D. (1989). The impact of mandatory reporting legislation on reporting behavior. *Child Abuse & Neglect, 13*, 471.
Layton, R. (2003). *Our best investment: A state plan to protect and advance the interests of children* (Review of Child Protection in South Australia). Adelaide: Government of South Australia.
Mathews, B. (2012). Exploring the contested role of mandatory reporting laws in the identification of severe child abuse and neglect. In M. Freeman (Ed.), *Current legal issues. Volume 14: Law and childhood studies* (pp. 302–338). Oxford: Oxford University Press.

Mathews, B. (2014). *Mandatory reporting laws for child sexual abuse in Australia – A legislative history* (Report for the Royal Commission into Institutional Responses to Child Sexual Abuse). Sydney: Commonwealth of Australia.
Mathews, B., & Bross, D. (2008). Mandated reporting is still a policy with reason: Empirical evidence and philosophical grounds. *Child Abuse and Neglect, 32*, 511–516.
Mathews, B., & Bross, D. (2014). Using law to identify, manage and prevent child maltreatment. In J. Korbin & R. Krugman (Eds.), *Handbook of child maltreatment* (pp. 477–502). Dordrecht: Springer Scientific.
Mathews, B., & Kenny, M. (2008). Mandatory reporting legislation in the USA, Canada and Australia: A cross-jurisdictional review of key features, differences and issues. *Child Maltreatment, 13*(1), 50–63.
Mathews, B., Walsh, K., Rassafiani, M., Butler, D., & Farrell, A. (2009). Teachers reporting child sexual abuse: Results of a three-state study. *University of New South Wales Law Journal, 32*(3), 772–813.
Mathews, B., Walsh, K., Butler, D., & Farrell, A. (2010). *Teachers reporting child sexual abuse: Towards evidence-based reform of law, policy and practice* (Report for New South Wales, Queensland and Western Australia). Brisbane: Queensland University of Technology.
Melton, G. (2005). Mandated reporting: A policy without reason. *Child Abuse and Neglect, 29*, 9–18.
Mikton, C., Power, M., Raleva, M., Makoae, M., Al Eissa, M., Cheah, I., Cardia, N., Choo, C., & Almuneef, M. (2013). The assessment of the readiness of five countries to implement child maltreatment prevention programs on a large scale. *Child Abuse & Neglect, 37*, 1237–1251.
Nelson, B. (1984). *Making an issue of child abuse*. Chicago: University of Chicago Press.
Paulsen, M. (1967). Child abuse reporting laws: The shape of the legislation. *Columbia Law Review, 67*, 1–49.
Paulsen, M., Parker, G., & Adelman, L. (1966). Child abuse reporting laws-some legislative history. *George Washington Law Review, 34*, 482.
Proctor, L., Aarons, G., Dubowitz, H., English, D., Lewis, T., Thompson, R., Hussey, J., Litrownik, A., & Roesch, S. (2012). Trajectories of maltreatment re-reports from ages 4 to 12: Evidence for persistent risk after early exposure. *Child Maltreatment, 17*(3), 207–217.
Putnam-Hornstein, E., & Needell, B. (2011). Predictors of child protective service contact between birth and age five: An examination of California's 2002 birth cohort. *Children and Youth Services Review, 33*, 1337–1344.
Runyan, D. (2014). Foreword. In J. Korbin & R. Krugman (Eds.), *C. Henry Kempe: A 50 year legacy to the field of child abuse and neglect* (pp. v–vii). Dordrecht: Springer Scientific.
Shamley, D., Kingston, L., & Smith, M. (1984). Health professionals' knowledge of and attitudes towards child abuse reporting laws and case management, in Victoria. *Australian Child and Family Welfare, 9*(1), 3–8.
Summit, R., & Kryso, J. (1978). Sexual abuse of children: A clinical spectrum. *American Journal of Orthopsychiatry, 48*, 237–251.
United States Department of Health and Human Services, Administration on Children, Youth and Families. (2001). *Child maltreatment 1999*. Washington, DC: US Government Printing Office.
United States Department of Health and Human Services, Administration on Children, Youth and Families. (2006). *Child maltreatment 2004*. Washington, DC: US Government Printing Office.
United States Department of Health and Human Services, Administration on Children, Youth and Families. (2007). *Child maltreatment 2005*. Washington, DC: US Government Printing Office.
United States Department of Health and Human Services, Administration on Children, Youth and Families. (2014). *Child maltreatment 2012*. Washington, DC: US Government Printing Office.
Victorian Law Reform Commission. (1988). *Sexual offences against children* (Report No. 18). Melbourne: Victorian Law Reform Commission.
Wald, M. (2014a). Taking the wrong message: The legacy of the identification of the battered child syndrome. In J. Korbin & R. Krugman (Eds.), *C. Henry Kempe: A 50 year legacy to the field of child abuse and neglect* (pp. 89–101). Dordrecht: Springer Scientific.

Wald, M. (2014b). Beyond maltreatment: Developing support for children in multiproblem families. In J. Korbin & R. Krugman (Eds.), *Handbook of child maltreatment* (pp. 251–280). Dordrecht: Springer Scientific.

Webberley, H. (1985). Child maltreatment reporting laws: Impact on professionals' reporting behavior. *Australian Journal of Social Issues, 20*(2), 118–123.

Wood, J. (1997). *Royal commission into the NSW Police Service Final Report (Volumes 4 and 5: The Paedophile Inquiry).* Government of the State of New South Wales, Sydney. http://www.pic.nsw.gov.au/OtherReportsAndPublications.aspx

Wood, J. (2008). *Report of the special committee of inquiry into child protection services in New South Wales*. http://www.lawlink.nsw.gov.au/cpsinquiry

Wurfel, L., & Maxwell, G. (1965). The battered child syndrome in South Australia. *Australian Paediatric Journal, 1*, 127–130.

Zellman, G., & Fair, C. (2002). Preventing and reporting abuse. In J. Myers et al. (Eds.), *The APSAC handbook of child maltreatment* (pp. 449–475). Thousand Oaks: Sage.

Chapter 2
Who Is Maltreated and How Mandated Reporting Might Help

Desmond K. Runyan

While mandated reporting was generated as a key prevention strategy for child abuse or neglect nearly 50 years ago, it is not widely recognized that reporting does not represent a primary prevention approach. In order to report maltreatment, maltreatment must be thought to have occurred. Secondary prevention (intervening in an occurrence) and tertiary prevention (rehabilitation) are the direct benefits of reporting. Mandatory reporting should have a strong benefit if there is a high likelihood of recurrence among maltreated children; if it increases the sensitivity of the diagnosis of maltreatment, finding more children who are maltreated; and if it leads to the improvement in the safety or outcomes of children. Mandated reporting of child maltreatment depends upon the recognition of the maltreatment by designated professionals in all states and by all citizens in some states. While state-mandated reporting has a more than 40-year history in the United States, child maltreatment remains a serious public health problem. Because of the limitations in science, the impossibility of any clinical trials of mandatory reporting, and the constant evolution of intervention approaches, clearly establishing which children are better off for having been reported is virtually impossible. However, in contrast to available evidence from other countries, the United States has seen a remarkable reduction in child abuse over 20 years (Finkelhor et al. 2014).

The harms resulting from child abuse and neglect and our understanding of the risks and benefits of intervention have become clearer in the years since the 1993 National Research Council report *Understanding Child Abuse and Neglect* (National Research Council 1993). The harms of death and disability described in the 1962 Battered Child Syndrome article in JAMA (Kempe et al. 1962) were described through cross-sectional studies. Better data on the harms of maltreatment came from cross-sectional and retrospective studies including the Adverse Childhood

D.K. Runyan, M.D., Dr.P.H. (✉)
Department of Pediatrics, The University of Colorado School of Medicine, Aurora, CO, USA
e-mail: des.runyan@ucdenver.edu

B. Mathews, D.C. Bross (eds.), *Mandatory Reporting Laws and the Identification of Severe Child Abuse and Neglect*, Child Maltreatment 4,
DOI 10.1007/978-94-017-9685-9_2

Experience or ACE studies (Anda et al. 2006). Only relatively recently have risk and protection from the harms of maltreatment been examined in longitudinal studies, with clear attention to temporal relationships and the proportion of outcome variance explained by the different type, chronicity, and severity of maltreatment experiences (National Research Council 2013; English et al. 2005; Barth et al. 2002). Child maltreatment has been incorporated into current thinking about toxic stress with associated brain changes[1] and directly linked to increased risky behaviors for sexually transmitted diseases (Jones et al. 2010), depression, aggression, substance abuse, and poor parenting.

In the LONGSCAN longitudinal study of children maltreated early in life or considered to be at risk for maltreatment, the majority of *reported* maltreatment occurred in early childhood (Proctor et al. 2012). This observation contrasts with parent self-reports of abusive or disciplinary behavior; children in the 5–9-year-old age group are more likely to actually experience physically abusive behaviors from their parents, whereas older children are more likely to be sexually abused (Theodore et al. 2005). Several studies have documented biases in child maltreatment reporting that appears to be associated with race and income (Laskey et al. 2012; Hampton and Newberger 1985) although child abuse and neglect are not classless or immune to income issues (Pelton 1978). Another important set of biases relate to the severity of child maltreatment reported by type of maltreatment. In the LONGSCAN studies, a set of severity criteria were applied that ranged from no visible injury to life-threatening injury or permanent disability for each form of maltreatment. Over 50 % of all maltreatment reports, except in the situation of sexual abuse, were classified as being characterized by the lowest forms of severity although 47 % of sexual abuse was classified as high severity as the definition of high severity included penetration (Litrownik et al. 2005).

Other systematic errors occur in the classification of type of maltreatment. Psychological or emotional maltreatment is rarely the official determination but is actually quite frequent. When child maltreatment allegations among children involved in the LONGSCAN study were reviewed and coded for type, severity, and chronicity of maltreatment by trained reviewers using specified research criteria for type of maltreatment, there is almost a tenfold increase in numbers of children who were classified as victims of psychological maltreatment from about 4 % of allegations to nearly 40 % of allegations (Runyan et al. 2005). Even the process of substantiation is an issue. Children with unsubstantiated allegations have outcomes that look more like the children with substantiated reports of child abuse than children who have not been reported (Husey et al. 2005). Unsubstantiation is clearly much more complicated than just that maltreatment did not occur.

In the past it may have been possible to dismiss societal intervention as there has been little evidence for effectiveness. However, intervention in child maltreatment has become more nuanced, and there have been major strides in evidence for effective mental health intervention. We have learned a great deal about foster care and other interventions. Rates of foster care placement are falling (Child Trends

[1] Glaser D. Child abuse and neglect and the brain - a review. Journal of Child Psychology and Psychiatry 2000 41:97–116.

Databank 2014), the use of congregate care is declining (The Annie E. Casey Foundation), and changes in policy include adoption of multiple or differential response (Kyte et al. 2013) and family-group decision making (National Center on Family Group Decision Making) by social service agencies. Evidence-based treatments are being adopted to address the traumas that the children have experienced (Aarons et al. 2011) and to maximize the quality of interventions such as *Fostering Health Futures* (Taussig et al. 2012) for children in foster care.

National data indicate a remarkable, and largely unrecognized, fall in rates of physical abuse and neglect in the United States since 1993 (Finkelhor et al. 2013). This decline parallels other changes including falls in the homicide and divorce rates (US Department of Justice, Bureau of Statistics 2011). The declines in child maltreatment rates appear to lag behind the remarkable 63 % decline in intimate partner violence against women in the United States (Catalano 2012). Longitudinal data on the occurrence of child abuse in households with domestic violence suggest that households with domestic violence have a 44 % increased chance of a child abuse report occurring in the household in the next year (English et al. 2009). It is possible, even likely, that a sizable portion of the decline in child maltreatment since 1993 is attributable to the decline in domestic violence. Research indicates children in domestic violence-filled households may not only be other victims of the perpetrator of the domestic violence. Women victims of maltreatment are also more likely to perpetrate maltreatment (Casanueva et al. 2009). When fewer men and women are either perpetrators or victims of intimate partner violence, a decline in violence against children is also likely.

Surveys of parents reveal that self-reports of abuse and neglect behaviors are likely 20–40 times more common than official substantiated reports. One specific form of maltreatment, shaking of children under the age of 2 to "discipline" or teach the child, may be 150 times more common than diagnosed *shaken baby syndrome* (Theodore et al. 2005). In North Carolina, the rate of harsh or abusive punishment (beating, choking, kicking, or hitting with an object someplace other than the buttocks) self-reported by parents was 4.3 % compared to an official rate of just 0.2 %. The parent-reported rate is likely to also be an underestimate. Parental knowledge that a child has been sexually victimized by an adult (1 %) can be contrasted to an official rate of reported sexual abuse in North Carolina; parents reported 15 times more sexual abuse than official statistics recorded (Theodore et al. 2005). Population surveys demonstrate widespread awareness and concern of the problems of child sexual abuse and physical abuse in society.

Studies of child maltreatment that ask the children directly about their experiences also demonstrate the limitations of official child maltreatment data. In the LONGSCAN study, children were asked directly about their maltreatment experiences at age 12. Children being followed actively by child protective services had their records reviewed for allegations at frequent intervals, and they were interviewed with a computer-based self-interview that enhanced privacy and gave the children the opportunity to reveal other maltreatment experiences (Knight et al. 2000). The number of children who self-reported physical abuse, sexual abuse, or neglect on the computer was more than double the number of children known to social services for each form of maltreatment (Runyan et al. 2005). For example, at age 12, just 3.2 %

of the children had substantiated reports of child sexual abuse, but an additional 14.2 % of the children self-reported child sexual abuse. At age 18, 38 % of the LONGSCAN cohort self-reported psychological or emotional maltreatment during their lifetimes. Investigations of the consequences of child maltreatment that rely on only official reports would have missed most of the exposures to either sexual abuse or psychological abuse, and the conclusions drawn from a study that relied on official reports would have significantly misrepresented the consequences.

Despite the limitations of mandatory reporting in bias and under-ascertainment, the ability of society to help children is enhanced by finding more of the children who have experienced child maltreatment and providing services. Greater sensitivity in screening or case finding means engaging more children in intervention. The trend lines for reduction of child maltreatment in the United States, and international data on harsh child discipline that suggest a larger problem in low- and middle-income countries without organized child protection systems, argue for mandated reporting as a part of the larger strategy to protect children and enhance child well-being.

References

Aarons, G., Hurlburt, M., & Horwitz, S. M. (2011). Advancing a conceptual model of evidence-based practice in public service sectors. *Administration and Policy in Mental Health, 38*, 4–23.

Anda, R. F., Felitti, V. J., Bremner, J. D., Walker, J. D., Whitfield, C., Perry, B. D., Dube, S. R., & Giles, W. H. (2006). The enduring effects of abuse and related adverse experiences in childhood. *European Archives of Psychiatry and Clinical Neuroscience, 4*, 174–186.

Barth, R. P., Biemer, P., Runyan, D. K., Webb, M. B., Berrick, J. D., Dowd, K., Griffith, J., Kinsey, S., Newman, J., Siebenaler, K., Weeks, M., Byron, M., Cano, G., Green, R., Herget, D., Langer, M., Liu, J., Lunghofer, L., Lytle, T., McCracken, R., Mierzwa, F., Shende, A., Suresh, R., Wall, A., & Wallace, I. (2002 June–July). Methodological lessons from the National Survey of Child and Adolescent Well-Being: The first three years of the USA's first national probability study of children and families investigated for abuse and neglect. *Children and Youth Services Review, 24*(6–7), 513–541.

Casanueva, C., Martin, S., & Runyan, D. K. (2009). Repeated referrals for child maltreatment among intimate partner violence victims: Findings from the National Survey of Child and Adolescent Well-Being. *Child Abuse & Neglect, 33*, 84–93.

Catalano, S. (2012). *Intimate partner violence 1992–2010*. Bureau of Justice Statistics 2012. http://www.bjs.gov/index.cfm?ty=pbdetail&iid=4934

Child Trends Databank. (2014). *Foster care*. Available at: http://www.childtrends.org/?indicators=foster-care. See more at: http://www.childtrends.org/?indicators=foster-care#sthash.IuXCfuk7.dpuf

English, D. J., Upadhyaya, M. P., Litrownik, A. J., Marshall, J. M., Runyan, D. K., Graham, J. C., & Dubowitz, H. (2005). Maltreatment's wake: The relationship of maltreatment dimensions to child outcomes. *Child Abuse & Neglect, 29*, 597–619.

English, D. J., Graham, J. C., Newton, R. R., Lewis, T. L., Thompson, R., Kotch, J. B., & Weisbart, C. (2009). At-risk and maltreated children exposed to intimate partner aggression/violence: What the conflict looks like and its relationship to child outcomes. *Child Maltreatment, 14*(2), 157–171.

Finkelhor, D., Jones, L., & Shattuck, A. (2013). *Updated trends in child maltreatment, 2011, crimes against children research center*. Durham: University of New Hampshire.

Finkelhor, D., Shattuck, A., Turner, H. A., & Hamby, S. L. (2014). Trends in children's exposure to violence, 2003–2011. *JAMA Pediatrics, 168*(6), 540–546. doi:10.1001/jamapediatrics.2013.5296.

Glaser, D. (2000). Child abuse and neglect and the brain – A review. *Journal of Child Psychology and Psychiatry, 41*, 97–116.

Hampton, R. L., & Newberger, E. H. (1985 January). Child abuse incidence and reporting by hospitals: Significance of severity, class, and race. *American Journal of Public Health, 75*(1), 56–60. doi:10.2105/AJPH.75.1.56.

Hussey, J. M., Marshall, J. M., English, D. J., Knight, E. D., Lau, A. S., Dubowitz, H., & Kotch, J. B. (2005). Defining maltreatment according to substantiation: Distinction without a difference? *Child Abuse & Neglect, 29*, 479–492.

Jones, D. J., Runyan, D. K., Lewis, T., Litrownik, A., Black, M., Wiley, T., English, D., Proctor, L., Jones, B. L., & Nagin, D. (2010). Violence exposure trajectories among high risk youth and their association with two subsequent HIV/AIDS risk behaviors. *Journal of Clinical Child and Adolescent Psychology, 39*, 667–680.

Kempe, C. H., Silverman, F. N., Steele, B. F., Droegemueller, W., & Silver, H. K. (1962). The battered-child syndrome. *The Journal of the American Medical Association, 181*(1), 17–24. doi:10.1001/jama.1962.03050270019004.

Knight, E. D., Runyan, D. K., Dubowitz, H., Brendford, C., Kotch, J., Litrownik, A., & Hunter, W. (2000). Methodological and ethical challenges associated with child self-report of maltreatment: solutions implemented by the LONGSCAN consortium. *Journal of Interpersonal Violence, 15*(7), 760–775.

Kyte, A., Trocmé, N., & Chamberland, C. (2013). Evaluating where we're at with differential response. *Child Abuse & Neglect, 37*, 125–132.

Laskey, A. L., Stump, T. E., Perkins, S. M., Zimet, G. D., Sherman, S. J., & Downs, S. M. (2012). Influence of race and socioeconomic status on the diagnosis of child abuse: A randomized study. *Journal of Pediatrics, 160*(6), 1003–1008.e1.

Litrownik, A. J., Lau, A., English, D. J., Briggs, E., Newton, R. R., Romney, S., & Dubowitz, H. (2005). Measuring the severity of child maltreatment. *Child Abuse & Neglect, 29*, 553–573.

National Center on Family Group Decision Making, Kempe Center, University of Colorado. http://www.ucdenver.edu/academics/colleges/medicalschool/departments/pediatrics/subs/can/FGDM/Pages/FGDM.aspx. April 4, 2012

National Research Council (NRC), & Commission on Behavioral and Social Sciences and Education, Panel on Research on Child Abuse and Neglect, Washington, DC. (1993). *Understanding child abuse and neglect*. Washington, DC: National Academy Press.

National Research Council: Institute of Medicine. (2013 September). *New directions in child abuse and neglect research*. Washington, DC: National Research Council.

Pelton, L. H. (1978 October). Child abuse and neglect: The myth of classlessness. *American Journal of Orthopsychiatry, 48*(4), 608–617.

Proctor, L. J., Aarons, G. A., Dubowitz, H., English, D. J., Hussey, J. M., Lewis, T. L., Thompson, R., Weisbart, C., Litrownik, A. J., & Roesch, S. (2012). Trajectories of maltreatment re-reports from ages 4 to 12: Evidence for persistent risk after early exposure. *Child Maltreatment, 17*(3), 207–217.

Runyan, D. K., Cox, C. E., Dubowitz, H., Newton, R. R., Upadhyaya, M., Kotch, J. B., Leeb, R., Everson, M. D., & Knight, E. (2005). Describing maltreatment: Do child protective service reports and research definitions agree? *Child Abuse & Neglect, 29*, 461–477.

Taussig, H. N., Culhane, S. E., Garrido, E., & Knudtson, M. D. (2012 July). RCT of a mentoring and skills group program: Placement and permanency outcomes for foster youth. *Pediatrics, 130*(1), e33–e39.

Theodore, A., Chang, J. J., Runyan, D. K., Hunter, W. M., Bangdiwala, S. I., & Agans, R. (2005). The epidemiology of the physical and sexual maltreatment of children in the Carolinas. *Pediatrics, 115*(3), e331–e337.

The Annie E. Casey Foundation. *Reducing congregate care: Worth the fight*. http://www.aecf.org/blog/reducing-congregate-care-worth-the-fight/. April 4, 2012

US Department of Justice, Bureau of Justice Statistics. (2011). *Homicide trends in the United States 1980–2008*. http://www.bjs.gov/content/pub/pdf/htus8008.pdf

Chapter 3
Competing Values and Evidence: How Do We Evaluate Mandated Reporting and CPS Response?

Brett Drake and Melissa Jonson-Reid

The purpose of this chapter is twofold. We will first explore the underlying rationales for reporting and CPS response. We will then move forward to examine the evidence around both mandated reporting and CPS responses and services. We conclude with suggestions for policy and future research to provide a conceptual framework for understanding the issue of mandated reporting and to provide information relevant to understanding its appropriateness and utility relative to the broader child protective services system.

Why Have a Child Protection System?

The legal concepts underlying parental and child rights have undergone numerous transitions in the last two centuries and remain in a state of some contention. Parents have been variously seen as having a divine right to raise their children as they see fit, natural rights based on heredity, property rights over their children, and a societal responsibility to parent their child well, which implies to many the right to parent as they best see fit (Woodhouse 1992). The state is seen as having a right and a responsibility to intervene in supporting the child's best interests under the doctrine of parens patriae, in which the state via the courts has a jurisdiction over the children which is even broader than parental power (Hart 2011). There is a general agreement that the innately powerless nature of childhood, best exemplified by the utter helplessness of the newborn, places children in a similar category to several other groups (e.g., severely cognitively incapacitated individuals) who are dependent on others to protect their rights.

B. Drake, Ph.D. (✉) • M. Jonson-Reid, Ph.D.
Brown School of Social Work, Washington University in St. Louis, St. Louis, MO, USA
e-mail: brettd@wustl.edu; jonsonrd@wustl.edu

B. Mathews, D.C. Bross (eds.), *Mandatory Reporting Laws and the Identification of Severe Child Abuse and Neglect*, Child Maltreatment 4,
DOI 10.1007/978-94-017-9685-9_3

We have therefore moved from a conceptualization of children as property wholly under parental authority to beings with autonomous and innate rights. These rights can be very specifically enumerated in principle (e.g., the Convention on the Rights of the Child (OHCHR 2015)) or can be operationally established in law (e.g., DHHS 2011). There can no longer be debate that the child's autonomous rights, independent of the parent, are, at least in theory, generally recognized in developed western nations.

Missions, Statements, and Visions

While child protection laws and policies can vary radically from nation to nation and even state to state (e.g., Australia, the United States), the core general principles *underlying* child maltreatment policy and legislation are remarkable in that they tend to be quite consistent across nations and states.

Child Safety Is Framed as the Single Paramount Goal of Child Protective Systems

Supporting the child's right to safety is unambiguously the paramount concern underlying virtually all international, national, and state child welfare legislation and policy. Clear examples abound, one representative example being: "The overriding principle of the Act is that the safety, welfare and wellbeing of children or young people must be paramount" (Australasian Legal Information Institute 2014). One could easily modify the opening line of this paragraph in substituting the phrase "safety and well-being" for "safety" as a large number of documents do refer to child well-being as a paramount goal.

The Paramount **Goal** *of Protecting the Child Is Best Pursued Through the* **Means** *of Working with the Family When Possible*

There is also apparently a universal concordance around the value that if it can be done safely, a child should be maintained in his or her family setting, and the family should assist in making the child's environment safe and supportive of well-being. Perhaps the most concise statement of this can be found guiding child welfare policy in the United States. The Child Abuse Prevention and Treatment Act (CAPTA) states, "The child protection system should be comprehensive, child centered, family-focused, and community-based" (DHHS 2011). The Convention on the Rights of the Child places a typical emphasis on the centrality of families, being "Convinced that the family, as the fundamental group of society and the natural environment for the growth and well-being of all its members and particularly children, should be afforded the necessary protection and assistance so that it can fully assume its responsibilities within the community" (OHCHR 2015). Here, we see shadows cast by long-standing ideas – both that the family has a standing to care for the child as they see fit rooted in natural or civil (DHHS 2011) law and that families have rights to make decisions about their children so that they can exercise their responsibility to society to produce the best possible next generation of citizens (Woodhouse 1992). Parental prerogative therefore must not be abridged frivolously, as this may both violate parental rights per se and may damage parents' ability to discharge their obligation to society to contribute to a functional next generation.

Child Maltreatment Occurs in a Community Context

The word "community" is commonly present in legislation and guidance around child protection (OHCHR 2015; DHHS 2011). There is recognition that the community is the context in which families live, and abuse and neglect occur; that the community has a key role in identifying maltreatment; and that the community is where many preventative, supportive, or ameliorative programs exist and is both a venue and a means for furthering CPS work. For example, "The mission of The Texas Department of Family and Protective Services is to protect children, the elderly, and people with disabilities from abuse, neglect, and exploitation by involving clients, families, and communities" (Texas DFPS 2013). While "community" is commonly mentioned, it is an unavoidably nebulous term and one which tends to defy ascription of responsibility. For these reasons, policy language around community context and involvement appears frequently to be less actionable and well operationalized than other policy elements.

Responding to Maltreatment Is a Universal Responsibility

This is generally recognized. "All elements of American society have a shared responsibility in responding to child abuse and neglect" (DHHS 2011, p. 6). This recognition occurs even in jurisdictions lacking mandated reporting – "There are no mandatory reporting laws in England, but guidance issued by professional bodies and Local Safeguarding Children Boards emphasize the duty to make a referral where there is a reasonable belief that a child is at risk of significant harm" (NSPCC 2015).

Prevention Is Desirable

The word "prevention" is used, by our count, 54 times in CAPTA, including, obviously, in the title. "Prevention is the best hope for reducing child abuse and neglect and improving the lives of children and families" (DHHS 2011). Prevention is implicit in the Convention on the Rights of the Child, in which children are to be free from negative situations rather than having a right to "escape from" or "be treated for" such problems. Such language championing prevention is present in all legislation we have reviewed. Some locales are suggesting a fundamental realignment from what might be termed an "ambulance-like" service to a more general "public health-like" program: "Australia needs to move from seeing 'protecting children' merely as a response to abuse and neglect to one of promoting the safety and wellbeing of children. Leading researchers and practitioners – both in Australia and overseas – have suggested that applying a public health model to care and protection will deliver better outcomes for our children and young people and their families" (Council of Australian Governments 2009).

We are left, therefore, with a situation in which international, national, and local visions share much clear commonality at a general level. Child protection's goals of safety, or perhaps "safety and well-being" as paramount, the preferred context of this being first the family and then community, the universality of responsibility, and the desirability of prevention, form a common vista.

Child Protective Services

In most countries, public child protective services agencies are tasked with identifying and serving children who need protection in accordance with the above policies. Child protective services vary markedly from place to place, but a series of core concepts do apply consistently across systems. It should be noted that relatively little attention has been paid to the following underlying concepts, and we hope to provide some clarification before moving forward.

Harm

Harm is a key concept in child maltreatment legislation and policy. It is not clear, however, that attention has been paid to thinking through what we mean by "harm" and whether CPS should be charged with providing services to protect from all forms of harm or more as an emergency response when there is a clear and critical safety issue. The most obvious exemplars of harm related to safety and threat of physical injury might include physical abuse or sexual abuse. These acute forms of maltreatment were the first popularly recognized (e.g., Kempe et al. 1962; Kempe 1978). By 1984, researchers were calling more attention to child neglect (Wolock and Horwitz 1984). Recent research indicates that similar levels of immediate harm can result from child neglect (Gilbert et al. 2009a, b). The need for a CPS role in regard to immediate safety or injury seems more generally accepted.

Harm, however, can also be understood in terms of denial of what is needed to establish healthy development or well-being (Davies et al. 2009; Noh and Talaat

2012). There are a number of ingredients that can be thought of as essential to healthy development, the absence of which potentially harms a child: (1) adequate food, shelter, and hygiene; (2) cognitive stimulation (particularly in the early years); (3) affection and nurturing; (4) supervision to help avoid hazards; (5) adequate health care; and (6) access to recreation for physical fitness and socialization with peers. The United Nations Convention on the Rights of the Child includes an even broader and more detailed set of needs. In terms of neglect and emotional harm, the idea of persistence is involved (Glaser 2011), meaning a single incident is unlikely to result in harm, but repetition or a pattern of incidents may have a cumulative impact. Various studies indicate that longer-term harm is equally likely from neglectful situations as it is from physical or sexual abuse (Gilbert et al. 2009a, b). It is unclear if this is the result of accumulated exposures to risk (Jonson-Reid et al. 2012). Harm can also be related to more indirect exposure such as domestic violence (Edleson 2004) or lack of adequate supervision of eating habits leading to obesity (Viner et al. 2010). There is much less consensus across states and countries about what constitutes the need for child protection when we expand the word harm to include the idea of future well-being.

Prevention

We have seen above how CPS is generally tasked with the prevention of harm. As we move toward a set of policies explicitly valuing well-being, it becomes important to not only prevent injury but to also prevent those circumstances which will interfere with healthy development. It is not clear that policy makers have taken this into account in designing child protective systems and preventative programs. We would therefore suggest that prevention can be thought of as an effort to reduce acute harm or an effort to interrupt ongoing circumstances likely to reduce well-being. Thankfully, a relatively small proportion of maltreatment reports involve serious immediate harm; many involve threats to well-being. Indeed, across most outcomes, relatively little difference is found in long-term outcomes according to system determination of harm in the United States (Drake et al. 2003; Jonson-Reid et al. 2009; Hussey et al. 2005; Kohl et al. 2009). Even when differences are found (e.g., Chiu et al. 2011), the relative number of unsubstantiated cases compared to substantiated cases makes this an important group. In the United States, among the three million unique children with screened-in reports in 2011, only about one in five (681,000) was "substantiated," "indicated," or classed as "alternative response victims" (U.S. Department of Health and Human Services, Administration for Children and Families, Administration on Children, Youth and Families, Children's Bureau 2012). These 681,000 children were proportionately more likely to receive post-response services, but due to their greater numbers, far more unsubstantiated children actually received such services. It seems clear that risk of harm, if one uses well-being as the metric, appears to apply to the majority of reported cases. The question becomes whether or not CPS is or should be tasked with providing more preventative services to this very large portion of cases. If protection from "harm" encompasses these broader long-term threats to development, this implies a response that will mitigate that harm.

How Do We Find Children Who Need Help?

If we move on with the assumption that children have a right to protection and we come to some form of consensus on what harm means, at least locally, then logically we need a response. This response would, at a minimum, assume there was a means of finding children who need help. We have already seen that virtually every society officially proclaims as a matter of policy that this is a priority. The method of identifying children who need help, however, differs.

There are essentially four potential means of identifying children who are experiencing some form of maltreatment, the first of which would be to avoid any mandatory reporting and formal state child welfare response (Melton 2005). While no rigorous test of such a model could be found in the literature, there is a trial of such a program in New Zealand (reported in Davies et al. 2009). Such a model requires the community to be knowledgeable enough to determine when a child needed protection and to be receptive to interacting with troubled families. Beyond this, there must be adequate resources and commitment to making these interactions effective. While the idea of a fully informal network has been identified among kin (Korbin 1994), there is some indication that this is not an insubstantial hurdle when it comes to identifying and caring for nonrelated children (Gaudin and Polansky 1986; Korbin 1994). Interestingly, in the section on detecting and reporting maltreatment in the World Health Organization's Guide to Child Abuse Prevention (Butchart and Harvey 2006), we find the following statement (p. 71): "The usefulness of mandatory reporting is particularly questionable in situations where there is no functioning legal or child protection system to act on a report. At the same time, there is extensive evidence that the public as well as professionals are reluctant to act on knowledge or suspicions of maltreatment." This would suggest that perhaps the early work on willingness to care for nonrelative children at risk is not without parallel in the international community.

In the current policy reality, there are three primary versions of reporting of abuse or neglect. In the first version, nobody is legislatively mandated to report (e.g., the United Kingdom). Typically, this involves a permissive or voluntary reporting system coupled with a state child protective services agency designed to respond to cases (Wallace and Bunting 2007). Permissive reporting relies on the adequate judgment of the reporter to know what and when to report. It also presumes that we are satisfied that enough of the children who need protection will become known to a permissive reporter. Such a system might, in theory, reduce the burden of having more reports than a system can handle. On the other hand, one might run a higher risk of missing children in need (Wallace and Bunting 2007). In the second version, some people, usually professionals whose work frequently brings them into contact with children, are mandated to report. This appears to be the most common form of mandatory reporting. In the third version, all people are required to report (e.g., Texas, Florida, and the Northern Territory in Australia). It is not clear how well this is operationalized for nonprofessionals. Other hybrid structures can be imagined and do exist in some places. For example, West Virginia would fit into the second version described above, except in the case of sexual abuse where all people are required to report.

While criticisms of mandated reporting abound, most of these are anchored in concerns that there is too much emphasis on investigation which seriously diminishes resources that could be provided for services (Melton 2005). As mentioned above, either having no formal policy or having only voluntary reporting could reduce the number of cases identified. It is not clear, however, whether voluntary or permissive systems might differentially place children unable or unlikely to disclose at greater risk, for example, infants or children with disabilities or victims of sexual abuse. Good empirical evidence, that a voluntary compared to mandatory system of detection is better or worse, is not yet available. So what do we know about mandated reporting? We will explore this partly by forwarding and replying to what we believe to be some popular misconceptions.

Myth: We have solved the problem of identifying maltreated children.
Reality: Most maltreatment still goes unreported.

One of the more difficult phenomena to accurately measure is the rate of actual maltreatment as compared to reported maltreatment. Some kinds of maltreatment, for example, physical abuse of preverbal children which leaves no visible injury, are impossible to identify absent self-reporting by the perpetrator. Many key child maltreatment studies (e.g., the National Survey of Child and Adolescent Well-Being (NSCAW)) do not even attempt to study maltreated children outside of the formal child welfare system. The largest studies to attempt to measure rates of actual maltreatment, as opposed to reported maltreatment, are the four waves of the National Incidence Studies in the United States (Sedlak et al. 2010). NIS-4 estimates that more than half of all maltreatment cases go unreported to CPS. There are several studies indicating that maltreatment is underreported by health-care professionals (Ben Natan et al. 2012; Flaherty et al. 2008; Markenson et al. 2007; Merrick et al. 2010). Studies of reporting in other countries have found similar problems among educators (Choo et al. 2013; Feng et al. 2010; Schols et al. 2013). It is difficult to know how this varies by type of maltreatment or victim profiles, at least in part due to deficits in current research. For example, a recent meta-analysis approach to estimating prevalence of sexual abuse found a dramatic difference between informant studies and self-report. This study suggests that underreporting was part of the reason for this difference (Stoltenborgh et al. 2011), but the same analysis could not be completed for neglect due to insufficient numbers of informant studies (Stoltenborgh et al. 2013). There is some indication that cultural beliefs may play a role in reporting in international studies (Ben Natan et al. 2012; Choo et al. 2013; Feng et al. 2010), but the magnitude of this impact in the United States appears to vary by type of reporter, region, and method of study (Ashton 2010; Ibanez et al. 2006; Krase 2013). Finally, there is some evidence to indicate that children with disabilities are underreported (Stalker and McArthur 2012). It is clear, however, that while some have asserted that "... whatever else one can say about child protection policy in the United States, it is clear that the primary problem is no longer case finding!" (Melton 2005, p. 10), this assertion is not supported by the evidence.

Myth: Mandated reporting laws cause large increases in report rates.
Reality: Evidence suggests reporting laws are not the main driver of report rates.

The United States offers a natural laboratory for understanding the degree to which mandated reporting laws cause increases in reports. One way to understand this phenomenon is to look at reports over time. The vast increases in reporting from the "discovery" of child abuse by Kempe until now happened well after mandated reporting laws were put into place. All states had mandated reporting by 1967 (AHA 1979), but the bulk of reporting increase happened more than 10 years after this. For example, between 1977 and 2003, reports per 10,000 children quadrupled (Drake and Jonson-Reid 2007; AHA 1979; U.S. Department of Health and Human Services, Administration on Children, Youth and Families 2005). Since 2003, the rate of child abuse reporting in the United States has only increased slightly moving from an estimated 2.9 million referrals in 2003 to 3.4 million estimated referrals in 2011 (U.S. Department of Health and Human Services, Administration on Children, Youth and Families 2005, 2012; CWIG 2012).

While reports from professional reporters increased faster than reports from non-professionals (4.88 times vs. 3.25 times), this could well be due to the proliferation of helping professionals (Finkelhor and Jones 2006) during this timeframe, rather than increased observance of mandated reporting laws which had already been on the books for a decade. Even if reports from professionals had escalated only at the (3.25 times) rate of nonprofessionals, total reports would only have been reduced by 19 % (Drake and Jonson-Reid 2007).

Another way to understand this problem is to look at the official report rates from those states in which everyone is a mandated reporter and compare them to the remaining states in which only designated professionals are mandated. Among the 18 states with universal mandated reporting, we found that the average report rate is 54.0 per 1,000, while the report rate for the remaining states is 52.8 per 1,000 – virtually identical numbers. These figures were calculated by averaging the report rates (U.S. Department of Health and Human Services, Administration for Children and Families, Administration on Children, Youth and Families, Children's Bureau 2012) from each of the 18 states with universal mandated reporting (CWIG 2012) and comparing them to the remaining states and the District of Columbia, while excluding West Virginia, which has universal mandated reporting for sexual abuse but only mandated reporting for professionals for other types. It should be remembered that in the United States as a whole with universal mandated reporting by professionals, almost half of all reports (42.4 %) were submitted by nonprofessional reporters.

The evidence presented by the historical data seems clear. The massive escalations in reporting happened more than a decade after mandated reporting laws were established, and expanding mandated reporting universally is not associated with any notable differences in reporting.

Another way we can look at these historical data is to understand how types of substantiated maltreatment have changed over time (data not being generally available for types of unsubstantiated reports). There are undoubtedly a number of factors which could influence changes, including different rates of actual maltreatment, different reporting tendencies, and different state policies regarding what kinds of reports are accepted. In comparing 1977 (AHA 1979, Figure 10) and 2011 data (U.S. Department of Health and Human Services, Administration for Children and Families, Administration on Children, Youth and Families, Children's Bureau 2012, Table 3.8), we can see that there were more multiple findings in 1977, with a total of 1.54 types of maltreatment recorded per case, compared to only 1.27 types of maltreatment reported per case in 2012. This is undoubtedly partly due to the fact that more subtypes of maltreatment were reported in 1977, with, for example, seven different types of physical abuse being broken out, as compared to simply "physical abuse" in the 2011 data.

Several types of maltreatment remained relatively stable across the years in terms of their proportion among substantiated reports. For example, physical abuse in 1977 was 23.7 % of substantiated reports and in 2011 it was 17.6 %. Neglect was present in 82.2 % of cases in 1977 and 78.5 % in 2011. Other/unknown cases stated stable at around 10 % (9.7 % in 1977, 10.6 % in 2011). The one type which rose dramatically was sexual abuse, being 5.8 % of substantiated reports in 1977 and 9.1 % of substantiated reports in 2011. Two kinds of maltreatment dropped, "emotional neglect" comprised 24 % of substantiated reports in 1977, but "psychological maltreatment" comprised only 9 % of all reports in 2011. It is unclear how similar these categories might actually be. Medical neglect also dropped from 9 % of all cases in 1977 to 2.2 % of all cases in 2011.

Interpretation of the above data requires awareness of several factors, such as the fact that neither timeframe includes 100 % of the states nor that the total number of reports has roughly quadrupled over time. However, it is interesting to note that the proportion of sexual abuse reports is now higher than in the past and that psychological maltreatment may be lower. This latter point is probably due to more restrictive agency guidelines regarding screening in or substantiating psychological maltreatment. No matter how these data are viewed, they do not seem to indicate a proliferation of lower risk or meaningless cases.

Myth: Child Protection is overwhelmed by investigative responsibilities.
Reality: Investigations are proportionately a very small burden on the system.

Based on available data, the evidence suggests that the cost of investigations to child protective service agencies is small, most likely below 10 % of total costs and possibly below 5 %. The most recent estimate of the total cost of child protective services in the United States dates from 2006 (DeVooght et al. 2008) and is 25.7 billion dollars per year. Adjusted for inflation, this would be 29.8 billion as of 2013. The Cost of Protecting Vulnerable Children IV (Scarcella et al. 2004) found that about half of the total child protection expenditures were for foster care and residential services. Investigative costs were so small as to not even comprise their own category, being included together with, among other things, "all prevention services, child protective services, family preservation services, reunification services, and in-home support services" (p. 5). These expenses together accounted for 14 % of all expenditures.

There have been several recent comprehensive workload studies done on caseload-carrying child protective service workers across the nation. In Washington (Washington State Department of Social and Health Services 2007), 18 % of caseworker effort was characterized as being spent on investigations and associated work (e.g., paperwork, travel), whereas the corresponding number in New York was 19 %. These numbers pertain to workers with caseloads only and exclude administration, management, support, research, and other staff. This 20 % figure therefore reflects time spent by only a portion of the workforce, and workforce costs are only a portion of the total child protective service expenses, with out-of-home care payments, and contracted services absorbing a higher level of resources. Even though about 20 % of state worker time is spent on investigations, the actual proportion of state child protective resources spent on investigations is clearly far lower.

We can use the data in these studies to approach this question from another perspective. For example, the New York workload study estimated that the average investigative case took about 5.2 h and that a reasonable monthly number of cases served per worker might be about 24, yielding an annual caseload of 288 cases. Given that there are about 2,000,000 cases investigated annually (DHHS 2011), this would imply a need for about 7,000 full-time employee equivalent investigative workers nationally. This number is useful to consider, even though investigative work is often parsed out as a "part-time" job for workers who have other responsibilities, especially in rural areas. A quick perusal of online employment and salary information websites suggests reimbursement commonly in the mid-$30,000 range for child protective workers, and, after adding fringe benefits to establish a cost-to-agency figure, we can confidently say that the average child protective services investigator costs the state something in the area of $50,000 per year. This implies a total salary cost associated directly with child abuse investigations of something like $350,000,000 dollars annually for the United States as a whole. Compared to the estimated total cost of child protective services nationally, we see that investigative worker salaries probably comprise slightly more than one percent of total expenditures. We must, of course, add costs of training and supporting services, such as supervision, but even then, this means of estimating the total percentage of resources spent on child abuse investigators can only yield an estimate in the single digits, probably the low single digits. These calculations are also confirmatory of the Urban Institute estimates. The conventional wisdom that child welfare agencies are being catastrophically drained of resources by overwhelming investigative responsibilities is a persistent one. In reality, the burden of investigations on the total child welfare system is probably proportionately less than the sales tax you pay on a cup of coffee at Starbucks.

Myth: Substantiated cases are "real" cases, and unsubstantiated cases are "bogus."
Reality: Unsubstantiated cases feature almost the same risk as substantiated cases.

It is perhaps natural to instinctively understand "substantiation" as meaning "abuse or neglect happened" and to assume that "unsubstantiated" means "there was no abuse and there is no risk." There may be a tendency for people to think of substantiated and unsubstantiated cases as being very different – polar opposites, in fact.

This perspective was challenged two decades ago (Leiter et al. 1994) by a study finding that children's outcomes were not very different by substantiation status. Since that time, there have been a large number of studies showing that substantiated and unsubstantiated cases are at similar risk of negative future outcomes and re-reports of child maltreatment (Drake et al. 2003; Kohl et al. 2009; Hussey et al. 2005; English et al. 2002; Fakunmoju 2009). This may be due, in part, to the fact that substantiation requires both demonstration of harm or risk and clear evidence of the cause of the harm (Drake 1996), meaning many cases with low evidence cannot be substantiated. It is also the kind of result you would expect if the majority of reports involve persons who are at risk of child maltreatment. While it is clear that not all studies find equal risk of untoward outcomes across all domains (Chiu et al. 2011), there is good evidence to believe that the group of children who are assessed by child protective services are at higher risk than other children, even after controlling for other factors (Jonson-Reid et al. 2009).

Another way to understand the importance of unsubstantiated cases in prevention efforts is by noting that far more unsubstantiated than substantiated cases receive state post-response services (U.S. Department of Health and Human Services, Administration for Children and Families, Administration on Children, Youth and Families, Children's Bureau 2012; CWIG 2012). Even though such services are only provided to about 30 % of unsubstantiated children, compared to 60 % of substantiated children, the far larger number of unsubstantiated cases means that more unsubstantiated children than substantiated children get post-response services (747,369 compared to 358,838 based on 46 states reporting both statistics, U.S. Department of Health and Human Services, Administration for Children and Families, Administration on Children, Youth and Families, Children's Bureau 2012; CWIG 2012). Since child protective services are tasked with a preventative role, and given that unsubstantiated cases are at similar risk for re-report and other negative outcomes, it is not rational to simply classify all unsubstantiated cases as "misses" or as examples of inappropriate reporting. Quite the opposite is true – they provide a genuine opportunity for CPS to execute its primary mission – the prevention of harm to children at risk.

How Do We Protect Children Once Identified?

Depending on the means of identification, the response might vary. In a world without any reporting system, the response (if any) would have to be fully community driven. Communities would require the resources to be a positive support for families. One of the dilemmas of such a system is that it has been clearly established that those communities with the highest rates of child maltreatment are also those which are most disorganized and least efficacious (Coulton et al. 1999; Drake and Pandey 1996). While the nature of a causal relationship between community level factors and maltreatment rates remains a matter of debate (Coulton et al. 2007), many people suggest that structural inequalities over time (geographically concentrated, persistent poverty) result in highly disadvantaged communities which in turn place additional strain on struggling families (Blackstock and Trocme 2005; Jack 2004). In order to radically change this, there would need to be a societal willingness to fund what Sampson called "changing places not people" (2003). It is certainly a worthwhile idea to invest in communities to build the informal infrastructure for families (see Davies et al. 2009), but until sufficient community-based supports can be achieved to address maltreatment informally, some type of formal detection and response seems warranted for those cases that meet the standards of maltreatment in a given region, even strong advocates for community-based prevention call on both community responsibility and a strong formal service infrastructure (Daro and Dodge 2009).

Most countries opt for some level of formal agency response either operated through a governmental agency or contracted private agencies. This is true even for countries in the early stages of developing a formal response to child maltreatment (e.g., Almuneef and Fadia Al Buhairan 2012; Choo et al. 2013). Even in a qualitative study advocating for increased recognition of informal community supports, there was no call for eliminating the formal response to child protection (Holland 2012). Currently, several types of systems exist. Relatively, well-funded and established national child and family service systems exist in some nations (e.g., the United Kingdom, the Netherlands), while some nations have only a rudimentary or patchwork child welfare system. The United States provides a good example of the diversity which can exist in service systems.

Mandated Reporting: A Linkage to Services?

Current thinking about mandated reporting policies cannot be understood without reference to the systems and services that receive and act upon these reports. Early on in the history of detecting maltreatment, however, it is clear that a formal linkage between existing institutions and the potential reporter did not exist. For example, Kempe et al. (1962) exhorts each physician to "acquaint himself with the facilities available in private and public agencies that provide services for children. These include children's humane societies, divisions of welfare departments and societies for the prevention of cruelty to children" (p. 111). While there has been a substantial change in infrastructure since that time, it is not clear that a fully evolved "system" has been achieved.

Myth: The US Public Child Welfare is a comprehensive child protection system.
Reality: The US child protection response is more like a patchwork quilt.

In the United States, while many systems contact children, the burden for assuring safety and well-being has fallen, by default, onto state and county departments of social services and the child protective system. This default assignment is now enshrined in law, for example, in CAPTA and in the Child and Family Service Reviews required by the US Government monitor states on how well their child protective service systems support child well-being. Child protective services are not currently charged with only protecting children from acute harm; they are also charged with supporting child well-being.

Perhaps because of these federal legislative efforts, child welfare systems are often conceptualized and evaluated as if they represent a comprehensive system of care. In most cases, they do not. Child welfare systems do have well-developed reporting protocols, established procedures for interfacing with the courts, and guidelines related to providing foster care. These are services virtually unique to public child welfare and are federally mandated and regulated. These services are remarkable for being reactive and represent tertiary rather than primary or secondary preventative roles. The more preventive service responses vary substantially by state and region.

When it comes to a preventative or early intervention role, the American public child welfare system is much more variable and tends to resemble a patchwork quilt rather than a comprehensive system. For example, the most common form of services is case management and referral, which are typically provided by public child welfare workers. The actual direct services or concrete supports, however, are delivered by other agencies (e.g., family counseling, housing assistance, addictions services, and parenting programs). This creates a unique dynamic where the outcomes of the "child protective services response" are actually dependent on agencies with whom they have little or no control and may or may not have a fiscal relationship. While this section is focused on the United States, it is worth noting that this natural dependence on other systems or services to produce positive outcomes for children is by no means limited to the United States (e.g., Almuneef and Fadia Al Buhairan 2012; Munro 2011). This is one of the key problems in holding the child welfare agency responsible for preventative functions and well-being outcomes (Barth and Jonson-Reid 2000). By way of comparison, other systems work very differently. For example, the 911 system – a general system in the United States of emergency telephone calls to police, ambulance, and fire services with many other countries using a 000 number – receives distress calls, clarifies the issue at hand, identifies the needed service, and responds to the problem. These intermediary responders (police, ambulance, fire) may then rely on further systems, courts and jails, hospitals, social service agencies, insurance companies, and the like to meet the more distal needs of the person served. How well this system works relative to the final outcome for an individual is, like child welfare, dependent on available resources and ability to triage to further intervention as needed. Unlike child welfare, however, the secondary response systems here are much more clearly aligned with the initial emergency responders. Some countries have child welfare systems that more closely align with this 911 approach with explicit protocols for government versus agency responsibility and data sharing to track cases (Angman and Gustafsson 2011; Wallace and Bunting 2007). There are a few regional examples of this type of close-knit collaboration in the United States (Daro and Dodge 2009). There are, however, no national or even consistent state-level models.

If we wish to have a system that is more like a 911-initiated system, then we must have adequately funded entities equivalent to a fire department, ambulance company, or police force and there must be an established secondary level (within or outside the public system) for taking over the case once the initial response is done. Likewise, the evaluation of such a system must be appropriately linked to the various roles and responsibilities so that improvements can be made. For example, if there is an increased rate of death from heart attacks, we would want to know if it was a training issue for responders, lack of quality care in hospital emergency departments, specialty cardiac services, or even something like traffic delaying the response time (Griffin and McGwin 2013). Calls for a comprehensive data system that allow for such tracking of services and outcomes have been made in both the United States and international literature (e.g., Jonson-Reid and Drake 2008; Munro 2011). This is critical as the remedy for the problem is very different based on where the problem lies. Arguably, we have a long way to go before we achieve this type of system.

Myth: Mandated reporters and parents receiving CPS intervention dislike CPS interventions and find them counterproductive.
Reality: They are generally satisfied with CPS interventions and think it helps assure child safety.

One of the strongest enduring myths in the mandated reporting debate is that mandated reporters are largely dissatisfied with the system as it exists. To the degree that dissatisfaction with the current reporting system does exist, the principal complaint is that child protective services do not take enough action or will not accept cases that the reporters consider serious, not that child protective services commonly overreach or are unnecessarily intrusive (Cocozza and Hort 2011; Drake and Jonson-Reid 2007). Various surveys of mandated reporters (Berlin et al. 1991; Compaan et al. 1997; Flaherty et al. 2006; Kalichman 1991; Kalichman and Craig 1991; Weinstein et al. 2000, 2001) have arrived at very similar findings, principally that reporting is helpful rather than harmful to families and that reporting aids in assuring child safety. While mental health professionals report some disruption to treatment in about a quarter of cases, "Several studies have found that making a report of suspected child abuse or maltreatment concerning a client in psychotherapy is more likely to have a positive outcome for the relationship or to effect no change, than to be damaging". In one survey, mandated reporters were asked directly if they believed mandated reporting laws were necessary, and almost all (94 %) responded that they believed they were (Kalichman and Craig 1991).

Perhaps surprisingly, clients are also generally pleased with CPS contact, with one large study showing that more than three quarters of investigated parents were "satisfied" or "very satisfied" with the investigation, two out of three saying their family was doing better after the investigation, and less than one in ten saying they were doing worse (English et al. 2002). These general findings have been replicated in numerous other studies (e.g., Chapman et al. 2003; Fryer et al. 1990, 1988). Of course, satisfaction and effectiveness and even adequate coverage are different things.

Do CP Services Work?

This is a difficult question. Most children and families that are reported (whether by permissive or mandated reporters) do not receive any response other than an assessment or investigation (Jonson-Reid 2011; U.S. Department of Health and Human Services, Administration for Children and Families, Administration on Children, Youth and Families, Children's Bureau 2012). Unless the situation is clearly one involving very serious abuse or very high risk to the child – for example, sexual abuse or physical abuse of an infant – typically, more than one report (and often a few) is required before the priority to provide services is high enough to trigger a child welfare response. If we assume that a large proportion of children (and their families) reported a need for something but most will get nothing, then it is difficult to assess the overall system impact unless there was a significant deterrence effect or other benefit of the report itself. The idea of deterrence is based on the fact that you have been made aware that you have violated an established societal norm and that an authority figure both is aware of this and is able to become aware of future violations. This is similar to the argument of building community responsibility related to the control of youth behavior (Sampson 2003). It is predicated, of course, on the child's parents or caregivers valuing the societal norm and the opinion or the response of the person who notices and having the capacity to alter their behavior toward the child. Second, there could be a value to the child. Perhaps there is a value for a child in knowing that what is happening is not acceptable or desirable separate from whether or not social agencies can effectively intervene (Wekerle 2013). Most would argue, however, that a positive outcome for a child protection response would more likely follow from some sort of service.

Current Models for In-Home Response

Differential Response

Sometimes termed "alternative response" or a "two-track system," differential response (DR) represents a structural redesign of child abuse investigations and services. Prior to DR, agencies had a single "track" wherein cases of suspected maltreatment, whether reported by mandated or non-mandated reporters, could be investigated, after which the more serious cases might involve removal of the children or other court action, and less serious cases might receive services or be closed. Differential response is an attempt to split out cases earlier, often at the initial agency telephone intake, and provide either "investigations" – generally in the case of sexual abuse or other serious cases – or "assessments" in other less serious cases to provide the appropriate service response for respective cases. In this way, a kind of triage system operates at an earlier stage to more promptly and efficiently refer families to necessary helpful service providers in appropriate cases and to reserve more formal investigations only for cases where a child is or is more likely to be in need of protection.

Differential response is being configured differently in different states, and many open questions exist, including, for example, the degree of substantial practical differences between investigative and assessment tracks. Differential response was employed in 18 states as of 2011 (U.S. Department of Health and Human Services, Administration for Children and Families, Administration on Children, Youth and Families, Children's Bureau 2012). This approach is also being explored internationally (Davies et al. 2009; Mathews and Bromfield 2012). The assessments are designed to trigger a case plan and connection to services. Early research (e.g., Siegel and Loman 2011) suggests that consumer satisfaction may be higher, while child safety appears not to be compromised.[1]

Family-Centered or Case Management Services

Following an assessment or investigation, families may be offered voluntary in-home services that are essentially a form of case management. Research on lower level in-home services is mixed. In a study of families with a first report of maltreatment, those families receiving the lowest intensity of in-home services had lower recurrence rates than those receiving more intense (family preservation or intensive in-home services or foster care) or no services in data that also control for interactions with substantiation and other parent-level services received (Drake et al. 2006). In another study that grouped all post-investigative services together, there was no significant effect of services among unsubstantiated case and a moderate increase in risk among substantiated cases (Connell et al. 2007). Another study found a moderate increased risk of recurrence for served unsubstantiated cases that was mostly offset for substantiated cases, but non-child welfare services were not controlled (Fluke et al. 2008). A recent study found higher risk among children receiving some form of child welfare services (Fuller and Nieto 2013), but there were no controls for poverty or other services nor was the type of in-home services clear.

Why such a range of findings? First, as mentioned above, there are variations in measurement that may result in different outcomes. Additionally, some research indicates that different forms of maltreatment and intensity of initial investigation are associated with particular service recommendations which may confound understanding recurrence (Bae et al. 2009). Further in studies that have included assessments of parental engagement and readiness for change, this factor has been significant in improvements in family functioning and reduced maltreatment (DePanfilis and Zuravin 2002; Hindley et al. 2006; Littell and Girvin 2005). Most studies of services and recurrence have been unable to also capture such family level variables. Dosage of services (frequency of contact) is also at issue. In an analysis of a nationally representative group of families engaged in child welfare

[1]For a general overview of some of these contentious issues, the reader is directed to the special issue of *Research on Social Work Practice*, September 2013, in which all sides of the debate are thoroughly discussed.

in-home services after investigation, only 66 % reported having seen their caseworker in the last month (Chapman et al. 2003). Finally, as mentioned earlier, the most common form of service is case management and referral, meaning that successful outcomes are frequently dependent on the other services offered and accessed.

Intensive In-home Services (IIHS)

Also known as family preservation services, this form of child protection response is designed for families that are at imminent risk of having a child removed from their care due to maltreatment but are diverted to these intensive services instead. Data regarding the effectiveness of IIHS are mixed. For example, the California Evidence-Based Clearinghouse on Child Welfare rates homebuilders, perhaps the best known IIHS program, as "supported by research evidence" but not "well supported by research evidence," despite a very large set of studies on IIHS over the past several decades. The research has been confused and contentious to the point where articles have been written on how best to evaluate IIHS evaluations (Jacobs 2001). A key problem is that it appears that IIHS effectiveness varies markedly by client characteristics. One recent meta-analysis (Channa et al. 2012) found that these programs "were effective in preventing placement for multiproblem families, but not for families experiencing abuse or neglect."

Thinking Ahead: How Do We Move to a Reporting and Response System Best Informed by Research Evidence?

More than 50 years after Kempe's groundbreaking article in 1962, several forms of reporting and response have developed throughout the world. There remain, however, many gaps in our understanding of mandated reporting and child protection system response. Further, much of our data that does exist is limited to studies in the United States, Canada, the United Kingdom, and Australia. We know very little about the types of reporting and response systems in other countries. What follows are suggested areas of research or methodological issues that need to be addressed to improve our evidence base to protect children. We begin with issues related to reporting and then focus on services to intact families.

Consensus on "Maltreatment"

What is the appropriate metric for determining what is "abuse" and "neglect"? In the United States, responsibility for "defining" maltreatment is left to the individual states and changes over time. This makes it very challenging to understand the prevalence of different types of maltreatment and to understand effective response methods. A first step in improving measurement requires the setting of boundaries regarding the concept of harm and what constitutes risk (Davies et al. 2009). It is clear that some countries cast a very wide net in terms of what the government or agencies are responsible for in terms of supporting child development (Angman and Gustafsson 2011). It is not clear that other countries like the United States are accepting such a broad mandate. In cases where definition change precedes such acceptance of responsibility and preparedness of response, there have been poor outcomes (Edleson 2004). What is "bad" for a child in the context of their family may not necessarily be the same as what we decide is abuse or neglect in terms of a CPS response. Whatever is included in the definition of maltreatment related to reporting should be connected to an adequately resourced response.

What Form of Reporting Is Better?

Ideally, we would have a better understanding of permissive reporting versus mandated reporting versus fully community-based approaches that have no formal system at all. As discussed earlier, there is substantial evidence that maltreatment is underreported even among those mandated to report. This confounds the ability to assess this type of policy. Some research indicates that mandated reporting improves case finding (Al Eissa and Almuneef 2010; Mathews et al. 2010). Pritchard and Williams (2010) compared child abuse-related deaths (CARD) in infants with non-child abuse fatalities and found that CARD rates dropped relative to other causes of death in England and Wales, whereas this was not true in other countries like the United States. As aforementioned, the United Kingdom has more of a permissive reporting system. Comparing countries – or jurisdictions within countries – with different systems may help in this matter but has to be done with extremely careful attention to maltreatment definitions and the perceived and real value of the response system in place. In countries with mixed systems like the United States, we also need to understand the impact of reporting in the context of whether reporter type influences the system response.

When Reporters Choose Not to Report, What Happens?

It is clear that even mandated reporters do not always report (Sedlak et al. 2010). Questions have been asked about professionals' comfort with reporting (Gilbert et al. 2009a, b), but this is not the same as asking what types of alternative actions were taken instead of reporting. There is also some indication that mental health-care professionals may not act on self-reported maltreatment because they do not believe it to be a priority issue in treatment (Read et al. 2007), but little work has been done in this area, nor is it clear whether or not most potential reporters who choose not to report have ongoing contact with the child and family and, if so, what (if anything) they did to help the child and the child's family and whether this was successful.

Similarly, we do not really know much about how known cases that went unreported fare. We have retrospective recall studies like the famous Adverse Childhood Experiences Study (Donga et al. 2004), but we do not know who was reported and who was not and what happened. There is indication that future death and injury might have been prevented if abusive head trauma had been properly identified and reported in some studies (Jenny et al. 1999). However, severe physical abuse is relatively rare among all cases of maltreatment. We have studies that have used official reports such as the National Study of Child and Adolescent Well-Being (OPRE 2013), but these do not capture unreported cases. NIS asks questions about unreported cases, but we do not know what happens to them in the long term (Sedlak et al. 2010). Only two studies could be found that compared children with self-reported maltreatment (in adolescence) to officially reported cases. Those children identified by both official and self-report methods generally experienced more incidences of maltreatment and had worse mental health outcomes (Cohen et al. 2001; Shaffer et al. 2008). Cohen and colleagues found higher rates of poor mental health among children with official reports compared to self-report or no reports. It should be noted that the Shaffer and colleagues (2008) study appeared to have drawn their sample from a higher-risk population. It is also possible that some of the children who remain unreported are served in other ways or find other resources.

Services

What Services Are for Whom?

There is no current widespread triage system that provides for families with different levels of need, outside of determining whether a child can safely remain within the home. In other words, for the 95 % of children who remain at home, we have no systematic way of understanding which families will need just a brief connection to services and will be adequately treated and which families will need support, possibly for many years. As aforementioned, many surveys of families involved at some level with child welfare reporting want more services rather than less. But how much is enough? Several calls have been made for matching long-term intervention with apparent long-term or multiple problem families (Munro 2011). But appropriate targeting of resources at the time a family first comes to the attention of child protection is still elusive. Length of services tends to be arbitrarily set by policies related to funding or some other time constraint, rather than by when we anticipate seeing a sufficiently powerful positive effect.

It is also often unclear whether child protection should focus on the child's needs, the parents' needs, and the community's capacity to support the child and the child's family or some combination of these. If the services are tied to child well-being, then service determination is not dependent only on the parents' needs or actions. So for example, a child who needs a developmental assessment would receive access to that even if the investigator did not see a risk of maltreatment because the goal is to promote child well-being. When there is a suspicion of maltreatment, the presumed assumption is that there is a need for parenting training and that this will improve the situation. While there are evidence-based and promising parenting programs, these are typically not delivered by child welfare, although some exceptions exist (e.g., Chaffin et al. 2012). It is also not clear that this is the best or sufficient response given the many other family level risk factors associated with maltreatment (Jonson-Reid and Drake 2008). Still others argue for a social capital or socio-economic approach targeting poverty rather than maltreatment per se (Blackstock and Trocme 2005). Different foci dictate different forms of measuring both services and outcomes.

What Would Have Happened Without Services?

Since we do not randomly assign families to services within the CPS context, it can be difficult to assess and easy to draw conclusions based on inadequate information. We tend to study etiology without consideration of services (Jonson-Reid 2004), and since services are rare, we are unlikely to accidentally see impact (Jonson-Reid 2011). As illustrated in the figure below, there are several steps to think through in improving our understanding of CPS services. First, there must be appropriate assessment of need. Earlier, we reviewed the current status of the literature about substantiation and discussed the notion that this particular metric is not ideal in terms of understanding whether or not a child is at risk of harm. A substantial literature exists regarding risk assessment in child protection, and early doubts as to the effectiveness of risk assessment tools (Wald and Woolverton 1990) have yet to be satisfactorily answered. It may instead be more useful to move away from attempting to predict an act of maltreatment, per se, and consider instead what the threats to safety and well-being are and how they are to be best served (Drake and Jonson-Reid 1999; Davies et al. 2009). This, however, is an empirical question requiring that services be available to make the evaluation of such an assessment worthwhile. It also suggests the need for a certain level of training to be present among those making such assessments. Currently, the degree of training required and the amount of training actually provided vary substantially by region, and few studies control for the level of preparation of the child protection staff. This is a little researched area, but there are theoretical and some empirical reasons to believe this has an important effect (Munro 2005; Ryan et al. 2006; Strolin et al. 2006). In the future, it will be important to better understand the degree to which the expertise of child protective services personnel plays a role in both appropriate decision making and improved case outcomes.

Assuming an adequate assessment process is in place, understanding outcomes means understanding who is providing what, and how well. If the need is met by CPS, then the family need only complies with CPS and the outcome is directly linked to the CPS intervention. If CPS is the case manager, however, the family must first agree with the referrals provided, then access the services, and then complete their engagement with the services in order to anticipate a positive outcome. Further, the services outside the CPS system must be examined in terms of quality since complying with a service that is ineffective is unlikely to result in positive change.

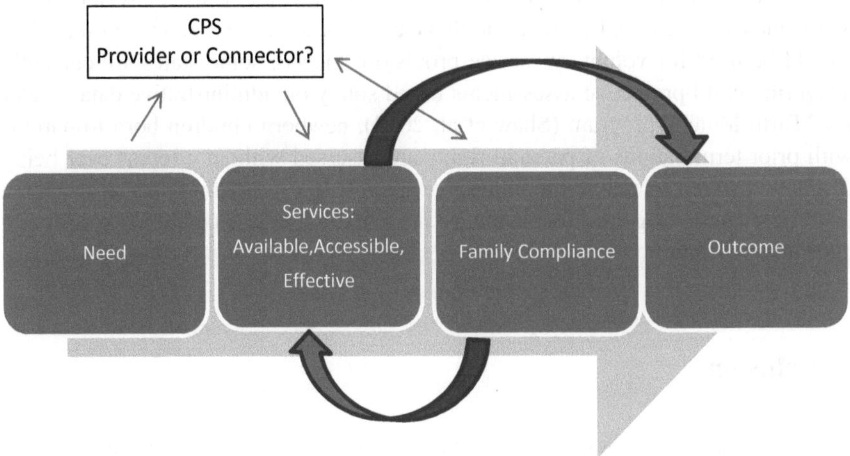

The Promise of Big Data

The general issue of reporting should be understood in a broader context. "No single professional can have a full picture of the child's needs and circumstances and, if children and families are to receive the right help at the right time, everyone who comes into contact with them has a role to play in identifying concerns, sharing information and taking prompt action" (Her Majesty's Government 2013, p. 8). Linkage of agency data systems and administrative data to survey data may hold particular promise in advancing our understanding of how to improve our responses to and prevention of maltreatment. This requires careful attention not only to the construction of linked data across public and private agencies but also to creating an ongoing feedback loop between data and policy (Jonson-Reid and Drake 2008). This will require that data systems include variables that are relevant to the logic models developed specific to the form of detection and CPS response in a given country or region.

We have already arrived at a place where technology exists to have some child welfare contacts be initiated automatically, without a report at all. One recent study (Putnam-Hornstein and Needell 2011) found that for a very small subpopulation with a large number of risk factors noted on their birth record, the likelihood of a child maltreatment report within the first 5 years of life was 89.5 %. It is an open question as to whether child welfare should consider taking a truly proactive stance and offering voluntary preventative services on the basis of such data. Such action might seem highly desirable or even inevitable if child protection is viewed as a public health issue. On the other hand, those persons persisting (wrongly we believe) in regard to child protective services as a punitive system might see such preemptive action as a violation of parental rights. As data systems are cross-linked, our ability to predict who will be referred in advance will increase, and if we are serious about a preventative role for CPS, there should be a discussion as to if and when such data should be used for voluntary service provision. Indeed, some states are currently triggering child protective assessments based solely on administrative data. Under the "Birth Match" program (Shaw et al. 2013), newborn children born to parents with prior terminations of parental rights are assessed without a report ever being filed. It may well be that in the future, we are able to use existing data to provide a level of accurate targeting for voluntary preventative services which is simply not currently possible.

Conclusion

In our view, many debates over the advisability of mandated reporting laws are clouded by two key problems. One has to do with the failure of the empirical literature to adequately undergird the current debate, and the second has to do with a failure to place mandated reporting laws within the broader framework of child protective services.

In some quarters, there is a long-standing and established "conventional wisdom" about the adverse consequences of mandated reporting. Unfortunately, much of it is contradicted by empirical data and properly nuanced, more precise, and more thorough analysis of concepts and issues. These contradictions range from simple misunderstandings (e.g., that unsubstantiated cases are equivalent to unnecessary reports) to inaccurate characterizations of the current system (e.g., that child protective services are overwhelmed by their investigatory responsibilities) to broader misconceptions about the system in general. In order for the mandated reporting debate to move forward and for improvements to be made to child protection systems, all relevant discussions must be far more evidence based. We believe that most policy makers would prefer engaging in evidence-based policy making to the alternatives and mandated reporting policy is one area in which the evidence is strong enough to support such an approach.

Despite a long history of child protection services, we know surprisingly little about the outcomes for children and families who receive the most common and least intensive forms of services. We also know relatively little about children who receive investigations and no further services. This is undoubtedly partly true to methodological difficulties, including difficulties in establishing control groups. Clearly, the need for services as indicated by children reported far outstrips the current system's ability to intervene. Without further evidence regarding what can be done within formal child protection, what can be done in conjunction with other agencies, and what can be done within the community, child protection practice will remain a disjointed system with a great deal of room for improvement.

References

Al Eissa, M., & Almuneef, M. (2010). Child abuse and neglect in Saudi Arabia: Journey of recognition to implementation of national prevention strategies. *Child Abuse & Neglect, 34*(1), 28–33.

Almuneef, M. A., & Fadia Al Buhairan, M. D. (2012, January). Child maltreatment prevention readiness assessment country report: Saudi Arabia. *Child Maltreatment, 11*, 12.

American Humane Association. (1979). *National analysis of official child abuse and neglect reporting, 1977* (DHEW publication # OHDS 79–30232). Washington, DC: U.S. Government Printing Office.

Angman, I., & Gustafsson, M. (2011). *Combating child abuse and neglect in Sweden*. The Netherlands Youth Institute, NJI. http://www.youthpolicy.nl/yp/downloadsyp/Daphne-report-Sweden.pdf

Ashton, V. (2010). Does ethnicity matter? Social workers' personal attitudes and professional behaviors in reporting child maltreatment. *Advances in Social Work, 11*(2), 129–143.

Australasian Legal Information Institute. (2014). *New South Wales children and young persons act*. Available online at http://www.austlii.edu.au/au/legis/nsw/consol_act/caypapa1998442/

Bae, H., Solomon, P., & Gelles, R. (2009). Multiple child maltreatment recurrence relative to single recurrence and no recurrence. *Children and Youth Services Review, 31*(6), 617–624. ISSN 0190–7409. http://dx.doi.org/10.1016/j.childyouth.2008.11.005

Barth, R. P., & Jonson-Reid, M. (2000). Outcomes after child welfare services: Implications for the financing and design of child welfare services. *Children and Youth Services Review, 22*(9/10), 787–810.

Ben Natan, M., Faour, C., Naamhah, S., Grinberg, K., & Klein-Kremer, A. (2012). Factors affecting medical and nursing staff reporting of child abuse. *International Nursing Review, 59*(3), 331–337.

Berlin, F., Malin, H., & Dean, S. (1991). Effects of statutes requiring psychiatrists to report suspected abuse of children. *American Journal of Psychiatry, 148*(4), 449–453.

Blackstock, C., & Trocme, N. (2005). Community-based child welfare for aboriginal children: Supporting resilience through structural change. *Social Policy Journal of New Zealand, 24*, 12–33.

Butchart, A., & Harvey, A. (2006). *Preventing child maltreatment: A guide to taking action and generating evidence*. World Health Organization and International Society for Prevention of Child Abuse and Neglect. http://whqlibdoc.who.int/publications/2006/9241594365_eng.pdf

Chaffin, M., Hecht, D., Bard, D., Silovsky, J., & Beasley, W. (2012). A statewide trial of the SafeCare home-based services model with parents in child protective services. *Pediatrics, 129*(3), 509–515.

Channa, M., Stams, G., Bek, M., Damen, E., Asscher, J., & Van Der Laan, P. (2012). A metaanalysis of intensive family preservation programs: Placement prevention and improvement of family functioning. *Children and Youth Services Review, 34*(8), 1472–1479.

Chapman, M. V., Gibbons, C. B., Barth, R. P., & McCrae, J. S. (2003). Parental views of in-home services: What predicts satisfaction with child welfare workers? *Child Welfare, 82*(5), 571–596.

Child Welfare Information Gateway. (2012). *Mandatory reporters of child abuse and neglect*. Washington, DC: U.S. Department of Health and Human Services, Children's Bureau.

Chiu, Y. L., Ryan, J. P., & Herz, D. C. (2011). Allegations of maltreatment and delinquency: Does risk of juvenile arrest vary substantiation status? *Children and Youth Services Review, 33*(6), 855–860.

Choo, W. Y., Walsh, K., Chinna, K., & Tey, N. P. (2013). Teacher reporting attitudes scale (TRAS) confirmatory and exploratory factor analyses with a Malaysian sample. *Journal of Interpersonal Violence, 28*(2), 231–253.

Cocozza, M., & Hort, S. (2011). Chapter 5: The dark side of the universal welfare state? Child abuse and protection in Sweden. In N. Gilbert, N. Parton, & M. Ikiveness (Eds.), *Child protection systems: International trends and orientations*. New York: Oxford University Press.

Cohen, P., Brown, J., & Smailes, E. (2001). Child abuse and neglect and the development of mental disorders in the general population. *Development and Psychopathology, 13*, 981–999.

Compaan, C., Doueck, H., & Levine, M. (1997). Mandated reporter satisfaction with child protection: More good news for workers. *Journal of Interpersonal Violence, 12*, 847–857.

Connell, C., Bergeron, N., Katz, K., Saunders, L., & Tebes, J. (2007). Re-referral to child protective services: The influence of child, family, and case characteristics on risk status. *Child Abuse & Neglect, 31*(5), 573–588.

Coulton, C., Korbin, J., & Su, M. (1999). Neighborhoods and child maltreatment: A multi-level study. *Child Abuse & Neglect, 23*(11), 1019–1040.

Coulton, C., Cramptin, D., Irwin, M., Spilsbury, J., & Korbin, J. (2007). How neighborhoods influence child maltreatment: A review of the literature and alternative pathways. *Child Abuse & Neglect, 31*(11–12), 1117–1142.

Council of Australian Governments. (2009). *The national framework for protecting Australia's children, 2009–2020*. Available online at: http://www.dss.gov.au/our-responsibilities/families-and-children/publications-articles/protecting-children-is-everyones-business

Daro, D., & Dodge, K. A. (2009). Creating community responsibility for child protection: Possibilities and challenges. *The Future of Children/Center for the Future of Children, The David and Lucile Packard Foundation, 19*(2), 67.

Davies, E., Rowe, E., & Hassall, I. (2009). *Approaches to defining child neglect and intervening to prevent it: A literature review*. Institute of Public Policy, Auckland University of Technology. Available online at: http://www.rowedaviesresearch.co.nz/media/neglect%20prevention%20and%20intervention.pdf

DePanfilis, D., & Zuravin, S. (2002). The effect of services on the recurrence of child maltreatment. *Child Abuse & Neglect, 26*, 187–205.

Department of Health and Human Services. (2011). *Child abuse prevention and treatment act*. Available online at http://www.acf.hhs.gov/sites/default/files/cb/capta2010.pdf

DeVooght, K., Allen, T., & Geen, R. (2008) *Federal, state, and local spending to address child abuse and neglect in SFY 2006*. Casey Family Programs Available at: http://www.ChildTrends.org/Files//Child_Trends-2009_02_17_FR_CWFinancePaper.pdf

Donga, M., Anda, R., Felitti, V., Dube, S., Williamson, D., Thompson, T., Loo, C., & Giles, W. (2004). The interrelatedness of multiple forms of child abuse, neglect and household dysfunction. *Child Abuse & Neglect, 28*, 771–784.

Drake, B. (1996). Unraveling unsubstantiated. *Child Maltreatment, 1*(3), 261–271.

Drake, B., & Pandey, S. (1996). Understanding the relationship between neighborhood poverty and specific types of child maltreatment. *Child Abuse & Neglect, 20*(11), 1003–1018.

Drake, B., & Jonson-Reid, M. (1999). Some thoughts on the increasing use of administrative data in child maltreatment research. *Child Maltreatment, 4*(4), 308–315.

Drake, B., & Jonson-Reid, M. (2007). A response to Melton based on the best available data. *Child Abuse & Neglect, 31*, 343–360.

Drake, B., Jonson-Reid, M., Way, I., & Chung, S. (2003). Substantiation and recidivism. *Child Maltreatment, 8*(4), 248–260.

Drake, B., Jonson-Reid, M., & Sapokaite, L. (2006). Re-reporting of child maltreatment: Does participation in other public sector services moderate the likelihood of a second maltreatment report? *Child Abuse & Neglect, 30*, 1201–1226.

Edleson, J. L. (2004). Should childhood exposure to adult domestic violence be defined as child maltreatment under the law. In *Protecting children from domestic violence: Strategies for community intervention* (pp. 8–29). New York: Guilford Press.

English, D. J., Marshall, D. B., Coghlan, L., Brummel, S., & Orme, M. (2002). Causes and consequences of the substantiation decision in Washington State Child Protective Services. *Children and Youth Services Review, 24*, 817–851.

Fakunmoju, S. (2009). Substantiation and adverse appeal outcomes: Content analysis and testing of Drake's harm/evidence model. *Child Maltreatment, 14*(1), 53–68.

Feng, J. Y., Huang, T. Y., & Wang, C. J. (2010). Kindergarten teachers' experience with reporting child abuse in Taiwan. *Child Abuse & Neglect, 34*(2), 124–128.

Finkelhor, D., & Jones, L. (2006). Why have child maltreatment and child victimization declined? *Journal of Social Issues, 62*(4), 685–716.

Flaherty, E. G., Sege, R. D., Price, L. L., Christoffel, K. K., Norton, D. P., & O'Connor, K. G. (2006). Pediatrician characteristics associated with child abuse identification and reporting: Results of a national survey of pediatricians. *Child Maltreatment, 11*(2006), 361–369.

Flaherty, E. G., Sege, R. D., Griffith, J., Price, L. L., Wasserman, R., Slora, E., Dhepyasuwan, N., Harris, D., Norton, D., Angelilli, M. L., Abney, D., & Binns, H. J. (2008). From suspicion of physical child abuse to reporting: Primary care clinician decision-making. *Pediatrics, 122*(3), 611–619.

Fluke, J., Shusterman, G., Hollinshead, D., & Yuan, Y. (2008). Longitudinal analysis of repeated child abuse reporting and victimization: Multistate analysis of associated factors. *Child Maltreatment, 13*, 76–88.

Fryer, G., Poland, J., Bross, D., & Krugman, R. (1988). The child protective service worker: A profile of needs, attitudes, and utilization of professional resources. *Child Abuse & Neglect, 12*, 481–490.

Fryer, G., Bross, D., Krugman, R., et al. (1990). Good news for CPS workers: An Iowa survey shows parents value services. *Public Welfare, 48*(1), 38–41.

Fuller, T., & Nieto, M. (2013). Child welfare services and risk of child maltreatment rereports: Do services ameliorate initial risk? *Children and Youth Services Review, 47*(1), 46–54.

Gaudin, J., & Polansky, R. (1986). Social distancing of the neglectful family: Sex, race, and social class influences. *Children and Youth Services Review, 8*(1), 1–12.

Gilbert, R., Kemp, A., Thoburn, J., Sidebotham, P., Radford, L., & MacMillan, H. (2009a). Recognising and responding to child maltreatment. *Lancet, 373*, 167–179.

Gilbert, R., Widom, C., Browne, K., Fergusson, D., Webb, E., & Janson, S. (2009b, January 3–9). Burden and consequences of child maltreatment in high-income countries. *The Lancet, 373*(9657), 68–81.

Glaser, D. (2011). How to deal with emotional abuse and neglect—Further development of a conceptual framework (FRAMEA). *Child Abuse & Neglect, 35*(10), 866–875.

Griffin, R., & McGwin, G., Jr. (2013). Emergency medical service providers' experiences with traffic congestion. *Journal of Emergency Medicine, 44*(2), 398–405. doi:10.1016/j.jemermed.2012.01.066. Epub 2012 Aug 9.

Hart, A. (2011). Child safety in Australian family law: Responsibilities and challenges for social science experts in domestic violence cases. *Australian Psychologist, 46*, 31–40.

Her Majesty's Government. (2013). *Working together to safeguard children*. Available online at: https://media.education.gov.uk/assets/files/pdf/w/working%20together.pdf

Hindley, N., Ramchandani, P., & Jones, D. (2006). Risk factors for recurrence of maltreatment: A systematic review. *Archives of Disease in Childhood, 91*(9), 744–752.

Holland, S. (2012). Trust in the community: Understanding the relationship between formal, semi-formal and informal child safeguarding in a local neighbourhood. *British Journal of Social Work, 44*(2), 384–400.

Hussey, J., Marshal, J., English, D., Knight, E., Lau, A., Dubowitz, H., et al. (2005). Defining maltreatment according to substantiation: Distinction without a difference? *Child Abuse & Neglect, 29*, 479–492.

Ibanez, E. S., Borrego, J., Jr., Pemberton, J. R., & Terao, S. (2006). Cultural factors in decision-making about child physical abuse: Identifying reporter characteristics influencing reporting tendencies. *Child Abuse & Neglect, 30*(12), 1365–1379.

Jack, G. (2004). Child protection at the community level. *Child Abuse Review, 13*, 368–383.

Jacobs, F. (2001). *What to make of family services evaluations* (Chapin Hall Center for children discussion paper). Available Online at: http://www.chapinhall.org/sites/default/files/old_reports/58.pdf

Jenny, C., Hymel, K. P., Ritzen, A., Reinert, S. E., & Hay, T. C. (1999). Analysis of missed cases of abusive head trauma. *The Journal of the American Medical Association, 281*(7), 621–626. doi:10.1001/jama.281.7.621.

Jonson-Reid, M. (2004). Child welfare services and delinquency: The need to know more. *Child Welfare, 83*(2), 157–174.

Jonson-Reid, M. (2011). Disentangling system contact and services: A key pathway to evidence-based children's policy. *Children and Youth Services Review, 33*, 598–604.

Jonson-Reid, M., & Drake, B. (2008). Multi-sector longitudinal administrative databases: An indispensable tool for evidence-based policy for maltreated children and their families. *Child Maltreatment, 13*(4), 392–399. PMC 2993509.

Jonson-Reid, M., Drake, B., & Kohl, P. (2009). Is the overrepresentation of the poor in child welfare caseloads due to bias or need? *Children and Youth Services Review, 31*(3), 422–427.

Jonson-Reid, M., Kohl, P., & Drake, B. (2012). Child and adult outcomes of chronic child maltreatment. *Pediatrics, 129*(5), 839–845. NIHMS 436968.

Kalichman, S. (1991). Laws on reporting sexual abuse of children. *Journal of Psychiatry, 148*, 1618–1619.

Kalichman, S., & Craig, M. (1991). Professional psychologists decision to report suspected child abuse: Clinician and situation influences. *Professional Psychology, 22*(1), 84–89.

Kempe, C. H. (1978). Sexual abuse, another hidden pediatric problem: The 1977 C. Anderson Aldrich lecture. *Pediatrics, 62*(3), 382–389.

Kempe, C. H., Silverman, F. N., Steele, B. F., Droegemueller, W., & Silver, H. K. (1962). The battered-child syndrome. *Journal of the American Medical Association, 181*, 17–24.

Kohl, P., Jonson-Reid, M., & Drake, B. (2009). Time to leave substantiation behind. *Child Maltreatment, 14*, 17–26.

Korbin, J. (1994). Sociocultural factors in child maltreatment. In G. Melton & F. Barry (Eds.), *Protecting children from abuse and neglect: Foundations for a new national strategy* (pp. 182–223). New York: Guilford Press.

Krase, K. S. (2013). Differences in racially disproportionate reporting of child maltreatment across report sources. *Journal of Public Child Welfare, 7*(4), 351–369.

Leiter, J., Meyers, K., & Zingraff, M. (1994). Substantiated and unsubstantiated cases of child maltreatment: Do their consequences differ? *Social Work Research, 18*(2), 67–82.

Littell, J., & Girvin, H. (2005). Caregivers' readiness for change: Predictive validity in a child welfare sample. *Child Abuse & Neglect, 29*(1), 59–80.

Markenson, D., Tunik, M., Cooper, A., Olson, L., Cook, L., Matza-Haughton, H., Treiber, M., Brown, W., Dickinson, P., & Foltin, G. (2007). A national assessment of knowledge, attitudes, and confidence of prehospital providers in the assessment and management of child maltreatment. *Pediatrics, 119*(1), e103–e108.

Mathews, B., & Bromfield, L. (2012). Australian laws and policies on child neglect. In H. Dubowitz (Ed.), *World perspectives on child abuse* (pp. 61–66). Aurora: ISPCAN.

Mathews, B., Walsh, K., Butler, D., & Farrell, A. (2010). *Teachers reporting child sexual abuse: Towards evidence-based reform of law, policy and practice* (Report for New South Wales, Queensland and Western Australia). Brisbane: Queensland University of Technology.

Melton, G. (2005). Mandated reporting: A policy without reason. *Child Abuse & Neglect, 29*, 9–18.

Merrick, M. T., Butt, S. M., Jent, J. F., Cano, N. M., Lambert, W. F., Chapman, A. V., & Sanders, L. M. (2010). No follow-up after positive newborn screening: Medical neglect? *Child Maltreatment, 15*(4), 315–323.

Munro, E. (2005). Improving practice: Child protection as a systems problem. *Children and Youth Services Review, 27*(4), 375–391.

Munro, E. (2011). *The Munro review of child protection. Part One: A systems analysis*. Available online at: http://dera.ioe.ac.uk/11434/1/TheMunroReviewofChildProtection-Part%20one.pdf

Noh, C. H. C., & Talaat, W. I. A. W. (2012). Verbal abuse on children: Does it amount to child abuse under the Malaysian law? *Asian Social Science, 8*(6), 224.
NSPCC. (2015). *Child protection system in Scotland at a glance*. Available online at http://www.nspcc.org.uk/preventing-abuse/child-protection-system/scotland/
OHCHR. (2015). *Convention on the rights of the child*. Available online at http://www.ohchr.org/EN/ProfessionalInterest/Pages/CRC.aspx
Office of Planning, Research and Evaluation. (2013). *National survey of child and adolescent well-being (NSCAW), 1997 – 2013: Project overview*. Available online at: http://www.acf.hhs.gov/programs/opre/research/project/national-survey-of-child-and-adolescent-well-being-nscaw-1
Pritchard, C., & Williams, R. (2010). Comparing possible 'child-abuse-related-deaths' in England and Wales with the major developed countries 1974–2006: Signs of progress? *British Journal of Social Work, 40*(6), 1700–1718.
Putnam-Hornstein, E., & Needell, B. (2011). Predictors of child protective service contact between birth and age five: An examination of California's 2002 birth cohort. *Children and Youth Services Review, 33*(11), 2400–2407.
Read, J., Hammersley, P., & Rudegeair, T. (2007). Why, when and how to ask about childhood abuse. *Advances in Psychiatric Treatment, 13*(2), 101–110.
Ryan, J. P., Garnier, P., Zyphur, M., & Zhai, F. (2006). Investigating the effects of caseworker characteristics in child welfare. *Children and Youth Services Review, 28*(9), 993–1006.
Sampson, R. J. (2003). The neighborhood context of well-being. *Perspectives in Biology and Medicine, 46*(3), S53–S64.
Scarcella, C., Bess, R., Zielewski, E., Warner, L., & Geen, R. (2004). *The cost of protecting vulnerable children IV: How child welfare funding fared during the recession*. Washington, DC: The Urban Institute.
Schols, M. W., De Ruiter, C., & Öry, F. G. (2013). How do public child healthcare professionals and primary school teachers identify and handle child abuse cases? A qualitative study. *BMC Public Health, 13*(1), 807.
Sedlak, A., Mettenburg, J., Basena, M., Petta, I., McPherson, K., Green, A., & Lee, S. (2010). *Fourth national incidence study of child abuse and neglect, report to congress*. Washington, DC: US Department of Health and Human Services.
Shaffer, A., Huston, L., & Egeland, B. (2008). Identification of child maltreatment using prospective and self-report methodologies: A comparison of maltreatment incidence and relation to later psychopathology. *Child Abuse & Neglect, 32*(7), 682–692.
Shaw, T. V., Barth, R., Mattingly, J., Ayer, D., & Berry, S. (2013). Child welfare birth match: The timely use of child welfare administrative data to protect newborns. *Journal of Public Child Welfare, 7*(2), 217–234.
Siegel, G., & Loman, L. (2011). *Minnesota permanency demonstration: Final evaluation report*. Available online at: http://www.iarstl.org/papers/MnPD%20Final%20Report-2011.pdf
Stalker, K., & McArthur, K. (2012). Child abuse, child protection and disabled children: A review of recent research. *Child Abuse Review, 21*(1), 24–40.
Stoltenborgh, M., van IJzendoorn, M. H., Euser, E. M., & Bakermans-Kranenburg, M. J. (2011). A global perspective on child sexual abuse: Meta-analysis of prevalence around the world. *Child Maltreatment, 16*(2), 79–101.
Stoltenborgh, M., Bakermans-Kranenburg, M. J., & van IJzendoorn, M. H. (2013). The neglect of child neglect: A meta-analytic review of the prevalence of neglect. *Social Psychiatry and Psychiatric Epidemiology, 48*(3), 345–355.
Strolin, J. S., McCarthy, M., & Caringi, J. (2006). Causes and effects of child welfare workforce turnover: Current state of knowledge and future directions. *Journal of Public Child Welfare, 1*(2), 29–52.
Texas Department of Family and Protective Services. (2013). *Our mission, vision and values*. Accessed online: https://www.dfps.state.tx.us/About_DFPS/mission.asp
U.S. Department of Health and Human Services, Administration on Children, Youth and Families. (2005). *Child maltreatment 2003*. Washington, DC: U.S. Government Printing Office.

U.S. Department of Health and Human Services, Administration for Children and Families, Administration on Children, Youth and Families, Children's Bureau. (2012). *Child Maltreatment 2011*. Available from http://www.acf.hhs.gov/programs/cb/research-datatechnology/statistics-research/child-maltreatment
Viner, R. M., Roche, E., Maguire, S. A., & Nicholls, D. E. (2010). When does childhood obesity become a child protection issue? *British Medical Journal, 341*(7769), 375–377.
Wald, M., & Woolverton, M. (1990). Risk assessment: The emperor's new clothes? *Child Welfare, 69*(6), 483–511.
Wallace, I., & Bunting, L. (2007). *An examination of local, national and international arrangements for the mandatory reporting of child abuse: The implications for Northern Ireland* (PDF, 544 KB). Belfast: NSPCC Northern Ireland Policy and Research Unit. ISBN 9781842280799.
Washington State Department of Social and Health Services. (2007). *Washington State Children's Administration workload study: Vol. I. Workload report*. Olympia: Washington State Department of Social and Health Services.
Weinstein, B., Levine, M., Kogan, N., Harkavy-Friedman, J., & Miller, J. M. (2000). Mental health professionals' experiences reporting suspected child abuse and maltreatment. *Child Abuse & Neglect, 24*(10), 1317–1328.
Weinstein, B., Levine, N., Kogan, J., Harkavy-Friedman, J., & Miller, J. (2001). Therapist reporting of suspected child abuse and maltreatment: Factors associated with outcome. *American Journal of Psychotherapy, 55*(2), 219–233.
Wekerle, C. (2013). Resilience in the context of child maltreatment: Connections to the practice of mandatory reporting. *Child Abuse & Neglect, 37*(2–3), 93–101.
Wolock, I., & Horowitz, B. (1984). Child maltreatment as a social problem: The neglect of neglect. *American Journal of Orthopsychiatry, 54*(4), 530–543.
Woodhouse, B. (1992). Who owns the child? Meyer and Pierce and the child as property. *William and Mary Law Review, 33*(4), 995–1122.

Chapter 4
An Inter-reporter Analysis of Mandated Child Maltreatment Reporting in the USA

John E. Kesner and Bridget V. Dever

Introduction

Mandatory reporting laws now exist in the USA in all 50 states, the District of Columbia, and the US territories. These laws require members of certain professional groups, who have contact with children in their work, to report to child protective services (CPS) when they have a reasonable suspicion that maltreatment has occurred. The US Department of Health and Human Services (DHHS) reports that of the roughly three million reports of maltreatment each year, the majority (60 %) come from professionals legally mandated to report suspected child maltreatment (US Department of Health and Human Services 2012).

Despite these laws, there is a lack of consistency in reporting by mandated reporters (Flaherty 2006; Webster et al. 2005). Mandated reporters face challenges in fulfilling reporting duties, including lack of knowledge about child maltreatment,

The National Child Abuse and Neglect Data System (NCANDS) Child File data were provided by the National Data Archive on Child Abuse and Neglect at Cornell University and have been used with permission. The data were originally collected under the auspices of the Children's Bureau, US Department of Health and Human Services. The collector of the original data, the funder, NDACAN, Cornell University, and the agents or employees of these institutions bear no responsibility for the analyses or interpretations presented here. The information and opinions expressed reflect solely the opinions of the authors.

J.E. Kesner, Ph.D. (✉)
Department of Early Childhood Education, College of Education, Georgia State University, 3987, Atlanta, Georgia, 30302-3987
e-mail: jkesner@gsu.edu

B.V. Dever, Ph.D.
Department of Education and Human Services, College of Education, Lehigh University, 111 Research Drive, A318 Iacocca Hall, Bethlehem, PA 18055, USA
e-mail: bdever@lehigh.edu

B. Mathews, D.C. Bross (eds.), *Mandatory Reporting Laws and the Identification of Severe Child Abuse and Neglect*, Child Maltreatment 4,
DOI 10.1007/978-94-017-9685-9_4

idiosyncratic interpretation of the law, and fear of retribution (Feng et al. 2012). Inconsistent reporting practices among mandated reporters result in inadequate protection of children. Many claim that the passage of these laws has produced an increase in unnecessary maltreatment reports as professionals make reports out of fear of legal action against them for not reporting (Takis 2008). Foreman and Bernet (2000) found confusion among mandated reporters, as some believed that the law required them to report even when their suspicion was based on a secondhand report of maltreatment. Other mandated reporters believed that they were only required to report suspected maltreatment based on their own personal observations.

It is unclear what effect the passage of mandated reporting laws has had on child protection. After an increase in total reports from 42.6 per 1,000 in 2004 to 43.9 per 1,000 children in 2005 (US Department of Health and Human Services 2006), the rate of reporting may be leveling off or even decreasing slightly as DHHS reports that the rate for 2010 was 43.8 per 1,000 children (US Department of Health and Human Services 2011). In addition, the number of children victimized, especially for physical and sexual abuse (Finkelhor and Jones 2006; Finkelhor et al. 2013), has been declining in recent years as evidenced by the declining number of substantiated cases of child maltreatment. Analysis of NCANDS data indicates that substantiated cases of maltreatment overall declined 2 % between 2010 and 2011, with a decline in sexual abuse of 3 %, while physical abuse and neglect evidenced a 1 % decline. In 2007, there were estimated 723,000 victims of child maltreatment but, by 2011, that number had decreased to 681,000 (US Department of Health and Human Services 2012).

However, changes in the number of reports from NCANDS data in either direction do not necessarily indicate an increase or decrease in child maltreatment. Recent trends may not indicate fewer children being victimized but, rather, a decline in the number of substantiated cases. Some researchers claim that serious maltreatment often goes unreported (Bensley et al. 2004; Kemp et al. 2009). Vague wording of mandated reporting laws, along with variations in states' requirements and differing criteria for substantiation, as well as perceived lack of response from CPS, can create frustration and confusion among mandated reporters. The net result is that many mandated reporters may choose not to report some suspected cases of maltreatment (Flaherty 2006; Zeman 2005).

Additionally, when data from official reports of suspected maltreatment are compared to the results of surveys of maltreatment experiences conducted with children, adolescents, and their parents, there seems to be a great deal of maltreatment that goes unreported (Gilbert et al. 2009). Webster et al. (2005) found that underreporting was more likely to occur in instances when maltreatment was more ambiguous and that it is more likely to occur than overreporting. While mandated reporters are under a legal mandate to report suspected child maltreatment, each comes into contact with children in different ways. Thus, issues such as client confidentiality, client autonomy, and the professional's code of ethical conduct manifest somewhat differently among the types of mandated reporters. Ultimately, unsure of whether their actions will do more harm than good, some professionals choose not to report some cases (Feng et al. 2012).

There has been a great deal of discussion and research about why and when mandated reporters choose to report suspected maltreatment. Yet, there is a dearth of research utilizing actual reporting data from Child Protective Services (CPS) to compare and contrast the reporting practices of mandated reporters. In order to understand these issues more clearly, it is critical to move away from the hypothetical and examine actual reporting data from mandated reporters.

Thus, the purpose of this paper is to describe and compare the reporting data of five mandated reporting groups across the USA. The mandated reporting laws require that individuals engaged in the following fields report to CPS suspected cases of significant child abuse and neglect: (1) education, (2) law and law enforcement, (3) medicine, (4) social services, and (5) mental health (Mathews and Kenny 2008). The present study compared the reporting practices of these five groups of mandated reporters in order to examine key differences in reporting practice. In particular, we explored these groups' reporting on the following variables: percentage of maltreatment reports, child characteristics, type of maltreatment reported, CPS response, and report outcome.

Methods

Design and Sample

Data from the 2010 National Child Abuse and Neglect Data System (NCANDS) were utilized for the analysis of reporting practices of mandated reporters. Each year states voluntarily contribute information related to maltreatment referrals and details of substantiated cases to the NCANDS (US Department of Health and Human Services 2011). It should be noted that it is not only the identification of substantiated cases which helps ameliorate the problem of child maltreatment. In many cases, simply making a report, even if not substantiated, brings the child to the attention of CPS and in many cases enables the provision of family services (Drake and Jonson-Reid 2007; Kohl et al. 2009). In 2010, approximately 3.5 million referrals were received to CPS agencies across the USA (US Department of Health and Human Services 2011). Three-fifths of the reports made to CPS alleging child maltreatment were made by professionals under a legal mandate to report. The remaining reports were made by others who were not under a legal mandate to report (e.g., family, friends, and neighbors). For more detailed demographic information about reports made by mandated reporters in 2010, see Table 4.1.

In working with datasets of this size, statistically significant differences may arise from a difference of a few hundredths of a percent. However, these differences may have little meaningful contextual significance. To provide more meaningful analyses, we selected a random sample of 1,000 cases for the ANOVA analyses comparing mandated reporters to one another as outlined below (Huck and Cormier 1996).

Table 4.1 Demographics of reports made by mandated reporters[a]

Report source	Percentage of all reports by these five mandated reporter groups (%)	Percentage of reports by each group that were substantiated (%)	Mean age of children involved in report (years)	Child gender	Child race	Child is Hispanic (%)	Child is prior victim (%)
Educational	29	19	9.6	Male 50 %	African American 24 %	26	28
				Female 49 %	White 58 %		
					Others 18 %		
Legal/law enforcement	30	44	7.6	Male 50 %	African American 25 %	22	28
				Female 50 %	White 61 %		
					Others 14 %		
Medical	13	33	6.2	Male 49 %	African American 27 %	23	17
				Female 51 %	White 58 %		
					Others 15 %		
Social service	20	29	8.0	Male 49 %	African American 30 %	17	38
				Female 50 %	White 55 %		
					Others 15 %		
Mental health	8	19	10	Male 49 %	African American 20 %	28	25
				Female 51 %	White 56 %		
					Others 24 %		

[a]Percentages may not equal 100 due to rounding

Statistical Analyses

Initial data analyses included creating a descriptive profile for each of the five mandated reporter groups from the NCANDS 2010 dataset. Profiles included demographics of the average child who was the subject of their report (age, gender, race, and ethnicity). Each profile also includes whether the report was substantiated, the type of maltreatment, whether the child had been a victim of maltreatment previously, the number of days necessary to investigate[1], and if an external agency had been contacted concerning the report and which agency.

Analyses of variance (ANOVA) were used to assess differences between reports of alleged maltreatment made by the mandated reporters on the target variables. Identical ANOVAs (with the exception of a substantiation rate variable, as this was used for selection into the second set of analyses) were conducted on only the substantiated cases of maltreatment made by the five mandated reporter groups. For the ANOVA analyses, only the 1,000 randomly selected cases were included, as described above. Categorical variables were dummy coded for use in the ANOVAs.

Results

Reporter Profiles

Reporter profiles were generated for each of the mandated reporter groups based on the complete NCANDS dataset (see Table 4.1). Educational personnel contributed 29 % of all reports made by the five groups combined. The average age of the child in their reports was 9.6 years and was almost evenly split between boys and girls. The majority of the children in education personnel's reports were White and African American.[2] The remaining children were members of other racial groups or unidentified racially. About one-fourth of the children in these reports were Hispanic.

Nineteen percent of the reports made by educational personnel were substantiated by CPS. Seventy-eight percent were not substantiated, and 3 % were either closed with no finding, unknown, or missing. An average of 2.3 days elapsed between the date of the beginning of the investigation and the date CPS made a determination in reports made by educational personnel. Twenty-eight percent of the children in these reports had been the victims of maltreatment previously. When an external agency was notified in cases reported by educational personnel,

[1] Days necessary to investigate were determined by the elapsed time, in days, between the date of CPS initial investigation and report disposition.

[2] Current estimates from the US Census Bureau (2012) of the racial makeup of children 0–17 in the USA are White, 73 %; African American, 15 %; Asian, 5 %; and others, 7 %. Hispanic origin is an ethnicity not a race. Children of Hispanic origin could be any race: 24 %.

the highest percentage involved notification of the police and/or prosecutor. The remaining notifications involved other agencies or were missing or unknown.

Legal or law enforcement personnel contributed 30 % of the reports made by mandated reporters in 2010. The children involved in their reports had an average age of 7.6 years. They were primarily White followed by African American. Twenty-two percent of the children in these reports were of Hispanic origin. Legal and law enforcement personnel reported an equal number of boys and girls as alleged victims of child maltreatment.

Forty-four percent of the reports made by legal or law enforcement personnel were substantiated by CPS. Two percent were classified as "indicated or reason to suspect," signifying that although there was strong suspicion that maltreatment was occurring, there was insufficient evidence to substantiate the case. Fifty-three percent were not substantiated, and the remaining 2 % were either closed without a finding or missing. CPS took an average of 2.4 days to begin an investigation and make a determination in reports made by legal or law enforcement personnel. Twenty-eight percent of the children were prior victims of maltreatment, and a majority involved a notification to some other agency.

Medical personnel contributed 13 % of the reports made by mandated reporters in 2010. In their reports, children were, on average, 6.2 years of age. They were primarily White followed by African American. The remaining children were members of other racial groups or of unknown racial origin. Twenty-three percent of the children in these reports were of Hispanic origin. Medical personnel reported slightly more girls than boys.

Thirty-three percent of the reports made by medical personnel were substantiated. One percent was classified as "indicated or reason to suspect." Sixty-three percent were not substantiated, and the remaining 3 % were either closed without a finding or missing. Reports made by medical personnel were investigated and a determination made in an average of 2.1 days. Seventeen percent of the children were prior victims of maltreatment, and when a notification was made to another agency, the police or prosecutor was most often notified.

Reports made by social service personnel comprised 20 % of the reports. They reported slightly more girls than boys. On average, children in these reports were 8 years of age and primarily White. The next largest racial group was African American, and the remaining children were of other races or of unknown racial origin. Seventeen percent of the children in these reports were of Hispanic origin.

Twenty-nine percent of the reports made by social service personnel were substantiated by CPS. Three percent were classified as "indicated or reason to suspect." The majority of reports were not substantiated by CPS, and the remaining cases were either closed with no finding, missing, or unknown. CPS took, on average, 2.2 days to investigate and make a determination regarding the reports made by social service personnel. Thirty-eight percent of the children in these reports were prior victims of maltreatment, and when notifications were made to outside agencies, most of the time it was to the police and/or prosecutor.

Mental health reporters contributed 8 % of the total reports. The average age of children involved in their reports was 10 years of age. They reported more girls than boys, and they reported more White children, with African American children comprising the next largest group. The remaining children were of other races or of unknown racial origin. Twenty-eight percent of the children in these reports were of Hispanic origin.

Nineteen percent of reports made by mental health personnel were substantiated by CPS, and 1 % were classified as "maltreatment indicated or reason to suspect." The remaining 80 % of the reports were unsubstantiated or closed with no finding. Reports made by mental health personnel took, on average, 3.8 days to investigate. Twenty-five percent of children in reports made by mental health personnel had a prior history of maltreatment. When it was known whether notifications were made to outside agencies, the majority of these notifications were made to the police and/or prosecutor.

Comparisons Between Mandated Reporters

Reports of Alleged Child Maltreatment

As detailed above, 1,000 cases were randomly selected from the full sample for the inferential analyses. Results of the analysis of variance (ANOVA), used to assess differences between the mandated reporter groups on their total reports of alleged maltreatment (i.e., including both substantiated and unsubstantiated reports), revealed some significant differences (see Table 4.2).

Age of Child. First, an ANOVA was conducted to test for differences across mandated reporters by age of child. The results indicated that there was a significant difference in child's age by reporter (F (4,999) =7.3, p<.001). Post hoc t-tests indicated that educational personnel differed significantly from all other reporters except mental health personnel. Educational personnel tended to report older children compared to social service, medical, and legal/law enforcement personnel. Medical personnel reported the youngest children and were found to be significantly different than all other reporters on child age in post hoc t-tests.

Other Child Demographics. There were no significant differences found between mandated reporters' reports of alleged maltreatment on the other target variables, i.e., child gender, child race, notifications, and the number of days taken by CPS to investigate the report (see Table 4.2).

Child's Prior Victimization. A third ANOVA indicated significant differences in reporting maltreatment of children who had been prior victims of maltreatment (F (4,864)=4.58, p<.01). Social service personnel were more likely to report a child who had been a prior victim of maltreatment and were significantly different from all other reporting groups on this variable. Thirty-eight percent of their reports of alleged maltreatment involved children who had been prior victims of maltreatment.

Reports of Different Types of Abuse and Neglect. Significant differences were also found between the reporters on all types of alleged maltreatment reported

Table 4.2 Means and standard deviations of study variables[a] and results of analyses of variance by report source (reports of alleged maltreatment)

	Legal/law enforcement		Education		Social service		Medical		Mental health		ANOVA[a] results	
	Mean	SD	Mean	SD	Mean	SD	Mean	SD	Mean	SD	*F*	*df*
Child's age	8.2	10.0	10.3	12.4	8.0	5.6	5.3	5.2	8.8	4.9	7.30**	4,999
Child is male	.47	.50	.47	.50	.52	.50	.51	.50	.51	.50	.413	4,995
Child is African American	.32	.46	.25	.44	.34	.46	.29	.46	.21	.41	1.80	4,947
Child is White	.61	.49	.62	.49	.60	.49	.61	.49	.61	.49	.076	4,949
Child is of other race	.03	.18	.05	.22	.03	.16	.05	.22	.05	.21	.61	4,999
Child is Hispanic	.28	.45	.32	.47	.20	.40	.29	.45	.22	.42	1.98	4,798
Number of days to investigate	2.4	6.5	2.3	7.5	2.2	5.9	2.1	2.5	3.8	7.1	1.1	4,999
Maltreatment substantiated	.44	.50	.20	.40	.24	.43	.29	.46	.16	.37	13.44**	4,998
Child is prior victim	.27	.45	.28	.45	.38	.49	.16	.37	.25	.44	4.58**	4,864
Physical abuse	.16	.37	.30	.46	.19	.40	.24	.43	.21	.41	4.51**	4,995
Neglect	.54	.50	.38	.49	.58	.50	.44	.50	.41	.50	6.57**	4,995
Medical neglect	0.0	0.0	.02	.12	.01	.10	.06	.23	.01	.11	5.23**	4,995
Sexual abuse	.15	.36	.10	.30	.15	.36	.18	.39	.22	.42	1.39	4,505
Psychological abuse	.15	.36	.06	.24	.03	.17	.03	.18	.10	.30	3.22*	4,432

** $p<.001$, * $p<.05$

[a]Categorical variables were dummy coded for use in the ANOVA

except for sexual abuse. Reports made by mandated reporters of alleged maltreatment differed on physical abuse (F (4,995)=4.51, p<.01), neglect (F (4,995)=6.57, p<.001), medical neglect (F (4,995)=5.23, p<.001), and psychological abuse (F (4,432)=3.22, p<.05). Mandated reporters also differed on the "other" category of maltreatment (F (4,269)=7.16, p<.001), but as this category was unspecified, it was difficult to interpret.

Although educational personnel reported the most physical abuse, they differed significantly only from legal/law enforcement and social service personnel. Legal/law enforcement personnel were the least likely to report physical abuse. Only 16 % of their reports involved physical abuse, but they were only significantly different from educational personnel.

Social service and legal/law enforcement were similar in regard to the percentage of their alleged cases which involved neglect. They differed significantly from all other mandated reporter groups, but not each other. Not surprisingly, medical personnel differed from all other reporters on the percentage of the cases of alleged medical neglect they reported. Legal/law enforcement personnel were more likely to report alleged psychological abuse and differed significantly from all other reporters except for mental health personnel.

Substantiation Rate. In addition, the mandated reporter groups also differed on the percentage of their reports which were substantiated by CPS (F (4,988)=13.44, p<.001). With the highest substantiation rate at 44 %, legal/law enforcement personnel were significantly different from all other mandated reporter groups. With the lowest substantiation rate at 16 %, mental health personnel were significantly different from medical and legal/law enforcement personnel.

Substantiated Reports of Child Maltreatment

The results of ANOVAs, which assessed differences between the mandated reporter groups on their substantiated reports of maltreatment on the target variables, revealed additional significant differences across the mandated reporters (F (4,999)=6.19, p<.001).

Age of Child. Children involved in substantiated cases of maltreatment reported by medical personnel were significantly younger than all other report sources. Medical personnel's substantiated reports involved children with an average age of 6.2 years. Mental health personnel's substantiated cases involved the oldest children at 10 years, but they differed significantly only from medical personnel.

Other Child Demographics. Although the race of the child involved in substantiated reports of maltreatment made by the five mandated reporter groups did not differ significantly (F (4,999)=0.90, p>.05), reports did differ in relation to the child's ethnicity (F (4,999)=4.60, p<.001). Substantiated cases reported by mental health personnel involved the highest percentage of Hispanic children compared to the other mandated reporters, and they were significantly different from all other reporters (Table 4.3). Substantiated cases reported by medical personnel were least likely to involve Hispanic children with just 18 % of their cases doing so.

Table 4.3 Means and standard deviations of study variables[a] and results of analyses of variance by report source (substantiated cases)

	Legal/law enforcement		Education		Social service		Medical		Mental health		ANOVA[a] results	
	Mean	SD	Mean	SD	Mean	SD	Mean	SD	Mean	SD	*F*	*df*
Child's age	7.9	8.5	9.7	9.8	8.9	9.5	5.3	5.5	7.6	5.0	6.2**	4,999
Child is male	.49	.50	.47	.50	.49	.50	.50	.50	.44	.50	0.3	4,999
Child is African American	.24	.43	.22	.41	.32	.47	.27	.45	.23	.42	1.9	4,999
Child is White	.66	.48	.62	.49	.58	.50	.60	.49	.49	.50	2.1	4,999
Child is of other race	.05	.23	.03	.17	.03	.17	.03	.18	.05	.22	0.9	4,999
Child is Hispanic	.24	.43	.30	.46	.25	.43	.18	.38	.45	.50	4.6**	4,999
Number of days to investigate	1.7	4.1	2.0	8.6	1.9	4.6	1.6	8.1	1.9	3.9	1.1	4,999
Child is prior victim	.26	.44	.24	.43	.32	.47	.15	.36	.28	.45	2.5**	4,833
Physical abuse	.14	.35	.37	.48	.18	.39	.13	.34	.18	.38	16.0**	4,997
Neglect	.53	.50	.35	348	.55	.50	.52	.50	.40	.49	7.4**	4,997
Medical neglect	.00	.00	.01	.08	.02	.15	.04	.20	.00	.00	4.4**	4,997
Sexual abuse	.17	.38	.07	.25	.17	.38	.14	.35	.19	.40	2.9**	4,519
Psychological abuse	.18	.38	.05	.21	.08	.27	.04	.21	.18	.39	4.7**	4,452

** $p<.001$, * $p<.05$

[a]Categorical variables were dummy coded for use in the ANOVA

However, they differed significantly only from mental health personnel and educational personnel. Educational personnel had the second highest percentage of Hispanic children. Medical personnel were the least likely to have substantiated cases that involved children with a prior history of maltreatment. With 15 % of their cases involving children with a prior history, they differed significantly from social service and legal/law enforcement personnel (F (4,833) = 2.47, $p < .05$).

Substantiated Cases of Different Types of Abuse and Neglect. The ANOVAs for the type of maltreatment that was substantiated showed significant differences between reporters on all types of maltreatment (F (4,997) = 15.96, $p < .001$). Substantiated cases may have involved multiple forms of maltreatment, but only the first maltreatment substantiated was used for these analyses. Educational personnel had the highest percentage of substantiated cases that involved physical abuse (37 %), and they differed significantly from every other mandated reporter (Table 4.3).

Substantiated cases reported by educational and mental health personnel had the lowest percentages of cases that involved neglect. They differed significantly from all other reporters but not each other (F (4,997) = 7.45, $p < .001$). Medical personnel and social service personnel were the only groups that had a significant number of substantiated cases that involved medical neglect. Thus, they were different from all other reporters, but not each other (F (4,997) = 4.36, $p < .05$). Educational personnel had the lowest percentage of substantiated cases that involved sexual abuse. They were significantly different from all other reporters except medical personnel. Mental health personnel had the highest percentage of substantiated sexual abuse cases (F (4,519) = 2.86, $p < .05$). Mental health personnel also had the highest percentage of substantiated cases that involved psychological abuse, and they were significantly different than all other reporters except for legal/law enforcement personnel, who had 17.6 % of their substantiated cases involving psychological abuse (F (4,452) = 4.67, $p < .05$) (see Table 4.3).

Discussion

The results of these analyses of the 2010 NCANDS data indicate some significant differences in the reporting practices of mandated reporters. Mandated reporters account for the majority of cases reported to CPS across the USA each year, making approximately 60 % of all reports (U.S. Department of Health and Human Services 2011). Rather than report them individually or in aggregate, it is critical to examine how these reports by professionals who work with children are similar to one another and how they differ between groups. Findings from such an examination can identify factors which either increase or decrease the effectiveness of a mandated reporter in reducing the incidence of child maltreatment. Results from these analyses can also inform training for specific mandated reporters, targeting the specific factors which characterize their reporting.

Overall Numbers of Reports and Rates of Substantiation, by Different Reporter Groups. Educational personnel were the second largest contributors of child maltreatment reports, yet they also had the second lowest substantiation rate. Conversely, legal/law enforcement personnel contributed the most reports of all the mandated reporters, and they had the highest substantiation rate. Educational personnel's high contribution rate and low substantiation rate argue against the idea that the more reports you make, the more likely they will be substantiated. It is more likely that the difference in substantiation rate between educators and those involved with the law has to do with training. Child maltreatment is a crime, and it is logical that those trained in the law would be better at providing reports that are more likely to meet the legal requirements for substantiation. Educators receive very little training in how to identify various types of abuse and collect the type of information needed to make a report (Hinkelman and Bruno 2008).

Numbers of Reports and Rates of Substantiation by Type of Abuse and Neglect, by Different Reporter Groups. As has been found previously, physical neglect was the most commonly reported maltreatment from all mandated reporters (Mennena et al. 2010). Social service personnel reported the most cases involving neglect, differing from all other reporters except for legal/law enforcement. While appearing to have a similar impact on reducing the number of neglect cases, social service and legal/law enforcement personnel actually differed significantly on the more important measure of substantiation. Approximately 1 in 4 reports of alleged maltreatment made by social service personnel were substantiated by CPS. However, legal/law enforcement personnel had a substantiation rate almost double that of social service personnel, making them more effective in identifying and reducing the incidence of neglect.

Educational personnel reported the most physical abuse but differed only from social service and legal/law enforcement personnel. In fact, legal/law enforcement personnel were the least likely group to report physical abuse, but, once again, with their substantiation rate more than double that of educational personnel, legal/law enforcement personnel are more effective in bringing cases of physical abuse to the attention of CPS.

It is difficult to explain why legal/law enforcement personnel reported the most psychological abuse. They differed significantly from all other reporters except for mental health personnel. Legal/law enforcement reported 5 % more cases compared to mental health personnel, but these differences virtually disappeared when examining substantiated cases. Although the differences in substantiated cases of psychological abuse between mental health personnel and legal/law enforcement personnel did not reach statistical significance, mental health personnel did have a higher percentage of substantiated cases than legal/law enforcement personnel. A higher percentage of substantiated cases, again, suggests more effective reporting by mental health personnel.

Child's Age and Ethnicity. Some of the differences among the mandated reporters found by age of the child involved in their reports are most likely a result of way some of the mandated reporters come into contact with children. Medical personnel tended to report the youngest children compared to all the other mandated reporters. Younger children are more likely to have frequent visits to the doctor (illness, vaccinations, etc.); thus, medical personnel are more likely to report younger children.

Although the majority of all reports made by all five mandated reporter groups involved White children, African American children appeared to be overrepresented in these data. According to the latest data from the US Census Bureau, African Americans comprised 15.3 % of the total US population under 17 years of age (US Census Bureau 2012). With approximately 25 % of the reports made by all mandated reporters involving African American children, they were involved at a rate that is 60 % higher than is expected based on their representation in the larger US population. African American children are most often involved in reports of neglect (46 %) followed by physical abuse (23 %). Despite this overrepresentation, there were no significant racial differences between reports of alleged or substantiated maltreatment made by mandated reporters.

However, significant differences were found on substantiated cases by child ethnicity. As noted previously, substantiated cases reported by mental health personnel involved a significantly higher number of Hispanics as compared to all other mandated reporter groups. These differences were not found in reports of alleged maltreatment involving Hispanic children, suggesting that the overrepresentation of Hispanics in child maltreatment may be more about substantiation by CPS and less about mandated reporter groups.

Child's Prior Victimization. Additionally, social service personnel were the most likely to have reports involving children with a prior history of maltreatment. They were significantly different from all other groups on reports of alleged maltreatment involving children with a prior history. This seems logical, as contact with a social worker is likely to increase following a substantiation of maltreatment. Increased family contact makes social service personnel better positioned to identify its reoccurrence.

Future Research

Although the findings from this study revealed some interesting differences in child maltreatment reporting among mandated reporters, future research should utilize a multi-year examination of reporting practices of mandated reporters. This will enable researchers to ascertain if the differences found in 1 year are indicative of trends in mandated reporting of child maltreatment and CPS response.

The analyses reported here represent an analysis of an extant administrative dataset. Thus, there are limitations to the research questions that can be addressed. In addition, there is variability in relation to the number of cases contributed by each state. With each state having its own definition and setting its own criteria for substantiation, some states end up contributing more reports to NCANDS each year. The issue of missing data is also a limitation that must be considered.

However, the results of these analyses reveal some interesting differences between mandated reporters. The legal mandate to report suspected cases of maltreatment applies to all five mandated reporter groups. However, the reporting practices of the five mandated reporter groups manifest somewhat differently between each reporter group. The two largest contributors of child maltreatment reports from these groups (educational and legal/law enforcement personnel) have distinctly different substantiation rates. Each reporter group has a unique reporting pattern related to how and why they come into contact with children. Thus, in order to accurately assess the effects of mandated reporting laws on identifying and ultimately reducing the incidence of child maltreatment, inter-reporter comparisons are essential. Such fine-grained analyses can also indicate where efforts need to be devoted to reporter training, response systems, and family support services in order to improve the effectiveness of mandated reporting in reducing the incidence of child maltreatment.

References

Bensley, L., Simmons, K., & Ruggles, D. (2004). Community responses and perceived barriers to responding to child maltreatment. *Journal of Community Health, 29*(2), 141–153.

Drake, B., & Jonson-Reid, M. (2007). A response to Melton based on the best available data. *Child Abuse & Neglect, 31*, 343–360.

Feng, J., Chen, Y., Fetzer, S., Feng, M., & Lin, C. (2012). Ethical and legal challenges of mandated child abuse reporters. *Children and Youth Services Review, 34*(1), 276–280.

Finkelhor, D., & Jones, L. (2006). Why have child maltreatment and child victimization declined? *Journal of Social Issues, 62*(4), 685–716.

Finkelhor, D., Jones, L., & Shattuck, A. (2013). *Updated trends in child maltreatment, 2011*. Durham: Crimes Against Children Research Center.

Flaherty, E. G. (2006). Does the wording of the mandate to report suspected child abuse serve as another barrier to child abuse reporting? *Child Abuse & Neglect, 30*(4), 341–343.

Foreman, T., & Bernet, W. (2000). A misunderstanding regarding the duty to report suspected abuse. *Child Maltreatment, 5*, 190–196.

Gilbert, R., Kemp, A., Thoburn, J., Sidebotham, P., Radford, L., Glaser, D., & MacMillan, H. L. (2009). Recognising and responding to child maltreatment. *The Lancet, 373*(9658), 10–16.

Hinkelman, L., & Bruno, M. (2008). Identification and reporting of child sexual abuse: The role of elementary school professionals. *Elementary School Journal, 108*(5), 376–391.

Huck, S. W., & Cormier, W. H. (1996). *Reading statistics and research*. New York: Harper Collins.

Kemp, G. R., Thoburn, A., Sidebotham, P., Radford, L., Glaser, D., & MacMillan, H. (2009). Recognising and responding to child maltreatment. *The Lancet, 373*(9658), 10–16.

Kohl, P., Jonson-Reid, M., & Drake, B. (2009). Time to leave substantiation behind: Findings from a national probability study. *Child Maltreatment, 14*(1), 17.

Mathews, B., & Kenny, M. (2008). Mandatory reporting legislation in the USA, Canada and Australia: A cross-jurisdictional review of key features, differences and issues. *Child Maltreatment, 13*, 50–63.

Mennena, F., Kimb, K., Sanga, J., & Trickett, P. (2010). Child neglect: Definition and identification of youth's experiences in official reports of maltreatment. *Child Abuse & Neglect, 34*, 647–658.

Takis, A. (2008). The mandatory reporting debate. *Macquarie Law Journal, 8*, 125–152.

U.S. Census Bureau (2012) Annual estimates of the resident population by sex, race, and Hispanic origin for the United States, 1 April 2010 to 1 July 2011 (NC-EST2011-03)

U.S. Department of Health and Human Services. (2006). *Child maltreatment 2005*. Washington, DC: U.S. Government Printing Office.

U.S. Department of Health and Human Services. (2011). *Child maltreatment 2010*. Washington, DC: U.S. Government Printing Office.

U.S. Department of Health and Human Services. (2012). *Child maltreatment 2011*. Washington, DC: U.S. Government Printing Office.

Webster, S. W., O'Toole, R., O'Toole, A. W., & Lucal, B. (2005). Overreporting and underreporting of child abuse: Teachers' use of professional discretion. *Child Abuse and Neglect, 29*, 1281–1296.

Zeman, L. (2005). Hotline tip to probable cause: Filling the gap between suspicion and physical abuse findings for mandated reporters. *The Journal of Long Term Home Health Care, 6*(2), 66–72.

Chapter 5
Privacy and Legal Duties to Warn About Unsafe Behaviors, Conditions, or Hazards: The Example of Child Abuse and Neglect Reporting

Donald C. Bross

Introduction

Child abuse reporting laws were not created nor do they continue without a context. A thorough examination of the context of child abuse reporting should reduce the opportunity for ad hominem attacks, but cannot eliminate positions that are staked out supporting or opposing mandatory reporting based primarily on personal perception rather than through continuing and careful empirical and policy research. One aspect of the context of mandatory child abuse reporting relates to whether the activity is unique to child welfare narrowly defined or whether the notion of identifying hazards, behaviors, and conditions dangerous to people has broad precedents and responds to rapidly changing modern life. The enactment of any mandatory notification requirement related to the condition or behavior of individuals, including children, necessarily implicates the many trade-offs between privacy and safety in daily life. These are issues addressed in this chapter.

Hazard and risk abound in modern life, coexisting with the many resources and benefits of civilization. In response to these dangers, one question that arises is: when to impose duties on individuals or organizations to recognize, notify or warn about hazards, risk, or immediate danger? Recognition of danger on behalf of one's fellow human beings has been considered a positive *value* and at times a *duty* across many centuries.[1] On the other hand, as technological capabilities have grown,

---

[1] Raising an alarm or raising a "Hue and cry." Soukhanov, A. H., ed. (1992), *American Heritage Dictionary of the English Language*, Boston, MA: Houghton Mifflin Company, p. 879; Select

D.C. Bross (✉)
Program in Pediatric Law, Policy and Ethics, Kempe Center for the Prevention and Treatment of Child Abuse and Neglect, Aurora, CO, USA

Department of Pediatrics, School of Medicine, University of Colorado Denver, Aurora, CO, USA
e-mail: donald.bross@ucdenver.edu; donald.bross@childrenscolorado.org

B. Mathews, D.C. Bross (eds.), *Mandatory Reporting Laws and the Identification of Severe Child Abuse and Neglect*, Child Maltreatment 4,
DOI 10.1007/978-94-017-9685-9_5

anxieties have increased about the standing of individuals within such complexity. More particularly, there are continuing concerns that the *sphere of privacy* for individuals is becoming more and more diminished and threatened. Given the intimacy of early human life, the value of personal privacy, as will be seen below, can also be seen as a value largely recognized for ordinary people only in limited settings until the past few centuries. Modern complexity created by population size, science, and intricate social organization can obscure how danger, privacy, and well-being coexist. The question posed in its broadest terms is: under what conditions and through what means are individuals expected, empowered, required or restricted from informing others of a perceived threat? The intrinsic and often overlooked embedded question is: how can society assure that information essential for individual and public functioning and benefit is made available when necessary? Coexisting with this question is: what are the limits of not only guarantees of safety but guarantees of privacy, either by individuals or corporate entities?

The reporting of suspected child abuse and neglect is one of many responsibilities that have been codified in a number of countries to assure that dangers to children of sufficient importance will be identified as soon as possible. The intent of such moral or legal duties is to assure that prevention, or at least a response "in time," will be made more likely. What follows is not a comprehensive analysis of legal duties to warn. This review, however, does have the purpose of providing examples of the range of duties to notify. For some of these examples, the apparent effects and countervailing effects will be described along with their range of possible benefits and detriments. Notwithstanding a necessarily brief review of privacy and accountability trade-offs, however, we can position child maltreatment reporting among the important practices by which human cultures can assure continuing recognition of child endangerment in the twenty-first century. The protection of children in particular is a special challenge because of their vulnerability, the dependence of modern societies on children who grow up successfully as citizens and fill highly demanding roles,[2] and the reality that the younger the children, the greater their reliance on the actions of others to keep them safe and well. The "case statement" for mandatory reporting of child abuse and neglect is, in many ways, similar to the argument for other reportable hazards and conditions: reporting of suspected child maltreatment increases the visibility of child endangerment, and maintaining visibility of harms to children increases the likelihood of response and successful prevention for one of the most significant threats to children's success in life.

Documents of English Constitutional History. Adams, G.B., Stephens, H.M. (eds.). When a fire, flood, or dramatic change in the environs of one's home or community was recognized, an alarm would be sounded. When an individual was thought to have committed a crime, villagers in England would be called to pursue the offender through the hue and cry.

[2] The importance of successful child rearing can be disputed, as perhaps being relatively insignificant to a nation's success or perhaps argued to be impossible except in fully modern societies. However, there are countering arguments that "investment" in children makes all the difference in terms of which societies succeed better than others. Bross, D.C. (1991). The rights of children and national development: Five models. Child *Abuse & Neglect* 15(Sup.I): 89–97.

Guaranteeing children's safety and well-being assures the well-being of human society.[3]

The Contending Values of Privacy and Accountability

In order to consider child maltreatment in context, it is necessary to at least briefly note both comparable current conflicts about privacy and accountability and historical antecedents for current practices. Some historical and cultural practices of mandating notifications have been abandoned. For example, kings and other monarchs afraid of revolt and even regicide supported laws punishing failure to notify the crown of possible acts of revolt or treason. The common law of England included the crime of misprision of a felony (failing to report knowledge of a felony to the authorities): *Sykes v DPP* [1962] AC 528. Such laws were intended to increase the chances of a monarch's survival by punishing any failure to warn crown officials of an impending treasonous act or plot. It is essential to recognize that there was a "privacy" being protected by such laws. It was the privacy of those in authority to be shielded from observation, questioning, and ultimately accountability for the behaviors being done in the name of the crown. Such laws stripped the rights of the plotters to be protected by concerns about their privacy. Challenges to the monarch through demands for greater transparency of policies and financial transactions were often invitations for suppression.

From the perspective of early civilizations, the survival of society through organized government was seen as being dependent on protecting the monarch. As the age of monarchies was replaced by other forms of government, the twentieth century in particular became an incubator for totalitarian governments, differentiated from earlier authoritarian governments by the completeness and efficiency of newer forms of tyranny. Modern totalitarian governments exploit modern technologies and powerful ideologies. Under the implicit notion of government survival, a totalitarian government can mandate the building of apartments with thin walls or built-in eaves dropping. When a totalitarian government imposes sanctions for individuals who refuse to spy on fellow citizens, the authorities can normalize laws that reach well beyond the "ordinary" identification of direct and immediate threats to the government. Totalitarian governments have been known to require notification to government functionaries of any statements of political or cultural opposition or dissent, no matter how mild or indirect. Privacy is greatly diminished or largely nonexistent with respect to many personal, cultural, and political activities in totalitarian countries. As it was under the culture of absolute monarchy, the "privacy" which exists in such cultures is primarily a "privacy" for governmental power. In such settings, there is little or no "accountability" for the misbehaviors of those in power. On the other hand, there is "accountability" for any individual who is sanctioned for anything done or said about the government that does not please the authorities.

[3] Bross and Mathews, 2012.

The hermetically sealed state can come close to abolishing most personal privacy for citizens, so that it can achieve nearly complete compliance with state policies. This is "accountability" that means citizens are completely accountable to authorities but with no reciprocal obligation owed to the citizens: an asymmetric power relationship ripe for abuse. Under such a culture, privacy as a value, even if not absolutely in practice, can be largely extinguished. Argued here is that "privacy" and "accountability" can be favored to extremes, with all of the accountability imposed on some within society who will have no privacy, while all of the privacy achieved is maintained primarily for the benefit of those in power, for whom there is little or no accountability.[4]

This broad introduction leads to the need for analysis of parallel changes in the culture, politics, and law of family life, issues which can only be acknowledged here. For example, in Roman law, children's complete lack of legal rights was embodied in the concept of patria potestas, which gave a father complete dominion over his children and his wife. Such was the extent of this power, and such was the nonchalance with which children were regarded, that in early Roman law the father had the right to expose infants to the elements if he chose to reject their existence[5]: A Borkowski (1994) *Textbook on Roman Law*, Blackstone Press, London, 103; J Gardner (1986) *Women in Roman Law and Society*, Routledge, London, 155. The father also had the right to punish his children, which could include imposing a penalty of death. Further rights included the power to sell one's children aged under seven. The Roman Law doctrine of *parens potestas* or "father rules" has been replaced in many societies that borrowed portions of Roman language and culture. While following *parens patriae in some ways*, doctrine in common law jurisdictions has produced a more nuanced perspective. To the extent that society endorses parental authority over a child, it should also impose duties and constraints on parents as a balancing condition for parental power to be legally sustainable.[6]

Viewed historically, the concept of "privacy" is prominent in both individual liberties law and criminal law. Privacy is a much more encompassing idea than

[4] One illustration of the present "large-scale conflict" over values of privacy versus disclosure is the twenty-first century debate about the extent to which spy agencies should or must be able to access private communications to keep a country's citizens free from terrorism. On one side are individuals who fear that concerns about terrorism are leading to excessive governmental power to track individual lives. On the other are individuals who see modern communications technology as a Trojan horse for enemies who would intrude into most of a nation's affairs, public *and* private, seeking to rob, e.g., trade secrets, or sabotage (e.g., long-distance electrical systems). On one hand, can the secret services of a country be "accountable" for the nation's safety if too many limits are placed on what data is sought? On the other hand, is privacy again being eroded or lost in the name of "protection"? And isn't "accountability" needed not only to make sure sufficient intelligence information is gathered for national safety but also to assure that the same agencies do not exceed spying authority?

[5] Borkowski, A. (1994) *Textbook on Roman Law*, Blackstone Press, London, 103; Gardner, J. (1986) *Women in Roman Law and Society*, Routledge, London, 155.

[6] Lehr v. Robertson (1983) 463 U.S. 248, 262.

concepts of confidentiality, nondisclosure, or testimonial privilege. The concept of privacy in the common law tradition has expanded to include personal rights of religious practice, political belief, choice of marriage or sexual partners, control of personal reproduction, and rights against government intrusion even when a crime is being investigated, requiring many due process safeguards for the constitutional validity of criminal investigations to be upheld. While privacy is indeed a very broad issue, the scope of this analysis is limited, touching only on the extent to which information in any form can be held away from other individuals, and under what circumstances, as well as when information must be conveyed. The purpose is to place reporting duties as a narrow area of policy within a very large realm of philosophical, legal, and practical issues.

Sources for the Meaning and Value of Privacy

In 1890, two famous Justices of the US Supreme Court, Samuel Warren and Louis D Brandeis, wrote a law review article on privacy that has been cited frequently since its publication.[7]

> Political, social, and economic changes entail the recognition of new rights, and the common law, in its eternal youth, grows to meet the new demands of society. Thus, in very early times, the law gave a remedy only for physical interference with life and property, for trespasses vi et armis. Then the "right to life" served only to protect the subject from battery in its various forms; liberty meant freedom from actual restraint; and the right to property secured to the individual his lands and his cattle. Later, there came a recognition of man's spiritual nature, of his feelings and his intellect. Gradually the scope of these legal rights broadened; and now the right to life has come to mean the right to enjoy life, – the right to be let alone; the right to liberty secures the exercise of extensive civil privileges; and the term "property" has grown to comprise every form of possession – intangible, as well as tangible.
>
> Thus, with the recognition of the legal value of sensations, the protection against actual bodily injury was extended to prohibit mere attempts to do such injury; that is, the putting another in fear of such injury. From the action of battery grew that of assault.* Much later there came a qualified protection of the individual against offensive noises and odors, against dust and smoke, and excessive vibration. The law of nuisance was developed.* So regard for human emotions soon extended the scope of personal immunity beyond the body of the individual. His reputation, the standing among his fellow men, was considered, and the law of slander and libel arose.* Man's family relations became a part of the legal conception of his life, and the alienation of a wife's affections was held remediable.* Occasionally the law halted, as in its refusal to recognize the intrusion by seduction upon the honor of the family. But even here, the demands of society were met. A mean fiction, the action per quod servitium amisit, was resorted to, and by allowing damages for injury to the parents' feelings, an adequate remedy was ordinarily afforded.* Similar to the expansion of the right to life was the growth of the legal conception of property. From corporeal property arose the incorporeal rights issuing out of it; and then there opened the wide realm

[7]Warren, S., Brandeis, L.D. (1890) *The right to privacy. Harvard Law Review* 4(December 15, 1990: 193.

> of intangible property, in the products and processes of the mind,* as works of literature and art, * goodwill,* trade secrets, and trademarks.*[8]
>
> This development of the law was inevitable. The intense intellectual and emotional life, and the heightening of sensations which came with the advance of civilization, made it clear to men that only a part of the pain, pleasure, and profit of life lay in physical things. Thoughts, emotions, and sensations demanded legal recognition, and the beautiful capacity for growth which characterizes the common law enabled the judges to afford the requisite protection, without the interposition of the legislature.

This long quotation presents as well as any summary, the change in the meaning of "privacy" during the most recent centuries. By describing the "intangible" as well as tangible, usually property related, rights, the Justices were announcing, at least in the USA, the legal recognition of an expanding sphere of personal privacy. Justices Warren and Brandeis, who are quoted in the lengthy excerpt found immediately above, refer to the innovative capacity of the Common Law. However, it is perhaps their obvious familiarity with the US Constitution that gave them a "head start" on expanding the concept of personal privacy. Specified protections for the "privacy of beliefs" are found in the First Amendment to the US Constitution[9] and are also found in the Fourth Amendment.[10] The thinking reflected in the very term "the Right of Privacy" reverberates in eventual, but later, rulings of the US Supreme Court, including Griswold v. Connecticut,[11] in which the seven member majority endorsed the concept of a "penumbra of privacy" as being a guarantee implicit in the US Constitution, as well as a considerable number of subsequent decisions on behaviors related to sexual choices.

Technology has liberated human beings from being limited to a few, relatively slow, and scarce modes of communications to seemingly ever-expanding ways to communicate. These vast developments challenge us to ask whether privacy related to "new technology" might be culturally distinct.[12] How will we understand any value for the "privacy" of a person's face, lifestyle, associates, or "financial records/ transactions"? In this arena, privacy can be priced to some extent.[13] Rather than any

---

[8] *Citations in the original text are omitted for the sake of brevity.

[9] Article I. Freedom of Speech, Press, Religion, and Petition. Congress shall make no law respecting an establishment of religion, or prohibiting the free exercise thereof; or abridging the freedom of speech, or of the press; or the right of the people peaceably to assemble, and to petition the Government for a redress of grievances.

[10] Article IV. Right of search and seizure regulated. The right of the people to be secure in their persons, houses, papers, and effects, against unreasonable searches and seizures, shall not be violated, and no warrants shall issue, but upon probable cause, supported by oath or affirmation, and particularly describing the place to be searched, and the persons or things to be seized.

[11] The US Supreme Court overturned the conviction of a Connecticut woman who used contraceptives in violation of a Connecticut state law prohibiting such use. (1965). 381 U.S. 479.

[12] Savage, S. and Waldman, D. M., The Value of Online Privacy (October 16, 2013). Available at SSRN: http://ssrn.com/abstract=2341311 or http://dx.doi.org/10.2139/ssrn.2341311

[13] Economists Scott J. Savage and Professor Donald M. Waldman and their team: "(S)urveyed 1,726 people in seven cities nationwide and found a "representative consumer" was willing to pay $2.28 to conceal browser history, $4.05 to conceal contact lists, $1.19 to conceal personal locations, $1.75 to conceal the phone's ID number, and $3.58 to conceal the contents of text messages

estimate of monetary cost, it is the very example of "paying for privacy" during online communications that is important for the discussion here, because it illustrates how context, and the role of the person seeking privacy, influences assumptions of how much privacy can be maintained as a practical matter against the counterbalance of other rights and interests, economic and personal.

As a next example, and as a prefatory transition to the theme of accountability, "privacy" analyzed from the perspective of news media advocates presents the issue as a question of finding justifications for releasing information to the public due to the specific characteristics of the information or the nature of the source of the information.[14] From this perspective, privacy is a secondary and frustrating consideration, as the media is constrained from carrying out its mission of accountability through exposure of facts, some of them arguably "private" but nevertheless newsworthy for reasons such as accountability and media profit. This leads media advocates to a search for the circumstances under which the release of information to the public can and cannot be justified.[15]

> The legal right of privacy has been defined as the right to be let alone, the right of a person "to withhold himself and his property from public scrutiny if he so chooses." Federal Trade Commission v. American Tobacco Co. 262 U.S. 276 (1923) However, unlike the First Amendment right to free speech, privacy (in the media context) is not a right explicitly guaranteed by the Constitution. Instead, privacy law has developed over the last 100 years.[16]

While "certain intimate details about people, even though true, may be "off limits" to the press and public," such as educational, health, or private sexual activities, the names of minors can be published "in newsworthy stories as long as the information is "lawfully obtained" and "truthfully" reported."[17] In other words, the press, being anxious to "serve the public" as well as make money, has a motivation to "push the envelope" in choosing to publish what others might consider private information. In the same light, US media companies must recognize that the very fact that the likeness or details about a child's life are published can cause a court to find that an "invasion of privacy" has occurred.[18] The special domain of family life and children's privacy occurs within the larger domain of privacy and confidentiality, as reviewed in the following section.

---

location, $1.75 to conceal their phone's identification number, and $3.58 to conceal the contents of their text messages." The researchers believe theirs is the first economic study to gauge the monetary value smartphone users place on privacy. That value is measured in the willingness to consumers to pay for five different kinds of digital anonymity.

[14] In general, see Reporters' Committee for Freedom of the Press. (2011). *The First Amendment Handbook*. 7th edition. http://www.rcfp.org/rcfp/orders/docs/FAHB.pdf.

[15] Student Press Center Legal Brief, Invasion of Privacy Law. ©2011 Student Press Law Center.

[16] Id.

[17] Id. citing the unanimous 1979 decision, Smith v. Daily Mail. (1979). 443 U.S. 97. As another example, note that through legislative enactments, privacy rights have been created for citizens of the UK. See the website of The National Council for Civil Liberties: http://www.yourrights.org.uk/yourrights/privacy/index.html

[18] Foretich v. Lifetime Cable. (D.D.C. 1991). 777F. Supp. 47

Privacy Specific to Children and Families

Beginning in the early twentieth century, US Supreme Court decisions related to the US Constitution have been supportive of parental authority, and hence "privacy," to make major decisions about their children's education and religion, essentially blocking unjustified state intervention in family life even if parental decisions do not conform to majority opinion.[19] However, the first decision to the effect that parental authority or privacy has some limits occurred in 1944. Prince v. Massachusetts involved a state law regulating child labor that the parents in question opposed on First Amendment grounds of the freedom to exercise their religion. The child in question was under 12 years of age and was working "voluntarily" selling religious tracts for "a guardian" in the evening. The Court upheld the Massachusetts child labor restriction despite the parents' religious beliefs. From the mid-twentieth century forward, the meaning of personal privacy and privacy within the setting of the family was expanded through decisions addressing contraception,[20] abortion,[21] homosexual behavior,[22] involuntary treatment for mental illness,[23] possession of obscenity,[24] and municipal ordinances defining nuclear families as not including "extended families" for the purposes of zoning for housing.[25] Despite a century of expansion of individual privacy rights, the position of children often continues the implicit assumption of the very earliest cases that stand for the "privacy of parents" when they make decisions for their children and imply a "home as castle" analogy with parents as the controlling individuals on behalf of "family privacy." Simultaneously, however, and notwithstanding many decisions expanding privacy protections of many types, US Supreme Court decisions subsequent to Prince v. Massachusetts have also made clear that parental authority to refuse to take certain measures for their children, for example, to seek and approve medical care, cannot always be legally justified under a privacy umbrella, even for religious reasons.[26]

While decisions of the US Supreme Court receive the widest attention because they can affect the entire USA, the 50 state courts have always been more likely to be presented with questions of family privacy, and questions of accountability for what happens within families. In the earliest years of American common law, "accountability" usually had a focus of preventing or punishing illegitimacy. Determining who was responsible for supporting a child meant a focus on preventing

---

[19] Meyer v Nebraska. (1923). 262 US 390. The US Supreme Court ruled that parents could teach their parents German, even during a time of war against Germany, despite a Nebraska law making the teaching of German illegal; Pierce v. Society of Sisters (1925) has won on appeal to the US Supreme Court by parents who wished to satisfy the Oregon law requiring that children be educated, by having their children educated in private parochial schools.

[20] Griswold v. Connecticut (1965). 381 U.S. 479.

[21] Roe v. Wade (1973). 410 U.S. 113.

[22] Lawrence v. Texas (2003) 539 U.S. 558.

[23] O'Connor v. Donaldson (1975). 422 U.S. 563; Addington v. Texas (1979) 441 U.S. 418.

[24] Stanley v. Georgia. 1969). 394 U.S. 557.

[25] Moore v. City of East Cleveland (1977) 431 U.S. 494.

[26] Jehovah's Witnesses, St., Washington v. King Cty. Hosp. (1968). 390 U.S. 598.

out of wedlock births, leading to paternity cases, and also stigmatization of orphans and children born out of wedlock generally. Early twentieth-century divorce law in the USA often focused on child support. With respect to privacy, most state court decisions deferred to parental authority to make decisions for their children. With the early twentieth-century advent of the "tender years" and ensuing "best interests of the child" standards for determining child custody, parental conflicts were for many years expressed primarily in terms of disagreements about custody and child support. However, from the 1980s on, disagreements about privacy and accountability arose with some frequency and most strongly when allegations of various forms of child abuse or neglect were raised by one parent, the other, or both. Yet, during all of the years leading up to the publication of the Battered-Child Syndrome in 1962, it is remarkable that decisions related to reporting suspected child maltreatment by individuals inside or outside of families do not appear in the appellate case law of the USA. One might reason that since parents held power to decide for their children what confidential information should be revealed, including maltreatment by someone within the family, a report by a physician about possible abuse to authorities would interfere with the parent's fundamental rights. Dean Monrad Paulsen refuted this position in 1967[27] just after all 50 American states sequentially and individually passed child abuse reporting laws. He reasoned that a person, including a parent, who held power over another had no authority to exercise such power in a way that kept in harm's way the person (child) for whom the power was exercised.

Children's Privacy Rights

State statutes requiring reports of suspected child abuse are not the only example of limiting parental authority to govern a child's exercise of privacy rights. Under the "police powers" reserved to them by the Constitution,[28] American states have individually decided for what purposes a person under 18 can give consent to therapeutic or preventive health care without consent by or notice to parents,[29] and the issues of children's competence and right to consent on their own have been addressed by UK court decisions.[30] These laws and decisions have addressed consent by persons under 18 years of age to diagnosis and treatment related to substance abuse, sexually transmitted infections, contraception, mental health care, the right of a minor parent to consent to the care of her or his own child, and consent by emancipated minors.[31] In most other areas, the states defer to parents. Thus, protecting the privacy of children in these narrow situations occurs at the cost of parents being entitled to know everything about their children's medical care.

[27] Paulsen, The Legal Framework for Child Protection, Colum. L. Rev. 66:679, 711 (1966).

[28] Sligh v. Kirkwood (1915) 237 U.S. 52. See also: Santiago Legarr, The historical background of the police power. J. of Constitutional Law 746–794.

[29] Holder, A.R. (1989). Children and health care *Philosophy and Medicine*. 33: 161–172.

[30] *Gillick v West Norfolk and Wisbech Area Health Authority* [1986] AC 112; *R (Axon) v Secretary of State for Health* [2006] EWHC 37 (Admin). See also: Taylor, R. (2007) Reversing the retreat from Gillick? R (Axon) v Secretary of State for Health. Child and Family Law Quarterly, 19(1): 81–97.

[31] See, for example, Colorado Revised Statutes §§19-3-101 et seq.

Parents can deliberately legally waive their child's right to confidentiality in a number of settings. Parents can also "waive consent" without meaning to. One example would be talking about their children's medical issues or school performance outside of a professional relationship, as in discussing their child's situation with a neighbor or a member of the media or talking about their child's court proceedings inside or outside of court.[32] Without a parent present, a journalist can argue that some children are old enough to consent to an interview even though the law provides no explicit standard. Thus, journalists in training can be instructed to obtain consent from minors when they are interviewed, while recognizing that if a child is as young as elementary school age, consent to newspaper interviews and other activities is likely to be treated like consent to contracts or many adult level activities, i.e., not legally recognized.

Parents should also be asked by police specifically to consent for a child to speak with police during an investigation, depending on the nature of the investigation. With respect to juvenile and family courts, the standard practice can be either to presume in favor of closed hearings or presume in favor of open hearings. Depending on the local presumption, motions can be made to close or open hearings by any person with standing to make the motion. The National Association of Counsel for Children has established a position that balances the many different interests served by either maintaining confidentiality or open proceedings in either child protection or delinquency proceedings, recognizing that the equities involved are often different depending on the nature of the litigation.[33]

With respect to many kinds of decisions about children's lives or their right to consent, the states have not acted uniformly to determine their privacy and confidentiality, in effect often defaulting to common law precedents. In some of these domains, Congress has filled the legislative vacuum. Federal laws provide for confidentiality of children's school records, allowing their use almost exclusively for educational purposes, while also creating a few exceptions, including for state laws that existed before the Federal law such as child abuse reporting (Buckley Amendments). The Federal Health Insurance Portability and Privacy ACT (HIPPA) now governs the exchange of protected health information (PHI)[34] including the PHI of children. For further information, see the Summary of the HIPAA Privacy

---

[32] As seen in the example of the following case, a family court from a common law jurisdiction can impose very strict rules of confidentiality on anyone who becomes privy to the information in the case. A county council, a mother, a father, and XYZ [2005] EWHC 31 (Fam), Case No: WR03C00142, http://www.familylawweek.co.uk/site.aspx?i=ed85

[33] National Association of Counsel for Children. Policy Statement. *Confidentiality of Juvenile Court Proceedings and Records.* Adopted by NACC Board of Directors April 25, 1998. http://c.ymcdn.com/sites/www.nacchildlaw.org/resource/resmgr/policy/policy_statement_-_confident.pdf?hhSearchTerms=%22court+and+confidentiality%22

[34] "Under the HIPAA Privacy Rule, protected health information (PHI) refers to individually identifiable health information. Individually identifiable health information is that which can be linked to a particular person. Specifically, this information can relate to:

- The individual's past, present or future physical or mental health or condition,
- The provision of health care to the individual, or,
- The past, present, or future payment for the provision of health care to the individual.

Rule: What Information is Protected – Developed by the Office for Civil Rights at the US Department of Health and Human Services (2003). This site provides a summary of the HIPAA Privacy Rule.[35]

Modern communications technology, particularly through the internet, has resulted in crimes that exploit new technology to target children. The Children's Online Privacy Protection Act (15 U.S.C. §§ 6501-6506) allows parents to control what information is collected online about their children (younger than 13 years old). Operators of websites that either target children or knowingly collect personal information from children must post privacy policies, obtain parental consent before collecting information from children, allow parents to determine how such information is used, and provide the option to not participate or to block some information.

US Federal law also regulates research with minors and extends the protections for minors beyond HIPPA to include specific requirements for both the nature of human subject research permitted and the process by which human subject research on children can be conducted.[36]

To this point, many illustrations have shown that privacy and confidentiality are cherished human values, widely recognized and supported and, in many instances, legally enforced. Numerous requirements for consent prior to release of private or confidential information demonstrate the extent to which privacy is valued and protected. At the same time, however, there are many, many exceptions to the values, rules, and laws that safeguard personal privacy. The following section outlines reasons for imposing limits on confidentiality and privacy.

Information and Accountability

Confidentiality is widely recognized as an important value, is widely supported, and is reasonably well understood. The risks of confidentiality, however, are often overlooked. Why create duties requiring that information be shared? Absent information, neither private nor public business, can continue. Beyond this obvious fact, without access to information, some situations are likely, if uninterrupted, to cause a variety of personal and property injuries. Situations in which lack of information can lead to disaster are not limited to wars; weather, epidemics, and crimes can lead

Common identifiers of health information include names, social security numbers, addresses, and birth dates.

The HIPAA Security Rule applies to individual identifiable health information in electronic form or electronic protected health information (ePHI). It is intended to protect the confidentiality, integrity, and availability of ePHI when it is stored, maintained, or transmitted." See: What is "protected health information" (PHI) and "electronic protected health information" (ePHI) under HIPAA?http://www.hrsa.gov/healthit/toolbox/HealthITAdoptiontoolbox/PrivacyandSecurity/underhipaa.html

[35] http://www.hrsa.gov/healthit/toolbox/HealthITAdoptiontoolbox/PrivacyandSecurity/underhipaa.html

[36] 45 Code of Federal Regulations §46 et al. See especially Subpart D. See also: Sieber, J. E.; Stanley, B. (1988) Ethical and professional dimensions of socially sensitive research. *American Psychologist*, 43(1)49–55. doi: 10.1037/0003-066X.43.1.49

to immediate death or avoidable injury to individuals who are foreseeable victims. More broadly, if with less urgency, economies can fall, public and private corruption can harm millions, and gradual exposure to hazards or behaviors often create irreversible, yet avoidable, injuries, because privacy allows hazard or injury to advance without interruption. Without information about the harmful behavior of individuals or groups, or information about the results of such behavior, accountability is not possible. Not only is information necessary to hold those accountable after harm has been caused, but prevention of harm sometimes may only occur when notifications or warnings are communicated in a timely way.

Reporters and editors insist that they should not be compelled to reveal their "sources." Their claim is based on a principle embedded in the First Amendment to the Constitution that in free societies a free media, "the press," is essential to maintain freedom. Explicitly and implicitly this is an endorsement of the value of accountability needing to outweigh privacy under certain circumstances. The press position is that, in general, not so much information should be kept secret from public disclosure. "The media" extends the argument to the effect that, in general, less information should be protected from public disclosure so that society knows when public and private business is being conducted well and that such revelations do not endanger, but advance, the public interest. This position, offered with legal, moral, practical, monetary, political, constitutional, and cultural supports, introduces the overall question of how to assure responsibility for the exercise of power in the current world.

The position taken by the "free press" across the world, a position that favors the release of more information and discourages many forms of privacy, finds support as soon as one conducts even minimal research seeking examples of laws that require release or reporting of information that some might prefer not to have discovered. Laws that require sharing of information go to the heart of modern economies and nation states; examples include taxation; regulation; economic management of national economies, e.g., through economic surveys; and licensing of businesses and individuals. All of these activities require individuals or organizations of individuals to make available information that they might prefer would remain private. All of these requirements that reduce privacy are performed, at least arguably, for necessary government and societal functioning.

One example, "The Civil War Income Tax of 1862," the first income tax in the US history, represented an early high point for the publicity of tax information. Pursuant to this statute, tax assessment information was posted on "courthoues doors and in newspapers,"[37] to assure "accountability," i.e., to assure compliance with the tax law.[38] Beginning in 1976, the US Congress created confidentiality for tax records but did so while also enacting many exceptions.[39] "The specific disclosure standards vary, but Congress generally crafts a given statutory test based on its sense

[37] Swartz, P. (2008) The future of tax privacy. *National Tax Journal*. 61(4):883–900, 884.

[38] Id.

[39] Id at 883.

of the necessary benefits and burdens of disclosure in a specific context."[40] This is an example of a governmental power that is generally considered essential for the existence of government: the power to tax. The example is also noteworthy in that the notion of "privacy" for tax records followed significantly later than the implementation of the Federal Income Tax.

Professional relationships are another area in which there are conflicts between access to information and the need for the essential service to be performed. Without disclosure to at least one other person, the benefits of the confessional, doctor-patient, mental health-client, or attorney-client relationship are not available. "Accountability" in this context means that without the revelation of "private information" the necessary services or care cannot be provided, or provided sufficiently. Unless the person being served is "accountable," the professional cannot be accountable to the client. A great deal of very personal information about a patient (including, today, even their genetic make-up) is often necessary for accurate diagnosis or treatment. The lawyer, the accountant, or the faith practitioner must know essential personal information about the person being helped, sometimes including embarrassing or humiliating details about the circumstances that led the person to seek assistance.

There is another practical reality. While some professional services are conducted on a "cash only" basis, reimbursement for therapy, legal representation, or other personal services not only encourages but demands extensive disclosure. Still, all services must be provided in a way that harm beyond the act of disclosure itself is minimized. Harms beyond "the act of disclosure itself" include the need to protect from unwarranted oversight or intrusion by government, groups, or individuals. The government might wish to employ sanctions for even trivial offenses if they are by individuals who oppose the government. There can be government and private "true believer" groups who wish to embarrass or undermine individuals with whom they do not agree by violating the privacy rights of targeted individuals who oppose them. There are some who will wish to intrude on the privacy of others for personal pleasure or profit, with the possibilities seemingly endless for voyeurism, blackmail, and exploiting foreknowledge of financial, health, or other personal decisions. Modern technology has magnified, but did not create, the challenge of maintaining a "private sphere of behavior" when there are times when at least limited disclosure is essential.

Unsafe Conditions, Behaviors, and Hazards: How Is Accountability Achieved?

In order to prevent or respond to the occurrence of endangerment, information about the situation is required. Some conditions, behaviors, and hazards are unarguably of a higher level of concern than ordinary business or ordinary life. Without discounting the economic and political harms of nondisclosure already discussed, some

[40] Id. 883–4.

conditions and behaviors create more immediate and severe forms of potential personal harm or monetary loss. These concerns include a greater than average prospect for preventable death, injury, or devastating loss of property, often accompanied by difficulty in assessing the immediacy or proximity of the threat. An often used illustration of a limitation on “free speech” is falsely crying “fire” in a crowded theatre. Here the exercise of the “private” right of free speech is limited by the concern for public safety. At the same time, the “fire in the theatre” example presents an implication: “shouting fire” is a behavior of great importance when justified by the facts, and any misuse or corruption of the “civic and moral good” of warning people of danger therefore creates its own form of egregious wrong.

Information is also needed to address situations that are not immediately drastic in their timing and results. There is a broader problem of dangers to individuals and populations from conduct or conditions that occur repeatedly but slowly over time, cumulatively, and eventually causing great harm. Society generally agrees that excess heavy metals in water, air, or gasoline must be controlled, even though such harms are neither immediately visible nor imminent in likely occurrence. If the dangers are not identified early, they will result eventually in extensive and perhaps devastating harm. However, the dilemma that often arises in such circumstances is that recognizing and responding to the problem depends on access to information thought by some to be, in some sense, “private.” Examples of this balancing between disclosure and accountability include decades of conflict related to disclosure of the effects of cigarettes and lead in gasoline and the continuing modern debate about “fracking.”

One way to begin evaluating the competing values of accountability and privacy is to differentiate and define harm, hazard, danger, and risk. These terms can represent different degrees of only potential or actual harm, and separately the terms can incorporate not only the nature of the harm but also the probability and immediacy of each. Among important modern practices with respect to reporting are public health and reporting of communicable diseases, as well as monitoring and reporting of hazardous wastes and release of toxins into the air or water. Notification that an individual appears to be mentally ill and as a result a direct danger to self or another, notification that a person has a substance abuse disorder of such severity that he or she poses a danger to self or others, as well as notification of apparent child maltreatment are all modern practices for dealing with immediate and prospective direct harm.

Primary Intent of Ameliorative or Preventive Reporting Is Not Punishment

The first reaction to reporting under mental health, child abuse, and public health traditions should not be to assume that the intent of reporting is to ensure punishment. Rarely are mentally ill, substance abusing, or even child-abusing individuals criminally prosecuted in countries where all of these reporting laws exist; this is consistent with child protection laws preferring the least intrusive response even in cases where significant abuse is identified.[41] During the HIV epidemic, many carriers of HIV and others at risk believed that their rights would be endangered if traditional sexually transmitted disease reporting was to include HIV. Since the discovery of HIV, the reader is challenged to find examples of the prosecution of individuals merely because of a positive HIV status in countries with (1) highly developed and scientific public health agencies along with (2) traditions of strong and enforced human rights.[42]

Trying to maintain accountability for harmful conduct is one function of the criminal law, and there is no need to list examples of the need for a system of criminal law in every human society. Yet many examples of harmful conduct do not typically result in criminal prosecution; in many cases, the criminal justice system through enforcement agencies are required to, and do, take the least intrusive course: in the criminal context, it is much more common for people to receive cautions and warnings for technically illegal conduct that does not reach a particularly serious threshold. One of the most important categories of behaviors that result in harm to self or others that are not typically prosecuted are behaviors that are harmful that occur because of the condition of the person who causes the harm. Driving with a medical impairment, such as limited vision or a seizure disorder, can be prosecuted but most individuals do not receive severe punishments or even punishments at all, unless they caused significant harm. A person with a substance abuse disorder is more likely to be prosecuted for driving under the influence, because the scale and scope of the problem is so clearly established as highly dangerous and prevalent. Moreover, substance abuse disorders can be notably resistant to other remedies, such as self-help or voluntary treatment.

As a further example, it is regulation and civil law suits, not criminal law, that are usually applied to achieve accountability for preventable fires, hazardous waste, toxic chemical releases, radiation exposure, gas explosions, and other events and exposures generally. Misbehavior of these kinds is most often managed through regulation, although criminal fines are an additional remedy. Most prosecutors of misbehaviors causing the events just noted reserve criminal charges for the most reckless or intentional circumstances. Public agencies such as the Office of Safety and Health Administration (OSHA), nongovernmental agencies including unions and public and private "watchdogs," and the media can bring to bear the requirements supported by law for changes in behavior, management, and acceptance of responsibility through negotiated settlements, publicity or law suits, and, rarely, criminal sanctions. When a plane crashes, many changes can be imposed, from many directions, on those who control the sources of the flaws, but criminal prosecutions rarely are viewed as necessary or useful for accountability.

---

[41] One of the few studies published on how many cases of maltreatment confirmed by a government case worker will be filed as a criminal charge yielded the result that only 4 % of founded cases result in criminal prosecution.

[42] A rare example of prosecution of an HIV-positive individual occurred in the state of Colorado. The prosecution involved a prostitute who continued in the sex trade while HIV positive, and who continued to be able unable or re-word?? was refusing to practice safe sex despite counseling.

Accountability Within the Personal Lives of Parents, Children, and Families

Does the concept of accountability have a place in the modern, and private, lives of parents and children? The mere suggestion of such a possibility calls to mind, for many, the specter of totalitarian states that recognize no individual liberties. Individual rights are replaced by the implicit "ownership" of individuals by the state. Further consideration recalls the centuries-long history of child welfare that focused most specifically on illegitimacy, bastards, orphanages, the "Scarlet Letter" of adultery, and paternity suits. A major concern addressed by the "Common Law" of Britain and its "offspring" nations (Canada, Australia, the USA, and New Zealand) has been the problem of unwanted births. The overwhelming commitment to avoiding unlicensed or unsupported pregnancy and resulting babies was largely aimed towards accountability. In such circumstances, the father's identity, the loss of control over the pregnancy by the mother, and intrusive proceedings to establish parentage of children (to ensure their financial support and care without reliance on public sources) eroded the privacy rights of the adults and children involved.

Psychiatric diagnosis and treatment of individuals are generally not publicized. The confidential relationship between patient and treating physician gained the usual common law expectations of confidentiality derived from nonpsychiatric medicine. The traditional protection of that relationship extended the doctor-patient privilege to courtroom proceedings, unless those proceedings involved the diagnosis, treatment, and possible commitment for care of the patient in question. The landmark Tarasoff decision of 1976 by the California Supreme Court, however, dramatically limited the general rule of privacy: confidentiality became limited by law in favor of a supervening duty to report situations in which the treating doctor knew or should have known that her or his patient was mentally ill and a direct danger to an identifiable person or persons.

Modern attention to child maltreatment, domestic violence, and elder abuse is shifting the value, law, and policy balance away from favoring parental "privacy" as against all other considerations. Autonomy of adults to the level that it excludes the safety of others is only a qualified endorsement. For example, domestic violence experts and advocates are split on the question of whether a victimized spouse, usually a woman, must be left to decide when to disclose her victimization. The argument in favor of this position is that, in essence, domestic violence involves victims who are powerless to stop it, and taking away their ability to decide when and how it is safe to reveal the abuse only adds to the victim's helplessness. When there is a vulnerable child in the family, however, mandatory reporting laws are generally viewed as prioritizing the child's safety above other concerns.

A final example of the possible erosion of personal privacy in favor of "accountability" relates to notifying individuals exposed to potentially deadly diseases, such as HIV, that are conveyed only or primarily through intimate contact and exchange of fluids or cells. Notifying a spouse or partner – unaware of their loved one's disease status – that she or he is at risk for infection often reveals the likely identity of the carrier. This is true even when anonymous "contact slips" are used. While HIV is considered treatable, it remains a very difficult disease to identify and manage, and the ethical and health arguments for preventing its spread through contact tracing are considered by many to be both powerful and hard to refute. Here again, changing science and technology are creating the need to address the trade-offs for accountability and privacy.

Finally, there is modern recognition that central governments, today's "sovereign," must give way to public demands for transparency under defined circumstances. Examples of this are legislation that creates defined rights for citizens to have access to what otherwise might be considered confidential government documents, as in the US, UK, and Australian Freedom of Information Acts (sometimes called "right to information").[43]

Balancing Privacy and Accountability

The reasons why confidentiality, secrecy, and privacy are treasured by people in public and private roles have been explored. Also introduced has been the idea of how often our need for responsibility and accountability require access to information and a degree of transparency in public and private life. Along with the importance of each of these human concerns, the point has been made that our understanding of the meaning of privacy has evolved through time. Finally, examples have been provided of how often concerns of privacy and accountability compete for priority, often in unavoidable ways.

How do societies and legal systems balance the often competing interests of privacy and confidentiality? In this section, solutions and partial solutions to resolving disputes between these competing rights are presented with a view to clarifying when either privacy or accountability outweighs the other. In the final analysis, it will be clear that both confidentiality and accountability are values that can be used to harm or to protect. In effect, both can be "shields" and "swords" for human behavior and human institutions.

Partial solutions are a common approach to resolving the inherent conflict between secrecy and accountability. No one solution for resolving the conflict between two such important values is likely. Numerous approaches, however, allow the analysis to move from a stark, black-and-white (and perhaps false) dichotomy. These include balancing the two interests, employing a doctrine like "need to know," recognizing supervening duties, and undertaking a "titrated analysis" in which hierarchies of enforcement and protection for the competing values can be analyzed in detail. This approach requires recognizing the mutability of values or concepts such as privacy and confidentiality. Context and facts, rather than immutable principles, must matter. Nothing asserted here means that either value can or should be ignored or not supported.

[43] U.S. http://www.foia.gov; U.K. http://www.legislation.gov.uk/ukpga/2000/36/contents

Balancing tests are well known in law. Whether a search can occur without a warrant depends on balancing many factors, such as whether there is time to obtain a warrant, whether an emergency involving life and death must be investigated promptly (even at the risk of reducing the chances for a criminal conviction), and whether the search has the intention of preparing a criminal charge, or is an administrative search for the general purpose of public safety, are among the many considerations in upholding a search as lawful or declaring a search to be unlawful. In an extensive article, Mark Hardin, while working for the American Bar Association Center on Children and the Law, examined the problem of obtaining information lawfully after a report of child maltreatment is received and protections once a report is made. While focused on searches after a child abuse report, Hardin's analysis is a classic exposition of the use of a balancing test to determine when such information can be obtained and when not.[44]

Need-to-know doctrine was fostered in large measure by the advent of nuclear weapons that intensified the gravity of managing military secrets. In particular, how could a government assure its citizens that the information necessary to employ the weapon would be available, but limited, to the Commander in Chief, and to all of the individuals necessary to manage such a complex task, on short notice, and to no one else. The US military applied the doctrine of "need to know," carefully specifying who, with what training, with what authority, and with what checks and balances, would be given compartmentalized information sufficient to act, without being easily corrupted or obtained by anyone who should not have the information.[45] This example is important for demonstrating that there must be exceptions to even the most important secrets. Without the exceptions, there would be no means to prevent devastating activities which otherwise could be undertaken without accountability.

Within family law, a parent deciding whether or not a child should receive a specified treatment for a diagnosed illness needs to know all of the elements of informed consent that any patient consenting should have. If the parent should not decide such an important matter without full disclosure, surely a judge asked by physicians to override parental judgment should not make such a decision without having at least the same information.[46] In this application of the doctrine, only the information specifically related to the decision at hand must be provided, and not details of the individual's situation irrelevant to the decision at hand.

Supervening, intervening duties that can override personal privacy are manifest in the Tarasoff[47] decision and the 1905 US Supreme Court decision upholding

---

[44] Hardin, M. (1988). Legal barriers in child abuse investigations: State powers and individual rights. 63 *Wash. L Rev.* 493 et seq.

[45] http://en.wikipedia.org/wiki/Need_to_know

[46] Bross, D.C., DeHerrera, N. (2005) Refusal of therapy for children: Factors affecting judicial decisions to override parental decisions. In: Amanda George Donnelly (Ed.) *State of the Art Advocacy for Children, Youth, and Families*. Denver: National Association of Counsel for Children, 147–158; Bross, D.C. (1982) Medical care neglect, *Child Abuse & Neglect* 5(4):375–382.

[47] Tarasoff v. Regents of the University of California. (Cal. 1976).17 Cal. 3d 425, 551 P.2d 334, 131 Cal. Rptr. 14.

mandatory immunization.[48] Overall, the doctor-patient relationship and by extension the psychiatrist-patient relationship have long been supported in common law countries. This legal support extends also, with qualifications, to clinician-patient relationships of psychologists[49] and many other therapists. However, when a reasonable therapist believes or reasonably should believe that a patient is mentally ill and as a result a direct threat to an identifiable person, then the safety of the prospective victim outweighs the privacy of the patient.[50] While consent to medical care is a fundamental requirement of the doctor-patient relationship, a communicable disease epidemic can create a need so great that individuals might be immunized, or at least quarantined, against their will.[51]

"Titrated analysis" involves analyzing hierarchies of duty and protection within the competing values of privacy and accountability. The concept is introduced here to provide a method for moving away from the dichotomous analysis of privacy *versus* safety. In analyzing the question of child abuse records gathered by child protection agencies in the USA under the heading of "central registries," the author proposed some years ago that there are at least seven different uses of such data. For each of these possible uses, there are different interests involved and the need for the data and the harm in its possible sharing vary from use to use.[52] The seven uses identified were:

1. To permit cross-checking of records and to adjust the clinical index of suspicion or to otherwise aid in the evaluation or diagnosis of cases on a clinical basis
2. To permit more efficient management of a state's social services system by providing data for managers and legislators on case loads and comparable information
3. To permit fundamental and evaluation research on the causes, consequences, and effective interventions for child abuse and neglect
4. To prevent a wrongly accused person from being charged or sued or to provide background information which will provide mitigating factors in a sentencing
5. To refuse an adoption
6. To refuse to license an individual for day care, foster care, or similar child care employment
7. To aid criminal investigations[53]

The monograph just cited concludes, in part: "From a legal perspective, 'how much process is due' depends on the particular way in which a registry is being

[48] Jacobson v. Massachusetts. (1905) 197 U.S. 11. See also: Parmet, W.E, Goodman, R.A. and Farber, A. (2005) Perspective: Individual rights versus the public's health – 100 Years after Jacobson v. Massachusetts. *N. E. J. M.* 652–654.

[49] Melton, G.B., Petrila, J., Poythress, N.G. et al. (2007) Constitutional, common-law, and ethical contours of the evaluation process: the mental health professional as double agent. *Psychological Evaluations for the Courts*. 3rd Ed. New York and London: The Guilford Press, pp. 83–84.

[50] See end note xx supra.

[51] See end note xix supra.

[52] Bross, D.C. (1988) Confidentiality, Due Process and the Business of Central Registries: Legal and Policy Considerations. (Monograph) Williamsburg, Va: National Center for State Courts.

[53] Id., 34.

used. Registries used primarily for case management and non-identifying research, for example, require relatively few safeguards beyond what is normally required of confidential governmental records. On the other hand, screening for denial of rights to a property license to provide care for children carries with it a need for more rigorous procedures of notice, review, and appeal."[54] A record sought in aid of criminal prosecution would have to meet the stringent safeguards of not only access to the data but also rigorous challenges of admissibility under the law of criminal procedure. Child abuse records are created by any system that identifies suspected child maltreatment, including mandatory reporting systems. As shown here, the use of reports must be and is very nuanced, and criticisms of mandatory reporting virtually never acknowledge how further safeguards, as well as management decisions about how to employ the information obtained for purposes of treatment, determine at least as much about the utility of reporting as the mere reports themselves.

Child welfare records and central registries provide a useful illustration for making analysis of reporting laws which "titrate" the interests involved and clarify that a raw dichotomy for making decisions about privacy-safety trade-offs often is insufficient for acceptable policy results. This example demonstrates that arguments about mandatory reporting should not be about whether such a law is never or always useful, but rather supports the principle that there should be a continuing process of objective research that establishes when reporting is useful, is harmful, or is in equipoise when viewed in terms of costs and benefits. It should be acknowledged by all involved that child safety is about minimally acceptable parenting as well as about privacy sufficient that child rearing is not disrupted or damaged without "due process" of moral and legal checks and balances. Child safety is not only about parenting or "family" privacy but also about every situation in which children are receiving care, such as day care, school, camps, clinics, club, religious, and sports activities. The right of children to have "access to society" should become a universal, enforced right, tempered by shelter from unwarranted, unjustified, spurious, and, most especially, malevolent "inquiries" by totalitarian agencies or predators on children.[55]

When analyzing duties to protect the public from hazards, what factors should be weighed in comparing duties to maintain confidentiality and duties to support safety? The policy challenge is to include factors such as severity of the harm to be prevented; ease of identification of the harm or hazard (so that what is to be reported is not unreasonably speculative); availability of practical interventions weighed against the change; whether any harms from interfering with either privacy or safety are quantifiable or not; and the availability of practical remedies for individual

---

[54] Id., 49.

[55] Civil rights for children can be seen as a statutory right not to be denied protection or entitlements due to their age. For example, under the UK Equality Act of 2010, the following forms of discrimination are prohibited: age, disability, gender reassignment, marriage and civil partnership, race, religion or belief, sex, sexual orientation, pregnancy or maternity discrimination in the work place, directly or indirectly. Equality Act of 2010. http://www.legislation.gov.uk/ukpga/2010/15/contents.

human and systematic errors. Surely the inherent vulnerability of children should be one of the factors weighted heavily during any balancing test.

Because vested interests will always be present on both sides of any policy divide related to privacy and accountability, the assumptions made and either being implied or overtly asserted must be carefully analyzed from the perspective of the lives of children. Since children as a group vary in their ability to express and advocate for their own health, economic, and political interests, the interests and rights of children are usually more difficult to sustain than the rights of adults. This is especially true for children without reasonably competent caregivers. Adults, including those with beneficent motivation, can easily overcome children's proper interests unless the adults act in ways that are thoughtful, nuanced, and organized. A possible way to militate against inimical acts by well-intentioned adults is to require, whenever possible, that those caring for or attempting to assist children should act through empowering alliances with all children to whatever extent they are able to participate ethically.

The act of reporting is only the first step in working for safety while minimizing intrusions on privacy. Factors that affect legal determinations to favor or disallow information sharing about reports of child abuse or other behaviors and conditions are numerous. A partial list includes: What is the nature of information acquired, by whom was it reported and by whom received and gathered, in what context, and about which individuals or situations does the data pertain? Who can determine and grant permissions to share or disseminate the gathered information, express or implied, and for what purpose? Some statements or claims of disseminated information can be prohibited if the public statement is sufficiently harmful to a person's reputation. Common law has recognized remedies for slander per se and defamation per se, as in a public statement alleging that an individual has syphilis during an age when there was no cure for the disease and its association with immoral behavior. A law can label the dissemination of certain information as ipso facto wrong even if the fact communicated is true. Eventually policies, some enforced by statute or rules, can create standards for specific types of required reports or information derived from reports. In the instance of communicable disease, legislators sometimes delegate to public health authorities the right to decide which diseases must be reported and when information should be disseminated so long as there is a basis in science, for example, as a function of epidemic trends. Other standards are created by case law, for example, what information the physician must tell the patient is governed by informed consent law.

In summarizing how decisions can be made about safety and confidentiality, there are alternative approaches being used. Among these are:

- Balancing Tests
  - Which require clarity about what is at stake for each value in the specific conflict at hand
  - Which require recognition that assertions are not the same thing as facts directly proven, for example, based on transparent research findings

- "Need to Know"
  - "Big secrets" (HIV status, nuclear codes) can and have been maintained.
  - While neither perfect safety nor perfect secrecy is possible, many challenging situations have been addressed by focusing on who does and who does not "need to know."
- "Supervening, intervening duties" are required when the foreseeable harm is severe, immediate, and reasonably predictable.
- "Titrated analysis," as in the use of child protection records and medical records, leads to layered and systematic review of data sharing versus privacy. Titrated analysis must be based on clarity about the science, or lack of science, supporting the particular policy. There must, as well, be as much clarity as possible about the various interests in conflict and solutions available for addressing the issues without ignoring either confidentiality or accountability.

Reporting and Beyond: The Need for Fully Effective Access to Society for Children

Privacy and Confidentiality at the Time of Reports of Maltreatment

Because the youngest children spend most of their time with their primary caregivers, safety in families is the most crucial place for child safety. Most deaths due immediately to child maltreatment occur in the first 4 years of life,[56] and while abuse is usually thought to be the primary reason for preventable child deaths due to maltreatment, neglect is actually the source for about half of these preventable deaths. As part of the security of the home as a place of refuge and nurturing, privacy is important and indeed, absent substantial countervailing factors, should be considered essential to healthy child development.[57] However, confidentiality can also be used as a sword and shield against observation with the result that devastating harm can be done in the name of confidentiality and privacy. Some homes and some families provide little or none of the care that is vital.

In balancing children's vulnerability and lack of autonomy on one hand, and the enormous power granted to parents over their children in most societies on the other, most will agree that parental prerogatives including the need for privacy in family life should be supported presumptively. However, privacy claims should not prevail under conditions in which a child is, or has a likelihood of, suffering from

[56] Child Abuse and Neglect Fatalities 2011: Statistics and Interventions. (2013) Child Welfare Information Gateway, Children's Bureau/ACYF February 2013, at page 4. https://www.childwelfare.gov/can/statistics/stat_fatalities.cfm

[57] Goldstein, J., Freud, A., Solnit, A.J. (1973) Beyond the Best Interests of the Child. New York: Free Press.

significant harm or possible death. Under such circumstances, the child's right to privacy exercised by a caregiver, including a parent, must be abrogated. If investigation is denied by a parent claiming the child's right to privacy, it should be determined when the behavior is in effect the wielding of a sword to defend the parent's interests rather than an action providing confidentiality as a shield for the benefit of the child. Reporting laws have proven to be a very narrow way for roughly 5 % of a given total population of children to be identified as maltreated.[58] Children ever identified in the records of child abuse agencies in the USA are up to four times more likely to be deceased by age 18 than others in their birth cohort.

Privacy and Confidentiality After Reports of Maltreatment

True "citizenship" means more than lip service to the ideas of connection, participation, and influence. The language of the United Nations Convention on the Rights of the Child is clear with respect to its aspiration that children should be treated as fully participating members of society whenever possible. Once a report of child maltreatment is received and a decision is made to evaluate the report thoroughly, new obstacles based on privacy can impede a proper examination of the child's situation. Thus, reporting laws are merely a first step in assuring accountability on behalf of children whose care can be proven to be inadequate.

Mark Hardin for many years served on the staff of the American Bar Association Center on Children and the Law. Mr. Hardin analyzed "Legal Barriers in Child Abuse Investigations: State Powers and Individual Rights"[59] and discussed many of US laws that govern investigation of child maltreatment reports in the context of parental, child, and family privacy. Among his conclusions was a recommendation that reporting laws assure that information to complete a proper evaluation of a child maltreatment report would be legally regulated and be required to be made available whenever justified:

> Child abuse reporting laws generally do not require, however, that the reporter provide information or records beyond those included in the original report. Nor do they require persons not reporting child abuse or neglect to cooperate with the investigation. (citation omitted). Accordingly, state laws should be amended to require both persons obligated to report, and the agencies and institutions for which they work, to provide any information that may be relevant or helpful to an investigation of child abuse or neglect. Where child abuse is reported by an individual who has no legal obligation to do so, the law should require the reporter to provide such relevant follow-up information as is requested by the agency. Confidentiality laws should be abrogated where necessary to accomplish these purposes, and persons or entities meeting these statutory obligations in good faith should also

[58] George E. Fryer, Tom Miyoshi. (1990). Kempe Center research combining a one-year Colorado birth cohort that followed all children born in the same year, matching names with children ever confirmed by the Colorado Department of Human Services as maltreated, and a search of the National Death Registry. Unpublished

[59] Id. 193, 586.

> be exempted from liability. The same statutory penalties that presently apply to willful failures to report child abuse and neglect should be extended to failures to provide obligatory follow-up information.[60]

Once a report is received, records of the child's investigation and evaluation are confidential under state law, and any related court proceedings are confidential or not depending on local practice. Access to state child protection records is limited and usually depends on who wishes to have access to the record and for what purpose.[61] Allegations that the process itself is inimical to children or families are based more often on belief than on rigorous study. The absence of valid research means that many current efforts might be more helpful than harmful. Relatively few child protection cases not brought to the criminal courts receive much, if any, public attention. Of the hundreds of thousands of cases of confirmed child maltreatment in the USA, one study found that only 4 % of those cases resulted in a criminal prosecution.[62] This can be read to imply that there is "overreporting" or it could be read to say that there are many more "speeding tickets" and fines than punishments for substantiated maltreatment. The data also imply that of all children ever identified by a report of suspected child maltreatment, relatively few have their identities or those of their family members revealed to the public. Involuntary evaluation by a case worker is unlikely to be welcome for most. At the same time, citing a list of horrible overreactions by caseworkers cannot be used to condemn the overall importance of the activity, absent empiric information about how most parents feel following a child protection intervention, and given evidence that many children need the intervention. Allegations of systematic and devastating harm to the 4–5 % of children and families ever reported can be studied. One study that asked parents in one American state whether their family was "worse off" or "better off" from two different protective services responses to reports resulted in three times more parents answering that their families were better off. Furthermore, the criticism that children are harmed by foster care must be made in the face of research that finds:

> Although children placed in foster care are at substantial risk for a host of mental health problems and a number of adverse outcomes, these findings do not necessarily suggest that foster care, per se, causes or contributes to these outcomes. In fact, we have found that maltreated children who were placed and remained in foster care demonstrated better functioning than maltreated children who reunified with their biologic families or maltreated children who were never removed from their homes (research citations omitted). The sequelae of maltreatment, described above (earlier in the article found in Pediatric Clinics of North America) likely contribute to the identified problems for foster youth. Studies that have interviewed youth currently and formerly placed in foster care generally have positive feelings about foster care. Most thought placement necessary and in their best interests, and

---

[60] Hardin, M. (1988) Legal barriers in child abuse investigations: State powers and individual rights. 63 *Wash. L Rev.* 493 et seq.

[61] Bross, D.C. (1988). *Confidentiality, Due Process and the Business of Central Registries: Legal and Policy Considerations.* (Monograph) Williamsburg, VA: National Center for State Courts.

[62] Tjaden, P. G., Thoennes, N. (1992) Predictors of legal intervention in child maltreatment cases, *Child Abuse & Neglect* 16:807–821.

> they reported that things would have gotten worse at home without child welfare intervention (research citations omitted).[63]

A very different and important discussion needs to take place as to how reporting laws might be better tailored, for example, with respect to neglect broadly defined, to allow a focus on cases that cry out for investigation even though they are "only neglect." Even more important if child protection is to be improved is valid research on agency response to reports. Creating "differential response" without an adequate scientific basis for triaging of reports is a poor substitute for promoting better science. Elevating support for clinicians should ensure that they have the training and qualities that allow them to use both experience and actuarial research to make better triaging and treatment decisions. Psychology, social work, psychiatry, and pediatrics have important contributions to make in this area.

Over time, those who would eliminate mandatory reporting of severe abuse and neglect might contribute most by devoting energy to (1) preventing child abuse and neglect, which will lead to much less maltreatment to report, and (2) developing science and practices that assure that when a report is made, there is both better triage and better treatment when needed for the reports that are confirmed. A willingness to accept these parameters would allow most who with integrity and intelligence discuss the policy of mandatory reporting, and to enter more informed discussions and related actions concerning why some maltreatment might not need to be reportable, while at the same time more clearly defining the types of situation that, in all good conscience, should not be ignored, no matter where they occur.

Conclusion

Both privacy and accountability (responsibility) are cherished values. Policy, law, and practice decisions must inevitably balance these competing values, in all aspects of life, including the family.

Those who must make decisions favoring privacy versus accountability necessarily must also weigh not only financial but also many hard to define costs of giving one value priority over the other. If the life or health of a child is being injured due to a parental condition, behavior, or even the lack of a parent or guardian, hermetic privacy perpetuates unacceptable harm through isolation of children from the notice and benefits of society at large. Until the life or health of a child is endangered, the child's and family's privacy should be supreme, absent other extraordinary factors. However, privacy considerations should not prevail once a reasonable level of concern has been raised and supported by observable facts.

Depriving a child or a child's parents or other caregivers of privacy absent reasonable concerns about harm or safety can cause harm from intrusion and

[63] Kim Shipman, Heather Taussig. (2009) "Mental health treatment of child abuse and neglect: The promise of evidence-based practice." *Pediatric Clinics of North America*. 56(2):417–428.

disruption. However, modern child abuse and neglect reporting laws have established a decades-long track record of being used, analyzed, and modified when necessary to balance the interests of children, parents, and communities involved. Neither abstract arguments with little or no supportive data nor philosophical objections based primarily on untested assumptions should receive much attention. Surely such arguments should not be given much weight until convincing research establishes that curtailing reporting laws will not prove more harmful than current practices. At the very least, mere speculation should not be sufficient to sway the perspective of objective individuals when little or no empirical evidence supports the argument, especially given that modification of practices with an ameliorative function often proves a better result than abolishing such practices entirely.

Child maltreatment reporting resides within a very large domain of efforts to guard against losses of great personal and societal consequence without disregarding or diminishing other values, social policies, and priorities. Child abuse reporting occurs within the circumscribed domain of reporting and response systems that focus on preserving or enhancing individual safety and well-being, notwithstanding that the situations addressed also have enormous society-wide implications. Communicable diseases, gunshot and knife wounds, driving impairments, mental health conditions in which an identifiable person is a risk to society[64], and "normal" police and ambulance service response systems are, in general, all situations in which an individual is a source or vector of harm threatening a foreseeable victim or victims. Before mandatory reporting, the full extent and importance of abuse of children was neither documented nor carefully studied. Notwithstanding an episodic history of child saving and "liberation," the most severe critic should acknowledge that only with the required visibility of child maltreatment has research, professional understanding, and public support brought continuing attention to a great many aspects of child victimization. Mandatory child abuse reporting is limited to situations of reasonable suspicion, and reporters who do not act in "good faith" can be punished through civil or criminal proceedings. Confidentiality requirements are imposed by the same laws that require reporting, as well as ancillary legislation and judicial precedents that limit the sharing of identifiable information related to specific child abuse reports and cases result in the general public rarely obtaining information about child maltreatment cases that do not lead to criminal charges.

Rather than turning our backs on information about children's safety and well-being, there should be better recognition that modern life has created risks to chil-

[64] In the UK, the Mental Health Act 1983 provides for: (2) An application for admission for assessment may be made in respect of a patient on the grounds that:

(a) He is suffering from mental disorder of a nature or degree which warrants the detention of the patient in a hospital for assessment (or for assessment followed by medical treatment) for at least a limited period.
(b) He ought to be so detained in the interests of his own health or safety or with a view to the protection of other persons. See: http://www.legislation.gov.uk/ukpga/1983/20/contents.

dren from elements that are difficult for parents to control. Given the existential importance of successful child rearing and the existence of dangers such as online predation, we should not be reducing the chances that devastating harm will be ignored. It is also clear that harms occur outside of the immediate sphere of the family. We must require attention also to the dangers for children from the variety of collective, organized, or corporate conduct and conditions that should be monitored. Newer forms of notification of hazards and duties to report might be needed, hopefully encouraged by shared concerns about the safety and well-being of children. Both current and proposed reporting and notification laws should be evaluated through rigorous and ongoing research.

How are reporting laws consistent with evolving interpretations of privacy and accountability, and what, in this high tech era, constitutes a realistic expectation of privacy? Modern life has continually shifted the discussion about confidentiality and sharing of data for reasons of accountability. Human society has grown in numbers, and the more people, the more "impersonality" that results. With many more visual, written, and physical records of different kinds available, privacy is inevitably much more difficult to maintain. The collection of vast, detailed personal information is the price virtually everyone pays to enjoy the advantages of the World Wide Web. Technology enables easy, inexpensive recording of images of everything from people's faces to people's public travel and transactions to easy copying and extensive methods for creating access – legal and illegal – to vast amounts of once private data. A common reaction from individuals within such societies is elevated concern that no one's life is "private" anymore.[65] Responses to such recognition include efforts to shield individuals from having their identities stolen, their personal information misused for the benefit of others, and increased attention to situations in which an expectation of privacy is viewed as being most important to individual well-being. Society's struggle to provide both safety and privacy to its members has included, in some countries, the enactment of child abuse reporting laws that are focused, specified, and limited in their approach to identifying children (1) in immediate danger or (2) experiencing accumulating risk from harm over time while yet maintaining the confidentiality of much that is undertaken in determining the degree of hazard and need for response on behalf of the children identified.

Respect for privacy is not omnipresent in the world, nor is it the only societal value, nor is it uniform in its application. Children deserve privacy within their families and lives as much as, and perhaps more than, adults. However, the obligations to warn about unsafe behaviors, conditions, or hazards, including child abuse and neglect, are in place to try to ensure that as far as is possible, children, as the future of the society in which they live, are protected. Children, in every society,

[65] It is interesting to me that, paradoxically, people are willingly and voluntarily revealing equally vast amounts of information about their personal lives through social media and about their travels and transactions through loyalty cards, credit cards, and EZ passes. Personal comment, Donald Woodhouse, April 2014.

deserve at least the minimal monitoring and access to society that creates the possibility of assuring that individuals, no matter who they are, might be held responsible if they are harming children or failing to provide children's necessities when the means to do so are at hand.

Acknowledgements The author acknowledges the editing help of Donald Edward Woodhouse, Antioch College, and Edward Richards, School of Law, Louisiana State University, both of the USA, and Dr Andrew Graeme Rowland, Emergency Department, North Manchester General Hospital, UK, who are of course not responsible for errors, omissions, or opinions found herein.

Chapter 6
The Historical Background for Mandatory Reporting Laws in Public Health

Edward P. Richards

Introduction

This chapter reviews the history and legal basis for public health surveillance, then looks at the modern world of big data and all pervasive surveillance. While specific legal references are from the United States, most countries follow a similar framework. Historically, there was little legal recognition of personal privacy. Yet the difficulty of collecting data – the administrative cost of surveillance – was so high that individuals generally had significant actual privacy. Through the 1970s, reporting depended on paper reports manually sent in by physicians, and few physicians took the time to file the reports.

Contemporary law recognizes more general privacy rights, but there are still few limitations on government access to data for public health surveillance. Technology and cultural changes have dramatically increased the volume of that data and made it extremely cheap to collect and analyze it. Now public health surveillance can include electronic data from laboratories, individual's Google searches for disease symptoms, grocery store checkout data that includes over-the-counter and prescription drug purchases, and Facebook updates on every aspect of personal behavior.

The traditional problem of public health surveillance was how to get physicians and others to report. Now the problem for public health authorities is to avoid being drowned in the sea of available data. Public health surveillance is no longer a question of getting everything available. Now authorities must decide what are the most cost-effective sources of information, how can they be handled to minimize unnecessary intrusions into personal privacy, and how to extract the data that needs action from the noise.

E.P. Richards, JD, MPH (✉)
LSU Law Center, Louisiana State University, Baton Rouge, LA, USA
e-mail: richards@lsu.edu

B. Mathews, D.C. Bross (eds.), *Mandatory Reporting Laws and the Identification of Severe Child Abuse and Neglect*, Child Maltreatment 4,
DOI 10.1007/978-94-017-9685-9_6

The Taxonomy of Public Health and Safety Reporting

The legal and ethical considerations in public health surveillance cannot be analyzed in isolation from the nature and uses of the data collected. There are three dimensions to reporting: Is the data collected from the individual with the target condition or from a third party? Does the data identify specific individuals, or is it anonymous? Finally, how will the data be used? Is it to benefit the target individual, to benefit the public's health, or to punish an individual for criminal conduct?

Who Provides the Data?

Agencies collect information from individuals about themselves, first-party reporting, and from others who hold information about the individual, third-party reporting. An example of first-party reporting would be interviewing HIV-infected individuals about their sexual partners so that their partners can be notified and counseled about their exposure to HIV. In some cases, medical tests or examinations are required, such as an x-ray for pulmonary tuberculosis or a blood test for syphilis. These are legally classified as searches and, if the individual does not consent, searches can be ordered by a court and administered against the individual's will.[1]

A regulation requiring physicians to report HIV-infected patients would be third-party reporting in that the data is obtained from someone (a third party in legal terms) other than the person with the condition being investigated. There are several legal tools to obtain information from third parties. The traditional tool for public health surveillance is a law that requires that the patient's HIV status (or other condition) be reported when it comes to the attention of the mandatory reporter. The agency can also use a subpoena which is a demand for existing information held by a third party. This can be used to investigate conditions that are covered by reporting laws. If the information is needed quickly or if the agency wants to assure an accurate report, an inspector can search the records and copy the necessary information. While the legal frameworks may differ among countries, all public health and safety agencies use these basic techniques.

How Intrusive Is the Reporting?

From a legal and ethical point of view, the least problematic data is anonymous data that provides information about the condition being tracked, but without identifying the individuals with the condition. Anonymous data is used to track widespread, common diseases or conditions, such as seasonal influenza. Reporting is often

[1] This is rare for public health testing, although a person who refuses testing for tuberculosis might face isolation until it can be shown that there is no risk of transmission. Testing will be ordered if it is a criminal matter, such as abuse of a child with possible transmission of an STI.

limited to the number of cases a healthcare provider has seen, with no additional information. Such data is used for epidemiological background information rather than for individual interventions. Even if the patient is not named, the more detail in the report, the higher the probability that this information can be linked to a target individual. This has become much more significant in the modern era when there is access to extensive personal information on social media and from third-party data aggregators. If individuals can be identified by linking the report with other available data sources, it will raise the same issues as identified data (Yakowitz 2011).

As long as it is collected properly, data such as influenza counts for epidemiologic purposes do not invade an individual's privacy. In contrast, reports of syphilis, a less common disease with more serious sequelae, include the identity of the patient so that the patient can be located by disease investigators. This is done to assure that persons infected with syphilis receive treatment. People who are infected with syphilis are not restricted, and treatment is not legally mandated in routine cases.[2] Disease investigators will contact sexual contacts whom the infected individual voluntarily identifies (Ogilvie et al. 2005). Thus, syphilis reporting raises some privacy issues, but is a limited intrusion into the individual's life.

Historically, most disease reporting was required to allow authorities to take action to prevent specific individuals from spreading a communicable disease. This requires reporting the name and address of the infected person. While there were cases litigating the right of the state to take the restrictive actions, there was no question about the reporting itself until 1977, when the United States Supreme Court decided a case challenging the right of New York to require the named reporting of persons receiving narcotics prescriptions (Whalen v. Roe 1977). Patient plaintiffs argued that this was an impermissible violation of their privacy, and their physicians argued that it was an improper intrusion into the physician-patient relationship. The court upheld the right of the state to require named reporting, only cautioning that the data should be protected from unnecessary disclosure. Despite the legality of named reporting and its importance in public health, it continues to be controversial for diseases which have a social stigma or which affect minority groups disproportionately.

The largest screening and named reporting program in the United States is the screening of newborns to detect genetic diseases. Newborn screening data is used to identify affected newborns so that they can be treated before the disease does irreversible damage (Moyer et al. 2008). It is the only large-scale, mandatory, systematic screening and reporting program for genetic diseases. (In some states, there is also mandatory HIV screening for newborns to assure that infected infants receive prompt treatment.) While mandatory screening and reporting of genetic diseases is very controversial, the justification for these programs in newborns is that the diseases being screened can only be mitigated by early treatment. Without screening at birth, the chance for early intervention would be lost, at a high cost in suffering and medical care costs.

Tuberculosis reporting raises significant personal privacy issues. While there is concern for the health of the tuberculosis carrier, the primary purpose of tuberculosis

[2] This could become an issue if a pregnant woman refused syphilis treatment.

reporting is to identify infected individuals who are a threat to the community. Infected individuals are subject to mandatory testing, treatment (or indefinite confinement in lieu of treatment), and restrictions until they are no longer infectious. Despite the level of intrusion, this is still a public health matter rather than a criminal matter – restricting tuberculosis carriers is not done as a punishment for being infected.[3] This limits the legal protections for the individual's liberty and privacy. While tuberculosis reporting is done to protect the community, it also benefits persons infected with tuberculosis by assuring that they receive evaluation and treatment.

Some public health surveillance programs only benefit the public. For example, in many states, healthcare providers are required to report individuals with mental or physical conditions that can impair driving to the state agency that licenses drivers. The public health threat is the risk of an automobile accident, not the transmission of a communicable disease. The individual's condition has already been diagnosed by a healthcare provider. The purpose of the report is to allow the state to evaluate whether the individual can safely drive a car. Since such a report will likely cost the individual the right to drive, this is a significant intrusion on individual liberty. This intrusion is justified by the risk the individual poses to others and to himself/herself. While the individual might choose to accept the personal risk of driving, the potential harm to others justifies denying the individual this choice.

Abuse reporting poses more complex issues because the purpose of the report is to prevent future harm to the victim of the abuse and to identify the abuser. The report is intrusive for the victim, but this is outweighed by the potential benefits of intervention to stop the abuse. The information may also identify criminal wrongdoing and trigger a criminal investigation and prosecution of the abuser. The abuser has no right of privacy in this data, so it cannot be said to intrude on his/her privacy. As will be discussed later, legal problems arise if the source of the information about the abuse is someone who has a legally privileged relationship with the abuser, such as his/her lawyer. In the United States, abuse laws were first aimed at child abuse and neglect. Many states now require reports of elder abuse.

Violent injury reporting (gunshot wounds, stab wounds, etc.) is done primarily for law enforcement purposes, not to benefit the wounded person or prevent future injuries. While the injury may be accidental, many wounds are due to criminal activity. While some physicians feel an ethical conflict when asked to make a report that may trigger the prosecution of their patient, physicians have no right to refuse to comply with violent injury reporting laws.

Vital statistics are records of births and deaths. These have been recorded for wealthy property owners for hundreds of years, since the information is critical to the inheritance of property and titles. The families themselves would keep records. The parish churches would record births, baptisms, marriages, and deaths. The church might also keep records on poorer parishioners. The state's interest in these was historically related to property and taxes. It is only more recently that states have passed laws requiring the systematic recording of births and deaths.

[3] Even if the isolation is done in a jail, the courts have not found that the purpose is punishment.

This required information now includes demographic and medical information that makes these records an indispensable source of epidemiologic information.

Since the primary purpose of collecting vital statistics records is legal, there are strict regulations on healthcare professionals to assure that vital statistics data is reported accurately. This makes vital statistics records the most robust of all traditional public health records. Individuals are not allowed to opt out of vital statistics reporting. In that sense, the reporting is intrusive – it is identified and you cannot opt out. But unlike most other forms of identified surveillance data, it is not used for individual public health or law enforcement interventions. Thus, the intrusion into autonomy is very limited and easily balanced against the benefit to the individual of having a reliable way to establish identity.

Unlike other public health records, birth and death records can be valuable to criminals. For example, the United States vital statistics recording system does not do a good job of matching death and birth records. This allows an individual to use a birth certificate of someone born about the time of their birth, but who died in infancy, as the basis for a false identity. The risk of improper use has been exacerbated in the online world. It may be necessary to include unique markers in vital statistics records, such as the DNA sample that was collected for screening for neonatal genetic diseases. Such enhanced records will raise significant privacy questions.

Comparative Law Issues

Reporting laws are part of administrative law, the law that governs the relationship between government agencies and the people for noncriminal matters. Unlike some aspects of the United States legal system, the administrative law system parallels those in many other countries. All systems must balance the protection of public health and safety against individual privacy and autonomy. In the United States, and most other democratic societies, protections for the individual's privacy increase when the purpose of gathering the information is to prosecute the individual for a crime. The individual's rights are much more limited when the information is needed to prevent future harm to others. The legal cases used as examples in this chapter will only be binding law in the United States, but they are representative of common solutions to this balancing question as stated in Article 8 of the European Convention on Human Rights (European Convention on Human Rights Act 2003):

1. Everyone has the right to respect for his private and family life, his home and his correspondence.
2. There shall be no interference by a public authority with the exercise of this right except such as is in accordance with the law and is necessary in a democratic society in the interests of national security, public safety or the economic well-being of the country, for the prevention of disorder or crime, for the protection of health or morals, or for the protection of the rights and freedoms of others.

The History of Public Health Power

The fear of plagues is as old as society. They were a threat to individual health and life and a threat to the state itself. Epidemics could destabilize a society and, if the society was naïve to the infection, might totally destroy it (McNeill 1976). Public health was part of national security and subject to the legal deference due to threats to the state. Public health and national security still merge in surveillance for bioterrorism and pandemic illness. Since the power of the state is strongest when its existence is threatened, it is not surprising that historic public health powers were very broad.

Some of the first public health laws are codified in the book of Leviticus in the old testament of the Bible. The word "quarantine" derives from *quadraginta*, meaning 40. It was first used between 1377 and 1403 when Venice and the other maritime cities of the Mediterranean adopted and enforced a 40-day detention for all vessels entering their ports (Bolduan and Bolduan 1949). This detention period allowed symptoms to develop among any infected persons so that they could be identified. The English statutory and common law recognized the right of the state to identify and quarantine plague carriers. Blackstone observed that disobeying quarantine orders merited severe punishments, including death (Blackstone 1769).

The American colonies followed this English law, and when the United States Constitution was written, the public health powers of the colonies were left with the states (Cooley 1987). Soon after the Constitution was ratified, the states were forced to exercise their police power to combat an epidemic of yellow fever that raged in New York and Philadelphia. The flavor of that period was later captured in an argument before the Supreme Court:

> For ten years prior, the yellow-fever had raged almost annually in the city, and annual laws were passed to resist it. The wit of man was exhausted, but in vain. Never did the pestilence rage more violently than in the summer of 1798. The State was in despair. The rising hopes of the metropolis began to fade. The opinion was gaining ground, that the cause of this annual disease was indigenous, and that all precautions against its importation were useless. But the leading spirits of that day were unwilling to give up the city without a final desperate effort. The havoc in the summer of 1798 is represented as terrific. The whole country was roused. A cordon sanitaire was thrown around the city. Governor Mifflin of Pennsylvania proclaimed a non-intercourse between New York and Philadelphia. (Smith v. Turner 1849)

A few years earlier, in 1793, a yellow fever epidemic killed 10% of the population of Philadelphia (Powell 1949). When individual rights were balanced against these threats to the public health and even to societal order itself, the courts found few limits to the public health power to protect the population, called the police power.[4] This basic legal analysis and the deference to public health police power persist today.

The state has a second source of power that is used for some forms of public health surveillance, the *parens patriae* power. This is the power of the state as a parent to protect individuals, sometimes against their will. The classic example is involuntary mental health commitment. When the commitment is because the patient is a danger to others, it is a police power commitment. When the commitment

---

[4] This usage predates the use of police to mean law enforcement agencies dealing with criminal law matters.

is because the patient is a danger to himself/herself, it is a *parens patriae* commitment. Programs to identify and report noncommunicable diseases, which contain a component of treatment or intervention to benefit the affected person, are at least partially justified by the *parens patriae* authority. Neonatal screening for genetic diseases to allow early treatment of the newborns is primarily a *parens patriae* intervention, although there is community benefit (police power) in the epidemiologic data that is generated.

In contemporary law, most public health programs, including disease surveillance and abuse reporting, are handled by state and local agencies under state law. The federal government collects data on environmental health, workplace safety, and occupational diseases. Some states run their own parallel programs that provide additional protections for the employees of the large employers covered by federal programs. These state programs also reach smaller employers that are not covered by the federal programs. National security issues, which implicate foreign powers or involve domestic terrorism, are handled by the federal government, in cooperation with local authorities.

Constitutional Restrictions on First-Party Data Collection

Obtaining first-party information through a search is the most intrusive form of public health surveillance.[5] While the modern notion of privacy was unknown to the drafters of the Constitution, they were familiar with intrusive searches of their homes by British troops. As a result, the only privacy interest that is explicitly protected in the text of the Constitution is the security of one's home and personal effects from a search. The 4th Amendment does not prevent these searches, but establishes a standard for legal process before a search can be done:

> The right of the people to be secure in their persons, houses, papers, and effects, against unreasonable searches and seizures, shall not be violated, and no warrants shall issue, but upon probable cause, supported by oath or affirmation, and particularly describing the place to be searched, and the persons or things to be seized. (Constitution 1789)

The core requirement is a warrant issued by a decision-maker who is independent of the agency that is doing the search. That decision-maker is usually a judge because judges are from a different branch of the government than the agency requesting the warrant. The judge must determine whether sufficient evidence has been presented to establish a reasonable probability that a search of a specific location will turn up identified evidence related to a purpose of the search. In criminal law cases, this means evidence related to a crime that has already been committed.[6] These requirements prevent the so-called fishing expeditions where the police

---

[5] Medical tests such as blood tests are considered searches for legal purposes; thus, the most intrusive search would be an involuntary medical test.

[6] This can include the criminal act of planning a future crime, such as conspiracy to commit murder. The court does not need to wait until the murder is carried out.

search for evidence that might alert them to a crime. They also prevent searches from being used as harassment.

The Constitution also prevents a person from being forced to testify against himself. Testimony means actual testimony, not facts collected through searches or tests. With certain limited exceptions, the privilege against self-incrimination only applies to testimony in criminal proceedings. Self-incrimination is seldom at issue in public health investigations because public health investigators do not force people to provide information. For example, in contact tracing for sexually transmitted infections, people are not coerced into identifying their contacts. Even in matters that touch criminal law, such as prostitution, public health investigators usually do not involve the police because they know that doing so would destroy community trust, making it difficult to do disease investigations in the future.

Exceptions to Search Warrant Requirements

The 4th Amendment seems to require a probable cause warrant for all searches of a person's home or effects. This makes sense for investigating crimes that have taken place, but does not fit with the public health goal of prevention. Most public health searches are fishing expeditions, in that they are looking for problems or data to try to understand some aspect of public health. Fortunately, public health searches were also known to the drafters. Colonial boards of health carried out warrantless searches for public health threats such as insanitary conditions or vermin. A homeowner who refused entry to a health inspector risked a fine and arrest. These searches continued after the ratification of the Constitution. The first case contesting these warrantless searches did not reach the United States Supreme Court until 1959 (Frank v. Maryland 1959). The court found that the 4th Amendment warrant requirements were limited to searches for evidence in criminal cases: warrantless public health searches were not unreasonable. The court stressed the long history of warrantless public health searches. They were considered a limited intrusion into individual rights because the evidence was only used to prevent future injuries, not for criminal prosecution.

The court revisited this question a few years later, during the political turmoil of the 1960s (Camara v. Municipal Court City and County 1967). It was concerned that health officials might abuse such unfettered discretion. The court recognized that public health searches were looking for conditions that might pose risks in the future, rather than looking for evidence of crimes that had already occurred. Thus, it would be impossible to specify the evidence that would be sought. Since many public health searches are based on general criteria such as the time elapsed since the last inspection, there is no specific probable cause based on individualized conditions for a given home. The Supreme Court created a relaxed warrant requirement that allowed a warrant to be issued based on criteria such as the neighborhood to be searched, the time since the last searches, or generalized factors such as an increase in rats in the area. There was no need for specific information about each place to be searched.

Since these non-probable cause warrants are used by administrative agencies, they are usually called administrative warrants to distinguish them from the warrants which are used for criminal investigations. Administrative warrants limit the possible misuse of searches without providing individualized protection for home or business owners. The Supreme Court also recognized that even this limited warrant was not necessary if it would unduly compromise the state's ability to carry out the search. For example, if there were no time to obtain a warrant or if the process of obtaining the warrant might alert the subject of the search and prevent an effective search, the agency could demand entry without a warrant. Since these administrative searches do not provide 4th Amendment protections, they are not to be used as a subterfuge to search for criminal evidence without a proper probable cause warrant.[7]

Warrants are not necessary if the subject of the search consents to the search. This is important in public health because most people will cooperate with public health inquiries. In most circumstances, public health officials ask for consent for searches and inquiries and only go to court for a warrant if there is no sufficient cooperation. The court has also recognized constructive consent through a reduced expectation of privacy. Thus, operators of regulated businesses whose operating permits or licenses include a notice that they are subject to warrantless searches and inspections were found to have a reduced expectation of privacy and could not refuse a warrantless search. Most businesses that have a public health permit, such as food handling permits, hospital licenses, etc., are subject to these warrantless search and inspection provisions. These same provisions also apply to businesses that affect public safety, such as firearm dealers.

Administrative searches are often used to discover information about public health and safety risks such as fire code violations and sanitation problems. Public health agencies can issue orders that require drawing blood or doing an x-ray to collect information about dangerous communicable diseases.[8] In child abuse and neglect investigation, an administrative search might be used to evaluate the condition of the home of a child who is suspected of being neglected. This would be a first-party search as regards actions taken against the caregiver for abuse, but a third-party search as regards the welfare of the child.

There are some cases where public health and safety investigators need to be aware of criminal due process rights. All child abuse and neglect cases are potentially criminal law matters as the information may be used for prosecuting the abuser. Sexually transmitted infection investigations can become criminal law matters if rape is at issue. If communicable disease agents or toxins are used as weapons or as terrorist agents, then there will be a hybrid criminal and public health investigation. In general, if criminal charges are a possibility, it may be necessary to get a probable cause warrant so the evidence can be used in a criminal trial. If there is an acute threat, like a toxic release, the agency must protect the public health first, even if it might limit the eventual use of the evidence that was gathered in a criminal trial.

---

[7] The courts have used this public health prevention rationale to authorize national security and counterterrorism searches based on general warrants that do not require probable cause.

[8] If the person consents to the test, no further action is needed. If the person refuses, then the public health agency will have to ask a court to enforce the order through the police or sheriff's office.

Third-Party Surveillance

Most public health surveillance is based on getting information from third parties, i.e., someone other than the person the information concerns. Laboratories are required to report positive tests for communicable diseases. Healthcare providers, teachers, and many others are required to report potential child abuse and neglect. Outside the public health realm, banks are required to report cash transactions over a certain amount, and there are many other institutions that must report activities that might be linked to criminal activity or terrorism.

The legal rule is simple: with a few exceptions, you have no expectation of privacy in information held by third parties. That means that individuals have no right to prevent the government from collecting information that has been given to third parties. The government does not have to get a warrant to collect the information, and individuals do not have the right to be informed that the information is being collected. This is contrary to most people's expectations, including those of many lawyers who do not work with administrative or national security law.

Legal Privileges

In the United States, there are two classes of exceptions to the general rule that there is no expectation of privacy in information held by third parties: common law legal privileges and protections provided by legislation.[9] There are three common law privileges: spousal privilege, priest-penitent privilege, and attorney-client privilege. Spousal privilege prevents one spouse from testifying against the other about the information he/she was told by the other spouse. This does not apply to information that the spouse gained independently, such as seeing a murder weapon. It would not include seeing the other spouse abuse a child, but it would include being told about the child abuse by the spouse. In many states, the spousal privilege has been abolished for child abuse reporting.

Priest-penitent privilege protects information given to a priest during confession. Information that the priest is told during pastoral counseling or during administrative duties, such as supervising other priests, is not privileged. Many states have specific laws construing priest-penitent privilege very narrowly for child abuse investigation and reporting. Some have abolished the privilege entirely for child abuse cases.

Attorney-client privilege protects information told to an attorney by a client.[10] Unlike the other two privileges, there is a constitutional basis for the attorney-client privilege in the constitutional right to be represented by counsel. Thus, the state cannot abolish the constitutional minimum attorney-client privilege. However, the

[9] These are mirrored in most Western countries.

[10] There is a separate, weaker privilege, called attorney work product doctrine, that protects information that the attorney finds out himself/herself about the case.

constitutional attorney-client privilege is only about past behavior, not information about future crimes. This is embodied in state codes of ethics for lawyers, which typically allow – but do not require – reporting of potential future crimes by clients that may cause death or serious bodily harm. Child abuse would likely come under this exception. This would allow the state to require lawyers to report ongoing abuse without infringing on the constitutional right of counsel or the professional code of ethics.

Attorney reporting is, and has been, very controversial. Some states list attorneys as mandatory reporters in their abuse reporting statute, and others have a general duty for anyone who suspects child abuse or neglect to make a report. In states where attorneys have reporting duties, some allow the attorney-client privilege to be claimed if the attorney found out the information from the client. In the states where attorneys have a duty to report and there is no exception for attorney-client privilege, there is the possibility that attorneys must report child abuse discovered in representing their clients and may be disciplined for failing to do so.

Divorce and custody battles pose unique legal and ethical problems for child abuse reporting. They are the rare situation where there is a substantial risk of false reports. Allegations of child abuse by one party can dramatically change the balance of power in the legal dispute. The court is unlikely to award custody to an abusing parent and may also find greater fault (and give a greater settlement) against such a parent (Coulson 2007). The lawyer's duty and the extent of privilege are also more difficult to determine because the information is about a wrongdoing by someone other than the client.

In almost all other arenas, persons who are given information that causes them to suspect child abuse are encouraged or required to report that information to child protective services. But when an attorney is told by his/her client that the opposing party in a legal dispute is abusing a child, the attorney must evaluate the truthfulness of the allegations. Failing to act on the information could prejudice the client's case and leave the child open to further abuse. Bringing out the information in the legal proceeding and/or reporting it to child protective services will likely generate a heated response to the court by opposing counsel and lead to careful scrutiny by the judge. If the allegation cannot be proved, the court can order harsh sanctions against the client, even if the attorney was acting in good faith. If the court believes that the attorney was not acting in good faith, but was using the allegation strategically, the attorney may also face disciplinary action.

Statutory Protections for Personal Medical Information

Information held by third parties other than those entitled to one of the traditional three privileges is available to the government without a warrant unless it is otherwise protected by statute. This includes medical information. While the literature often speaks of a physician-patient privilege, this is not a traditional legal privilege. It exists only to the extent that it has been created by statute. Before the 1960s, few states had any specific legal protection for the physician-patient relationship. A physician who violated a patient's confidence broke no law, and it was difficult for patients to win damages in private lawsuits for breach of privacy.

At this point in time, all states have some form of medical privacy law, and there is a federal law, the Health Insurance Portability and Accountability Act (HIPAA), that also protects and regulates the disclosure of personal health information (PHI). HIPAA does not create a federal physician-patient privilege, nor does it allow state medical privacy laws to be enforced by the federal courts (Northwestern Memorial Hosp. v. Ashcroft 2004). None of these laws protect PHI from public health reporting. As summarized by the Centers for Disease Control and Prevention (CDC), HIPAA has a broad exception for public health reporting and investigation:

> Without individual authorization, a covered entity may disclose PHI to a public health authority that is legally authorized to collect or receive the information for the purposes of preventing or controlling disease, injury, or disability including, but not limited to:
>
> reporting of disease, injury, and vital events (e.g., birth or death); and;
> conducting public health surveillance, investigations, and interventions.
>
> PHI may also be disclosed without individual authorization to:
>
> report child abuse or neglect to a public health or other government authority legally authorized to receive such reports; and …
>
> an individual's employer, under certain circumstances and conditions, as needed for the employer to meet the requirements of the Occupational Safety and Health Administration, Mine Safety and Health Administration, or a similar state law. (CDC 2003)

More generally, HIPAA provides an exception for any request from an administrative agency or from a court with a court order. Those administrative agency requests could include requests for medical records to audit billing, quality, or any other parameter of regulatory interest. This would preempt any contrary state laws if the request came from a federal agency. State privacy laws also allow reporting to public health and other authorities. These laws usually include immunity provisions for persons making reports to prevent lawsuits by persons who claim the report defamed them or invaded their privacy. Some protections are absolute, and others depend on the report being made in good faith.

Access to Reported Data Held by the Government

Governments have great power to collect information about individuals, with or without their permission. Some of this information, such as information about sexually transmitted infections, is very sensitive and could cause both personal distress and economic consequences if it was improperly disclosed. Concerns about such release have driven opposition to reporting programs of all kinds. Despite these ongoing concerns, public health agencies have a good record of preserving the privacy of reported information.

The public and the media do not have a constitutional right to information that is held by the government. The federal government did not create a statutory right of public access to government-held information until 1967. This is called the Freedom of Information Act (FOIA). States have their own versions of public access laws, which are often called open records laws. While these laws allow wide access to government-held data, they limit public access to personal information held about identified individuals. Most identified public health reporting data is held at the state level and only reported to the Centers for Disease Control and Prevention (CDC) as aggregate numbers. The Occupational Safety and Health Administration (OSHA) collects extensive identified public health data on workers exposed to toxic chemicals and other workplace hazards. This data is available to employers and worker groups to facilitate safer workplaces.

Public health information is sometimes at issue in litigation. All reported public health data, as opposed to data developed by the agency through its own investigations, comes from sources that are not held by the government, such as patient medical records. A judge can order custodians of these original records to provide copies of the records to the courts in appropriate cases. It is much more difficult to get individual reported data from public health agencies, but not impossible, unless the state specifically protects information by statute.[11]

Child abuse and neglect reports are hybrids, with some aspects of a public health record, but also aspects of a criminal law investigation report. While some of the information may be available in the child's medical records, often there is information that is only recorded in the report or that was developed in the agency's investigation of the case. Child abuse and neglect information is often at issue in legal proceedings and will be available to both the prosecutor and the defendant. It may be available to the press through trial proceedings, depending on state law. Outside of legal proceedings, the information is not generally available to the public.

A primary purpose of public health surveillance is to build datasets for epidemiologic research. This requires some level of access for researchers and for the public itself. Traditionally this was managed by the release of data without personal identifiers such as names and addresses. The data would have general information about the individuals such as age, zip code, and information about the disease condition. If necessary for the use of the data, other physiologic information such as age, weight, and lab test results and others and demographic information such as race or gender might be included. With the advent of social media, data aggregators,[12] and other Internet resources, it is possible to find out the identities of many persons in the anonymous data provided by the state.

[11] Most states allow patients to request the release of information held about them by the state. This allows third parties such as employer or prosecutors to force the patient to sign a release, thus allowing access to the information. It is more protective to have an absolute statutory prohibition on release of public health information.

[12] Data aggregators are private companies that collect and sell personal information about individuals. This information is obtained from credit card companies, retailers, public databases such as police records, financial institutions, Internet business, and any other legal sources of information. This aggregated data is a detailed profile of the individual and can contain very specific medical information obtained from drug purchases and other sources of medical information not covered by HIPAA.

In one case, the health department tried to limit public access to cancer registry data because it was concerned that the identities of persons with rare cancers could be determined by matching the data with other sources of information. It argued that this would violate the law that prevented the release of identified public health report data. The court sympathized with the agency's concerns but found that blocking public access to the registry data would undermine a primary purpose for its collection (Southern Illinoisan, a Div. of Lee Enterprises, Inc. v. Department of Public Health 2001). This will be a growing problem as social media and data brokers undermine the notion of personal privacy, making it possible to identify at least some individuals in public health datasets that are detailed enough for serious epidemiologic research.

Ethical Concerns

Healthcare providers are often shocked by the government's broad powers to require reporting of patients' confidential information and the limits on patient's authority to control this reporting. This illustrates the conflict between public health ethics and medical ethics (bioethics). Public health ethics and communicable disease reporting evolved when communicable diseases were a threat to the state, as well as to the health of the public, and privacy was not a well-developed concept. The rights of the state to protect itself and the public outweighed the individual's right to complete autonomy.

The medical ethics movement arose from the Nuremberg trials that prosecuted physicians who ran experiments on Nazi captives. It is focused on protecting individual autonomy (Trials of War Criminals 1949). The core value is that patients are entitled to control their own care and anything that is done to their bodies (World Medical Association 2013). More recently, this has come to include control over information about their bodies and their mental health: patients must consent to the collection and release of their medical information unless otherwise specified by law (Health Insurance Portability and Accountability Act 1996).

HIV and the Breakdown of Public Health Reporting

The most ethically and epidemiologically difficult question is whether people should be allowed to opt out of reporting. From the individual-oriented bioethics view, patient autonomy should always be respected. This means that the patient should control whether the information is reported to the government. In contrast, traditional public health values reporting and its benefits to the community over individual autonomy, and so it does not allow an individual to opt out.

These policies coexisted into the 1980s. When the first cases of unusual infections and rare cancers were seen in gay men in 1981, they were investigated and managed with classic public health disease reporting and contact investigation. This was not seen as unethical or an invasion of privacy by the gay community. They had been cooperating in a large-scale reporting and contact tracing study of hepatitis B in bathhouses since the 1970s. As the epidemiology of the disease was elucidated, it was named acquired immunodeficiency disease syndrome – AIDS. Reporting and contact investigation continued and soon showed an identical epidemiology to hepatitis B, strongly suggesting that it was a blood-borne pathogen spread by sexual contact, injection drug abuse, and blood transfusions.

It was not until the HIV virus was identified and a screening test was developed that resistance to named reporting of infected persons surfaced. The concern was that health departments would leak the information to employers and others who would use the information to discriminate against asymptomatic persons who were infected with the virus. Civil libertarian groups pressured the states and CDC to allow anonymous testing of persons with HIV. Most states and the CDC agreed to this. The CDC pressured states that continued to require named reporting to allow anonymous testing. This undermined the ability to track and understand the spread of the disease and its natural history.

More troublingly, this opposition to HIV reporting became a general opposition to public health reporting. Many states weakened their disease control laws and made it more difficult to identify and manage persons with diseases such as tuberculosis.[13] In the 1990s, states such as New York faced a resurgence of tuberculosis secondary to their weakened disease control programs (Brudney and Dobkin 1991). This led many states to reinstate some of the lost powers of their health departments. It took another decade for the CDC to realize that HIV could not be effectively understood and managed without named reporting and contact investigation. In 2006, the CDC began to require states to reinstate mandatory disease reporting for HIV and to encourage voluntary testing. The conflicts over HIV reporting and contact investigation have been largely resolved in favor of the traditional disease control model. But the suspicion of reporting engendered by the controversy has empowered broader resistance to public health reporting, such as the collection of disease registry data.

Disease Registries

Disease registries are population-based datasets: a record of every person who is diagnosed with a disease. These are typically genetic and environmental diseases, not communicable diseases, and are usually rare conditions. The registry is used to accumulate as many cases as possible to help understand the epidemiology of the disease. This can allow the identification of specific genetic markers or the causal agents for rare cancers. While disease registry reporting could be mandated under

[13] The opposition to vaccination also increased during this period, and many states responded by making it very easy for parents to opt their children out of mandatory childhood vaccinations.

the police power, many registries allow patients to opt out, and some require patients to opt in (Beskow et al. 2006). Both opt-out and opt-in requirements make it much more difficult to get a full dataset. If the disease is rare, these provisions can make proper analysis impossible because of the loss of data points and the possible selection bias of individuals who opt out.

Allowing patients to control access to information gathered by public health agencies makes large-scale epidemiologic studies much more difficult. It is very hard to track down all the patients to get their consent. This is particularly difficult with death certificate-based research where the legal representative of the estate must give permission. Since many people die without a will and have no formal representative for their estate, there is no effective way to get consent for the study. The national medical privacy law in the United States (HIPAA) has provisions to allow death certificate research without the consent of all the subjects.

The Future of Public Health Surveillance

Reporting has traditionally been seen as an exception to the private world of medical information. This private world was not a creature of law, but a result of the costs of physical access. Almost all medical information was written, usually handwritten, on unstructured paper records. Bits of information about a patient were scattered through records held by multiple medical care providers. Each provider only held the information generated in that practice or facility. Security was lax, with a white coat often being the only identification necessary to get a record. But getting that record meant finding the patient's providers and physically going to their offices. For individual targets of reporters or investigators, there was little privacy. For the average patient, who was not being individually investigated, there was very effective privacy.

As medical information is collected in standardized electronic formats, it becomes much cheaper to obtain data on individuals and whole populations. Laws governing access, and technological protections against unauthorized access, take the place of the inherent security of paper records. A major objective of federal health policy is to move all medical information to electronic records. These records will be used as a massive resource for doing research for evidence-based medicine. At the same time, individuals are using social media and Internet-based health forums to share personal medical information and to search for medical information. Google searches for information about the flu and flu remedies show the beginning of flu outbreaks before the official flu reporting systems (Cook et al. 2011; Ginsberg et al. 2009; Chan et al. 2011).

While there are ethical and legal issues in treating all personal medical information as part of a research database, it is likely that these will be overcome through promises of better medical treatments at lower costs. Patients will be incentivized/coerced into participating as a condition of insurance or access to desirable care systems. Most traditional public health reporting will become part of the "big data" analysis of all individual medical information. A harbinger of this is the New York

City Health Department reporting regulation requiring hemoglobin A1C testing and reporting on persons with diabetes (Chamany et al. 2009). Diabetes is an important disease, and proper management is a critical personal health issue, but unlike communicable diseases, it only threatens society economically. Congress is also using economic justifications for allowing health insurers to monitor people's weight and other risk factors and assess penalties against them.

The notion that individuals give up the right to medical privacy because their medical conditions will increase the cost of medical care and thus burden society is a profound philosophical shift. Traditional reporting was based on the notion of direct threats such as infection or abuse. Economic risk-based surveillance and intervention are based on a communitarian notion of shared societal costs as justifying limits on individual rights. This implies a blurring of the distinction between public and private data, as is already happening with social media. Social media such as Facebook make their income by collecting personal information about their members and selling it to advertisers and others. Some of this data comes from the individual and some from their network of friends. Anyone who uses these media has no legal expectation of privacy in the information that they provide to the service.

There are other services called data aggregators that collect very detailed dossiers on every individual by buying data from merchants and credit card companies and other data services. Data aggregators started as credit reporting services but have expanded their business to collecting as much data as possible about every individual who uses credit, credit cards, or is otherwise trackable through available data. For example, you can learn a lot about a person's medical conditions through their supermarket and pharmacy purchases. Women who purchase prenatal vitamins learn this when their email starts to fill with ads for baby-related products. If you include a person's Facebook data and Google searches, you may get more information than if you had the person's medical records. Add in the data that will be available in electronic medical records, and it will be possible to do very detailed public health and safety epidemiology without the need for anyone to generate reports and send them to the government. It will be possible to mine public health and safety data from the general universe of medical and personal information available about individuals.

Legally, the big data world does not present any new privacy issues. The data is all held by third parties, and the individual does not have any expectation of privacy. Technically, the major limitation of a data mining model over a reporting model is the excluded populations. Less technologically advanced countries will have much less data available. In the United States, many of the poor do not have Internet access and do not use credit, which limits the data available on them. But these populations are also difficult to monitor through the traditional reporting systems because they have fewer interactions with healthcare providers and others who have reporting duties. There are also people who do not use social media or the Internet but still seek medical care and otherwise participate in the economic system. While there may be less data on these two populations, there will still be the traditional medical record, which will now be electronic and subject to data mining.

Just as there are populations that are excluding from data mining, there are populations that could be data mined that are invisible to traditional reporting.

There are a significant number of persons who avoid traditional medical care. They self-medicate with drugs and herbals bought over the Internet, sometimes illegally, and they seek information from persons outside the regulated medical care world. Most of this activity now takes place on the Internet and through social media, making information available through data mining that could not be captured through traditional reporting and investigation.

Making the transition from reports triggered by the specific medical diagnoses or events to data mining for public health information will require new legal arrangements between data vendors and agencies doing public health surveillance. In some cases, this might mean broadening who has a reporting duty. In most cases, it will require developing new ways of analyzing data to identify public health information. Police departments are already monitoring social media to identify pedophiles. This could be expanded to look for child abuse, perhaps even creating ways for victims to reach out for help through social media. Public health agencies could contract with sources such as Google to obtain disease control information mined from Internet searches.

Conclusions

The modern world of electronic data will transform public health reporting and surveillance. Traditional disease and child abuse reports generated by healthcare providers and caregivers are still the core data source, but it has always been an incomplete and imperfect source of information. The challenge for future data collection will be finding a way to retrieve valuable information from the ocean of data that is now available without becoming overwhelmed. National security agencies have learned the hard lesson that too much data can make it impossible to see patterns and identify risks in a timely manner. Public health agencies, with much more limited capability to manage large datasets, will have to develop partnerships with private data sources to effectively use new resources such as social media and Internet search data. Doing so successfully will greatly enhance their ability to protect the public's health and safety.

References

Beskow, L. M., Sandler, R. S., & Weinberger, M. (2006). Research recruitment through US central cancer registries: Balancing privacy and scientific issues. *American Journal of Public Health, 96*(11), 1920–1926.

Blackstone, W. (1769). *Commentaries on the laws of England* (Vol. 4). Oxford: Clarendon Press.

Bolduan, C. F., & Bolduan, N. W. (1949). *Public health and hygiene …* (4th ed., illustrated). Philadelphia/London: W.B. Saunders Co.

Brudney, K., & Dobkin, J. (1991). Resurgent tuberculosis in New York City: Human immunodeficiency virus, homelessness, and the decline of tuberculosis control programs. *American Review of Respiratory Disease, 144*(4), 745–749.

Camara v. Municipal Court City and County, 387 U.S. 523 (1967).
CDC. (2003). HIPAA privacy rule and public health: Guidance from CDC and the U.S. Department of Health and Human Services. *MMWR, 52*, 1–20.
Chamany, S., Silver, L. D., Bassett, M. T., Driver, C. R., Berger, D. K., Neuhaus, C. E., et al. (2009). Tracking diabetes: New York City's A1C Registry. *Milbank Quarterly, 87*(3), 547–570.
Chan, E. H., Sahai, V., Conrad, C., & Brownstein, J. S. (2011). Using web search query data to monitor dengue epidemics: A new model for neglected tropical disease surveillance. *PLoS Neglected Tropical Diseases, 5*(5), e1206.
Constitution of the United States, 4th Amendment (1789).
Cook, S., Conrad, C., Fowlkes, A. L., & Mohebbi, M. H. (2011). Assessing Google flu trends performance in the United States during the 2009 influenza virus A (H1N1) pandemic. *PLoS One, 6*(8), e23610.
Cooley, T. M. I. (1987). *Constitutional limitations*. Birmingham: Legal Classics Library.
Coulson, R. C. (2007). Professional responsibility and false accusations of child abuse. *Journal of Contemporary Legal Issues, 16*, 233.
European Convention on Human Rights Act, Section 8 (2003).
Frank v. Maryland, 359 U.S. 360 (1959).
Ginsberg, J., Mohebbi, M. H., Patel, R. S., Brammer, L., Smolinski, M. S., & Brilliant, L. (2009). Detecting influenza epidemics using search engine query data. *Nature, 457*(7232), 1012–1014.
Health Insurance Portability and Accountability Act of 1996, Codified at 42 U.S.C. § 300gg and 29 U.S.C § 1181 et seq. and 42 USC 1320d et seq.
McNeill, W. H. (1976). *Plagues and peoples*. Garden City: Anchor Press.
Moyer, V. A., Calonge, N., Teutsch, S. M., & Botkin, J. R. (2008). Expanding newborn screening: Process, policy, and priorities. *Hastings Center Report, 38*(3), 32–39.
Northwestern Memorial Hosp. v. Ashcroft, 362 F. 3D 923 (2004).
Ogilvie, G., Knowles, L., Wong, E., Taylor, D., Tigchelaar, J., Brunt, C., et al. (2005). Incorporating a social networking approach to enhance contact tracing in a heterosexual outbreak of syphilis. *Sexually Transmitted Infections, 81*(2), 124–127.
Powell, J. H. (1949). *Bring out your dead: The great plague of yellow fever in Philadelphia in 1793*. Philadelphia: University of Pennsylvania Press.
Smith v. Turner, 48 U.S. (7 How.) 283, 340–341 (1849).
Southern Illinoisan, a Div. of Lee Enterprises, Inc. v. Department of Public Health, 319 Ill.App.3d 979, 747 N.E.2d 401 (Ill.App. 5 Dist. 2001).
Trials of War Criminals before the Nuremberg Military Tribunals under Control Council Law No. 10, Vol. 2 (1949) Washington, DC: U.S. Government Printing Office.
Whalen v. Roe, 429 US 589 (1977).
World Medical Association. (2013). World Medical Association declaration of Helsinki: Ethical principles for medical research involving human subjects. *JAMA, 310*(20), 2191–2194.
Yakowitz, J. (2011). Tragedy of the data commons. *Harvard Journal of Law and Technology, 25*, 1.

Part II
Theoretical/Ideological Debates and Issues

Debates about *whether the laws should be enacted, and why*: (1) political philosophy including 'rights' theories, (2) economics, (3) ethics, and (4) law

Chapter 7
A Theoretical Framework for Designing and Evaluating Strategies to Identify Cases of Serious Child Abuse and Neglect

Ben Mathews

Introduction

A central dimension of the State's responsibility in a liberal democracy, and arguably any just society, is the protection of individuals' central rights and freedoms and the creation of the minimum conditions under which each individual has an opportunity to lead a life of sufficient equality, dignity and value. A special subset of this responsibility is to protect those who are unable to protect themselves from genuine harm. Substantial numbers of children suffer serious physical, emotional and sexual abuse and neglect at the hands of their parents and caregivers or by other known parties. Child abuse and neglect occurs in a situation of extreme power asymmetry characterised by physical, psychological, emotional, cognitive, social and economic inequality and dependency. The physical, social, behavioural and economic costs to the individual, and the social and economic costs to communities, are vast and often endure through the lifespan. Children are not generally able to protect themselves from serious abuse and neglect. This enlivens both the State's responsibility to protect the child and the debate about how that responsibility can and should be discharged.

The Hidden Nature of Serious Child Abuse and Neglect: Nondisclosure

It is extremely significant that for many reasons, serious maltreatment is largely hidden and undisclosed by the child and perpetrator. It occurs in the family sphere,

B. Mathews (✉)
Australian Centre for Health Law Research, Faculty of Law,
Queensland University of Technology, GPO Box 2434, 4001 Brisbane, QLD, Australia
e-mail: b.mathews@qut.edu.au

B. Mathews, D.C. Bross (eds.), *Mandatory Reporting Laws and the Identification of Severe Child Abuse and Neglect*, Child Maltreatment 4,
DOI 10.1007/978-94-017-9685-9_7

and apart from sexual abuse, it is most frequently inflicted on infants who are preverbal and young children who cannot resist, represent themselves, resolve the situation or disclose the experience (Mathews 2012). Neonates, infants and very young children are clearly at the highest risk of fatality and serious harm from severe abuse and neglect – Kempe et al. (1962) remarked that severe physical abuse was mostly inflicted on children aged under 3 – and this influenced some of the first mandatory reporting laws being limited to reports of abuse of children aged under 12 (Mathews 2014). Sexual abuse is characterised by numerous features so that it too is typically undisclosed by the child and the perpetrator. It is unsurprising then that children rarely disclose their own suffering, and in severe cases, which clearly constitute fundamental breaches of children's rights and which often constitute criminal conduct, those who inflict the abuse or neglect are also unlikely to do so. This hidden nature of serious abuse and neglect, and the silence which accompanies it, is a central factor which must be acknowledged in any discussion of theory and social policy about responding to child maltreatment.

Public Health, Economics, Political Philosophy

Critical tasks for a liberal society and for any public health approach in responding to serious child maltreatment must be to employ strategies for primary prevention (population-wide approaches to prevent it occurring in the first place), secondary prevention (approaches focusing on particular subsets of the population known to be loci of higher prevalence) and tertiary prevention (Turnock 2009; Gostin 2008). In the context of serious child maltreatment that has already been inflicted, this tertiary response aspect of the public health approach dovetails with the goals of a liberal society to protect fundamental rights. A core question arises for society, given that most serious child maltreatment occurs in the family sphere and is hidden, is unlikely to be disclosed by the child or by the person who inflicted it, causes substantial personal and economic harm to both individual and community and infringes fundamental individual rights and freedoms. The question is: How can society identify these situations so that the maltreatment can be interrupted, the child's needs for security and safety, and health and other rehabilitation can be met and the family's needs can be addressed to reduce the likelihood of recurrence?

A Theoretical Framework for Evaluating Policy Approaches to Identifying Cases of Serious Child Abuse and Neglect

This chapter proposes a theoretical framework applicable for any society that is considering justifiable and effective policy approaches – including decisions whether or not to adopt mandatory reporting laws – to identify and respond to cases of serious child abuse and neglect. The core of the theoretical framework is based on major principles from both classical liberal political philosophy and leading political philosophers from the twentieth century and the first part of the new millennium. The principles are also seen to be consistent with long-established fundamental principles recognised by both civil and criminal law. In addition, these principles are situated within and informed by health and economics disciplines.

Thinking about the theoretical basis of a mandatory reporting law is necessary for several reasons. While many jurisdictions have adopted mandatory reporting laws of varying dimensions, detailed consideration of their theoretical justifiability is seldom undertaken, either by those who support or oppose the laws, both within and outside jurisdictions having the laws. Debates about the laws are sometimes not adequately informed and proceed under incorrect assumptions about the nature of the laws and without sufficient consideration being given to their theoretical justifications. In addition, consideration of theoretical bases for the laws rarely takes place in relation to different types and extents of child maltreatment. In some jurisdictions which do not yet have mandatory reporting laws – both industrialised countries and developing countries – there are discussions about the normative status of these laws in the sense of whether they *should* be adopted in any form and why or why not, but these discussions tend not to include detailed theoretical examination. Such discussions also extend beyond normative debates to consider what different forms the law *can* practicably take, in light of competing social priorities and resource constraints; these conversations also should be grounded in a theoretical framework. As well, even among those who support the basic principles underpinning the laws, some may have questions about their appropriate scope and implementation and the place they occupy within any broader child welfare and child protection apparatus, which itself can be seen as a component of a public health system.

In human affairs, normative questions about what should be done and the reasons it should be done are unable to be finally settled to the satisfaction of every person. Any theoretical account moves from certain points of departure and must adopt certain philosophical preferences and reject or ascribe less value to others. Accordingly, in this chapter I do not claim to set down a theory that resists every alternative theory. Other perspectives adopting different social, philosophical and economic preferences would privilege other goals and outcomes. However, the theory I propound here is animated by the genuine principles inherent in liberal theory. My argument is that other views which do not do so are fundamentally inconsistent with the genuine principles of liberalism and just societies, are not consistent with the claims and objectives of those societies, and that the framework proposed here – or something close to it – constitutes a legitimate model which is compatible with the central goals of a liberal society. Advocates of other approaches inconsistent with these principles must account for that incompatibility.

By developing a reasoned theoretical framework which is compatible with defining concepts from law, public health and economics, this proposed theory can constitute a useful guide and evaluative measure for social policy generation and decisions in the context of preventing, identifying and responding to child abuse. In the first instance, I am here concerned with a primary goal: of identifying cases of severe abuse which otherwise would remain hidden. Part 1 of this chapter first briefly situates the context: it identifies the appropriate parameters of the discussion and proposes some working definitions of child abuse and neglect; identifies key social, health and economic costs of serious abuse and neglect; and explains the nature and provenance of mandatory reporting laws and their place and function as one component of a broader child welfare and child protection apparatus. It also acknowledges key rights enshrined in the common law and criminal law which protect children's physical security (which relate to physical and sexual abuse) and rights to a minimum standard of care (which relate to neglect). In Part 2, I explore key principles from liberal political theory, drawing on the classical thought of Locke and Mill and more recent work by Rorty, Rawls, Okin and Nussbaum. I draw together strands of liberal thought to develop a framework within which the key social policy of mandatory reporting laws can be situated and evaluated, focusing on the individual rights and needs of the child to dignity, equality, freedom, security and, ultimately, a minimal opportunity in life. Nussbaum's *capabilities framework* (2011) is particularly useful in this endeavour, and I draw on and extend this approach in considering social and legal policy in the context of serious abuse of children who cannot protect themselves or their own interests. It will be concluded that against this framework, and in the absence of a demonstrably superior alternative, mandatory reporting laws are a theoretically justified and necessary component of a just society's strategy for child welfare and community flourishing.

Part 1

Parameters of the Discussion: What Types and Extents of Abuse and Neglect Are We Talking About?

Two major parameters need to be made clear. First, while the types of child maltreatment have in recent years been extended in some jurisdictions, most notably to include exposure to domestic violence and prenatal exposure to maternal substance abuse, this discussion refers to the four classical forms of child maltreatment: physical abuse, sexual abuse, emotional abuse and neglect. This does not mean that theorising about other familial-caused trauma to children and social and legal responses to those traumas cannot be informed by this model; but for the purposes of this chapter, I will confine the discussion to the four main maltreatment types.

Second, it needs to be made clear that in dealing with the topic of mandatory reporting legislation, this chapter does not deal with any and all extents of 'abuse' and 'neglect', but only with abuse and neglect that is of a *serious or severe nature and extent*. This parameter needs to be made clear for two reasons. In the first place, mandatory reporting duties in legislation are generally – despite some arguably ill-advised exceptions – premised on a duty to report only significant or serious maltreatment and harm to children (Mathews and Kenny 2008; Mathews 2012). They do *not* require reports of trivial incidents or experiences, isolated discomfort or upset, poverty in and of itself, 'less than ideal parenting' or *any* 'risk' of suffering abuse or harm. The context of significant actual abuse (with accompanying or likely harm) having already been suffered – and clear cases where such abuse/harm has not yet been suffered but is at demonstrably clear risk of being suffered – is the one to which mandatory reporting laws are relevant, and this discussion proceeds on this basis. This was the original context which animated the first reporting laws: Kempe et al. (1962) and the 'battered-child syndrome' were concerned with doctors' failure to report cases of intentional serious physical injury to children through assaults causing fractures to the long bones, fractures to the skull and subdural haematoma. These were indisputably serious injuries and clear and profound breaches of the child's individual rights to safety and security; the abuse and its harm had already occurred and the child was at clear risk of future further injury. This does not imply that 'lesser' forms of harm and risk of harm are not important and should receive no response by social, health and welfare systems to prevention or intervene; it simply marks the appropriate terrain of some forms of social and legal response that are central to this discussion. In the second place, this point is often missed in debates about mandatory reporting, meaning that misapprehensions occur about the nature, scope and likely consequences of mandatory reporting legislation, which can lead some commentators to making inaccurate statements and drawing unwarranted conclusions about both factual and theoretical matters.

Definitions of Each Type of Abuse and Neglect

For the purpose of discussion and operationalisation of the theory, it is also necessary to use some definitions of each type of maltreatment. Adopting the basis of a previous model (Mathews and Bross 2014), I will use the following definitions of discrete abuse types, which draw on those proposed by leading scholars and which are consistent with rights and obligations in criminal law, civil law and child protection law:

- *Physical abuse* includes acts of physical assault by parents or caregivers which result in death or serious physical harm or which present an imminent risk of doing so; it excludes lawful corporal punishment.[1]
- *Sexual abuse* includes acts not only of penetrative abuse but also acts of masturbation, oral sex, fondling, voyeurism, exposure to sexual acts, exposure to or involvement in pornography and other forms of commercial sexual exploitation, all of which are acts done to sexually gratify the abuser; it is usually inflicted by an adult, but is often and can be inflicted by another, usually older child, where the victim is not developmentally capable of understanding the acts or is not able to provide true consent (World Health Organisation 2006).
- *Psychological or emotional abuse* exists when the relationship between the parent or caregiver and the child is characterised by pervasive or persistent acts

[1] A clear challenge is presented by the question of whether and when corporal punishment is 'physical abuse'. This chapter does not intend to explore this question in detail.

or omissions which result in serious emotional harm or present an imminent risk of doing so (Glaser 2002, 2011).[2]

- *Neglect* is constituted by omissions by parents or caregivers to provide the basic necessities of life such as food, shelter, clothing, supervision and medical care, which result in serious harm or present an imminent risk of doing so (Dubowitz 2000).

It can readily be seen that each definition clearly includes a dimension of 'severity' or 'seriousness'. In the case of sexual abuse, all sexual abuse is seen as immediately having such severity. For the other three types, the abuse or neglect must have already been of sufficient severity to cause serious harm or to involve acts which have already been committed which may not yet have caused such harm but present an imminent risk/likelihood of causing such harm.

In each maltreatment subtype, a range of acts and harms can be present on a spectrum of severity. Some brief and by no means exhaustive examples of kinds of abuse/harm at each end of the spectrum for illustrative purposes will make it clear that some manifestations of 'abuse' and the harm caused by it will clearly be within the purview of theory and practice relating to a mandatory reporting duty, while others clearly will not.

	Abuse/acts and/or harm(s) of clearly sufficient severity	Abuse/acts and/or harm(s) of clearly insufficient severity
Physical abuse	Physical assaults on neonates and infants; serious assaults on older children especially if using an implement; beating, whipping, burning	Minor physical acts for discipline, control or prevention of danger (e.g. crossing the road); reasonable (minor) corporal punishment where legally permissible
Sexual abuse	All sexual abuse is of sufficient seriousness[a]	Not applicable; all sexual abuse is seen as being of sufficient seriousness. Note that consensual peer activity is not classed as sexual abuse
Emotional abuse	Serious denigration and rejection of the child, persistent and profound lack of emotional interaction/attachment especially for neonates and infants	Occasional name-calling, shouting

(continued)

[2] According to Glaser's (2011) typology, there are five categories of such harmful acts and omissions: first, emotional unavailability, unresponsiveness and neglect; second, interacting with the child with hostility, blame, denigration, rejection or scapegoating; third, developmentally inappropriate or inconsistent interactions with the child; fourth, failure to recognise or acknowledge the child's individuality and the psychological boundary between the parent and the child; and fifth, failure to promote the child's socialisation within the child's context, by either active mis-socialisation or corruption, by isolating the child or by failing to provide adequate stimulation and opportunities for learning.

	Abuse/acts and/or harm(s) of clearly sufficient severity	Abuse/acts and/or harm(s) of clearly insufficient severity
Neglect	Serious medical neglect especially of very young children, serious malnutrition especially of neonates and infants, clearly inadequate supervision, persistent failure to ensure child attends school, household featuring clearly dangerous conditions, e.g. faecal matter and other infection hazards	Occasional failure to provide desirable nutrition or clothing, without clear serious damage to health/well-being; purely poverty-related circumstances which do not cause severe harm

[a]When discussing the concept of sexual abuse, a benefit of the WHO definition above is that it enables accommodation of cultural practices which, for example, may involve nudity, but which lack a defining component necessary to constitute 'sexual abuse'. For example, some cultures may practice family bathing or naturism, but such activities would lack the element of sexual gratification which is a defining and essential feature of 'abuse'.

Key Features of Serious Child Abuse and Neglect Which Must Be Considered by Any Theoretical Framework: The Nature and Costs of Serious Child Abuse and Neglect

There are central features of the phenomena and sequelae of child abuse and neglect which must be taken into account by any theoretical discussion. Chief among these are children's developmental vulnerability, meaning that the youngest children are most frequently victimised; the breach of fundamental rights to bodily inviolability and security; the broad range of serious harms and health consequences to the child, which are both immediate and which endure, thus destroying or fundamentally impeding the development in the child of core capabilities which compromises functioning and flourishing throughout childhood and adulthood; the massive economic cost; and the limited window of opportunity within which important disabling harms can be remedied.

It is important to first acknowledge that there are various dimensions of heterogeneity across and within both the types of maltreatment and their consequences for individuals. The matrix above clearly shows the differences between the kinds of abusive acts constituting maltreatment. Neglect in particular has several different subspecies: medical, nutritional, emotional, educational and supervisory. Different kinds of maltreatment are more likely to present different kinds of consequences for the child; but even within types, and even where the acts are the same kind, duration and chronicity, it is widely accepted that not all individuals will experience the same type or extent of all kinds of physical, social and behavioural consequences (Putnam 2003; Widom 2014).

However, we do know the age profile of victimisation. Evidence from the USA of the incidence of maltreatment and the ages of victims show that for each type of maltreatment except sexual abuse, there is a *developmental vulnerability*. That is, in general, the youngest children are most often victimised, which is unsurprising since they are the most vulnerable. Hence, infants aged under 1 year of age are most often victimised, followed by infants aged 1, then infants aged 2; approximately one third of all victims are under 4 years old; another quarter are aged 4–7; and three quarters of all victims are aged under 12 (United States Department of Health and Human Services 2006).

In addition, it is broadly accepted that the adverse physical and mental health, behavioural, educational, social and economic consequences of respective kinds of serious abuse and neglect, and coexisting types, are extremely substantial (Gilbert et al. 2009; Paolucci et al. 2001). There are numerous studies and reviews of these consequences, especially in relation to physical abuse (see, e.g. Gershoff 2002; Landsford et al. 2002), sexual abuse (see, e.g. Chen et al. 2010; Nelson et al. 2002; Paolucci et al. 2001; Putnam 2003) and neglect (Hildyard and Wolfe 2002; Perry 2002; Veltman and Browne 2001). There are fewer studies of the effects of emotional abuse, but there is still convincing evidence of its deleterious effects (Egeland 2009). Overall, in addition to fatalities, prominent common effects, which in many cases inherently compromise critical development or which persist through the lifespan, include failure to thrive; impaired brain development; impaired social, emotional and behavioural development; reduced reading ability and perceptual reasoning; depression; anxiety; post-traumatic stress disorder; low self-image; physical injuries; alcohol and drug use; aggression; delinquency; long-term deficits in educational achievement; and adverse effects on employment and economic status. For the purpose of this discussion, what is particularly notable is that it is not simply the physical insults and consequences to the child that are significant; it is the impacts both direct and indirect, immediate and prolonged, on the child's development as a human – their *core capabilities* (Nussbaum 2011) – which are crucial. This central point will be returned to in Part 2.

In total, the economic costs to survivors, both in the short term and long term, and to families and communities, are profound. Direct and indirect economic costs at a national level in various countries have been estimated in the billions (Fang et al. 2012; Fromm 2001; Taylor et al. 2008). What is also of fundamental importance, and exacerbated by the fact that developmental vulnerability means that it is the youngest infants and children who are most affected, is that for young children who suffer compromised capacity as a result of this type of disadvantage, the ensuing cost is not only massive but is probably *irremediable* later in life or is made extremely difficult and costly to remedy. The Nobel Prize winning economist James Heckman and others have highlighted this fact and the necessity of intervening at as early a stage in life as possible (Heckman 2006, 2008, 2013; Heckman et al. 2003; Shonkoff and Phillips 2000). The family environment is a critical predictor of early cognitive and noncognitive ability, and gaps in these skills emerge by age 4–6 (Carneiro and Heckman 2003). Environments that do not develop these skills place children at a disadvantage which may never be restored. Economic return from early intervention is very high compared with later attempts to redress imbalances resulting from deficient family environments (Heckman 2006). Heckman (2012) urged public investment in the provision and development of cognitive skills and socio-emotional and character skills (e.g. attentiveness, impulse control, persistence) for disadvantaged children from birth to age 5.

The need for early identification of serious cases of child maltreatment before the capacity to intervene diminishes or expires appears so evident as to be unassailable. It also seems that intervening with the 'hardest' cases of disadvantage offers greatest value. It makes sound economic sense to invest in these domains; while the initial cost may appear high, it is far less than the costs which will otherwise accrue to the individual and society. In addition, addressing early disadvantage in children may also diminish intergenerational cycles of disadvantage.

The Hidden Nature of Serious CAN: Nondisclosure and the Need for Case Identification by Others

Serious child abuse and neglect is inflicted in the family sphere. In general, it is unwitnessed by others outside the family, and it is rarely disclosed by the child victim or the adult wrongdoer. Children rarely report their own situation to welfare agencies, accounting for 0.5 % of substantiated reports in the USA in 2004 (US Department of Health and Human Services 2006, p. 20) and 2 % of substantiated reports in Canada (excluding Quebec) in 2003 (Trocmé et al. 2005, p. 876). Parents and caregivers who inflict maltreatment (and perpetrators of sexual abuse) very rarely report their wrongdoing: in the USA in 2004, only 0.1 % of substantiated reports were made by alleged perpetrators and a further 4 % by non-perpetrating parents (US Department of Health and Human Services 2006, p. 20). Without a system where people outside abused or neglected children's families bring the children's circumstances to the attention of authorities, many and perhaps most cases will remain hidden. Case finding remains a massive and central challenge.

This is further borne out by the mismatch between the true incidence of serious maltreatment as indicated by population studies and the number of cases brought to light in societies, including those that have adopted mandatory reporting legislation. Even where mandatory reporting schemes exist, many cases evade the attention of authorities for numerous reasons (Mathews and Bross 2014). As well, a large reservoir of cases will not become known to any authority figure (Sedlak and Broadhurst 1996). Population studies of maltreatment generally (May-Chahal and Cawson 2005; Radford et al. 2011; Sedlak et al. 2010),[3] and of discrete types such as sexual

[3] In the USA, the fourth National Incidence Study by Sedlak et al. (2010) (NIS-4) found an overall numerical decrease of 19 % in actual harm to children since NIS-3 in 1993. Nevertheless, in the study year 2005–2006, over 1.25 million children were significantly harmed by abuse or neglect (this uses the very stringent actual harm standard, not the endangerment standard; as acknowledged by Sedlak et al. (p 3), this actual harm standard exceeds even the standard used by CPS agencies as the substantiation threshold). The breakdown by maltreatment type was physical abuse (323,000), sexual abuse (135,300), emotional abuse (148,500) and neglect (771,700). Neglect included educational neglect (360,500), physical neglect (295,300) and emotional neglect (193,400). These numbers can be compared with those identified by government child welfare agencies in that year: 899,454, which includes those endangered, not actually harmed (US DHHS 2007). In the UK, May-Chahal and Cawson (2005) found 16 % prevalence during childhood of

abuse (Dunne et al. 2003; Finkelhor et al. 1990; Rosenman and Rodgers 2004; Stoltenborgh et al. 2011)[4] and physical abuse (Rosenman and Rodgers 2004; Straus et al. 1998),[5] show that the number of cases which becomes known to government agencies is a small fraction of the real incidence.

Nondisclosure by parents and caregivers can be explained by the fact that serious maltreatment is a class of legal and moral wrongdoing which clearly constitutes fundamental breaches of children's rights, and in many cases the behaviours in question will be criminal acts which also engage the power of the State. Children's nondisclosure is often caused by the extent of their vulnerability; due to their infancy they are simply unable to do anything to protect themselves. Yet even when older, children's nondisclosure is influenced by their vulnerability and their situation within a multifactorial and asymmetric power dynamic characterised by the child's vastly inferior physical, cognitive, psychosocial, emotional and economic capacities. In the case of sexual abuse, which is sometimes inflicted by parents and caregivers, this power dynamic will operate; but even when inflicted by others – most usually, another trusted adult known to the child or an older child – nondisclosure or long-delayed disclosure is still typical (Arata 1998; Paine and Hansen 2002; Smith et al. 2000), due to an inherent power asymmetry and further entrenched by its inherent secrecy; feelings of shame, guilt and embarrassment (Kogan 2004; Ney et al. 1986); threats; and fear of reprisals to the child or other family members (Palmer et al. 1999; Berliner and Conte 1990). Nondisclosure is also strongly indicated in clerical abuse, a situation also characterised by multifactorial power dynamics (John Jay College of Criminal Justice 2004; Parkinson et al. 2010).

The Nature and Purpose of a Mandatory Reporting Law

As outlined in more detail elsewhere in this book (see Chap. 1), mandatory reporting legislation refers to specific kinds of legislative provisions which impose a duty on specified groups of persons to report designated types of child maltreatment. These designated persons are usually named occupational or professional groups who frequently encounter children in the course of their work. The underlying concept is to impose a requirement on designated people who are well placed to detect cases of severe child abuse and neglect to report known and suspected cases to the attention of government welfare agencies, so that measures can be taken to ensure the child is safe, that the maltreatment stops, that rehabilitation can be provided and that the

self-reported serious maltreatment, with the following breakdown by type: physical abuse (7 %), sexual abuse (16 %), emotional abuse (6 %) and neglect (11 %).

[4] Finkelhor et al. (1990) found that sexual abuse was suffered by 27 % of girls and 16 % of boys; Rosenman and Rodgers (2004) found that before age 16, 1.1 % experienced sexual abuse by a parent. Dunne et al. (2003) found that before age 16, 12 % of girls and 4 % of boys experienced penetrative abuse and 33.6 % of girls and 15.9 % of boys experienced non-penetrative abuse.

[5] Straus et al. (1998) found that 4.9 % suffered severe physical abuse in a year. Rosenman and Rodgers (2004) found that before age 16, 5.2 % experienced physical abuse (punched, kicked, hit with an object or needed treatment).

needs of the child and the family can be identified and supported. For example, if in the course of their work a doctor or a police officer or a teacher encounters a 3-year-old child who has suffered severe intentional physical injury, or injuries suggesting sexual abuse or severe neglect, the legal obligation requires the professional to report their knowledge or reasonable suspicion that the child has been abused and has suffered harm to a government child welfare agency so that the agency can assess the child's situation to determine what protective and supportive actions need to be taken. The legislation provides the reporter with protections as well: their identity as the reporter is confidential, and they cannot be liable in any civil, criminal or administrative proceeding for any consequences of the report (Mathews and Kenny 2008).

The first primary objective of these laws is to identify cases of serious child abuse and neglect. This remains so, whether the mandatory reporting law adopted in any given jurisdiction is of broader or narrower scope. There are two main ways in which the scope of these laws differs across jurisdictions (both between countries and within countries): which types of abuse and neglect must be reported and by which persons? Hence, there is a spectrum of mandatory reporting laws. At one extreme, a law such as Western Australia's requires reports only of sexual abuse and limits the reporter groups to teachers, doctors, nurses, midwives and police. At the other extreme, jurisdictions require reports of all four forms of child abuse and neglect, as well as exposure to domestic violence, and apply this duty to a much broader range of reporter groups. After the report is made, it is then up to the relevant child welfare agency to determine the appropriate assessment approach and response to the particular case. In one sense, the reporter's task is complete once the report has been made, although if the reporter is in a continuing relationship with the child, such as a teacher, the person will have their normal duty to support the child in an appropriate way.

Provenance of Mandatory Reporting Laws: Kempe, the 'Battered-Child Syndrome' and Gaze Aversion

The concern to identify cases of serious child abuse and neglect, and to use the expertise and availability of numerous persons who deal with children in the course of their work, and who can thus act as protective 'sentinels' for the child's welfare (Sedlak and Broadhurst 1996), is the central concept underpinning mandatory reporting laws. This concept remains as true today as it did in animating the first reporting laws. As discussed in more detail in Chap. 1, the first mandatory reporting laws were enacted in the USA between 1963 and 1967 (Paulsen 1967; Nelson 1984). Motivated largely by the recognition of the 'battered-child syndrome' (Kempe et al. 1962), these laws were initially limited to requiring medical professionals to report suspected physical abuse inflicted by a child's parent or caregiver. Kempe had identified not only the situation of severe intentional injury being inflicted on parents but also the widespread reluctance and/or seeming inability of many doctors to recognise it and deal with it appropriately by reporting it to authorities (Bross and Mathews 2014). Doctors' repeated failure to act on clear cases of violent assault to infants embodied the phenomenon of 'gaze aversion'; they looked away when they encountered a situation which caused them discomfort or psychological confusion.

Hence, one function of the mandatory reporting law was to place in law the ethical and moral obligations to act on behalf of a vulnerable child who one knew or suspected was the subject of serious abuse or neglect. The law represents the will of the people as represented by Parliament and as such sets down principles of acceptable and unacceptable conduct. The mandatory reporting law states to the community that child abuse and neglect, and children's rights to security and safety and adequate chance in life, is taken seriously.

Extension of Mandatory Reporting Laws in Some Jurisdictions: After Kempe and CAPTA 1974

The scope of the initial legislation in all states soon expanded in three ways, spurred in part by the 1974 federal legislation: the Child Abuse Prevention and Treatment Act (CAPTA), which allocated funds to states based on the parameters of their laws. First, State laws were amended to require members of additional professional groups to report suspicions of abuse (some states would require all citizens to make reports). Second, the types of reportable abuse were expanded to include not only physical abuse but sexual abuse, emotional or psychological abuse and neglect. Third, the extent of harm required to have been caused or suspected to have been caused to activate the reporting duty was required by CAPTA to be unqualified by expressions such as 'serious harm', and this accompanied many states abandoning such qualifications (Kalichman 1999).

The Most Recent Revision of CAPTA

This can be contrasted with the current version of CAPTA which, since 1996, defines 'child abuse and neglect' as meaning 'at a minimum, any recent act or failure to act on the part of a parent or caretaker, which results in death, *serious* physical or emotional harm, sexual abuse or exploitation, or an act or failure to act which presents an imminent risk of *serious* harm' (5106g(2)). The emphasis is clearly on, at a minimum, acts of abuse and neglect which have caused serious harm. The focus on significant or serious harm is explicitly found in the legislation across Australia and in most US State laws. However, some jurisdictions in the USA and Canada have a less explicit focus on significant harm. Some jurisdictions also restrict the duty to cases where not only is the harm qualification present, but in addition, the child does not have a parent able to protect them from the harm.

Rights Enshrined in the Common Law and Criminal Law Which Protect Children's Rights to Physical Security and a Minimum Standard of Care

In their concern to protect children from serious abuse and neglect, mandatory reporting laws clearly parallel other legal remedies in both civil and criminal law. This is particularly the case of physical abuse, sexual abuse and serious neglect, although it is perhaps not as clear in the case of emotional abuse.

To first consider criminal law, both common law jurisdictions and code jurisdictions contain numerous provisions making it an offence to commit various kinds of physical and sexual assault, and these apply where the victim is a child. Examples of offences related to physical assault include common assault, assault occasioning bodily harm, grievous bodily harm, torture, manslaughter and murder. One exception commonly made is to allow corporal punishment, although over 30 countries now prohibit this (Durrant and Smith 2011), and even where it remains permitted, there are limits on its acceptable use so that it must generally be for legitimate discipline or control and must not be unreasonable. Examples of offences related to sexual assault include prohibitions on sexual activity with children, distinct from other sexual offences between adults, including indecent dealing with a child, unlawful carnal knowledge of a child and maintaining a sexual relationship with a child; and general sexual offences will also apply to child victims, including rape and incest. New categories of criminal offence have also recently been created to deal with offences related to the creation, distribution and possession of child pornography (often referred to as 'child exploitation material').

Finally, examples of criminal offences related to neglect of children also feature in various forms in virtually all jurisdictions. These offences include criminal neglect and failure to provide necessaries of life.[6] Some jurisdictions also have the offences of failing to protect a child from harm (see, e.g. the *Children, Youth and Families Act 2005* (Vic) s 493), of leaving a child unattended (s 494) and of endangering the life of a child by exposure[7] – all also being species of neglect.

[6] For example, under the Criminal Codes of the Northern Territory, Queensland, Tasmania and Western Australia, it is the duty of every person who has the care of a child under 16 years old to provide necessaries of life to the child (Criminal Code (NT), s 149; Criminal Code (Qld), s 286; Criminal Code (Tas), s 145; Criminal Code (WA), s 263). Comparable provisions exist in the other non-Code Australian jurisdictions, including *Crimes Act 1900* (ACT), s 39; *Crimes Act 1900* (NSW), s 43A; and *Criminal Law Consolidation Act 1935* (SA), s 30. For a case example of fatal neglect, see Ebony's case: R v BW and SW (No 3) [2009] NSWSC 1043.

[7] Criminal Code 1899 (Qld) s 326; *Crimes Act 1900* (NSW), s 43; *Crimes Act 1900* (ACT), s 41 (child under the age of 2 years); *Criminal Code* (NT), s 184 (child under the age of 2 years); and *Criminal Code* (Tas), s 178 (child under the age of 14 years).

Civil Law

As with all criminal offences, the criminal offences noted above primarily recognise that these duties are owed not only to the child victim, but are duties owed to the State. This remains so even with modern victims of crime compensation schemes. Yet, alongside the criminal offences, the law clearly recognises the rights possessed by the child victim as having their equivalent in civil law, with this branch of law giving the child victim the right to a personal remedy to gain access to compensation for harm, injury, pain and suffering and other loss (such as lost opportunity and economic loss) and to facilitate health rehabilitation. For both physical and sexual assaults, the relevant causes of action lie in tort law, in trespass to the person (common law assault and battery) and in negligence.[8] For neglect, the cause of action would lie in the tort of negligence.

These rights and remedies in civil law rest on foundational concepts resonating with the individual rights and liberties recognised by liberal theory. The basic right underpinning all these is the general legal right to bodily inviolability, or bodily integrity, clearly recognised for at least three centuries.[9] The philosophical concept underpinning this legal principle is autonomy (self-rule); that is, an individual has a right to choose what happens regarding his or her own body, and this entails a right to bodily integrity. The principle of autonomy heavily informs the common law in general.[10] Autonomy is an interest held not only by parents, but by children. The very basis of tort law is that one individual has interfered with the 'autonomy' of another person's body or private interests, either by an intentional act, a negligent manner of acting or a failure to act when under a legal duty to do so.

The Nature and Scope of Parental Power at Law

As between parents and children, these legal principles are consistent with and flow from the duties of parents which have been recognised at common law for centuries. Parents do not have untrammelled power over their children's lives, liberties and freedoms; children are not the chattels of their parents. As observed by Locke in

[8] In *AB v Victoria* (Unreported, Supreme Court of Victoria, Gillard J, 15 June 2000), a Victorian jury found a government school principal and deputy principal liable for failure to report what was found should have amounted to a reasonable suspicion that the child had been and was being sexually abused. The action was pleaded in negligence, with the failure to report occurring in 1991–1992. This was before Victoria introduced legislation in 1993 requiring teachers to report suspected child sexual abuse. The student was awarded $494,000 in damages for the contribution of the failure to report to her subsequent suffering of abuse by her stepfather and consequential injury. A common law duty has been held to coexist with mandatory reporting obligations in the USA (*Landeros v Flood* (1976) 551 P 2d 389) and Canada (*Brown v University of Alberta Hospital* (1997) 145 DLR 4th 63).

[9] *Cole v Turner* (1704) 6 Mod 149; *Collins v Wilcock* [1984] 1 WLR 1172.

[10] *Stuart v Kirkland-Veenstra* (2009) 237 CLR 215 at 248.

1690 – which we will come to shortly – parents had duties at common law to maintain, protect and educate their children. These duties were reinforced by leading text writers such as Blackstone (1765) and have been reinforced by the House of Lords[11] and the High Court of Australia.[12] More recent examples of common law authorities referring generally to the duty owed by parents towards their young children can be found in cases of severe child abuse and neglect leading to the child's death and parental liability for murder or manslaughter.[13] Indeed, parental power over their children is exceeded by the Supreme Court in its *parens patriae* jurisdiction; this recognises that the State is the supreme parent of children for the reason that it has the necessary power to look after those who cannot look after themselves and sometimes has to exert power over children's lives when parents should not have that power or are otherwise unable to wield it (Seymour 1994).

Part 2

In a just society, including any liberal democracy, law is a tool for regulating conduct to promote and secure social justice, equality, dignity and fundamental human rights and for creating human capabilities. In Part 2, I will draw together strands of liberal thought to develop a theoretical framework within which the key social policy of mandatory reporting laws can be situated and evaluated. Landmark liberal theories have at their core a focus on the rights and needs of the individual – including the child as an individual – to dignity, equality, freedom, security and, ultimately, a minimal opportunity in life. It will be seen that, alongside the factual situation articulated in Part 1, the theoretical perspectives and concepts fundamental to liberal thought, and hence to a legitimately ordered liberal society, are entirely consistent and compatible with, and in fact require, a device such as a form of mandatory reporting law as part of a functioning child welfare apparatus.

Social Justice and Individual Rights

The conceptual basis for any law or policy in human affairs in a liberal democratic state must be to promote the key principles with which a liberal polity is concerned. The fundamental position is that individuals, including children, are free and equal and have rights to security and should have equal opportunities which are not unfairly limited by chance or by the typical dimensions of personhood which have

[11] *Gillick v West Norfolk and Wisbech Area Health Authority* [1986] AC 112.

[12] *Secretary, Department of Health and Community Services (NT) v JWB and SMB (Marion's Case)* (1992) 175 CLR 218.

[13] *R v BW [No 3]* [2009] NSWSC 1043; *Sam v The Queen* (2011) 206 A Crim R 67.

historically been used to discriminate against people and perpetrate injustice and undesirable power imbalances: gender, race, religion and class. The essence of the modern liberal project is to promote fundamental ideals of equality, freedom, dignity and autonomy and in an applied sense to do this by creating social conditions that better advance these priorities. Social and legal measures can be devised to help create conditions of lived experience so that these goals are more likely to be achieved for more individuals, and especially those in traditional dimensions of vulnerability, overcoming the natural imbalance in opportunity bestowed by the pure chance of birth and the inequality that flows from that lottery. The creation of better opportunities for those born into less equal conditions translates to provision to these individuals of a higher chance of attaining these core attributes of personal security, equality of opportunity, autonomy and dignity. The benefits of such opportunity creation flow to individuals, communities and the entire society.

In the context of child maltreatment, core ideas and ideals animating this approach can be found in many of the most prominent thinkers from liberal thought and related theoretical positions. While children's welfare and relations between parents and children have not explicitly occupied a great deal of time in these writings, both classical and more recent, there are sufficient acknowledgments of children's place in this theory on which we can construct an applied framework. These observations can be seen to resonate with legal principles in common law, which were noted earlier. While the theorists discussed below expound various principles over a time span of more than 300 years, a common strand uniting their ideas is evident: that a genuinely liberal society must not ignore wrongs committed against children by adults, including most significantly by parents and caregivers. Notions of parental liberty should not be unduly privileged over children's rights to personal security. A just society must include measures to address the vulnerability of children to abuse and neglect and to promote children's rights to dignity, security, egalitarian treatment and a decent opportunity in life.

John Locke: Within Liberal Society, Parental Power Is Limited and Conditional; Children Have Rights

John Locke's *Second Treatise of Government* (1690) has as a starting point that people are born free and equal, meaning not that this is so in reality, but that a legitimate government must be arranged so as to promote this value. For Locke, the legitimacy of government in a political society rested on its central concern to secure individuals' 'property', with 'property' embracing not only goods and realty, but the individual's life, liberty and security. The very reason for government's existence was to protect and secure the rights of the individual. This purpose of government marked the justifiable parameters of State action. Within the family context, Locke stated that parental power extended only to govern children for their own 'help, instruction, and preservation' (Locke 2003, p. 176); it did not extend to life or death or the child's liberties. The child's rights were acknowledged: 'The power of the father doth not reach at all to the lives, liberties and estates of the child, which is only in [the child's] own disposing'. Parental guardianship was conditional on being appropriately exercised and so could be forfeited (pp. 126–127). These principles were groundbreaking at the time, given the social realities of children's lived experience and given that, on a broader scale, an institution as fundamental as education did not become compulsory in England until the 1880s. However, the principle of the child's liberty and right to security of the person – while often breached – can be seen as a logical and long-articulated principle in the liberal framework.

John Stuart Mill: Liberalism Must Protect Children in the Family Sphere

Possibly the most prominent and influential next proponent of children's fundamental rights in the family and social context was the influential theorist and campaigner John Stuart Mill. In 1859, in his famous work *On Liberty*, Mill demanded the protection of children from external injury (Mill 1998, p. 14). Significantly, despite all the other contexts in which children suffered various depredations – workplaces such as mines and factories, the street for the homeless and destitute and other institutions such as orphanages – Mill identified the family sphere as the most important domain requiring State control to prevent abuse of power (1998, p. 116). Fundamental to this insight was Mill's recognition of the link between a distorted sense of parental liberty over their children and the State's neglect to secure children's safety (1998, p. 116). These principles were consistent with Mill's harm principle, in which he formulated a concept demarcating the limit of the State's justifiable sphere of action and, as a corollary, the individual's sphere of protected activity. Mill's harm principle posited that the State may not intervene in an individual's behaviour provided it is only self-regarding and causes no harm to others. For Mill, the State could intervene to respond to a parent's behaviour that harmed her or his child, but not in relation to behaviour that did not. The parameters of what can be said to constitute sufficient 'harm' are slippery, and the methods of State intervention are numerous and may involve measures which are supportive as well as coercive; but one example Mill provides relates to the parental duty to ensure their child is educated (the reason being that the child has a right to be provided by their parent with an education and hence an opportunity to succeed in life; society also has a right not to have to support an uneducated child). If a parent could not pay for their child's education, this should be subsidised by the State. Mill is notable for being particularly attentive to children's rights and needs; it is no coincidence that he also broke new ground in advocating for the rights of women, another marginalised group, in *The Subjection of Women*.

International Legal Instruments Increasingly Recognise Children's Rights

Since Locke's and Mill's writings, major social developments occurred to translate some of these principles into practice. One example is the provision of universal compulsory education – the failure to ensure one's child attends school would now be seen as a species of parental neglect, i.e. educational neglect, and under the mandatory reporting law in New South Wales, this is a form of child maltreatment. Others include broader healthcare for children (failure to secure aspects of which would be another species of neglect, i.e. medical neglect) and extension of criminal laws regarding various assaults to children.

In addition, these fundamental rights expressed in political philosophy have since been translated into several core human rights instruments. These can be traced to the League of Nations' *Declaration of the Rights of the Child* 1924, the *Universal Declaration of Human Rights* 1948 recognising childhood as requiring special care and assistance and the *Declaration of the Rights of the Child* 1959 articulating the need for children's rights: 'the child, by reason of his [or her] physical and mental immaturity, needs special safeguards and care, including appropriate legal protection' (Pr. 2). Most recently, the *United Nations Convention on the Rights of the Child* 1989 contains various children's rights. Most specifically in this context, Article 19 obliges States parties to take all appropriate legislative, administrative, social and educational measures to protect children from all forms of abuse and exploitation. There are also rights to life, a minimum standard of health and an education. These rights can clearly be seen to involve rights to certain things and rights against certain things: 'negative liberties' and 'positive liberties'. These rights map clearly onto the recognised forms of child abuse and neglect:

- The right to life, liberty and security (physical abuse, sexual abuse)
- Freedom from abuse, freedom from exploitation (physical abuse, sexual abuse)
- The right to health (nutritional neglect, medical neglect, prenatal substance abuse)
- The right to an education (educational neglect)

Richard Rorty: A Philosophical Pragmatist Concerned with Decreasing Suffering and Giving Children an Equal Chance of Happiness

In more recent theoretical work, the core concerns of earlier liberal theorists are adopted, explored and extended. While the context for such theoretical work is somewhat different to that inhabited by Locke and Mill, the central concerns for individual equality, fairness and a reasonable opportunity at a decent life – including an adequate start in life – are readily apparent. Some of this thought emanates from thinkers such as Richard Rorty, an avowed pragmatist in the tradition of Charles

Peirce, William James and John Dewey, for whom a philosophy of hope became more useful and meaningful for lived experience than the aridity of philosophical debates about the existence of fundamental truths. Rorty used as a standard for weighing the goodness of an action whether it is 'more useful' for creating a better future by 'containing more of what we consider good and less of what we consider bad' – with the goods embodied by such goals as variety, freedom and growth (1999, pp. 27–28) and other concrete advantages for lived experience. In this vein, Rorty also stated that (1999, p. xxix): 'What matters for pragmatists is devising ways of diminishing human suffering and increasing human equality, increasing the ability of all human children to start life with an equal chance of happiness'. Hence, while having shelved any attempt to solve the traditional 'reality/appearance' dispute, Rorty adopted as an evaluative measure of conduct and policy the central tenets of liberal society: freedom, egalitarianism, increasing respect and equality and diminishing suffering. For Rorty, this approach is embedded in an ability to sympathise with others' pain, sensitivity to that pain, and a feeling that we owe a moral obligation to those who endure that pain (p. 14).

John Rawls: The Fundamental Conditions of a Just Society

For Rorty and fellow pragmatists, the test of the goodness of an idea is in part its ability to generate consensus. This impulse towards the generation of a consensus about what is fair and just, and a sound plan for action, can also be seen in the work of John Rawls, often seen as the most significant political philosopher of the twentieth century. In *A Theory of Justice* (1971), Rawls devised the tool of a thought experiment, using the twin concepts of the original position and a veil of ignorance, as a means of contemplating and arriving at the fundamental conditions of a society which would provide its citizens with a reasonable chance of equality and human flourishing. Rawls posited that if a group of rational people were placed in the 'original position' of having to design the fundamental characteristics of the society into which they were born, with these persons being situated behind a 'veil of ignorance' such that they did not know any of their personal or familial attributes on being born – such as their race, gender, creed, wealth or class – then they would choose organising political and economic principles for that society which would ensure equal basic liberties for all citizens (on Rawls's conception, confined to civil and political rights), equality of opportunity and the 'difference principle': that social and economic inequalities are only just if they produce compensating benefits for all and especially for the least advantaged members of society.

The Benefits and Limitations of Rawls's Theory

The benefit of Rawls's theory is that it reveals at least part of the essence of what a just society must contain, stripped of the contaminated motivations flowing from more advantaged accidents of birth. However, some have observed that the actors in

Rawls's original position – as in other social contract theories – are assumed to be in a position of rough physical and cognitive equality; they are adults possessing rationality and agency. While they are contemplating what features a just society should possess to enable each rational agent to flourish to a minimal level, the group of actors does not contain those without moral or prudential rationality, and it appears that the task set does not include the requirement to ensure justice and equality for those who lack these attributes. Curiously, perhaps indicating that the theory reflected its time, those in the original position were also stated to be 'heads of families', a fundamentally limiting factor which has been trenchantly criticised (Okin 2004); additionally, sex was not a characteristic placed behind the veil of ignorance, so that issues of gender equality and oppression were neither acknowledged nor considered. Furthermore, surprisingly and problematically, as it is fundamentally inconsistent with the spirit of the exercise and with the core concepts of liberalism itself, Rawls conceded (at least initially) that those who cannot enter agreements or contracts – including children – are not owed political justice.[14]

While it is perhaps reasonable to conclude that even this more limited group of actors in the original position would choose principles of social organisation which neither permit severe child maltreatment nor allow it to go unaddressed, this gap in Rawls's model presented a conundrum that others would identify and confront, including Susan Moller Okin (1989, 2004). Of particular relevance to this discussion, Rawls has been strongly and persuasively criticised for simply assuming that family relations are just (Okin 1989, 2004, p. 1550). These criticisms prompted Rawls to turn his attention to some but not all familial injustices and power asymmetries.

Rawls's Response to Criticisms of Ignoring Familial Injustice, and Statements on Children's Rights

In 1997 Rawls provided several responses to these points in *The Idea of Public Reason Revisited* (1999, pp. 156–164). Of particular relevance are Rawls's statements about justice in the family sphere and children's rights. Rawls acknowledges that the family is part of the basic structure of society to which the core principles of justice apply because a central role – and therefore a duty – of parents is to raise and care for their children, so as to ensure their moral development and education so that they can develop into responsible adult citizens. Rawls disputes Okin's claim that his theory applies to the family as a structure itself but does not apply to the internal workings of the family, hence leaving inequality for women unattended. He does this by maintaining that while political principles do not apply *directly* to the

[14]This might have been based on a view that only a 'reciprocator' can possess a right. On that view, rights and duties are correlative and reciprocal so to every right you have there is a corresponding duty that you owe. On this view, children owe no duties, so could not have rights. On this view, having an interest is not the same as having a right, and we might well have obligations to children based on their capacity to have interests, but these obligations cannot be cashed out in terms of corresponding rights. Others, with whom I agree, would argue that possession of interests is sufficient to bear rights, and one does not need to be a reciprocator to have rights.

internal life of the family, they 'impose essential constraints on the family as an institution and so guarantee the basic rights and liberties, and the freedom and opportunities, of all its members...by specifying the basic rights of equal citizens who are the members of families. The family as part of the basic structure cannot violate these freedoms' (p. 159).

Significantly, Rawls continued that (pp. 159–161):

> These principles do not inform us how to raise our children, and we are not required to treat our children in accordance with political principles...Surely parents must follow some conception of justice (or fairness) and due respect with regard to their children, but, within certain limits, this is not for political principles to prescribe. *Clearly the prohibition of abuse and neglect of children, and much else, will, as constraints, be a vital part of family law*...Just as the principles of justice require that wives have all the rights of citizens, *the principles of justice impose constraints on the family on behalf of children who as society's future citizens have basic rights as such*...the principles of justice still put essential restrictions on the family...adult members of families [are] equal citizens first...No institution or association in which they are involved can violate their rights as citizens...*The equal rights of women and the basic rights of their children as future citizens are inalienable and protect them wherever they are*...If the so-called private sphere is alleged to be a space exempt from justice, then there is no such thing.

Rawls's Revised Model: Children's Rights as Citizens

These statements indicate that if he had not previously done so, Rawls had come to accept that children possessed fundamental rights both within and beyond the family and that it was important to recognise this. His statements about children's rights within the family, including the right to be free from abuse and neglect, are particularly notable. They show beyond any doubt that on his approach, there were fundamental limits on what parents were permitted to do in relation to their children and that abuse and neglect should neither be permitted nor allowed to go unaddressed.

In one immediate respect, however, Rawls's revised outlook can and should be readily modified. Wherever Rawls refers to children's rights as *future* citizens, the reference must be simply to *children as citizens*. This is so because there is no doubt that children are citizens, each being entitled to protection by the laws of their country and being bound by legal duties themselves. Children's duties and entitlements do not accrue on majority; they are present throughout childhood. This is embodied in legal principles, and some rights are even present before birth. It would be plainly inconsistent with liberal theory to deny children these rights to safety and security in the family sphere.

Other theorists identified issues with the mechanics of Rawls's approach, while supporting its overall usefulness as a device for identifying principles of social justice. Okin (2004) herself defended liberalism as the organising framework for society, arguing that 'liberalism properly understood, with its radical refusal to accept hierarchy and its focus on the freedom and equality of individuals, is crucial to feminism…consistent and fully developed liberalism, quite radically revised so as to include women, has great potential for feminism' (p. 1546). Similarly, Nussbaum (1999) observed that, rather than being too focused on the individual, liberalism needed to pay *more* attention to the individuals within the family sphere. Some of these other theorists have since further developed notions of what characteristics must be supported in individuals' lives to enable a minimum standard of equality and opportunity, with these theories being far more cognisant of injustices in spheres Rawls left less well attended: especially gender and the family. In this regard, the most prominent and useful among these thinkers is the work of Martha Nussbaum.

Martha Nussbaum's 'Capabilities Approach' to Social Justice and Human Development

The sensitivity to others' pain identified by Rorty finds an echo in Martha Nussbaum's 'capabilities approach' to social justice and human development (Nussbaum 2011). At its core, this approach is concerned with ensuring that government secures, protects and fosters certain capabilities in each individual citizen, as without a certain level of these capabilities, it is not possible for an individual to lead a life of sufficient equality, dignity, autonomy and freedom. On this approach, the central duty of a legitimate government is to generate and secure the circumstances under which the individual's capabilities are created.

There are ten stated core capabilities which are seen as necessary for an individual to live a decent life. The attainment of these capabilities does not require an equal measure of each capability across all individuals in society. Rather, it requires an 'ample threshold' (p. 36) or minimum measure of each capability for each individual, without which the individual's dignified existence and capacity to flourish is unjustly compromised, and *those who require more help should receive that help* (p. 24). Significantly, each person is seen as *an end in themselves* and is not a means to an end (p. 35). The consequence of this is that social policy – which can sometimes enhance individuals' capabilities even when focused on groups, namely, families – must *primarily* be focused on the needs of the individual. This focus on the individual person's needs is required precisely because the group-based structures within society may in fact be the context and cause of individual injustice and suffering.

Accordingly, the fundamental inequalities that may subsist within core societal structures such as the family must be addressed. An example of this is that to the extent that a traditional patriarchal family and the actions occurring within it cannot be reconciled with attainment by individuals within the family of the capabilities, then that structure must be radically reassessed and its adverse effects remedied. Within the family context, Nussbaum maintains correctly, with Mill, that those views within classical liberal thought which sought to preserve the family sphere as private and therefore immune from intervention aimed at overcoming injustice inflicted in the private sphere were *inconsistent* with true liberalism (Nussbaum 2011, pp. 146–147); and it is clear that such injustices must be addressed in any fair society.

The ten capabilities, in summary form (pp. 33–34), are:

1. Life: being able to live a life of normal length
2. Bodily health: being able to have good health, nourishment and shelter
3. Bodily integrity: being able to be secure against violent assault including sexual assault and domestic violence, being able to move freely, having opportunities for sexual satisfaction and reproductive choice
4. Senses, imagination and thought: being able to think and reason in a way informed by education, being able to use thought in connection with material of one's own choice, being able to use one's mind freely and to have freedom of expression and choice
5. Emotions: being able to have attachments to people, to have feelings and to love; freedom from impediments to emotional growth
6. Practical reason: being able to form one's own conception of the good and to critically reflect on one's own life plan, freedom of conscience and religion
7. Affiliation: being able to live with and interact with others and to imagine another's situation (empathic development); freedom of assembly, freedom of speech; being able to enjoy social bases of self-respect through being seen as equal to others (freedom from discrimination on grounds of race, sex, sexual orientation, ethnicity, caste, religion, nationality)
8. Other species: being able to live with concern for the natural world
9. Play: being able to laugh, play, enjoy leisure and recreation
10. Control over one's environment: being able to participate in political choices, to possess property rights and to seek employment on an equal basis with others

Some instances of a lack of a key capability will be particularly disadvantageous, creating what some have termed 'corrosive disadvantage' (Wolff and de-Shalit 2007) which produces a cascade of disadvantage by compromising or destroying other of the core capabilities; in these areas Nussbaum urges particular investment of scarce resources (pp. 99–100). In addition, affiliation and practical reason are seen as being especially important capabilities that promote, and are necessary for, the attainment and use of others. What is also highly significant in the practical application of these principles is that Nussbaum refuses to accept that in a context of apparently limited resources, there must always be trade-offs between these capabilities; it is simply the task of government to find a way to attain the necessary minimum standard. This may not entail the immediate securing of all capabilities (p. 39); but what should happen is that government should explore all possible avenues by which the capabilities can be secured and how people can more closely realise a capability even if it cannot be satisfactorily secured.[15]

[15] Nussbaum notes that creative solutions may play a part. An example from the Indian state of Kerala, which combined provision of education with a midday meal to children; this overcame a social obstacle presented by children's wage-earning for families previously outweighing the advantage seen in allowing children to attend school. Subsequently, illiteracy has been almost eradicated and India's Supreme Court requires all government schools in the country to provide such a meal.

Nussbaum Extending Rawls

Nussbaum's approach is substantially consistent with much of Rawls in its concern with a just ordering of society to overcome the inequalities and hence the injustices created by the accident of birth. In this sense, it is of the same liberal lineage in its concern to overcome traditional divisions of reality and opportunity based on class, gender, race and religion and instead to enable a fairer conferral of opportunity to obtain meaningful values inherent to a dignified human life.

However, Nussbaum moves beyond Rawls's consensus approach to the social contract limited to those in symmetrical relationships of power, by being not only concerned with inequality generally (even in the traditional senses acknowledge by liberal thought), but by being more explicitly and consciously concerned with several dimensions of *inherent inequality*, including those in which there is a clear asymmetry of power, which are not commonly central to the liberal project. One of these is the treatment of the disabled, which would cover a broad population including children with cognitive impairments, to elderly persons with dementia and other neural conditions. In essence, this concern constitutes an attempt to ensure that those with an innate lack of power are adequately represented in ways beyond Rawls's exercise.

Nussbaum's expansion of the circle of human concern is highly significant because it clearly embraces not only the interests of those with cognitive impairments; it also embraces a clear consideration of children's interests. In 2012 (Dixon and Nussbaum 2012), Nussbaum would explicitly identify children's rights as a new fourth frontier of justice, after the three she had identified earlier in *Frontiers of Justice* (2006).[16] The basis for this was children's *special vulnerability* and the fact that the social contract model does not adequately cater for theorising entitlements in domains characterised by marked power asymmetry; children's special vulnerability means they are not the free independent and equal agents in the social contract model; their 'unusual vulnerability and powerlessness' requires a new approach to basic rights.[17]

The Capabilities Approach, Children's Rights and Child Maltreatment

At the core of Nussbaum's capabilities approach is a striving to nurture each individual's potential as a human being by ensuring the protection of a sufficient amount of the core capabilities required for each individual to deploy those attributes in

[16] Justice between nations, justice for the disabled and justice for animals.

[17] In my view this is consistent with an even more developed version of Rawls's social contract, original position and veil of ignorance. If the rational actor in the original position was approaching the situation with knowledge that certain conditions were required in childhood to enable development and flourishing, then those conditions would have to be adequately considered. That is, they would have to consider the position not just of adults 'fallen from the sky fully formed' into such a society; they would have to consider also and especially the developmental requirements of humans from birth. Hence, the exercise requires a second dimension of imaginativeness and a third dimension of empathy.

their own life. The way in which the individual uses those capabilities is determined by their own choice; the concern is therefore to arrange social policy to ensure that all individuals have an adequate 'set of opportunities, or substantial freedoms' (p. 18) to exercise genuine autonomy. This has a similar motivation to Rorty's core goal, but adds multiple layers of practical content to the ambition.

Nussbaum comments that 'capability-destruction in children is a particularly grave matter and as such should be off-limits' (p. 27), meaning that those charged with the care of children should not be at liberty to destroy their capabilities. As well, while accepting that parents have some degree of freedom to make decisions regarding their children, there are some types of activity which should not remain guarded by this private sphere: 'Some issues are, or should be, easy: we should all agree that domestic violence and child sexual abuse should be aggressively policed by the state' (p. 148). While being a much broader and more nuanced theory, it is possible to discern a resonance between the capabilities approach and what Kempe described as 'the child's right of access to society' which animated the first mandatory reporting laws. It is notable that Nussbaum recognises that while the capabilities approach is concerned with the situation of all individuals in a society, as befits a theory flowing from political liberalism, it is 'concerned with entrenched social injustice and inequality, especially capability failures that are the result of discrimination or marginalization' (p. 19) and charges government and public policy with the urgent task of improving the quality of all people's lives. Children who experience severe maltreatment are a particularly vulnerable and marginalised group.

One of the most prominent social goods on an application of the capabilities approach is the right to education (152ff) as this is not only a good in itself, but it enables the securing and advancement of other goods. However, we can readily view the entire set of capabilities as a useful and apposite matrix. It is plain that many of the core capabilities are integral to this proposed theoretical framework in the context of child abuse and neglect. The first three capabilities clearly map onto direct rights and freedoms (1, 2, 3) and are relevant to protection from physical abuse, sexual abuse and neglect. The others (4, 5, 6, 7, 9) are also relevant because the typical social, behavioural and psychological consequences of serious abuse and neglect either compromise or destroy these capabilities. The way in which the capabilities approach connects with child abuse and the fourth frontier of justice is to focus on the developmental aspect. Without a minimum amount of certain goods, an individual child is unable to develop a cascade of other attributes, particularly cognitive and emotional skills. These then flow down into compromised development of other core capabilities.

Conclusion

This theoretical framework indicates fields of political, legal and social activity to protect children from certain types of fundamental breaches to their rights as citizens and actions which destroy and compromise their core capabilities. These capabilities have their roots in the ideals promoted by liberal society and are demonstrably concrete and suggest the kinds of measures justified in responding to them. The framework evinces a robust theoretical basis which supports the development and implementation of a mechanism to identify cases of serious child abuse and neglect.

The theoretical discussion alone does not of necessity indicate the conclusion that 'a mandatory reporting law is required'; this would clearly be too prescriptive. However, when taken together with other key features of the context of child maltreatment identified in Part 1 – the often severe effects; its hidden nature; its criminal nature; the age of victims; the likelihood that it will not be voluntarily brought to the attention of welfare agencies by parents or the child; the evidence that at least before law and policy were first created, even professionals whose ethical role required care for patients would ignore obvious cases; the lack of demonstrable evidence that another method is superior in bringing such cases to light; and economic wisdom in early capacity building in the disadvantaged – then a strong normative conclusion crystallises. If we are genuine about promoting children's rights and if we take these matters seriously, then *some* measure should be adopted to identify these cases, so that the child's situation can be identified and addressed.

This requirement leads to the question: *what* measure should be adopted to identify these cases? This is where Dr. Kempe and his colleagues found themselves in the late 1950s. Their solution was to respond to a particular type of child abuse – severe physical abuse – and the inaction of a professional group, by advocating for a mandatory reporting law: a legal obligation to report suspected serious cases of child abuse, together with associated mechanisms to support such a scheme. This would only be one part of a system of child and family support – Kempe strongly advocated for secondary prevention (1976) – but nevertheless an essential part. To date, the evidence of case finding in jurisdictions with such an approach, compared with their counterparts, indicates that on balance it is practically far superior than other alternative methods (see further Chap. 1).

The *capabilities approach*, and its fidelity to the core principles of liberal society, children's rights as citizens and children's special vulnerability and suffering of serious abuse and neglect in the family sphere, complements and is consistent with a public health approach to child maltreatment. Just as the public health approach is consistent with mandatory reporting as one element of such an approach, so too is the capabilities approach consistent with governmental measures (in this case, via legislation and associated measures such as reporter training, intake agencies, response services and provision of health and rehabilitative services) to respond to the child's needs and enable the protection of and fostering of the child's core capabilities. Hence, the tertiary prevention aspect (a mandatory reporting law for existing serious harm and for clear and high risk for serious harm) is necessary because of the asymmetric power dynamic and other features characterising the context of serious child abuse and neglect, including the child's special vulnerability and inability to do anything to remedy the problem. This response is focused on protecting certain of the child's core capabilities in an immediate sense (e.g. life, bodily health and bodily integrity: capabilities 1–3) and on creating the conditions under which other of the child's core capabilities can be nurtured and sustained in future (e.g. senses, emotion, practical reason, affiliation). Without an intervention facilitated by a report by a sentinel reporter, these will not be possible (this assumes the parent will not seek assistance, an assumption borne out by the evidence). In addition, the secondary prevention aspect (reporting of children at clear risk of severe harm) also has similar effects, as well as having as a focal point of concern the development of capabilities in the parent. An approach to child and social welfare which contains as one strategy a mandatory reporting law for serious child abuse and neglect is consistent with and, on this theoretical approach, is required, to advance a genuine commitment to the true principles of liberal theory and children's rights and the flourishing of children, future generations and broader society.

Acknowledgements I am grateful to colleagues for comments on an earlier draft of this paper: Dr. Andrew McGee from QUT's Australian Centre for Health Law Research, Dr. Kerryann Walsh from QUT's Children and Youth Research Centre and my co-editor of this volume Professor Don Bross.

References

Arata, C. (1998). To tell or not to tell: Current functioning of child sexual abuse survivors who disclosed their victimization. *Child Maltreatment, 3*, 63–71.

Berliner, L., & Conte, J. (1990). The process of victimization: The victims' perspective. *Child Abuse & Neglect, 14*, 29–40.

Blackstone, W. ([orig 1765] 1830). *Commentaries on the laws of England* (15th ed.). London: Cadell and Davies.

Bross, D., & Mathews, B. (2014). The battered child syndrome: Changes in the law and child advocacy. In R. Krugman & J. Korbin (Eds.), C. Henry Kempe: A 50 year legacy to the field of child abuse and neglect (pp. 39–50). Dordrecht: Springer Scientific.

Carneiro, P., & Heckman, J. (2003). Human capital policy. In J. Heckman, A. Krueger, & B. Friedman (Eds.), *Inequality in America: What role for human capital policies?* (pp. 77–239). Cambridge, MA: MIT Press.

Chen, L., et al. (2010). Sexual abuse and lifetime diagnosis of psychiatric disorders: Systematic review and meta-analysis. *Mayo Clinic Proceedings, 85*(7), 618–629.

Dixon, R., & Nussbaum, M. (2012). Children's rights and a capabilities approach: The question of special priority. *Cornell Law Review, 97*, 549–593.

Dubowitz, H. (2000). What is child neglect? In H. Dubowitz & D. DePanfilis (Eds.), *The handbook for child protection*. Thousand Oaks: Sage.

Dunne, M., Purdie, D., Cook, M., Boyle, F., & Najman, J. (2003). Is child sexual abuse declining? Evidence from a population-based survey of men and women in Australia. *Child Abuse & Neglect, 27*(2), 141–152.

Durrant, J., & Smith, A. (Eds.). (2011). *Global pathways to abolishing physical punishment: Realizing children's rights*. New York: Routledge.

Egeland, B. (2009). Taking stock: Childhood emotional maltreatment and developmental psychopathology. *Child Abuse & Neglect, 33*, 22.

Fang, X., Brown, D., Florence, C., & Mercy, J. (2012). The economic burden of child maltreatment in the United States and implications for prevention. *Child Abuse & Neglect, 36*, 156–165.

Finkelhor, D., Hotaling, G., Lewis, I., & Smith, C. (1990). Sexual abuse in a national survey of adult men and women: Prevalence, characteristics, and risk factors. *Child Abuse & Neglect, 14*, 19–28.

Fromm, S. (2001). *Total estimated cost of child abuse and neglect in the United States: Statistical evidence*. Prevent Child Abuse America. Retrieved October 22, 2007, from http://www.preventchildabuse.org/site/DocServer/cost_analysis.pdf?docID=144

Gershoff, E. (2002). Corporal punishment by parents and associated child behaviors and experiences. *Psychological Bulletin, 128*, 539.

Gilbert, R., et al. (2009). Burden and consequences of child maltreatment in high-income countries. *Lancet, 373*(9657), 68–81.

Glaser, D. (2002). Emotional abuse and neglect (psychological maltreatment): A conceptual framework. *Child Abuse and Neglect, 26*, 697–714.

Glaser, D. (2011). How to deal with emotional abuse and neglect – Further development of a conceptual framework (FRAMEA). *Child Abuse and Neglect, 35*, 866–875.

Gostin, L. (2008). *Public health law: Power, duty, restraint* (2nd ed.). Berkeley: University of California Press.

Heckman, J. (2006). Skill formation and the economics of investing in disadvantaged children. *Science, 312*, 1900–1902.

Heckman, J. (2008). Schools, skills, and synapses (IZA Discussion Paper No. 3515). Bonn.

Heckman, J. (2012). The Heckman equation. www.heckmanequation.org

Heckman, J. (2013). *Giving kids a fair chance*. Cambridge, MA: Massachusetts Institute of Technology Press.

Heckman, J., Krueger, A., & Friedman, B. (Eds.). (2003). *Inequality in America: What role for human capital policies?* Cambridge, MA: MIT Press.

Hildyard, K., & Wolfe, D. (2002). Child neglect: Developmental issues and outcomes. *Child Abuse & Neglect, 26*(6–7), 679–695.

John Jay College of Criminal Justice. (2004). *The nature and scope of sexual abuse of minors by Catholic priests and deacons in the United States, 1950–2002*. Washington, DC: United States Conference of Catholic Bishops.

Kalichman, S. (1999). *Mandated reporting of suspected child abuse: Ethics, law and policy*. Washington, DC: American Psychological Association.

Kempe, C. H. (1976). Approaches to preventing child abuse: The health visitors' concept. *American Journal of Diseases of Children, 130*, 941–947.

Kempe, C. H., Silverman, F., Steele, B., Droegemueller, W., & Silver, H. (1962). The battered-child syndrome. *Journal of the American Medical Association, 181*, 17–24.

Kogan, S. (2004). Disclosing unwanted sexual experiences: Results from a national sample of adolescent women. *Child Abuse & Neglect, 28*, 147–165.

Landsford, J., et al. (2002). A 12 year prospective study of the long-term effects of early child physical maltreatment. *Archives of Pediatrics and Adolescent Medicine, 156*, 824.

Locke, J. ([orig 1690] 2003). Two treatises of government. In I. Shapiro (Ed.). *Two treatises of government and a letter concerning toleration* (pp. 1–209). New Haven: Yale University Press.

Mathews, B. (2012). Exploring the contested role of mandatory reporting laws in the identification of severe child abuse and neglect. In M. Freeman (Ed.), *Current legal issues. Volume 14: Law and childhood studies* (pp. 302–338). Oxford: Oxford University Press.

Mathews, B. (2014). Mandatory reporting laws for child sexual abuse in Australia – A legislative history: Report for the Royal Commission into Institutional Responses to Child Sexual Abuse. Sydney: Commonwealth of Australia.

Mathews, B., & Bross, D. (2014). Using law to identify, manage and prevent child maltreatment. In J. Korbin & R. Krugman (Eds.), *Handbook of child maltreatment* (pp. 477–502). Dordrecht: Springer Scientific.

Mathews, B., & Kenny, M. (2008). Mandatory reporting legislation in the USA, Canada and Australia: A cross-jurisdictional review of key features, differences and issues. *Child Maltreatment, 13*(1), 50–63.

May-Chahal, C., & Cawson, P. (2005). Measuring child maltreatment in the United Kingdom: A study of the prevalence of child abuse and neglect. *Child Abuse & Neglect, 29*(9), 969–984.

Mill, J. ([orig 1859] 1998). On liberty. In J. Gray (Ed.), *John Stuart Mill on liberty and other essays* (pp. 5–128). Oxford: Oxford University Press.

Nelson, B. (1984). *Making an issue of child abuse*. Chicago: University of Chicago Press.

Nelson, E., et al. (2002). Association between self-reported childhood sexual abuse and adverse psychosocial outcomes: Results from a twin study. *Archives of General Psychiatry, 59*, 139–145.

Ney, P., Moore, C., McPhee, J., & Trought, P. (1986). Child abuse: A study of the child's perspective. *Child Abuse & Neglect, 10*, 511–518.

Nussbaum, M. (1999). *Sex and social justice*. Oxford: Oxford University Press.

Nussbaum, M. (2006). *Frontiers of justice*. Cambridge, MA: Harvard University Press.

Nussbaum, M. (2011). *Creating capabilities*. Cambridge, MA: Harvard University Press.

Okin, S. M. (1989). *Justice, gender, and the family*. New York: Basic Books.

Okin, S. M. (2004). Gender, justice and gender: An unfinished debate. *Fordham Law Review, 72*(5), 1537.

Paine, M., & Hansen, D. (2002). Factors influencing children to self-disclose sexual abuse. *Clinical Psychology Review, 22*, 271–295.

Palmer, S., Brown, R., Rae-Grant, N., & Loughlin, M. (1999). Responding to children's disclosure of familial abuse: What survivors tell us. *Child Welfare, 78*, 259–282.

Paolucci, E., Genuis, M., & Violato, C. (2001). A meta-analysis of the published research on the effects of child sexual abuse. *The Journal of Psychology, 135*, 17–36.

Parkinson, P., Oates, K., & Jayakody, A. (2010). Breaking the long silence: Reports of child sexual abuse in the Anglican Church of Australia. *Ecclesiology, 6*(2), 183–200.

Paulsen, M. (1967). Child abuse reporting laws: The shape of the legislation. *Columbia Law Review, 67*, 1–49.

Perry, B. (2002). Childhood experience and the expression of genetic potential: What childhood neglect tells us about nature and nurture. *Brain and Mind, 3*(1), 79–100.

Putnam, F. (2003). Ten-year research update review: Child sexual abuse. *Journal of the American Academy of Child and Adolescent Psychiatry, 42*, 269–278.

Radford, L., Corral, S., Bradley, C., Fisher, H., Bassett, C., et al. (2011). *Child abuse and neglect in the UK today*. London: NSPCC.

Rawls, J. (1971). *A theory of justice*. Cambridge, MA: Harvard University Press.

Rawls, J. (1999). *The law of peoples, with "The Idea of Public Reason Revisited"*. Cambridge, MA: Harvard University Press.

Rorty, R. (1999). *Philosophy and social hope*. London: Penguin.

Rosenman, S., & Rodgers, B. (2004). Childhood adversity in an Australian population. *Social Psychiatry and Psychiatric Epidemiology, 39*(9), 695–702.

Sedlak, A., & Broadhurst, D. (1996). *Third National Incidence Study of child abuse and neglect*. Rockville: Westat.

Sedlak, A. J., Mettenburg, J., Basena, M., Petta, I., McPherson, K., Greene, A., et al. (2010). *Fourth National Incidence Study of child abuse and neglect (NIS-4): Report to congress, executive summary*. Washington, DC: U.S. Department of Health and Human Services, Administration for Children and Families.

Seymour, J. (1994). Parens Patriae and wardship powers: Their nature and origins. *Oxford Journal of Legal Studies, 14*, 159.

Shonkoff, J., & Phillips, D. (2000). *From neurons to neighbourhoods: The science of early childhood development*. Washington, DC: National Academies Press.

Smith, D., Letourneau, E., Saunders, B., et al. (2000). Delay in disclosure of childhood rape: Results from a national survey. *Child Abuse & Neglect, 24*(2), 273–287.

Stoltenborgh, M., van Ijzendoorn, M., Euser, E., & Bakermans-Kranenburg, M. (2011). A global perspective on child sexual abuse: Meta-analysis of prevalence around the world. *Child Maltreatment, 16*(2), 79–101.

Straus, M., Hamby, S., Finkelhor, D., Moore, D., & Runyan, D. (1998). Identification of child maltreatment with the parent-child Conflict Tactics Scales: development and psychometric data for a national sample of American parents. *Child Abuse and Neglect, 22*, 249–270.

Taylor, P., Moore, P., Pezzullo, L., Tucci, J., Goddard, C., & De Bortoli, L. (2008). *The cost of child abuse in Australia*. Melbourne, Vic: Australian Childhood Foundation and Child Abuse Prevention Research Australia.

Trocmé, N., Fallon, B., MacLaurin, B., Daciuk, J., Felstiner, C., Black, T., et al. (2005). *Canadian incidence study of reported child abuse and neglect – 2003: Major findings*. Ottawa, ON: Minister of Public Works and Government Services.

Turnock, B. (2009). *Public health: What it is and how it works* (4th ed.). Sudbury: Jones and Bartlett.

United States Department of Health and Human Services, Administration on Children, Youth and Families. (2006). *Child maltreatment 2004*. Washington, DC: US Government Printing Office.

United States Department of Health and Human Services, Administration on Children, Youth and Families. (2007). *Child maltreatment 2005*. Washington, DC: US Government Printing Office.

Veltman, M., & Browne, K. (2001). Three decades of child maltreatment research: Implications for the school years. *Trauma, Violence and Abuse, 2*, 215–239.

Widom, C. (2014). Longterm consequences of child maltreatment. In J. Korbin & R. Krugman (Eds.), *Handbook of child maltreatment* (pp. 225–250). Dordrecht: Springer Scientific.

Wolff, J., & de-Shalit, A. (2007). *Disadvantage*. Oxford: Oxford University Press.

World Health Organisation. (2006). *Preventing child maltreatment: A guide to taking action and generating evidence*. Geneva: World Health Organisation and International Society for Prevention of Child Abuse and Neglect.

Chapter 8
Ethics and the Identification and Response to Child Abuse and Neglect

Jacqueline J. Glover and Lisa M. Justis

Introduction

Child abuse and neglect continues to be a growing concern around the globe (Hart et al. 2011). To some, the ethics related to child maltreatment may seem to be relatively straightforward – maltreatment is wrong so don't do it, and if you witness it, report it. But for professionals, communities, and families struggling to make good choices on behalf of children, the ethical issues are not so easy (Levi 2008). They involve conflicting obligations and require an ethical framework to think through the issues. What follows is the identification of an ethical framework and its application to clinical issues involving the thresholds of mandatory reporting, family as decision makers, end-of-life decision making, visitation and placement, funding priorities, research, and the two emerging controversial issues of reporting pregnant women whose substance use behaviors put their fetuses at risk and obesity as medical neglect.

J.J. Glover, Ph.D. (✉)
Department of Pediatrics, University of Colorado School of Medicine, Aurora, CO, USA

Center for Bioethics and Humanities, University of Colorado,
Anschutz Medical Campus, 13080 E. 19th Ave, Aurora, CO, USA
e-mail: Jackie.Glover@ucdenver.edu

L.M. Justis
Kempe Child Protection Team Faculty, The Kempe Foundation for the Prevention and Treatment of Child Abuse and Neglect, Aurora, CO, USA

B. Mathews, D.C. Bross (eds.), *Mandatory Reporting Laws and the Identification of Severe Child Abuse and Neglect*, Child Maltreatment 4,
DOI 10.1007/978-94-017-9685-9_8

An Ethical Framework

An ethical framework includes the articulation of the values of the stakeholders, identifying where they may be in alignment, and developing an argument for what values should take precedence when they are in tension. By definition, an ethical issue arises when values are in tension and people need to think through how best to balance their conflicting obligations. The concern about child abuse and neglect arises out of the deeply held values of non-maleficence (not harming) and beneficence (promoting well-being). Other important values include respect for the autonomy (self-rule) of patients and families and respect for the family relationships themselves. Privacy, confidentiality, compassion, promoting trust, and fidelity (promise-keeping) are also central. Justice is also a very important value, although it is one of the hardest values to agree about, especially in the sense of fair allocation of scarce resources. But justice is also central to our concept of advocacy on behalf of vulnerable children and undergirds the criminal justice system's concerns about due process, fair punishment, and rehabilitation.

There has been a recent call to switch from a welfare framework in child abuse and neglect identification and treatment to a child's rights or human rights framework (Hart et al. 2011). In the USA, where rights language predominates, one would expect that the ethical dialogue would already consider basic human rights. But that is not necessarily the case. There is much disagreement about which rights take precedence and rights language itself can be very polarizing. Consider, for example, the seemingly endless debate between a "right to life" on the one hand and a "right to choose" on the other hand. A call for universal healthcare in the USA prompts a debate between negative rights of noninterference (liberty interests) and a positive right to education, public safety, healthcare, and other necessary elements of an equal opportunity to flourish (Gostin 2010). Rights language tends to be used as a kind of trump card, thrown down as if it already answers the ethical questions. But what is a moral right in the first place? There is general agreement about legal rights – the processes and procedures guaranteed in constitutions, laws, and common law. But a moral right is different. It is a justified claim, and if you have a justified claim, there is a correlative obligation on the part of someone to refrain from doing it or to provide it. To call something a right is to identify something as being so supremely important that people must attend to these specific obligations. If rights language can be so polarizing in dialogue, why not simply discuss our obligations – what is owed and to whom?

This difference in ethical dialogue reflects some deep cultural differences, between an emphasis on the independent individual and his or her free choice, and an emphasis on interdependence in a community, and the obligations we share to promote a life well lived for all together. To some, the only rights are rights of noninterference (Sade 2012). But for others, rights are associated with positive welfare claims (Gostin 2010). Ethical dialogue in many parts of the world identifies human rights and human dignity as basic components of an ethical framework and ethical decision making. Article 19 and the General Comment 13 of the UN Convention on the Rights of the Child seek to use a child rights approach "to promote a worldwide reformulation of child protection priorities, policies and practices" (Hart et al. 2011). Underreporting and underfunding is a basic problem everywhere. And if rights language succeeds in drawing attention to these issues, it has served a very good purpose. And if rights language succeeds in bringing the issues of justice front and center, it also has served a very good purpose. At a policy level, what kind of society do we want to be? What do we owe our children, especially in an environment of limited resources to meet seemingly limitless needs?

Child rights language is used to highlight the importance and significance of children and the appreciation of the particularity of each and every individual child. "The particular child has never existed before and will not again…..Every child deserves respect and promotion of its unfolding/emerging added value to life" (Hart et al. 2011). This is a far cry from the history of children as replaceable chattel – only valued instrumentally for what they could do for their parents (Murray 1996).

In the clinical setting, obligations toward the child have to be balanced with obligations toward the family. In the USA, there are movements promoting both patient-centered care and family-centered care (AAP, Committee on Hospital Care and Institute for Patient- and Family-Centered Care 2012). In pediatrics, the decision framework is referred to as the "best interest" standard. In the absence of an adult patient with values and preferences of his or her own, parents are presumed to be the most appropriate decision makers for their children. Out of love and a deep sense of responsibility, it is assumed that parents will act in their children's best interests. But as we have been discussing, children don't only belong to their families. They are also members of communities and the broader society who are concerned for their welfare and providing them an open future (Feinberg 1980) and a fair chance to participate in community life (Glover and Caniano 2011). Healthcare professionals, acting on behalf of these larger societal values, often have to challenge parents who seem to be making decisions or are behaving in ways that are not in their children's best interests. Parents and families are important, but their decisions and actions are not unqualified. This balancing of obligations to families with independent obligations to children is the ethical framework identified by the Committee on Bioethics of the American Academy of Pediatrics (1995). So the stakeholders in the ethical framework include the child, siblings, parents, other family members and friends, healthcare professionals, and social institutions like hospitals, clinics, the criminal justice system, social services, and other governmental entities.

Mandatory Reporting

Some in the literature have argued that this "best interest" standard is too vague and subjective to guide decision making in pediatrics and that something more like the "harm threshold" should be used instead (Diekema 2004). Parents should be given wide latitude to make decisions on behalf of their children unless it reaches the threshold of "harm." But Diekema's harm standard assumes that we can more readily calculate harm than benefit. That may be true, but there still are remaining questions about how much harm is enough to trigger a report of child abuse or medical neglect, which would be the mechanism to override parental decision-making authority.

Levi identifies uncertainty about what counts as abuse or reasonable suspicion that abuse has occurred as being at the heart of the ethical issues in child abuse and neglect (Levi 2008). At stake are the values of not harming, promoting benefit, respecting cultural differences, and justice. He gives the example of spanking to illustrate cultural differences in the use of corporal punishment. Intention and proportionality play a role. But in spite of the fact that there may be gray zones, "….no reasonable person would dispute the notion that an adult who non-accidentally inflicts serious harm on a child commits an act of abuse" (Levi 2008). And although intention plays a role in some contexts (injuring a child by pushing the child out of the way of an oncoming car), good intentions do not render any practice immune from being judged abuse (Levi 2008).

Where should the threshold be for mandatory reporting? If the threshold is too low, we risk violating principles of justice and not harming. Mandated reporters are more likely to suspect and report children whose ethnic and socioeconomic profiles are different from their own (Levi 2008). Reports and investigations of child abuse can destroy families and careers (Levi 2008). The ideal would be sensitive and careful investigations and help for at-risk families, but often the reality can be very different and families are damaged in the process (Levi 2008). Additionally, some are concerned that reporting is not the best way to protect a child's interests. Levi's discussion of these factors is meant not to suggest that reporting is wrong, but the counterbalancing values should be included in a calculus of when to report (Levi 2008). Also, setting the threshold too high for mandatory reporting risks not protecting children from harm and losing the opportunity to intervene on behalf of an at-risk family.

One of the most interesting discussions in the Levi chapter is about your obligations when you genuinely think that reporting is not going to help the child. Your obligations to support the law and protect the child from harm are at odds. Conscientious refusal is only justified when certain conditions are met: (1) you genuinely believe that reporting suspected abuse will result in net harm, (2) you are confident that the child is not at risk for subsequent harm and you are willing to take responsibility for their safety, (3) all other law-abiding options are also conducive to significant harm, and (4) you are willing to defend your choice publicly and accept the legal penalties for not reporting (Levi 2008). A possible concern with this approach is overconfidence in your ability to protect a child. "However imperfect, CPS agencies provide the only systematic approach for investigating and safeguarding a child's well-being" (Levi 2008). The American Medical Association's Code of Medical Ethics recognizes the values underlying the law. Principle III states, "A physician shall respect the law and also recognize a responsibility to seek changes in those requirements which are contrary to the best interests of the patient" (http://www.ama-assn.org/ama/pub/physician-resources/medical-ethics/code-medical-ethics.page).

The literature has shown that there are a constellation of concerns and barriers to reporting. A concern that the response will be worse than the status quo is only one of potentially many. Professionals are also concerned about what will happen to their relationships with patients and families. They also identify a need for further education and raising general awareness of these issues (Pietrantonio et al. 2013). Rather than relying solely on the mandatory reporting mechanism, some would propose switching the ownership of the problem of abuse from just some to all of us. A colleague, when talking with students, identifies this preemptive approach. He teaches, "When you see a stressed mom in the grocery store screaming at one of her children and threatening to hit the other because the child is pulling candy from the shelf, we, as caring citizens/neighbors should intervene and say something like "you seem really stressed – can I help you by picking up the candy?" and then put yourself between the child and the mom while –picking up the candy" (Krugman 2014, School of Medicine, University of Colorado, Researcher in Child Abuse and Neglect, personal communication). It seems overly simple and very difficult to measure in an evidence-based way, but it could change the culture and be a visible sign that we value *our* children and we won't let them be treated badly.

Another approach is to view mandatory reporting not as the problem to be solved but as an opportunity of sorts in that it can be a gateway to services. It represents the identification of people at risk and could be associated with various primary prevention strategies. If you fail to report a situation where a child may be at risk – if there are other children in that home – they could be harmed as well. Reporting can also be viewed as part of the resilience process, where the law sets the stage for child safety and child and family well-being planning (Wekerle 2013).

Finally, to address concerns about the values of trust and preserving relationships with patients and families, some are proposing that it is possible to partner with families through the reporting process. Professionals need to develop certain communication skills, akin to the SPIKE method for breaking bad news. They report that it is possible to preserve the relationship even through reporting (Pietrantonio et al. 2013).

SPIKE (Pietrantonio et al. 2013) stands for:

Setting – It is important that the setting be private with little chance of interruptions. It should be away from the child(ren). Providing privacy and respecting confidentiality preserves caregiver dignity. Conversations about the limits of confidentiality at the beginning of the relationship could help mitigate concerns further down. If there are concerns for physical reprisal (which is rare), additional support (staff or security) can be nearby.

Perception – The first step is to assess the caregiver's percepts of the concerns. "What have you been told? What is your understanding?" A health professional who shows patience and a willingness to take the time to ensure that the caregiver has understood, can aid in lessening confusion. By engaging the caregiver in a discussion of what might happen to the child with a report to CPS and soliciting their opinions, professionals can suggest a non-judgmental and collaborative approach.

Invitation – It is not appropriate to ask permission to make a report to CPS. The goal is to maintain honest and open communication by sharing with the caregiver your concerns and what your obligations are in light of them. "I'm afraid that someone has hurt your child and these are my responsibilities." It may be helpful to negotiate the scope of information to be shared with CPS or to even have the caregiver present for the call.

Knowledge – It is important to share information about clinical findings that led to the decision to report in a clear and understandable way. Among the information to be shared is information about possible outcomes.

Emotions – Responding to emotions is essential throughout the conversation. It is important to observe any emotions, identify them and the reason for the emotion and perhaps most importantly, let caregiver know that the emotion has been understood. Although it may be difficult to withhold judgment, an empathic response toward the caregiver and withholding criticism strengthens the therapeutic relationship. (Pietrantonio et al. 2013)

Ethically, this partnership is the ideal way to respect all of the values at stake – promoting well-being of the child and family by beginning the opportunity to build resiliency, not harming by failing to report, reducing the harm by the way you report, and respecting the family and the family relationship. It also respects the professional and societal values that undergird the law of mandatory reporting.

Three Case Examples

The above more theoretical discussion could benefit from the description of three kinds of clinical cases in which a decision about reporting has to be made. The first case is paradigmatic when it is clear that you should report:

1. An infant is brought in for care with unexplained physical findings. There are bruises and fractures and/or an unexplained head injury. The caregiver's story is not consistent with the physical findings. For example, the baby was described to be fine before a nap and simply didn't wake up from the nap. Or injuries are attributed to a fall in an infant who is not yet crawling or walking. The caregiver is a young single parent who has recently lost her job and lives in a high-stress environment. The decision to report is based on a calculus of physical findings, observed behavior, and risk factors (Levi 2008).
2. A second kind of case is not so clear-cut. Family members are telling the care team that there is something going on with another family member. This is a high-risk family known to social services, and one relative is accusing another relative of harming the child. The child hasn't been seen in the clinic recently and the family members want you to report. But it is hearsay and they are unwilling to report themselves for fear of alienating the family. If you can't get them to report and if the other family is already in the social service system, perhaps a call to social services just to check and see if the child has been seen recently would be warranted. And if the child is a patient, perhaps a reminder call to get the child in for a checkup is also a prudent action.

   Another gray zone in Colorado, where the authors reside, is the presence of marijuana in a household with children. Since possession and use of marijuana is legal in Colorado, it would seem to take something more to trigger a report. Clearly, ingestion of edibles and caregivers smoking so much marijuana that they become unsafe caregivers are examples of where reporting would be necessary.
3. The issue of homelessness is very difficult for healthcare professionals to deal with. Being homeless is not ideal. But it is not illegal either and homelessness in itself is not a sufficient reason to report neglect. As with marijuana use in the home, homelessness has to be accompanied by some tangible harm such as

failing to make clinical appointments for a child needing care, a child not being sufficiently nourished, or a child having bruises or fractures that are unexplained.

Family as Decision Makers

For many professionals, allowing families to make healthcare decisions on behalf of their children who they may have abused, or allowed the abuse to happen, is counterintuitive and the source of much moral distress. The practice of relying on parents as decision makers is based on the assumption that parents will make decisions that promote their children's well-being, based on their love and sense of responsibility. For parents who are suspected of abuse or being complicit in abuse, this assumption is believed to be false. Abuse is the opposite of protection and promoting well-being. Many staff ask, "why are they even involved since they have proven that they can't act in their child's best interest?"

It is first the value of justice in the sense of due process that we seek to honor when we involve parents as decision makers. At the beginning of a case, none of them have been proven to be responsible for the abuse of their children and parental rights have not been terminated. It seems impossible for some staff to believe, but many and probably most parents involved in abuse cases still love their children. Their parenting skills may be very limited, and they need assistance beyond what they may have experienced or learned in their own families growing up. Our ethical framework requires compassion and presence with these families – working with them for the benefit of their children in the context of the family. The values of beneficence and non-maleficence require support to preserve the family in so far as possible because it affords us a better chance to protect this child, to break the cycle, and to prevent problems in the future for this child and other children.

But the obligation to work with families is not unqualified. Sometimes a decision needs to be made that a parent simply cannot make good choices on behalf of their children. Some parents love their children very much but are unable to love them well or even keep them safe. In these times of money concerns and decreased staffing, it is increasingly difficult to get Child Protective Service (CPS) agencies to assume custody. They regard the children as safe as long as they are in the hospital. They avoid making medical and custody decisions until the child is ready for discharge. This pattern of delay makes it even more difficult for professionals to believe that they are being advocates for their patients when they make decisions about the limitations of parental decision making, only to face resistance from CPS. It is important to remember that even in cases where you believe that family are not the best decision makers, it is critical to try to maintain a compassionate presence, even while continuing to advocate for what you believe is in the patient's best interest. This balancing of obligations toward the patient and toward the family is the source of much moral distress on the part of the staff, and hospitals must provide resources to help them deal with the distress.

Visitation and Placement

This same tension between obligations to the child and obligations to the family is apparent in decisions regarding visitation and placement. It is sometimes the perception of the staff that the family shouldn't even come and visit the child since they are responsible for the child being hospitalized in the first place. While understandable, there are justice concerns as mentioned previously. There is also benefit for the family from seeing the reality of what has occurred. It is necessary for them to gain this perspective for their own future healing and for decision making as appropriate. It is also important, but often difficult, to maintain a nonjudgmental presence while the family visits. Staff who cannot fulfill this professional obligation should be allowed to seek other assignments. Support must be provided to the staff who are struggling and to all members of the unit who find they are balancing obligations among patients. It is also a matter of justice as fairness when certain staff members bear the brunt of the burden of taking care of challenging patients (Fowler 2008).

Placement decisions reflect and carry some of these same tensions between staff and families and are often complicated by the addition of conflicts among family members viewing the situation of the child and parents from any number of different perspectives. If certain family members don't really believe that their loved one can be a perpetrator, are they really the best place for the child to live? Even if the family says that they will follow the directions of the staff, will they undermine in a more subtle way the therapeutic plans? The reality is that sometimes this is the least bad option. There are situations where the child is ready for discharge and the rest of the family is much disrupted and there is no foster care placement available. Or sometimes foster care is available and the presumption is that the family is better than foster care. This presumption can be driven by the added pressure of preserving the scare resource of foster care providers. In the face of this difficult balancing act to promote the child's best interests, sometimes diligent and caring professionals must choose the least bad option. They make the best decision based on good information and good clinical judgment, and then perhaps they attempt to limit any harm by an increase in the frequency of the monitoring.

End-of-Life Decisions

The ethical framework of working with families to make good decisions is even more challenging in the face of end-of-life decisions. Staff can be very bothered by what they see as a conflict of interest when families have to make decisions that may result in a more serious criminal charge of child abuse resulting in death or even murder. Because end-of-life decisions are hard for any family to make and values can differ markedly among families and professionals, it can be difficult to sort out when families have unacceptable conflicts of interest. Families should not be identified as automatically having an unacceptable conflict of interest and be excluded when making end-of-life decisions. The Academy of Pediatrics supports a parent's right to make decisions about withdrawing life-sustaining treatment, even in cases of suspected child abuse (Committee on Child Abuse and Neglect and Committee on Bioethics 2000).

CPS agencies also have a type of conflict of interest. CPS often does not want to make these decisions to avoid the conflict associated with making a decision when the death of the child would result in fewer resources being expended from their budgets. The prosecutor may have conflicts of interest out of concern for weakening their case or "making the case" for a more serious criminal charge. Courts also may not want to be involved in making a decision about forgoing life-sustaining treatment, given the notoriety that often accompanies these cases. These considerations often lead to the presumption that continuing treatment is in the best interest of the child, when it may not be. When unacceptable conflicts are present, the AAP recommends that a guardian ad litem for medical decision making be appointed (Committee on Child Abuse and Neglect and Committee on Bioethics 2000). They can serve as an unbiased but compassionate advocate for the child's best interests and often as a fact finder for the judge. Ultimately, a judge makes the final decision about the withdrawal of life-sustaining treatment if there are conflicts that rise to the level of court involvement (Arias and Weise 2012).

In situations with so many possible conflicts, decisions should be made according to what is best for the child. Decisions to forego life-sustaining medical treatments should be made using the same guidelines as those used for any critically ill child (Committee on Child Abuse and Neglect and Committee on Bioethics 2000). Consulting with the hospital's ethics committee can be very helpful (Arias and Weise 2012).

It is important to remember that most parents still love their children and should be offered all of the support services available to any family facing the death of a child. These services include the ethics committee, bereavement counselors, chaplains, or other persons identified by the parents as providing important psychological and spiritual support (Committee on Child Abuse and Neglect and Committee on Bioethics 2000).

Funding Priorities

The ethical framework that has been identified supports the funding of even broader services to include primary prevention, early identification, more family services that support mental health and resiliency, and effective follow-up (Hart et al. 2011). In this era of cost constraints, it is understandable that priority is normally given to helping the children and families who have already been identified. Prioritizing those with the greatest need or at the greatest risk is a well-known and understandable principle of the allocation of scare resources (Cookson and Dolan 2000). But this allocation scheme is ultimately not sustainable. It is a recipe for needing even more money if prevention is never or hardly ever undertaken and if research into more effective prevention and treatment is not adequately funded.

Leventhal and Krugman have identified three salient lessons learned over the past five decades since the publication of "The Battered Child Syndrome" by Henry Kempe and others: (1) Many children and families are affected, (2) the consequences can be lifelong and intergenerational, and (3) treatment and prevention can work but need to be expanded (Leventhal and Krugman 2012). Among the things that they list that would have concerned Dr. Kempe are "the lack of any committed federal funding dollars for research and training focused on child maltreatment… and a child protection system that often fails to provide adequate treatment services for children and families" (Leventhal and Krugman 2012).

As intended by a child's rights perspective, funding for the identification, prevention, and treatment of child abuse and neglect should reflect our deeply held professional and societal values that prioritize our obligations to promote the well-being of children and their families.

Research

Research into child abuse and neglect is a high priority and needs to occur. Under the principle of maximization of scarce resources, it is important to use scarce resources in the best way possible, as determined by evidence of best practices. These obligations of justice are joined by obligations to do good and prevent harm, which assumes that we can tell the difference. But research into child maltreatment raises some challenging ethical questions. The major methodological challenge is to get good data by promising confidentiality, in the face of the ethical and legal requirement to report suspected abuse and neglect that may be identified through the research (Socolar et al. 1995). One method to preserve confidentiality requires obtaining a certificate of confidentiality, which may protect the data from being obtained for many types of legal proceedings (Cashmore 2006). However, it is not clear that the certificate would protect the researcher from the obligation to report child abuse (Socolar et al. 1995). Other possible methodological approaches to avoid the legal obligation of reporting include (1) anonymous data collection in the form of encoded random responses where the researcher is blinded to the data, (2) transmission of the data out of state or country, or (3) direct data entry into a computer by subjects so that the researchers are not aware of the responses of any individual (Socolar et al. 1995). Although this may help with the legal requirements, it is not clear that it answers the ethical question of whether it is ethically appropriate to design a protocol where you have good evidence to suspect that abuse may be happening and you intentionally blind yourself to any specifics so you cannot report. It seems a pointed violation of the ethical obligations to prevent harm and promote benefit to the child. Can the potential for direct harm to a child be acceptable in light of the benefits of the information to be gained from the research? For that balancing to be ethically acceptable, it would have to be an acceptably low risk of harm compared with a very high probability of benefit from the research information. One possible solution that doesn't involve this balancing of potential harms and benefits is to blind the study to the immediate researchers but have the data coded and an independent observer to watch the data and trigger a report if necessary.

This raises the second challenge in research, getting informed consent and telling prospective subjects that this reporting could occur. Researchers will worry about the quality of the data if they cannot preserve total confidentiality. But research ethics requires truth-telling and respect for the subject's autonomy in choosing to participate or not. And who gives the consent for this research? If the children are the subjects, is it even appropriate to get consent for research from their parents who may be the perpetrators of the abuse? The absence of parental consent may prevent children's views from being heard in research to the detriment of the quality of the research. One possible solution is to use "passive consent" or "opt out consent." A general letter is sent to parents which clearly outlines the nature and process of the research and that it will go forward if parents do not choose to opt out (Cashmore 2006). It is unclear whether this approach would be approved by many Institutional Review Boards (IRBs) in the USA who favor a more active consent process.

A third challenge comes with subject recruitment. Children are a vulnerable population and require special protections against harm. Children who are involved in abusive and/or neglectful home environments may be even more vulnerable to the psychological harms of answering sensitive questions (Black and Ponirakis 2000). It is often difficult to identify who is the actual subject of the research, the children or their caregivers. Subjects may feel coerced into participation, especially if recruitment takes place in the context of social services. The family may think that participation in research will help their case with social services or law enforcement.

Further challenges with confidentiality in child maltreatment research include when parents ask about what their children have said about them. Because of the emotional nature of this research, professionals may be tempted to discuss the cases to process their own emotions. Professional obligations to preserve privacy and confidentiality must be emphasized. Third, when data sets are shared, there is an increased risk for privacy and confidentiality violations. And finally, individuals who are involved in legal proceedings may seek research information if it helps their cases. Researchers must be diligent in handling the boundaries of confidentiality in a clear way before the research ever begins (Socolar et al. 1995).

Because this research can be so ethically challenging, it may be useful to work with your human subjects Institutional Review Board (IRB) to discuss these issues and involve them in the protocol development. Also, research ethics consultation services are growing in the USA and internationally, and if they are available at your institution, they could be a valuable resource (Cho et al. 2008).

Emerging Controversial Issues

To some, the whole area of child abuse and neglect is controversial enough in that it raises issues of parental rights and authority and pits them against children's rights and the power of the state (Meyer 2000). Recently, two even more controversial issues have emerged to challenge the ethical framework that has been identified. These issues involve two very vulnerable populations, namely, pregnant women with substance use disorders and obese children and their families.

Pregnant Women, Substance Use Disorders, and the Protection of Fetuses

If our ethical framework is encouraging primary prevention, many people are asking: Why not start with pregnant women (ACOG Committee on Ethics 2008)? Beginning in the 1990s, there have been an increasing dialogue about how to treat pregnant women with substance use disorders and a building controversy about putting pregnant women in jail as happened in South Carolina (Nelson and Marshall 1998). Among the professional community, clear guidance is offered by the American College of Obstetricians and Gynecologists (ACOG) in the 2008 report of the ACOG Committee on Ethics opinion, "At-Risk Drinking and Illicit Drug Use: Ethical Issues in Obstetrics and Gynecological Practice." Based on the ethical principles/values of beneficence, non-maleficence, respect for autonomy, and justice, they strongly recommend universal screening questions, brief interventions, and referral to treatment (ACOG Committee on Ethics 2008). They state, "Criminal charges against pregnant women on grounds of child abuse have been struck down in almost all cases because courts have upheld the right to privacy, which includes the right to decide whether to have a child, the right to bodily integrity, and the right to "be left alone", and have found that states could better protect fetal health through education and making available medical care and drug treatment centers for women" (ACOG Committee on Ethics 2008). Additional concerns include that pregnant woman may not seek the care that they need if they fear legal involvement. For this reason, the State of Colorado enacted a statute that prohibits information about substance abuse shared by a woman with her doctor or nurse during pregnancy from being used in any criminal prosecution (§13-25-136, Colorado Revised Statutes). Justice issues are also implicated in that punitive measures are not applied evenly across sex, race, and socioeconomic status (Nelson and Marshall 1998).

Even though the issue of treating pregnant women is "solved" as a matter of professional practice and perhaps legally in many jurisdictions, reporting practices still vary widely and the issues themselves raise much moral distress among staff. For example, the law in Colorado quite clearly states that fetuses are not persons for reporting of child abuse (in the interest of H., 74 P.3d 494 Colorado Court of Appeals 2003). But many efforts have been made to increase obligations toward fetuses, including the recent so-called "personhood" laws (Collins and Crockin 2012). Many Departments of Human Services (DHS) in Colorado will do nothing with a potential child abuse report until the baby is born. But some DHS agencies will take the report and inform the area hospitals so they can intervene at the earliest point following birth. This logic of not intervening until the baby is born does not make good clinical and ethical sense. The impact on fetuses is quite clear, and more harm can be prevented if you intervene early (Goler et al. 2008). There is increasing evidence that substance abuse treatment linked with prenatal visits improves perinatal outcomes (Goler et al. 2008) and especially if the partner participates (Chang et al. 2005).

But is the child abuse reporting system the best way to help prevent harm to fetuses and future children? It seems it is not, given the evidence for the efficacy of clinical interventions and the harms associated with using criminal justice mechanisms. The limited child abuse resources also favor keeping this population out of the child abuse reporting system. Here is another opportunity for greater awareness of the issues and best practices for clinical care. An ethically grounded and holistic approach would be substance use treatment for the pregnant woman and support services for her family.

Obesity as Medical Neglect

"In 2008, the Child Welfare League of America reported that many state courts have expanded their definition of medical neglect to include morbid obesity and then ruled certain children were victims of neglect because of their obesity" (Perryman 2011). In a recent article in the Yale Journal of Health Policy, Law, and Ethics called "Tipping the Scale: A Place for Childhood Obesity in the Evolving Legal Framework of Child Abuse and Neglect," the authors argue that obesity should fit into the child abuse and neglect framework and offer suggestions for future judicial interpretations and future legislative developments. The authors support the notion and call for clear guidance of when morbid obesity, not just obesity or being overweight, should trigger a child abuse or neglect report (Garrahan and Eichner 2012).

In the clinical setting, pediatricians are familiar with the concept of failure to thrive and its possible association with child abuse and medical neglect. But what about the other end: life-limiting obesity? The clinical and ethical logic seem to be present, to prevent harm and promote benefit to the child. The health consequences of obesity are known and severe (Deckelbaum and Williams 2001).

Critics raise concerns about what exactly is in the family's control when their children are obese. There are plenty of possible contributing environmental issues, including economic and cultural ones. "Obesogenic" food environments and sedentary behaviors abound, some due to economics and locations without safe places to exercise and others due to the overabundance of food deserts. Other observers point to the genetic factors that predispose children to obesity.

The increasing epidemic of obesity is certainly a cause for concern. But is labeling it a problem of child abuse and neglect going to be an effective way to treat the issue? The same justice issues of bias and discrimination that were discussed with pregnant woman using drugs apply here, too. Some would argue that family intervention is a more ethically justified way to proceed (Perryman 2011). It assumes that there are things to change in a family's behavior. That's not the point of disagreement. Having a legal intervention is not necessarily the way to promote that change and may, in fact, have negative consequences in that families may not seek that care that they need. Not only does family intervention respect parents as decision makers, but it includes a concern for the whole family's well-being, not just the child's well-being.

If calling obesity a concern for child abuse and neglect raises the dialogue about the epidemic of obesity and provides some incentives for change, maybe that's a good thing. But given the limits of child abuse budgets, the downside is that it could take away needed resources from other children and families. It could also raise further distrust in a system that on the one hand is accused of not helping enough and on the other hand is accused of taking children away from their families unnecessarily.

Summary/Conclusion

There are many ethical issues that arise in the identification and response to child abuse and neglect. Careful attention to the values of the stakeholders, where they are in tension and where they align, can be useful in determining how best to balance competing obligations. Open discussion among a multidisciplinary team is often a useful way to proceed. Consultation with institutional ethics committees or other resources can be helpful.

References

American Academy of Pediatrics, Committee on Bioethics. (1995). Informed consent, parental permission, and assent in pediatric practice. *Pediatrics, 95*(2), 314–317.

American Academy of Pediatrics, Committee on Child Abuse and Neglect and Committee on Bioethics. (2000). Forgoing life-sustaining medical treatment in abused children. *Pediatrics* 106(5), 1151–1153.

American Academy of Pediatrics, Committee on Hospital Care and Institute for Patient and Family-Centered Care. (2012). Patient-and family-centered care and the pediatrician's role. *Pediatrics, 129*(2), 394–404.

American College of Obstetricians and Gynecologists Committee on Ethics. (2008). At-risk drinking and illicit drug use: Ethical issues in obstetric and gynecologic practice. *Obstetrics and Gynecology, 112*(6), 1449–1460.

American Medical Association Code of Ethics. Council on Ethical and Judicial Affairs. Current Opinions with Annotations (2014/2015 Ed.). http://www.ama-assn.org/ama/pub/physician-resources/medical-ethics/code-medical-ethics.page

Arias, J. J., & Weise, K. L. (2012). Pediatric end-of-life decisions when abuse is suspected. *Virtual Mentor, 14*(10), 767–770.

Black, M. M., & Ponirakis, A. (2000). Computer-administered interviews with children about maltreatment: Methodological, developmental, and ethical issues. *Journal of Interpersonal Violence, 15*(7), 682–695.

Cashmore, J. (2006). Ethical issues concerning consent in obtaining children's reports on their experience of violence. *Child Abuse & Neglect, 30*, 969–977.

Chang, G., McNamara, R. K., Orav, E. J., et al. (2005). Brief intervention for prenatal alcohol use: A randomized trial. *Obstetrics and Gynecology, 105*(1), 991–998.

Cho, M. K., Tobin, S. L., Greely, H. T., et al. (2008). Strangers at the benchside: Research ethics consultation. *American Journal of Bioethics, 8*(3), 4–13.

Collins, L. R., & Crockin, S. L. (2012). Fighting 'personhood' initiative in the United States. *Reproductive BioMedicine Online, 24*, 689–691.

Colorado Revised Statutes – 13-25-136, C.R.S.

Cookson, R., & Dolan, P. (2000). Principles of justice in health care rationing. *Journal of Medical Ethics, 26*, 323–329.

Deckelbaum, R. J., & Williams, C. L. (2001). Childhood obesity: The health issue. *Obesity Research, 9*(4), 239S–243S.

Diekema, D. S. (2004). Parental refusals of medical treatments: The harm principle as threshold for state intervention. *Theoretical Medicine and Bioethics, 25*, 243–264.

Feinberg, J. A. (1980). A child's right to an open future. In W. Aiken & H. LaFollette (Eds.), *Whose child? Parental rights, parental authority and state power* (pp. 124–153). Totowa: Littlefield.

Fowler, M. D. M. (Ed.). (2008). *Guide to the code of ethics for nurses: Interpretation and application* (pp. 67–69). Silver Spring: ANA.

Garrahan, S. M., & Eichner, A. W. (2012). Tipping the scale: A place for childhood obesity in the evolving legal framework of child abuse and neglect. *Yale Journal of Health Policy, Law, and Ethics, 12*(2), 336–370.

Glover, J. J., & Caniano, D. A. (2011). Ethical considerations in newborn surgery. In P. Puri (Ed.), *Newborn surgery* (3rd ed.). London: Hodder Arnold Health Sciences.

Goler, N. C., Armstrong, M. A., Taillac, C. J., & Osejo, V. M. (2008). Substance abuse treatment inked with prenatal visits improves perinatal outcomes: A new standard. *Journal of Perinatology, 28*, 597–603.

Gostin, L. O. (2010). *Public health law & ethics: A reader* (p. 17). Berkeley: University of California Press.

Hart, S. N., Lee, Y., & Wernham, M. (2011). A new age for child protection – General comment 13: Why it is important, how it was constructed, and what it intends? *Child Abuse & Neglect, 35*, 970–978.

In the Interest of H., 74 P.3d 494, Colorado Court of Appeals, 2003.

Leventhal, J. M., & Krugman, R. D. (2012). "The Battered-Child Syndrome" 50 years later: Much accomplished, much left to do. *JAMA, 308*(1), 35–36.

Levi, B. H. (2008). Child abuse and neglect. In P. A. Singer & A. M. Viens (Eds.), *The Cambridge textbook of bioethics* (pp. 132–140). New York/Cambridge: Cambridge University Press.

Meyer, D. D. (2000). *The paradox of family privacy*. 53 Vand.L.Rev.525.

Murray, T. H. (1996). *The worth of a child* (pp. 59–62). Berkeley: University of California Press.

Nelson, L. J., & Marshall, M. F. (1998). *Ethical and legal analyses of three coercive policies aimed at substance abuse by pregnant women*. Charleston: Medical University of South Carolina, Program in Bioethics.

Perryman, M. L. (2011). Ethical family interventions for childhood obesity. *Preventing Chronic Disease: Public Health Research, Practice and Policy, 8*(5), 1–3.

Pietrantonio, A. M., Wright, E., Gibson, K. N., et al. (2013). Mandatory reporting of child abuse and neglect: Crafting a positive process for health professionals and caregivers. *Child Abuse & Neglect, 37*, 102–109.

Sade, R. M. (2012). Health care reform: Ethical foundations, policy and law. *Journal of the American College of Surgeons, 215*(2), 286–296.

Socolar, R. R. S., Runyan, D. K., & Amaya-Jackson, L. (1995). Methodological and ethical issues related to studying child maltreatment. *Journal of Family Issues, 16*(5), 565–586.

Wekerle, C. (2013). Resilience in the context of child maltreatment: Connections to the practice of mandatory reporting. *Child Abuse & Neglect, 37*, 93–101.

Chapter 9
Medical Perspectives: Bioethics/Ethics and the Duties of Medical Professionals and the Nature, Advantages, and Limits of Public Health Approaches

Donald Woodhouse

Introduction

Mandatory reporting of suspected child abuse highlights the intersection of clinical practice and public health, underscoring that medicine is practiced within a social context. "Child abuse did not exist in meaningful societal terms until it was named and measured." Mandatory reporting also highlights the intersection of law, professional standards, and ethics. Ethical issues associated with mandatory reporting include breaching confidentiality and perceived adverse consequences of reporting.

Effective prevention requires the linked efforts of individual clinicians who observe – and report – suspected maltreatment on a case-by-case basis and robust public health monitoring, intervention and prevention strategies at the family, community and societal level.

The bioethical principles of autonomy, beneficence, non-maleficence, and justice as reflected in professional codes and the values articulated in the evolving ethics of public health define the obligations and duties of each. While clinical medicine focuses on the individual patient and public health serves the entire community, they intersect in preserving the dignity of the human person and protecting the vulnerable. Society is ethically justified in imposing limits on the confidential relationship between patient and provider to prevent maltreatment, and clinicians may ethically honor mandatory child abuse reporting laws to protect individuals and advance the public good. Not reporting is not ethical; "professional involvement in the area of child abuse can be thought of as part of a professional's responsibility to the community he or she serves."

D. Woodhouse, J.D., M.P.A. (✉)
Antioch University New England, Keene, NH, USA
e-mail: dwoodhouse@antioch.edu

B. Mathews, D.C. Bross (eds.), *Mandatory Reporting Laws and the Identification of Severe Child Abuse and Neglect*, Child Maltreatment 4,
DOI 10.1007/978-94-017-9685-9_9

The Intersection of Clinical Medicine and Public Health

Henry Kempe alerted the medical community to the clinical indicators of child abuse and catalyzed the national response that led to mandatory reporting of suspected abuse (Kempe et al. 1962). In the words of Jonathan Mann "...child abuse did not exist in meaningful societal terms until it was named and measured" (Mann 1997, p. 10). Mandatory reporting thus highlights the intersection of clinical practice and public health and underscores the reality that medicine is always practiced within a social context (Pellegrino and Thomasma 2004). Public health resources complement and supplement the care and expertise of medical providers in treating and preventing child maltreatment.

Mandatory reporting also highlights the intersection of – and potential conflicts between – law and professional ethical standards:

> With few exceptions, reporting statutes place limits on confidentiality and privileged communications. Professional discretion and judgment are rarely given consideration in reporting requirements. As a result, laws that require reporting suspected child abuse and neglect in professional contexts often conflict with basic professional values and ethical principles. (Kalichman 1999) Providers who are fully aware of their legal obligation to report suspected abuse, however, may choose not to report when they believe that doing so is unethical. (Kalichman 1999, p. 42)

Clinicians[1] see and focus on individual patients, with clear obligations to those patients stemming from professional standards, law, and general ethical principles. The legal obligation to report maltreatment stems from an equally clear recognition of society's collective responsibility to protect children and the corollary need to assess the nature and magnitude of risks to children and to evaluate the efficacy of interventions:

> The clinical relationship centers on a vulnerable, anxious, dependent, often suffering individual person.... For public health physicians and nurses the relationship is with the whole society. The end or purpose of the relationship is the good of humans as a collectivity, the common good.... Their [public health physicians and nurses] "patient" is society and its ills. They serve the good of society's individual members secondarily by assuring a healthy community in which the individual can flourish. (Pellegrino and Thomasma 2004, p. 21)

It's been stated that the central dilemma in public health is balancing the rights of the individual against those of society (Richards and Rathbun 1999), and it cannot be disputed that clinical medicine and public health have different immediate ends. Not infrequently, these ends compete or conflict. Some go so far as to suggest that this conflict is inevitable and that "to ignore the ethical tensions between communal and individual interests would be, *prima facie*, poor professional practice" (Hester 2004, p. 1). "A truly dynamic philosophy of society recognizes the necessity of a continuously negotiated struggle to balance individual and common good" (Pellegrino and Thomasma 2004, p. 19). Historic challenges to compulsory

[1] References to clinicians throughout, unless otherwise noted, include not only physicians but other healthcare providers (nurses, dentists, and psychologists) who are required to report.

vaccination[2] and contemporary controversies about HIV/AIDS testing, partner notification (Bayer and Toomey 1992), directly observed therapy for tuberculosis (Bayer and Dubler 1993), and access to scarce health resources all underscore that such conflicts are real and not theoretical.

To reconcile the interests of individuals and the community when they conflict (or, realistically, to decide and to act in the face of this tension) requires, inter alia, an understanding of the ethical values that underlie clinical decision making and those of public or social health. In the specific instance of child protection and mandatory reporting, it is suggested these interests converge and are arguably more complementary rather than antagonistic: "Clinical medicine and social medicine intersect in preserving the dignity of the human person" (Pellegrino and Thomasma 2004, p. 16). "Despite personal feelings about the reporting process, practitioners are urged to maintain compliance with their legal mandate and function as child advocates. Professional involvement in the area of child abuse can be thought of as part of a professional's responsibility to the community he or she serves" (Alvarez et al. 2005, p. 326).

Societal acknowledgment of and response to child abuse, the emergence of biomedical ethics as a distinct field, and the evolution of a corresponding ethics of public health all occurred fairly recently – within the past 50–60 years. During this period the boundary around the individual therapeutic encounter between physician and patient eroded as medical technology introduced new therapies but also posed challenging questions about who should have access to these therapies and who should decide.[3] During the same period Kempe and others shifted the focus of child protection beyond the responsibility of medical providers to include a wide range of "mandated reporters" inside and outside the medical community and demanded a societal response. Child protection is often characterized as the conflict between parental rights and society's duties to protect its vulnerable members. Among Kempe's contributions was the recognition that child welfare is not an exclusively private, family matter but an important public health concern, i.e., that child welfare is the parents' responsibility unless and until they breach that obligation, at which point the community can and must intervene.

This chapter describes the public health role in preventing violence and abuse, the benefits and limitations of that approach, and the interplay with mandatory reporting. The principles of biomedical ethics and the ethical standards and values underlying both clinical practice and public health practice are summarized as they apply to mandatory reporting. Clinical ethics and the ethics of public health lead to the same conclusion about mandatory reporting, albeit from different perspectives. Society is ethically justified (if not obligated) in imposing limits on the confidential relationship between patient and provider to prevent child maltreatment. And

[2] See Jacobson v. Massachusetts, 197 U.S. 11 (1905) upholding compulsory immunization statutes at the beginning of the twentieth century.

[3] In the biomedical research universe, corresponding ethical issues arise concerning who should bear the risk of testing new clinical interventions.

clinicians may ethically honor mandatory child abuse reporting laws to protect individuals and advance the public good. Not reporting is not ethical.

What Is Public Health?

Definitions of public health range from detailed descriptions of the many and varied roles of public health workers (sanitation, restaurant inspections, vital statistics, disease control, environmental monitoring, education, health promotion) to the broad Institute of Medicine definition: "Public health is what we, as a society, do collectively to assure the conditions for people to be healthy" (National Research Council 1988, p. 1). Thus framed, it is clear that the focus of public health is on populations and communities, rather than on individuals. Generally (though not exclusively) a function of state, federal, and local government, the public health workforce includes clinicians – physicians, nurses, mental health workers – and a range of other specialists, not all of whom belong to a distinct profession or are bound by a professional code of standards like those for the healing professions (physicians, nurses, psychologists) (AMA 2004; APA 2010; ANA 2009).

The Role of Public Health in Preventing Violence and Child Maltreatment

Public health's responsibility to prevent child maltreatment arises from two sources: First, there are practical and professional limits on an individual clinician's ability to provide the spectrum of services needed to fully protect children who may have been maltreated and to prevent further abuse and, second, from the realization that intentional violence in all forms (e.g., domestic partner violence, elder abuse, child abuse, homicide, and suicide) is in fact a public health issue amenable to traditional (and creative new) public health interventions.

Physicians are bound to address maltreatment and other forms of violence as they present in the clinical setting, within the limits of their professional competence and the immediate case. Some are concerned about a perceived trend toward "medicalizing" the wide range of social factors which contribute to violence and suggest that going beyond the parameters of the clinical case drains resources from others and dilutes their professional roles. By reporting suspected abuse (i.e., without the need to investigate or prove intent), clinicians can enlist and engage the resources and expertise of child protective services, public health, and, rarely, law enforcement. "Handing off" cases by reporting enables clinicians to adhere to what's been termed "clinical parsimony" and focus on delivering services they are prepared to do best: caring for individual patients.

Violence, including violence against children, was once perceived as primarily a law enforcement matter. It is now recognized as a public health problem that can be studied, understood, and prevented. It was not always so. Public health traditionally dealt with aspects of infectious disease: identifying agents that caused or transmitted it and reducing or eliminating conditions that facilitated its spread through immunization, environmental, and educational campaigns. Only within the last decades of the twentieth century was violence – including child abuse, elder abuse, and domestic partner violence – recognized as a public health problem. Public health interventions and strategies were adapted and applied to prevent violence and change social norms surrounding it. In the words of former US Surgeon General C. Everett Koop, "[P]ublic health is in the business of continually redefining the unacceptable" (Rosenberg and Fenley 1991, p. v.).

Initial public health concerns about violence and abuse centered on the immediate consequences and the human, societal, and economic costs of intentional injuries and deaths. Research about the long-term consequences of abuse now furnishes additional justification for addressing child maltreatment as a public health issue and for invoking the tools of public health, including reporting and surveillance. It is now known that early childhood trauma has lifelong health consequences.

Given the observed associations with childhood trauma and a range of problems – substance abuse, teen pregnancy, depression, anxiety, sexually transmitted diseases, smoking, and obesity – in later life, Mercy and Saul (2009) cited in Zimmerman and Mercy (2010) conclude:

> [P]reventing maltreatment has come to be seen as an important factor in enhancing the overall health and wellness of the population. [A]buse, neglect and other traumatic events can take a serious toll, contributing to health problems over a lifetime. (Zimmerman and Mercy 2010, pp. 4–5)

The US Surgeon General's 1979 report, *Healthy People*, outlined a national prevention strategy with specific objectives for reducing homicide, suicide, and child abuse rates and identifying associated risk factors; the report also called for improving the reliability of data on child abuse and family violence (HEW 1979). Essential to this strategy is surveillance, a basic public health tool for collecting and analyzing data to define and measure the scope and magnitude of the problem, develop intervention strategies, and evaluate their efficacy (Rosenberg and Fenley 1991, p. ix). Mandatory reports[4] form the cornerstone of these surveillance efforts. Despite jurisdictional variation in who must report and questions about the extent of underreporting, public health reports provide baseline data, the starting point for assessing the extent and magnitude of the problem and the ability to observe and monitor trends.

Initial public health initiatives addressed homicide and suicide, especially among young people:

> The early successes in youth-violence prevention paved the way for a public health approach to other violence problems, such as intimate partner violence, sexual violence, and child maltreatment. Efforts were made to document each problem, understand the risk and pro-

[4] In addition to suspected child abuse, medical providers in many jurisdictions are also required to report other forms of violence, including gunshot and stab wounds.

> tective factors associated with each type of violence, and begin building the evidence base for prevention. (Dalhberg and Mercy, February 2009, p. 169)

By shifting the focus from individual and family dynamics to community-based and societal strategies, public health initiatives complement and supplement patient-level interventions. Education and promotion efforts inform, educate, and raise societal awareness of maltreatment and define (and redefine) the limits of the unacceptable (as, e.g., with parental attitudes toward corporal punishment). Consistent, uniform ongoing surveillance (building on mandatory reports) and the application of epidemiologic techniques support new interventions and monitor and assess their efficacy. By virtue of their local, state, and national presence, public health agencies can be, on the one hand, accessible and responsive and, on the other, capable of assimilating and analyzing national-level data. Public health officials can monitor shifts in the many conditions that put children at risk and develop prevention strategies at the individual, family, community, and societal levels. Reporting and other surveillance data monitor and measure these initiatives.

The goal of public health is to establish a continuum of services that extends beyond individual families to include "…public education efforts to change social norms and behavior, neighborhood activities that engage parents, and public policies and institutions that support families" (Zimmerman and Mercy 2010, p. 6). Initiatives promote collaboration among community partners such as early childhood education, schools, police, faith-based organizations, libraries, and neighborhood recreation centers with the shared aim of prevention. These approaches reflect a societal shift from reactive to proactive strategies that can reach more families, in non-stigmatizing settings, and prevent maltreatment and other forms of violence before they occur.

The Centers for Disease Control and Prevention (CDC) Public Health Leadership Initiative, a multiyear project launched in 2009 with funding from the Doris Duke Charitable Foundation, identified best practices to promote "…safe, stable, and nurturing relationships…" for all children, to support a strong national public heath prevention system. Public health agencies are uniquely qualified for addressing maltreatment:

- There is compelling scientific research base that makes the case for preventing maltreatment as a strategy to promote health and prevent disease across the lifespan.
- The child protection system sees only a fraction of the total number of children who experience abuse or neglect, and its involvement is after the fact.
- It is not practical, financially feasible, or even appropriate to provide individualized social services to all families.
- Public health efforts have successfully addressed other health concerns by using a mix of education, communication, and policy changes: Consider the use of bike helmets or "back-to-sleep" campaigns.
- Public health is experienced at addressing complex health issues (e.g. smoking, substance abuse) that require sustained, multiprong strategies that have been adapted to changes over time.
- Public health campaigns are often multidisciplinary, cutting across several service systems and engaging a variety of professionals as well as "regular" people.
- Public health agencies already have access to young children through immunization programs, as well as WIC (Women, Infants and Children), home visiting, and other maternal/child health initiatives. (CDC 2012; Zimmerman and Mercy 2010)

Limitations of Public Health

Public health's role in child maltreatment is necessary but not sufficient. The factors that make public health an effective complement to clinical medicine with regard to abuse are among its limitations:

> [A]lthough the final aim of health protection is to assist and safeguard the individual human being, public health is instrumentally and strategically committed to perform at the level of populations, seeking epidemiological knowledge and proposing health care measures that can only be achieved at the social level. (Kottow 2012, p. 37)

Effective prevention requires the linked efforts of the clinicians who observe – and report – suspected maltreatment on a case-by-case basis and robust public health monitoring and prevention strategies.

Ethical Considerations

The initial clinical encounter leading to a differential diagnosis that includes possible maltreatment is the catalyst for all subsequent protective and preventive services. Clinicians who suspect abuse must, by law, report it to initiate protective services for the benefit of the index case, to engage child protective services, and to contribute to community-level surveillance. A substantial proportion of mandated reporters – 40 % is the most commonly cited datum (Alvarez, Donahue, Kenny, Cavanagh, and Romero 2005)[5] – however, indicate that on at least one occasion they did not report suspected abuse. Many who acknowledge not reporting cite what they believe to be overriding ethical concerns: the duty of confidentiality[6] to patients or families, which is most commonly cited, potential "double agentry" (i.e., perceiving reporting as "service to the state" that compels them to serve the interests of someone other than the client) (Stadler 1989), concerns that reporting will undermine or abrogate the trust required to establish and maintain a therapeutic relationship, and fears that reporting will cause greater harm than good to the abused individuals.[7]

[5] Surveys of physicians and psychologists summarized by Kalichman (1999, p. 13) indicate that from 29 to 63 % of surveyed physicians and psychiatrists acknowledged not reporting at least one case of suspected abuse.

[6] The terms confidentiality, right to privacy, and privilege are used (sometimes interchangeably) to explain or justify not reporting. While all impose or justify restrictions on disclosing private information, each has a distinct origin and meaning. "Confidentiality" generally refers to ethical duties placed on professionals to maintain client confidences (considered to be essential to enable patients to candidly describe their conditions); "privacy" is an individual's right, recognized at common law (and in certain instances constitutionally protected), to be left alone and avoid governmental interference in intimate affairs. "Privilege" involves rules of evidence that preclude introduction of information revealed within specified relationships (e.g., physician-patient or lawyer-client) from being admitted or used in legal proceedings. All involve safeguards of information and all are subject to limitations or qualifications which permit disclosure under certain circumstances.

[7] Other reasons given for failing to report include mistrust of or prior negative experiences with child protective services and ignorance about the requirements and procedures for reporting.

The healing professions (physicians, nurses, and psychologists) have codes of conduct that articulate aspirational goals and enforceable standards of practice for members of the profession. The codes commonly require achieving and maintaining professional competence (with legal corollaries in licensing and credentialing regulations) and affirmative obligations to prevent harm. The American Medical Association *Code of Medical Ethics* (AMA 2004), the American Psychological Association (APA) *Ethical Principles of Psychologists and Code of Conduct* (APA 2010), and the American Nurses Association (ANA) *Nursing Code of Ethics* (ANA 2009) all emphasize the primacy of the duty to protect patient confidence, yet all explicitly acknowledge that there are legitimate limitations on that duty, most notably when required by law to report.

Professional Codes and the Law

The AMA Code of Medical Ethics defines the term "ethical" to mean matters "involving (1) moral principles or practices and (2) matters of social policy involving issues of morality in the practice of medicine," and "unethical" refers to professional conduct which fails to conform to these moral standards (AMA 2004, p. 1). The code acknowledges that, while ethical values and legal principles are closely related, ethical obligations typically exceed legal duties and that, in some cases, law mandates unethical conduct. "In general, when physicians believe a law is unjust, they should work to change the law. In exceptional circumstances of *unjust* laws, ethical responsibilities should supersede legal obligations" [emphasis supplied]. Principles are "standards of conduct which define the essentials of honorable behavior for the physician." The relevant principles with regard to mandatory reporting state:

> A physician shall respect the law and also recognize a responsibility to seek changes in those requirements which are contrary to the best interests of the patient. (Principle III.)
>
> A physician shall respect the rights of patients, colleagues, and other health professionals and shall safeguard patient confidences and privacy within the constraints of the law. (Principle IV.)

In explicating the principles, the Council on Ethical Judicial Affairs Opinions recognizes clear exceptions or limits on confidentiality:

> The physician should not reveal confidential communications or information without the express consent of the patient, *unless required to do so by law. The obligation to safeguard patient confidences is subject to certain exceptions which are ethically and legally justified because of overriding social considerations.* (emphasis supplied) (AMA 2004)

Examples provided include patients who threaten to inflict serious bodily harm on others, communicable diseases, and gunshot and knife wounds "as required by applicable statutes or ordinances."

With specific regard to abuse, the Council on Ethical and Judicial Affairs acknowledges that reporting laws "often create a difficult dilemma for the physician" because suspected offenders and victims alike may plead with the physician to keep the matter confidential, but the opinion concludes: "The physician should comply with the laws requiring reporting of suspected cases of abuse of spouses, children, elderly persons, and others" (AMA 2004, p. 130).

The American Psychological Association's corresponding "Ethical Principles of Psychologists and Code of Conduct" delineates five general principles which are "aspirational goals" for professional psychologists:

(a) Beneficence and non-maleficence
(b) Fidelity and responsibility
(c) Integrity
(d) Justice
(e) Respect for people's rights and dignity

The principles are detailed and clarified in ethical standards which are enforceable rules of conduct. Relevant standards are:

> 4.01 Maintaining Confidentiality "Psychologists have a primary obligation and take reasonable precautions to protect confidential information … recognizing that the extent and limits of confidentiality may be regulated by law…."

With regard to those limits, Standard 4.05 reads in pertinent part:

> 4.05 Disclosures
>
> (b) Psychologists disclose confidential information without the consent of the individual only as mandated by law for a valid purpose such as to … (3) protect the client/patient, psychologists or others from harm….

In that regard, psychologists are ethically obligated, as part of obtaining voluntary informed consent at the outset of therapy, to inform clients about the limits of confidentiality:

> 4.02 Discussing the Limits of Confidentiality
>
> (a) Psychologists discuss with persons (including, to the extent feasible, persons who are legally incapable of giving informed consent and their legal representatives) and organizations with whom they establish a scientific or professional relationship (1) the relevant limits of confidentiality and (2) the foreseeable uses of the information generated through their psychological activities. (See also Standard 3.10, Informed Consent.)
> (b) Unless it is not feasible or is contraindicated, the discussion of confidentiality occurs at the outset of the relationship and thereafter as new circumstances may warrant.[8] (APA 2010)

The American Nurses Association Nursing Code of Ethics sets out nine provisions with accompanying interpretive statements that describe the primary goals, values, and obligations of the profession. Here too, while stressing the critical importance of protecting patient confidences, the profession explicitly acknowledges that there are legal and ethical limits to that duty:

---

[8] This standard also requires psychologists who comply with the law and file a mandated report to advise clients of the fact of that report ("…as new circumstances may warrant").

> Provision 3 The nurse promotes, advocates for, and strives to protect the health, safety, and rights of the patient.
>
> 3.2 Associated with the right to privacy, the nurse has a duty to maintain confidentiality of all patient information. The patient's well-being could be jeopardized and the fundamental trust between patient and nurse destroyed by unnecessary access to data or by the inappropriate disclosure of identifiable patient information. The rights, well-being, and safety of the individual patient should be the primary factors in arriving at any professional judgment concerning the dispositions of confidential information received from or about the patient ... *Duties of confidentiality, however, are not absolute and may need to be modified in order to protect the patient, other innocent parties and in circumstances of mandatory disclosure for public health reasons.* (emphasis supplied) (ANA 2009)

Bioethics

While standards of professional conduct have centuries-old roots, "bioethics" as a distinct field is only decades old, emerging first in response to revelations of egregious research misconduct and expanding and adapting to help researchers, practitioners, and policy makers address challenges posed by such advances such as organ transplantation, hemodialysis (and related access issues), assisted reproduction, genetic sequencing, stem cell research, and the like.

In the research context, the National Commission for the Protection of Human Subjects of Biomedical and Behavioral Research identified three basic ethical principles – respect for persons, beneficence, and justice – articulated in the Belmont Report (DHHS 1979):

> Respect for persons incorporates at least two ethical convictions: first, that individuals should be treated as autonomous agents, and second, that persons with diminished autonomy are entitled to protection. The principle of respect for persons thus divides into two separate moral requirements: the requirement to acknowledge autonomy and the requirement to protect those with diminished autonomy. (DHHS 1979)

Fundamentally, bioethics and the respective professional codes are grounded in respect for persons ("A fundamental principle that underlies all nursing practice is respect for the inherent worth, dignity and human rights of every individual" (ANA 2009)), manifested in the requirement in both research and clinical practice to obtain the voluntary informed consent of individual patients or research participants before exposing them to potential risks.

Four principles of biomedical ethics (Beauchamp and Childress 2009) are now commonly[9] accepted: respect for autonomy, non-maleficence, beneficence, and justice. All four principles are considered prima facie binding; that is, they are binding if they do not conflict with other principles in a given case or situation. In theory, each principle has independent value, without assigning weight or priority to any one. These "principles," which are explicitly incorporated or otherwise reflected

[9] Though not universally, see Ebbeson (2010).

in each of the professional codes described above, are believed to reflect a common morality across all cultures.

Stated most simply *respect for autonomy* requires respect for all persons and imposes both affirmative and negative obligations on clinicians and researchers: Individuals are entitled to respectful treatment, and medical professionals must provide full, adequate, accessible information to enable individuals (whether patients or research participants) to make voluntary, informed decisions about treatment or participation. As noted above, this includes information about all potential risks, including limits to confidentiality. Conversely, the autonomous actions of individuals should not be controlled or constrained by others, unless the individuals pose a threat to the community:

> Autonomy is limited when it results in the identifiable, probably grave, harm to others. . . [W]henever the good of the patient, as perceived by the patient, poses a definable, grave, or probable risk to identifiable third persons, the physician's covenant with her patient is superceded by her duty to avoid a greater threat to third parties or to society at large. (Pellegrino and Thomasma 2004, p. 31)[10]

The tension between liberty in personal choice protected by respect for autonomy and the general "social good" advocated by medical or public health professionals is evident in continuing controversies about public health "paternalism": proposed gun restrictions, laws addressing mandatory use of motorcycle helmets, smoking in public settings, and even in the recent and highly publicized (and ultimately unsuccessful) efforts of the City of New York to limit the size of sugar-based soft drinks (Grynbaum 2013).

The principle of *beneficence* has several aspects: One should prevent evil or harm to another, one should remove sources of evil or harm to others, and one should do and promote good.

Non-maleficence (considered by some to be within the principle of beneficence) holds that one should not cause evil or harm.

The principle of *justice* is most often invoked in the healthcare setting in terms of distributive justice and equal access to resources. In the research context, it means, inter alia, that the burdens or potential risks of research should not be disproportionately placed on those who will not benefit from the research findings.[11]

While each of these prima facie principles is considered to have equal significance, autonomy was and largely remains the emphasis or dominant theme, at least in the United States. This reflects in part the era – the 1960s and 1970s – during which bioethics as a field developed. Deference to individual rights was evident in

---

[10] In the realm of child abuse, this obligation to protect third parties is codified in mandatory reporting statutes; in other contexts a common law "duty to warn" imposes the same responsibility on physicians and mental health providers to prevent harm to identifiable third parties; see Tarasoff v. Regents of California, 551 P.2d 332 (Cal. 1976).

[11] This arises most visibly in the case of clinical research trials conducted in impoverished areas of the world (such as parts of Africa), where the costs of any resulting therapeutic agents would be beyond the reach of the trial participants, and also comes into play where research is proposed that excludes significant portions of the population.

controversies about confidential vs. anonymous HIV testing, partner notification, and directly observed therapy for tuberculosis. Concerns about quarantine as a tool to limit the spread of multidrug-resistant (MDR) TB and other virulent and contagious agents periodically refocus this debate.

The resurgence of some infectious diseases (arguably due to declines in immunization rates) and the emergence of new (or new to human) agents, as well as the explicit extension of public health into "new" areas such as violence prevention, highlighted the need to articulate public health's core values and frame a distinct ethics of public health.[12] That public health is intrinsically linked to government and that it has and exerts police powers (e.g., required reporting of suspected abuse, civil and criminal penalties for failure to do so, immunity for good faith reporters, quarantine, mandatory restaurant inspections, and the like) (Richards 2009) make it essential to articulate and define the underlying values.

> In a liberal, pluralistic democracy, the justification of coercive policies, as well as other policies, must rest on moral reasons that the public in whose name the policies are carried out could reasonably be expected to accept. (Childress et al. (2002) citing Nagel (1995))

Various formulations have been proposed, some critical of the "interpersonal principlist approach" described above and others building on, adapting, or incorporating those principles into a framework more suited to public health's "utilitarian, paternalistic, and communitarian orientations" (Callahan and Jennings, Feb 2002):

> Public health bioethics must deal with a brand of principlism that evolved, for better or worse, as an interpersonal form of ethics mainly concerned with the clinical encounter and the physician-patient relationship, but ill-equipped to face the challenges presented by the collective issues of public health which differ substantially from those of clinical medicine. . . . . Although the four principles of doctrine [autonomy, beneficence, non-maleficence, and justice] are more relevant to clinical ethics, they cannot be dismissed in approaching the bioethical quandaries of public health precisely because, acting as check-lists, these moral tenets must always be incorporated into ethical reflection, nuanced to find their places in different cultural environments and adapted to the practices they address. (Kottow 2012, p. 34)

A working group of bioethicists who examined the parallels and the differences between clinical bioethics and public health practice identified the following "general moral considerations" believed to capture and describe the moral content of public health:

- Producing benefits;
- Avoiding, preventing, and removing harms;
- Producing the maximal balance of benefits over harm and other costs ("utility");
- Distributing benefits and burdens fairly ("distributive justice") and ensuring public participation;
- Including the participation of affected parties ("procedural justice");
- Respecting autonomous choices and actions, including liberty of action;
- Protecting privacy and confidentiality;

[12] See, e.g., Gostin (2001) who discusses three aspects of public health ethics: an ethics *of* public health (professional ethics), an ethics *for* public health (advocacy ethics), and an ethics *in* public health (applied ethics).

- Keeping promises and commitments;
- Disclosing information as well as speaking honestly and truthfully (often grouped under transparency); and
- Building and maintaining trust. (Childress et al. 2002, pp. 171–172)

While offering guidance these considerations (some of which conflict and some of which limit public health activities at times) must be considered in context and may not – likely will not – have the same moral weight in different situations. With regard to child maltreatment and mandatory reporting, for example, the most obvious conflicts arise between commitments to keep privacy and maintain trust, on the one hand (to encourage individuals to seek care), and the requirement that caregivers disclose information acquired in the context of therapy. Weighting each of these considerations equally would result in inaction.

The authors thus propose a series of "justificatory conditions" to consider when determining whether the ends of the public health activity (here child protection) warrant coercive policies or justify overriding certain specific values for the benefit of the greater good. These justificatory conditions are:

- *Effectiveness* ("showing that … infringing one or more moral considerations will probably protect public health")
- *Proportionality* (showing that the probable public health benefits outweigh the infringed moral considerations)
- *Necessity* ("…proponents must have a good faith belief, for which they can give supportable reasons, that a coercive approach is necessary")
- *Least infringement* ("public health agents should seek to minimize the infringement of general moral considerations"; for example, when public health activity "infringes confidentiality, they should disclose only the amount and kind of information needed, and only to those necessary")
- *Public justification* (public health agents should justify or explain infringements on moral considerations to the relevant parties) (Childress et al. 2002, p. 173)

Examining reporting from a public health ethics perspective, therefore, involves identifying applicable moral considerations which are infringed when medical providers are required to report suspected abuse. Critics of mandatory reporting cite infringements of privacy and confidentiality, promise keeping, and the maintenance of a trustful relationship between patient and provider as compelling reasons not to report.[13] All are legitimate concerns.

The question becomes whether adequate "justifications" counterbalance these concerns. The *effectiveness* of reporting in terms of protecting children and advancing public health (by illuminating the incidence, nature, and magnitude of abuse) is clear: In 2011 the US child protective services (CPS) received 3.7 million referrals of children being abused or neglected (Centers for Disease Control and Prevention

[13] A common reason given for failing to report is concern that the act of reporting will jeopardize the therapeutic relationship between provider and patient and breach any trust that has developed, thus disrupting therapy and causing greater harm than good. This is of greatest concern where the maltreatment has been revealed by the abusing individual in the course of therapy.

2013). In terms of both immediate protection, and by preventing long-term (lifetime) effects, the benefits of reporting also appear *proportional* to the infringements. "Society's averted gaze" described and challenged by Kempe, and subsequent data on the incidence and prevalence of abuse (681,000 children were estimated to be victims of maltreatment and an estimated 1,750 children died from maltreatment in 2011) argue that required reporting is indeed *necessary* to bring cases to light and protect children.

While the specific content, format, and procedures for reporting vary by jurisdiction, all limit the required information and the designated recipients to essential data. Clinicians are not required to investigate to establish intent or actual maltreatment (i.e., they are not required to dilute their professional role). Thus while justificatory conditions impose limits on confidentiality, they do not waive or abrogate that duty. Practitioners remain ethically obligated to release only that information required by the reporting statute; they are not obligated and in the spirit of *least infringement* should not provide more background information on families or clients than is required.

Yet another approach to public health ethics was proffered by the late Jonathan Mann, who argued that medicine, public health, ethics, and human rights are linked and that:

> [M]odern human rights . . .because they were initially developed entirely outside the health domain and seek to articulate the societal preconditions for human well-being, seem a far more useful framework, vocabulary, and form of guidance for public health efforts to analyze and respond directly to the societal determinants of health than any inherited from the past biomedical tradition. (Mann 1997)

Mann noted that, despite differences, there is "substantial overlap" between medicine and public health:

> Medicine and public health are two complementary and interacting approaches for promoting and protecting health . . . Yet medicine and public health can, and must also be differentiated, because in several important ways they are not the same. The fundamental difference involves the population emphasis of public health, which contrasts with the essentially individual focus of medical care. Public health identifies and measures threats to the health of populations, develops governmental policies in response to these concerns, and seeks to assure certain health and related services. In contrast, medical care focuses upon individuals – diagnosis, treatment, relief of suffering, and rehabilitation. (Mann 1997, p. 6)

Acknowledging that medical practice operates within a context highly influenced and governed by law and public policy, and that at times human rights and public health are confrontational (citing the early years of the AIDS epidemic and controversies about mandatory testing, quarantine, and isolation), Mann observed that:

> [W]hile modern human rights explicitly acknowledges that public health is a legitimate reason for limiting rights, more recently the underlying complementarity rather than the inherent confrontation between public health and human rights has been emphasized. (Mann 1997)

Mann asserted that because ethics and human rights derive from similar core values, they can be viewed as a continuum:

> [P]ublic health work requires both ethics applicable to the individual public health practitioner and a human rights framework to guide public health in societal analysis and response. (Mann 1997)

With regard to child maltreatment, both public health and human rights emphasize the well-being of children as autonomous individuals entitled to be free from violence and strive to eliminate the effects of child maltreatment on society as a whole.

Theory vs. Practice

Applying values and ethical principles in theory is easy; applying them in practice is less so and often uncomfortable. When clinicians have established relationships with families or when a therapeutic relationship may be jeopardized by reporting, doing the right thing can be difficult. Various models have been proposed that incorporate ethical principles into the decision process. Greipp's "Model for the Analysis of Under Reporting Child Abuse" (Greipp 1997), for example, is a nursing practice model that requires caregivers to be aware of and sensitive to "learned inhibitors" (i.e., their own personal and professional experiences, culture, and belief systems) that influence thoughts and actions about abuse and to progress through an ethical decision framework. At the center of the framework is the ethical duty to maintain professional competence, which includes knowing applicable child abuse laws and diagnostic procedures. Other elements of the framework include the general ethical principles (autonomy, beneficence, non-maleficence, and justice).

The total ethical framework rests on its deontological base, defined here as:

> A fundamental belief in and respect for one's obligations to other human beings (infants, children and adolescents) – one's duty. A belief that individuals are ends in and of themselves. To act morally in cases of suspected child abuse is to do what is rational and legal and desirable (child protection) for each child, independent of the caregiver's biases, inclinations, or inconvenience. (Greipp 1997, p. 262)

Applying this analysis, the author concludes

> To ignore a suspected situation of abuse would be a violation of beneficence and nonmaleficence. It certainly would violate the principle of justice, because no human being deserves to be abused. Justice mandates that nurses protect children from abuse. (Greipp 1997, p. 263)

Greipp further contends that justice also requires that all those involved in abuse cases "must be cognizant of and follow reporting laws." (Greipp 1997, p. 263)

Kalichman (1999), observing that "Professional ethics codes have not been particularly helpful in resolving conflicts created by the differences among standards of confidentiality and legal requirements to report suspected child abuse," (p. 162) lists a number of "points of ethical consideration" to guide practices in mandated reporting. These include: having accurate knowledge of state reporting laws, providing clients with informed consent information that includes the limits of confidentiality at the outset of a professional relationship, always reporting verbal revelations of child abuse, limiting practice to areas of competence, and informing parents or guardians before reporting unless doing so endangers children (pp. 162–164).

Challenges for Mental Health Providers

The scope of early reporting laws focused on medical practitioners and physical signs or radiographic evidence of abuse. Over time, the definitions of abuse and those mandated to report expanded to include mental health providers, who face different challenges:

> The problem with mandatory reporting laws is their application in mental health service settings without regard to the nature of these services. The settings and relationships within which suspected child abuse occurs in mental health services are qualitatively different from those of emergency medicine and pediatrics, the original targets of mandatory reporting legislation. Mental health professionals, and other nonmedical human service professionals, are unlikely to detect the battered child syndrome, although it is likely that they may be exposed to those circumstances that raise suspicions of child abuse. In addition, mental health professionals frequently rely solely on their observations of behavior in making determinations about child abuse. Concerns about privacy, trust, and respect play crucial roles in mental health professionals' dissatisfaction with mandated reporting. (Kalichman 1999, pp. 41–42)

Possible abuse is often revealed to mental health workers – psychiatrists, psychologists, social workers – during the course of therapy or family counseling, sometimes by the adult perpetrator. New and controversial research on "recovered" or false memories of child abuse and the general challenges of interviewing and eliciting accurate histories from very young children pose additional challenges for mental health workers. Ethical obligations of confidentiality and considerations of promise keeping and trust are thus deemed paramount and frequently cited reasons for not reporting. The principle of autonomy, however, requires that mental health workers fully disclose the limits of confidentiality – namely, the requirement to report threatened harm or abuse – at the outset of therapy and obtain fully informed consent before proceeding.

Stadler (1989) presents a "reporting decision tree" that can be used which involves giving adult clients opportunities to make the report themselves during the session, to report while the client listens, to report from another room while the client waits, and, if none of these options is acceptable to the client, to reaffirm the mental health worker's mandated reporter status and the intent to make the required report after the session.

The legal and ethical responsibility to report (i.e., to break confidentiality by providing the specific information required in that jurisdiction) does *not* relieve the provider of the duty of confidentiality altogether:

> There are, however, additional ethical considerations to make when determining what to include in a report. The level of detail released in a report should be limited to an amount

> that minimizes breaches in confidentiality while maximizing child protection (Melton and Limber, 1989). It is not necessary to release information in a report unless it will assist the social service agency in making determinations of abuse or will help the agency to take action on behalf of the child and family. As stated in the Ethical Principles of Psychologists and Code of Conduct (APA, 1992), "In order to minimize intrusions on privacy, psychologists include in written and oral reports, consultations, and the like, only information germane to the purpose for which the communication is made" (Standard 5.03a). In reporting suspected child abuse, the purpose of the information released is to protect children. Information should therefore be limited to the degree to which child protection will be achieved. (Kalichman 1999, p. 148)

There is also an ethical obligation to inform parents when confidentiality is breached by making a required report. The Ethical Principles of Psychologists and Code of Conduct (APA 2010) require discussions of confidentiality should be renewed with clients "as new circumstances may warrant" (Principle 5.1). Telling parents and children that a breach of confidentiality is necessary is easier when an informed consent policy has already fully explained the limits to confidentiality.

Conclusion

The AMA Code of Medical Ethics, the APA Ethical Principles of Psychologists and Code of Conduct, and the ANA Nursing Code of Ethics all emphasize the primacy of the duty to protect patient confidence, yet all explicitly acknowledge limitations on that duty, most notably when required by law to report. The values and principles underlying these professional codes and the evolving ethics of public health also make clear that society is morally justified in encroaching on the duty to protect patient confidences for the public good. Requiring clinicians and others to report and complying with reporting laws can be seen as ethical and appropriate exercise of both public health power and clinical discretion. "Not reporting" known and suspected child maltreatment is unethical.

References

Alvarez, K. M., Donahue, B., Kenny, M. C., Cavanagh, N., & Romero, V. (2005). The process and consequences of reporting child maltreatment: A brief overview for professionals in the mental health field. *Aggression and Violent Behavior, 10*, 311–331.

AMA. (2004). *Code of medical ethics current opinions with annotations*. Chicago: American Medical Association Press.

ANA. (2009). *Code of nursing ethics*. Washington, DC: American Nurses Association.

APA. (2010). *Ethical principles of psychologists and code of conduct*. Washington, DC: American Psychological Association.

Bayer, R., & Dubler, N. N. (1993). The dual epidemics of tuberculosis and AIDS: Ethical and policy issues in screening and treatment. *American Journal of Public Health, 83*, 649–654.

Bayer, R., & Toomey, K. E. (1992). HIV prevention and the two faces of partner notification. *American Journal of Public Health, 82*, 1158–1164.

Beauchamp, T. L., & Childress, J. F. (2009). *Principles of biomedical ethics* (6th ed.). Oxford: Oxford University Press.

Callahan, D., & Jennings, B. (2002, February). Ethics and public health: Forging a strong relationship. *American Journal of Public Health, 92*, 169–176.

CDC. (2012, October 16). *Public health leadership initiative.* Retrieved from Centers for Disease Control and Prevention: www.cdc.gov/violenceprevention/phl/

Centers for Disease Control and Prevention. (2013, September 17). *Child maltreatment facts at a glance 2013.* Retrieved from CDC Injury Prevention and Control: www.cdc.gov/violenceprevention/childmaltreatment/datasources.html

Childress, J. F., Faden, R., Gaare, R., Gostin, L. O., Kahn, J., Bonnie, R. J., & Nieburg, P. (2002). Public health ethics: Mapping the terrain. *Journal of Law, Medicine & Ethics, 30*, 170–178.

Dalhberg, L. L., & Mercy, J. A. (2009). History of violence as a public health problem. *Virtual Mentor: American Medical Association Journal of Ethics, 11*, 167–172.

DHHS, C. f. (1979). *The Belmont report: Ethical principles and guidelines for the protection of human subjects of research.* Washington, DC: U.S. Government Printing Office.

Ebbeson, M. (2010). Two different approaches to principles of biomedical ethics: A philosophical analysis and discussion of the theories of Tom L. Beauchamp and James F. Childress and the Danish philosophers Jakob Rendtorff and Peter Kemp. In T. N. Pace (Ed.), *Bioethics: Issues and dilemmas* (pp. 95–111). Hauppauge: Nova.

Gostin, L. O. (2001). Public health, ethics, and human rights: A tribute to the late Jonathan Mann. *Journal of Law, Medicine & Ethics, 29*(2), 121–130.

Greipp, M. E. (1997). Ethical decision making and mandatory reporting in cases of suspected child abuse. *Pediatric Health Care, 11*, 258–265.

Grynbaum, M. M. (2013, March 11). Judge blocks New York City's limits on big sugary drinks. *New York Times*, p. 1. Retrieved from Judge Block: www.bloomberg.com/news/2013-03-11/new-york-city-soda-size-limitations-barred-by

Hester, D. (2004). Professing public health: Practicing ethics and ethics as practice. In M. Boylan (Ed.), *Public health policy and ethics* (pp. 1–16). Dordrecht: Kluwer Academic.

Hew, U. D. (1979). *Healthy people: The surgeon general's report on health promotion and disease prevention.* Washington, DC: U.S. Government Printing Office.

Kalichman, S. C. (1999). *Mandated reporting of suspected child abuse: Ethics, law, & policy* (2nd ed., xiv, 235 pp.). Washington, DC: American Psychological Association.

Kempe, C., Silverman, F., Steele, B., Droegemueller, W., & Silver, H. (1962). The battered child syndrome. *Journal of the American Medical Association, 181*, 4–11.

Kottow, M. (2012). *From justice to protection: A proposal for public health bioethics* (Springer briefs in public health). New York: Springer. doi:10.1007/978-1-4614-2026-2_4.

Mann, J. (1997). Medicine and public health, ethics and human rights. *The Hastings Center Report, 27*(3), 6–13.

Mercy, J. A., & Saul, J. (2009). Creating a healthier future through early interventions for children. *JAMA: Journal of the American Medical Association, 301*, 1–3.

Nagel, T. (1995). Moral epistemology. In R. E. Bulger, E. M. Bobby, & H. V. Fineburg (Eds.), *Society's choices: Social and ethical decision making in biomedicine* (pp. 201–214). Washington, DC: National Academy Press.

National Research Council. (1988). *The future of public health.* Washington, DC: The National Academies Press.

Pellegrino, E. D., & Thomasma, D. C. (2004). The good of patients and the good of society: striking a moral balance. In M. Boylan (Ed.), *Public health policy and ethics* (pp. 17–37). Dordrecht: Kluwer Academic.

Richards, E. P. (2009). Dangerous people, unsafe conditions. *The Journal of Legal Medicine, 30*, 27–50.

Richards, E. P., & Rathbun, K. C. (1999). The role of the police power in 21st century public health. *Sexually Transmitted Diseases, 26*(6), 350–357.

Rosenberg, M. L., & Fenley, M. (1991). *Violence in America: A public heath approach*. New York: Oxford University Press.

Stadler, H. A. (1989). Balancing ethical responsibilities: Reporting child abuse and neglect. *The Counseling Psychologist, 17*, 102–110.

Zimmerman, F., & Mercy, J. L. (2010). A better start: Child maltreatment prevention as a public health priority. *Zero to Three, 30*, 4–10.

Chapter 10
Economic Issues in the Community Response to Child Maltreatment

Leonie Segal

Establishing the Case for a Government Role in Child Maltreatment

The economic discipline is concerned with maximising community well-being for available resources. Underpinning economics is a study of markets, market failure and the role of government. That the unfettered operation of the private market will *rarely* solve the resource allocation questions optimally is not widely understood. Rather, markets typically suffer from 'market failure' such that the self-interested behaviour of individuals (as providers and consumers of goods and services) does not work in the best interest of society at large. In these circumstances, some level of intervention by government is desirable to generate better outcomes for the community. In this context, the role of government is to improve efficiency. The primary sources of market failure are (1) *externalities*, when producers (or consumers) do not fully bear the costs or fully reap the benefits of their actions, (2) *imperfect information* held by consumers/citizens and/or producers especially about the consequences of their actions, (3) *public goods attributes* whereby consumers cannot be efficiently excluded from consumption, and (4) *restrictions on entry* creating the conditions for exercise of monopoly power. The unfettered operation of the private market will also result in a level of inequity in income, health, opportunity, education, access to food and housing that most citizens would find unacceptable.

The efficiency of markets also assumes a rational consumer or agent, able to make decisions that are in their own best interest judged by them ex post and also able to make favourable choices for others whom they represent. There is a large literature contesting the assumption of the rational consumer or agent. This is

L. Segal, B.Econ. (Hons)., M.Econ., Ph.D. (✉)
School of Population Health, University of South Australia, Adelaide, SA, Australia
e-mail: Leonie.segal@unisa.edu.au

B. Mathews, D.C. Bross (eds.), *Mandatory Reporting Laws and the Identification of Severe Child Abuse and Neglect*, Child Maltreatment 4,
DOI 10.1007/978-94-017-9685-9_10

observed especially in impulsive, risk-taking and addictive behaviours, the potentially destructive behaviours of those who are mentally ill, and in parents who make what seem to be very poor choices for their children, even in the face of adequate information, or who abuse or neglect their children.

Taken together, the three factors, namely, (1) pervasive market failure, (2) 'irrational' behaviour of individuals and (3) a societal concern with equity, create a very powerful argument for interventionist public policy in multiple spheres. Put simply, the self-interested behaviours of individuals will result in total societal well-being that is considerably less than is theoretically achievable, and government intervention is justified on the basis of adding to the common good. Especially where children and other vulnerable people are adversely affected by the destructive behaviours of others, there is a growing view that society has an obligation to intervene. However, as some individuals and businesses will do better under an unfettered system, there can be strong opposition to government intervention, especially where powerful business interests are at stake, captured in the catchcry of 'nanny state' (Segal 2010). For example, restrictions on alcohol sales are strongly resisted, supposedly to protect citizen freedoms, but of course the protection of profits is the real concern. (Businesses are perfectly happy with government intervention in support of their industry.)

Governments have a range of policy options at their disposal to promote desired behaviours and restrict undesirable behaviours. The first of these options are *regulatory and legislative measures*, such as those relating to the wearing of seat belts, a minimum drinking age, regulations for safe food preparation and sale, occupational health and safety, the disposal of toxic substances, restriction on gambling outlets and the criminalisation of certain substances. Laws for the mandatory reporting of child maltreatment cases are also such a measure. The aim of mandatory reporting legislation is to bring cases of concern to the attention of child and family welfare agencies with the purpose of protecting the child and improving child outcomes.

The second option is *direct service provision* – delivery of desired services that would not be provided by the market (or at too low a level) funded entirely or in part through taxation (to ensure zero- or low-direct payment by consumers). The defining feature is that it is not in the broad societal interest to restrict access to these services on the basis of capacity or willingness to pay. They can be delivered by governments or contracted out under defined service agreements to ensure government objectives are met. Examples are public housing, free/subsidised education (preschool, school, universities), health care (hospitals, infant welfare services, vaccinations), family support services, employment services, child protection services and domestic violence services.

The third option is *financial incentives* – taxes and subsidies aimed at influencing behaviours by changing relative prices facing the consumer. This includes punitive taxes, for example, on tobacco products or high excise taxes on petrol or excluding fresh food from GST or support payments to assist selected industries such as farmers, selected manufacturers, etc.

The fourth option is *benefit/welfare payments*, primarily to address equity objectives by redistributing income. A priority is children living in extreme poverty.

In Australia, there are/have been a myriad of payments to support families, including the supporting parents pension, family tax benefits, parental leave provisions, the 'baby bonus' and rent subsidies. Pension payments generally leave the recipient with complete freedom in how monies are spent. In Australia, there are programmes that seek to restrict spending for some welfare recipients. This includes selected families with substantiated child neglect cases, who are put on child protection income management (70 % of their pension tied to a basics card), in an attempt to ensure spending on staples. The challenge for government is to determine the optimal set of policy options to address the specific problem in the best way possible. The aim is then, given the particular context, to find the solution that will improve individual and societal outcomes to the greatest extent possible, given budget constraints.

Child Maltreatment as 'Market Failure'

The phenomena of child maltreatment could be viewed as an example of 'market failure'. The growing child is from conception into adolescence entirely dependent on their parents for their survival and development. The family is absolutely central in determining whether or not the child has the opportunity to realise their full potential and live a long and productive life. The physical and emotional development in the early years has far-reaching consequences through neurobiological, developmental and evolutionary pathways. The early environment affects the child's way of understanding and being in the world, as observed in attributes such as exercise of impulse control, the ability to learn, sense of agency, levels of distress and anxiety and resilience (Shonkoff et al. 2009; Anda et al. 2006).

Early childhood experiences influence the likelihood of adopting healthy and protective behaviours or unhealthy and destructive behaviours, through childhood and across the lifespan (Chapman et al. 2007; Dube et al. 2006; Edwards et al. 2007). While the community and broader society in which the family lives are also important, as is the child's inherent personality traits, the family environment has a core influence and specifically the parents' interactions with the child (Bowlby 1982; Amos et al. 2011). In the modern democratic welfare state, where the rule of law is well established and a safety net (income support, etc.) is in place to address severe poverty and ensure access to health care and education, the family relationship environment will almost certainly have the biggest influence on children's life outcomes.

In extreme, but not rare, cases, the quality of the family environment can directly threaten survival itself, via the direct fatal effects of maltreatment but also through the ongoing consequences of trauma. Persons with a child maltreatment history have a *several fold* (up to 15 times) rate of suicide compared to children with no such history (Duke et al. 2010) (see Table 10.1). A vastly lower life expectancy of 20 years is also reported for persons experiencing multiple (>5) childhood adversities. These cover emotional, sexual and physical abuse, witnessing domestic

Table 10.1 Child maltreatment and risk of suicide attempt – odds ratio for suicide attempt children subject to maltreatment relative to no maltreatment

Type of maltreatment	Odds ratio for suicide attempt	
	Female	Male
Physical abuse by an adult living in the household	5.1	6.9
Sexual abuse by a family member	4.3	15.0
Drug or alcohol abuse by family	2.9	3.5
Witnessing physical violence (family member on another family member)	11.1	4.9

Source: Duke et al. (2010)
Note: Derived from a 2007 survey of 136,549 Minnesota school students

violence, parental incarceration, parental mental illness, parental divorce/separation and parental substance abuse (Brown et al. 2009). Unfortunately this level of adversity is not uncommon in highly vulnerable populations and in communities where rates of child maltreatment are very high.

The role for government to intervene in relation to child abuse and neglect is thus absolutely clear and rests on three core arguments:

1. *The ethical argument*

   There is a clear ethical imperative to protect highly vulnerable members of our society from the damaging actions of others. Children are absolutely defenceless, unable to understand or articulate their distress and can be somewhat invisible. Concerns about equity are also pertinent. Child maltreatment is considerably more common in lower socio-economic sectors of society and is also likely to perpetuate social and economic disadvantage. Low educational attainment, teen pregnancy, unemployment, welfare dependency, involvement in crime, drug and alcohol abuse and mental illness are all consequences of child maltreatment. For any society that has a 'closing the gap' agenda related to income, educational or health disparities, addressing child maltreatment to ensure harms are minimised is a logical strategy component.
2. *Violation of the assumption of the rational consumer/agent or skills/knowledge gap*

   The inability of the parent to act in the best interests of their child, even though this is what every parent would want, can be considered irrational behaviour warranting government intervention. This argument does not require maltreatment to be extreme but simply that parental behaviour is other than that consistent with creating a safe and nurturing environment for the child as the parent would wish. The appropriate response would depend on the level of harm and the reason for the inappropriate parenting behaviour. This might start with parenting classes for expectant or new parents, an infant welfare centre/infant visiting programme to improve knowledge and skills or social supports for very isolated parents advancing to a more therapeutic approach or a more intrusive regulatory approach for more chaotic and disturbed families where the situation for the child is of serious concern. In the more serious cases of abuse or neglect, poor parenting is unlikely to reflect a simple knowledge or skills gap, but rather the effects of unresolved childhood trauma on the capacity for intimate relationships such as that between a mother and her child (Amos et al. 2011, 2014a, b). Amos and colleagues argue convincingly that the child acts as a potent trauma trigger for the mother. The mother's behaviour in neglecting or abusing her child is a logical response given the distorted perspective created by her own trauma history, but irrational from the perspective of an undamaged individual or the wider societal good. (While the model explicitly refers to mothers, it almost certainly applies also to fathers.) Some of the known consequences of child maltreatment, such as drug and alcohol abuse, mental illness and inability to develop healthy relationships, directly impact on the capacity of parents with a history of maltreatment to adopt behaviours that are protective of others in their care.

It is also the case that the private market will inherently exploit, for profit the more vulnerable in society who experience poor impulse control. This can exacerbate the unfavourable conditions for these parents by fuelling their abuse of alcohol, tobacco, illicit drugs, gambling and the like, which further compromise their capacity to parent in a safe manner.

3. *Externalities (costs on others) – considerable costs incurred by society of failing to intervene*

   The dominant costs of child maltreatment are borne not by the perpetrator but by others; in the first place the child and secondly society. These costs are considerable. For the child, there is the immediate and acute distress, which can result in an ever-present fear, anxiety and hypervigilance, morbidity and, in cases of fatality, a life cut short. There are in addition ongoing or downstream consequences of developmental delay, drug and alcohol abuse or other addictive behaviours, risk taking/adoption of harmful lifestyle behaviours (such as tobacco smoking and poor nutrition), poor mental health/serious mental illness (e.g. up to 12 times the rate for schizophrenia[13]), compromised physical health, placement in care, involvement in crime as victim and / or perpetrator, low educational attainment, welfare dependency, unemployment, difficulty with intimate relationships, teenage pregnancy, likelihood of maltreating their own children and premature death. These consequences are reported to have from 1.5 to 12 times the relative risk for persons with a child maltreatment history relative to those without. See, for example, Table 10.1 above. The odds ratios for child maltreatment for poor mental health vary by study, but large excess risk is uniformly reported (Chapman et al. 2007; Duke et al. 2010; Norman et al. 2012). Studies also report a more than doubling the risk for physical conditions (e.g. stroke 1.7–3.00 times (Norman et al. 2012); obesity 1.3–9.8 times (Gilbert et al. 2009)).

In short, child maltreatment imposes large negative health, social and economic consequences, both contemporaneous with the maltreatment and ongoing (Shonkoff and Garner 2012). These consequences result in huge budgetary impacts in the form of additional expenditure on services and lost production. Expenditure is incurred to address the consequences of child maltreatment particularly on hospital in-patient services and Emergency Department presentations, drug and alcohol programmes, suicide prevention and response, rehabilitation, on the criminal justice system, housing support, income support/welfare payments, remedial education and on the child protection system. These consequences are expensive. A child placement in 24 h out-of-home care can cost more than $300,000/year (for residential care) (ROGS 2014a); involvement in crime is also costly (prison > $80,000 per prisoner year and more for juveniles) (ROGS 2014b). A life of welfare dependency, drug and alcohol addiction or serious mental illness involves ongoing government expenditures as well as impacts on social cohesion. Child maltreatment is also responsible for a considerable reduction in the productive potential of society and thus lower gross domestic product as a consequence of premature death, low workforce participation and educational failure limiting skills and knowledge formation.

The total societal burden of child maltreatment is undoubtedly very large with several published estimates, for example an estimated total cost of child maltreatment in the USA of US$124 billion, or a cost per nonfatal case of US$210,000 (Fang et al. 2012). But the full costs are difficult to quantify, given the wide scope of impacts. None of the published studies provide a fully comprehensive estimate. For example, studies fail to incorporate the effect of child maltreatment on harmful behaviours such as smoking or morbid obesity (themselves being large source of disease burden). They also ignore the intergenerational nature of abuse, which in effect attaches an infinite stream of costs to child maltreatment.

It is increasingly understood that the observed relationships between child maltreatment and the health, social and economic consequences can be taken as causal, not merely correlational. There are well-defined causal mechanisms that predict the serious consequences of child abuse and neglect that are observed. These mechanisms are found in the attachment and trauma literature (Bowlby 1982; Amos et al. 2011), evolutionary theory (Amos et al. 2014a, b), developmental psychology and neural biology (Shonkoff et al. 2009).

The results of randomised controlled trials confirm that it is possible to intervene with families to reduce rates of maltreatment and that this has the expected impact on health, social and economic outcomes (Reynolds et al. 2002; Olds et al. 1997; Mikton and Butchart 2009; Berry et al. 2007).

This means that there are effective interventions to reduce rates of child maltreatment and reduce the consequent harms, both in families at risk (no contact with the child protection system) and in families where abuse or neglect is already present.

Not surprisingly, given the ethical and efficiency arguments for a government role in addressing child maltreatment and the existence of effective strategies, governments across countries and jurisdictions have policies to protect children. The question is not whether a formal child protection system should exist, but what should it look like? How should maltreatment be defined? At what point is intervention warranted? Is there to be a different system response for different maltreatment thresholds? What are the strategy components? What is the balance between investigation, child removal and family support? And in relation to family support, what is the balance between case management and practical support and a therapeutic approach incorporating treatment for past and current trauma?

If we had full information about (1) the consequences of child maltreatment, including budgetary impacts, and (2) the effectiveness and cost of all possible intervention strategies, it would be possible to develop an evidence-driven child protection strategy. In the interim, the challenge is to draw on the best available evidence to inform the policy response and determine the evidence that we should be gathering to better inform future policy.

Determining the Optimal Policy Response to Child Maltreatment and the Role of Mandatory Reporting

Overview

This section considers how governments might respond to families where there is a level of concern about the welfare of the child such that cases should be brought to the attention of the child protection system for specific action to protect children from harm. It is assumed in this discussion that a regulatory child protection system is part of a broader system of family support, incorporating a suite of options of varying intensities to offer families the necessary supports for creating a nurturing environment for their children.

In understanding the performance of the child protection system, it is necessary to think through *how to define child maltreatment*. Definitions of child abuse and neglect (CAN) vary considerably, partly reflecting varying contexts and the purpose of the definition. The cut point, in terms of what constitutes a case of maltreatment of sufficient severity to warrant action – which may be a family support rather than a formal child protection investigation – is ideally determined by (1) evidence of harms, (2) source of harms and (3) capacity of the system to improve outcomes for children and families. Evidence around all three aspects is pertinent where the definition is designed to trigger a government response. In contrast, if a definition is for use in epidemiological research into the risks for and/or consequences of child maltreatment, the capacity for and impact of a response is irrelevant.

A common premise underpinning the statutory system is that the highest risk cases offer the greatest potential for benefit through government intervention (e.g. immediate life-saving), with progressively lower potential for benefit as extent and likelihood of harm falls. This is consistent with a recent review of intervention studies of family support/preschool/infant visiting that identify greatest benefit in programmes that target the most vulnerable families (Segal et al. 2013).

Interestingly, this model contrasts with the population health maxim that greatest benefits are to be found in 'shifting the entire population' (Rose 2001) cited in favour of population approaches and universalism and against the targeting of services to those at highest risk. While this maxim is very popular, it needs to be understood as an empirical question. Whether a targeted or population approach will be the most efficient depends on the particular health or social problem being addressed, the cost of case finding those at high risk, the profile of harms and the costs and effectiveness of interventions across the risk spectrum.

That is, an approach based on the evidence of what works is what is required, not one that privileges a particular stage in risk creation or level of vulnerabilities. But that said, it is invariably desirable to offer something to populations wherever they sit on the primary, secondary and tertiary prevention continuum, with an approach proportional to the level of risk and potential for benefit. Further, contrary to popular wisdom, the level of benefit is typically proportional to level of risk; the higher the risk and expectation of harms, the greater the capacity for benefit. It is also clear that for children trapped in situations of serious harm, however that is defined, a policy response by government to protect children is paramount and must incorporate, at a minimum: (1) an efficient mechanism for case finding and (2) an effective multifaceted approach for protecting at-risk children.

Case Finding/Reporting

We are concerned here with understanding the optimal mechanism for encouraging an 'ideal' level of reporting of suspected cases of serious child maltreatment. The options for such a mechanism fall into three categories: (1) *legislative*, involving mandatory legislation requiring specific occupations to report suspected cases of child abuse or neglect to the appropriate bodies, with protections for reporters, and usually (but not always) with penalties for failure to comply, (2) *professional obligation* under designated codes of practice for nominated professions to report suspected cases of child abuse or neglect, and (3) *citizen option* to report suspected cases. Any of these mechanisms presume an associated administrative process for receiving and acting on reports.

When mandatory reporting was first introduced in the USA in the 1960s, there was no formal mechanism to identify and respond to children subject to even extreme levels of abuse or neglect. This left many children at extreme and imminent risk, as societal action was rarely invoked to protect even those children who had been repeatedly and clearly subject to grievous harm. This was presumably a reflection of the pervading culture internationally, of nonintrusion into the lives of families by government and a perceived limit on the role of clinicians and others working with children. This culture of nonintrusion into family life is complex and arguably still limits the societal response to issues such as domestic violence and child maltreatment (leaving many of the most vulnerable citizens without protection). The reporting requirements or professional obligations are focused on the child experiencing significant harm and therefore also apply to cases of non-parental child maltreatment occurring outside the family, typically cases of sexual abuse. Again, social convention, in dealing with respected organisations, compounded by a high level of defensiveness from these same organisations has in the past demonstrably failed children experiencing harm.

It seems certain that the introduction of mandatory reporting in the 1960s has been instrumental in driving culture change in the behaviour of core professional groups in contact with vulnerable families and children. Mandatory reporting in bringing suspected cases of maltreatment to the attention of the child protection authorities demands a response and ultimately greater resourcing of the child protection system. For example, in Australia, resources allocated to child protection have more than doubled in real terms (2012–2013 dollars) from AUD 1,511.1 million in 2003–2004 to AUD 3,521.7 million in 2012–2013 (ROGS 2014a). (The benefit achieved by this increase in funding is hard to measure, but it was certainly aimed at advancing child and family welfare.)

Determining the best approach to case finding is complex. Historically, it is almost certain that mandatory reporting has been central in driving culture change and encouraging greater social responsibility in reporting children suspected to be at grave risk. However, it may be asked whether, in societies which have had mandatory reporting for some decades, such a model is still required? Where this has driven a culture shift, it may be that mandatory reporting and professional obligation are not very different in terms of outcomes. For example, in some contexts, certain reporter groups who only have a policy-based obligation (which is not covered by legislation), such as police, do make substantial numbers of reports. However, in other contexts and subsets of abuse, it is also known that some professional groups having only a policy-based duty make significantly fewer reports and identify far fewer cases than their counterparts who do have a legislative duty to report (Mathews et al. 2010). This can reflect a fear of reporting, lacking the protections provided by legislation, while being subject to identification, complaints and civil and disciplinary proceedings (Mathews et al. 2009). It is difficult to generalise because of the considerable variation in operational detail, such that there may be as much variation within a system type as across system types, relating to the precise reporting obligations and the administrative system for receiving and responding to reports.

Another way of considering this question of case finding is to assess whether the system for reporting currently in place in the particular jurisdiction performs 'well enough'. Desirable performance in this context is concerned with identifying a 'high' proportion of cases of *severe* maltreatment or risk of maltreatment reported to a child protection agency and followed up appropriately and 'low' reporting of cases involving lower levels or no maltreatment. What constitutes 'high' and 'low' is a matter for debate and discussion and might reasonably vary by level and type of abuse, given some abuse types are less hidden (e.g. serious physical abuse) than others (e.g. sexual abuse).

The aim is for a good overlap of the populations of 'severely' maltreated children and a child abuse and neglect report, which is then actioned appropriately. A reporting system that has a high proportion of reported cases (which after assessment are determined to require a child protection and/or family support response), and a low proportion of reports that require neither, may indicate a well-performing system, but it is also consistent with a system which is failing to detect too many serious cases. Assessing performance in terms of a match between reports and substantiated cases is fraught and further complicated by the contested nature of how to define a case of child maltreatment warranting intervention. In short, the claim of 'over-reporting' under a system of mandatory reporting is difficult to test (Mathews 2012) and certainly cannot be established by reference to rates of unsubstantiated reports or rates of unsubstantiated investigations (Drake 1996; Drake and Jonson-Reid 2007; Kohl et al. 2009).

The primary role of reporting (notification) under mandatory reporting systems is to identify children who have been significantly harmed by abuse or neglect or who are at imminent risk of being so harmed; a secondary function or consequence of such reports is to identify families in need of support to facilitate the provision of assistance. Measuring system success or failure simply by the proportion of abuse or neglect reports that are substantiated, does not address the possibility of children at considerable risk within the community about whom no reports have been made or the value of identifying highly vulnerable families in need of assistance. Child protection systems increasingly have an alternate pathway to the statutory route through which vulnerable families are offered a range of family support services, which may include case management (e.g. to support access to income support, housing, employment, practical and social supports), therapeutic trauma-based counselling and parenting programmes designed to improve the parent/child relationship (such as 'circle of security' or incredible years). Having such a referral occur through a child protection system may well increase the uptake of such services for more vulnerable families, who might otherwise not engage, creating an 'early intervention' pathway. Even for families who are referred to and progressed through the statutory child protection system, a finding of 'not substantiated' would not necessarily mean that the child was (is) not at serious risk of harm.

As in any legal process, a finding reflects on the evidence able to be gathered. In Australia 8–18 % of children – depending on jurisdiction – who were the subject of an unsubstantiated investigation were within 12 months subject to a substantiated investigation (ROGS 2014a).

Further, a statutory system with constrained capacity is likely to focus on abuse or neglect associated with a serious risk of imminent harm deemed to require immediate action. Cases of potentially serious harms, but of longer-term onset such as major developmental delay, risk of drug and alcohol abuse and a life of mental illness or of crime may be less likely to be investigated or substantiated. In short, a decision not to investigate a child harm report, or a non-substantiation of a report after investigation, does not necessarily mean the report was not appropriate. And as a matter of logic, given the challenges of accurately identifying cases, any system that had a very low rate of non-cases could be assumed to be missing many serious cases. Knowledge of the prevalence of child maltreatment of seriousness that would justify a report would be useful in considering whether the reporting regime is resulting in an appropriate number of reports, whether too few or too many (Fig. 10.1).

Estimates of prevalence of child maltreatment are generated from two distinct sources: (1) child protection data and (2) survey data. Both are interesting and provide distinct perspectives on likely underlying rates:

1. Child protection data – reports, investigations, substantiation, family support services

Data on the Australian child protection system are reported in detail by the Productivity Commission in their annual Report on Government Services (ROGS)

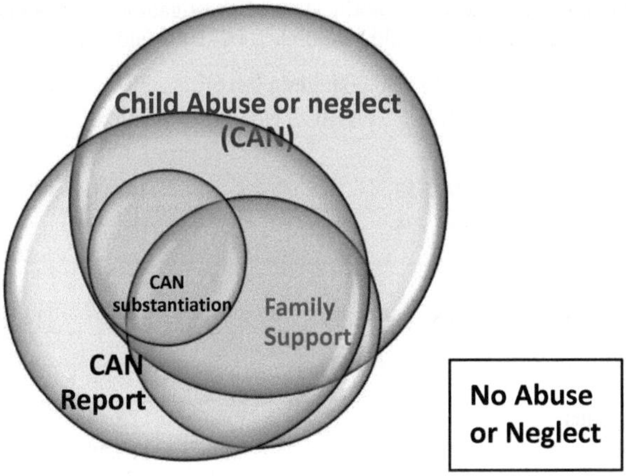

Fig. 10.1 Depiction of prevalence of child abuse and neglect (CAN), report, substantiation

(2014a). Selected data from this extensive report is presented in Table 10.2. This shows that in 2012–2013, 184,284 children were the subject of a notification and that 40,685 or 22.1 % had a substantiated notification. But we also note that the majority of notifications (55 %) were dealt with by 'other means', often through an alternate family support pathway. A 'not substantiated' finding was recorded for just 21.8 % of notifications, or only 19 %, if we adjust for those for whom a substantiated finding would be delivered within 12 months.

We can also observe that rates of notification, investigation and substantiation are much higher in Aboriginal and Torres Strait Islander (ATSI) peoples. For example, again from ROGS (2014a), in 2012–2013, 143.9 per 1,000 ATSI children aged 0–17 years were the subject of a notification, more than double that of a decade earlier and 5.7 times the rate for non-ATSI children. Rates of notification in non-ATSI children peaked in 2008–2009 at 37.8 per 1,000 children, falling back to 25.3 per 1,000 children by 2012–2013, which is just below 2002–2003 levels. Much of this fall is attributable to changes in child protection policies in NSW, a previously high notifying jurisdiction, which instituted an alternate family support pathway for vulnerable families. This can be seen in the high proportion of reports in 2012–2013 'dealt with through other means' and large increase in referrals to intensive family support services. Another consequence has been a sharp fall in nonfinalised investigations. Current rates of notification in ATSI children of just over 14 % in 2012–2013 would translate into well over 50 % of ATSI children with a notification over their childhood. (See South Australian study of cumulative notification rates for Indigenous and non-Indigenous Australians from three birth cohorts (Delfabbro et al. 2010).)

The conversion of completed investigations to substantiation was 47.3 % in 2012–2013 (53,634÷113,307), the same rate for the ATSI and non-ATSI population. This is considerably higher than the low rate of 33 % in 2008–2009, driven by low rates in NSW, which resulted in a change in the reporting criteria in NSW to one

Table 10.2 Child protection services: notifications, investigations, substantiations, Australia, ATSI and non-ATSI, number and rate/1,000 children 2002–2003 and 2012–2013

	2002–2003 (children 0–16)			2012–2013 (children 0–17)		
	All	ATSI	Non-ATSI	All[a]	ATSI	Non-ATSI
Notifications						
Number of notifications	198,353			273,004	**57,794**	**215,210**
Number of *children* subject to a notification	130,224			184,284		
Children in notifications rate/'000	28.8	62.6	27.2	35.2	143.9	25.3
Investigations						
Total investigations	66,456			122,545	30,619	79,606
N finalised				**113,307**	**32,923**	**74,708**
Finalised N children	50,063			85,455		
Investigations rate rate/'000 children	11.1	32.8	10.1	16.3	86.2	11.4
Outcome of finalised investigation						
Not substantiated number	25,412			59,673		
Substantiated investigations	40,416			**53,634**	**15,655**	**35,973**
Children				40,685		
Children with a substantiated investigation rate/'000 children	6.8	21.6	6.1	7.8	45.1	5.6
Investigations in progress, closed no outcome	28,922			9,160		
Notifications dealt with by other means	NA			150,537[b]		
Children in out-of-home care on June 30						
Number	20,297	4,750	15,547	40,624	13,914	26,454
Rate per/'000 children	4.5	22.5	3.4	7.7	56.9	5.3
Children in 1+ OHC placement during year						
Number	19,399	4,026	15,373	50,097	16,597	33,057
Rate/'000 children	6.1	27.0	5.0	9.6	68.3	6.6
Children commencing intensive family support services	2,217	313	1,904	22,116[c]	4,826	14,467

Source: ROGS (2003, 2014a, Tables 15A 8 and 15A 18)

Notes

ATSI Aboriginal and Torres Strait Islander

[a]Includes unknown Indigenous status

[b]Highly variable by jurisdiction – 0 % in Queensland, 27.5 % in Western Australia, 48 % in New South Wales, 62 % in the Northern Territory, 72 % in South Australia, 74 % in Victoria and 83 % in the ACT and Tasmania

[c]Includes unknown Indignous status and data for SA and Tas for which data not available by Indigenous status.

of 'serious' harm, together with the introduction of a family support diversionary pathway. But at 47 % from a common sense perspective, this does not suggest that the mandatory reporting system is encouraging an excessive rate of notifications and investigations, relative to case finding.

2. Community surveys of the prevalence of child abuse and neglect

Ideally child protection data would also be compared with the actual prevalence of child abuse and neglect in the community, to assess the performance of the child protection system in relation to rates of notification and case finding. However, even though rates or prevalence of child abuse and neglect have been reported in numerous surveys, there are inherent problems in any survey-based estimates of child maltreatment. This arises from likely selection and retention bias in longitudinal or cross-sectional studies and challenges in defining a population which has/has not experienced child maltreatment. Maltreatment is not inherently dichotomous, but exists along a spectrum, and there is no consistency in the definitions used in surveys. Some of these issues in estimating the prevalence of child abuse and neglect are discussed below.

Definition and Scope There is little agreement internationally about how to define child maltreatment, in the context of a child protection system. While the historic focus of mandatory reporting was children faced with imminent risk of serious injury or death, evidence has been accumulating of the profound long-term consequences of neglect and abuse, even when the risk of imminent death or serious injury is low. While a society may accept an obligation to 'protect children' and enhance their life possibilities, the determination of the point at which, and the ways in which, to intervene can only be answered if we understand the consequences of intervening or failing to intervene. It cannot be taken as a given that intervening will always result in better outcomes or that a specific strategy will represent a worthwhile investment for the society, given competing calls on resources.

For example, a child witnessing domestic violence on a regular basis may have a small risk of imminent death or serious physical injury, but in the context of potential harms such as developmental delay, risk of drug and alcohol dependence, poor educational outcomes, unemployment, involvement in crime/incarceration, poor mental and physical health, risk of suicide and premature death, they may warrant protection. Refining definitions of child maltreatment to reflect the levels and severity of harms is desirable, and further refining these in terms of capacity to improve outcomes for the child, family and society is not well advanced. What is known is that multiple sources of ongoing maltreatment tend to be considerably more harmful to the child, as is maltreatment combined with other adverse childhood experiences, such as parental divorce/separation, homelessness or extreme poverty. The challenge is to refine definitions of abuse and neglect, both to reach some shared understanding of what constitutes maltreatment but most crucially to better match the service response to the nature of current harms and expected future consequences.

Ideally operational definitions will reflect evidence of harms. While it is well established that maltreatment across more than one category and of an ongoing nature will have the most severe consequences, the data quality is insufficient to establish precise evidence-based cut points that reflect expected levels of harm. In considering the ideal threshold, the likely benefit/harm ratio from intervening also needs to be considered. Again the data needs here are considerable.

Bias in the Data Collection Process There are two ways of generating estimates of the prevalence of child maltreatment: surveys and child protection records. Child protection records cannot provide an independent estimate unrelated to the operation of the child protection system, which leaves surveys, longitudinal cohort studies or cross-sectional studies. Survey estimates will be flawed for several reasons:

- Reliance on memory – compromised by the young age at which abuse can occur (frequently as a baby or infant), recognition of abuse or neglect when this might have represented normative behaviour in the immediate community, possible difficulty in recording disturbing childhood experiences – the more distressing of which may be unconsciously suppressed.
- The representativeness of study samples – many of those most affected by maltreatment, for example, who have become homeless, experience severe mental illness, have been incarcerated and have low levels of literacy, or died prematurely will be missing from population surveys. They may fit exclusion criteria (many studies exclude persons living in institutions), be less likely to respond and be amongst the 'lost to follow-up' group in longitudinal studies, before questions about maltreatment are asked.
- Studies employ a wide range of questions in describing abuse or neglect, which not surprisingly have changed over time, with varying levels of comprehensiveness across types of abuse and varying levels of precision in how abuse is described. The precise questions, the sample frame and response rate need to be well understood in order to better understand what a prevalence estimate derived from a particular survey might mean.

Any confusion in the classification of persons as cases (subject to child maltreatment) and comparators (no maltreatment history) and absence from the survey data of those who have suffered the most severe consequences of child abuse and neglect will also affect the accuracy of estimates of relative risks of the postulated consequences of child maltreatment.

3. Prevalence of child maltreatment in Australia – survey-based estimates

Table 10.3 provides a summary of estimates of the prevalence of child maltreatment in Australia, across the four recognised categories. The material is drawn from a recent review by the Australian Institute of Family Studies (AIFS 2013). The estimates of prevalence are based on respondent recall, using a number of questions. Estimated prevalence by type of abuse varies widely depending on the questions used to elicit responses and survey population. In general, the more questions used to explore the issue, the higher the rates that are reported, especially pertinent in relation to neglect or witnessing family violence.

It is clear from the Australian studies and the international literature (WHO 2010) that child maltreatment is not uncommon. It is experienced by at least 20 %

Table 10.3 Estimated rates of child maltreatment in Australia by type of abuse % (source study)

			Witness DV	Sexual abuse
	Physical abuse	Neglect	Emotional abuse	(3, 5, 6,7,9)
Prevalence	5.0–10 % (1,2,7,10,11)	1.6–2.7 % (10,11)	4.3–23.0 %	*M* 1.4–8 %, *F* 4–12 % penetrative
	18.0 % (8)	12.2 % (12)	(2,4,10,11)	*M* 5.7–16 %, *F* 13.9–36 % non-penetrative
Example of questions (related to childhood)	Were you physically mistreated	I was neglected (11)	Verbally abused	Penetrative sexual contact by family
	Harsh physical punishment effects till at least next day	Parents watched out for you, fed you, gave you attention (reverse-scored) (10)	Physical violence between adults caring for you	A range of specific sexual behaviours
	Deliberate physical injury by an adult	A number of Qs covering cognitive, emotional, physical and supervisory neglect (12)	Witnessed physical or sexual abuse of others in family	
	Physical abuse		Suffered humiliation, ridicule, bullying, or mental cruelty by a parent	
	Was parent physically violent?			
	Exposed to moderate to severe violent behaviours			

Source: AIFS (2013)

Source studies from which rates drawn

1. ABS (2005). $n=16{,}500$ (18+)
2. Cohen et al. (2006). $n=1{,}296$ (18–70) – community 'self-selected sample'
3. Dunne et al. (2003). $n=1{,}784$ (18–59)
4. Indermaur (2001). n = 5,000 (12–20 years)
5. Mamun et al. (2007). $n=2{,}578$ (21 years)
6. Moore et al. (2010). $n=1{,}745$ (24 years)
7. Mazza and Dennerstein (2001). $n=362$ (*F* 51–62 years)
8. Mouzos and Makkai (2004). $n=6{,}677$ (F 18–69 years)
9. Najman et al. (2005). $n=1{,}793$ (18–59)
10. Price-Robertson et al. (2010). $n=1{,}000$ (23–24 years)
11. Rosenman and Rodgers (2004). $n=7{,}485$ (20–24 years, 40–44 years, 60–64 years)
12. Straus and Savage (2005). $n=270$,81 % *F* (mean age 23 years)

of children in many developed western nations and considerably more in some countries and communities. The reported level of abuse and neglect suggests a rate of failure of families to provide a safe and nurturing environment for the child that poses a serious challenge for governments seeking to protect children, even recognising that not all maltreatment warrants state intervention.

It is possible to compare estimated prevalence rates with rates of child protection notifications. As reported in Table 10.2, 3.5 % of children attracted a child protection notification in 2012–2013 (ROGS 2014a). As notifications accrue across childhood up till age 17, cumulative rates of notification over a child's life will be several times the annual rate, suggesting a cumulative rate of at least 25 % (based on longitudinal cohort data for South Australia (SA)) (Delfabbro et al. 2010). Interestingly, it seems that the rate of children with a notification in Australia is in the same ballpark as reported rates of child maltreatment. While actual maltreatment and reports are unlikely to be exactly aligned, but with ~50 % of investigations resulting in a substantiation and most other reports referred for family support services, it seems that reports and maltreatment are likely in reasonable alignment. The fact that rates of notifications for Aboriginal and Torres Strait Islander children are several times higher is also consistent with indicators of higher rates of abuse and neglect in this population. For example, there are higher rates of hospitalisation for assault (in New South Wales the rate for Indigenous Australians is ~7 times that for non-Indigenous Australians at 5.1/1,000 vs. 0.75/1,000), and higher rates of imprisonment (in NSW the rate for Indigenous Australians is 14 times the non-Indigenous rate, 198.5/10,000 vs. 14.6/10,000), and there are patterns of very low school attendance (often <50 % of days attended) and low school retention (43 % to year 12 for Indigenous children in NSW compared with 76 % for non-Indigenous Australians) despite free education (AIHW 2013).

The Child Protection Response

Any serious attempt at case finding will identify at-risk children and families that are struggling, demanding a response from the child protection and family support system. The failure of so many families to create a safe and nurturing environment for their children creates a considerable challenge for government, but one that is ignored at its cost. The high risk of intergenerational abuse and neglect means that the problem will not resolve of its own accord. In fact, high rates of child maltreatment can be seen in part, as a reflection of past failures of the child protection and family support service system.

The approach to case finding sits within a wider response system and needs to be considered in the broader policy context. It is the suite of policies and how they are implemented, including the level of resourcing that will determine their effectiveness. Australia has adopted mandatory reporting across the country (albeit with jurisdictional variation in types of abuse covered and reporter categories), but what happens after the report is made will also have a major impact on the outcomes for children. Even given system variation, mandatory reporting would seem to offer the best chance of ensuring that serious cases are brought to the attention of the authorities for the purpose of protecting children.

The service response post report is highly variable across the country and even within jurisdictions depending on the abuse type. For example, the use of investigation and possible removal or 'dealt with by other means' such as diversion to family support programmes differs widely across jurisdictions. (In 2012–2013 reports dealt with by 'other means' accounted for 0 % in Queensland, 27.5 % in Western Australia, 48 % in NSW, 62 % in the Northern Territory, 72 % in SA, 74 % in Victoria and 83 % in the ACT and Tasmania (ROGS 2014a).) A recent inquiry into the child protection system in Queensland has recommended changes in that jurisdiction to bring it more in line with the other states (QCPCI 2013).

Expenditure per child in the population (aged 0–17) on various child protection activities varied hugely as is illustrated in Table 10.4. For example, expenditure on general child protection activities varied from $142 per child aged 0–17 in the ACT to 1,012 in the NT and on out-of-home care from $294 in Victoria to $1,204 in the NT and on intensive family support services from a low of $8.65/child in the NT to $89/child in NSW (ROGS 2014a, Table 15.A1). For children commencing family support services, spending varied from a high $35,000 per child in WA to only $3,588 per child in the NT (ROGS 2014a, Table 15.4). It is also clear that the translation between a notification, investigation and substantiation varies considerably across jurisdictions. For example, the ACT had the second highest rate of children in a notification at 76.8/1,000 but with less than a quarter subject to an investigation and 5.9/1,000 with a substantiation, contrasting with Queensland with only 19/1,000 notified but a similar 6.4/1,000 children with a substantiated investigation (see Table 10.4). The fact that there is such variation suggests considerable uncertainty about what is the best child protection system response. This level of variation provides a natural experiment ripe for study.

The wide variation in the child protection and wider system context with which the reporting system interfaces means that the context as much as the reporting mode itself will determine its performance (cost and effectiveness). And the variability in context is not even fully captured in the matters considered above. There is also the cost of delivery of child protection services, the operational model of service delivery, the skill level and competence of staff, ability to attract suitable carers into the foster care or kinship care system, quality of residential care, extent and quality of family support services and access to quality mental health services and early childhood services in the wider service system as well as within the child protection system.

Discussion

The underpinning causes of maltreatment dictate what is needed to disrupt current and future maltreatment. The extent to which the child protection system is reflective of that understanding will determine how effective it will be in working with

Table 10.4 Indicators of major child protection system differences across jurisdictions expenditure by broad activity category and rates of selected case finding actions 2012–2013

Jurisdiction	Expenditure $/head popn 0–17 years on child protection			Rates per 1,000 children 0–17			
	Receive notifications, conduct investigations, case management	Out-of-home care	Intensive family support services	Children notified	Children in completed investigation	Children in a substantiated investigation	Children in OHC on June 30
NSW	218	461	89.1	38.8	19.1	9.6	10.5
Vic	156	294	52.7	41.2	13.1	7.9	5.0
Qld	274	367	35.8	19.0	17.1	6.4	7.2
WA	223	371	50.2	22.7	15.8	5.0	6.3
SA	144	435	30.6	34.6	9.0	5.1	7.4
Tas	181	359	61.8	68.5	13.3	7.8	9.1
ACT	142	364	11.5	76.8	16.6	5.9	6.7
NT	1,013	1,204	8.7	104.4	43.9	19.0	11.8

Source: ROGS (2014a, Tables 15A.1, 15A.8, 15A.21)

these highly vulnerable families and children brought to their attention. A trauma-based explanation that understands maltreatment as part of a pattern of intergenerational abuse and neglect suggests a trauma-informed treatment response is required. This will differ markedly from a response where the underlying theoretical model presumes that a skills and knowledge deficit is the core barrier to safe parenting. While it is increasingly recognised that trauma will affect the capacity for parenting, this may look like a skills and knowledge deficit; but a simple educational or behavioural approach is unlikely to be successful and can even exacerbate the situation for the child if it is perceived by parents to be shaming and judging (Amos et al 2014a, b).

It is important that we get the child protection and wider service response right. Because of the severe consequences of child maltreatment, costs will be incurred by society *regardless* of the service response. It is rather a matter of *where* those costs fall, on which portfolio and programme area. Will it be the child protection and criminal justice systems, social security (income support), drug and alcohol services or hospital services? And who will primarily bear the costs, the child, the family or the community, and which government agencies and level of government? Table 10.5 provides a schematic representation of this observation.

A set of mutually reinforcing policy elements are necessary to effectively address the disturbing social problem of child maltreatment. No single policy lever will suffice and individual policy components can perform poorly or well, depending on other elements of the policy framework and level of resourcing. If a child protection system is under-resourced relative to rates of child abuse and neglect (serious enough to warrant intervention) and societal norms incorporate a concern for vulnerable and at-risk children, the system will almost certainly be overwhelmed, regardless of the reporting model. An overwhelmed child protection system only tells us that the system is overwhelmed, not whether the reporting system is wrong. Or the converse: if the child protection system is coping with current demands, it does not mean that the reporting system is right.

The balance of resourcing between case finding and family support is a matter of considerable interest. Case finding by itself does nothing to improve outcomes for children and families. It must interface with an effective evidence-based response model if child outcomes are to be improved. However, solving the problem of child abuse and neglect is highly complex, in part because the ideal place for any child is with their birth family *if* that setting can be made adequately safe and nurturing. Certainly experience of placing a child in an alternative environment where safety cannot be assured is the worst of all possible worlds. In short, determining the optimal policy mix and the role of mandatory reporting within that is challenging.

Conclusion

Many families struggle to provide the nurturing environment conducive to optimal or even 'good enough' child development and growth. And this cannot be ignored. Child abuse and neglect is a profound form of trauma with serious and wide-ranging

Table 10.5 Schema indicating cost consequences of child maltreatment under alternative policy scenarios

	Alternative policy scenarios		
Cost category	Minimal child protection response	Evidence-driven response: preventive/ family support[a]	Maximal response investigative/ OHC placement
Child protection/family support services			
Case finding (mandatory reporting or occupational policies+logging/triaging)	$	$$$	$$$
Family support services	$	$$$$$	$$
Investigation/court preparation, etc.	$	$$	$$$$$
Out-of-home care placement/case management	$	$$$	$$$$$
Consequences of abuse and neglect			
Mortality/morbidity (premature death, loss of quality of life/disability)	$$$$$	$$	$$
Health-care costs	$$$$$	$$	$$$
Criminal justice costs	$$$$$	$$	$$$
Welfare dependency/unemployment/loss to gross domestic product	$$$$$	$$	$$$
Intergenerational abuse cycle	$$$$$	$$	$$$
Drug/alcohol dependence, other risky behaviours	$$$$$	$$	$$$
Domestic violence	$$$$$	$$	$$$

[a]Assuming an effective evidence-informed trauma-focused service delivery model

consequences for the child, the family and society. The consequences of child maltreatment such as drug and alcohol abuse, mental illness, incarceration, failure in intimate relationships, teenage pregnancy, low educational attainment, welfare dependency, homelessness and involvement in crime are all predictors of maltreatment and perpetuate a destructive cycle of abuse and neglect, unless this can be disrupted with effective strategies. There is no advantage in finding children who are being maltreated if the outcomes for them and their family cannot be improved. Reflecting on previous failures with the removal of children and mixed success of family support programmes, we need better evidence of the capacity of the child protection system to improve outcomes for children and families.

The theoretical model that informs our understanding of maltreatment needs to be continually revisited to ensure it reflects current thinking on this issue. If this is not correct, it is unlikely that the child protection system will work effectively to protect the child or address the pattern of intergenerational abuse, a considerable preventive opportunity. There seems limited recognition in the child protection system and related policy context in Australia that child abuse and neglect is a form of trauma for the child, and that parents invariably suffer from their own unresolved trauma history.

We need to be asking: Where is the trauma-informed response to the children and the families involved in the child protection system? Who is doing routine mental health assessments for all children and parents involved with the child protection system and where is the evidence-informed treatment response? An emphasis on knowledge and skills and case management (FaHCSIA 2011) within a punitive framework such as income management (Macklin 2010) is simply to misunderstand these families. If the response system fails to acknowledge the high levels of mental illness, drug and alcohol abuse and unresolved trauma in this population of struggling parents, it will almost certainly fail.

That is, until there is a better understanding of the reasons for child maltreatment and its intergenerational pattern, the system will fail these most vulnerable of families with consequences also for the wider society. Current research adopting a trauma lens is of considerable interest (Amos et al. 2011; Amos et al. 2014a, b) but implies the need for longer-term intensive trauma-based psychotherapy services.

The sector requires highly trained professionals to deliver a quality service to what is a very challenging population. With increasing funding to the NGO sector, ensuring adequate skill levels, training and mentoring of staff will be critical. In order to devise an optimal system for responding to child maltreatment, we need to understand better what works for these families and put in place a system that is resourced to meet the needs, not just in terms of budget allocation but also in terms of a well-trained, highly skilled professional workforce that has the necessary level of mentoring and supervisory support.

Total costs of child maltreatment can be reduced over the longer term by adopting an evidence-based and cross-portfolio system response. Child maltreatment is too complex an issue for any single agency to carry; a number of programmes and agencies must work in concert drawing on a sound theoretical model and understanding of the genesis of maltreatment if we are to make progress.

References

ABS (Australian Bureau of Statistics). (2005). Personal safety survey. ABS. http://www.ausstats.abs.gov.au/ausstats/subscriber.nsf/0/056A404DAA576AE6CA2571D00080E985/$File/49060_2005%20(reissue).pdf

AIFS (Australian Institute of Family Studies). (2013). *The prevalence of child abuse and neglect*. Canberra: Australian Government. www.aifs.gov.au/cfca/pubs/factsheets/a144254/index.html. Accessed 30 Jan 2014

AIHW (Australian Institute of Health & Welfare. (2013). *Aboriginal and Torres Strait Islander Health Performance Framework 2012 report: New South Wales. Cat no IHW 88*. Canberra: AIHW.

Amos, J., Furber, G., & Segal, L. (2011). Understanding maltreating mothers: A synthesis of relational trauma, attachment disorganization, structural dissociation of the personality and experiential avoidance. *Journal of Trauma and Dissociation, 12*(5), 495–509. doi:10.1080/15299732.2011.593259.

Amos, J., Segal, L., & Cantor, C. (2014a). Entrapped mother, entrapped child: Agonic mode, hierarchy and appeasement in intergenerational abuse and neglect. *Journal of Child and Family Studies*. doi:10.1007/s10826-014-9950-3

Amos, J., Furber, G., & Segal, L. (2014b, December). An exposure and response prevention based treatment for chronic mother-child relational trauma, neglect and abuse: Parallel parent and child therapy (P-PACT). *Journal of Marital and Family Therapy* (submitted).

Anda, R. F., Felitti, V. J., Walker, J., Whitfield, C. L., Bremner, J. D., Perry, B. D., Dube, S. R., & Giles, W. H. (2006). The enduring effects of abuse and related adverse experiences in childhood: A convergence of evidence from neurobiology and epidemiology. *European Archives of Psychiatry and Clinical Neurosciences, 56*(3), 174–186.

Berry, M., McCauley, K., & Lansing, T. (2007). Permanency through group work: A pilot intensive reunification program. *Child Adolescent Social Work Journal, 24*(5), 477–493. doi:10.1007/s10560-007-0102-0.

Bowlby, J. (1982). *Attachment* (2nd ed.). New York: Basic Books. (First published 1969)

Brown, D. W., Anda, R. F., Tiemeier, H., Felitti, V. J., Edwards, V. J., Croft, J. B., & Giles, W. H. (2009). Adverse childhood experiences and the risk of premature mortality. *American Journal of Preventive Medicine, 37*(5), 389–396. doi:10.1016/j.amepre.2009.06.021.

Chapman, D. P., Dube, S. R., & Anda, R. F. (2007). Adverse childhood events as risk factors for negative mental health outcomes. *Psychiatric Annals, 37*(5), 359–364.

Cohen, R. A., Hitsman, B. L., Paul, R. H., McCaffery, J., Stroud, L., Sweet, L., Gunstad, J., Niaura, R., MacFarlane, A., Bryant, R. A., & Gordon, E. (2006). Early life stress and adult emotional experience: An international perspective. *The International Journal of Psychiatry in Medicine, 36*(1), 35–52. doi:10.2190/5R62-9PQY-0NEL-TLPA.

Delfabbro, P., Hirte, C., Rogers, N., & Wilson, R. (2010). The over-representation of young Aboriginal or Torres Strait Islander people in the South Australian child protection system: A longitudinal analysis. *Children and Youth Services Review, 32*, 1418–1425. doi:10.1016/j.childyouth.2010.06.011.

Drake, B. (1996). Unraveling "unsubstantiated". *Child Maltreatment, 1*(3), 261–271. doi:10.1177/1077559596001003008.

Drake, B., & Jonson-Reid, M. (2007). A response to Melton based on the best available data. *Child Abuse & Neglect, 31*, 343–360.

Dube, S. R., Miller, J. W., Brown, D. W., Giles, W. H., Felitti, V. J., Dong, M., & Anda, R. F. (2006). Adverse childhood experiences and the association with ever using alcohol and initiating alcohol use during adolescence. *Journal of Adolescent Health, 38*(4), 444.e1–444.e10. doi:10.1016/j.jadohealth.2005.06.006.

Duke, N. N., Pettingell, S. L., McMorris, B. J., & Borowsky, I. W. (2010). Adolescent violence perpetration: Associations with multiple types of adverse childhood experiences. *Pediatrics, 125*(4), e778–e786. doi:10.1542/peds.2009-0597.

Dunne, M. P., Purdie, D. M., Cook, M. D., Boyle, F. M., & Najman, J. M. (2003). Is child sexual abuse declining? Evidence from a population-based survey of men and women in Australia. *Child Abuse & Neglect, 27*(2), 141–152. doi:10.1016/S0145-2134(02)00539-2.

Edwards, V. J., Anda, R. F., Gu, D., Dube, S. R., & Felitti, V. J. (2007). Adverse childhood experiences and smoking persistence in adults with smoking-related symptoms and illness. *Permanente Journal, 11*, 5–7.

FaHCSIA (Department of Families Housing Community Service and Indigenous Affairs). (2011). *Fact sheet – Intensive family support services in the northern territory*. Canberra: Australian Government.

Fang, X., Brown, D. S., Florence, C. S., & Mercy, J. A. (2012). The economic burden of child maltreatment in the United States and implications for prevention. *Child Abuse & Neglect, 36*(2), 156–165. doi:10.1016/j.chiabu.2011.10.006.

Gilbert, R., Widom, C. S., Browne, K., Fergusson, D., Webb, E., & Janson, S. (2009). Burden and consequences of child maltreatment in high-income countries. *The Lancet, 373*(9659), 68–81. doi:10.1016/S0140-6736(08)61706-7.

Indermaur, D. (2001). *Young Australians and domestic violence* (Trends and issues in crime and criminal justice, no. 195). Canberra: Australian Institute of Criminology.

Kohl, P. L., Jonson-Reid, M., & Drake, B. (2009). Time to leave substantiation behind: Findings from a national probability study. *Child Maltreatment, 14*(1), 17–26. doi:10.1177/1077559508326030.

Macklin, J. MP. (2010). *The Bath inquiry into the Northern territory child protection system, Attachment B. Media Release*. Canberra: Australian Government. http://www.formerministers.dss.gov.au/14020/bath-inquiry-into-the-northern-territory-child-protection-system/. Accessed 20 Jan 2014.

Mamun, A. A., Lawlor, D. A., O'Callaghan, M. J., Bor, W., Williams, G. M., & Najman, J. M. (2007). Does childhood sexual abuse predict young adult's BMI? A birth cohort study. *Obesity, 15*(8), 2013–2110. doi:10.1038/oby.2007.250.

Mathews, B. P. (2012). Exploring the contested role of mandatory reporting laws in the identification of severe child abuse and neglect. In M. Freeman (Ed.), *Law and Childhood Studies* (pp. 302–338). Oxford: Oxford University Press.

Mathews, B., Payne, H., Bonnet, C., & Chadwick, D. (2009). A way to restore British paediatricians' engagement with child protection. *Archives of Disease in Childhood, 94*(5), 329–332.

Mathews, B., Walsh, K., Butler, D., & Farrell, A. (2010). *Teachers reporting child sexual abuse: Towards evidence-based reform of law, policy and practice (Report for New South Wales, Queensland and Western Australia)*. Brisbane: Queensland University of Technology.

Mazza, D., & Dennerstein, L. (2001). The physical, sexual and emotional violence history of middle-aged women: A community-based prevalence study. *MJA, 175*(4), 199–201.

Mikton, C., & Butchart, A. (2009). Child maltreatment prevention: A systematic review of reviews. *Bulletin of the World Health Organization, 87*, 353–361. doi:10.2471/BLT.08.057075.

Moore, E. E., Romaniuk, H., Olsson, C. A., Jayasinghe, Y., Carlin, J. B., & Patton, G. C. (2010). The prevalence of childhood sexual abuse and adolescent unwanted sexual contact among boys and girls living in Victoria, Australia. *Child Abuse & Neglect, 34*(5), 379–385. doi:10.1016/j.chiabu.2010.01.004.

Mouzos, J., & Makkai, T. (2004). *Women's experiences of male violence: Findings from the Australian Component of the International Violence Against Women Survey (IVAWS)* (Research and public policy series no. 56). Canberra: Australian Institute of Criminology.

Najman, J. M., Dunne, M. P., Purdie, D. M., Boyle, F. M., & Coxeter, P. D. (2005). Sexual abuse in childhood and sexual dysfunction in adulthood: An Australian population-based study. *Archives of Sexual Behavior, 34*(5), 517–526.

Norman, R. E., Byambaa, M., De, R., Butchart, A., Scott, J., & Vos, T. (2012). The long-term health consequences of child physical abuse, emotional abuse and neglect: A systematic review and meta-analysis. *PLoS Medicine, 9*(11), e1001349. doi:10.1371/journal.pmed.1001349.

Olds, D. L., Eckenrode, J., Henderson, C. R., Jr., Kitzman, H., Powers, J., Cole, R., Sidora, K., Morris, P., Pettitt, L. M., & Luckey, D. (1997). Long-term effects of home visitation on mater-

nal life course and child abuse and neglect: Fifteen-year follow-up of a randomized trial. *JAMA, 278*(8), 637–643. doi:10.1001/jama.1997.03550080047038.
Price-Robertson, R., Smart, D., & Bromfield, L. (2010). Family is for life: Connections between childhood family experiences and wellbeing in early adulthood. *Family Matters, 85*, 7–17.
QCPCI (Queensland Child Protection Commission of Inquiry). (2013). *Taking responsibility: A roadmap for Queensland Child Protection*. Brisbane: Queensland Child Protection Commission of Inquiry.
Reynolds, A. J., Temple, J. A., Robertson, D. L., & Mann, E. A. (2002). Age 21 cost-benefit analysis of the Title I Chicago Child-Parent Centers. *Educational Evaluation and Policy Analysis, 24*(4), 267–303.
ROGS (Steering Committee for the Review of Government Service Provision). (2003). Report on Government Services. Canberra: Productivity Commission. http://www.pc.gov.au/gsp/rogs/2003.
ROGS (Steering Committee for the Review of Government Service Provision). (2014a). *Report on government services 2014, volume C*. Canberra: Productivity Commission. http://www.pc.gov.au/gsp/rogs/community-services. Accessed 31 Jan 2014.
ROGS (Steering Committee for the Review of Government Service Provision). (2014b). *Report on government services 2014, Volume F*. Canberra: Productivity Commission. http://www.pc.gov.au/gsp/rogs/justice. Accessed 29 Jan 2014
Rose, G. (2001). Sick individuals and sick populations. *International Journal of Epidemiology, 30*(3), 427–432. doi:10.1093/ije/30.3.427.
Rosenman, S., & Rodgers, B. (2004). Childhood adversity in an Australian population. *Social Psychiatry and Psychiatric Epidemiology, 39*(9), 695–702. doi:10.1007/s00127-004-0802-0.
Segal, L. (2010). The role of government in preventative health: 'Nanny state' or redressing market and policy distortions. *Australian Medicine, 22*(4), 32–33.
Segal, L., Dalziel, K., & Papandrea, K. (2013). Where to invest to reduce child maltreatment – A decision framework and evidence from the international literature. In Appendix F in *Taking responsibility: A roadmap for Queensland Child Protection* (pp. 619–641). Brisbane: Queensland Child Protection Commission of Inquiry. http://www.childprotectioninquiry.qld.gov.au/__data/assets/pdf_file/0017/202625/QCPCI-FINAL-REPORT-web-version.pdf. Accessed 4 July 2013.
Shonkoff, J. P., & Garner, A. S. (2012). The lifelong effects of early childhood adversity and toxic stress. *Pediatrics, 129*(1), e232–e246. doi:10.1542/peds.2011-2663.
Shonkoff, J. P., Boyce, W. T., & McEwen, B. S. (2009). Neuroscience, molecular biology, and the childhood roots of health disparities: Building a new framework for health promotion and disease prevention. *The Journal of the American Medical Association, 301*(21), 2252–2259.
Straus, M. A., & Savage, S. A. (2005). Neglectful behavior by parents in the life history of university students in 17 countries and its relation to violence against dating partners. *Child Maltreatment, 10*(2), 124–135. doi:10.1177/1077559505275507.
WHO (World Health Organization). (2014). Child maltreatment fact sheet number 150. http://www.who.int/mediacentre/factsheets/fs150/en/. Accessed 30 Jan 2014.

Part III
Legal and Conceptual Debates/Issues

Issues concerning *legal and conceptual challenges* posed by the nature of the laws – e.g. problems in the concepts of ‘reasonable suspicion’, ‘reasonable belief’, ‘serious harm’, ‘significant harm’, and other definitional problems which cause uncertainty and may influence failure to report, and unnecessary reporting

Chapter 11
Neglect: Should There Be Mandatory Reporting?

Edward Goldson

Introduction

In the recent past, there has been discussion as to whether there should be mandatory reporting for child abuse and neglect, and most specifically whether there should be reporting of neglect. Worley and Melton (2013) maintain that mandatory reporting in general has not worked and that the concept is flawed. They maintain that it has not served to protect children nor to prevent child maltreatment. I would agree that there are a number of failures, but these are failures not because the concept is flawed. It is rather that the flaws and failures reside in the system designed to respond to the reports. The examples offered by the critics of reporting of inadequate resources and services currently available to Child Protective Services are well taken. However, this is a very different issue from doing away with mandated reporting. For example, one does not stop diagnosing autism because there are inadequate resources to meet the needs of children with that diagnosis. Does a physician not diagnose Tay-Sachs disease because there is no known cure? In the medical and child development arena, the answer would be no. What will be addressed in this chapter is a similar question. Namely, do you discard a concept because you have not put in adequate resources and thought to operationalizing it? Wald is more nuanced in his criticism of the results of policy of mandatory reporting, focusing on neglect as a great expansion from the original focus on severe abuse. It is easier to accept Wald's position that there needs to be changes in how the response,

Appreciation is extended to Howard Dubowitz MD and Donald Boss JD, PhD, for their contributions to the writing of this chapter.

E. Goldson, M.D. (✉)
University of Colorado School of Medicine, Children's Hospital Colorado,
13213E 16th Ave, Aurora, CO, USA
e-mail: Edward.goldson@childrenscolorado.org

B. Mathews, D.C. Bross (eds.), *Mandatory Reporting Laws and the Identification of Severe Child Abuse and Neglect*, Child Maltreatment 4,
DOI 10.1007/978-94-017-9685-9_11

treatment, and monitoring of neglect are organized. The question then becomes what do we do after we evaluate and diagnose neglect? (Wald 2013)

If one reviews the most recent reports from the National Child Abuse and Neglect Data System (NCANDS), neglect is considered a form of maltreatment. Moreover, it is the most commonly reported manifestation of child maltreatment (U.S. Department of Health and Human Services et al. 2012). At the same time, neglect presents the clinician with enormous challenges in terms of considering, identifying, evaluating, diagnosing, and managing this form of maltreatment. Moreover, it raises many questions about disposition and can involve the social, medical, and legal systems. Mandatory reporting becomes an even more challenging issue in the face of scarce resources and the fact that even in discussing and writing about neglect, it is often separated from abuse. For example, in discussing maltreatment, one usually hears the phrase "abuse and neglect" rather than child maltreatment. For some, neglect may not be as "serious" as inflicted trauma or sexual abuse (Wald 2013). For others, it may be considered the result of, or associated primarily with, poverty and the ripple effects of poverty, including poor access to health care, undernutrition, dysfunctional families, and toxic environments. Neglect is much more rarely associated with socioeconomically advantaged families (Slacks et al. 2004). Thus, neglect is considered by many not as a manifestation of "abuse" but rather a condition almost always resulting from poverty. In order to revisit mandatory reporting as an issue of controversy when neglect is suspected, it might be helpful to return to basic definitions of maltreatment and neglect more specifically.

Because the definition of "reportable" neglect became law across the USA early in the modern effort to address child maltreatment worldwide, early efforts at definition of both maltreatment generally and neglect specifically serve as a good beginning point for defining neglect that should result in a legal duty to address the plight of a specific child. Since the 1970s, notwithstanding variations, every state in the USA has a child maltreatment definition and a reporting system. The definition in the federal code published in 1974 was part of an early effort to "standardize" national definitions so that all the states would be more similar in their approach, and the early effort remains a simple statement for what has evolved in much of the USA as the definition of child maltreatment:

> "Child maltreatment" means the physical or mental injury, sexual abuse or mental injury, or maltreatment of a child by a person who is responsible for the child's welfare under circumstances which indicate harm or threatened harm to the child's health or welfare. (Federal Child Abuse Prevention Treatment Act 1974)

Because the American approach has based its definitions on child maltreatment, and child neglect, that might lead to reporting and even involuntary intervention by state child protection services agencies, American laws of reporting are frequently more detailed in terms of what is reportable child maltreatment and what is not. For that reason later in this chapter, we will return to the definitions of child maltreatment and neglect specifically.

Before looking to specific examples of neglect that are reportable in the USA, it should be noted that the framing and definition of maltreatment provided by the World Health Organization (WHO) (World Health Organization 1999) in the 1990s tends to parallel the original US national definition even while expressed in different languages:

> Child abuse or maltreatment constitutes all forms of physical and/or emotional ill-treatment, sexual abuse, neglect or negligent treatment or commercial or other exploitation, resulting in actual or potential harm to the child's health, survival, development or dignity in the context of a relationship of responsibility, trust or power.

In addition to this broad definition of child maltreatment, WHO provided a more focused definition of neglect:

> Neglect and negligent treatment
>
> Neglect is the failure to provide for the development of the child in all spheres: health, education, emotional development, nutrition, shelter, and safe living conditions, in the context of resources reasonably available to the family or caretakers and causes or has a high probability of causing harm to the child's health or physical, mental, spiritual, moral or social development. This includes the failure to properly supervise and protect children from harm as much as is feasible.

It should be noted that WHO also provides definitions of emotional abuse.[1] It can be argued, and it is the view of the author that many forms of maltreatment, whether characterized as physical abuse or neglect, can immediately and ultimately harm the child through a failure of caregivers, or society. Thus, neglect is a failure to provide not only the obvious necessities of life that include food, shelter, and health care but to look at children's rights more generally and address children's interests and even rights to an environment of emotional safety and development free from the injurious effects of factors such as a lack of access to society or exposure to "patterns of belittling, denigrating, scape goating, threatening, scaring, discriminating, ridiculing or other non-physical forms of hostile or rejecting treatment." In order not to enlarge the argument of this chapter, and thus risk distracting from the basic position taken here, that reporting of neglect is essential to children's safe and full development, this broader argument for a fuller appreciation and enforcement of children's rights will await another manuscript.

---

[1] Emotional abuse includes the failure to provide a developmentally appropriate, supportive environment, including the availability of a primary attachment figure, so that the child can develop a stable and full range of emotional and social competencies commensurate with her or his personal potentials and in the context of the society in which the child dwells. There may also be acts toward the child that cause or have a high probability of causing harm to the child's health or physical, mental, spiritual, moral or social development. These acts must be reasonably within the control of the parent or person in a relationship of responsibility, trust or power. Acts include restriction of movement, patterns of belittling, denigrating, scapegoating, threatening, scaring, discriminating, ridiculing or other nonphysical forms of hostile or rejecting treatment (Garbarino et al. 1986; Garbarino and Gilliam 1980).

Enforceable Definitions of Neglect: An Example

Turning back from the definitions offered from the international perspective by WHO, to a national perspective (that of the USA), what about the definition of neglect in a state or local environment? The World Health Organization and national legal standards defining neglect generally can be enforced only through voluntary or official actions taken in the community where a child lives. Given that the response to a report of child neglect is likely to be handled, if at all, within local communities, it is useful to examine what a local government has defined as enforceable standards of child neglect. After all, it is at the local level that enforcement of standards of care is realized as a practical matter. The law of the State of Colorado in the USA provides an example of enforceable definitions of neglect (Colorado Children's Code 2012):

> Colorado Revised Statutes §19-1-103(1)(a)(III) defines child neglect as, "Any case in which a child is a child in need of services because the child's parents, legal guardian, or custodian fails to take the same actions to provide adequate food, clothing, shelter, medical care, or supervision that a prudent parent would take." In addition, CRS 19-3-102 (1) (c) states that a child is neglected or dependent if, "The child's environment is injurious to his or her welfare."

Basically, the state's law defines child neglect as a failure on the part of a caregiver to provide basic things to the child that a prudent parent would provide to keep his or her child alive, physically healthy, and safe from harm. Carefully examined, these "basic things" are also essential for a child's survival. Child Protective Services breaks neglect down into six basic categories to help clarify different ways in which a caretaker may not be providing minimally well for the child. These categories are:

- Deprivation of necessities
- Injurious environment
- Educational neglect
- Medical care neglect
- Failure to protect from harm
- Lack of supervision/supervision inconsistent with child's needs

These named types of neglect can lead not only to a caseworker deciding that a child is neglected under the state's law, but can in theory lead to a judge deciding that a child is dependent or neglected because of one or more of these occurrences. These definitions can be usefully elaborated in turn.

A deprivation of necessities is probably what most people think of when they think of child neglect. In this category, a caretaker is neglecting a child by not providing necessary things like food, appropriate clothing, shelter, and a place to sleep. An injurious environment is an environment that is unhealthy or unsafe for a child. The child may not have been harmed yet from the environment, but the environment is such that if something is not done to change the environment or circumstances, or remove the child from the environment, the child is at risk of severe harm. Some factors that could create an injurious environment for a child would be domestic violence, parental drug and alcohol abuse, and uncontrolled, explosive, or violent behavior by a parent(s)/caretaker that another adult has not or cannot be expected to manage. The physical residence of the family might also create the injurious environment with conditions such as a bug or rodent infestation, animals that are not properly cleaned up after or cared for, rotting food, access to chemicals, exposed wiring or other hazards, piles of items that could fall and injure a small child, dirty diapers, piles of trash, etc. When looking at physical health or safety hazards to a child, Child Protective Services takes into account the safety hazards, as well as the ages of the children in the home.

Educational neglect occurs when a child is not receiving educational services because of an action or omission of the parent, not because of the actions of the child. Child Protective Services can work with the school district when dealing with allegations of educational neglect, and often these reports are first forwarded to the district attendance director for follow-up, as the attendance director has the ability to follow up with the family and even pursue court action if appropriate. In many communities, child protection services do not address school nonattendance but truancy is handled instead by the schools or law enforcement.

Medical neglect occurs when a parent or caretaker does not get a child needed medical attention, as determined by a medical professional. Medical neglect could include not getting a child treated for an injury or illness and also could include not getting a child needed dental care if that lack of dental care is seriously affecting the child's health, ability to eat, or if it will cause the child these kinds of problems in the future.

A parent or caretaker fails to protect a child when he or she knowingly allows someone else to harm or neglect the child. Failure to protect can also occur if a parent or caretaker knowingly allows the child to be unsupervised or inadequately supervised around someone who is known to have abused or neglected children previously or is known to be dangerous.

Lack of supervision or supervision inconsistent with a child's needs occurs when a parent or caretaker leaves a child alone and without an adequate older caregiver. The child's age and developmental level are crucial to determining if there is lack of supervision, along with the dangerousness of the immediate environment, regardless of whether or not the child is injured as a result. There is no specific age at which a child can legally be left alone in Colorado, and parents or caretakers must consider the choice to leave a child unsupervised for periods of time carefully. To elaborate, things that need to be taken into consideration include not only the child's chronological age but also the child's maturity level, resources, and ability to act in case of emergency. Other things to consider would be who else will know the child is alone, the presence of neighbors or relatives in close proximity who will check on the child, whether the child in question also is the child watching other children, whether the child knows where the parent or caretaker is and when they will return, and whether the child can contact the parent, caretaker, or other responsible adults easily if needed. Enforcement of this law has encouraged the development of Red

Cross courses that offer babysitting classes to children beginning at age 11. Given that the age of emancipation in Colorado is 18 years old, parents are responsible for the care of their children until the child is 18 years old.

The Clinical Presentation of Neglect

Physicians who diagnose and treat children are presented with many symptoms. Symptoms of severe neglect can include a child who is underweight for age, is experiencing poor growth, or who is diagnosable for failure to thrive. Among factors that might be provided when obtaining a child's medical history are consistent hunger, poor hygiene, and improper dress for the weather or setting. Unattended physical problems or medical needs, consistent lack of supervision, and even abandonment might be discerned.

Behavioral Indicators of neglect can include begging or stealing food, poor school attendance, constant fatigue, assuming adult responsibilities well beyond the child's capabilities, and developmental delays not otherwise explained.

Legal definitions can serve as guidelines for those working in the area of identification and management of children's health and behavioral health who are suspected of having been neglected. In addition, as will be noted later, these laws also set the stage for the concept of the rights of the child. Neglect of a child and, I would suggest, the failure to report neglect is one way of denying the child her or his rights. Before addressing that issue, however, there are nonlegal definitions of neglect that should inform medical practice. These pediatric definitions can be less detailed than the legal ones but nevertheless inform the way in which pediatrics frames the broad concept of neglect as it falls under the umbrella of child maltreatment. Central to the pediatric perspective is recognition that neglect can threaten or directly cause "harm to the child's health or welfare."

> Neglect occurs when those responsible at whatever level for meeting the basic needs of children fail to do so. (Helfer 1990)

> Neglect occurs when the basic needs of children are not adequately met, regardless of cause, resulting in actual or potential harm. (Dubowitz et al. 1993)

> Neglect as a form of child maltreatment is widely defined as the omission of proper care by caretakers and/or the community – either deliberate or due to extraordinary inattentiveness – that leads to avoidable suffering and/or failure in the child to reach her or his physical, intellectual and/or emotional developmental capacity. (Dubowitz et al. 2005)

From the pediatric perspective, there is no judgment as to which is "worse" physical abuse or neglect. Neglect can be just as negative, dangerous, and, at times, fatal as can any other form of maltreatment including inflicted trauma or sexual abuse. At the same time, neglect, as it is for any other manifestation of maltreatment, presents unique challenges to those working in this field. The prevalence of neglect raises obvious questions of limited resources.

Neglect from an Epidemiological Perspective

Recent data on the incidence of maltreatment as reported by the National Child Abuse and Neglect Data System (NCANDS) for the USA in 2012 reveals the following:

Incidence of child maltreatment, USA, 2012 (Child Maltreatment 2012)

Basic data	
Child population of 52 jurisdictions	74,577,627
Child population of 51 reporting jurisdictions	74,150,798
Reported unique children who	3,165,572
Received a CPS response	
Unique victims from reporting	678,810
Type of abuse	
Medical neglect	15,705
Neglect	531,241 (78.3 %)
Physical abuse	124,544 (18.3 %)
Psychological maltreatment	57,880 (10.6 %)
Sexual abuse	62,936 (9.3 %)
Perpetrator	
Mother	250,553
Father	127,654
Mother and father	132,557
Other (combinations)	46,894
Total parents	557,658 (81.5 %)
Total nonparent	81,816 (12.0 %)
Total unknown	44,774 (6.5 %)
Fatalities	
Child population of reporting states	72,483,465
Fatalities	1,593

These data confirm that neglect is the most common manifestation of child maltreatment identified and reported. This then leads us to return to the question of whether neglect should be reported using the usual models of reporting which tend to be categorical and adversarial. If the answer is "yes," then should the reporting mechanism continue with the current process? If the answer is "no," then should the reporting be different and the response different and what should be done to address the needs of the population of children who are neglected and not reported? What mechanisms are in place to protect them and thereby safeguard and preserve their rights as citizens of the country?

From the pediatric and epidemiological perspectives, the term neglect is an umbrella for various acts of omission and even commission, and this is codified in law to some extent at least in the State of Colorado. Thus, the encompassing pediatric definitions of child neglect easily include deprivation of necessities; the presence of an injurious environment or environmental neglect; medical, educational, and emotional neglect; the failure to protect a child; and a lack of supervision or supervision inconsistent with the child's needs or capabilities. The importance of neglect is demonstrated in a recent article in which Welch and Bonner (2013) reviewed child fatalities in Oklahoma spanning the years 1987–2008. During that period, they identified 372 deaths associated with neglect among children ranging from 0 to 17 years. The categories of death identified included supervisory/environmental neglect, deprivation of needs, and medical care neglect. Deaths associated with neglect occurred most commonly among boys (58.1 %), with 58.7 % of all of the deaths occurring among children ≤ 2 years of age. Women, in 80.4 % of the deaths, were the responsible party and in 71.2 % of the deaths it was the mother. The primary cause was supervisory/environmental neglect rather than deprivation of needs or medical neglect. The most common events associated with these deaths were unintentional drowning (23.9 %) and smoke inhalation (13.4 %). Of interest, 12.4 % of the children in the study had current involvement with Child Protective Services, and 41.9 % had had contact with another section or division in the Department of Human Services.

What can be learned from this study? It is currently the largest data set of child mortality associated only with neglect. Infants and young children require close supervision. This is driven home by deaths of children left at home without smoke detectors and those left unsupervised who drowned. Given that neglect can be fatal, and in many cases might be prevented, should neglect be regarded as a "less important" manifestation of child maltreatment? This translates to a policy in which children will be recognized as neglected, but not reported. Why not determine with greater reliability and validity if the most severe risk for neglect and nonfatal neglect can be identified so that death may indeed be avoided and further neglect be prevented?

How to Improve Policy and Practice: There Is Usually More than One Possible Approach

In the current framework, many assume that the result of the "systems" in play is that someone is culpable or responsible for the neglect. The newer model first subscribes to the view that neglect of a child's needs should be identified and shown as not being addressed for whatever reasons. Second, this model recognizes that there are multiple factors contributing to neglect while acknowledging parents and/or other caregivers often play a significant role (Dubowitz et al. 2005). In Dubowitz's model, the goal is not only in identifying neglect and making the appropriate authorities aware of its presence but working to avoid unnecessarily imputing blame. The proper focus should be to understand the causes of the neglect and to correct them. If we can understand the causes and conditions associated with neglect, which will be framed in terms of the child's needs not being met, then perhaps methods can be designed and supported to prevent or ameliorate the effects of neglect. This change of emphasis must recognize both the core elements and variations among current definitions while working to address how the concept of neglect is framed. The local conditions in which children are raised do vary from country to country, community to community, and from one socioeconomic class to another. The response to neglect will reflect the way a society or community perceives the child as an individual, not merely an appendage of others even in the midst of family, and the child's rights as being separate and unique from those of the parents or caregivers.

Dubowitz and his colleagues (2005) identify 12 types of basic needs which, if not addressed, constitute neglect. They include inadequate food, exposure to household hazards, inadequate personal hygiene, inadequate health care, inadequate mental health, inadequate emotional support and/or affection, inadequate parental structure and/or guidance, inadequate cognitive/stimulation/opportunity, unstable caregiver relationship, unstable living situation, exposure to family conflict and/or violence, and exposure to community violence and/or lack of neighborhood safety. These types of neglect can be used in an attempt to conceptualize neglect not as specific categories but from an ecological perspective, recognizing there are multiple and interacting factors that contribute to neglect and perhaps define it. One of the fundamental aspects of neglect that came out of this study was the concept of neglect as a continuum based on a variety of measures and reports from multiple sources including the parent and child.

Culture that Emphasizes the Rights of Children as Individuals Even While Living in Families

Embedded in the above framing of neglect is actually a list of children's rights. It is noteworthy that in the beginning of the twentieth century, before the Geneva Convention or the United Nations addressed the need for a declaration of children's rights, Janusz Korczak, a Polish pediatrician, spoke of the need for such a document. Korczak died in 1944 in Treblinka, one of the death camps in Poland. Before his death, he started to identify what those rights were. A partial list of these rights includes the child has a right to love, the child has a right to respect, the child has a right to optimal conditions in which to grow and develop, and the child has a right to an education (Lifton 1988). It is noteworthy that some 50 to 60 years later these values are again expressed, in more depth in the World Health endorsement of the Children's Bill of Rights.

The Children's Bill of Rights

April 20, 1996

We, Children from seven countries and three continents, having communicated with each other over the Internet, agree that the following are natural rights of Children all over the world, and hereby ratify them:

Articles of the Children's Bill of Rights

Section I: Articles that are implemented immediately

1. Children's universal rights

As compared to adults, children until the age of 18 have the right to receive special care and protection.

Children all have the same rights, no matter what country they were born in or are living in, what their sex is, what their race is, or what their religion is.

2. Right to inherit a better world

Children have the right to inherit a world that is at least as good as the one their parents inherited.

Children have a responsibility to think about how they will leave a better world to their children, and, when they become adults, they have the right and duty to act on this.

3. Right to influence the future

Children have the right to participate in discussions having to do with the directions our society is taking -- on the large political, economic, social, and educational issues and policies -- so that children can help create the kind of world they will grow up in.

Adults have an obligation to communicate their views of these large issues in terms that children can understand, and provide children with the same information that is available to all adults.

Children have the right to understand how things change within society, and to learn how to influence these changes.

4. Right to freedom of thought, opinion, expression, conscience, and religion

Every child has the right to express his or her opinion freely, and adults should address that opinion with the child in every decision that affects him or her. Children have the right to carry out research to help form these opinions.

Children have the right to express their views, obtain information, and make ideas or information known.

Children have the right to form their own views in matters of conscience and religion.

5. Right to media access

Children have guaranteed access to all important communications media so that they may communicate nationally and internationally amongst themselves and with adults.

6. Right to participate in decisions affecting children

Children have the right to participate in all committees and decisions that make plans and set policies that directly or indirectly affect children.

7. Right to privacy

Children have the right to privacy to the same extent adults have.

8. Right to respect and courtesy

Children should be treated with respect and courtesy by adults, as well as by other children.

9. Right to an identity

Children separated from their birth parents at birth or at an early age have the right to know that this happened. Children have the right to know their name, who their birth parents are, and when and where they were born.

10. Right to freedom of association

Children have the right to meet with others, and to join or form associations, equivalent to that held by adults.

11. Right to care and nurturing

Children have the right to have nurturing and caring parents or guardians.

12. Right to leisure and play

Children have the right to leisure, play, and participation in cultural and artistic activities. Children have the right to a enjoy at least a few hours every day when they are free from worries.

13. Right to safe work

Children have the right to be protected from work that threatens their health, education, or development.

Children have the right to have pocket money so that they may learn to manage money.

14. Right to an adequate standard of living

Every child has the right to a standard of living adequate for his or her physical, mental, spiritual, moral, and social development, no matter how wealthy his or her parents are.

15. Right to life, physical integrity and protection from maltreatment

Children have the right to be protected from all forms of maltreatment by any adult, including a parent. This includes but is not limited to: physical abuse, including torture, violence, hitting and slapping; harmful drugs, including alcohol and tobacco; mental abuse; and sexual abuse.

Infanticide is prohibited.
No child shall be forced into marriage.

16. Right to a diverse environment and creativity

Children have the right to have many different things, people, and ideas in their environment.

Children have the right to listen to music of their choice.

Children have the right NOT to have their creativity stifled.

17. Right to education

Every child has the right to education, education that aims to develop his or her personality, talents, and mental and physical abilities to the fullest extent, no matter how wealthy the child's parents are.

Education should foster respect for a child's parents, for the child's own cultural identity, language and values, as well as for the cultural background and values of others.

Children have the right to an excellent education in any school. Schools will differ not in the quality of the education they offer, but only in their philosophies of teaching, and what professional specializations they stress.

18. Right to access appropriate information and to a balanced depiction Of reality

Adults have the obligation to provide children with information from several different sources.

Children should be protected from materials adults consider harmful.

Children have the right to have reality presented to them in a balanced and accurately representative fashion.

19. Right not to be exposed to prejudice

Children have the right NOT to be taught that one group (racial, national, religious, etc.) is superior to another.

Section II: Articles that require social or national policies

20. The right to a clean environment

Children have a right to a clean environment (water, air, ground, sea).

21. Right to a small national debt

Governments and countries must decrease national debt which will have to be paid for by future generations.

22. Right to vote

Children over 14 have the right to vote on issues that directly affect children, in all local, regional, national and international elections.

23. Right to medical care

Children have the right to be kept alive and in the best health and medical care science can provide, no matter how wealthy their parents are.

24. Legal rights

Children accused of crimes have at least the same legal rights as adults.

No child shall be institutionalized against her or his will without due process rights.

25. Right not to participate in war

Young people under 21 have the right NOT to go to war. [17]

A review of the above statement by children from seven countries makes apparent that the rights articulated by Korczak, the World Health Organization, the United Nations Convention on the Rights of the Child, and the 12 needs identified by Dubowitz et al. have much in common. They all lead to the awareness that if children are denied basic rights to have their needs met, then by definition, they are being neglected. This is of course easy to say on paper, but how does it play out in the multiple countries and communities in the real world? Does it apply to all socioeconomic, racial, and religious groups? If one considers the literature on neglect, there is a common implication that neglect occurs primarily (and perhaps only) among the poor. There are data demonstrating that neglect occurs more commonly among the poor (Slacks et al. 2004). However, neglect does also occurs among the more advantaged in our communities, including failures to provide loving care and attention that are probably never reported. Why shouldn't emotionally unavailable parents, a lack of committed nurturing, and withdrawal of support constitute forms of neglect? How should the plight of "latchkey" children be characterized?

What of children who come home every day from school to empty if affluent homes with perhaps only a pre-prepared meal waiting to be warmed in the microwave? Can this also be considered a failure to meet the child's needs? These children might have their physical needs met, but what about their emotional and developmental needs? This behavior appears to be emotional neglect, as defined above.

Cultural and Policy Tradeoffs

The consequences of neglect and the consequences of not reporting neglect should be considered together. How serious are the effects of neglect versus the prevalence of harm to families due to intervention attempting to identify and help treat neglect? How much of the research now available on neglect has resulted from studies of children who were identified through reports of neglect, and how many resources flow to addressing neglect due to annual reports of the incidence and prevalence of neglect? There is much more research on the costs to children's health and well-being from neglect than research on the downsides from reporting, evaluation, and treatment, both when provided and not provided after a report.

An important place to begin the analysis on the importance of neglect for identified victims is to consider the impact of neglect on infants (Wotherspoon and Gough 2008). Infants from their birth learn affect regulation and are dependent on caretakers to help them modulate their responses to stress. The needs of the infant include a nurturing, responsive, consistent, and available caretaker, for as much time as possible. If caretakers are inconsistent, intrusive, or violent in their responses to the infant, or "merely" unavailable, the stress to the infant can be almost intolerable. Neglect at this age, aside from physical neglect (including under nutrition which can lead to death), is known to have adverse social, emotional, and intellectual consequences. Neglect occurs when the caretaker cannot or does not read the infant's cues and so is unable or unwilling to respond appropriately and contingently. Signs in infants having these experiences include inconsolable crying, passivity or listlessness, altered sleep patterns, feeding disorders – often associated with problems with digestion – and an absence or very limited repertoire of self-soothing behaviors. Among the consequences of emotional neglect are cognitive delays and poor academic functioning, social withdrawal, and poor peer interactions along with a greater incidence of internalizing problems such as depression and anxiety (Wotherspoon and Gough 2008). The early work on hospitalism by Rene Spitz (1946) and the later work by John Bowlby (1988) on the importance of attachment for normal instead of abnormal infant development both demonstrate that at least minimally competent, loving care that includes the characteristics just described is essential for good child development and can be the difference between life and death.

The effects of neglect extend beyond infancy, producing long-term consequences (Goldson and Bonner 2008). With or without experiences of neglect during infancy, older children can experience many forms of neglect including (1) a lack of adequate food and nourishment; (2) failure to support school attendance, achievement, and activities or allowing or encouraging truancy; (3) leaving children unattended, not providing adequate supervision, or failing to protect children from maltreatment or dangerous situations; (4) failure to provide safe housing or appropriate clothing; (5) failure to meet a child's needs for nurturance and interaction (see psychological maltreatment below); and (6) failure to adhere to medical or therapeutic procedures recommended for serious diseases, injuries, or emotional and behavior problems (Erickson and Egeland 2002). The experience of child neglect at different stages of development creates the risk of cumulative injury to development.

In many cases, infants and children suffer from several forms of neglect, concurrently, increasing the risk of serious consequences on the child's development and behavior. Although physical and sexual abuse currently receive more public and professional attention, the majority of substantiated cases of maltreatment in the USA are for a form of neglect or multiple forms of neglect (Welch and Bonner 2013).

Neglect can be chronic, such as long-standing lack of adequate nutrition or episodes of leaving children unattended for periods of time. This is an example that reflects the Dubowitz model which speaks to a failure of meeting the needs of the child. For example, data reveal children are most likely to die in child-set fires that occur when appropriate adult supervision is lacking (Bonner et al. 1999). Other forms of fatal neglect occur when caregivers fail to provide necessary medical care (Geffken et al. 1992) or fail to meet the nutritional and emotional needs of the child, resulting in failure to thrive (Oates and Kempe 1997).

Over the long term, the main focus in research on neglected children has been on physical and emotional neglect. In one of the first studies to specifically study neglected children, they were found to have learning problems, low self-esteem, and as they grew older, a high rate of delinquency (Steele 1977). Subsequent research showed that neglected children were less interactive with their peers (Hoffman-Plotkin and Twentyman 1984), were passive, tended toward helplessness in stressful situations, and evidenced significant developmental delays (Crittenden and Ainsworth 1989). They had severe language delays and disorders (Katz 1992) and experienced a significant decline in school performance upon entering junior high school (Kendall-Tackett et al. 1993). Longitudinal studies have shown the negative effects of physical neglect, particularly during preschool and primary grades for the children's school behavior (Erickson and Egeland 2002). These problems related to physical neglect continued into adolescence, with these youth having low school achievement scores, heavy alcohol use, and school expulsions and dropouts. Clearly, physical neglect can have devastating effects on children's and adolescents' functioning and adjustment.

In the past decade, studies have focused on the neurobiological consequences of maltreatment and suggest that maltreatment leads to compromised central nervous system and brain development (Perry 1997). Studies have documented impairments in physiological functioning (Lewis 1992) characterized by smaller intracranial and cerebral volumes in maltreated children with PTSD versus controls (DeBellis et al. 1999a, b). Perry (2002) discussed the severe, long-term consequences for brain function if a child's needs for stable emotional attachments, physical touch from primary adult caregivers, and interactions with peers are not met. He suggests that if the necessary neuronal connections are lacking, the brain development for both caring behavior and cognitive capacities is damaged in a "lasting fashion."

The current research reveals neglect is a major social problem affecting thousands of children across the USA. Those neglected children who survive have problems developing adequate confidence, concentration, and social skills necessary to successfully adapt to school and to develop and sustain interpersonal relationships (Erickson and Egeland 2002). Without appropriate intervention in the family and with the child, the prognosis for these children is guarded.

Expanding the discussion slightly, the effects of psychological maltreatment are often difficult to separate from those of other types of maltreatment, as children are often victims of multiple forms of abuse. Psychological maltreatment is considered by many professionals to be a core component of all forms of child abuse and neglect (Binggeli et al. 2001; Claussen and Crittenden 1991; Brassard et al. 1987). Findings from longitudinal, prospective research, cross-cultural research, and studies designed to compare the impact of different forms of abuse have served to support this concept and document the severe outcomes associated with chronic child neglect.

The Minnesota Parent-Child Project followed a cohort of children from birth to adulthood whose mothers were at risk for parenting problems (Egeland 1997; Egeland and Erickson 1987; Erikson et al. 1989). When compared with children from the control group, the maltreated children, including those who were psychologically maltreated, showed serious consequences. Children whose mothers were hostile or verbally abusive demonstrated anxious attachments, lack of impulse control, distractibility, hyperactivity, angry and noncompliant behavior, difficulty in learning and problem-solving, negative emotions, and lack of persistence and enthusiasm. However, the effects of a psychologically unavailable mother, i.e., one who denied emotional responsiveness to the child, was the most devastating. The outcomes for the children with psychologically unavailable caregivers included a decline in competency from infancy through the preschool years, anxious avoidant attachment, noncompliance, lack of impulse control, low self-esteem, high dependence, self-abusive behavior, and serious psychopathology. Other longitudinal studies have shown that parental rejection and lack of positive parent-child interactions are significant predictors of childhood aggression and delinquency (Lefkowitz et al. 1977; Loeber and Stouthammer-Loeber 1986).

Psychological maltreatment includes both acts of commission, i.e., parental hostility and verbal aggression, and acts of omission, i.e., parental neglect and indifference and denying emotional responsiveness to a child's cues. A multi-method study of dozens of anthropology studies found that parental rejection had negative effects on children in every culture and existed in many of the world's cultures (Rohner and Rohner 1980). Children who were rejected tended to be aggressive, have poor self-esteem, be emotionally unstable and unresponsive, and have a negative worldview.

Other research has compared the differential effects of psychological maltreatment with other forms of abuse. Claussen and Crittenden (1991) found that psychological maltreatment more accurately predicted problematic developmental outcomes than the severity of physical injury to the children, indicating that treatment plans should emphasize intervening in the psychological aspects of the child's environment. In comparing the effects of psychological maltreatment with those of physical and sexual abuse, studies have found strong associations between psychological maltreatment and bulimia (Rorty et al. 1994), depression, and low self-esteem (Briere and Runtz 1990; Gross and Keller 1992). While psychological harm is more difficult to observe and clearly document, research has established that it is a recognizable and serious condition that warrants increased attention to legal and child welfare policies and practices in order to intervene more effectively on behalf of children (Hart et al. 2002).

It is apparent from the evidence presented in the child maltreatment and child development literature that neglect, independent of other forms of maltreatment, is harmful to the physical, emotional, and cognitive development of individuals of all ages. It must also be considered that neglect is very heterogeneous and comes in many forms. In addition, neglect often appears concurrently with other forms of child maltreatment. Moreover, the outcome for these children is made worse if neglect is accompanied by other forms of maltreatment and/or if the neglect is chronic.

Much of what we know about the identification of many kinds of neglect, and its treatment, results from studies of children reported for neglect. Many children confirmed to be neglected receive little or no treatment, and neither do their parents. At the same time, a great number of neglected children and parents who neglect do receive treatment. Programs like Safe Care (Edwards and Lutzker 2008) have been developed specifically to respond to neglecting families and children, and the program is both successful and characterized as "evidence based." All of the families receiving intervention through the Safe Care program were referred after formal reports to child protection agencies. More recently, research has begun to determine if the intervention works with voluntary families. It is also suggested in the literature that if neglect can be prevented or identified early on, there is a greater chance for its effects to be ameliorated with intervention directed toward the victim as well as the individual responsible for meeting the child's needs. Another way of framing this issue would be to prevent neglect by closely attending to the needs of the child. If this is not possible, for any reason, then seeking to identify in what way the child's needs have not been met would be the first goal to assessing the nature of the neglect. The second would be to correct the failure to meet the child's needs in whatever way is possible. Thus, in most circumstances, a non-accusatory approach should be maintained whenever possible in working with those who are responsible for the care of the child. This approach is very different from what can occur in a child protection culture or system in which the responsible individual (or individuals) can be found "guilty" of an omission of care and punished rather than being offered voluntary or required treatment.

Central to addressing the failure to meet the needs of children is a longer and more complex framing and discussion of what we call neglect. The larger conversation should recognize that there is no "single" cause for neglect. There can be a single event that might lead to a child's death. However, a child's death due to neglect is imbedded in multiple contexts which are influenced by multiple conditions. If one were to follow the approach offered by Dubowitz and his colleagues, the identification of the risk factors associated with a failure to meet the child's needs becomes the point of evaluation, rather than waiting for a report to be submitted. Proctor and Dubowitz (2014) offer these types of facts as relevant for early identification of risk for neglect:

Societal context

- Poverty
- Child welfare and health professions

Community/neighborhood context

- Social capital

Family context

- Parent-child relationship
- Stressful life experiences
- Family chaos and violence

Individual parent factors

- Caregiver depression
- Substance abuse
- Isolation and lack of social support
- Developmental history, personality, and level of functioning
- Information processing

Child factors
Protective factors
General factors
Context specific factors

Needless to say, this is a long list to consider. However, it can be argued that if we do not consider these variables (factors), we will not truly be able to address neglect, and instead we may eventually become involved in an adversarial relationship resulting if those who are responsible for not meeting the child's needs have, for whatever reason, failed to do so. This latter approach is another and arguably better way to address the cultural and policy tradeoffs associated with addressing child neglect than eliminating child neglect reporting and hoping that communities will assume responsibility for preventing a sufficient number of individual children from neglect.

The Medical or Public Health Approach to Child Neglect

In considering strategies for evaluating and intervening in neglect, let us consider a more traditional medical context. If one is caring for a family with a child with a chronic illness, the categorical or individual systems approach is not effective. Central to meeting the needs of a child with a chronic illness is the model of collaborating rather than "accusing" or "blaming." One does not blame the child for being born prematurely, or for being an individual with Down syndrome or fragile X syndrome or for falling on the autism spectrum. One does not approach treatment by dividing the child into categories (mental health, developmental, physical) and addressing them individually, by "carving" the child up, but one rather seeks to understand all of the factors – medical, developmental, emotional, societal, institutional, and educational – that may have an impact on the child's well-being. This requires collaboration between the various stakeholders including the child's parents or caregivers. For example, the parent is not blamed if the child with chronic lung disease does not gain weight as well as one would like or expect. Instead one needs to consider the child's pulmonary status and function, the role it plays in her/his ability to feed without becoming fatigued or aspirating the food, and the strategies the parent may use in feeding the child and/or supporting the child in her/his activities, providing medication, rest, and encouragement. This is not to say the parent may not be contributing to the problem, but they are not "the culprit." The parents' role needs to be considered, but they should not be "blamed." On the contrary, the parents need to be included in the process of assessment and treatment and be involved in collaborating with physicians and therapists as they all seek to find ways to optimize the child's health and more specifically their pulmonary function. Furthermore, the parents would have to link with institutions and programs where they could access the services and resources necessary to sustain interventions and supports dedicated to helping the child and family address her/his medical, social, emotional, educational, and cognitive needs.

Let us then change the term "chronic lung disease" to "potential (at risk)" for neglect or a child who has been neglected. The risk factors associated with child neglect are listed above and are summarized here. The first would be the societal context which includes poverty and the organization of child welfare and health-care systems. Second is the community/neighborhood context which includes its social capital. Third is the family context which includes parent-child relationships, life experiences, family chaos, and violence. The fourth consists of individual parent factors including caregiver depression and substance abuse, isolation and lack of social support, developmental history, personality and level of functioning, and information processing. These factors may be independent of poverty and may play a role in neglect among the more affluent. These factors would also apply to the successful care of a child with a chronic illness (or even an acute illness). In our consideration of the burden of illness anywhere in the world, we do not discard certain conditions, i.e., intellectual impairment, systemic lupus erythematosus, recurrent urinary tract infection, epilepsy, etc. because they occur either frequently or infrequently. In addition, we do not blame the child or the parents for being sick. On the contrary, we seek to diagnose, evaluate, and seek to treat, such that the child can achieve optimal function and participation in her/his environment.

Taking into consideration the data already presented, I would suggest now is the time to reframe how neglect is conceptually addressed. Should we not move to an ecological view of neglect that eschews an accusatory, adversarial view as to who is culpable for the neglect, to one which asks the questions, how and why were the child's needs not met? How can that failure be corrected so that the child and her/his family have the opportunity to address the salient issues and to correct them? The basic reasons to identify risk factors associated with neglect and to report suspected or actual neglect are (1) to prevent neglect and (2) to ameliorate the negative consequences of neglect. Critical to achieving this goal is to bring all stakeholders, including parents, into a conversation that seeks to meet the needs of the child rather than place blame and exact retribution from those who have not met the child's needs. This is not trivial since we are talking about the most commonly occurring manifestation of maltreatment with the greatest number of children being affected. It has been reported that among very young children investigated by US welfare agencies for alleged maltreatment, there is persistence of mental health problems, and many opportunities for early identification and early intervention by effective parent-based programs are missed (Proctor and Dubowitz 2014). Thus, our current system is not necessarily working if we seek to achieve the goals noted above. This is not a function of mandated reporting. On the contrary, it is a function of the fact we have not considered other strategies to respond to neglect once it has been reported, recognizing that the current paradigm is inadequate and has not met the needs of these children and their families or other caregivers.

It is my opinion that neglect should be reported for the following reasons: First, if the risk for and recognition of neglect or suspected neglect does not take place, the child is left in a vulnerable position. The chances for future neglect and more devastating consequences increase (McCue et al. 2013). In a word, if the risk for neglect or the presence of neglect is not reported, or somehow identified, there is a significant chance that these children will "fall through the cracks" and suffer more severe neglect and perhaps experience other forms of maltreatment. Second, if the neglect is reported, there is a chance of preventing more damage and injury to the child and family. Third, with reporting and assessment, one has a greater chance to identify and understand the factors contributing to the neglect and thereby identify and access resources and supports that can correct or treat the circumstances that contributed to the failure to meet the child's needs. We have learned a great deal by conducting research with families reported for neglect, in terms of what interventions can help children receive ameliorative care and parents become better parents. Fourth, if the issues contributing to neglect can be addressed, then the negative consequences for the child and family can possibly be prevented or ameliorated. Reporting is never an easy task, even for the most experienced. Nevertheless, in order to accomplish the tasks identified above, some kind of report must be made. Usually, under the current system, a report suspecting neglect has occurred is made by a health professional, social worker, teacher, or other individual involved in the care of the child or associated with the child.

In most states in the USA, the law mandates that if one has reason to suspect maltreatment has occurred, a report should be made either to child protective services (CPS) or to a law enforcement agency. Most typically an investigation ensues, almost always with neglect cases evaluated by protective services, but often with an implicit goal of identifying the perpetrator (s) and bringing them to justice. Reporting by itself does not ineluctably lead to such a result, and we can change our individual behaviors and our cultures. By the nature of any system which frames neglect in strict categorical terms, we risk creating an adversarial encounter with the model of "guilty until proven innocent." Under these circumstances, someone must be "guilty" and punished. Supports are provided in many cases, although there is increasing evidence that referrals for interventions are not made, much less provided (Pietroantonia et al. 2013). Unfortunately, under the current system, we do not really meet the needs of many children nor those of their families. In addition, the system does not accept "risk" as a category. Thus, if one is concerned that the child, based on observation, past history, and/or report, is at risk for not having his needs met, there is really no recourse for prevention unless it is stated that the failure is suspected. (It should be noted that current experimentation with the Safe Care program is attempting to find out if "risk" cases, rather than "reported" cases, will benefit from the program.) Too often we are forced into being reactive rather than proactive with respect to neglect. We are not able to anticipate and respond to concerns formally unless there is enough to justify a report, rather than just a referral for services. As a result we often must wait until we suspect something untoward has occurred. Thus, what if we would agree under the facts of a specific case that there are risks of devastating consequences from a developing pattern of neglect and that generally clearly established and harmful neglect should be reported as neglect; but that the facts of the cases also merit a different approach than investigation and response to the failure to meet the child's needs? In a word, one would want to identify those at risk and prevent neglect rather than have to deal with the neglect after it has occurred.

If one again considers the rights of children, one must be mindful that every child has the right to be protected and to live in a safe environment. She or he has the right to be heard and to be respected. If we do not bring our concerns about neglect to the appropriate and responsible agencies in the community, we are denying a child his or her rights as a human being. This perspective seems to fit the goals of the relatively new approach to evaluating children at risk for or strongly suspected of not having their needs met through a process of "differential response" (Kyte et al. 2013). Differential response (hereinafter DR) under most of its definitions does not take place as a substitute for, or in the absence of, mandated reporting. In order for a Child Protective Service (CPS) to be considered a DR system, it must have the capability to provide both protection and other resources and approaches to evaluation and intervention. There is, in the most extreme circumstances, the protective and sometimes investigative mode which is the traditional CPS orientation.

The traditional approach when used under dire circumstances for the child is absolutely reasonable. On the other hand, there are circumstances when a "non-investigative" DR pathway should be employed. The response in a DR pathway is to engage the family in looking at the child's and family's needs, determining if they have been met; if they have not been met, how they can be met; and where they may be having difficulty or even failed. This pathway is family focused, rather than being primarily focused on the child and the injuries she/he has received. This pathway seeks to engage the family as well as other stakeholders as they seek, together, to address the barriers – environmental, emotional, financial, developmental, and educational. In other words, systematic steps are taken toward meeting the child's needs. This model reaches out for community resources to develop informal and formal support networks. This approach is far more complex than the traditional one, and a set of core values has been suggested (Kaplan and Mekel-Holguin 2008) to guide the development, implementation, and evaluation of the efficacy of the DR approach. These values include (a) engagement versus adversarial approach, (b) services versus surveillance, (c) label of "in need of services/support versus perpetrator," (d) encouraging versus threatening, (e) identification of needs versus punishment, and (f) continuum of response rather than one size fits all. The key to considering DR as a model for addressing the needs of children is clearly summarized in Kyte's article. "Differential response is a fairly new and innovative approach to responding to the dual mandate of CPS. While in some instances it becomes paramount for CPS to intervene in protection of the child. In other instances it becomes imperative to collaborate with the family and respond to their needs to ensure child well being. DR represents a compromise between competing tensions of child protection and family support by allowing CPS the flexibility to meet both of these mandates" (McCue et al. 2013, p. 130). I would also add that within this model, the institutions – legal and other agencies and professions – are held accountable for the process and the outcome and are themselves monitored.

In the 1970s the author was involved in a pilot program developed in a low income population to respond to all forms of maltreatment. The results from the program were never published, yet are worth describing briefly. Exactly 100 children who had been adjudicated as maltreated along with their families were referred to a hospital-based child development center by social services and the courts. The children, ages birth to 10 years of age, and their families were evaluated, their strengths and weaknesses assessed, and their needs identified. All families were assigned a social worker, and the children were referred for needed therapy, e.g., physical and speech therapy. Mental health supports were available to the adults, and the children had access to health care provided by three pediatricians involved in the program. Over a 2-year period, there was no recurrence of maltreatment, many of the mothers were able to leave abusive relationships, a number of the mothers completed their high school education, and many obtained satisfying work. Central to the concept of both this program and what the author understands DR to be is the needs assessment and the coordinated "wraparound" approach. The goal was to identify strengths, focus on them, and utilize them to positively influence behavior rather than to look for who was "guilty" or who was the "perpetrator" and punish them. In addition, access to consistent medical care was critical, which was what families reported to us. The fact that the physicians were an integral part of the program and communicated with other providers may well have been an important factor leading to success, at least in the short term.

This discussion has as its goal to ask the reader to rethink how neglect is defined and addressed within the context of the child's rights. A review of the current incidence data in the USA is presented demonstrating that neglect is the most commonly reported form of child maltreatment and acknowledging that neglect can be fatal. What is of significance is there are programs that demonstrate we can have a positive effect on neglect through mandatory reporting. Examples of these programs include the positive effect of Safe Care (Edwards and Lutzker 2008) and the program in Memphis developed by David Olds (Donelan-McCall et al. 2009). Donelan-Mcall et al. (2009) conducted the home visiting program at three experimental sites. The positive effects of this program, where they did not have official records from child protective services (CPS) but had striking evidence from children hospitalized for neglect. They found a four to five times greater mortality among children whose mother's had not been visited as compared to those who had been in the program. Thus, we have at least two evidence-based programs – Safe Care and the Olds study – demonstrating a positive effect of these kinds of interventions. Children and families would probably not have accessed these programs unless there had been mandatory reporting. Therefore, the idea that "there's nothing known that we can do" does not hold. These programs are not perfect and are not the end all with respect to neglect. What is being suggested here is a reframing of neglect appears to be in order, allowing a move away from a categorical approach to neglect with there being a perpetrator and victim. The new approach to child neglect would be addressed through the following questions. "How have the child's needs not been met" and "How can someone do something about this failure?" This approach moves from an accusatory and adversarial paradigm to one of collaboration and support for the child and family.

To advance the conversation, it is useful to incorporate the possibilities offered by new models of support and intervention. These include the relatively new approach called differential response (DR) and the developing Safe Care model. These programs may offer alternative means of immediately protecting the child or, when necessary, choosing traditional methods. With these possibilities in mind, CPS and other helping agencies can have the option to use less adversarial approaches to address the child and family's needs. The reader is encouraged to enter into open-minded discussions and consider other strategies to meet the needs of the child and family when neglect has occurred or a high risk of harm exists. It is not suggested that DR or any other single program is the only or final answer to this challenging work. There is much to be done to establish relative strengths and weaknesses of programs that are currently being replicated and, fortunately, also being evaluated as a matter of course and for quality assurance purposes. It will also be necessary to determine if this approach is cost effective, whether there are adequate resources to accomplish the required tasks, and to what extent such approaches can be utilized by most CPS agencies.

Are communities willing to expend the time, energy, training, and evaluation of preventive programs? There are multiple other questions to be raised about introducing different paradigms for preventing child neglect. It is a departure from the way we have been approaching neglect but one that needs to take place. New approaches become more pressing to the extent that the old approaches have not been working. This is not the time to not report or respond to neglect but rather a time to enforce the need to report. It is a time to rethink our approaches to identification, intervention, support, and ongoing monitoring and to evaluate new models that may be more effective, less adversarial, and which can establish more open lines of communication and collaboration. Just as abandoning hospitals and medicine in the late 1800s, due to the poor quality of both, would have slowed the scientific advances of modern medicine, it is likely that reducing identification and public recognition of child neglect by eliminating reporting would result in delayed understanding and investment in the problem. Neglect is challenging as its various manifestations are the result of the interaction between multiple cultural, social, political, psychological, medical, and legal factors. Child neglect has been largely ignored historically, and reporting raises awareness of child neglect within the consciousness, and perhaps even the conscience, of the community. Ignoring neglect by not reporting it does not really resolve the issue and, in reality, tramples on the rights and needs of the most vulnerable members of our community.

References

Binggeli, N. J., Hart, S. N., & Brassard, M. R. (2001). *Psychological maltreatment: A study guide*. Thousand Oaks: Sage.

Bonner, B. L., Crow, S. M., & Logue, M. B. (1999). Fatal child neglect. In H. Dubowitz (Ed.), *Neglected children* (pp. 156–173). Thousand Oaks: Sage.

Bowlby, J. (1988). *A secure base: Parent child attachment and healthy human development*. New York: Basic Books.

Brassard, M. R., Germain, R., & Hart, S. N. (Eds.). (1987). *Psychological maltreatment of children and youth*. New York: Pergamon.

Briere, J., & Runtz, M. (1990). Differential adult symptomatology associated with three types of child abuse histories. *Child Abuse & Neglect, 14*, 357–364.

Child Maltreatment. (2012). *National child abuse and neglect data system*. Washington, DC: U.S. Department of Health and Human Services.

Children's Bill of Rights. lenar@tenet.edu, or debivort@umd5.umd.edu

Claussen, A. H., & Crittenden, P. M. (1991). Physical and psychological maltreatment: Relations among types of maltreatment. *Child Abuse & Neglect, 15*, 5–18.
Colorado Children's Code (Titles 19–21). (2012). http://rchive.org/details/govlawcocode21121921
Crittenden, P. M., & Ainsworth, M. D. S. (1989). Child maltreatment and attachment theory. In D. Chcchetti & V. Carlson (Eds.), *Child maltreatment: Theory and research on the causes and consequences of child abuse and neglect* (pp. 432–463). New York: Cambridge University Press.
DeBellis, M. D., Baum, A. S., Birmaher, B., Keshavan, M. S., Eccard, C. H., Boring, A. M., Jenkins, F. J., & Ryan, N. D. (1999a). Developmental traumatology Part I: Biological stress systems. *Biological Psychiatry, 45*(10), 1259–1270.
DeBellis, M. D., Keshavan, M. S., Clark, D. B., Casey, B. J., Giedd, J. N., Boring, A. M., Frustaci, K., & Ryan, N. D. (1999b). Developmental traumatology Part II: Brain development. *Biological Psychiatry, 45*(10), 1271–1284.
Donelan-McCall, N., Eckenrode, J., & Olds, D. L. (2009). Home visiting for the prevention of child maltreatment: Lessons learned during the past twenty years. *Pediatric Clinics of North America, 56*(2), 389–404.
Dubowitz, H., Black, M., Starr, R. H., Jr., & Zuravin, S. (1993). A conceptual definition of child neglect. *Criminal Justice and Behavior, 20*, 8–26.
Dubowitz, H., Newton, R. R., Litrownik, A. J., Lewis, T., Briggs, E. C., Thompson, R., et al. (2005). Examination of a new conceptual model of child neglect. *Child Maltreatment, 10*(2), 173–189.
Edwards, A., & Lutzker, J. R. (2008). Iterations of the SafeCare Model: An evidence based child maltreatment prevention program. *Behavior Modification, 32*, 736–756.
Egeland, B. (1997). Mediators of the effects of child maltreatment on developmental adaptation in adolescence. In D. Cicchetti & S. L. Toth (Eds.), *Rochester symposium on developmental psychopathology, volume VIII. The effects of trauma on the developmental process* (pp. 403–434). Rochester: University of Rochester Press.
Egeland, B., & Erickson, M. (1987). Psychological unavailable caregiving. In M. R. Brassard, R. Germain, & S. N. Hart (Eds.), *Psychological maltreatment of children and Youth* (pp. 110–120). New York: Pergamon.
Erickson, M. F., & Egeland, B. (2002). Child neglect. In J. E. B. Myers, L. Berliner, J. Briere, C. T. Hendrix, C. Jenny, & T. A. Reid (Eds.), *The APSAC handbook on child maltreatment* (2nd ed., pp. 3–20). Thousand Oaks: Sage.
Erikson, M. F., Egeland, B., & Pianta, R. (1989). The effects of maltreatment on the development of young children. In D. Cicchetti & V. Carlson (Eds.), *Child maltreatment theory and research on the causes and consequences of child abuse and neglect* (pp. 647–684). New York: Cambridge University Press.
Federal Child Abuse Prevention Treatment Act 42. United States Code 5106g(4): 1974
Garbarino, J., & Gilliam, G. (1980). *Understanding abusive families* (p. 7). Lexington: Lexington Books.
Garbarino, J., Guttman, E., & Seeley, J. (1986). *The psychologically battered child: Strategies for identification, assessment and intervention* (p. 5). San Francisco: Jossey-Bass.
Geffken, G., Johnson, S. B., Silverstein, J., & Rosenbloom, A. (1992). The death of a child with diabetes from neglect: A case study. *Clinical Pediatrics, 31*, 325–330.
Goldson, E., & Bonner, B. L. (2008). Child maltreatment: Developmental consequences. In M. L. Wolraich, D. D. Drotar, P. H. Dworkin, & E. C. Perrin (Eds.), *Developmental-behavioral pediatrics: Evidence and practice* (pp. 699–709). Philadelphia: Mosby/Elsevier.
Gross, A. B., & Keller, H. R. (1992). Long-term consequences of childhood physical and psychological maltreatment. *Aggressive Behavior, 18*, 171–185.
Hart, S. N., Brassard, M. R., Binggeli, N. J., et al. (2002). Psychological maltreatment. In J. E. B. Myers, L. Berliner, J. Friere, et al. (Eds.), *The APSAC handbook on child maltreatment* (2nd ed., pp. 79–103). Thousand Oaks: Sage.

Helfer, R, E. (1990). The neglect of our children. *Pediatric Clinics of North America, 37*, 923–942

Hoffman-Plotkin, D., & Twentyman, C. T. (1984). A multimodal assessment of behavioral and cognitive deficits in abused and neglected preschoolers. *Child Development, 35*, 794–802.

Kaplan, C., & Mekel-Holguin, L. (2008). Another look at the national study on differential response in child welfare. *Protection Children, 23*, 5–21.

Katz, K. (1992). Communication problems in maltreated children: A tutorial. *Journal of Childhood Communication Disorders, 14*(2), 147–163.

Kendall-Tackett, K. A., Williams, L. M., & Finklehor, D. (1993). Impact of sexual abuse on children: A review and synthesis of recent empirical studies. *Psychological Bulletin, 113*, 164–180.

Kyte, A., Tocmė, N., & Chamberland, C. (2013). Evaluating where we're at with differential response. *Child Abuse & Neglect, 37*, 125–132.

Lefkowitz, M., Eron, L., Walder, L., et al. (1977). *Growing up to be violent: A longitudinal study of the development of aggression*. New York: Pergamon.

Lewis, D. O. (1992). From abuse to violence: Psychophysiological consequences of maltreatment. *Journal of American Academy of Child and Adolescent Psychiatry, 31*, 383–391.

Lifton, B. J. (1988). *The king of children: The life and death of Janusz Korczak*. New York: St Martin's Press.

Loeber, R., & Stouthammer-Loeber, M. (1986). Family factors as correlates and predictors of juvenile conduct problems and delinquency. In M. Tonry & N. Morris (Eds.), *Crime and justice, an annual review of the research* (7th ed., pp. 29–149). Chicago: University of Chicago Press.

McCue, S., Hurlburt, M. S., Heneghan, A., Zhang, J., Rolls-Reutz, J., Landsverk, J., & Stein, R. E. K. (2013). Persistence of mental health problems in very young children investigated by US child welfare agencies. *Academic Pediatrics, 13*, 524–530.

Oates, R. K., & Kempe, R. S. (1997). Growth failure in infants. In M. E. Helfer, R. S. Kempe, & R. D. Krugman (Eds.), *The battered child* (5th ed., pp. 374–391). Chicago: University of Chicago Press.

Perry, B. D. (1997). Incubated in terror: Neurodevelopmental factors in the "cycle of violence". In J. D. Osofsky (Ed.), *Children in a violent society* (pp. 124–149). New York: Guilford.

Perry, B. D. (2002). Childhood experience and the expression of genetic potential: What childhood neglect tells us about nature and nurture. *Brain & Mind, 3*, 79–100.

Pietroantonia, A. M., Wright, E., Gibson, K. N., Alldred, T., Jacobson, D., & Niec, A. (2013). Mandatory reporting of child abuse and neglect: Crafting a positive process for health professionals and caregivers. *Abuse & Neglect, 37*, 102–109.

Proctor, L. J., & Dubowitz, H. (2014). Child neglect: Challenges and controversies. In J. E. Korbin & R. D. Krugman (Eds.), *Handbook of child maltreatment* (pp. 27–61). Dordrecht: Springer (In Dubowitz, H. (2013). Neglect in children. *Pediatric Annals, 42*, 73–77).

Rohner, R. P., & Rohner, E. C. (1980). Antecedents and consequences of parental rejection: A theory of emotional abuse. *Child Abuse & Neglect, 4*, 189–198.

Rorty, M., Yager, J., & Rossotto, E. (1994). Childhood sexual, physical, and psychological abuse in bulimia nervosa. *American Journal of Psychiatry, 151*, 1122–1126.

Slacks, K. S., Holl, J. L., McDaniel, M., Yoo, J., & Bolger, K. (2004). Understanding the risks of child neglect: An exploration of poverty and parenting characteristics. *Child Maltreatment, 9*, 395–408.

Spitz, R. A. (1946). Anaclitic Depression. *Psychoanalytic Study of the Child, 2*, 313–342.

Steele, B. F. (1977, February). *Psychological dimensions of child abuse*. Paper presented to the American Association for the Advancement of Science, Denver, CO.

U.S. Department of Health and Human Services, Administration for Children and Families, Administration on Child, Youth and Families, Children's Bureau. (2012). *Child maltreatment*.

Wald, M. S. (2013). Taking the wrong message: The legacy of the identification of the Battered child syndrome. In R. D. Krugman & J. E. Korbin (Eds.), *C. Henry Kempe: A 50 year legacy of child abuse and neglected* (pp. 89–101). Heidelberg/New York/London: Springer.

Welch, G. L., & Bonner, B. L. (2013). Fatal child neglect: Characteristics, causation and strategies for prevention. *Child Abuse & Neglect, 37*, 745–752.

World Health Organization. (1999, March 29–31). Report on the Consultation on Child Abuse Prevention Geneva.

Worly, N. K., & Melton, G. B. (2013). Mandated reported laws and child maltreatment: The evolution of a flawed policy response. In R. D. Krugman & J. E. Korbin (Eds.), *C. Henry Kempe: A 50 year legacy to the field of child abuse and neglect* (pp. 103–118). Heidelberg/New York/London: Springer.

Wotherspoon, E., & Gough, P. (2008). *Assessing emotional neglect in infants*. Centre of Excellence for Children's Well-Being (CECW) Information Sheet #59E. Toronto: University of Toronto, Faculty of Social Work.

Chapter 12
Mandatory Reporting and the Difficulties Identifying and Responding to Risk of Severe Neglect: A Response Requiring a Rethink

Bob Lonne

Introduction

Neglect of children is a significant social issue worldwide and is typically the most frequently reported form of maltreatment in Western nations, with its severe forms sometimes resulting in significant illness and disablement or death. Yet, paradoxically, it remains 'neglected' and largely in the shadow of physical and sexual abuse, often being viewed as less serious despite the real-life consequences of its insidious and compounding nature and the lasting damage it causes to intergenerational familial relationships and the life outcomes of those affected. This chapter explores the many complex forms of child neglect, its causes and impacts and the strategies to prevent it.

In particular, a critical standpoint is taken in analysing the rationale and merits of mandatory reporting of neglect and their effects, systemically and for children. It is argued that with respect to neglect, and severe neglect in particular, that mandatory reporting is counterproductive to our efforts to prevent maltreatment because it has too many unintended consequences that hinder system and family responses to access necessary preventative programs and supports, particularly concerning the social structural factors at play. Examples are used to highlight the characteristics of system failures regarding severe neglect and to understand why our reporting system responses can fail. Finally, key practice and policy issues regarding mandatory reporting of severe neglect are unpacked and examined, exploring the ways in which we can enhance our efforts to prevent child neglect, render support in timely and effective ways and thereby protect children from its more profound impacts.

B. Lonne (✉)
Faculty of Health, School of Public Health and Social Work, Queensland University of Technology, Brisbane, QLD, Australia
e-mail: b.lonne@qut.edu.au

B. Mathews, D.C. Bross (eds.), *Mandatory Reporting Laws and the Identification of Severe Child Abuse and Neglect*, Child Maltreatment 4,
DOI 10.1007/978-94-017-9685-9_12

What Is Neglect?

Differing Social Constructions

Despite long-standing attention there is not yet available a universally accepted definition of 'neglect', although Dubowitz (2007) rightly notes that there is 'a surprising level of agreement about what constitutes neglect' (p. 604). Essentially, definitions of neglect are socially constructed and are, therefore, dependent upon localised individual, collective and normative processes that take account of a diverse array of considerations (Dubowitz 2012; Horwath 2007; Moran 2009; Tanner and Turney 2003). These include cultural, religious, community and societal beliefs, values and ethics, not to mention a myriad of interpretations applied to specific behaviours and events and their situational and circumstantial contexts.

Many personal, professional and organisational influences are at play when practitioners make determinations about neglect, with one study identifying that the assessment task is as much a practice – moral activity as a technical – rational one, that is, both their head and heart are used in the process (Horwath 2007). Moreover, many of those with an interest in determining whether or not social interventions should be undertaken come from different organisational and disciplinary backgrounds with their own distinct discourses and perspectives (Horwath 2007). Hence, what is defined as neglect in one community may not be defined as such in another, even though they are in the same country or region, perhaps with a shared language and other cultural characteristics.

Neglect is a global term for quite different phenomena. Stein et al. (2009) identified important differences in the way neglect might be defined at the various stages of childhood, positing that more age-sensitive definitions were required. Scott (2014) in an Australian Institute of Family Studies (AIFS) review identified neglect types including physical, supervision, medical, educational, abandonment and emotional which have distinct aetiologies.

Further, the characteristics and causes of neglect are dissimilar to physical abuse and sexual abuse in particular ways including its sometimes chronic nature; definitional difficulties that mean its occurrence is less binary compared to abuse; different intentions of parents/carers; and that neglect increases the risk of exposure to other forms of harm (Mennen et al. 2010; Scott et al. 2012). Neglect is also harder to prove than abuse incidents because it requires establishing that something is missing and that its absence will cause an observable harm or risk of harm in the future, a feature that makes reporting potentially speculative. These differences require differentiated responses, whereas most child protection systems treat them as the same.

Viewpoints about child abuse and neglect are evolving and highly contested within social policy, not the least because of the variety of understandings about children and their needs, the role of the state in ensuring their safety and well-being and families' rights to privacy (Ferguson 2004). Nigel Parton (2006) has explored various social constructions of children and childhood in England and how these have changed over time, along with understandings of child abuse and neglect and governance of the family. He noted heightened social surveillance and wider regulation and intervention into families under the rubric of protecting children from risk of harm within 'the preventive state'.

Many organisational and legislative definitions of neglect are actually contained within broad definitions of 'child abuse and neglect' with no attempt to distinguish these different concepts. Despite these differing social constructions and definitional issues, there is a dominant theme within most definitions of neglect, and this is the assigning of responsibility and fault with the parent/carer. This blaming aspect is problematic (Dubowitz 2013; Harries and Clare 2002) because it individualises the events and places responsibility for social structural factors with parents/carers and, arguably, hinders them taking up voluntary support services. Whilst it is evident that finding fault with parents is more likely to occur in situations where their own actions are central to the maltreatment, what is at issue here is the extent to which this happens within forensic approaches to child protection. The emphasis placed on blaming here stems from the deficit-oriented features of such investigatory systems (Lonne et al. 2009) and leads to many service users feeling stigmatised and fearful (Shemmings et al. 2012), which is quite different to their typical responses when voluntary services are provided through differential response approaches (Kyte et al. 2013; QUT and Social Research Centre 2013; Winkworth et al. 2010).

Nonetheless, fault is present in criminal legislation in many jurisdictions, particularly with severe neglect being a criminal offence (Mathews and Bross 2014). Fault, or at least a 'failure' to provide the child with a basic necessity, is also implied in definitions used in professional circles. For example, the US National Child Abuse and Neglect Data System defines neglect as 'a type of maltreatment that refers to the failure by the caregiver to provide needed, age-appropriate care although financially able to do so or offered financial or other means to do so' (see American Humane Society 2014). The Australian Institute of Family Studies (AIFS 2014) refers to neglect as 'the failure by a parent or caregiver to provide a child (where they are in a position to do so) with the conditions that are culturally accepted as being essential for their physical and emotional development and wellbeing'. Finally, the Department of Children and Families Connecticut (2014) defines neglect as 'the failure, whether intentional or not, of the person responsible for the child's care to provide and maintain adequate food, clothing, medical care, supervision, and/or education'.

Uncertainty and Complexity in Determinations of Neglect

In many ways, dealing with neglect captures many of the tensions, challenges and complexities of working in child protection. Neglect is a very complex phenomenon to definitively determine (Dubowitz 2007; Gaudin 1999; Mennen et al. 2010; Stoltenborgh et al. 2013) and personal beliefs play a role (Horwath 2007). A recent meta-analysis of prevalence rates in 13 studies of physical neglect and 16 of emotional neglect found 'a disturbingly high prevalence of physical neglect (163/1,000 cases) and emotional neglect (184/1,000 cases)' (Stoltenborgh et al. 2013, p. 354).

There are, however, a multitude of definitional, methodological and data system issues present, and comparing different studies is not a precise science as assumptions do need to be made in reaching conclusions (Gilbert et al. 2009a; Scott 2014; Stoltenborgh et al. 2013). Nonetheless, this meta-analysis puts neglect in the vanguard to protect children and reflects its dominance as a maltreatment type within formal child protection data around the globe (AIHW 2013; Child Trends 2012; Gilbert et al. 2009b, 2011; Mennen et al. 2010; Stein et al. 2009; US Department of Health and Human Services 2010).

When operationally defining neglect we must take into account a messy and uncertain interplay of risk indicators at the child, family, community and societal levels, knowing that these are understood within a normative framework of what is 'reasonable' in light of the circumstances and the general expectations of relevant social roles, such as being a father and mother. Dubowitz (2013) has depicted neglect as being on a continuum, with 'optimal' and 'grossly inadequate' being polar ends, and determinations of adequate care being variable dependent upon a range of contextual factors. Where exactly the threshold point is for severe neglect is unclear, and the available literature tends to focus on those matters that entail children's deaths or significant illness and disablement, but does not provide much guidance on the many other examples of neglect that entail a potential risk for dire consequences but no actual current presentation of serious harm.

The development of poor care events into neglect and the emergence of signs of demonstrable harm is an insidious process. The challenge of identifying the early signs of neglect, and particularly severe neglect, in advance of tangible signs and outcomes of harm is very difficult indeed and may be impossible. There is a huge difference between the prospective and the retrospective as we shall see later in some tragic examples.

The consequences of neglect are sometimes profound and are often experienced well after the neglectful event or behaviour occurs (Gaudin 1999; Gilbert et al. 2009a, b). Tanner and Turney (2003) identify that neglect can be occasional and reactive or entail a sustained and chronic breakdown in the relationship of care. Scott et al. (2012) highlight that when making determinations about neglect, we need to take into account both the level of severity and chronicity along a continuum and to also assess the cumulative effects of multiple relatively low-level events that may compound over time. For example, a lack of emotional response from a parent may not be significant if it is a one-off event, but continuing emotional absence can have significant impacts on children.

Moreover, neglect does not just concern what someone, typically a parent or carer, has done to a child in a particular situation or over time, such as recklessly placing them in harm's way, but what they also might not have done but should have. Hence, acts of commission as well as omission are relevant, but always within a normative understanding as to what was the 'proper thing to do' – what ought to have been done in the particular circumstances but was missing.

The parents'/carers' failure to provide an appropriate aspect or level of care for a child of a particular developmental level also entails the assignment of responsibility upon the parent/carer to do so in order to prevent unwanted and potentially dangerous events occurring. Here the concept of risk plays a central part. That is, the neglect must involve either a demonstrable and significant negative consequence upon the child's health and well-being or an unacceptable risk of this eventuating. Determining prospective risk is replete with suppositions about future events or impacts that might, or might not, be able to be reliably and accurately measured, but are nonetheless perceived as real.

These usually entail moral judgments about the level of adult behaviour and responsibility displayed by the carer, a key feature of many definitions. Assigning responsibility can also spill over into blaming parents, which can hinder the opportunities for working collaboratively with health and welfare professionals (Shemmings et al. 2012). In light of this, Dubowitz (2013) has argued for definitions of neglect to focus on when a child's basic needs are not being met rather than parental omissions. Yet, there are limits to moral expectations of parents because neglect also entails definitions and assessments about 'good enough care' rather than a good or high standard of care.

In its more severe examples, though, neglect may entail a legal and criminal response such as when there has been a 'failure to provide the necessities of life', or the neglectful act is deemed to have entailed a degree of behaviour, or the consequences are so serious as to constitute criminal negligence. The task of setting these standards is one shared by many within particular cultures, communities and societies. This includes extended family, elders, community leaders and people of eminence such as the judiciary and health and welfare professionals. Gender is often at the heart of these frameworks for child-rearing behaviours and caring, with women usually carrying primary caregiving roles. On the broader front there is the United Nations Convention on the Rights of the Child that sets particular standards and which most nations have ratified (Reading et al. 2009).

There is 'strong evidence linking neglect to poverty' (Dubowitz 2007, p. 605; Carter and Myers 2007; Jonson-Reid et al. 2013). This factor makes for real complexity when trying to determine whether children are being neglected because of their parents'/carers' actions or primarily because of social and economic deprivations. For example, McSherry (2007) and Dubowitz (2007) explored the issues surrounding a 10-year-old caring for younger siblings due to their parents being at work and identified many grey areas in determining whether or not neglect was occurring and even whether this may in some circumstances be the 'lesser of two evils' and a positive learning experience for the child in the caring role.

Cultural relativism is also at play when matters of child abuse and neglect are at issue (Gilbert et al. 2011; Reading et al. 2009). There is any amount of evidence from around the globe that illustrates the critically important part that culture plays in the determination of what does, and does not, constitute a situation of child abuse and neglect (Dubowitz 2012; Jonson-Reid et al. 2013; Saunders et al. 1993), although some US studies have identified general agreement about what constitutes neglect across different racial/ethnic and socio-economic groups (Dubowitz et al. 1998).

Of particular note are the issues that arise for immigrants, people of colour and indigenous peoples as well as other groups who are socially excluded, such as people with intellectual and mental health disabilities, and single parents, particularly those households headed up by women (Bilson et al. 2013; Daniel et al. 2010; Child Trends 2012; Gilbert et al. 2011; Gillespie et al. 2010; Kaplan 2013; Jonson-Reid et al. 2013; LaLiberte and Lightfoot 2013; MacLaurin et al. 2005; McConnell 2013; Saunders et al. 1993; Scott 2014). These groups experience overrepresentation in most child protection and welfare systems and in the case of indigenous peoples profound overrepresentation. Whilst the reasons for indigenous overrepresentation are complex and interrelated, the Australian Institute of Health and Welfare (AIHW) has identified one of the factors as 'perceptions arising from cultural differences in child-rearing practices' (2012, p. 14). There are major social, economic and health disparities evident for indigenous peoples that both contribute to this overrepresentation and are also made worse by it (see Steering Committee for the Review of Government Service Delivery 2013).

Neglect is the most frequently reported type of harm for indigenous Australian children (AIHW 2013, p. 54). The largest groups of notifiers are primarily those who are subject to mandatory reporting requirements: police, school authorities and health and welfare personnel (AIHW 2013, p. 55). Recent Australian inquiries into state child protection systems have identified the increasing overrepresentation of Aboriginal and Torres Strait Islanders, despite a raft of policies aimed at reducing it (Cummins et al. 2012; Queensland Child Protection Commission of Inquiry 2013; Wood Inquiry 2008). Further, aggregated child protection data identifies increasing overrepresentation of Australia's indigenous children who are subject to reports of alleged maltreatment, substantiated harm and children under orders and in alternative care – their overrepresentation increases the further they progress into the care system (AIHW 2013). The situation is similar in Canada for First Nations children (Blackstock et al. 2004; Gillespie et al. 2010; Sinha et al. 2010, 2011) and elsewhere (Child Trends 2012; Gilbert et al. 2011).

This overrepresentation by reporting and intervention systems should not be viewed as arbitrary. Rather, these are patterns associated with poverty, marginalisation and race, and we find that groups with these characteristics find themselves targeted within our reporting systems – that is, they are significantly overrepresented and, as we shall see later, increasingly so as they go further into the care system. Mandatory reporting within such systems cannot be properly seen as a benign policy affecting all equally, but should be seen as part of an overall system that accentuates overrepresentation for groups that already experience substantial inequality and disadvantage (Bywaters 2013). One could perhaps conclude differently if mandatory reporting and investigation led to effective helping that specifically addressed the influential social structural factors, but they do not and are instead fashioned around individualising the matter and emphasising interventions that reinforce parental responsibility within a blaming and stigmatising orientation.

Moreover, not only are these social structural dimensions not taken account of and corrected within our mandatory reporting systems, they are reinforced by it, with a preponderance of reporters being those who are required either legislatively or organizationally to report suspected harm (AIHW 2013). The evidence overall is strong that the overrepresentation results from more than just social disadvantage (Doolan et al. 2013; Sinha et al. 2011; Steering Committee for the Review of Government Service Delivery 2013), although some evidence is mixed (Sinha et al. 2010). These situations are very difficult for people and groups feeling alienated and distrustful of societal support structures, even to the point of being unwilling to access needed assistance, particularly if they fear being reported to child protection authorities and losing their children (Bilson et al. 2013). This is an important point and highlights the inadvertent consequences of mandatory reporting, namely, that such approaches promote investigation but are far less successful in providing helpful assistance and guidance to struggling families, particularly when they fall just short of the reporting thresholds or just short of being a substantiated outcome and therefore remain ineligible for ongoing support.

In this author's view, when determining whether neglect of children is occurring and its level, a range of contextual factors are pertinent, such as the:

- Child's characteristics, including their age, developmental level, vulnerability and the presence of any special needs, particularly disability
- Levels of capacity of the parent/carer, including their maturity, mental health, resourcefulness and commitment to their children's well-being
- Severity and chronicity of neglectful events and the risk of cumulative harm
- Approaches taken to child-rearing practices within the family, cultural group and community, including influences such as ethnicity, religion and gendered responsibility
- Family environment, including relationship quality and the levels of conflict and interpersonal violence present
- Community context, including the relative levels of poverty and social exclusion experienced by particular groups; the access to resources, supports, and services; and the perceptions of safety and well-being within the neighbourhood
- Actual harm experienced and the risk of potential harms evident, neglect often involving an insidious process of harm accumulation over time

Before examining the merits of mandatory reporting for neglect, including its severe manifestations, it is important to understand the diversity found across the various types, forms and continuum of neglect, which is often conflated within the literature into a global maltreatment category. It is argued that this can result in a loss of the different aetiologies present and a push for generalised interventions that take no account of these important differences. Moreover, the complexities inherent when making prospective assessments of risk of future harm and outcomes are often ignored within assessments where the thresholds for intervention are blurry at best and assumptions about the supposed predictability of relatively low-level neglect escalating to become severe. Further, as described earlier, those needy families that fall just short of the mandatory reporting and investigation thresholds often find themselves ineligible for supportive services, or more often, health and welfare staff are focused on reporting the matter rather than offering direct universal support (Daniel et al. 2010). In this chapter the argument is made that in light of the difficulties and unreliability of such professional assessments, that mandatory reporting of neglect and severe neglect are counterproductive.

Types of Neglect and Impacts

The literature suggests many different types of neglect and specific forms within each of these; however, there are various findings regarding the ability to accurately assign particular impacts to specific acts, types and forms of neglect (Jonson-Reid et al. 2013). Indeed, most professional literature on neglect depicts it as a global category of maltreatment, with the sequelae undifferentiated as to their origins and specific types of neglect or abuse (Gaudin 1999; Gilbert et al. 2009b; Stoltenborgh et al. 2013). This reflects and compounds the 'neglect of neglect' within the literature and hinders recognition of its impacts (Dubowitz 2007; McSherry 2007; Stoltenborgh et al. 2013). Further, there are numerous definitional and methodological variations that make it hard to compare research findings (Dubowitz 2012; Gilbert et al. 2009b; Stein et al. 2009; Stoltenborgh et al. 2013; Tanner and Turney 2003).

Scott's review (2014) highlighted the frequently identified types as:

- Physical
- Supervisory
- Medical
- Educational
- Abandonment
- Emotional neglect

Physical Neglect This pertains to the child's needs for adequate food, nutrition, clothing and shelter. Each of the forms within this type of neglect is distinguishable and has different impacts, but is nonetheless viewed as the 'necessities of life', and parents/carers are deemed responsible to provide them. Yet, the linkage here to poverty is clearly apparent, and parents may be unable rather than unwilling to do so. Severe neglect will often be associated with physical neglect and entail serious consequences for children's health and well-being, including death or significant illness and disablement.

Supervisory Neglect According to Scott et al. (2012, p. 6), supervisory neglect occurs when 'inadequate supervision leads to or has the potential to lead to harm to the child. The difficulty in adequately defining supervisory neglect is compounded by a lack of clarity of what constitutes adequate supervision in a given situation, combined with the lack of clarity in defining neglect'. It entails inadequate supervision for a relatively short period where there are unacceptable risks of harm for the child, such as young children being unsupervised around water or a dependent child being left alone at home whilst the parent is elsewhere. For example, recent studies of fatal maltreatment identified supervisory neglect as critical in determining child drowning as neglect rather than 'accidents' (Damashek et al. 2013; Welch and Bonner 2013). Determination of supervisory neglect is dependent upon a range of factors including the child and parent/carer's abilities, capacity (including impairment) and relationship; accessibility of help and resources; the danger present and potential consequences; and the nature of the circumstances in which the supervision was inadequate.

Medical Neglect This entails a failure to provide appropriate and necessary health care in a timely manner, which has a material impact on the child's health, and where a reasonable parent would have sought such care. It can involve medical recommendations being ignored and treatment not being accessed, but, again, it is not straightforward as not all recommendations for treatment are essential, not all parental behaviour will have a significant impact on the child, and poverty may be a factor in making medical care unaffordable. Religious beliefs may also be present, and many states in the USA, for example, allow religious exemptions in their civil codes for child abuse and neglect (Dubowitz 2013), although most other jurisdictions around the world do not.

Educational Neglect Scott (2014) has identified this as a failure to provide a child with 'an education and the necessary tools to participate in an education system' (p. 4), where parents/carers take decisions to either prevent the child accessing education or support the child's decision to refuse to attend school. Educational neglect can result in significant detriment to a child's life chances of securing sustainable employment and may trap them into ongoing poverty, which is also an important factor for consideration because low-income households may not have the resources available to adequately support children's education. We will later examine high-profile Australian cases where educational neglect was at issue.

Abandonment This involves a parent/carer leaving a child alone or in the care of another person for a lengthy period and either a prolonged separation or severing of the relationship with the child. In essence, the child is left to their own devices to care for themselves, or is left with an inappropriate person who has an uncaring relationship with them, or who does not have the capacity or commitment to undertake a caring role.

Emotional Neglect This occurs when there is significant inconsistency in, or the absence of, nurturance and affection within the caring relationship to the point where the parent/carer is unable to meet the child's needs. Research indicates that its impacts can be very severe upon the child's emotional and psychological health and well-being and their social development (Dubowitz 1999; 2013; Gaudin 1999; Gilbert et al. 2009a, b; Stoltenborgh et al. 2013), as well as the ongoing familial relationships and children's behaviour and identify formation, particularly with attachment disorders (Crittenden 1999; Howe et al. 2000). Longer-term effects include adolescents demonstrating a higher likelihood of substance abuse, risky and aggressive behaviours and poorer physical and mental health (Gaudin 1999; Scott 2014; Stoltenborgh et al. 2013). However, there are considerable methodological limitations in the research undertaken of emotional neglect, and further detailed studies are required to fully understand the short-term and long-term impacts (Gaudin 1999).

Longer-Term Impacts The literature identifies that effects can be compounding and cumulative, with a multifarious array of harm sometimes evident and featuring physical, emotional, psychological and relational aspects. Damage to a child's emotional and psychological well-being can occur, leading to difficulties developing wholesome relationships with others (Crittenden 1999; Howe et al. 2000; Tanner and Turney 2003), with failure in parent–child attachment being replicated across generations (Reder and Duncan 2001). There is evidence that children who were neglected are more likely than others to experience poor economic circumstances as adults and to need higher levels of social support (Gilbert et al. 2009a; Scott 2014; Stoltenborgh et al. 2013). However, these consequences are often insidious and only become clearly evident over the long term, making earlier predictions difficult.

What can also occur is an intergenerational transmission of powerful life narratives that children build to explain and understand themselves, their situations and relationships. These can entail an overt sense of hopelessness and despair, becoming a pervasive influence through life because the messages they contain are used to guide their interactions with others, their feelings about themselves and their emotional investments into relationships. The sorts of narratives can include messages such as:

- 'I am unloved and unlovable'.
- 'I am damaged goods, needy, vulnerable and downtrodden'.
- 'Family members will always hurt you, and they only like you when they want something'.
- 'People cannot be trusted as they will always let you down and use you'.
- 'There is no use trying as you can never get ahead'.
- 'My life will never get any better because people like me are destined to be losers'.
- 'For people like me, life is full of tragedies and disappointments. That's just the way it is and will always be'.

Carrying these sorts of negative narratives can have the effect of sapping their energy for living a full and rewarding existence – their life force is reduced by powerful self-messages that make it difficult to aspire or to see a better future. Hence, mental health issues are observable, including PTSD and substance abuse, along with relationship difficulties and other adverse outcomes (Gilbert et al. 2009b; Jonson-Reid et al. 2013). It is unsurprising that their lack of trust in others and reduced life expectations should spill over into their relationships with health and welfare personnel who intervene in relation to their care of their own children (Crittenden 1999; Howe et al. 2000; Tanner and Turney 2003).

Why Does Child Neglect Happen?

The early work of Crittenden (1999) and Dubowitz (1999) was important in developing conceptual understandings about why people neglect children and shaping intervention approaches, such as working in the longer-term rather than brief interventions (Jonson-Reid et al. 2013; Tanner and Turney 2003). Putting aside the already identified issues around definitions and the types of neglect, and the influence of poverty, there are a number of reasons postulated for neglect occurring.

Tanner and Turney (2003, pp. 27–29) identified the causes as being within the intrapersonal, interpersonal, social and ecological domains. These are too complex and interrelated to go into detail within this chapter, but generally involve the following factors, and typically there are multiple combinations at play:

- Personalistic – e.g. immaturity, sense of powerlessness
- Psychiatric/psychological – e.g. information processing, mental health and substance abuse, learned helplessness
- Psychological/psychosocial – family functioning, communication, conflict resolution, leadership, role and characteristics of extended family
- Attachment – e.g. disordered parent–child relationships
- Child development – e.g. impacts of developmental history and disability
- Sociological – e.g. poverty, social exclusion, community impoverishment
- Ecological – interplay between the intra- and interpersonal and social/societal factors
- Parental environment – links between parental skills, social support, resource management

The literature indicates that a range of typical factors, whilst not necessarily causal, can affect how chronic and severe neglect manifestations may present, including parent/carer illness and mental health disability, alcohol and drug abuse, child illness and disability, low income, ethnicity, domestic violence, prior history of maltreatment and being in care and poor access to social supports (Daniel et al. 2010; Dubowitz 1999, 2007; Fallon et al. 2013; Gilbert et al. 2009a, b; Jonson-Reid et al. 2013; Kaplan 2013; LaLiberte and Lightfoot 2013; McConnell 2013; McSherry 2007; Saunders et al. 1993; Scott 2014; Sinha et al. 2010, 2011; Stoltenborgh et al. 2013).

Most families, at one stage or another in their history, experience significant events or stressors that either challenge or overwhelm their own resources and lead them to seek support and assistance from family, friends, neighbours and community (Melton 2010). This is part and parcel of living within a web of social care in a community or neighbourhood. However, neglecting families often have limited access to support sources, either because of damaged relationships and engagement with others or reduced community capacity resulting from poverty and social exclusion.

Crittenden (1999) highlighted that notwithstanding the presence of macro factors such as poverty and social marginalisation, parents/carers have critical responsibilities which they fail to uphold, whether it be due to psychological/emotional matters or otherwise. She proposed three 'forms' of neglect, namely:

- Disorganised
- Emotional
- Depressive

These partly result from parents'/carers' interpersonal problems, leading to a failure to establish and maintain relationships with their children that are productive, nurturing and enduring. Importantly, the underlying problems need to be addressed for the neglecting behaviour to change and for the caring relationships to be refashioned and renewed, if not restored. This requires longer-term interventions that are empathic and supportive rather than brief, incident-specific ones (Dubowitz 2013; Jonson-Reid et al. 2013; Scott 2014; Tanner and Turney 2003).

Disorganised Neglect These families typically have multiple life problems and respond chaotically and primarily through displaying highly variable emotional feelings and affect that create unpredictable responses to, and relationships with, the children in their care. Children learn to exaggerate their emotional responses and develop reactive relationships. Intervention is challenging and focuses upon structured involvements that seek to reassure, support and provide guidance to enable the parent/carer to become cognitively organised and to regulate their emotions (Scott 2014).

Emotional Neglect According to Crittenden (1999), this is least likely to be associated with poverty and is notable by parent/carer behaviours and relations that are primarily cognitive and do not engage with emotional and affective responses but instead focus on meeting children's physical and material needs and adherence to normative rules and expectations. Hence, these families do not necessarily attract adverse attention as the emphasis on compliance with rules, achievement and independence in the children can come across as 'normal' and mask the lack of emotional content within the relationships (Scott 2014). Chastisement of overt emotional responses can be common. Crittenden (1999) argued for further research on intervention efficacy and that these should aim to have the child remain within the home so that they do not feel separation stress and further abandonment.

Depressive Neglect This is the most common form of neglect, with families appearing passive, disengaged and disinterested in change or ameliorative interventions. Their life narratives reflect ever-present struggle to address the needs of the children and they 'doubt that anything will change the current situation' (Scott 2014, p. 12). Parents/carers are frequently unresponsive to environmental cues or pressures, and their children's needs and demands are frequently ignored (Crittenden 1999). Hence, particularly when children are very young, their basic physical and emotional needs can be left unaddressed, resulting in them learning to shut out their own feelings and wants and become passive and unresponsive (Scott 2014). If chronic, depressive neglect can result in cumulative harms and a potential, in its severe forms, to result in death, significant illness including malnutrition and disablement. Interventions are aimed at both reshaped cognitive processes and learning new behavioural processes and structures and addressing the mental health sequelae in therapy and with medical assistance.

What Is Severe Neglect?

The significant difficulties in prospectively determining the existence and future consequences of severe neglect in any given case have been outlined as well as the problems with assigning parental neglect. In contrast, there is less uncertainty when there is substantial evidence of current severe neglect, for example, in cases of profound malnutrition. Ambiguities become less of an issue, albeit within a continuum that nonetheless does not have clear thresholds. Rather, the term 'severe' depicts events and outcomes that clearly do not meet community standards and which have wholly unacceptable and serious consequences for the child's health and well-being. For the purposes of this chapter, and based on Dubowitz's work (2013), I have defined severe neglect as occurring when:

> A child's basic needs are not met and present a serious threat for the child's health and wellbeing, with high and unacceptable risk of, or demonstrable impacts including, death or significant injury, illness and disablement. The impacts upon the child have a significant disabling effect upon their short-term or long-term physical, emotional and psychological wellbeing, and profoundly affect their capacity to engage in emotionally nurturing social and familial relationships.

This definition tries to steer away from the negative implications of accentuating parental/carer responsibility and fault which, as Dubowitz (2013) acknowledges, can have detrimental effects upon engagement with them that hinders or prevents the effective helping relationships and interventions. This compounds the fact that some parents/carers have great difficulty in developing trusting relationships with health and welfare professionals. Nonetheless, most definitions of neglect, particularly criminal ones, do assign culpability and an associated allegation of fault. Perhaps more importantly, mandatory reporting approaches and subsequent forensic investigation can be perceived as coming from such a position because they embrace an individualisation of neglect situations, hold parents/carers entirely responsible for addressing it and simultaneously minimise or ignore the social and structural dimensions.

The argument here strongly promotes families receiving supports and assistance to address the contributing factors and impacts of severe neglect. However, there are consequences from going down the path of delivering services only following a report and investigation, usually a substantiated one, with attendant stigmatisation and reinforcement of negative life narratives. Reporting is not a benign process of inquiry resulting in better access to services for needy people. There is evidence of investigators being confrontational and disrespectful communicators, which fosters parental alienation (Shemmings et al. 2012). Investigation can also lead to service user hostility and suspicion that child protection workers have acted unethically concerning private information parents provided (QUT and Social Research Centre 2013). Too often investigation results in limited or no support being provided other than the reporting (Daniel et al. 2010; Melton 2005). Further, it affects trust levels in the practitioner–service user relationship when the former has made the mandated report (Harries and Clare 2002; Steinberg et al. 1997), potentially damaging the take-up of available support.

Severe and fatal neglect involves a range of types (Welch and Bonner 2013) including starvation and malnutrition; inadequate shelter, clothing and control of the climate and environment; failing to provide adequate supervision and guidance to a child resulting in serious injury from foreseeable environmental dangers and causes; abandonment that places the child at risk of significant harm; and failing to provide a child with affection and nurturance sufficient to meet their emotional and relational needs, which has a significant impact upon their psychological and social well-being and behaviour.

These examples are determined in line with local community norms and standards, but because the consequences are severe, they will likely involve statutory interventions that are based on legal definitions in keeping with community child development and protective expectations (Scott 2014). Hence, interventions do not occur randomly or arbitrarily but, rather, on a clear legal definition outlined in local statutes.

Severe Neglect Examples

Understanding the types and nature of severe neglect can assist in understanding how policy and practice failures occur, but also what the system limitations are. Two high-profile Australian tragedies illustrate different aspects of the types and forms of neglect, as well as the limitations and consequences of mandatory reporting. The first, the death in New South Wales of 7-year-old 'Ebony' in 2007, was investigated by the Ombudsman but also triggered the Wood Inquiry (2008) into the state's child protection system. The second case involved the deaths of 18-month-old twins in Brisbane, Queensland, in mid-2008.

Ebony, Aged 7 Years

On 3 November 2007, Ebony, who was autistic, died of chronic starvation shortly after her family relocated. Her mother was convicted of murder and sentenced to life imprisonment, whilst her father was found guilty of manslaughter and received a sentence of 16 years imprisonment. The Ombudsman's report details both the events leading to Ebony's death and the significant issues that arose with inter-agency organisation, including communication, roles, responsibilities and poor coordination (NSW Ombudsman 2009).[1] The Ombudsman's report made a wide range of observations and recommendations to the Departments of Community Services (DoCS); Education and Training; Ageing, Disability and Home Care; Housing; and the NSW Police Force, which in combination with the Wood Inquiry report (2008) have guided the restructuring and ongoing reform of the state's protective system and policy and practice frameworks.

Whilst the broad mandatory reporting laws were not recommended to be rescinded, they were recognised by the Wood Inquiry (2008) as leading to the child protection system being strained with increasing reports and investigations, yet reducing substantiation levels, and with over 70 % coming from mandated reporters

[1] Further information is available on this case from the judgement of the New South Wales Supreme Court: R v BW & SW (No 3) [2009] NSWSC 1043.

(Wood Inquiry 2008, p. 172). The Inquiry found increasing reporting (more than half the reports) involved around 20 % of the families and that 'the level of seriousness of reports has decreased' (p. 181). Examples were identified of mandatory reporters making repeated reports because of a lack of response by DoCS (Wood Inquiry 2008, pp. 171–172) and of more than 10 % of mandated reports not reaching the legislated thresholds. The Inquiry (2008) concluded that 'it is clearly a waste of police, health, school/child care and DoCS resources to make and process thousands of reports which DoCS believes do not amount to a risk of harm as defined in the Care Act' (p. 176).

An overhauled system resulted from the Inquiry recommendations and government's *Keep Them Safe* initiatives. These included a new differential response model for the intake and referral of reports through Child Wellbeing Units within six key government agencies that filter and assess these, ensuring direct referral to early intervention and prevention services without the need for reporting and statutory investigation and narrowing the law to make mandatory reports only in cases of significant abuse or harm. Reports, including from those mandated, and investigations have subsequently decreased dramatically. For example, prior to the Wood Inquiry, New South Wales, Australia's largest state with around one third of the population, had 61 % of the reports nationally, 79 % of the investigations and 63 % of the substantiated outcomes, with staggering increases of more than 350 % in each during the 5 years to 2006–2007 (Bromfield and Holzer 2008). These authors noted the growth and that the demand increases were far and away greater than other Australian jurisdictions and that there was flow through to the rates per 1,000 children under protective orders which were also substantially higher than elsewhere. Following the Inquiry and associated reforms, notifications fell from 213,686 in 2008/2009 to 98,845 in 2010/2011, with commensurate falls in investigations and substantiations (AIHW 2012, pp. 17–19).

Ebony, who had global developmental delay as a result of failure to thrive, was the third child of four to parents who were aged 32 years (father) and 18 years (mother) when they became a couple. They were estranged from their families and experienced many issues including mental health, prescription drug dependence, relationship problems, domestic violence and income support for health reasons – poverty was an issue. Disorganised and possibly depressive forms of neglect presented in this case (Crittenden 1999). Whilst accessing a range of health and welfare services, generally speaking, they were seen as being very difficult to engage into helping services and sometimes obstructive. For example, the Department of Ageing, Disability and Home Care records described them as 'chronic non-attendees for appointments' (NSW Ombudsman 2009, p. 32).

From 1993 to 2007, there were 17 reports of suspected risk of harm, but few of these were mandatory notifications under the NSW Children and Young Persons (Care and Protection) Act 1998. For example, the Department of Ageing, Disability and Home Care made a mandatory notification of Ebony in 2006 because of not accessing therapy services. The Ombudsman (2009) advised that 'DoCS' involvement with the family prior to 2000 was minimal. During this period, the department received three reports, two of which it investigated … (that) did not identify significant concerns regarding risks to the children' (p. 10). The Ombudsman's investigations raised concerns about DoCS' responses to reports about 'Ebony and her sisters from 2005 onwards' (p. 9).

Over the long term, the primary protective issues were the chronic nonattendance at school by the two older children and, subsequently, Ebony and the failure to thrive of Ebony and her younger sibling. Parental difficulty in coping with Ebony and her sibling's behaviour and squalor in their Department of Housing rental accommodation are also noted. Protective action was at times minimal and at other times intensive (2001–2003), with the removal of her younger sibling in 2002 as a result of failure to thrive and other court action to ensure that the parents utilised appropriate health, educational and support services. The Ombudsman (2009) noted 'the department's repeated failure to respond to these same concerns when they re-emerged over a two year period from 2005. In this regard, between 2005 and 2006, DoCS received nine risk of harm reports concerning the three older children. During this period the two eldest girls' attendance at school was poor and in June 2005 they ceased attending school altogether' (pp. 11–12). On occasions, there was parental resistance to letting the workers see Ebony, which was likely to be related to their fear of investigation and removal of the children.

What is clear is that whilst the educational neglect of the two older siblings was seen as significant, as was the failure to thrive of the youngest child, the health, educational and protective interveners did not usually perceive Ebony's situation to entail severe neglect, but to be at a lower threshold and more about parental refusal to access appropriate services to deal with her disabilities.

Crucially, the Ombudsman (2009) identified numerous system and human issues within DoCS including heavy workloads and other organisational pressures, information system and communication failings, staff performance and turnover issues, individual judgement errors and supervision lapses, the result being 'critical information about what actions had occurred and what needed to be done, was lost' (p. 14). In this overstretched organisational environment, the Ombudsman reported that 'we were told that in these circumstances the case of the three children was not a priority in the caseworker's caseload', resulting in inadequate follow-through that may have detected Ebony's deteriorating condition and intervened to address this.

All these system issues in Ebony's case have been identified in other major inquiries as resulting from the system pressures associated with workload demands that are driven by mandatory reporting and forensic approaches to child protection that see investigation as the primary service and which operate in risk-averse ways (see Cummins et al. 2012; Queensland Child Protection Commission of Inquiry 2013).

But this is only part of the issue. The statutory system, overburdened by demand pressures of reports and investigations, was in no position to either assign a higher priority to Ebony compared to other cases or to allocate the resources necessary to ensure a proper follow-up and intervention. Viewing Ebony's tragic death as merely the result of poor staff performance and judgement ignores the systemic issues and the role of mandatory reporting in overwhelming the protective responses.

Unnamed Twins Aged 18 Months

On 16 June 2008 in Brisbane, Australia, toddler twins were found dead in their bedroom by their 11-year-old sibling. They had died from malnutrition approximately a week earlier, but their mother, who was suffering from a major depressive illness, had hidden this knowledge from her four other children and her estranged husband who also lived in the house. Depressive and, potentially, disorganised forms of neglect were evident (Crittenden 1999). According to a treating psychiatrist, the woman's fear of being discovered was 'one of the drivers of not seeking help' (*Courier Mail* 8 August 2013 p. 21). Both the mother and father were charged with murder for failing to provide the twins with the necessities of life, but had pleas of manslaughter accepted by the prosecution after the trial had commenced, with both receiving 8-year custodial sentences.

There was extensive media coverage and the court heard that the twins were infrequently seen by family and friends, and 'the last sighting of them at a healthy weight was in February or March 2008' (*Courier Mail* 25 July 2013, p. 15). The mother, who had her first child at 17, had a complex history including suffering abuse as a child and being fostered (*Courier Mail* 17 August 2013, p. 48). Following relocation in 2007, the family situation deteriorated with a marital relationship breakdown, her husband drinking and gambling heavily and she disengaging and secluding the twins in their closed bedroom.

One psychiatrist attributed her actions to feeling ashamed, resulting from the depressive illness that 'substantially impaired capacity to control her actions' (*Courier Mail* 7 August 2013, p. 14). In her evidence, the mother said that she knew it was wrong to underfeed the twins but 'was too frightened to seek help in case they were taken from her' (*Courier Mail* 6 August 2013, p. 12). The court heard evidence of squalor in the house, high levels of school absenteeism by the other children, behavioural issues and the 11-year-old having to step up, prepare meals and look after her siblings. There was, however, no reporting history to the child protection authorities.

The father's disengagement from the family and his responsibilities (apart from working) and the mother's enveloping depression and absorption into computer games and extricating from contact with family, friends and other supports are notable. She told the court she wanted to avoid criticism of her parenting skills – 'I was ashamed of my situation' (*Courier Mail* 6 August 2013, p. 12). 'When the mother reached out to her own mother for help, she was assured that she was a wonderful mother and told not to worry', and the grandmother said, 'we should have picked a lot more up but we just didn't' (*Courier Mail* 17 August 2013, p. 65).

Whilst Queensland's mandatory reporting system is narrower than NSW, there were nonetheless health and education personnel involved, as well as family and friends, and of note is the mother's own childhood experiences of being in care which clearly had a bearing on her fear of, and desire to avoid, statutory intervention.

Fear of Being Reported

In many respects these cases are similar, not just because of deaths by starvation but with regard to associated factors such as mental illness, alcohol and drug abuse, disengagement from accessible supports, fear of statutory intervention, behavioural issues with the children, school absenteeism and squalor in the house and the general form of the neglect. These are all quite typical factors in disorganised and depressive neglect situations. However, in Ebony's case there was considerable reporting, mandatory and otherwise, which was associated with the parents' unwillingness to be further involved. The mandatory reporting in place did not prevent the tragedy and contributed to parental avoidance of voluntary assistance and statutory intervention. In the twins' case there was no reporting, mandatory or otherwise, and their mother was fearful of seeking help that might lead to the further involvement of child protection in her life. Anxiety over determinations of parental fault was present. Fear of being reported was clearly present in both cases and had a bearing on not accessing helping services. Fear of losing one's children and avoidance of helping services are outcomes of mandatory reporting regimes, albeit unintended (Daniel et al. 2010; Harries and Clare 2002).

Predicting Future Outcomes

It is arguable on the facts of these cases that the neglect was not perceived as severe by those who knew the situation, but as something far less serious until, that is, the deaths of the children. This is a key point and relates to the earlier discussion about the fuzziness of the definition of neglect and its many types and forms, and determination of the thresholds for reporting, and determining what exactly severe neglect is. Prospectively determining severe and fatal outcomes is quite different to retrospectively doing this.

Perhaps more importantly, these cases involve predictions of risk – that is, potential harm at an indeterminate future point. Those involved were placed in a position that required them to foresee a situation of severe neglect and tragic consequences in circumstances where this was at odds with the neglect that had so far been evident. This raises the question of whether or not it is actually possible, in operational terms, to accurately and reliably assess such future outcomes. Is the assessment task, in reality, so speculative and future oriented as to render such conclusions as having unacceptable reliability?

Or is it as Dubowitz (2013, p. 74) notes, just 'difficult to predict the likelihood and nature of future harm', but still achievable with a reasonable degree of accuracy? Does mandatory reporting actually lead to any appreciable level of increased protection for children in such fuzzy and uncertain circumstances as are found in typical neglect cases? Or does it just trigger feelings of threat and fear by parents/carers that leads to decreased prospects for help seeking? And does it merely overwhelm already stretched systems, sending them into a situation where, paradoxically, the more they undertake risk-averse investigations of reports, the less likely they become able to render the sorts of early intervention and help to prevent neglect?

Can forensic child protection systems geared to mandatory reporting in the hope of preventing neglect respond to it in any ways other than removal of children that meet the thresholds? Because of the clear threat they entail, is child protection able to provide any services to fearful parents that are realistically going to be taken up voluntarily when the threshold for removal has not been met? And, to what extent does mandatory reporting influence professionals, subtly and otherwise, to reject and resist reporting matters because it takes it out of their hands, does not guarantee improved outcomes and may make matters significantly worse?

The Merits of Mandatory Reporting of Severe Neglect

Mandatory reporting, whether by statute or policy, has become increasingly controversial since its inception, not the least because it extends the role of the state into the privacy of family life and requires a range of health, education and welfare personnel, depending on specific requirements, to report suspected harm of children to the authorities, thereby altering their role from helping to surveillance. Systems are quite varied across jurisdictions depending on their scope, who is involved, and the processes for reporting and assessing thresholds (Gilbert et al. 2011). Much has been written about the scope and relative merits of such laws and organisational policies, including in this text (see, e.g. Gilbert et al. 2009b; Harries and Clare 2002; Lonne et al. 2009; Mathews et al. 2009; Mathews and Bross 2008; Melton 2005). It is beyond the scope of this chapter to fully examine these as the focus here is on severe neglect, but the key arguments can be summed up as:

- When there is adequate resourcing and effective implementation, mandatory reporting is a necessary measure to help families and prevent harm to children from abuse and neglect, which is often hidden, through early advice to protective authorities that facilitates coordinated protective interventions whilst quantifying the problem and addressing legal and ethical issues (Mathews 2012).
- Mandatory reporting is counterproductive because it net widens social surveillance, particularly of marginalised groups, leading to overburdened systems that infringe family privacy through unnecessary intrusive investigations, and hinders children's protection by overwhelming available resources, alienating reporters in positions to help those in need and frightening parents from seeking help (Harries and Clare 2002).

Unfortunately, mandatory reporting has also changed the role of community members, making them more of a bystander who has become a tool of social surveillance and provider of information to authorities, rather than an active helper building community social care capacity (Daniel et al. 2010; McLeigh 2013; Melton 2005,

2013). Social surveillance is central to mandatory reporting, a mechanism by which behaviour assessments and intervention regimes are targeted to errant citizens. In doing so, it can be perceived as doing more harm than good, at least from the perspective of those who are reported and by mandated reporters who resist because of fears of unintended consequences in their professional relationships.

The crucial importance of relational practice and working with people in empathic and humane ways has received increasing attention, not the least because of pejorative discourses and the 'othering' of parents within child protection systems and recognition of the alienating experiences that many families experience from investigation and involuntary interventions (Featherstone et al. 2014). Pervasive neo-liberal discourses that emphasise punishment, social surveillance and behavioural compliance of particular groups and refashion governance of the family and the role of the state are part and parcel of our contemporary approaches to protecting children – mandatory reporting in its various forms needs to be understood within this macro political context (Parton 2014).

Nonetheless, it is arguable that mandatory reporting is justifiable in situations of severe physical and sexual abuse of children, which are tantamount to criminal conduct and have profound impacts on children's health, well-being and safety, and where a failure to report can have tragic consequences. However, there are important differences between the presentations of abuse and neglect, with the latter typically being insidious in its development and very difficult, if not impossible, to both recognise current sequelae and reliably predict potential harm. The aetiology of these maltreatment forms is quite different, for example, the part that poverty plays in neglect.

This author believes that, on balance, mandatory reporting of neglect is counterproductive to the interests of protecting children because it reduces the likelihood that families will engage with protective and helping supports, which paradoxically increases the risk of harm to child populations. Reasons for this include:

- Defining neglect and its thresholds is complex and prone to variable influences that make it too subjective and likely to be prejudicial to marginalised groups, thereby contributing to their overrepresentation in protective systems.
- The inherent difficulties in accurately identifying neglect and predicting the risk of future severe harm make the process of mandatory reporting too unreliable.
- Mandatory reporting is highly stigmatising and thereby counterproductive because it reinforces social marginalisation.
- The mandatory reporting approach is always in danger of focusing on the individual 'perpetrator' and is unable to focus on the ecological and social context except to reduce these to individualistic risk factors.
- When employing mandatory reporting, child protection agencies are prone to ignore or minimise the social structural dimensions of neglect, potentially undermining public health approaches that promote early intervention and prevention.
- Mandatory reporting feeds significantly increased service demands onto already stretched systems and thereby overwhelms their capacity to provide holistic assessments and interventions because resources are devolved to unnecessary and counterproductive investigations.

- Mandatory reporting entails significant disruption to the relationship between the reporter and the parent/carer that can cause irreparable damage to the helping and protective processes for all those involved.
- Many parents/carers who neglect carry powerful negative life narratives that entail a sense of hopelessness, fatalism and shame, and mandatory reporting feeds these narratives with a renewed sense of distrust of other's motives and fear of the consequences, thereby decreasing self-referral and help seeking.
- Propensity to not access, or withdraw from, services is sometimes characteristic of neglecting parents/carers and is exacerbated by mandatory reporting, thereby placing children at greater risk – coercion makes them increasingly avoidant and transitory in their relationships with support networks.
- Differential response systems, rather than mandatory reporting intrusions, divert needy families to accessible support services and have a lot more going for them with regard to positive family responses.
- The nature and form of most types of neglect require a longer-term protective and helping intervention that is distinctly at odds with mandatory reporting and risk-averse regimes which emphasise investigation as the service and short-term intensive involvement.
- Whilst neglect typically has the highest incidence of harm, most of this is at relatively low levels that do not meet intervention thresholds, and mandatory reporting wastes limited resources spent on unnecessary investigations in order to assuage organisational and community anxieties.

There are reasons for the historical 'neglect of neglect' within our forensically oriented child protection approaches. Whilst there is evidence that statutory approaches are largely successful in addressing the most egregious forms of harm (Finkelhor and Jones 2006; Melton 2010, p. 94), there is little evidence that these have been successful in reducing the prevalence or impact of neglect (Cummins et al. 2012; Gilbert et al. 2009a, b; Stoltenborgh et al. 2013). A recent longitudinal study in six developed countries found little support for concluding that there was a decline in child maltreatment despite massively increased resources (Gilbert et al. 2012).

What neglecting families need is mandatory support rather than reporting and investigation. We know that parents appreciate and take up non-stigmatising help when it is accessible where they need it (QUT and Social Research Centre 2013; Winkworth et al. 2010). Yet, we also know that our systems are labouring under the expectations of prioritising investigation of reports of suspected harm and that this impacts negatively on our capacity to provide ameliorative and supportive assistance to vulnerable families and children. For example, recent Australian judicial inquiries all concluded that the systems were struggling to cope with the demands for statutory investigations of alleged harm and that this was threatening system sustainability, financially and otherwise (see Cummins et al. 2012; Queensland Child Protection Commission of Inquiry 2013; Wood Inquiry 2008).

It is important to understand the reasons why our protective systems are structured and delivered in particular ways. There is an ingrained punitive, stigmatising and blaming aspect to our forensic approaches (Lonne et al. 2009), and Dubowitz (2013) notes how counterproductive this can be for neglecting families. Mandatory reporting is a key strategy of the forensic orientation of child protection, which is different to approaches in other parts of the globe (Gilbert et al. 2011; Kojan and Lonne 2012). Yet, there is increasing evidence that differential response works (Kapland and Merkel-Holguin 2008; Kyte et al. 2013).

Mathews (2012) has identified a number of reasons for maintaining mandatory reporting regimes, but fails to distinguish between the differences and merits for both abuse and neglect cases. Whilst the claim is made that most substantiated cases 'are identified as a result of a report by a mandated reporter' (p. 337), his argument does not properly take account of the skews that occur with regard to reporting by police, health and welfare personnel and the negligible rates of self-referral by parents/carers in child protection systems compared to the substantial rates in some Scandinavian countries such as Norway (Kojan and Lonne 2012). The Norwegian parents identified a range of high needs about their inability to care including poor home conditions, mental illness, drug abuse, domestic violence and behavioural/psychological problems for their child, but did so within an approach that prioritises voluntary interventions and access to resources and support rather than investigation.

Mathews (2012) has, in my view, correctly differentiated the necessity for legislation and mandated authorities to identify contextually relevant thresholds and to respond appropriately to different kinds of cases. In explanation of the overreporting that has occurred, he has identified implementation issues and the need for governments to provide adequate resources and to educate reporters about which cases should and should not be reported. However, the analysis provided has not, in my view, sufficiently drawn the link between systemic mandatory reporting behaviours by front-line staff and the subsequent demand increases that threaten system sustainability. Over the past decade in Australia, there have been huge increases in spending on child protection yet little evidence of a reduction in the incidence or impact of maltreatment (Cummins et al. 2012; Queensland Child Protection Commission of Inquiry 2013). Whilst in the USA there is evidence of declining abuse rates (Finkelhor and Jones 2006), there is little evidence of the same occurring for neglect, which is associated with inequality and disadvantage (Gilbert et al. 2009a).

Again, whilst Mathews' work correctly identifies that many multiple reports are made for a small proportion of families, he does not fully explore how this can rightly be perceived as evidence of gross systemic failure to address their problems. Nor does it properly explain the fact that many Australian jurisdictions now do investigations on more than a quarter of all children, with far higher rates being experienced by indigenous children (Bilson et al. 2013; Cummins et al. 2012; Gilbert et al. 2012; Queensland Child Protection Commission of Inquiry 2013; Wood Inquiry 2008). In my view, the unrelenting service demands resulting from risk-averse mandatory reporting make it necessary to prioritise time and resources to the most risky cases, and as the Ebony example showed, this can often be neglect cases that are, for a variety of reasons, generally seen as less serious. Further, the social and other costs of these levels of surveillance of the population are astonishing. It is little wonder that parents/carers can end up feeling threatened and fearful and subsequently unwilling to seek help.

Being investigated has an impact on how people perceive themselves and their family life. For example, a recent Victorian study of over 500 parents/carers of children who received services either via an investigation of alleged harm or by voluntary referral through the differential response path of community-based family service agencies identified staggering differences in their perceptions of the intervention outcomes (QUT and Social Research Centre 2013). Approximately 85 % of the family service participants rated their parenting skills and the children's health, safety and well-being as having improved, whereas around half that proportion of the child protection, parents/carers felt the same. Both groups had high and complex needs including drug and alcohol services, disability, family violence, mental health and family support programs. Around a quarter of the child protection, parents believed that information they had provided to the department had been used inappropriately.

Which door families use to access support and services makes a difference and investigating parents does impact (QUT and Social Research Centre 2013). Further, socially isolated and disadvantaged sole parents of young children said they felt judged and under surveillance by formal social support agencies in a recent study in Australia, identifying that they were most likely to be assisted in everyday non-stigmatising environments (Winkworth et al. 2010).

The Key Practice and Policy Issues

As noted earlier, neglect captures many of the tensions, challenges and complexities of working in child protection because of its definitional variations and ambiguities, and the complexity and uncertainty in operationalising these in real-life situations replete with contextual and cultural considerations. Further, there are a number of pressing questions with regard to severe neglect and the ways in which our practices and policies attempt to deal with it.

For many years sexual and physical abuse has been centre stage in our quest to prevent harm to children, whilst neglect has been largely sidelined, despite its dominant incidence. A clearer focus on neglect entails a broader mission than just micro investigations into families and instead requires an ecological framework to address social structural factors including the drivers of poverty, social exclusion and alienation (Scott 2014). Successful interventions are far more likely to be longer-term programs and service delivery which are based around effective and ethical helping relationships (Dubowitz 2013; QUT and Social Research Centre 2013; Winkworth et al. 2010).

Neglect is a global term with various definitions that mostly entail the assigning of fault to parents/carers, which fits squarely within the individually oriented mandatory reporting regimes of many child protection systems. But neglect entails a wide spectrum of types and forms and much of the limited extant research has often not differentiated in regard to these or even from abuse. We need a stronger research focus to understand better the aetiology and sequelae of the types, spectrum and forms of neglect and to develop interventions that are more specifically targeted to address particular associated issues and factors. Public health approaches and systems that provide a collaborative joined-up network of services and programs are much more likely to be successful in addressing the multiple facets of neglect and also the intergenerational aspects, such as the damage to familial relationships. Such interagency systems require collaborative communication networks and protocols to facilitate family access to needed resources and services, but may still be problematic (McDonald and Rosier 2011a, b).

A robust evidence base will assist practitioners by indicating what works, when and for whom, but will also help to build confidence about helping approaches and becoming more resilient to the sense of hopelessness that can surround many chronic neglect situations. Knowing more about how best to help places us in a position where we can emphasise the real lifelong benefits of voluntary services and supports that work, rather than enforcing social surveillance through mandatory reports, investigations and enforced behaviour plans that entail many negative impacts. We do not need to go down the path of having improved early intervention and prevention services that are part of an extended social surveillance system that enforces behavioural plans for members of groups deemed troublesome (Featherstone et al. 2013). Rather, we can have accessible and non-stigmatising public health approaches that address the ecological and structural factors at play (Tanner and Turney 2003).

Mandatory reporting regimes are now widespread in the Western world, either by statute or policy/contractual requirement, and they are hard to remove once implemented (Harries and Clare 2002). Yet, neglect is different to abuse of children, notwithstanding that in many cases they coexist. We need to differentiate our responses to these different phenomena and not resile from the task of refining our protective approaches and ensuring that the unintended consequences to mandatory reporting are limited, if not eliminated.

A serious flaw of mandatory reporting regimes, however, is that to a large degree their effectiveness relies upon robust interagency collaboration, system integration, role clarity, clear policy and procedure, regular cross-agency training and mindful management to ensure that the whole system shares responsibility for the welfare of children and providing assistance to struggling families. There is little evidence of this being evident in most jurisdictions, although improvements are occurring. As outlined earlier, there are numerous unintended consequences and critical system failures that require us to rethink the merits of basing our approaches primarily on social surveillance and mandatory reporting of neglect situations rather than providing more accessible help and less blaming and stigmatising through a public health approach that addresses social structural factors.

In this chapter an argument has been put forward to question the utility of mandatory reporting concerning severe neglect and also its less serious manifestations. Misdirecting resources to undertake innumerable fruitless investigations of low-grade neglect might not be the intention of mandatory reporting laws but is nonetheless the result as amply demonstrated by substantiation rates that are now very low in most jurisdictions. Such a system is counterproductive to children's health and well-being because it impacts negatively on parent's propensity to voluntarily seek assistance and support.

To repeat, what vulnerable and stressed families where neglect is an issue need is mandatory support rather than reporting. Neglect can have profound impacts and in its severe manifestations can result in death, ill health and disablement. Its impacts upon children emotionally, psychologically, relationally and physically can seriously harm their life outcomes. Yet, the aetiology of neglect is quite varied across its different types and forms, being defined in normative processes that in themselves are highly subjective and variable.

The severity and chronicity of neglect often mean that longer-term strength-based interventions are more suitable than intensive investigations that are deficit oriented. Mandatory reporting of neglect can make matters worse than they were, not the least because it reinforces strong negative life narratives of struggling parents/carers. Health, welfare and educational authorities are far better to be 'agents of hope' for struggling families than feared tools of system surveillance (Featherstone et al. 2013).

Perhaps most importantly, mandatory reporting is a key component of risk-averse forensic systems that individualise the factors at play, yet patterns of the resultant statutory intervention have significant associations with inequality, poverty and race, which frequently lead to increasing overrepresentation as children go further into the care system. There are very clear social structural dimensions to neglect that mandatory reporting not only largely ignores, but potentially reinforces. A compassionate civil society has to balance multiple needs and interests, and render aid in ethical and humane ways, that are mindful of the rights of all. Mandatory reporting is a hindrance to these aims and needs to be seriously rethought if it is to play a purposeful and humane role in correctly detecting, discerning and preventing harm to children at significant risk of severe neglect, particularly in its less serious but cumulative forms.

Acknowledgements I am grateful for the discussions and guidance offered by Prof. Nigel Parton, Dr. Debbie Scott and Christopher Boyle, not the least being to try to capture both the macro and micro realities of mandatory reporting of severe neglect.

References

American Humane Society. (2014). *Child neglect*. Washington, DC: American Humane Society. Viewed 6 February 2014 from http://www.americanhumane.org/children/stop-child-abuse/fact-sheets/child-neglect.html

Australian Institute of Family Studies. (2014). *What is child abuse and neglect*? Melbourne: AIFS. Viewed 6 February 2014 from http://www.aifs.gov.au/cfca/pubs/factsheets/a142091/

Australian Institute of Health and Welfare. (2012). *Child Protection Australia 2010–11* (Child Welfare series no. 53, Cat. no. CWS 41). Canberra: AIHW.

Australian Institute of Health and Welfare. (2013). *Child Protection Australia 2011–12* (Child Welfare series no. 55. Cat. no. CWS 43). Canberra: AIHW.

Bilson, A., Cant, R. Harries, M,. & Thorpe, D. (2013). A longitudinal study of children reported to the Department of Child Protection in Western Australia. British Journal of Social Work, 1–21. Advanced access doi:10.1093/bjsw/bct164

Blackstock, C., Trocmé, N., & Bennett, M. (2004). Child maltreatment investigations among aboriginal and non-aboriginal families in Canada: A comparative analysis. *Violence Against Women, 10*(8), 901–916.

Bromfield, L., & Holzer, P. (2008). *Australian Institute of Family Studies Submission to the Special Commission of Inquiry into Child Protection Services in NSW*. Melbourne: Child Protection Clearinghouse, Australian Institute of Family Studies.

Bywaters, P. (2013). Inequalities in child welfare: towards a new policy, research and action agenda. *British Journal of Social Work*. First published online: May 3, 2013, 1-18. doi:10.1093/bjsw/bct079

Carter, V., & Myers, M. (2007). Exploring the risks of substantiated physical neglect related to poverty and parental characteristics: A national sample. *Child and Youth Services Review, 29*(1), 110–121.

Child Trends. (2012). *Child maltreatment*. Viewed 6 July 2013 from http://www.childtrends.org/?indicators=child-maltreatment

Crittenden, P. (1999). Child neglect: Causes and contributors. In H. Dubowitz (Ed.), *Neglected children: Research, practice and policy* (pp. 47–69). Thousand Oaks: Sage.

Cummins, P., Scott, D., & Scales, B. (2012). *Report of the Protecting Victoria's Vulnerable Children Inquiry*. Melbourne: Department of Premier and Cabinet. Retrieved 24 June 2012, from http://www.childprotectioninquiry.vic.gov.au/report-pvvc-inquiry.html

Damashek, A., McDiarmid Nelson, M., & Bonner, B. (2013). Fatal child maltreatment: Characteristics of deaths from physical abuse versus neglect. *Child Abuse & Neglect, 37*(10), 735–744.

Daniel, B., Taylor, J., & Scott, J. (2010). Recognition of neglect and early response. *Child and Family Social Work, 15*, 248–257.

Department of Children and Families Connecticut. (2014). *Definitions of child abuse and neglect*. Hartford, CT: Department of Children and Families Connecticut, Hartford Conneticut. Viewed 6 February 2014 from http://www.ct.gov/dcf/cwp/view.asp?Q=316956

Doolan, I., Najman, J., Mills, R., Cherney, A., & Strathearn, L. (2013). Does child abuse and neglect explain the overrepresentation of Aboriginal and Torres Strait Islander young people in youth detention? Findings from a cohort study. *Child Abuse & Neglect, 37*(5), 303–309.

Dubowitz, H. (Ed.). (1999). *Neglected children: Research, practice and policy*. Thousand Oaks: Sage.

Dubowitz, H. (2007). Understanding and addressing the "neglect of neglect:" Digging into the molehill. *Child Abuse & Neglect, 31*(6), 603–606.

Dubowitz, H. (Ed.). (2012). *World perspectives on child abuse* (10th ed.). Aurora, CO: ISPCAN, Colorado.

Dubowitz, H. (2013). Neglect in children. *Pediatric Annals, 42*(4), 73–77.

Dubowitz, H., Klockner, A., Starr, R., & Black, M. M. (1998). Community and professional definitions of neglect. *Child Maltreatment, 3*(3), 235–243.

Fallon, B., Ma, J., Allan, K., Pillhofer, M., Trocmé, N., & Jud, A. (2013). Opportunities for prevention and intervention with young children: Lessons from the Canadian incidence study of reported child abuse and neglect. *Child and Adolescent Psychiatry and Mental Health, 7*(4), 1–13. doi:http://dx.doi.org/10.1186/1754-2000-7-4

Featherstone, B., Morris, K., & White, S (2013). A marriage made in hell: early intervention meets child protection. *British Journal of Social Work*, Advance access. doi:10.1093/bjsw/bct052

Featherstone, B., White, S., & Morris, K. (2014). *Re-imagining child protection: Towards humane social work with families*. Bristol: Policy Press.

Ferguson, H. (2004). *Protecting children in time: Child abuse, child protection, and the consequences of modernity*. Basingstoke: Palgrave Macmillan.

Finkelhor, D., & Jones, L. (2006). Why have child maltreatment and child victimization declined? *Journal of Social Issues, 62*(4), 685–716.

Gaudin, J. (1999). Child neglect: Short-term and long-term outcomes. In H. Dubowitz (Ed.), *Neglected children: Research, practice and policy* (pp. 89–109). Thousand Oaks: Sage.
Gilbert, R., Kemp, A., Thoburn, J., Sidebotham, P., Radford, L., Glaser, D., & Macmillan, H. L. (2009a). Recognising and responding to child maltreatment. *Lancet, 373*(9658), 167–180.
Gilbert, R., Widom, C., Browne, K., Fergusson, D., Webb, E., & Janson, S. (2009b). Burden and consequences of child maltreatment in high-income countries. *Lancet, 373*, 68–81.
Gilbert, N., Parton, N., & Skivenes, M. (2011). *Child protection systems: International trends and orientations*. Oxford: Oxford University Press.
Gilbert, R., Fluke, J., O'Connell, M., Gonzalez-Izquierdo, A., Brownell, M., Gulliver, P., Janson, S., & Sidebotham, P. (2012). Child maltreatment: Variations in trends and policies in six developed countries. *Lancet, 379*, 758–772.
Gillespie, J., Whitford, D., & Abel, M. (2010). Community networking: A policy approach to enhance Aboriginal child welfare in off-reserve communities. *Indigenous Policy Journal, 21*(3), 1–19.
Harries, M., & Clare, M. (2002). Mandatory reporting of child abuse: Evidence and options – Report for the Western Australian Child Protection Council, Perth, Western Australia, Discipline of Social Work and Social Policy, University of Western Australia. Viewed 24 August 2013 from http://www.celt.uwa.edu.au/__data/assets/pdf_file/0009/1102131/MRFinalReport.pdf
Horwath, J. (2007). The missing assessment domain: Personal, professional and organisational factors influencing professional judgements when identifying and referring child neglect. *British Journal of Social Work, 37*, 1285–1303.
Howe, D., Dooley, T., & Hinings, D. (2000). Assessment and decision making in child abuse cases: An attachment perspective. *Child and Family Social Work, 5*, 143–155.
Jonson-Reid, M., Drake, B., & Zhou, P. (2013). Neglect subtypes, race and poverty: Individual, family and service characteristics. *Child Maltreatment, 18*(30).
Kaplan, K. (2013). Child welfare involvement among parents with mental illness. *CW360⁰ the intersection of child welfare and disability: Focus on parents*, 6–7. Retrieved from http://cascw.umn.edu/portfolio-items/cw360-the-intersection-of-child-welfare-and-disability-focus-on-parents/
Kapland, C., & Merkel-Holguin, L. (2008). Another look at the national study on differential response in child welfare. *Protecting Children, 23*(1–2), 5–21.
Kojan, B., & Lonne, B. (2012). A comparison of systems and outcomes for safeguarding children in Australia and Norway. *Child and Family Social Work, 17*(1), 96–107.
Kyte, A., Trocmé, N., & Chamberland, C. (2013). Evaluating where we are at with differential response. *Child Abuse & Neglect, 37*(2–3), 125–132.
LaLiberte, T., & Lightfoot, E. (2013). Parenting with disability. *CW360⁰ the intersection of child welfare and disability: Focus on parents*, 4–5.. Retrieved from http://cascw.umn.edu/portfolio-items/cw360-the-intersection-of-child-welfare-and-disability-focus-on-parents/
Lonne, B., Parton, N., Thomson, J., & Harries, M. (2009). *Reforming child protection*. London: Routledge.
MacLaurin, B., Trocmé, N., Fallon, B., McCormack, M., Pitman, L., Forest, N., Banks, J., Shangreaux, C., & Perrault, E. (2005). *Alberta incidence study of reported child abuse and neglect, AIS-2003: Major findings*. Calgary: University of Calgary.
Mathews, B. (2012). Exploring the contested role of mandatory reporting laws in the identification of severe child abuse and neglect. In M. Freeman (Ed.), *Law and childhood studies: Current legal issues* (pp. 302–338). Oxford University Press: Oxford.
Mathews, B., & Bross, D. (2008). Mandated reporting is still a policy with reason: Empirical evidence and philosophical grounds. *Child Abuse & Neglect, 32*, 511–516.
Mathews, B., & Bross, D. (2014). Using Law to Identify, Manage and Prevent Child Maltreatment. In R. Krugman & J. Korbin (Eds.), *Handbook of Child Maltreatment* (pp. 477–502). Dordrecht: Springer.
Mathews, B., Goddard, C., Lonne, B., Short, S., & Briggs, F. (2009). Developments in Australian laws requiring the reporting of suspected child sexual abuse. *Children Australia, 34*(3), 18–23.

McConnell, D. (2013). The out-of-home placement of children born to parents with intellectual disability. *CW360⁰ the intersection of child welfare and disability: Focus on parents*, 8–9. Retrieved from http://cascw.umn.edu/portfolio-items/cw360-the-intersection-of-child-welfare-and-disability-focus-on-parents/

McDonald, M., & Rosier, K. (2011a). *Interagency collaboration – Part A: What is it, what does it look like, when is it needed and what supports it?* Melbourne: Australian Institute of Family Studies.

McDonald, M., & Rosier, K. (2011b). *Interagency collaboration – Part B: Does collaboration benefit families? Exploring the evidence*. Melbourne: Australian Institute of Family Studies.

McLeigh, J. (2013). How to form alliances with families and communities. *Child Abuse & Neglect, 37*(S), 29–40.

McSherry, D. (2007). Understanding and addressing the "neglect of neglect": Why are we making a molehill out of a mountain? *Child Abuse & Neglect, 31*(6), 607–614.

Melton, G. B. (2005). Mandated reporting: a policy without reason. *Child Abuse & Neglect, 29*(1), 9–18.

Melton, G. B. (2010). Angels watching over us: Child safety and family support in an age of alienation. *American Journal of Orthopsychiatry, 80*(1), 89–95.

Melton, G. B. (2013). Programs aren't enough. *Child Abuse & Neglect, 37*(S), 1–7.

Mennen, F., Kim, K., Sang, J., & Trickett, P. (2010). Child neglect: Definition and identification of youth's experiences in official reports of child maltreatment. *Child Abuse & Neglect, 34*(9), 647–658.

Moran, P. (2009). *Neglect: Research evidence to inform practice*. London: Action for Children.

NSW Ombudsman. (2009). *The death of Ebony: The need for an effective interagency response to children at risk. A special report to Parliament under section 31 of the Ombudsman Act 1974*, Sydney: NSW Ombudsman.

Parton, N. (2006). *Safeguarding childhood: Early Intervention and surveillance in a late modern society*. Basingstoke: Palgrave Macmillan.

Parton, N. (2014). *The politics of child protection: Contemporary developments and future directions*. Basingstoke: Palgrave Macmillan.

Queensland Child Protection Commission of Inquiry. (2013). *Taking responsibility – A roadmap for Queensland Child Protection*. Brisbane: Queensland Child Protection Commission of Inquiry. Viewed 24 August 2013 from http://www.childprotectioninquiry.qld.gov.au/__data/assets/pdf_file/0017/202625/QCPCI-FINAL-REPORT-web-version.pdf

Queensland University of Technology (QUT) & Social Research Centre. (2013). *The child and family services outcomes survey 2012 final report*. Melbourne: Department of Human Services. Viewed 24 August 2013 from http://www.dhs.vic.gov.au/about-the-department/documents-and-resources/reports-publications/the-child-and-family-services-outcomes-survey

Reading, R., Bissell, S., Goldhagen, J., Masson, S., Parton, N., Pais, M. S., Thoburn, J., & Webb, E. (2009). Promotion of children's rights and prevention of maltreatment. *Lancet, 373*, 332–343.

Reder, P., & Duncan, S. (2001). Abusive relationships, care and control conflicts and insecure attachments. *Child Abuse Review, 10*, 411–427.

Saunders, E., Nelson, K., & Landsman, M. (1993). Racial inequality and child neglect: Findings in a metropolitan area. *Child Welfare, 72*(4), 341–354.

Scott, D. (2014). *Understanding child neglect.* Melbourne: Australian Institute of Family Studies. Viewed 3 April 2014 from http://www.aifs.gov.au/cfca/pubs/papers/a146596/index.html

Scott, D., Higgins, D., & Franklin, R. (2012). *The role of supervisory neglect in childhood injury*. Melbourne: Australian Institute of Family Studies. Viewed 14 October 2013 from http://www.aifs.gov.au/cfca/pubs/papers/a142582/cfca08.pdf

Shemmings, D., Shemmings, Y., & Cook, A. (2012). Resistant families and attachment research. *Child and Family Social Work, 17*, 130–137.

Sinha, V., Trocme, N., Fallon, B., & MacLaurin, B. (2010). Understanding the investigation-stage overrepresentation of First Nations children in the child welfare system: An analysis of the First Nations component of the Canadian Incidence Study of Reported Child Abuse and Neglect 2008. *Child Abuse & Neglect, 37*(10), 821–831.

Sinha, V., Trocme, N., Fallon, B., MacLaurin, B., Fast, E., Prokop, S., et al. (2011). *Kiskisik Awasisak: Remember the children. Understanding the overrepresentation of First Nations children in the child welfare system*. Ottawa: Assembly of First Nations.

Steering Committee for the Review of Government Service Provision. (2013). *Report on Government Services 2013, Indigenous compendium*. Canberra: Productivity Commission.

Stein, M., Rees, G., Hicks, L., & Gorin, S. (2009). *Neglected adolescents – Literature review*. London: Department of Children, Schools and Families.

Steinberg, K., Levine, M., & Doueck, H. (1997). Effects of legally mandated child-abuse reports on the therapeutic relationship: A survey of psychotherapists. *American Journal of Orthopsychiatry, 67*(1), 112–122.

Stoltenborgh, M., Bakermans-Kranenburg, M., & van Ijzendoorn, M. (2013). The neglect of child neglect: A meta-analytic review of the prevalence of neglect. *Social Psychiatry and Psychiatric Epidemiology, 48*, 345–355.

Tanner, K., & Turney, D. (2003). What do we know about child neglect? A critical review of the literature and its application to social work practice. *Child and Family Social Work, 8*, 25–34.

US Department of Health and Human Services, Administration on Children Youth and Families. (2010). *Child maltreatment 2010*. Washington, DC: US Government Printing Office.

Welch, G., & Bonner, B. (2013). Fatal child neglect: Characteristics, causation, and strategies for prevention. *Child Abuse & Neglect, 37*(10), 745–752.

Winkworth, G., McArthur, M., Layton, M., Thomson, L., & Wilson, F. (2010). Opportunities lost – Why some parents of young children are not well connected to the service systems designed to assist them. *Australian Social Work, 63*(4), 431–445.

Wood Inquiry. (2008). Report from the Special Commission of Inquiry into Child Protection Services in NSW, Sydney, State of New South Wales. Viewed 24 August 2013 from www.dpc.nsw.gov.au/publications/news/stories/?a=33794.

Chapter 13
The Sins of the (Irish) Fathers: Is Mandatory Reporting the Best Response?

Helen Buckley and Roni Buckley

Introduction

This chapter will consider the likely impact of imminent mandatory reporting legislation in Ireland and ask if, given the intelligence available to us, it is likely to achieve beneficial outcomes. It will deal with the question principally from the viewpoint of professionals from the various sectors who are likely to be scheduled as reporters. This perspective has been explored through the recent Irish empirical research conducted for a doctoral thesis by one of the authors (Buckley 2013). The study challenged the notion that a technical solution such as legislating for reporting can be effectively applied to such an inconsistent, dynamic and divisive social issue as child abuse. First, however, the proposed legislation will be briefly described, and the context in which the legislation has been developed will be explained, followed by an examination of three contextual factors in order to provide a backdrop for the exploration of the main question. These factors are the Catholic Church and its link with national politics, the formal child protection system and the perspective of service users whose interests the law proposes to address.

Proposed Mandatory Reporting Legislation

The Children First Bill was published in April 2014, and the legislation is still progressing through the necessary debate stages prior to enactment. A Heads of Bill document had been published in 2012 and put out for consultation. That document had contained proposals that were extremely broad, covering all services provided

H. Buckley (✉) • R. Buckley
School of Social Work and Social Policy, Trinity College Dublin, Dublin, Ireland
e-mail: hbuckley@tcd.ie

B. Mathews, D.C. Bross (eds.), *Mandatory Reporting Laws and the Identification of Severe Child Abuse and Neglect*, Child Maltreatment 4,
DOI 10.1007/978-94-017-9685-9_13

to children whether educational or recreational and imposed responsibility for reporting on designated persons, who would be held liable for the failure of the service to report suspected child abuse. It also provided for significant penalties including imprisonment for up to 5 years for failure to report. Following the publication of the Heads of Bill, a number of organisations made submissions, and a series of oral hearings was conducted by a government subcommittee which subsequently published a report.

The subsequent Children First Bill was a considerably watered-down version of the Heads and reflected widespread concern, particularly from doctors, youth services and teachers about some of the measures originally proposed. In the 2014 Bill, the sanctions had been deleted, the number of services to be included had been reduced and the role of designated persons had also been removed. Instead, the Bill proposed to mandate defined categories of persons who would be required to make a report to the statutory child protection service when they know or believe that a child has been harmed, is being harmed or is at risk of being harmed. 'Harm' is defined in section 2 of the Bill as 'to assault, ill-treat, neglect or sexually abuse the child, whether caused by a single act, omission or circumstance or a series or combination of acts, omissions or circumstances or otherwise'. The concept of 'ill treatment' is defined as 'to abandon or cruelly treat the child, or to cause or procure or allow the child to be abandoned or cruelly treated, in a manner that seriously affects or is likely to seriously affect the child's health, development or welfare' and 'neglect' is defined as 'to deprive the child of adequate food, warmth, clothing, hygiene, supervision, safety or medical care in a manner that seriously affects or is likely to seriously affect the child's health, development or welfare'. In an attempt to promote inter-agency collaboration, the Bill requires reporters to assist the Agency in the assessment of child protection risk and stipulates the establishment of an interdepartmental group to be placed on a statutory footing.

The Context in Which Mandatory Reporting Will Be Introduced

The recent move towards adopting a mandatory reporting law in Ireland was heavily motivated by consecutive revelations of child abuse scandals within the Catholic Church about which not only the actuality that priests and members of religious orders had sexually abused children, but the denial and feeble efforts of the Church authorities to deal with the problem caused considerable disquiet. One of the earliest cases of child sexual abuse by a cleric to be revealed in Ireland was that of Fr Brendan Smyth. In 1994, this Norbertine priest received widespread media attention after he was charged on 74 counts of indecent sexual assault and sentenced to 12 years in prison. It was revealed that the superiors in his order had responded to earlier reports of sexual misconduct with children by simply moving him through different locations in the republic and in Northern Ireland. Culpability was also attributed to the State; the failure to extradite Smyth to Northern Ireland for similar charges resulted in the resignation of the then Prime Minister as well as the President of the High Court. As Keenan (2012, pp. 19–20) has pointed out, the case highlighted the extent to which strong affiliations existed between the State and Church in Ireland. It brought to light the influence of the Church hierarchy over Irish political process but equally the protection afforded to the Church by the State when one of its members was accused of a serious crime.

Further, controversy and scandal continued to plague the Catholic Church in Ireland for the following two decades during which a series of TV documentaries exposed instances of physical and sexual abuse by the catholic clergy. These documentaries provoked public concern around the mismanagement of cases at the time they were reported and the lack of accountability by those who were in authority (Goode et al. 2003, pp. 8–9).

However, by the late 2000s, the establishment of a number of Commissions into the occurrence and handling of child abuse by the Catholic Church in Ireland revealed a new history of ill treatment of children. The Commission to Inquire into Child Abuse (2009) exposed a multitude of physical, emotional and sexual abuses of children as well as their consistent neglect, whilst the Commissions of Investigations into the Archdiocese of Dublin (2009) and Cloyne Diocese (2010) concentrated on child sexual abuse and the Church authorities' failure to notify the appropriate public bodies when an accusation was made against a priest. In response, the Minister for Justice stated in the Seanad Eireann debates:

> The Members in this House would be well aware of the content of published reports, such as the Ryan, Murphy and, more recently, Cloyne reports. These provide a litany of quite shocking revelations concerning the sexual abuse of children and failure to respond to that abuse…It is clear from these revelations and the various published reports that if those who had knowledge in the past of sexual offences committed against children had informed the Garda, many children who subsequently became the victims of abuse may have been protected from clerical sexual predators. There is a compelling argument, therefore, for closing the current loophole in the law.[1]

The impetus for introducing mandatory reporting legislation could also be seen as part of the evolution children's services in Ireland. Over the past four decades, the Irish child protection system has developed from what was quite an embryonic service to one which is today comparable to others in the Anglophone world and based on similar principles. Social policy analysts have tended to classify child protection systems in terms of their orientation, identifying some countries having a 'welfarist' approach underpinned by universal services, early intervention and family focused solutions, and others with a 'child protection' approach, based on the residual service provision and a regulated, investigative approach. The former approach is more commonly found in the mainland Europe, whereas the latter is more prevalent in the English-speaking world (Hill et al. 2002; Lonne et al. 2009). However, closer examination of the jurisdictions that operate different approaches indicates an increasing

[1] Alan Shatter, *Seanad Éireann Debates vol. 215, no.6, 10 May 2012.*

homogenisation as the formerly investigative regimes become more family support oriented, and the welfarist systems adopt more regulation and procedure (Gilbert 2012). The Irish child protection system never consciously adopted a strong or polarised orientation on which to develop. Its nearest comparator would probably be the 'family focused child protection' approach described by Connolly (2007) in respect of New Zealand. Ireland signed the United Nations Convention on the Rights of the Child (UNCRC) in 1992. The *Child Care Act 1991*, following the example of other signatories of the convention, was based on underpinning principles of early intervention, prevention, family support and collaborative service provision. Implementation of these measures is not compelled under domestic law, and they are followed more in spirit than the latter. Similarly, whilst the law emphasises the need for inter-agency collaboration, children's services in Ireland have remained divided between statutory and non-statutory providers, with only the former perceived to be under any legal obligation in respect of the protection of children.

National child protection reporting procedures of one type or another have been operating in Ireland since the 1980s. These, however, have had the status of guidelines, and whilst they were considered to be 'overarching' and 'administratively mandatory' (Department of Health & Children 1999; Murphy et al. 2005, p. 54), they had no legal basis, although certain professionals could be considered legally negligent if they failed to exercise a duty of care to a child in their charge. As in other jurisdictions, the system was subject to what have been called 'radical ruptures' (Foucault 1975, p. 96) instigated by a combination of scandals and increasing awareness of the prevalence and impact of harm to children. A series of inquiries into highly publicised child protection failures, including the aforementioned clerical sexual abuse scandals, have led to what have generally been regarded as 'predictable' responses (Buckley and O'Nolan 2013; Parton 2004) identifying, amongst other failures, low standards of communication between disciplines and agencies. Following the ubiquitous trend of child protection inquiries worldwide in assuming that increased regulatory measures have the capacity to rationalise an unwieldy arena of work, a number of Irish reports recommended legislative reform including the introductions of sanctions for failure to report suspected child abuse (Buckley and O'Nolan 2013).

After an initial flurry of activity in the mid-1990s, the matter of mandatory reporting lay dormant through several political administrations, some of which reconsidered and subsequently rejected it because the evidence of its advantages was equivocal. This was in the context of a growing concern that most investment in the child protection services was being expended in the investigation of cases at the expense of preventative interventions at a community level; there were concerns that mandating reporting of suspected child abuse would deepen this imbalance (Department of Health 1996). However, the publication in 2009 and 2010 of further reports documenting abuse by priests and religious in the dioceses of Dublin and Cloyne (Commission of Investigation 2009, 2010) together with the ensuing public anger at Church authorities provided a political opportunity in 2011 for the newly formed government to take a strong position on child protection. For the first time, a full government department was established to deal with child and youth affairs, and a reform agenda was established. In this context, the government decided to revive the debate on mandatory reporting and in 2012 began the process of legislating. A constitutional referendum was held in Ireland in late 2012, with the objective of enshrining the rights of children in the Irish Constitution; the government used the term 'child protection' extensively in its campaign and implied that its own record of introducing reform was a step towards achieving the goal of the referendum, thereby attempting to unify the twin concepts of responsibility to report and children's rights in the mind of the voter. In effect, the main outcome of the referendum (which at the time of writing is still being contested in the Supreme Court) will be a change in the adoption law and an obligation on Courts to hear the views of children, neither of which have much bearing on child protection per se.

The Catholic Church and Irish Politics

In Ireland, historical links have bound the Church and government together since the foundation of the state (Raftery and O'Sullivan 1999). However, a speech made in the Irish parliament by the Prime Minister Enda Kenny in July 2011, in which he stated 'This is not Rome … this is a republic of laws, of rights, of responsibilities' (Oireachtas debate 2011), was seen by many as representing a severance in relations between the Irish State and the Church that had been building up for at least a decade as more instances of abuse by Church members were uncovered. Despite this schism, the activities of one cannot be viewed separately from the other where a topic like child abuse is concerned, and the connection between the two has been a major preoccupation of the government in its considerations about legislation and policy. Undoubtedly, the more recent response of the government was provoked by the recalcitrance of the Catholic Church. In the same speech which has since been considered to encapsulate the current Irish government attitude to the Church, the Taoiseach (Prime Minister) responded to the publication of the Cloyne report in July 2011, identifying it as the exposure of 'an *attempt by the Holy See, to frustrate an Inquiry in a sovereign, democratic republic…*' He went on to offer an assurance that *'through our Government's action [to put child protection guidance on a statutory footing] those who have been abused can take some small comfort in knowing that they belong to a nation, to a democracy where humanity, power, rights, responsibility are enshrined and enacted, always….always…. for their good'* (Oireachtas debate 2011).

Outside the domain of the Church, however, there was actually no empirical basis for arguing that the absence of legislation supported the reluctance to report on the part of health and welfare professionals. The number of reports made to the statutory child protection system has been growing consistently and doubled between 2007 and 2012. The principal reporters have been police, schools and health and welfare professionals who account for three quarters of referrals made (HSE 2014). Reviews and inquiries into cases of intra-familial child abuse which occurred during the period of 'modern' child protection service provision showed that most cases where deficiencies or errors were evident had been referred to the services on many occasions over the years. The principal weaknesses were related to delayed or inadequate responses, failures in inter-agency collaboration and incompetence in coordinating interventions (see, e.g. Brosnan 2008 and Gibbons 2010).

Whilst it is now known that Church authorities in Ireland had been aware of the problem of child sexual abuse by priests for a considerable period (Raftery and O'Sullivan 1999; Commission to Inquire into Child Abuse 2009), its extent has only been made clear in the past 20 years in Ireland through the publication of the aforementioned Commissions of Inquiry. The Church has responded by establishing a National Safeguarding Board for Children in the Catholic Church, one of whose functions is to audit the conformity of different dioceses and religious orders with the national policy and procedure. Almost all of the cases highlighted occurred more than 15 years ago, and most of the alleged perpetrators are deceased or have left the Church at this point (NBSCCC 2013). Despite this, scrutiny of the child protection activities of the Church endures primarily because of their history of unashamed noncompliance with protocols requiring them to report misdemeanours to the authorities.

Two important factors have to be borne in mind when considering the Church's apparently errant earlier response to reports that their members had committed sexual, physical and emotional abuse as well as neglect. Firstly, the fact that this was an institution that effectively determined the moral code of individuals and families inevitably elicited an extreme and angry reaction. However, it also has to be acknowledged that the number of children that were abused by religious is very low when compared to the maltreatment that has been inflicted on children by their families. Since the year 2000, approximately 300,000 reports have been made to child protection services; the vast majority of which concerned neglect or welfare issues occurring within families. In comparison, during the same period, eight allegations have been made against priests or members of religious orders pertaining to current (as opposed to historical) abuse (NSBCCC 2012, 2013). This is not to deny the individual significance of the alleged incidents but to demonstrate that the overall political response to child abuse is not being determined by what will be most effective for the majority of victims and vulnerable individuals but instead by a number of isolated cases. The political considerations on which mandatory reporting has been based are therefore not representative of the current scenario in Ireland which is evidenced in the statistics outlined above.

The second issue is more complex, and it is basically that even if a requirement to report suspected child abuse had been made legally mandatory decades ago, it would probably have had limited effect within the Church. The Church's own procedures for reporting child protection concerns, first established in the *Framework Document* (1996) and later updated by *Our Children Our Church* (2005), were inconsistently followed, as evidenced by the Ferns Report (Murphy et al. 2005) and the alter Murphy report (Commission of Investigation 2009). The Church reporting guidelines, known as the 'Framework Document' operating from the mid 1990s (Irish Catholic Bishops Conference 1996), set out a clear mandate that all complaints of child sexual abuse were to be reported to the police and the health boards, and a low threshold of 'reasonable suspicion' was to be applied. Despite this, both the Ferns and Murphy reports revealed that the guidelines were never implemented to an effective standard by Church officials. The later Cloyne Report (Commission of Investigation 2010, pp. 71–72) reiterated this, observing that too much concern was placed on attending to the needs of the alleged priest, at the expense of the victim. Importantly, communication from the Congregation of the Doctrine of the Faith in Rome expressed reservation about the contents of the Framework Document; this was seen to give tacit permission to those in positions of authority within the Irish Church to ignore it.

There was also a verbal evidence of the Church's sense of disconnectedness from the regulation by civil authorities; commenting on a news story in 2010 which revealed that the Catholic Primate of Ireland had failed to report an incident to the authorities during the 1970s, a professor of canon law commented that the Primate had been 'under no obligation whatsoever' to make a report at the time (Irish Times 16th March 2010). The perception held by the Church of their own exemption from the civil law had by that time been very firmly dismissed by the Irish Minister for Justice in 2002 famously comparing the status of the canon law to 'the rules of a golf course' (Irish Independent, 24 October 2002).

It can, however, now be claimed that the Church's former attitude has been utterly eradicated, and the Catholic hierarchy has accepted the very firm message conveyed to them that they are subject to the same obligations, legal or otherwise, as any other body. This began in 2002 with the announcement from the Irish Bishop's Conference of a nationwide independent audit of the handling of the child sexual abuse complaints from 1940 onwards. This review was later subsumed into the Commission to Inquire into Child Abuse run by the State, on the basis that it was duplicating the work of the Commission, but did signal the intention of the Church to clean up its act. The Primate of All Ireland Cardinal Brady recently reiterated in public that 'Vigilance is our watch word' (Irish Catholic Bishops Conference 2013) in respect of child protection and has opened safeguarding activities in the Church up for public scrutiny. The National Board for Safeguarding Children in the Catholic Church conducts and publishes audits, measured against rigorous standards and holds individual bishops to account for any deficits in their safeguarding activity. All community and institutional activities that involve the Church, even where their contact with children is small, are obliged to comply with the standards (NBSCCC 2009). Each diocese is subject to audit by the Child and Family Agency as per the recommendations of the Ferns inquiry (HSE 2013). As a consequence of their previous insubordination, the child protection measures operated by the religious in Ireland are subject to far greater levels of formal surveillance and audit than any other organisation in the state.

The Current State of Irish Children's Health, Education and Welfare Services

Irish child protection services have become increasingly regulated in the recent past, with a heavy concentration on the standardisation of the processes used and a restructuring of the sector. Elements of the new public service management have been introduced with key performance indicators based on the most quantitative aspects of the work. As in many other countries, there is a drive towards introducing alternative or differential response systems to deal with cases not requiring a statutory response; however, this has been compromised by deep budgetary cuts. As outlined above, statistical information indicates a steady escalation in referrals to statutory child protection services. Concern was raised in a recent government debate about the long waiting list of child protection cases waiting to be processed and allocated (Oireachtas debate 25th September 2014). This strongly indicates a limited capacity not only to respond but to fully investigate child protection reports.

Other indicators of the state of the child protection and welfare system indicate weakness in the early intervention and general welfare sphere; a recent report commissioned by Barnardos, a children's advocacy service, indicated that Irish family support services lacked coherence and fell short on a number of benchmarks including the provision of timely child and adolescent mental health services, access to general health care and school retention. The standards of early childhood care were considered to be low amongst Organisation for Economic Cooperation and Development (OECD) countries (Harvey 2011). Annual 'report cards' issued by the Children's Rights Alliance also cited 'consistent shortcomings and the lack of real progress in the areas of poverty, health and discrimination' (Children's Rights Alliance 2013, p. 1). Annual reports from the Office of the Ombudsman for children also highlight serious deficits in the provision of children's services, particularly in respect of access to education and therapeutic interventions. The 2013 report urged particular vigilance in respect of the anticipated pressure mandatory reporting would put on the system (Office of the Children's Ombudsman 2013). Following a recent structural reform, the CEO of the statutory Child and Family Agency acknowledged that the service currently had insufficient resources to meet its targets and was experiencing pressure due to the rising number of children in the country (Sunday Business Post, 6 July, 2014). Taken together, these external barometers portray a fragile system which may not easily withstand the anticipated impact of the added pressure in an economic environment where further investment is unlikely to be forthcoming for some time yet.

The Perspective of Service Users

The stakeholder groups which have the most influence on child protection reform rarely include service users, i.e. family members including children, despite official aspirations to include them (Buckley et al. 2008). No Irish service user groups were consulted about their views on the proposed legislation, yet it cannot be assumed that their ultimate response will be without a consequence. An English child protection academic David Howe (1992) once described service users as 'the jokers in the pack', commenting that children and families are not merely passive recipients of services and often exercise considerable agency in respect of the effectiveness of interventions. Irish studies which took place between 2006 and 2008 provided insight into what it is like to be on the receiving end of child protection services. Unsurprisingly, the attitude to statutory social work was ambivalent at best, and one of the studies in particular demonstrated the negativity with which the services were viewed, the stigma attached to becoming a client and the sense of powerlessness which that engendered (Buckley et al. 2008, 2011). The sort of quality benchmarks applied by service users in these studies reflected those from previous research (De Boer and Cody 2007), namely, that the *quality of relationships* forged with workers and the *manner in which services were delivered* were the mediating factors which determined their acceptability. They cited issues such as reliability, accessibility, respect, tolerance and friendliness as factors which could mitigate the perceived harshness of some of the more coercive actions of the child protection services. These, however, are the factors which some researchers believe are likely to be eroded by further proceduralisation and legalisation (Devaney 2004; Tilbury 2004). For example, Eileen Munro pointed out in her review of child protection services in the UK that services have become so standardised and prescriptive that they are unable to provide the required range of responses, which include trusting relationships as well as flexibility (Munro 2011). Writing about Irish reforms, Featherstone et al. (2012, p. 59) urge policymakers to attend to the concept of 'trust' in the delivery of services, rather than following the example of jurisdictions which 'privilege the management of institutional risk over the improvement of practice'.

The Irish studies also reflect a worrying trend previously identified in Australia (Humphreys 2007; Connolly 2009) and in the US (Friend et al. 2008) where exposure to domestic violence becomes a reportable child protection matter; rigid adherence to the regulation in other jurisdictions has resulted in the alienation of domestic violence victims and has acted as a disincentive to seek assistance. Evidence indicates that it also overburdens systems which are then constrained in their capacity to address child maltreatment of a more serious nature (Humphreys 2007). As already outlined, Irish child protection policy has acknowledged the importance of adopting a variety of responses to child welfare and protection issues, including the use of less formal routes to community services (Jeyes 2013), but the evidence that exists in Ireland and elsewhere indicates that the balance required to maintain helping relationships with families in trouble will become increasingly delicate in an environment that becomes more legalistic and the capacity to respond in a less formal manner will be constrained. This will be a particular challenge in a community-based family support and domestic violence services, where practitioners and managers who currently use a degree of discrimination will now be faced with a duty to report once they suspect harm to a child.

In summary, then, the setting in which mandatory reporting is to be introduced is one where there is a strong political desire to show that action is being taken, but also one which is brittle, under pressure and teetering between a child protection and welfarist orientations. This has been tacitly acknowledged by the government in their decision to dilute their original broad-ranging proposals in relation to a mandatory reporting, but despite attempts at damage limitation, the impact is still likely to be significant, as the next section will demonstrate.

The Potential Impact of Mandatory Reporting: Findings from an Irish Research Study

The success or failure of the proposed legislation will ultimately depend on the adherence to it by those who will be bound by it. The earlier part of this chapter focused on three different constituencies, i.e. the Catholic Church, the child protection and welfare services and the service users that come into contact, voluntarily or otherwise, with the child protection system. The remainder of this chapter will focus in depth on the likely impact that sanctioned reporting will have on attitudes and actions of a key stakeholder group, the professionals who will be scheduled as reporters. This topic was examined in depth by one of the authors (R. Buckley) in a doctoral study conducted in Ireland between 2011 and 2013 (hereafter referred to as the current study). Data for the research was gathered from individual and group interviews[2] with 156 participants from the sectors of health, education, social work, childcare and youth services including sports organisations and youth justice. Whilst the research question was being posed in a specific context, i.e. one where reporting of suspected child abuse had up to this point been administratively but not legally required, the findings that it elicited could have relevance for jurisdictions where mandatory reporting is already in operation and may explain variations in its operation.

The core purpose of the current study was to explore the potential impact of a mandatory reporting law on existing child protection reporting practices and processes in Ireland. In order to set a context for the examination of the main question, the study first established the degree to which frontline professionals are, at this juncture, equipped to respond to child abuse. It focused on their level of awareness about child harm and of their own responsibilities in that regard, on the basis that these were essential precepts that would determine the effectiveness or otherwise of any regulation. It also examined in some depth how professionals experienced the trajectory from the awareness of its probability to the identification of its existence through to reporting it to the authorities.

[2] 27 individual interviews were held, and 24 focus groups were conducted with a total of 129 individuals.

Openness to the Concept of Abuse

Child protection procedures tend to assume a uniform capacity amongst professionals to exercise reasonable judgement about child abuse once they are in possession of basic information and a set of instructions to follow. However, findings from the current study show that, despite all the recent media attention on historical and current abuse, professionals in children's services carry varying conceptualisations and constructions of child harm that are likely to shape their response to it.

Understandably, the level of understanding held by individuals in the study was linked to the amount of contact they had with children and the context in which they met them. The professional frameworks within which some of them worked tended to determine their openness to the possibility of abuse, for example, public health nurses saw themselves as having a duty to promote a child's general wellbeing by not only identifying abuse but intercepting any recurrence of it in the future. On the other hand, general medical practitioners (GMPs) acknowledged that the narrow clinical perspective that they operated within, as well as their lack of training, was unlikely to facilitate easy identification of anything outside the physical spectrum and even then only the most clear cut symptoms. As one GMP commented '*When I was training as an undergraduate…child sexual abuse…was unheard of*'. Some professionals worked in youth services where it was difficult to distinguish neglect from adversity or worrying behaviour from normal adolescent 'limit testing'; they observed that distorted understandings of child harm can have the paradoxical effect of lowering professional sensitivity. Other professionals' perspectives fell some way in between these extremes, but their ability to recognise child abuse was complicated by other factors which will be discussed below.

Data from the current study showed that many of the third-level courses that prepare students to work with children, including nursing, teaching, youth work, police work, sport and child care, have very little input on child protection, reflecting a finding by Buckley and McGarry (2011) which indicated that the average time spent on this topic in teacher education in Ireland was 3 h over the entire course. One third of the sample of graduate teachers in that particular study could not actually recall whether or not they had received any child protection training in their teacher education. As a result, most experiences were gained from placements during training as well as practical exposure later, but were considered by many to be insufficient to instil a sense of professional responsibility into their professional discourse. There is a clear implication in respect of the ability of teachers to discriminate between concerns that are reportable and those which are not.

Possibly connected to a deficient formative education in child protection, willingness to take 'ownership' of the relevant responsibilities varied considerably between different services. It was affected by a number of additional dynamics and perceived conflicts of interest that are likely to endure even when reporting becomes mandatory. For example, some professionals tended to resist moving from being a 'carer' to a 'conspirator'; others showed a tendency to 'abstract' the issue of child abuse, that is, to regard it as something that occurs outside a person's own reality, sometimes relegating it to the past or to other domains. Some jobs, it appeared, were not vocationally inclined towards the consideration of maltreatment; a neonatologist described her profession as 'Walt Disney ... it's lovely', insinuating that practitioners in her discipline would find it difficult to countenance how a tiny baby could be harmed.

In certain cases, the source of abstraction went beyond the frontline professionals and could be traced to the managerial structures in organisations, some of which kept their distance from the issue. The example was given of designated child protection officers in schools who were sometimes left solitary and unsupported by colleagues and line managers. This appeared to give rise in some cases to a sense, as one participant puts it, of being 'ambushed' by the weighty responsibilities they carried. Interviewees working in sports organisations confirmed the low motivation of individuals to sign up to a formal child protection role and the difficulty in filling those positions.

Detecting Child Abuse

The literature indicates that many professionals place their concerns along a 'continuum of severity that separates suspected abuse from reportable abuse' (Kennel and Agresti 1995, p. 612). The professionals who participated in the current research upheld that notion, confirming that 'straightforward' cases are rare and those with the more subtle indicators like emotional abuse and neglect are less likely to be confidently identified. The notion of 'theoretical' concerns was mooted; these were signs that arose in the context of chaos and turbulence which characterises how some families live. It was argued that confusion and dissent over thresholds for reporting would not be assisted by placing guidelines on a statutory footing; as one practitioner put it, the need to 'philosophise' whilst making a judgement would not be eradicated. Professionals argued that they will still be presented with symptoms that are often too intangible and obscure to define and so will continue to struggle with determining the appropriateness of making a report, despite the presence of mandatory reporting legislation. The ambiguity of medical and clinical signs was cited as a difficulty, partly because of the potential for alternative explanations but also as a result of the limited contact that some clinicians have with children. Participants commented on the difficulty of discerning whether sexualised language is a result of abuse, peer influence or social media. It was noted that some professionals have 'vantage points' unavailable to others, such as the opportunity to observe a child over a longer period or in more intimate circumstances, though the availability of these becomes limited as children mature.

Participants outlined the sort of obstacles that would challenge a straightforward application of the law and their own compliance with it. For example, presentations of abuse can be complicated by the contrivance of families to conceal it and avoid detection; doctors in the study pointed out that abusive families are less visible, tend to 'service hop' and are often transient, taking their 'histories' with them. Service evasion was noted as having the most significant effect for non-physical forms of abuse such as emotional abuse and neglect because detection of these forms of abuse was most reliant on the evidence building over a period of time to collate minor suspicions into a bigger body of evidence that provided more concrete proof of abuse. Service hopping and evasion inhibit the collation of such evidence. Some participants in the current study believed that the expectation that they would be able to form judgements about potential harm in respect of families who avoid contact is unrealistic.

Willingness to engage was cited as another improbable concept where abusive or potentially abusive families were concerned. For example, public health nurses are still reliant on the willingness of parents to engage with them and admit them into their homes and have no legal basis for insisting on entry. The concept of 'disguised compliance' identified by Reder et al. (1993) was also recognised by research participants who commented on how children could be presented in a certain way or conditioned to behave in a certain manner to conceal signs of abuse.

Whilst most professionals displayed commitment to protect children from abuse, the study showed that their motives were also permeated with anxiety about overstepping boundaries and 'jumping to conclusions'. The term 'balance' featured frequently in their narratives illustrates a reluctance to appear intrusive. Overall, it became apparent that whilst the 'case building' involved in detecting child abuse is evolutionary in how it progressed, it was not linear or consistent in the day-to-day work of professionals working with children who had to navigate a great deal of complexity and ambiguity to establish whether there was sufficient basis for concern.

Reporting Child Abuse

Interviewees in the current study were asked about their reporting practices once the suspicion of child abuse entered their consciousness. Their responses once again challenge the notion that adherence to reporting requirements is a straightforward business and illustrate the complex interplay of cognitive reasoning and risk assessment by professionals, most of whom are aware of the potentially life-altering consequences it may elicit for all stakeholders. The findings confirm that where presentations of suspected abuse are clear, i.e. physical manifestations such as bruises or direct disclosures by the child, reporters are driven by concern for the child to make reports and usually do so quickly. However, where concerns are more 'theoretical' as described above, responses tend to be delayed because of the multiplicity of anticipated positive and negative outcomes including adverse consequences. Particularly in terms of neglect where evidence may be ambiguous, professionals were more tentative about the prospect of reporting and recounted adopting a number of responses such as delayed reporting, rationalising of parental behaviour and second-hand reporting, where the concern was passed onto another professional instead of the statutory authorities. This finding is supported in a US study of the compliance of psychologists with child abuse reporting laws by Kalichman and Brosig (1993, p. 89) which found that most professionals tried to find supportive information about the occurrence of abuse before reporting. Anxiety about 'getting it wrong' and the potential consequences for themselves and for families of making an invalid report also impacts on the willingness of participants in the current study to make reports, a finding echoed by Lazenbatt and Freeman (2006) in Northern Ireland. Some professionals expressed the 'fear' factor and anticipation of personal retaliation from the persons they reported, particularly when they had reputations for violence.

Child protection guidance normally exhorts potential reporters to refrain from promising confidentiality, which most experienced professionals would agree is a worthy aspiration, but which is 'easier said than done'. Several participants demonstrated the inherent conflict in this counsel, identifying how efforts to encourage young people to be open and honest about their difficulties is paradoxically encouraging a trust that has to be later diminished by the act of telling someone else.

Confidence in the child protection system is recognised as a facilitator to reporting (Vulliamy and Sullivan 2000) and was evident in the current study, where practitioners who worked near to or had interconnected relationships with social workers claimed to feel 'safer' making reports. The lack of feedback from social work was one of the most resounding negative observations made by research participants. It was generally felt that the combination of the labour involved in the process of detection and the struggle to approach families prior to making a report warranted an assertive response from the system, but many had been left feeling disappointed and abandoned to deal with the aftermath of reporting without support. It was believed that such absence of reciprocity could act as a deterrent to future reporting, reflecting an earlier finding by Nayda (2002, p. 176) who found that nurses, disillusioned by the previous lack of response, tended to vary their reporting practices even though they were mandated.

The Anticipated Impact of Mandatory Reporting

The existence of a law is based on a reasonable expectation of compliance with whatever action or procedure is regulated by it; however, research on other aspects of child protection, for instance, a ban on corporal punishment of children, has found that adherence to the law is often variable in nature and very dependent on a range of variables including pre-existing positive attitudes and cultural readiness (Zolotor and Puzia 2010). Findings from the current study indicate similar ambiguities, illustrated in the varying attitudes of unconditional support, opposition, ambivalence or indifference to the possibilities offered by the legislation. Those who were wholly supportive of mandatory reporting tended to think of it as 'legitimate', or through a 'normative goal frame' as conceptualised by Etienne (2011), seeing the law as a foolproof method for protecting children and as a mechanism for redressing violations that occurred in the past whilst making a symbolic gesture about the importance of child protection in society. Some saw it as a mechanism for liberating themselves from any doubts or misgivings about the veracity of their concerns, allowing them to automatically report any suspicion and shift the onus on to the statutory system to ascertain its validity, as an interviewee pointed out:

> it takes all responsibility from you then … you can't start debating it intellectually at a staff meeting…I think it's great, it's the best thing that ever could happen.

However, some participants expressed cynicism about the proposed law, seeing it as an excessive and disproportionate response to scandal, creating a 'smoke-screen' which would not tackle the critical weaknesses in child protection. It was their opinion that the new law was designed to protect the State from further reprimand without addressing the real issue of a compromised child protection system. As one teacher opined:

> Who does this serve, this mandatory reporting? It serves the legislators… it covers them, so they're wiping their hands clean of it. Well, does it serve the pupil and the family of that pupil and even the school in which they're in, well I don't think so.

The current study illustrated how perspectives on the potential impact of mandatory reporting depended on the way that professionals believed it would impact on themselves and their services, on the child protection system generally and on children and families. Some clinicians outside the mainstream statutory service believed that it would increase their workload; requiring families to attend their services more often and monitoring the compliance of less experienced staff were seen as adding pressure. There were concerns that the law would deflect their attention away from a child's needs to the process of reporting which was more likely to be motivated by a fear of penalty than the child and family's welfare. Risk aversion was predicted and was seen not only in terms of its impact on professionals but the hazardous effect on child protection services who would be overwhelmed. A worst-case scenario was envisaged whereby professionals might be inclined to distance themselves from managing risk in their work with vulnerable families by either defensive reporting or 'turning a blind eye'.

Fear of 'swamping' the system was raised in a context where existing confidence in the capacity of services was already low. Increasing bureaucracy and a disproportionate investment of resources in processing reports was anticipated to the point where more time may be spent on administrative functions than actual interface with service users. The move to penalise failures to report was considered by some interviewees to be subordinate to the need for services to aid families once a concern is substantiated. Social workers commented pessimistically on the possibility, cited above, that professionals would use the legislation as an excuse to make reports based on inconsequential and insubstantial information without taking the time to consider the facts or discriminate between reportable and non-reportable incidents or indications.

> I've seen it… the professional rings up to give you the report and then they think they're work is done… 'dumping' on social workers, could actually increase

Apprehension was also expressed by interviewees from the NGO sector that further pressure would fall on them to case manage child protection concerns that the statutory services could not reach.

Perspectives on the potential impact of the mandatory reporting on children and families were mixed. A general medical practitioner commented on the possibility of more families being ‘dragged’ into the system, and a speech and language clinician also expressed concern about the ‘massive ordeal’ some families could experience because a practitioner was afraid not to report something which later turned out to be unfounded. It was suggested that families may be deterred from seeking help for fear that it may lead them into a child protection investigation.

Ironically, whilst most participants implied that the threat of sanctioning would motivate professionals who had hitherto been indifferent or ambivalent to become more aware of child protection issues and report them, considerable scepticism was expressed about the enforceability of the law. This was in the knowledge that very few cases had ever been prosecuted, but also because of the perceived difficulty in proving that an individual actively withheld information and the challenge involved in attempts to ‘legislate individual opinion’.

Overall, findings from the current study indicate that whilst the introduction of reporting legislation is likely to result in increased awareness about child abuse and a higher rate of engagement of families and professionals with the statutory child protection system, it will not eradicate the factors that currently challenge professionals in their ability and willingness to take what is perceived by many as a critical step in reporting a suspected child abuse to the authorities.

Conclusion

This chapter has focused on Irish children’s services at a transitional point between optional and mandatory reporting requirements. From a macro perspective, it has argued that public outrage about the conduct of the Catholic Church has dominated the child protection discourse and has fuelled the impetus for a political backlash against not only past abuse and mismanagement but also religious domination of social affairs in Ireland. The assumption that reporting legislation is either appropriate or timely in the current context has been challenged. It has also been argued that the renewed focus on regulation and legislation runs contrary to recent aspirations towards providing a proportionate response to the continuum of child welfare and protection matters that come to official attention. Recent research evidence in respect of the Irish system has been interrogated to demonstrate its limited capacity and somewhat fragile state, inferring that the additional pressure which will inevitably follow new legislation may well render the system untenable.

From a micro perspective, fresh empirical research findings have been used to highlight significant factors in the wider landscape of children’s services which may hinder the effectiveness of the proposed law. The research illustrates that many of the soon-to-be scheduled reporters lack knowledge and expertise in respect of child harm. It has highlighted the scant formative child protection education available to many professionals, but even more significantly, it has exposed limited professional motivation and managerial ambivalence about ‘owning’ the issue, which is regarded as complex and fraught with ambiguity. Reflecting previous findings from Ireland and other countries, the empirical evidence has also illustrated that despite official assumptions about likely compliance with regulations, actions are often inhibited by the doubts and personal challenges experienced by potential reporters which will be difficult to assuage. It has demonstrated mixed feelings about whether the proposed legislation will achieve more benefits than harm. Importantly, it has illustrated that the human and emotional costs of complying with legislation, both to reporters and families, are quite significant but rarely debated openly.

The principal argument laid out in this chapter is that in the present context, compelling uncertain professionals to make reports into a struggling child protection system is unlikely to serve children better. The worst-case scenario would be a high rate of false negatives, whereby child protection practitioners are too overwhelmed to discern between cases that require an immediate investigative response and those which can wait or may be best met by alternative services. If this occurs, the resulting diminution of confidence in the services is likely to deter reporters who may have otherwise reported serious abuse. A high rate of false positives would be equally detrimental; this could result from overzealous reporting from insecure professionals and would have the effect of undermining families and discouraging vulnerable parents from seeking help. If such adverse outcomes are to be avoided when mandatory reporting is introduced, measures will be required to increase confidence on two levels. Firstly, professionals' personal capacities to appropriately identify and respond to signs that children need help need to be enhanced, and secondly, the ability of the statutory system to respond appropriately and expeditiously must be strengthened so that reporters can anticipate that their concerns will be heard. The achievement of these will require training at pre- and post-qualifying levels for professionals likely to be working with children, particularly those in professionals that will be implicated by reporting legislation. Responsibility for child protection, together with commensurate resources, will need to be allocated to relevant government departments so that organisations such as schools, hospitals, youth and community services will assume ownership of the issue, create a safe culture and support the staff that are likely to encounter child abuse. The statutory system will need to be adequately supported by the full range of services that families require so that the most appropriate responses will be forthcoming when reports are made.

Mandatory reporting is internationally recognised as a symbol of government commitment to addressing the harms perpetrated on children; however, without attending to the complex processes that will determine its efficacy, the benefits of its introduction may only be rhetorical. The proposed solution is somewhat paradoxical; for mandatory reporting to work, the system needs to be well resourced and in good shape, with well-trained and competent practitioners and managers who are ready to take on child protection responsibilities and are confident in their judgement. It would also require sufficient services at preventive as well as interventive levels and good governance of statutory services. The irony is that were this healthy state to prevail, the necessity for legislation would be greatly diluted and mandatory reporting as a solution to the sins of the fathers would thus become a semi-redundant concept.

References

Black, F. (2002, October 24). Canon law has same status as golf rules, *Irish Independent*. http://www.independent.ie/irish-news/canon-law-has-same-status-as-golf-rules-26032154.html. Accessed 5 Dec 2013.

Brosnan, K. (2008). *Monageer inquiry*. Report presented to Ms Mary Harney T.D. Minister for Health and Children and Mr Dermot Ahern T.D. Minister for Justice Equality and Law Reform, 6th October 2008.

Buckley, R. (2013). *Child abuse reporting in Ireland and the socio-legal implications of introducing a mandatory reporting law.* PhD thesis, School of Social Work and Social Policy, Trinity College Dublin.

Buckley, H., & McGarry, K. (2011). Child protection in primary schools: A contradiction in terms or a potential opportunity? *Irish Educational Studies, 30*(1), 113–128.

Buckley, H., & O'Nolan C. (2013). *An examination of recommendations from inquiries into events in families, their interactions with State services and their impact on policy and practice*. Dublin: Department of Children and Youth Affairs. http://dcya.gov.ie/documents/publications/FamilyInquiries2013.pdf. Accessed 5 Dec 2013.

Buckley, H., Whelan, S., Carr, N., & Murphy, C. (2008). *Service users' perceptions of the Irish child protection system.* Dublin: Office of the Minister for Children and Youth Affairs. http://www.dcya.gov.ie/documents/publications/CF_service_users.pdf

Buckley, H., Carr, N., & Whelan, S. (2011). 'Like walking on eggshells': Service user views and expectations of the child protection system. *Child and Family Social Work, 16*, 101–106.

Children's Rights Alliance. (2013). *Report card 2013: Is Government keeping its promises to children?* Dublin: Children's Rights Alliance. http://www.childrensrights.ie/sites/default/files/submissions_reports/files/ReportCard2013.pdf. Accessed 9 Dec 2013.

Commission of Investigation. (2009). *Report into the Catholic Archdiocese of Dublin*. Dublin: Government Publications.

Commission of Investigation. (2010). *Report into the Catholic Diocese of Cloyne*. Dublin: Government Publications.

Commission to Inquire into Child Abuse. (2009) Report of the Commission to inquire into child abuse (Vols. 1–5). Dublin: Stationery Office.

Connolly, M. (2007). Practice frameworks: Conceptual maps to guide interventions in child welfare. *British Journal of Social Work, 37*(5), 825–837.

Connolly, M. (2009). Professional responses: Who does what in domestic violence and child protection? *Communities, Children and Families Australia, 4*, 34–37.

Dail Eireann Debate. (2011, Wednesday 20 July). *Commission of investigation report in the Catholic Diocese of Cloyne*. http://debates.oireachtas.ie/dail/2011/07/20/00013.asp. Accessed 5 Dec 2013.

De Boer, C., & Cody, N. (2007). Good helping relationships in child welfare: Learning from stories of success. *Child and Family Social Work, 12*, 32–42.

Department of Health. (1996). *Putting children first: Discussion document on mandatory reporting*. Dublin: Department of Health.

Department of Health and Children. (1999). *Children first: National guidelines for the protection & welfare of children*. Dublin: Department of Health & Children.

Devaney, J. (2004). Relating outcomes to objectives in child protection. *Child and Family Social Work, 9*(1), 27–38.

Etienne, J. (2011). Compliance theory: A goal framing approach. *Law and Policy, 33*(3), 305–333.

Featherstone, B., White, S., & Wastell, D. (2012). Ireland's opportunity to learn from England's difficulties? Auditing uncertainty in child protection. *Irish Journal of Applied Social Studies, 12*(1), Article 5.

Foucault, M. (1975). *Discipline and punish: The birth of the prison*. New York: Penguin.

Friend, C., Shlonsky, A., & Lambert, L. (2008). From evolving discourses to new practice approaches in domestic violence and child protective services. *Children and Youth Services Review, 30*, 689–698.

Gibbons, N. (2010). *Roscommon child care case*. Report of the Inquiry Team to the Health Service Executive, 27 October 2010. Dublin: HSE. http://www.hse.ie/eng/services/Publications/services/Children/RoscommonChildCareCase.html. Accessed 18 Nov 2012.

Gilbert, N. (2012). A comparative study of child welfare systems: Abstract orientations and concrete results. *Children and Youth Services Review, 34*, 532–536.

Goode, H., McGee, H., & O'Boyle, C. (2003). *Time to listen: Confronting child sexual abuse by Catholic clergy in Ireland*. Dublin: The Liffey Press.

Harvey, B. (2011). *A way forward for delivering children's services*. Dublin: Barnardos. http://www.barnardos.ie/assets/files/Advocacy/Brian%20Harvey%20Mar%202011%20_2_.pdf. Accessed 9 Dec 2013.

Health Service Executive. (2013). *Review of adequacy for HSE children and families services 2011*. Dublin: Health Service Executive.

Health Service Executive. (2014). Childcare performance indicators: Child protection and welfare referrals and sources of referrals 2012. Internal HSE document.

Hill, M., Stafford, A., & Green Lister, P. (2002). International perspectives on child protection. Appendix B of Scottish Executive *It's Everyone's Job to Make Sure I'm Alright: Report of the Child Protection Audit and Review, Edinburgh, Scottish Executive.*http://www.scotland.gov.uk/Resource/Doc/1181/0009926.pdf. Accessed 5 Dec 2013.

Howe, D. (1992). Child abuse and the bureaucratisation of social work. *Sociological Review, 40*, 490–508.

Humphreys, C. (2007). *Domestic violence and child protection: Challenging directions for practice* (Issues paper 13). Sydney: Australian Domestic & Family Violence Clearinghouse. http://www.adfvc.unsw.edu.au/pdf%20files/issuespaper_13.pdf. Accessed 5 Dec 2013.

Irish Catholic Bishop's Conference. (1996). *Child sexual abuse: Framework for a church response*. Dublin: Veritas.

Irish Catholic Bishops Conference. (2013). *Statement of Cardinal Brady, Primate of all Ireland.* http://www.catholicbishops.ie/2013/12/10/statement-cardinal-brady-publication-nbscccireport-archdiocese-armagh/. Accessed 30 Jan 2014.

Irish Times. (2010, March 15). *Brady insists he will not resign over Smyth case*. http://www.irishtimes.com/news/brady-insists-he-will-not-resign-over-smyth-case-1.854673. Accessed 5 Dec 2013.

Jeyes, G. (2013). *Change in a cold climate: Reform in a time of austerity*. Keynote speech delivered at the *13th ISPCAN European Regional Conference*, Burlington Hotel, Dublin, 18th September 2013.

Kalichman, S., & Brosig, C. (1993). 'Practicing psychologists' interpretation of and compliance with child abuse reporting laws. *Law and Human Behavior, 17*(1), 83–93.

Keenan, M. (2012). *Child sexual abuse and the catholic church: Gender, power and organizational culture*. New York: Oxford University Press.

Kennel, R., & Agresti, J. A. (1995). 'Effects of gender and age on psychologists' reporting of child sexual abuse. *Professional Psychology: Research and Practice, 25*(6), 612–615.

Lazenbatt, A., & Freeman, R. (2006). Recognising and reporting child physical abuse: A survey of primary health care professionals. *Issues and Innovations in Nursing Practice, 56*(3), 227–236.

Lonne, B., Parton, N., Thomson, J., & Harries, M. (2009). *Reforming child protection*. Abingdon: Routledge.

Munro, E. (2011). *Munro review of child protection: Final report – a child centred system*. London: Department for Education.

Murphy, F., Buckley, H., & Joyce, L. (2005). *The Ferns Report*. Dublin: Government Publications.

National Board for Safeguarding Children in the Catholic Church. (2009). *Standards and guidance document for the Catholic Church in Ireland*. Maynooth: NBSCCC. http://www.safeguarding.ie/wp-content/uploads/2011/11/Standards-and-Guidance.pdf. Accessed 30 Dec 2014.

National Board for Safeguarding Children in the Catholic Church. (2012). *Annual Report 2011*. http://www.safeguarding.ie/wp-content/uploads/2011/11/Annual-Report-2011.pdf. Accessed 5 Dec 2013.

National Board for Safeguarding Children in the Catholic Church. (2013). *Annual Report 2012*. http://www.safeguarding.ie/wp-content/uploads/2013/05/NBSCCCI_Report_2012.pdf. Accessed 5 Dec 2013.

Nayda, R. (2002). 'Influences on registered nurses' decision-making in cases of suspected child abuse. *Child Abuse Review, 11*, 168–178.

Oireachtas Debate. (2011). *Oireachtas debate on the publication of the Commission of Inquiry into the Catholic Diocese of Cloyne*. http://oireachtasdebates.oireachtas.ie/debates%20authoring/DebatesWebPack.nsf/takes/dail2011072000023?opendocument&highlight=Cloyne. Accessed 30 Jan 2014.

Oireachtas Debate. (2014). *Update on child and family Services*. http://oireachtasdebates.oireachtas.ie/debates%20authoring/debateswebpack.nsf/committeetakes/HEJ2014092500007#. Accessed 30 Dec 2014.

Ombudsman for Children. (2013). *Annual report 2012*. Dublin: Office of the Ombudsman for Children. http://www.oco.ie/assets/files/annual-report/OCOAnnualReport2012.pdf. Accessed 9 Dec 2013.

Parton, N. (2004). From Maria Colwell to Victoria Climbie: Reflections on public inquiries into child abuse a generation apart. *Child Abuse Review, 13*(2), 80–94.

Raftery, M., & O'Sullivan, E. (1999). *Suffer the little children: The inside story of Ireland's industrial schools*. Dublin: New Island.

Reder, P., Duncan, S., & Gray, M. (1993). *Beyond blame: Child abuse tragedies revisited*. London: Routledge.

Sunday Business Post. (2014, July 6). *Children's agency busts its budget in first year*. http://www.businesspost.ie/#!story/Home/News/Children's+agency+busts+its+budget+in+first+year/id/996e8c13-d229-41c4-8704-b134a12b09e0. Accessed 8 July 2014.

Tilbury, C. (2004). The influence of performance measurement on child welfare policy and practice. *British Journal of Social Work, 34*, 225–241.

Vulliamy, A., & Sullivan, R. (2000). 'Reporting child abuse: Paediatricians' experiences with the child protection system. *Child Abuse and Neglect, 24*(11), 1461–1470.

Zolotor, A., & Puzia, M. (2010). Bans against corporal punishment: A systematic review of the laws, changes in attitudes and behaviours. *Child Abuse Review, 19*, 223–227.

Chapter 14
Mandatory Reporting of Child Sexual Abuse by Religious Leaders

Patrick Parkinson

In recent years, an increasing amount of attention has been given to the problem of child sexual abuse in church communities. Churches are very vulnerable to this problem since they have an extensive involvement in work with children and young people. There are Sunday Schools, youth groups, church-affiliated boys and girls' associations, holiday clubs, church camps and other such activities. Other faith communities also involve children in different ways in the life of their congregations. Faith-based organisations have also been very involved in caring for children in institutional settings such as boarding schools and – in the past – children's homes.

It should not be surprising that faith communities contain within their ranks those who otherwise have a predisposition towards the sexual abuse of children. The tendency to sexually abuse children crosses all sectors of the population and includes people with a great variety of beliefs – and no belief. It is not surprising then that religious communities have a problem with child sexual abuse. It would be surprising if they did not.

Clergy are included in many jurisdictions as one of the categories of professional groups that are required to report child sexual abuse. Michigan provides an example. It has mandated members of the clergy to report among 22 listed categories of professional who might have contact with children in the course of their professional work (Mich. Comp. Laws. Ann. §722.623). It exempts a member of the clergy who receives a legally privileged communication in his or her professional character in a confession or similarly confidential context (Mich. Comp. Laws. Ann. §722.631). However, the inclusion of clergy among the categories of professional mandatory reporters is far from universal either in North America or elsewhere (Goldenberg 2013).

P. Parkinson (✉)
Faculty of Law, University of Sydney, Sydney, NSW, Australia
e-mail: patrick.parkinson@sydney.edu.au

B. Mathews, D.C. Bross (eds.), *Mandatory Reporting Laws and the Identification of Severe Child Abuse and Neglect*, Child Maltreatment 4,
DOI 10.1007/978-94-017-9685-9_14

This chapter considers the arguments for requiring clergy and other such religious leaders to report concerns about the sexual abuse of children and the different options for so doing. It sets the debate within the context of the seemingly high level of child sexual abuse within certain faith communities and the cultural impediments to reporting of abuse which are specific to certain religious groups.

The Context for Considering Mandatory Reporting

While sex offenders are found in all denominations and in people of many different theological persuasions (John Jay College 2011, p. 21; Parkinson 1997), it needs to be acknowledged that the problem of child sexual abuse is not evenly spread across all faith communities. All the evidence suggests that the Catholic Church has experienced a disproportionate problem in relation to child sexual abuse. Around the western world, case after case has emerged of Catholic priests and male members of religious orders being charged with sex offences against children. Perhaps for this reason, almost all of the research on child sexual abuse in churches has focused on abuse by Catholic priests and members of religious orders (Dale and Alpert 2007; Falkenhain et al. 1999; Farrell and Taylor 2000; Haywood et al. 1996a, b; Isely et al. 2008; John Jay College 2004; Langevin et al. 2000; Rossetti 1995; Smith et al. 2008; Terry 2008; Terry and Ackerman 2008).

The most comprehensive account of child sexual abuse in the US Catholic Church has come from the John Jay College of Criminal Justice. It found that 4 % of all priests who had served in the United States from 1950 to 2002 had allegations of child sexual abuse made against them (John Jay College 2004; Terry 2008). Most victims were male and older in age compared to victims in the general population (Terry and Ackerman 2008). Some evidence in Australia appears to indicate a higher level of offending than this. Prof. Des Cahill identified 378 priests who graduated from a particular seminary in Melbourne and who were ordained between 1940 and 1966. Of these, 14 (3.7 %) were convicted of sex offences against children and another four were acknowledged to have abused children after their deaths. That is, 18 priests or 4.76 % of the total who were ordained between those years sexually abused children. Taking a later cohort of seminarians, the 74 priests who were ordained between 1968 and 1971 from that seminary, 4 (5.41 %) had been convicted of sex offences against children (Cahill 2012). Another 20 had resigned the priesthood, and so as a proportion of those priests ordained in those three periods who had long-term careers in the priesthood, the percentage is rather higher.

The proportion of Catholic priests who had been convicted in criminal trials in the Cahill studies is very much greater than in the John Jay study. Only 3 % of all priests against whom allegations were made were convicted in the period of that study (John Jay College 2004). Arguably, the level of convictions of Catholic priests and religious in Australia is rather higher than for men in the general population, although reliable baseline data on levels of offending in the general population is hard to find (Parkinson 2013).

Any data on proportions of clergy who have abused children is, in any event, likely to be an underestimate because so many victims do not disclose abuse at all or do so decades after the events. Australian research indicates that the levels of disclosure of abuse are closely correlated with media exposure of the issue as a consequence of high-profile cases or public inquiries (Parkinson et al. 2010).

In comparison with the Catholic Church, prosecutions of clergy from other Christian traditions for child sexual abuse are much less common (Keenan 2012, p. 11). A study of child sexual abuse in the Anglican Church of Australia provides some evidence of levels of reported abuse in a Protestant faith community (Parkinson et al. 2009, 2010, 2012). The study was based on church files of all allegations of child sexual abuse by ministers, youth workers or other pastoral staff in parish settings in which the allegation has been made since 1990. Seventeen out of 23 dioceses in Australia took part in the study. Three rural dioceses declined to participate. The remaining 3 dioceses did agree to participate but were omitted from the study because they had no cases falling within the study criteria. The 6 dioceses that did not take part were all dioceses with comparatively small numbers of clergy in regional and rural areas of Australia.

This study was not a census of all reported cases of child sexual abuse within the Anglican Church but covered the great majority of the known cases that were within scope in the 17 dioceses that participated in the study. On a rough estimate, the proportion of Anglican clergy accused of sexual abuse in parish settings appears to be well below 1 % (Parkinson et al. 2012).

The statistics from the Victoria Police (2012), giving evidence to a Parliamentary Inquiry, also provide some evidence of the incidence of child sexual abuse in the Catholic Church compared with other faith communities. The Police identified all criminal convictions for sexual abuse of minors in Victoria between January 1956 and June 2012 involving members of religious organisations. Three hundred and seventy were victims of abuse in the Catholic Church. There were 37 victims in the Anglican Church, 36 in relation to the Salvation Army and 18 involving Judaism. While the Catholic Church has the largest number of adherents in Australia and priests and religious brothers often worked in boarding schools and children's homes which offered particular opportunities for abuse, the rate of convictions of Catholic Church personnel does seem to be strikingly out of proportion with the size of this faith community compared with other faith communities (Parkinson 2013).

The Catholic Church has not only been the major focus of attention regarding child sexual abuse in faith communities because of the apparently high incidence of such abuse. It has attracted attention also because of widespread allegations that it has covered up these offences and has otherwise failed to respond appropriately to victims. In Australia, a national Royal Commission is currently examining these issues and a Parliamentary Inquiry in the State of Victoria reported on the subject in November 2013 (Parliament of Victoria 2013). The pattern of cover-up has been an international one (Robertson 2010). In the United States, awareness of the extent of that cover-up is generally traced to reports in the *Boston Globe* newspaper in 2002 concerning the Boston Archdiocese (Smith et al. 2008; Plante and McChesney 2011). In Ireland, the reports of the Ryan and Murphy Commissions, together with other inquiries, also lifted the lid on much that had previously been hidden (Ryan Report 2009; Murphy Report – Dublin 2009; Murphy Report – Cloyne 2010). There have also been similar accounts in inquiries from other countries (Robertson 2010).

The Murphy Report into the Archdiocese of Dublin (Murphy Report – Dublin 2009, pp. 3–4) summarised its findings on the history of cover-up as follows:

> The volume of revelations of child sexual abuse by clergy over the past 35 years or so has been described by a Church source as a "*tsunami*" of sexual abuse. He went on to describe the "*tsunami*" as "*an earthquake deep beneath the surface hidden from view*". The clear implication of that statement is that the Church, in common with the general public, was somehow taken by surprise by the volume of the revelations. Officials of the Archdiocese of Dublin and other Church authorities have repeatedly claimed to have been, prior to the late 1990s, on 'a learning curve' in relation to the matter. Having completed its investigation, the Commission does not accept the truth of such claims and assertions.
>
> The Dublin Archdiocese's pre-occupations in dealing with cases of child sexual abuse, at least until the mid 1990s, were the maintenance of secrecy, the avoidance of scandal, the protection of the reputation of the Church, and the preservation of its assets. All other considerations, including the welfare of children and justice for victims, were subordinated to these priorities.

While the main focus has been on the Catholic Church, no church or other organisation with a significant work among children is free from reproach. In Australia, for example, there have been inquiries established by the Anglican Church into its past failings in dealing appropriately with child sexual abuse cases (Kohl and Crowley 1998; O'Callaghan and Briggs 2003; Olsson, and Chung 2004). There have also been significant issues in Orthodox Jewish communities in the United States (Resnicoff 2012).

Religious Barriers to Reporting

A major reason for having mandatory reporting laws is to overcome religious barriers to reporting that place at risk the well-being of children (Smith 1994) and which cannot be justified in the name of religious freedom.

Barriers to Reporting in Catholicism

The Catholic Church around the world is far from a monolithic institution with uniform policies and approaches to issues. In different countries and at different times, the Catholic Bishops Conferences have sought to deal with the issue of clerical sexual abuse in ways that have involved more or less transparency and cooperation with civil authorities. In Australia, for example, a protocol published by the Catholic Bishops Conference and leaders of religious orders in 1996 concerning the Church's responses to sexual abuse made it clear that it was the policy of the Church to cooperate with the police on such matters and to encourage those who complained of criminal misconduct by clergy and religious to make a formal report to the police (Towards Healing 1996). Since 2010 there has been a formal requirement in *Towards Healing* to notify the police of the complaint concerning the alleged offender even if the complainant declines to go to the police (Towards Healing 2010). Section 37.4 of *Towards Healing* states:

> In the case of an alleged criminal offence, if the complainant does not want to take the matter to the police, all church personnel should nonetheless pass details of the complaint to the Director of Professional Standards, who should provide information to the police other than giving those details that could lead to the identification of the complainant.

This is to ensure transparency and also because the police may be able to use the intelligence gained if other complaints emerge against the same alleged offender. One of the other obligations in *Towards Healing* is that no victim should be bound by any pledge of secrecy in relation to their account of the abuse.

However, as the Irish experience demonstrates, such a policy has not always had the support of the Catholic leadership in Rome. At about the same time as *Towards Healing* was being developed in Australia, the Irish bishops developed a policy which included mandatory reporting to the police of all credible reports of abuse. However, they were rebuked for so doing by the Vatican. On January 31, 1997, the Irish apostolic nuncio wrote to the Irish bishops, conveying the position of the Congregation for Clergy, that the policy of mandatory reporting 'gives rise to serious reservations of both a moral and a canonical nature'. The letter also instructed that the procedures established by the Code of Canon Law must be 'meticulously followed' (Storero 1997).

Evidence has also emerged of a view, attributed to Pope John Paul II, that bishops should protect priests from the authorities. In 2001, Bishop Pierre Pican of Bayeux was given a 3-month suspended prison sentence for not reporting Fr René Bissey, who had been sentenced to 18 years in prison in 2000 for sex offences against children. Cardinal Castrillón Hoyos, the Prefect of the Congregation for the Clergy, wrote to the Bishop, congratulating him on not denouncing a priest to the civil authorities. He was said to have acted wisely in preferring to go to prison rather than denounce his priest-son. Cardinal Hoyos advanced a theological reason for this position. He explained that the relationship between priests and their bishop is not professional but sacramental and forges very special bonds of spiritual paternity. He drew the analogy with rules of law in various countries which excused one close relative from testifying against another.

The letter concluded that in order to 'encourage brothers in the episcopate in this delicate matter', a copy of the letter would be forwarded to all the conferences of bishops. The Cardinal said at a conference in 2010 that he wrote the letter after consulting Pope John Paul II and that it was the Pope who authorised him to send this letter to all the bishops. It appears that the bishop indicated at his trial that the admission of guilt by the priest had not been in the confessional (Heneghan 2010a, b; Robertson 2010, para [53]).

Barriers to Reporting in Orthodox Judaism

There are also barriers to reporting as a consequence of some interpretations of the Jewish law. There is a view, held particularly by Haredi Jews, that Jews should not denounce fellow members of the community to secular authorities for wrongdoing (Resnicoff 2012) and that this includes not reporting the sexual abuse of children. This is because of the doctrine of *mesira*.

According to the leading twelfth-century rabbi Mosheh ben Maimon (Maimonides), *mesira* requires that Jews should always protect each other from the Gentile governments, and informants should be punished (Maimonides 1997, pp. 8, 9–10):

> Halacha 9
>
> It is forbidden to inform about a colleague to the gentiles and endanger his physical person or his property. This applies even when the person concerned is a wicked person who commits sins, and even if he causes one irritation and discomfort. Anyone who actually informs about a Jew and endangers his person or his property to the gentiles will not receive a portion in the world to come.
>
> Halacha 10
>
> It is permissible to kill a *moseir* [informer] in any country, even in the present age, when the court no longer metes out capital punishment.
>
> It is permitted to kill him before he informs. When he says: "I will inform on so and so and endanger his person and/or his property" – even property of minimal value – he has made it permissible for others to kill him.
>
> He should be warned and told: "Do not inform." If he says brazenly, "No. I will inform about him," it is a mitzvah to kill him, and whoever kills him receives merit.

Daniel Eidensohn, an Israeli psychologist and Haredi scholar, comments that the greatest reason for people refusing to get involved in cases of suspected child sexual abuse 'is that they are afraid of the serious crime of informing. It is one of the worst crimes a Jew can do' (Eidensohn 2010, p. 108). Other Orthodox Jewish scholars disagree that this doctrine requires that one Jew should not report child sexual abuse by another Jew to the authorities. Prof. Michael Broyde (2002, p. 7), for example, writes that 'serial killers, armed robbers, sexual predators or muggers… should all be informed upon if that is needed to protect society'.

While Jewish scholars may disagree on the application of *mesira* in a society governed by the rule of law, the belief that it is forbidden to inform upon another Jew seems to have a powerful influence on the actions of some. There have been numerous reports of retaliation against members of the Orthodox community in the United States who have spoken publicly about the problem of child sexual abuse in Orthodox Jewish families and communities (Resnicoff 2012). Orthodox rabbinical teaching on this subject in the United States has accommodated secular reporting laws to some extent, but the position taken by Agudath Israel is that even mandated reporters must consult the rabbi first before making a report and should do so only if the rabbi considers that the evidence is such that the legal duty to report arises (Berger 2011).

Different Bases for Mandatory Reporting

It is in this context, that consideration has to be given to the idea of mandating clergy, pastors, rabbis and other such authoritative religious leaders to report suspected sex offences against children to the police.

There are three forms that such mandatory reporting could take. The first is to add ministers of religion to the list of professionals who are required to report any reasonable concerns they have about the sexual abuse of a child. The arguments for and against such an inclusion are perhaps the same as for mandatory reporting generally. There needs to be a cost-benefit analysis of the gains to be made from identifying more children who have been sexually abused, or are at risk of sexual abuse, against the resources involved in training a new category of mandatory reporters and investigating cases where such concern was not warranted.

Arguably, few clergy have as much interaction with children and young people as certain other professional groups who typically are included in lists of mandatory reporters. If the aim of mandatory reporting were to identify children in the general community who are being abused or at risk of abuse, then the most obvious mandated reporters in church communities would be Sunday School teachers and youth leaders, not clergy. Nonetheless, these teachers and leaders – typically volunteers – might be expected to report concerns to the priest or minister with responsibility for the congregation. If that assumption is valid, then the case for mandating clergy as reporters might be that they would better ensure that there are reporting mechanisms within the life of the congregation or parish and that they are made aware of any serious concerns about the well-being of a child. They could then fulfil their obligation to report to authorities accordingly.

A second option is to mandate reporting only of child abuse concerns where the alleged perpetrator is another member of the religious organisation. The rationale for this would be to identify child abuse by clergy and other religious leaders in situations where, without compulsion, the church leader receiving the information about the abuse, or otherwise developing a reasonable suspicion about it, would be reluctant to report. An Inquiry in Victoria, Australia, into the protection of vulnerable children (PVVC 2012) recommended that:

> The Crimes Act 1958 (Vic) should be amended to create a separate reporting duty where there is a reasonable suspicion a child or young person who is under 18 is being, or has been, physically or sexually abused by an individual within a religious or spiritual organisation. The duty should extend to:
>
> - A minister of religion; and
> - A person who holds an office within, is employed by, is a member of, or a volunteer of a religious or spiritual organisation that provides services to, or has regular contact with, children and young people.
>
> An exemption for information received during the rite of confession should be made.

This reporting obligation would only extend to suspicions concerning abuse of a child or young person who was currently under 18. The Inquiry Panel was 'mindful of the right of an adult who was previously abused as a child to be able to choose whether or not they wish to lodge a complaint of criminal abuse' (PVVC 2012, p. 355). The Panel also considered, but did not recommend, the option of adding ministers of religion to the list of mandated reporters under child protection legislation on the basis that, in its view, the cost-benefit analysis did not justify that inclusion.

The Inquiry's recommendation, if adopted, would create a very limited obligation. A member of a religious organisation or a volunteer within it would be required to report if he or she reasonably suspects another member of sexual abuse but not if he or she had certain knowledge of sexual abuse of a child when the abuse was not occurring within a religious or spiritual organisation.

If the Inquiry's recommendation were to be adopted, then there would need to be a clearer definition of what is meant by 'an individual within a religious or spiritual organisation'. Presumably what is meant is that the abuse has occurred, or is occurring, within the context of the life of the congregation, for example, in the Sunday School or youth group, and that the alleged perpetrator is in a position of leadership or otherwise involved in that religious activity. The difficulty with creating a new criminal offence of this type is that the boundaries of the obligation may be difficult to draw. Parents, who are formally church members, may be 'individuals within a religious organisation', but if the concern about abuse or neglect arises in the care of their own children at home, there is no nexus with the life of the congregation. The distinction between abuse by a parent in the home and by a leader at a youth camp is arguably clear enough; but how would one classify a member of the music group or choir who meets a teenager in the course of that ministry but who is suspected of engaging in a sexual relationship with him or her in his own home? Criminal offences need to be defined with great clarity.

A third position is to mandate reporting to the police by any person, including members of the clergy, who knows or believes a criminal offence has been committed involving the sexual abuse of a child, whether or not the complainant is still a child, but subject to defences. This is essentially the position that has been taken in Ireland, following the various commissions of inquiry into abuse within the Catholic Church and in institutional care. The *Criminal Justice (Withholding of Information on Offences Against Children and Vulnerable Persons) Act 2012* provides that:

> 2.—(1) Subject to this section, a person shall be guilty of an offence if—
> (a) he or she knows or believes that an offence, that is a Schedule 1 offence, has been committed by another person against a child, and
> (b) he or she has information which he or she knows or believes might be of material assistance in securing the apprehension, prosecution or conviction of that other person for that offence, and fails without reasonable excuse to disclose that information as soon as it is practicable to do so to a member of the Garda Síochána [police].
> (2) Subsection (1) applies only to information that a person acquires, receives or becomes aware of after the passing of this Act irrespective of whether the Schedule 1 offence concerned was committed before or after that passing.
> (3) The child against whom the Schedule 1 offence concerned was committed (whether or not still a child) shall not be guilty of an offence under this section.

There is a similar offence in section 3 for failure to report an offence against a vulnerable person, which includes adults suffering an intellectual disability, mental illness or dementia or severe enduring physical impairment or injury which is of such a nature or degree as to severely restrict the capacity of the person to guard himself or herself against serious exploitation or abuse.

What this enactment does is to impose, prospectively, a duty to report on anyone who has material information which may lead to the apprehension, prosecution or conviction of a person for committing certain criminal offences against children, subject to defences. The Schedule 1 offences which form the basis of the reporting obligation include not only sex offences against children but also murder, manslaughter, physical assault and reckless endangerment. The focus of the Irish legislation is therefore evidently on a law enforcement response to child abuse, in contrast to the common form of mandatory reporting law which requires notification to the relevant child welfare department whether or not the notifier knows the identity of the perpetrator. The Irish provision therefore has, as its central focus, the prohibition of conscious concealment of evidence to assist a wrongdoer, whereas the central focus of most mandatory reporting laws is on the identification of children who may be victims of sexual abuse. While mandating reporting, the section preserves the rules of evidence concerning privileged communications (section 2(4)), which may prevent the admissibility of any such report in a criminal trial. The available penalties for failing to report include imprisonment.

Section 4 provides the defences:

> **4.**—(1) Subject to this section, in any proceedings for an offence under section 2 or 3, it shall be a defence for the accused person to show—
> (*a*) that the child or vulnerable person against whom the Schedule 1 offence or the Schedule 2 offence, as the case may be, concerned was committed made known his or her view (provided that he or she was capable of forming a view on the matter) that the commission of that offence, or information relating to it, should not be disclosed to the Garda Síochána [police], and
> (b) that he or she (the accused person) knew of and relied upon that view.
> (2) Without prejudice to the right of the child or vulnerable person against whom the Schedule 1 offence or the Schedule 2 offence, as the case may be, concerned was committed to disclose the commission of that offence, or information relating to it, to the Garda Síochána, it shall be presumed for the purposes of subsection (1), unless the contrary is shown, that if—
> (*a*) the child concerned has not attained the age of 14 years, or
> (*b*) the vulnerable person concerned falls under paragraph (a) of the definition of vulnerable person in section 1(1) (whether or not he or she also falls under paragraph (b) of that definition),
> he or she does not have the capacity to form a view as to whether the commission of that offence, or information relating to it, should be disclosed to the Garda Síochána.

Further provisions in this section state that if a child or vulnerable person does not have the capacity to make that decision, then the parent has a defence if he or she formed the view, on reasonable grounds, and taking account of the wishes of the child or vulnerable person that it was not in their best interests for the commission of the offence, or information relating to it, to be disclosed to the police. However, this defence is not available if the alleged offender is a family member, unless the parent relied upon the view of a doctor, nurse, psychologist or social worker who provided services to the child or vulnerable person concerned that the information should not be disclosed to the police. The professional giving that opinion is also protected if he or she had reasonable grounds for forming that view and acted in accordance with the standards of care that could reasonably be expected of a member of that profession in forming such a view in the circumstances concerned. Staff in certain prescribed organisations working with victims of abuse who are children or vulnerable persons have a similar defence for a reasonably based and good faith determination that it would be best, in order to protect the health and well-being of that child or vulnerable person, not to make a report to the police.

It may be that the Irish law is too complex. Laws which impose obligations on the general public need to be clear enough to be easily understood. The defences provided to parents and professionals rely on interpretations about reasonable beliefs and actions taken in accordance with appropriate professional standards; but where there is disagreement among professionals concerning the circumstances when it may be better not to report, the parent or professional risks being charged with an offence and finding that a court second-guesses his or her good faith judgment, leading to conviction on a serious charge.

It may be better, if the law is to take this pathway, for there to be a broadly based duty to report child sexual abuse and other serious criminal offences against children subject to good faith professional judgments of health professionals and social workers involved with children that it would be damaging to the health or safety of the child for such a report to be made. If parents are to be compelled to report, then this should be subject to rules or guidelines dealing with a parent's objection, expressed in good faith, to the effect that it is not in the best interests of the child, for the child to be required to give evidence in a criminal trial.

The Issue of the Confessional

In the Irish law, it is no defence to a charge of failing to report that the communication that led to receipt of the information was received in the context of sacramental confession. In Catholic doctrine, the confessional gives rise to particular difficulties, because, according to Canon 1388 of the Church's (universal) Canon law, intentionally breaching the seal of the confessional will lead to excommunication of the priest. The reason was explained by the Catholic Church in Victoria, Australia, in a submission to a Parliamentary Inquiry (Catholic Church in Victoria 2012, p. 106):

> The confession is understood as being made to God. The priest to whom the confession is made is representing the person of Christ. Consequently, admissions made to God through the priest are not the priest's to reveal.

Disclosures in the confessional are, in some jurisdictions, subject to privilege and a person may not be compelled to give evidence in court in breach of this obligation of confidentiality (Mabey 2006; Thompson 2011).

In the context of dealing with child sexual abuse, the significance of the confessional should not be exaggerated. Bishop Geoffrey Robinson, a leader in dealing with the issue of child sexual abuse in the Australian Catholic Church, comments as follows (Robinson 2012):

> Concerning the confessional, the first point to make is that paedophile priests simply do not go to confession. Partly this is because of the distorted thinking that is commonly part of their offence, that they have convinced themselves that what they are doing is not wrong. Partly, it is due to a fear that any priest they approach would not give them an easy absolution, but instead be very demanding indeed in terms of a 'purpose of amendment'.
>
> If any ever did go to confession, they'd make sure it was in circumstances where they would not be recognised.
>
> The priest hearing the confession would probably not know of the identity of the offender or of the victim, and so would have no specific crime to report. Furthermore, if a single priest broke the seal of confession and reported the matter to the police, that would be the last time any paedophile priest confessed to anything anywhere.

In 52 years as a priest, he had never had to deal with the situation of a person using the confessional to reveal the sexual abuse of children.

The balance between respect for religious beliefs and the rights and freedoms of others is not always an easy one to find, and while it might be the easy answer to the problem to insist that the protection of children trumps all other concerns, it is submitted that the same balancing exercise needs to be conducted in this area as in all other conflicts of rights and interests. In the case of the confidentiality of the confessional, how compelling is the evidence that overriding a religiously based objection will lead to a material improvement in the protection of children? Might it also have negative effects in preventing people going to confession and therefore depriving the priest of the opportunity to persuade the person to give himself up to the police as a condition for absolution? What impact does it have on social cohesion and respect for the law if the law refuses to accommodate genuinely and deeply held beliefs and religious practices which have long been respected in the past? Arguably, the case for overriding the seal of the confessional has not been made out.

Conclusion

The issues concerning mandatory reporting by clergy are, to some extent, similar to the issues involved in mandating other professionals but in other respects different. The case is quite weak for clergy to be required to report suspected child sexual abuse generally, if the objective is to identify sexually abused children and for the child protection authorities to respond accordingly. The decision about including a class of professional within the list of mandated reporters has typically been made on the basis of the likelihood that, in the course of their professional work, they will become aware of, or suspicious of, abuse of a child and are in a position to make sensible professional judgments concerning the nature and seriousness of the possible abuse so as to determine whether a report is justified.

The case for mandating ministers of religion to report knowledge and reasonable suspicions of criminal sexual offences by a member of the religious organisation to the police is strong, particularly in the light of the history of non-cooperation with the police seen, at the highest levels, in the Catholic Church and as a consequence of certain interpretations of Jewish law. These institutional barriers to reporting are, with the exception of the Catholic doctrine of the confessional, not doctrinal but cultural. Put differently, imposing an obligation on religious leaders to report criminal sexual offences against children, subject to the exception of sacramental confession, would not interfere with the right given in Article 18 of the International Covenant on Civil and Political Rights (ICCPR) which states:

> Everyone shall have the right to freedom of thought, conscience and religion. This right shall include freedom to have or to adopt a religion or belief of his choice, and freedom, either individually or in community with others and in public or private, to manifest his religion or belief in worship, observance, practice and teaching.

Mandatory reporting to police would improve the likelihood that offenders will be charged and convicted, with resulting benefits in terms of child protection. There remains, however, the difficult issue of how far the reporting obligation should extend. Mandatory reporting typically requires notification of concerns about children while they remain children for the purposes of intervening to protect them. Should clergy be under a duty to report even when the adult complainant does not want them to do so and indicates that he or she does not intend to make a statement to the police?

There is now sufficient evidence from around the world that some religious leaders have actively discouraged devout believers from going to the police and have sought to enforce that silence as a matter of religious obligation. If so, the appropriate balance in the law might best be found if clergy are required to report the suspected criminal offence, including the source of their information (which may be statements by the complainant), and then for the police to talk to the complainant about his or her concerns or fears about making a statement. The complainant ought to be able to say no; but in the light of the history that has emerged in recent years, there may need to be legislation that requires disclosure to the police of at least sufficient details that the police and complainant can have that conversation directly.

References

Berger, P. (2011, May 25). Ultra-orthodox group affirms abuse cases go first to Rabbi. *Jewish Daily Forward*. http://forward.com/articles/138131

Broyde, M. (2002). Informing on others to a just government: A Jewish Law view. *The Journal of Halacha & Contemporary Society, 41*, 5–48.

Cahill, D. (2012). *Parliamentary Inquiry*, Victoria, submission, September 2012 at http://www.parliament.vic.gov.au/images/stories/committees/fcdc/inquiries/57th/Child_Abuse_Inquiry/Submissions/Cahill_Professor_Desmond.pdf

Catholic Church in Victoria. (2012). *Facing the truth*. Parliamentary Inquiry, Victoria, submission, September 2012 at http://www.parliament.vic.gov.au/images/stories/committees/fcdc/inquiries/57th/Child_Abuse_Inquiry/Submissions/Catholic_Church_in_Victoria.pdf

Dale, K., & Alpert, J. (2007). Hiding behind the cloth: Child sexual abuse and the Catholic Church. *Child Abuse and Neglect, 16*, 59–74.
Eidensohn, D., (2010). *Child and domestic abuse* (Vol. I). https://www.createspace.com/en/community/message/47365
Falkenhain, M., Duckro, P., Hughes, H., Rossetti, S., & Gfeller, J. (1999). Cluster analysis of sex offenders: A validation with Roman Catholic priests and brothers. *Sexual Addiction and Compulsivity, 6*, 317–336.
Farrell, D., & Taylor, M. (2000). Silenced by God – An examination of unique characteristics within sexual abuse by clergy. *Counselling Psychology Review, 15*, 22–31.
Goldenberg, R. (2013). Unholy clergy: Amending state child abuse reporting statutes to include clergy members as mandatory reporters in child sexual abuse cases. *Family Court Review, 51*, 298–315.
Haywood, T., Kravitz, H., Grossman, L., Wasyliw, O., & Hardy, D. (1996a). Psychological aspects of sexual functioning among cleric and non-cleric alleged sex offenders. *Child Abuse and Neglect, 20*, 527–536.
Haywood, T., Kravitz, H., Wasyliw, O., Goldberg, J., & Cavanaugh, J. (1996b). Cycle of abuse and psychopathology in cleric and non-cleric molesters of children and adolescents. *Child Abuse and Neglect, 20*, 1233–1243.
Heneghan, T. (2010a). Cardinal hailed bishop for hiding predator priest: Report, April 15, 2010. Available at http://www.reuters.com/article/2010/04/15/us-pope-abuse-france-idUSLDE63E-2H420100415, Reuters.
Heneghan, T. (2010b). John Paul backed praise for hiding abuse: Cardinal, April 17, 2010. Available at http://www.reuters.com/article/2010/04/17/us-pope-abuse-cardinal-idUS-TRE63G1SH20100417, Reuters.
Isely, P. J., Isely, P., Freiburger, J., & McMackin, R. (2008). In their own voices: A qualitative study of men abused as children by Catholic clergy. *Journal of Child Sexual Abuse, 17*, 201–215.
John Jay College of Criminal Justice. (2004). *The nature and scope of sexual abuse of minors by Catholic priests and deacons in the United States, 1950–2002*. Washington, DC: United States Conference of Catholic Bishops (USCCB).
John Jay College of Criminal Justice. (2011). *The causes and context of sexual abuse of minors by Catholic priests in the United States, 1950–2010*. Washington, DC: United States Conference of Catholic Bishops (USCCB).
Keenan, M. (2012). *Child sexual abuse and the Catholic Church: Gender, power, and organizational culture*. Oxford: Oxford University Press.
Kohl, T., & Crowley, M. (1998). *Not the way of Christ. Independent pastoral inquiry into sexual misconduct by clergy or officers of the Anglican Diocese of Tasmania with particular reference to paedophilia*. Hobart: Anglican Diocese of Tasmania.
Langevin, R., Curnoe, S., & Bain, J. (2000). A study of clerics who commit sexual offenses: Are they different from other sex offenders? *Child Abuse and Neglect, 24*, 535–545.
Mabey, R. (2006). The priest-penitent privilege in Australia and its consequences. *Murdoch University Electronic Journal of Law, 13*, 51–79.
Maimonides, M. T. (1997). *The laws of injury and damages* (E. Touger, Trans.). Brooklyn: Moznaim Publishing. Available at http://www.chabad.org
Murphy Report – Cloyne. (2010). Commission of Investigation, Report into the Catholic Diocese of Cloyne, 2010. Available at http://www.justice.ie/en/JELR/Pages/Cloyne_Rpt
Murphy Report – Dublin. (2009). Commission of investigation. Report into the Catholic Archdiocese of Dublin, July 2009. Available at http://www.justice.ie/en/JELR/Cover%20Part%201.pdf/Files/Cover%20Part%201.pdf
O'Callaghan, P., & Briggs, F. (2003). *Report of the Board of Inquiry into past handling of complaints of sexual abuse in the Anglican Church Diocese of Brisbane*. Brisbane: Queensland State Parliamentary Papers. Available at http://www.parliament.qld.gov.au/AnglicanReport.pdf
Olsson, T., & Chung, D. (2004). *Report of the Board of Inquiry into the handling of claims of sexual abuse and misconduct within the Anglican Diocese of Adelaide*. Adelaide: Anglican Diocese of Adelaide.

Parkinson, P. (1997). *Child sexual abuse and the churches*. London: Hodder and Stoughton.
Parkinson, P. (2013). *Suffer the teenage children: Child sexual abuse in church communities*. Paper for the Center for the Study of Law and Religion, Emory University, January 2013; Sydney Law School Research Paper No. 13/09. Available at SSRN: http://dx.doi.org/10.2139/ssrn.2216264
Parkinson, P., Oates, K., & Jayakody, A. (2009). *Study of reported child sexual abuse in the Anglican Church*. Sydney: General Synod, Anglican Church of Australia.
Parkinson, P., Oates, K., & Jayakody, A. (2010). Breaking the long silence: Reports of child sexual abuse in the Anglican Church of Australia. *Ecclesiology, 6*, 183–200.
Parkinson, P., Oates, K., & Jayakody, A. (2012). Child sexual abuse in the Anglican Church of Australia. *Journal of Child Sexual Abuse, 21*, 553–570.
Parliament of Victoria. (2013). *Betrayal of trust: Inquiry into the handling of child abuse by religious and other non-government organisations*. Melbourne: Family and Community Development Committee.
Plante, T. G., & McChesney, K. (Eds.). (2011). *Sexual abuse in the Catholic Church: A decade of crisis, 2002–2012*. Santa Barbara: Praeger.
PVVC. (2012). *Report of the protecting Victoria's vulnerable children inquiry*. Melbourne: Government of Victoria.
Resnicoff, S. (2012). Jewish law and the tragedy of sexual abuse of children: The dilemma within the Orthodox Jewish community. *Rutgers Journal of Law and Religion, 13*, 281–362.
Robertson, G. (2010). *The case of the Pope: Vatican accountability for human rights abuse*. London: Penguin.
Robinson, G. (2012). On breaking the seal of confession. *Eureka St*, 22, no 23. Available at http://www.eurekastreet.com.au/article.aspx?aeid=34262#.UlX5hIZBN9g
Rossetti, S. (1995). The impact of child sexual abuse on attitudes toward God and the Catholic Church. *Child Abuse and Neglect, 19*, 1469–1481.
Ryan Commission. (2009). The Commission to inquire into child abuse, 2009. Available at http://www.childabusecommission.com/rpt/
Smith, L. (1994). Lifting the veil of secrecy: Mandatory child abuse reporting statutes may encourage the Catholic Church to report priests who molest children. *Law & Psychology Review, 18*, 409–421.
Smith, M., Rengifo, A., & Vollman, B. (2008). Trajectories of abuse and disclosure: Child sexual abuse by Catholic priests. *Criminal Justice and Behavior, 35*, 570–582.
Storero, L. (1997). 'Strictly confidential' letter from the Apostolic Nuncio to the members of the Irish Catholic Episcopal Conference. Published in 2011 and available at: http://graphics8.nytimes.com/packages/pdf/world/Ireland-Catholic-Abuse.pdf?ref=europe
Terry, K. (2008). Stained glass: The nature and scope of child sexual abuse in the Catholic Church. *Criminal Justice and Behavior, 35*, 549–569.
Terry, K., & Ackerman, A. (2008). Child sexual abuse in the Catholic Church: How situational crime prevention strategies can help create safe environments. *Criminal Justice and Behavior, 35*, 643–657.
Thompson, K. (2011). *Religious confession privilege and the common law*. Leiden: Martinus Nijhoff.
Towards Healing. (1996). *Towards Healing Australian Catholic Bishops' conference and Australian Conference of Leaders of Religious Institutes*, Sydney.
Towards Healing. (2010). *Towards Healing Australian Catholic Bishops' conference and Catholic religious Australia*, Sydney.
Victoria Police. (2012). *Parliamentary inquiry*, Victoria, Evidence, October 19, 2012 at http://www.parliament.vic.gov.au/images/stories/committees/fcdc/inquiries/57th/Child_Abuse_Inquiry/Transcripts/Victoria_Police_19-Oct-12.pdf

Part IV
Practical Issues and Challenges for Reporters

(Informed by and focussing on empirical studies)

Chapter 15
Practical Issues and Challenges for Physicians Reporting Suspected Child Maltreatment

Emalee Flaherty

Introduction

Child maltreatment, including physical abuse, sexual abuse, emotional abuse, and neglect, affects an estimated 10–35 % of children each year (Gilbert et al. 2009). These numbers are based on individuals' self-reports and parents' reports of maltreatment (Finkelhor and Dziuba-Leatherman 1994). Unfortunately, even in jurisdictions with mandatory reporting laws, only a minority of these children are brought to the attention of Child Protective Services or other state agencies who can provide intervention and services. In one study, only 5 % of children who had been physically abused and 8 % of children who had been sexually abused reported that they had contact with Child Protective Services (CPS) (MacMillan et al. 2003). Without intervention, many of these children will continue to suffer severe harm.

Child maltreatment has significant consequences. It is estimated that about 30,000 children around the world die each year because of child maltreatment, not including fatalities caused by malnutrition (World Health Organization 2010). All forms of severe child abuse, whether physical, sexual, or emotional, and neglect also produce significant short-term and long-term morbidity and disability. These adverse childhood events are associated with poor health in childhood, adult disease, shortened life expectancy, lower educational achievement, increased risk of behavior problems, depression, and other mental health problems (Chartier et al. 2007; Felitti et al. 1998; Flaherty et al. 2006b, 2009; Jonson-Reid et al. 2012; Leeb et al. 2011). To prevent these outcomes, it is important to identify children who have been maltreated, provide treatment, and protect them from further harm.

E. Flaherty, M.D. (✉)
Ann & Robert H. Lurie Children's Hospital of Chicago,
225 E. Chicago Ave, 16, Chicago, IL, USA
e-mail: eflaherty@luriechildrenshospital.org

B. Mathews, D.C. Bross (eds.), *Mandatory Reporting Laws and the Identification of Severe Child Abuse and Neglect*, Child Maltreatment 4,
DOI 10.1007/978-94-017-9685-9_15

The UN Convention on the Rights of the Child requires that all signatory nations have integrated systems that coordinate the response to child maltreatment (Svevo-Cianci et al. 2010). Some countries have enacted legislation that mandates designated professionals to report suspected child abuse, while other countries make it voluntary for professionals to report (Mathews and Kenny 2008). The United States was the first country to enact mandated reporting legislation; it is one of several countries that have statutes mandating the report of suspected child maltreatment to Child Protective Services (CPS), law enforcement, or both (Oswald 2013). All 50 states in the United States have laws that mandate that physicians must report to the state Child Protective Services or law enforcement if they have *reasonable suspicion* or *reasonable cause to suspect* that a child may have been abused or neglected. The exact language of these laws varies from state to state, but all have kept the mandate intentionally vague to allow room for discretionary judgment (Mathews and Kenny 2008). Physicians are mandated reporters in all states, and a substantial number of states require that all persons who suspect child maltreatment must make a report. Although laws may vary from country to country, many of the issues and challenges surrounding child maltreatment reporting appear to be similar.

Physicians are an important source of CPS reports. Pediatricians and family physicians are often the first to identify child maltreatment in children at all ages. They are particularly well positioned to identify child maltreatment in infancy, because they evaluate the infant multiple times during the first year of life. These frequent examinations may be critical to the outcome of these children, because young children are more vulnerable to suffer serious injuries that can lead to permanent disabilities and even death. In addition, physicians are in a unique position to identify families where there may be a significant risk of future abuse, because they are often aware of family stressors such as unemployment and may know of other family dysfunctions such as drug abuse, alcoholism, and interpersonal violence.

Underreporting of Suspected Child Maltreatment: Physicians and Other Reporter Groups

Physicians

Even when laws mandate reporting, physicians admit that they do not always report suspected child abuse (Borres et al. 2007; Flaherty et al. 2000; Offer-Shechter et al. 2000; Van Haeringen et al. 1998). In a number of surveys of physician practice in the United States, physicians have said that they report most, but not all, suspected abuse and neglect. Injury severity and the risk for serious harm appear to positively influence reporting behavior (Benbenishty and Schmid 2013), as physicians are more likely to report more serious injuries (Flaherty et al. 2008a; Morris et al. 1985; Zellman 1992). A survey of Chicago primary care clinicians found that 95 % said they had reported all physical abuse (Flaherty et al. 2000). In a similar survey conducted nationally, 3 % of physicians said they had not reported all injuries they suspected were caused by child abuse (Flaherty et al. 2006a).

In a survey of Virginia physicians, 91 % said they reported all physical abuse and 92 % responded that they reported all sexual abuse, while far fewer reported all physical neglect, emotional abuse, and medical neglect that they suspected (58 %, 45 %, and 43 %, respectively) (Saulsbury and Campbell 1985). It is not clear why physicians are less likely to report neglect, both physical and medical, and emotional abuse, but physicians in this study did say they were reluctant to report if they were not certain that it was abuse or neglect. They also indicated that they were less likely to report if they thought they could solve the problem without outside intervention. Another possible explanation for less frequently reporting these types of maltreatment is that they did not perceive them as harmful to the child as physical abuse and sexual abuse.

The Child Abuse Reporting Experience Study (CARES) was a national study that examined prospectively physicians' reporting practices (Flaherty et al. 2008a, b). Four hundred and thirty-four primary care practitioners collected data about 15,003 child injury visits. The practitioners indicated their level of suspicion that an injury was caused by child abuse using a five-point Likert scale (*very unlikely*, *unlikely*, *possible*, *likely*, *very likely*) and also indicated whether they reported a suspicion of physical abuse to CPS. CARES found that physicians did not report suspected child abuse far more commonly than they indicated in retrospective surveys. In summary, the physicians in the CARES study did not report 27 % of the children they suspected had injuries *likely* or *very likely* caused by child abuse. They also did not report 75 % of the injuries they assessed to be *possibly* caused by abuse. The term *reasonable suspicion* is intentionally vague, and one could argue that considering that an injury was *possibly* caused by abuse is not *reasonable suspicion* and so should not activate the reporting duty. However, considering an injury *likely* or *very likely* caused by abuse should be *reasonable cause to suspect* that child abuse has occurred, and in principle these situations should have been reported.

Other Mandated Reporter Groups

Other groups of mandated reporters also admit that they do not report all suspected child maltreatment to CPS. About 25–50 % of clinical psychologists, social workers, child care providers, elementary principals, and secondary principals said that they had failed to report all child abuse they suspected (Zellman 1990). The participants also reviewed an equal mix of vignettes describing cases of possible neglect, possible physical abuse, and possible sexual abuse. They rated the sexual abuse vignettes as most serious, and they indicated they were most likely to report sexual abuse than physical abuse and neglect. Asked how they had typically responded if they suspected child maltreatment, dentists, dental hygienist, nurses, and psychologists responded that they would most commonly consult with another professional, chart and observe, or discuss with the family rather than report to CPS, while physicians most frequently said they would report their suspicion to CPS (Tilden et al. 1994). In a survey of Taiwan nurses, 21 % responded that they had failed to report suspected child abuse (Feng and Levine 2005). An Australian study of nurses found an identical rate of failure to report (Mathews et al. 2009). Teachers also admit that they have failed to report all children that they suspected had been maltreated, including failure to report suspected child sexual abuse (Kenny 2001; Mathews et al. 2009).

Reasons Physicians Do Not Report Child Maltreatment

A number of studies have examined why mandated reporters do not report suspected child maltreatment, and many of these studies have explored physicians' experience. The most common reason physicians give for not having reported a suspicion of maltreatment is that they were not "certain" that the child was abused (Badger 1989; Flaherty et al. 2000; Offer-Shechter et al. 2000; Saulsbury and Campbell 1985). They fail to report despite the language of the laws which does not require certainty. In a particularly notable example, physicians admitted that they do not report caregiver-fabricated illness (Munchausen-by-proxy; Medical Child Abuse) in a child unless they are *virtually certain* of the diagnosis (McClure et al. 1996). These physicians estimated that, to report, they would need to feel the probability their diagnosis was correct as being greater than 90 %.

Perceived Disruption to the Family

Sometimes, mandated reporters express concern that a report to Child Protective Services will disrupt the family (Jones et al. 2008). However, for some categories of case in particular, this attitude fails to consider that the investigation triggered by a report may lead to information that allows Child Protective Services to determine with certainty that a child has or has not been abused. When discussing why they did not report suspicious injuries, physicians frequently mention their concern about harming the family, but they appear to omit any consideration of the potential harm to the child. Their failure to report may leave an abused child unprotected and vulnerable to further injury and even death (King et al. 2006; Oral et al. 2008; Ravichandiran et al. 2010; Jenny et al. 1999).

Inadequate Education and Training

The lack of certainty referred to above may be influenced by a lack of knowledge about child maltreatment and reporting duties. Physicians, like all mandated reporters, require excellent training to equip them with the knowledge, attitudes, and skills to be able to comply with their reporting duties. The reporting laws are complex, and the nature of the various forms of child abuse and neglect are also complex and can be very difficult to detect, even for doctors who can conduct physical examinations. Yet, physicians often receive little education about child maltreatment (Woolf et al. 1988). Physicians who have received education about child abuse expressed more confidence in their ability to identify and manage child abuse (Badger 1989; Flaherty et al. 2006a). Likewise, physicians with high confidence in their abilities were more likely to suspect and report child abuse in vignettes (Flaherty et al. 2006a). More education about abuse also correlates with appropriate thresholds for when suspected abuse must be reported (Crowell and Levi 2012).

Pediatric training programs provide more child abuse education than emergency medicine and family medicine programs (Starling et al. 2009). Pediatric residents in programs with an interdisciplinary child abuse assessment team and programs that used a written curriculum and had mandatory training scored significantly better on a test of child abuse knowledge (Starling et al. 2009). The majority of pediatric training programs do not require mandatory clinical rotations in child maltreatment (Narayan et al. 2006; Ward et al. 2004). Although some programs offer electives, some training programs offer no rotation in child maltreatment (Narayan et al. 2006). Residents who completed a mandatory rotation indicated they were better prepared to identify and evaluate child maltreatment than those without this mandatory training. As would be expected, residents' self-rating of competency correlated with the amount of training they received and the number of cases of child maltreatment they assessed (Ward et al. 2004).

Similarly, medical professionals have also indicated that they did not report suspected maltreatment, because they lacked knowledge about reporting laws and did not understand the reporting mechanism or process (Ashoor et al. 2012; Feng and Levine 2005; Gunn et al. 2005; Offer-Shechter et al. 2000). Particularly in countries without laws mandating reporting, physicians may be uncertain how to make a report to the proper authorities (Al-Moosa et al. 2003).

Familiarity with the Family

Several studies have found that physicians are less likely to report families that they know well and more likely to report families they do not know well (Flaherty et al. 2008a; Jones et al. 2008; Morris et al. 1985). In deciding whether to report a suspicious injury, clinicians were influenced by the length of their relationship with the family, by a family's attentiveness to other health needs, and by their familiarity with other children in the family. In some cases their familiarity with a family made them more likely to report a suspicion that the child had been abused. In those cases, because of their long relationship with a family, they were aware of family stresses, previous reports to CPS, or had previous concerns about parenting skills.

Physicians may sometimes have so much confidence in their knowledge of the family that they become angry with others who report suspected maltreatment to CPS. Child abuse pediatricians describe how primary care physicians have told them that they have "no business" reporting the family, because they are a "nice" family (Flaherty et al. 2012). Pollak suggested that countertransference may play a role in the physician's strong feelings and their subsequent failure to report suspected child maltreatment (Pollak and Levy 1989). This countertransference includes sympathy for the family and fear that the family will become angry with them.

Socioeconomic and Racial/Ethnic Biases

Socioeconomic and racial/ethnic biases may consciously or unconsciously affect the physician's identification and report of child maltreatment. African American children are more likely to be reported to CPS and substantiated as victims of maltreatment, but it is unclear whether they are more likely to be abused (Putnam-Hornstein et al. 2013). It is clear, however, that the possibility of abuse is more likely to be considered if the child is African American (Lane et al. 2002; Rangel et al. 2009; Wood et al. 2010). In the CARES study, the practitioners were more likely to report African American children with private insurance than non-African American children with insurance. The reporting rate was no different between racial groups without insurance. Insurance status served as a proxy for socioeconomic status (Flaherty et al. 2008a). These results suggest that Caucasian patients were underreported. Other studies also suggest that physicians may underreport Caucasian patients rather than overreport African American patients (Hampton and Newberger 1985). In Carole Jenny's study, the children with abusive head trauma whose diagnosis was initially missed were more likely to be Caucasian (Jenny et al. 1999). Other studies have found that social class influenced the identification and reporting of child abuse, but that race did not (Lane and Dubowitz 2007; Laskey et al. 2012).

Perceptions About Efficacy of CPS

Physicians may decide not to report child maltreatment, because they think that they can do a better job of managing and handling a family's dysfunctions than CPS. They may believe that reporting to CPS accomplishes little (Al-Moosa et al. 2003; McDonald and Reece 1979). Previous experience with CPS may influence whether a physician decides to report suspected abuse or neglect (Flaherty et al. 2000; Gunn et al. 2005; Zellman 1990). In one study examining physician experience reporting child abuse, the majority of physicians indicated that the children they had reported previously had not benefitted from CPS intervention. Almost half of these physicians said that this experience would make them less likely to report child abuse in the future. The majority of physicians complained that CPS did not keep them informed about the progress of the investigation (Flaherty et al. 2000; Socolar and Reives 2002; Vulliamy and Sullivan 2000). In the CARES study, physicians frequently anticipated the outcome of CPS intervention when deciding whether to report a suspicious injury to CPS (Jones et al. 2008). If they felt that the child and family would benefit from the intervention, they reported, and conversely, they did not report if they felt that CPS would not provide effective intervention (Finkelhor and Zellman 1991).

Fears Involving the Family

Physicians also express concern that a family and maybe other families in the community will leave the practice if they make a report to CPS (Jones et al. 2008; McDonald and Reece 1979; Vulliamy and Sullivan 2000). Some physicians fear that if the family leaves the practice because they report to CPS, they will no longer be able to provide help and necessary intervention and that the child may "get lost" to follow up (Jones et al. 2008). It is significant that in the CARES study, this fear was not justified as families did not leave the practice after they were reported (Jones et al. 2008). Some physicians do not report because they want to avoid conflict with the family or fear angering a patient (Ashoor et al. 2012; Jones et al. 2008). Some said they "feared precipitating a crisis which could result in harm to the child" (Gunn et al. 2005).

Concern About Involvement in Legal Proceedings

Some physicians express concern that they will have to testify in legal proceeding if they report suspected child maltreatment (Badger 1989). Some said that they are "afraid to go to court" (Vulliamy and Sullivan 2000). Others express concern about the time that testifying takes away from their medical practice. They also said they fear a lawsuit if they report (Gunn et al. 2005; Vulliamy and Sullivan 2000), despite legislative protections in all jurisdictions clearly protecting reporters from liability (Mathews and Kenny 2008). Some complain that attorneys did not provide them with adequate preparation prior to their giving testimony and that the court system has no respect for their time (Socolar and Reives 2002).

Overreporting of Suspected Child Maltreatment by Physicians

Although underreporting of suspected child abuse is more common, overreporting also occurs. This can be influenced by misdiagnosis or by misunderstanding of the legislative reporting duty. In the CARES study, the primary care clinicians reported seven children, 0.5 % of the total sample, who had injuries they indicated were *unlikely* caused by child abuse (Flaherty et al. 2008a). Child abuse experts who reviewed a subset of 92 cases from the CARES study indicated that they would not have reported two children – an infant with a clavicle fracture and a 5 year old with a penile adhesion (Sege et al. 2011). Some mandated reporters misunderstand their obligation to report and make reports when they do not suspect abuse (Foreman and Bernet 2000). Some professionals believe that they must report all allegations of abuse they hear from third parties. Anecdotally, I have reviewed cases that were reported to CPS because the professional said a hospital policy required that they report all such injuries but that they personally did not suspect child maltreatment.

Physicians' Interpretation of Mandatory Reporting Laws

Physicians demonstrate great variability in their interpretation of the laws mandating that child abuse be reported. In the CARES study, physicians reported only 64 % of the injuries they indicated were *very likely* caused by child abuse, but they reported 86 % of the injuries they assessed as *likely* caused by abuse (Flaherty et al. 2008a). Levi and Brown examined how physicians interpreted the meaning of "reasonable cause" to suspect child abuse (Levi and Brown 2005). When physicians were asked how high child abuse should rank on a list of differential diagnosis to be reported, 12 % of the physicians responded that it should be first or second on the list, while 47 % said that it should be considered reasonable suspicion and reported if it ranked as low as fifth to tenth on the differential diagnosis. In this same study, physicians were also asked to estimate the probability that abuse had occurred for reasonable suspicion to exist. While 35 % said the probability had to be (only) between 10 and 35 %, 15 % of the respondents indicated that the probability had to be ≥75 % to be considered a reasonable suspicion. The physicians' responses to the two scales were also inconsistent. Physicians who indicated that reasonable suspicion required 50–60 % probability also said that child abuse could rank as low as fourth or fifth on their list of differential diagnosis. Discussing these inconsistencies, Levi and Loebén (2004) argue that physicians better understand suspicion as a *feeling* rather than a *belief*.

The benefits of mandatory reporting laws have been debated (Oswald 2013). Some professionals advocate for alternative systems that would allow certain professionals with more experience managing child maltreatment to defer reporting while they work with the family or collect more information (Delaronde et al. 2000; Finkelhor and Zellman 1991). The majority of mandated reporters, however, support maintaining the existing reporting policies. It is concerning that in New Zealand, where laws do not mandate that child abuse be reported, a survey of professionals found that respondents who did not want mandatory reporting were more certain of their reporting decisions, but less accurate in their assessment of 12 child abuse scenarios (Rodriguez 2002).

Mathews and Bross (2008) argue that the benefits of these laws outweigh the disadvantages, especially for severe cases of abuse and neglect where the child's situation will not otherwise come to the attention of protective agencies. They point out that substantiation rates are higher in countries with mandated reporting laws when compared to jurisdictions where reporting is not mandated. Also, they point out that mandatory reporting is not the main problem for child protection systems but rather the poor response to reports. Inadequate responses are often related to insufficient funding of the investigative agencies and treatment programs. They also note that child maltreatment has been shown to be costly and argue that without mandated reporting, the economic burden would be even greater (Brown et al. 2011). In addition, if reporting laws and their associated supportive mechanisms did not exist, even more children would likely be left unprotected.

Recommendations to Improve Physicians' and Other Professionals' Reporting of Child Maltreatment

Because insufficient knowledge about child maltreatment is associated with poor confidence and competence, education of all mandated professionals who interact with children is needed. One such general education effort was initiated in New York State. In 1988, the state began to require that professionals take a course about identification and reporting of child abuse before they could receive a state license (Reiniger et al. 1995). Professionals who took the course reported that they learned new information about indicators of abuse and neglect, reporting procedures, legal liabilities, and legal responsibilities (Reiniger et al. 1995). Although there is no requirement that professionals receive further education after this initial course, a majority of physicians recommended that they should receive a refresher course every 5 years (Khan et al. 2005). Education about child maltreatment has been shown to significantly improve detection. After all health and social service agencies and school professionals in the Balearic Islands received training about child maltreatment, detection rates increased (Cerezo and Pons-Salvador 2004).

All medical students should receive training about child abuse. Rotations in Child Abuse Pediatrics should be mandatory in pediatric postgraduate training. After residency, physicians should continue to receive continuing education about child abuse. The education curriculum should be tailored to the specific needs of the professional. Physicians have indicated they would like more training about the subtle findings of child abuse, child neglect, interviewing, and court testimony (Anderst and Dowd 2010). Mandated reporters should also receive education about countertransference issues that may arise around the reporting process (Pollak and Levy 1989). Specifically, they should be taught about the fear, shame, and sympathy that may be evoked when considering the possibility of child maltreatment. All mandated reporters should also receive more education about CPS systems (including differential responses systems where children may be referred for service provision without being investigated) and the role and limits of CPS. The education should help the trainees understand the investigative process, the roles of the different professionals involved in the protection of children, and the outcomes for children who receive intervention and those who for whom there is no intervention (Flaherty et al. 2008b).

Chart flags or protocols may improve screening by reminding the clinician to consider the possibility of abuse. The systematic screening of children in emergency departments for child abuse has been demonstrated to improve the detection of child abuse (Louwers et al. 2010, 2012). When hospital-based clinicians were provided with specific, operational criteria for reportable child abuse, their assessment and reporting behavior improved. (Paradise et al. 1995) Checklists may make decision making more objective, by reducing bias and other errors leading to missed cases of child abuse (Ely et al. 2011). Rangel et al. (2009) found that a guideline determining a child should receive a skeletal survey to screen for occult fracture decreased the disparity in screening between black and nonblack patients.

Mandated reporters need to be taught the meaning of *reasonable suspicion* and *reasonable cause to suspect.* Providing mandated reporters with a threshold for reporting may make reporting decisions more consistent by providing a framework for decision making (Levi and Loeben 2004). Some have suggested that reporters should consider using 25 % probability as a threshold for reporting (Crowell and Levi 2012).

Mandated reporters should be taught how to discuss with caregivers their concerns about child abuse and the need to report suspected abuse to CPS. The "SPIKES" protocol for breaking bad news (Baile et al. 2000) is one protocol that has been successfully taught to medical students in an academic setting (Pietrantonio et al. 2013). This protocol was initially developed for use with oncology patients but has been successfully adapted for teaching others how to deliver "bad news" to patients. The protocol was successfully taught to medical students who then practiced their skills with a standardized patient and received feedback. The trainees reported increased confidence in their ability to deliver unfavorable medical information to patients (Baile et al. 2000).

Some presentations are complex and require more expertise to distinguish maltreatment from other causes. Mandated reporters should identify resources in their community who can help them when they are uncertain how to evaluate or whether they should suspect child maltreatment. Some hospitals have multidisciplinary teams. The collaborative assessment provided by the team is helpful, particularly in complex cases of child abuse, because different professionals bring different perspectives to the discussion. A broader range of viewpoints should lead to better decision making and more effective interventions (Kolbo and Strong 1997; Thun-Hohenstein 2006). To function successfully, teams need to trust each other, recognize and respect the different roles of their team members, and communicate effectively (Feng et al. 2010).

Child abuse pediatricians also can provide mandated reporters with help in their assessments and support in their decision making. In 2009, the American Board of Pediatrics offered the first certification examination in Child Abuse Pediatrics. There are now more than 200 board-certified child abuse pediatricians in the United States and many pediatricians in other countries with similar expertise. Mandated reporters may need the assistance and expertise of child abuse pediatrician to move them from considering abuse as a possibility to a probability (Sege and Flaherty 2008). After children are reported to CPS, the expertise of a child abuse pediatrician may be needed to assist investigators in determining whether a child has been maltreated (Anderst et al. 2009).

Summary

Child maltreatment is significantly underreported. Without CPS investigation and intervention, it is unlikely that a child will be protected from further harm. Professionals who work with children should seek out education about how to best recognize child maltreatment. They should consider the possibility of child maltreatment when caring for children without regard to the child's race, ethnicity, or socioeconomic status. They should recognize that some cases are complex and identify child abuse experts in their community who can assist them with evaluation and decision making.

References

Al-Moosa, A., Al-Shaiji, J., Al-Fadhli, A., Al-Bayed, K., & Adib, S. M. (2003). Pediatricians' knowledge, attitudes and experience regarding child maltreatment in Kuwait. *Child Abuse & Neglect, 27*(10), 1161–1178.

Anderst, J., & Dowd, M. D. (2010). Comparative needs in child abuse education and resources: Perceptions from three medical specialties. *Medical Education Online, 15*(1), 1–8. doi:10.3402/meo.v15i0.5193.

Anderst, J., Kellogg, N., & Jung, I. (2009). Is the diagnosis of physical abuse changed when Child Protective Services consults a Child Abuse Pediatrics subspecialty group as a second opinion? *Child Abuse & Neglect, 33*(8), 481–489. doi:10.1016/j.chiabu.2009.05.001.

Ashoor, A., Al Nasir, F., & Grant, N. (2012). Children abuse: Factors affecting case reporting by physicians. *Bahrain Medical Bulletin, 34*(3), 1–8.

Badger, L. W. (1989). Reporting of child abuse: Influence of characteristics of physician, practice, and community. *Southern Medical Journal, 82*(3), 281–286.

Baile, W. F., Buckman, R., Lenzi, R., Glober, G., Beale, E. A., & Kudelka, A. P. (2000). SPIKES – A six-step protocol for delivering bad news: Application to the patient with cancer. *The Oncologist, 5*(4), 302–311. doi:10.1634/theoncologist.5-4-302.

Benbenishty, R., & Schmid, H. (2013). Public attitudes toward the identification and reporting of alleged maltreatment cases among social groups in Israel. *Children and Youth Services Review, 35*(2), 332–339. http://dx.doi.org/10.1016/j.childyouth.2012.11.013

Borres, M. P., Hagg, A., Borres, M. P., & Hagg, A. (2007). Child abuse study among Swedish physicians and medical students. *Pediatrics International, 49*(2), 177–182.

Brown, D. S., Fang, X., & Florence, C. S. (2011). Medical costs attributable to child maltreatment: A systematic review of short- and long-term effects. *American Journal of Preventive Medicine, 41*(6), 627–635. doi:10.1016/j.amepre.2011.08.013.

Cerezo, M. A., & Pons-Salvador, G. (2004). Improving child maltreatment detection systems: A large-scale case study involving health, social services, and school professionals. *Child Abuse and Neglect, 28*(11), 1153–1169. http://dx.doi.org/10.1016/j.chiabu.2004.06.007

Chartier, M. J., Walker, J. R., Naimark, B., Chartier, M. J., Walker, J. R., & Naimark, B. (2007). Childhood abuse, adult health, and health care utilization: Results from a representative community sample. [Research Support, Non-U.S. Gov't]. *American Journal of Epidemiology, 165*(9), 1031–1038.

Crowell, K., & Levi, B. H. (2012). Mandated reporting thresholds for community professionals [Article]. *Child Welfare, 91*(1), 35–53.

Delaronde, S., King, G., Bendel, R., & Reece, R. (2000). Opinions among mandated reporters toward child maltreatment reporting policies. *Child Abuse & Neglect, 24*(7), 901–910.

Ely, J. W., Graber, M. L., & Croskerry, P. (2011). Checklists to reduce diagnostic errors. *Academic Medicine, 86*(3), 307–313.

Felitti, V. J., Anda, R. F., Nordenberg, D., Williamson, D. F., Spitz, A. M., Edwards, V., Koss, M. P., & Marks, J. S. (1998). Relationship of childhood abuse and household dysfunction to many of the leading causes of death in adults. The adverse childhood experiences (ACE) study. *American Journal of Preventive Medicine, 14*(4), 245–258.

Feng, J.-Y., & Levine, M. (2005). Factors associated with nurses' intention to report child abuse: A national survey of Taiwanese nurses. *Child Abuse & Neglect, 29*(7), 783–795. doi:10.1016/j.chiabu.2004.11.006.

Feng, J. Y., Fetzer, S., Chen, Y. W., Yeh, L., & Huang, M. C. (2010). Multidisciplinary collaboration reporting child abuse: A grounded theory study. *International Journal of Nursing Studies, 47*(12), 1483–1490.

Finkelhor, D., & Dziuba-Leatherman, J. (1994). Children as victims of violence: A national survey. *Pediatrics, 94*(4 Pt 1), 413–420.

Finkelhor, D., & Zellman, G. L. (1991). Flexible reporting options for skilled child abuse professionals. *Child Abuse & Neglect, 15*(4), 335–341.

Flaherty, E. G., Sege, R., Binns, H. J., Mattson, C. L., & Christoffel, K. K. (2000). Health care providers' experience reporting child abuse in the primary care setting: Pediatric Practice Research Group. *Archives of Pediatrics & Adolescent Medicine, 154*(5), 489–493.

Flaherty, E. G., Sege, R., Price, L. L., Christoffel, K. K., Norton, D. P., & O'Connor, K. G. (2006a). Pediatrician characteristics associated with child abuse identification and reporting: Results from a national survey of pediatricians. *Child Maltreatment, 11*(4), 361–369. doi:10.1177/1077559506292287.

Flaherty, E. G., Thompson, R., Litrownik, A. J., Theodore, A., English, D. J., Black, M. M., Wike, T., Whimper, L., Runyan, D. K., & Dubowitz, H. (2006b). Effect of early childhood adversity on child health. *Archives of Pediatrics & Adolescent Medicine, 160*(12), 1232–1238. doi:10.1001/archpedi.160.12.1232

Flaherty, E. G., Sege, R. D., Griffith, J., Price, L. L., Wasserman, R., Slora, E., Dhepyasuwan, N., Harris, D., Norton, D., Angelilli, M. L., Abney, D., & Binns, H. J. (2008a). From suspicion of physical child abuse to reporting: Primary care clinician decision-making. *Pediatrics*, peds.2007–2311. doi:10.1542/peds.2007-2311

Flaherty, E. G., Sege, R. D., & Hurley, T. P. (2008b). Translating child abuse research into action. *Pediatrics*, peds.2008–0715c. doi:10.1542/peds.2008-0715c

Flaherty, E. G., Thompson, R., Litrownik, A. J., Zolotor, A. J., Dubowitz, H., Runyan, D. K., English, D. J., & Everson, M. D. (2009). Adverse childhood exposures and reported child health at age 12. *Academic Pediatrics, 9*(3), 150–156. doi:10.1016/j.acap.2008.11.003

Flaherty, E. G., Schwartz, K., Jones, R. D., & Sege, R. D. (2012). Child abuse physicians: Coping with challenges. *Evaluation and the Health Professions*. doi:10.1177/0163278712459196

Foreman, T., & Bernet, W. (2000). A misunderstanding regarding the duty to report suspected abuse. *Child Maltreatment, 5*(2), 190–196.

Gilbert, R., Widom, C. S., Browne, K., Fergusson, D., Webb, E., & Janson, S. (2009). Burden and consequences of child maltreatment in high-income countries. *Lancet, 373*(9657), 68–81.

Gunn, V. L., Hickson, G. B., & Cooper, W. O. (2005). Factors affecting pediatricians' reporting of suspected child maltreatment. *Ambulatory Pediatrics, 5*(2), 96–101.

Hampton, R. L., & Newberger, E. H. (1985). Child abuse incidence and reporting by hospitals: Significance of severity, class, and race. *American Journal of Public Health, 75*(1), 56–60.

Jenny, C., Hymel, K. P., Ritzen, A., Reinert, S. E., & Hay, T. C. (1999). Analysis of missed cases of abusive head trauma. *JAMA, 281*(7), 621–626 [erratum appears in JAMA 1999 Jul 7;282(1):29].

Jones, R., Flaherty, E. G., Binns, H. J., Price, L. L., Slora, E., Abney, D., Harris, D. L., Christoffel, K. K., & Sege, R. D. (2008). Clinicians' description of factors influencing their reporting of suspected child abuse: Report of the child abuse reporting experience study research group. *Pediatrics, 122*(2), 259–266. doi:10.1542/peds.2007-2312

Jonson-Reid, M., Kohl, P. L., & Drake, B. (2012). Child and adult outcomes of chronic child maltreatment. *Pediatrics, 129*(5), 839–845. doi:10.1542/peds. 2011-2529.

Kenny, M. C. (2001). Child abuse reporting: Teachers' perceived deterrents. *Child Abuse & Neglect, 25*(1), 81–92.

Khan, A. N. G. A., Rubin, D. H., & Winnik, G. (2005). Evaluation of the mandatory child abuse course for physicians: Do we need to repeat it? *Public Health, 119*(7), 626–631.

King, W. K., Kiesel, E. L., & Simon, H. K. (2006). Child abuse fatalities: Are we missing opportunities for intervention? *Pediatric Emergency Care, 22*(4), 211–214.

Kolbo, J. R., & Strong, E. (1997). Multidisciplinary team approaches to the investigation and resolution of child abuse and neglect: A national survey. *Child Maltreatment, 2*(1), 61–72. doi:10.1177/1077559597002001007.

Lane, W. G., & Dubowitz, H. (2007). What factors affect the identification and reporting of child abuse-related fractures? [Article]. *Clinical Orthopaedics and Related Research August, 461*, 219–225.

Lane, W. G., Rubin, D. M., Monteith, R., & Christian, C. W. (2002). Racial differences in the evaluation of pediatric fractures for physical abuse. *JAMA, 288*(13), 1603–1609.

Laskey, A. L., Stump, T. E., Perkins, S. M., Zimet, G. D., Sherman, S. J., & Downs, S. M. (2012). Influence of race and socioeconomic status on the diagnosis of child abuse: A randomized study. *The Journal of Pediatrics, 160*(6), 1003–1008.e1001. doi:10.1016/j.jpeds.2011.11.042.

Leeb, R. T., Lewis, T., & Zolotor, A. J. (2011). A review of physical and mental health consequences of child abuse and neglect and implications for practice. *American Journal of Lifestyle Medicine, 5*(5), 454–468. doi:10.1177/1559827611410266.

Levi, B. H., & Brown, G. (2005). Reasonable suspicion: A study of Pennsylvania pediatricians regarding child abuse. *Pediatrics, 116*(1), e5–e12.

Levi, B. H., & Loeben, G. (2004). Index of suspicion: Feeling not believing. *Theoretical Medicine & Bioethics, 25*(4), 277–310.

Louwers, E. C. F. M., Affourtit, M. J., Moll, H. A., Koning, H. J. D., & Korfage, I. J. (2010). Screening for child abuse at emergency departments: A systematic review. *Archives of Disease in Childhood, 95*(3), 214–218. doi:10.1136/adc.2008.151654.

Louwers, E. C. F. M., Korfage, I. J., Affourtit, M. J., Scheewe, D. J. H., van de Merwe, M. H., Vooijs-Moulaert, A.-F., van den Elzen, A. P., Jongejan, M. H., Ruige, M., Manaï, B. H., Looman, C. W., Bosschaart, A. N., Teeuw, A. H., Moll, H. A., & de Koning, H. J. (2012). Effects of systematic screening and detection of child abuse in emergency departments. *Pediatrics*. doi:10.1542/peds.2011-3527

MacMillan, H. L., Jamieson, E., & Walsh, C. A. (2003). Reported contact with child protection services among those reporting child physical and sexual abuse: Results from a community survey. *Child Abuse and Neglect, 27*(12), 1397–1408. http://dx.doi.org/10.1016/j.chiabu.2003.06.003

Mathews, B., & Bross, D. C. (2008). Mandated reporting is still a policy with reason: Empirical evidence and philosophical grounds. *Child Abuse and Neglect, 32*(5), 511–516. http://dx.doi.org/10.1016/j.chiabu.2007.06.010

Mathews, B., & Kenny, M. C. (2008). Mandatory reporting legislation in the United States, Canada, and Australia: A cross-jurisdictional review of key features, differences, and issues. *Child Maltreatment, 13*(1), 50–63. doi:10.1177/1077559507310613.

Mathews, B., Walsh, K., Rassafiani, M., et al. (2009). Teachers reporting suspected child sexual abuse: Results of a three-State study. *University of New South Wales Law Journal, 32*(3), 722–813.

McClure, R. J., Davis, P. M., Meadow, S. R., & Sibert, J. R. (1996). Epidemiology of Munchausen syndrome by proxy, non-accidental poisoning, and non-accidental suffocation. *Archives of Disease in Childhood, 75*(1), 57–61.

McDonald, A. E., & Reece, R. M. (1979). Child abuse: Problems of reporting. *Pediatric Clinics of North America, 26*(4), 785–791.

Morris, J. L., Johnson, C. F., & Clasen, M. (1985). To report or not to report: Physicians' attitudes toward discipline and child abuse. *American Journal of Diseases of Children, 139*(2), 194–197.

Narayan, A. P., Socolar, R. R. S., & St Claire, K. (2006). Pediatric residency training in child abuse and neglect in the United States. *Pediatrics, 117*(6), 2215–2221. doi:10.1542/peds. 2006-0160.

Offer-Shechter, S., Tirosh, E., & Cohen, A. (2000). Physical abuse – Physicians knowledge and reporting attitude in Israel. *European Journal of Epidemiology, 16*(1), 53–58. doi:10.2307/3582047.

Oral, R. M. D., Yagmur, F. M. D., Nashelsky, M. M. D., Turkmen, M. M. D., & Kirby, P. M. D. (2008). Fatal abusive head trauma cases: Consequence of medical staff missing milder forms of physical abuse. *Pediatric Emergency Care, 24*(12), 816–821.

Oswald, M. (2013). Mandatory reporting of child abuse – Necessary medicine for 'nervous Nellies' or a remedy too far? *International Data Privacy Law*. doi:10.1093/idpl/ipt026

Paradise, J. E. M., Bass, J. M., Forman, S. D. M., Berkowitz, J., Greenberg, D. B. M., & Mehta, K. M. (1995). Minimum criteria for reporting child abuse from health care settings. *Pediatric Emergency Care, 11*(6), 335–339.

Pietrantonio, A. M., Wright, E., Gibson, K. N., Alldred, T., Jacobson, D., & Niec, A. (2013). Mandatory reporting of child abuse and neglect: Crafting a positive process for health professionals and caregivers. *Child Abuse and Neglect, 37*(2–3), 102–109. http://dx.doi.org/10.1016/j. chiabu.2012.12.007

Pollak, J., & Levy, S. (1989). Countertransference and failure to report child abuse and neglect. *Child Abuse & Neglect, 13*(4), 515–522. doi:10.1016/0145-2134(89)90055-0.

Putnam-Hornstein, E., Needell, B., King, B., & Johnson-Motoyama, M. (2013). Racial and ethnic disparities: A population-based examination of risk factors for involvement with child protective services. *Child Abuse and Neglect, 37*(1), 33–46. http://dx.doi.org/10.1016/j. chiabu.2012.08.005

Rangel, E. L., Cook, B. S., Bennett, B. L., Shebesta, K., Ying, J., & Falcone, R. A. (2009). Eliminating disparity in evaluation for abuse in infants with head injury: Use of a screening guideline. *Journal of Pediatric Surgery, 44*(6), 1229–1235.

Ravichandiran, N., Schuh, S., Bejuk, M., Al-Harthy, N., Shouldice, M., Au, H., & Boutis, K. (2010). Delayed identification of pediatric abuse-related fractures. *Pediatrics, 125*(1), 60–66. doi:10.1542/peds. 2008-3794.

Reiniger, A., Robison, E., & McHugh, M. (1995). Mandated training of professionals: A means for improving reporting of suspected child abuse. *Child Abuse & Neglect, 19*(1), 63–69.

Rodriguez, C. M. (2002). Professionals' attitudes and accuracy on child abuse reporting decisions in New Zealand. *Journal of Interpersonal Violence, 17*(3), 320–342. doi:10.1177/0886260502 017003006.

Saulsbury, F. T., & Campbell, R. E. (1985). Evaluation of child abuse reporting by physicians. *American Journal of Diseases of Children, 139*(4), 393–395.

Sege, R., & Flaherty, E. (2008). Forty years later – Inconsistencies in reporting of child abuse. *Archives of Disease in Childhood*, adc.2006.100545. doi:10.1136/adc.2006.100545

Sege, R., Flaherty, E., Jones, R., Price, L. L., Harris, D., Slora, E., Abney, D., & Wasserman, R. (2011). To report or not to report: Examination of the initial primary care management of suspicious childhood injuries. *Academic Pediatrics, 11*(6), 460–466. doi:10.1016/j. acap.2011.08.005

Socolar, R. R. S., & Reives, P. (2002). Factors that facilitate or impede physicians who perform evaluations for child maltreatment. *Child Maltreatment, 7*(4), 377–381. doi:10.1177/107755902237268.

Starling, S. P., Heisler, K. W., Paulson, J. F., & Youmans, E. (2009). Child abuse training and knowledge: A national survey of emergency medicine, family medicine, and pediatric residents and program directors. *Pediatrics, 123*(4), e595–e602. doi:10.1542/peds.2008-2938.

Svevo-Cianci, K. A., Hart, S. N., & Rubinson, C. (2010). Protecting children from violence and maltreatment: A qualitative comparative analysis assessing the implementation of U.N. CRC Article 19. *Child Abuse and Neglect, 34*(1), 45–56. http://dx.doi.org/10.1016/j. chiabu.2009.09.010

Thun-Hohenstein, L. (2006). Interdisciplinary child protection team work in a hospital setting. *European Journal of Pediatrics, 165*(6), 402–407.

Tilden, V. P., Schmidt, T. A., Limandri, B. J., Chiodo, G. T., Garland, M. J., & Loveless, P. A. (1994). Factors that influence clinicians' assessment and management of family violence. *American Journal of Public Health, 84*(4), 628–633.

Van Haeringen, A. R., Dadds, M., & Armstrong, K. L. (1998). The child abuse lottery–will the doctor suspect and report? Physician attitudes towards and reporting of suspected child abuse and neglect. *Child Abuse & Neglect, 22*(3), 159–169.

Vulliamy, A. P., & Sullivan, R. (2000). Reporting child abuse: Pediatricians' experiences with the child protection system. *Child Abuse & Neglect, 24*(11), 1461–1470.

Ward, M. G. K., Bennett, S., Plint, A. C., King, W. J., Jabbour, M., & Gaboury, I. (2004). Child protection: A neglected area of pediatric residency training. *Child Abuse & Neglect, 28*(10), 1113–1122. doi:10.1016/j.chiabu.2004.05.002.

Wood, J. N., Hall, M., Schilling, S., Keren, R., Mitra, N., & Rubin, D. M. (2010). Disparities in the evaluation and diagnosis of abuse among infants with traumatic brain injury. *Pediatrics, 126*(3), 408–414. doi:10.1542/peds. 2010-0031.

Woolf, A., Taylor, L., Melnicoe, L., Andolsek, K., Dubowitz, H., De Vos, E., & Newberger, E. (1988). What residents know about child abuse: Implications of a survey of knowledge and attitudes. *American Journal of Diseases of Children, 142*(6), 668–672.

World Health Organization. (2010). *Addressing violence against women and HIV/AIDS*. Geneva: World Health Organization.

Zellman, G. L. (1990). Child abuse reporting and failure to report among mandated reporters. *Journal of Interpersonal Violence, 5*(1), 3–22. doi:10.1177/088626090005001001.

Zellman, G. L. (1992). The impact of case characteristics on child abuse reporting decisions. *Child Abuse & Neglect, 16*(1), 57–74.

Chapter 16
Training in Reporting of Child Maltreatment: Where We Are and Where We Need to Go

Maureen C. Kenny

Introduction

Child maltreatment is an international societal issue. The United Nations Convention on the Rights of the Child (United Nations General Assembly 1989) emphasized the need for countries worldwide to recognize the importance of children's rights and to take action to promote these rights. Among these was the right to freedom from child abuse and neglect (Article 19). Unfortunately, despite this dictate, child maltreatment continues to be a pervasive issue in both developing and industrialized nations. Many countries have implemented extensive policies and legislation and responsive approaches, often known as child protection systems, with the goal of safeguarding children from maltreatment (Carter et al. 2006). While exact rates are impossible to report, between 500 million and 1.5 billion children are estimated to experience violence annually (UNICEF 2010). Even in those countries where there are strict laws against abuse and mandatory reporting of abuse, maltreatment occurs at alarming rates. For example, in the USA, 3.4 million referrals to child protection were estimated to include 6.2 million children (U.S. Department of Health & Human Services, Administration of Children and Families 2012), with victims hailing from all socioeconomic groups and ethnicities. From the referrals received, 61 % were screened in (indicating the allegation of child maltreatment met the state's standards for acceptance and became a report), which resulted in two million reports. In National Child Abuse and Neglect Data System (NCANDS), a child is considered a victim of maltreatment if he or she receives a disposition of substantiated, indicated, or alternative response victim. For 2011, the national estimate of victims was 681,000. The national number of victims who received services was approximately 366,000, and the national number of non-victims who received

M.C. Kenny (✉)
College of Education, Florida International University, Miami, FL, USA
e-mail: kennym@fiu.edu

B. Mathews, D.C. Bross (eds.), *Mandatory Reporting Laws and the Identification of Severe Child Abuse and Neglect*, Child Maltreatment 4,
DOI 10.1007/978-94-017-9685-9_16

services (in home or foster care) was approximately 747,000. Although it remains a complex social issue that has been addressed in many prevention models, increased focus on training and education of professionals is critical to provide early detection, identification, and referral to treatment.

The purpose of this chapter is to review the current literature on training professionals, reflect on the ongoing need for training, and propose training and education guidelines for mandated reporters. As Chen et al. (2013) state in regard to reporting child abuse, "education is required before achieving clinical competence" (p. 168) emphasizing that training is necessary to ensuring competence in identifying and reporting child abuse. The crucial need to protect children from abuse and neglect combined with their inherent vulnerability makes this an area of utmost importance in training professionals who will work with them.

It is important to note that the term *child abuse* will be used to cover the most commonly identified and researched forms of abuse and neglect (e.g., neglect, physical, sexual, and emotional abuse). While the author recognizes that countries vary in their definitions of abuse and neglect, and culture plays a role in defining such actions, for the purpose of brevity, it is assumed that the reader will apply the term accordingly in one's own context and environment. In addition, many countries are addressing issues of training for professionals. Eissa and Almuneef (2010), for example, wrote about the expanding recognition of child abuse and neglect in Saudi Arabia, which has led to mandatory reporting and improved child abuse data collection strategies. Still, this chapter will draw heavily on the work in the USA and Australia as these countries have the most developed systems of reporting (Mathews and Kenny 2008) and have produced a large body of research on training efforts. This work may serve as information relevant to other countries that have also begun to adopt mandatory reporting.

Mandated Reporters and Reporter Training in the USA

In most States, mandated reporters include educators, medical personnel (primarily physicians and nurses), and mental health professionals (psychologists, counselors) (Mathews and Kenny 2008). While these professionals vary greatly in their professional activities, they share some commonalities including having direct contact with children, serving as confidants or role models to children, and in most countries require a minimum level of university education. They are also viewed as child advocates, safeguarding children and possessing concern for children's welfare by virtue of their professional role, ethics, and activities. These professionals play an important role in the detection of maltreatment, enabling the provision of services to victims and their families, and the development and conduct of research in the area of maltreatment (Crettenden and Zerk 2012).

While many professional organizations in the USA deem child abuse to be a crucial issue for their members and many professionals are mandated reporters in all US states, there is currently no national standard governing the amount and content of child abuse training across the major professional groups – educators, physicians, and mental health professionals. Unfortunately, as Alvarez and colleagues (2010) state, "There has not been widespread dissemination of training programs to assist professionals in mandated reporting of suspected child maltreatment" (p. 211). This has meant that training programs differ across jurisdictions and across occupational groups even within jurisdictions, may not exist within some jurisdictions or for some professions within jurisdictions, may not be of high quality, may not be well administered, and thus leave professional groups untrained and victims vulnerable.

The Need for Training

Training is critical since the first professional who comes into contact with a victim is the one to direct the child's access to the resources of the child protection team and ultimately the victim's pathway to recovery (Hicks and Tite 1998). If professionals who are working with children and youth are appropriately trained, they may contribute to breaking the cycle of abuse (Swann 2000). Professionals will be in positions where they may have a legal and professional duty to report suspected abuse and neglect and will require training to develop the specialized knowledge and confidence needed to deal with this complex issue (Mathews 2011). As Lidchi (2007) states, "training needs to …transfer knowledge, improve research methods and develop practical skills" (p. 354). In addition to a need for training, there appears to be willingness for individuals to attend training as evidenced by the results of Orelove et al. (2000). They found that 92 % of educators and 96 % of investigators (including child protection workers and law enforcement) said they would attend specialized training if it were made available to them.

Proper, well-planned, and executed training is critical for professionals to assist in identification and reporting of child maltreatment. Given the high incidence, as well as the various and complex types of child maltreatment (e.g., sexual, physical, emotional, neglect), and often debilitating, long-term consequences for child victims, professionals need to be equipped to confront this social issue. Detection is frequently difficult due to the nature and context of some types of abuse as well as the secrecy surrounding them. Training allows for an exploration of the often complicated ethical, legal, and *moral* duties involved in the protection of children. The professional reporter plays a pivotal role in protecting seriously abused and neglected children, and they have the potential to make an impacting difference to the child's and family's life.

Widespread Variation in Training Efforts

Educators

While it is recognized that educators and early interventionists can play a pivotal role on child protection teams (Orelove et al. 2000), there is also an international consensus that most educators are ill equipped to perform their duties as mandated reporters. For example, although all of the educators and investigation workers in the Orelove et al. (2000) study in the USA were mandated reporters, less than a third reported being very knowledgeable about the process to report child abuse to child protection services (CPS). Seventy-nine percent of the educators said that their employers had a policy on reporting abuse, but only 25 % of them had received training on the policy within the past 3 years. According to Kenny (2004), almost two-thirds of the teachers surveyed in the USA reported having no training in child abuse during their preservice training, and very few teachers were aware of their school's procedures for reporting abuse. In addition, teachers claimed inadequacy in their ability to detect and identify all types of child abuse even when they had training. This lack of training has been documented in other countries as well. Buckley and McGarry (2011) found that 61 % of their beginning teachers in Ireland reported their training in child protection while pursuing their degree to be inadequate. Similarly, McKee and Dillenburger (2009) found that undergraduate students in Ireland in initial teacher education, early childhood studies, and health and leisure studies had some basic awareness of child abuse and neglect (CAN) issues, but their knowledge base was inconsistent and did not reach the levels required for those who will work directly with children.

The findings from a study by Walsh et al. (2008) in Australia, although conducted on solely neglect and physical abuse, bear reporting here. They found that teachers with no formal child protection training were more likely to both detect and report child physical abuse and neglect than those with formal training. They hypothesize that training may, in fact, provide teachers with increased awareness of the complexities of child maltreatment, such that "the more teachers know, the more they may realise they do not know" (p. 991). This is consistent with the findings of Buckley and McGarry (2011) who found that many of those teachers who recall having no training (51 %) considered themselves confident, while the majority of those who had training (59 %) were not confident or certain about their ability to identify abuse. This lack of confidence may indicate the inadequacy of their training as well as a misperception of one's abilities despite lack of education.

Many countries have begun to make programmatic efforts to provide training to teachers. In Queensland, Australia, teacher training includes a 3 h school-based interactive workshop using a standard package comprised of audiovisual segments, activities, question and answer clarification, and small group discussions on case scenarios (Walsh et al. 2008). Training is delivered by school leaders, generally principals and school/guidance counselors rather than child protection specialists.

In 2001, Hawkins and McCallum sought to evaluate the South Australian Education Department Mandated Notification Training (Hawkins and McCallum 2001). The training is a 1-day workshop designed to prepare educators and other mandated reporters to fulfill their reporting obligations. It includes an examination of one's values, attitudes, and experiences, the importance of maintaining a child/young person's focus and perspective when considering the possibility of child abuse and neglect, legal responsibilities, and recognition and notification of suspected child abuse and neglect. Using a control group, they found that, comparatively, participants in the workshop had increased confidence in their ability to recognize the indicators of abuse as well as increases in awareness of their reporting responsibilities, knowledge of what constitutes reasonable grounds, and of how to respond appropriately to a child's disclosure of abuse.

The literature on educators demonstrates that while they often make many reports of child abuse, they may also lack proper training to carry out their duties. Training is sporadic and inconsistent at best. The extent to which teachers are trained in child abuse seems to vary significantly across countries.

Physicians

Physicians, especially pediatricians, are often the first to come in contact with cases of suspected child abuse and neglect (Yehuda et al. 2010). However, it has been well documented that they may not receive adequate training in medical school (Johnson 1993). The majority of medical residents, pediatric program directors, and child protection program directors, in Canadian pediatric academic centers, rated their training in child maltreatment as "somewhat adequate, needs improvement" (Ward et al. 2004). Cavanagh et al. (2004) found that fewer medical staff (nurses and psychiatrists) had received training in asking about abuse than the nonmedical staff (therapists/psychologists). In addition, Kenny (2001b) found that slightly more than half (52 %) of the medical residents in her study reported having some education in child abuse in their training. Further, physicians may be ill informed about specifics related to abuse. For example, it was found that they tend to associate certain factors with child sexual abuse (such as religion, race, and family size), despite research demonstrating a lack of connection between these variables and a risk of experiencing child sexual abuse (Lentsch and Johnson 2000).

There is currently no specific mandated training in child abuse and neglect as a required subspecialty experience in pediatric residency education in the USA as per the Pediatric Residency Review Committee of the Accreditation Council for Graduate Medical Education (Narayan et al. 2006). For residency programs that offer didactic training in abuse issues, the majority (52 %) have been found to offer 3–6 h of training, and sessions were taught by physician experts (87 %) in child abuse and neglect. Overall, many pediatric residents leave residency with limited clinical training in child abuse and neglect, having been exposed to less than five cases of abuse. Narayan et al. (2006) found that 59 % of pediatric residency programs offer no mandatory rotation and 25 % offered no rotations at all in child abuse and neglect. However, 75 % did offer a mandatory, elective, or both rotations. Interestingly, elective rotations appeared to provide more comprehensive coverage of abuse and neglect.

In New York (USA), where there is a mandatory 4 h child abuse and maltreatment course for professionals (including physicians, mental health counselors, nurses, school service personnel, etc.) prior to licensure, Khan et al. (2005) surveyed physicians who had completed the course. On average, 90 % of the physicians answered the ten test items on child abuse correctly. Fifty to 85 % stated that the course made a significant difference in their knowledge and practice. However, results revealed that almost half of the surgeons and internists did not know how to initiate a report of abuse. The authors conclude that while the course may improve awareness, it may not increase reporting.

Palusci and McHugh (1995) utilized a child sexual abuse training for physicians (fellows, students, residents) that consisted of 3 h of didactic training and 6–12 h of patient care exposure and found that participants had a significant increase in their test scores on knowledge of various aspects of child sexual abuse (pre-post). The training utilized a multidisciplinary approach including video, direct patient care, supervision, interview, and medical examination. They believe that this approach had advantages over lectures and case discussions. This is consistent with Ward et al. (2004) who found that only 7 % of their medical residents reported didactic training as a strength, when being taught about child maltreatment.

The extent of training received by physicians seems to vary according to specialty. Starling et al. (2009) found that pediatric programs provide far greater training and resources in child maltreatment than emergency medicine and family medicine programs. In addition, pediatric programs were more likely to have a medical provider who specializes in child abuse, have physician faculty responsible for child abuse training, use a written curriculum for child abuse training, and offer an elective rotation in child abuse, than the emergency and family medicine programs. Residents who reported more training and patient experiences performed better on the knowledge quiz than those who did not have such experiences. This resulted in pediatric residents being more knowledgeable, more comfortable, and better trained in child abuse than their emergency and family medicine peers. While they performed better than their peers, their average score was still 73 %.

Donohue et al. (2002) utilized an abuse reporting skills checklist in a study in order to measure professionals' ability to master these steps when making a child abuse report. The study employed a single subject (third-year medical student) who participated in six training sessions (45 min each) over a 4-week period. The first two sessions focused on education regarding the state reporting laws and rules. The remaining sessions taught skills relevant to initiating child abuse reports, handling upset during child abuse reports, role-play of making reports, and handling reports with clients. A controlled multiple baseline design across behaviors was used to evaluate skills acquisition. Results demonstrated that the participant improved her skills in the area of initiating abuse reports (from baseline to follow-up) and an improved ability to resolve upset by the caregiver to the abuse report. With regard to participant feedback, the participant strongly agreed that the program contributed to her professional development, knowledge in reporting child maltreatment, and confidence in reporting child maltreatment.

McCauley et al. (2003) trained physicians and other professionals by utilizing a 35 min video, Ask-Sympathize-Safety-Educate-Refer-Treat (ASSERT), and a pre- and posttest measuring both knowledge and attitudes. The video, which featured role-plays to demonstrate different approaches to difficult clinical encounters, such as suspected abuse, was created in conjunction with a multidisciplinary team. Physicians were found to have significantly improved knowledge and attitudes about abuse after the training and the video was rated highly. Compared to the other professionals (nurses and social workers), physicians were found to show improvement in knowledge related to the legal requirements to report abuse and neglect.

As Christian (2008) concludes, much of the literature on physician training in child abuse suggests that improving knowledge, while not easy, is simpler than influencing medical practice. She contends that clinical competence in medicine is based both in knowledge and experience. Thus, if the aim of medical education is to improve practice, rather than simply just improve knowledge, education must focus not only on knowledge but skill development. These skills would be in the area of identification of child abuse, addressing concerns with families, reporting suspected child abuse, managing consequences of abuse, advocating for families, and working with families affected by child maltreatment.

Mental Health Professionals

Mental health professionals are likely to see many cases of suspected abuse as they often work with families in crisis. Clinical and counseling psychologists reported that their graduate training programs and internships were deficient in training them to address abuse issues, but those who were trained more recently rated their training more positively than did earlier graduates (Pope and Feldman-Summers 1992). However, overall the ratings were still low. More recent graduates reported that their programs provided little coverage of abuse issues, but it was an improvement from previously trained psychologists. In Australia, Crettenden and Zerk (2012) found that most psychology programs exposed students to issues related to child abuse and neglect as part of or integrated into other units of study. This is consistent with Champion et al. (2003) who also found that doctoral programs in psychology included information on child maltreatment in several courses in their curriculum, most often in ethics courses. Crettenden and Zerk (2012) conclude that there needs to be some agreement on the minimum level of information on child maltreatment required for psychology students, both at the undergraduate and graduate levels.

Alvarez and colleagues (2010) utilized an in-person 3 h workshop for mental health professionals that included a PowerPoint presentation and video vignettes, dissemination of state and federal laws on child abuse reporting, common indicators of child abuse, and a review of misconceptions resulting in the failure to report suspected child maltreatment. After random assignment to the control or training group, it was found that participants who were assigned to the training group improved their knowledge of laws, were able to identify child maltreatment scenarios, and evidenced knowledge of skills required to make a report of child maltreatment compared to controls.

Cavanagh et al. (2004) report on a 1-day training program in New Zealand developed to train professionals (nurses, psychologists/therapists, psychiatrists) on physical and sexual abuse inquiry and response. This was developed in response to recommended best practices for trauma and sexual abuse. Evaluations completed on this training at the end of the day found that 94 % of participants found some benefit to the training, including increased confidence in ability to inquire about and respond to abuse. Aspects of the training that were rated favorably by participants included role-playing, written handouts, and research summaries. Many wanted more time for the training, including an extra day. Six weeks after the training, the majority of participants reported that the training changed their clinical practice. The training had a self-reported positive effect on confidence and self-perceived abilities both in asking about abuse and responding to disclosures. These authors recommend a combined skills and knowledge-based program.

Law Enforcement

Law enforcement plays an important role in identification and responding to child maltreatment. In some jurisdictions, police officers respond along with social services to reports of child abuse, while in other instances they may recognize child maltreatment when investigating other crimes. While police officers are not required to attend university, they typically are trained in police academies. Thus, training in child abuse generally takes place during academy training. In the USA, the Police Training Commission sets the minimum standards that must be achieved, and the topic of child abuse falls into those standards, under the criminal statute of endangering the welfare of children (Rick McGarry, personal communication, December 1, 2013). Frequently, child protection workers will be utilized during these trainings to emphasize policies and procedures. In addition, there may be in-service training classes provided by child protection workers for experienced officers and for officers and detectives assigned to police department patrol and juvenile bureaus. Currently in the USA, there is no mandatory retraining on child abuse during the tenure of an officer, and the focus of training in the academy is often on the criminal aspects of child abuse.

The majority of law enforcement officers in the Portwood et al. (2000) study reported at least minimal amounts of training relative to the identification and investigation of cases of child maltreatment. However, this training seemed to have little effect in enhancing their duties. It seems that officers receive little formal training relative to the identification and/or investigation of child maltreatment beyond basic training courses at the beginning of their careers. In addition, it appears that this training focuses on legal standards, rather than more practical skills and indicators of abuse.

Patterson (2004) describes an 8 h training (including 2+ hours of role-playing) for police academy recruits that consists of the signs and indicators of all types of maltreatment, procedures for emergency removal of a child from a home, interviewing child victims, and reporting child abuse to child welfare authorities. Results indicated that those who had the training reported significantly more positive attitudes of sympathy and caring toward abusive parents, acquired more knowledge about child abuse and neglect, and developed more skills than those in the comparison group, who did not get the training. Portwood et al. (2000) report on the need for law enforcement to understand child development in order to be able to identify child maltreatment and make a report. In their evaluation of law enforcement workers' decision to report sexual abuse, they found that "whether the act is sexual in nature" emerged as the chief determinant in a worker's assessment of whether a particular act constitutes abuse. The authors conclude that law enforcement training may emphasize sexual abuse more than neglect or other types of abuse.

Overall, the research demonstrates a lack of systematic training with professionals as programs vary in length, content, and method of delivery. When training is provided, it is often not evaluated properly to ensure learning gains. Further, there appears to be a discrepancy between the number of reports made by professionals and the number of victims of maltreatment suggesting many victims are "missed." These data support the need to provide more effective training.

Hallmarks of Sound Training Approaches

Based on over 15 years of working with victims of maltreatment, scholarship and experience designing, and delivering reporter training, this author recommends a training model that would include training at multiple points in one's career including preservice (university based), in-service (on the job), and continuing education for professionals.

Recommended Training at Multiple Career Points

Most experts agree that training should be ongoing rather than a single information-giving course (Johnson et al. 1990). In past work, Alvarez et al. (2004) proposed that training preprofessionals should involve providing the trainees with a broad knowledge base that has been incorporated throughout the curriculum, whereas training of currently practicing professionals should focus on specific issues (e.g., legal definitions, symptoms) and be a part of continuing education. This approach also advocates for multiple training at various points in a professional's career.

Preservice Training

Training needs to take place early in one's academic career. Future educators and other professionals, for example, often engage in a variety of practicum experiences in the community early in their studies where they may potentially come into contact with abused children (McKee and Dillenburger 2009). It is imperative that preservice training programs include child abuse awareness and reporting laws in their curriculum (Skarbek et al. 2009). Training should begin in university classes and include not only information but case presentations. McKee and Dillenburger (2009) recommend that higher education colleges and universities need to support the necessity of preservice training by "having clear, accessible, written policies for academic personnel, students, and others involved in relevant curriculum delivery" (p. 328). Many respondents in the Baginsky and Macpherson (2005) study stated that trainers should not make the assumption that students have had any personal or professional experience with abuse, and so no prior knowledge should be assumed. This would require very basic information as an introduction to the topic of child maltreatment. If preservice training is not required, some students (future professionals) will graduate without the knowledge, skills, and attitudes required to effectively protect children (McKee and Dillenburger 2009).

While training at the preservice level is necessary, there are many barriers to implementing such training. The concept of an overcrowded curriculum is common. Baginsky and Macpherson (2005) make the argument that "too much competes for too little time" (p. 326) in most teacher training curriculums. Similarly, Crettenden and Zerk (2012) found that the respondents in their survey (heads of psychology programs in Australia) acknowledged the limited opportunities for faculty to teach child maltreatment issues due to the amount of material that has to be covered in already full curriculums. They further recommend that accreditation bodies for the various professions may want to address the issue of child maltreatment, thus ensuring its inclusion.

The lack of a faculty expert may also impede the implementation of child abuse training. Baginsky and Macpherson (2005) reported that 17 % of the courses for teachers that dealt with child protection and abuse issues were taught by a nonspecialist. However, there are ways to overcome the lack of faculty expertise. Changes to curriculum do not have to be overburdening, but rather programs can draw on existing resources (Champion et al. 2003). Champion et al. (2003) contend that some programs that may not have a course or faculty expert in child maltreatment may be able to utilize a child abuse course that is taught in a different department, which may also help with interdisciplinary training. Bryant (2009) recommends the use of CPS staff when training school counselors or inviting CPS staff to school for training of all faculty.

In many fields there appear to be resources available but not being utilized. For example, there is a published core content for residency training in child abuse as well as a video series available from the American Academy of Pediatrics to assist in curricular development for physicians (Narayan et al. 2006; Starling et al. 2009). For psychologists, Miller-Perrin and Malloy (2006) have suggested child abuse curriculum for both the graduate and undergraduate levels as well as the practice guidelines of the Professional Practice Board of the British Psychological Society (British Psychological Society 2007). McKee and Dillenburger (2009) describe "Learning to Protect," a child protection resource package for teacher education in England. Unfortunately, at many schools, training may come down to one dedicated faculty member who ensures that training takes place.

Initial Training on the Job

Formal training in school represents only one dimension of what needs to be a multifaceted approach to education and training for all professionals. Agencies need to emphasize the seriousness of the issue of child maltreatment. There needs to be a budgetary commitment to the development and maintenance of child protection training (Buckley and McGarry 2011). Agencies need to embrace the role of promotion of child safety and welfare. It is critical for administrators to provide continuous training on these issues and "keep the conversation alive" regarding child abuse. For some positions, it is essential to provide training once an individual is employed for several reasons. First, the agency may have their own policies and procedures in addition to those established by law. Second, providing on-the-job training will ensure that all employees have been instructed, regardless of the training that may or may not have taken place at the preservice level. Third, agencies that provide training are sending a message to employees about the value of children and the importance they place on mandatory reporting. Training can give employees a heightened awareness of an agency's commitment to protecting youth and their intolerance of unethical behavior (Wurtele 2012).

It is recommended that training on child abuse policies and procedures be provided initially when an individual is hired. Just as there is often a new employee orientation that covers employment policies, information regarding the policies and practices of the agency surrounding child abuse reporting should be delivered early in one's employment. McCauley et al. (2003) used this approach by requiring a video of various forms of family violence to be shown as part of their standard orientation process by human resources. It is not enough to simply mandate that employees be given a copy of child protection policies. Simple distribution or access to guidelines and material may not be sufficient in improving knowledge. Buckley and McGarry (2011) found that even when state guidelines mandate that all staff be given a copy of the child protection guidelines, this may not be the case. Only 22 % of the sample reported that they read the guidelines. Another 49 % said that they were not aware if their school had a child protection policy and 49 % had not read it. Eighty-three percent reported that they had no induction at their current school (place of employment) to child protection. Botash et al. (2005) found that only 20 % of their medical participants reported access to the New York state protocol regarding sexual abuse. As these authors conclude, "This is not a very effective method of providing lasting information" (p. 564).

Role of Agency Expert

As Buckley and McGarry (2011) state, training is not a guarantee of learning; however, it can provide a foundation that is supported by other initiatives. The role of an agency expert is one initiative that can be employed at sites. In addition to providing on-the-job training, it is recommended that each professional setting (school, agency) should have a team of key personnel with whom employees can consult on abuse cases (Hinkelman and Bruno 2008). McKee and Dillenburger (2009) advise that a child protection coordinator should be appointed to implement and supervise differential training procedures, as well as provide support to faculty and students; this individual would be responsible for ensuring ongoing, integrated preservice child protection training geared to the needs of each professional group. Assisting professionals with developing contacts with these key players can help build rapport among organizations, which may in turn increase the likelihood that professionals will report suspected abuse.

Buckley and McGarry (2011) report that in Ireland, each school has a designated liaison person (DLP) who has been trained by child protective services and acts as a resource to school staff. The DLP is responsible for receiving reports from school staff and passing them onto child protection. However, this resource is only good if staff is aware of and take advantage of it. Buckley and McGarry (2011) found that less than half of the teachers in their schools were aware of the presence of the DLP. Baginsky and Macpherson (2005) reported on the Education Act 2002 in the UK, which required every state-funded school to have a designated teacher responsible for child protection (ostensibly having received training in the area). The training for this teacher has been well established, but the extent to which other teachers are trained in identification and reporting varies and thus may affect their ability to utilize this resource. Narayan et al. (2006) found that 84 % of the physicians (chief residents) in their study reported that there was an easily identifiable expert in child abuse at their facility.

Continuing Education/Annual Training

Given the changes that take place and new developments in the field of child maltreatment, regular, continued education will be necessary. Chen et al. (2013) state that continuing education helps "bridge the gap" (p. 169) between the need for clinical competence in child maltreatment and the lack of sufficient training in curriculums. Given that some research has found that the longer teachers are teaching, the less likely they are to recognize the signs of child abuse (O'Toole et al. 1999), it is critical to reintroduce training annually. Also, annual presentations are necessary to ensure all employees are trained and kept informed of potential legal changes in reporting. While Botash et al.'s (2005) comments are related to medical continuing education, they are applicable here. "Continued medical education has been an accepted strategy for ongoing learning once medical providers have left the structured educational venues of medical school and is intended to improve medical provider knowledge and lead to improved patient outcomes" (Botash et al. 2005, p. 561).

While some states in the USA have instituted mandatory training for some professionals, it is critical that new content and information be included as well as more creative methods for training are implemented. For instance, Khan et al. (2005)

report that the New York mandatory child abuse course for physician licensure has not changed since its inception in 1988. McCauley et al. (2003) cite barriers to professionals obtaining continuing education credit, including lack of time and limited funds to travel to conference. Thus, innovative approaches, such as video and the Internet, may need to be utilized. This may be particularly relevant as mandates require ongoing training. Baginsky and Macpherson (2005), for instance, describe provisions of the Department for Education and Skills in the UK which requires training for teachers at the initial level, but also refresher training every two years.

Yehuda et al. (2010) conclude that a "one size fits all" training program will not work. They found different needs among the various professionals in their study (physicians, nurses, psychologists, social workers). Programs will need to be tailored to both the profession and the setting (e.g., hospital based, community based). Most importantly, it seemed that those professionals who are significantly involved in child abuse in their daily work express fewer needs for training, than those who do not face such cases regularly. Those with little contact may need foundational knowledge in signs, symptoms, and reporting procedures, while those who work more closely may need supervised practice and simulation.

Chen et al. (2013) found that a multidisciplinary sample of child abuse experts from various fields (medicine, nursing, social work, psychology) reached consensus on the need for child abuse education and what that education should entail. The most important competencies were deemed to be skills and knowledge of child abuse, specifically child protection laws. Training should include both information on the types of abuse, signs and symptoms of each type, and specific policies and procedures for reporting child abuse. Instruction should stress the importance of reporting suspected abuse and explain the steps to follow in reporting abuse. Given the rise of child abuse in youth-serving organizations (schools, sports clubs), information on how to report concerns of a colleague's behavior should also be covered. Baginsky and Macpherson (2005) reported that less than two-thirds of courses included information on how to deal with allegations made against a member of staff.

The use of a multidisciplinary team, including workers from law enforcement and child protection, to deliver training can be useful to provide multiple perspectives (Chen et al. 2013). McKee and Dillenburger (2009) state that this can help build resources among professionals and provide knowledge of different experiences. The use of these existing professional resources in the community also eliminates the need for faculty expertise.

Christian (2008) provides some guidelines for training with physicians that are applicable here with other professionals. She recommends highlighting and repeating essential messages, encouraging participation in educational interactions, using concise graphic educational materials, and providing positive reinforcement of improved practices in follow-up. Alvarez and colleagues (2010) state that best practices for teaching child abuse reporting include interactive exercises involved in practicing the reporting process in real-world scenarios and specifying how and when to involve clients when making a report in such a way that minimizes negative effects on the family and professional relationship. In some cases, the decision to involve clients may be necessary too such as in cases of extreme danger or sexual abuse. Role-playing allows for the practice of complex skills that the professional needs to master. Because reporting can be a stressful situation, role-playing these techniques will also allow professionals to receive feedback and potentially decrease their anxiety when making reports.

Discussion

There have been several attempts to utilize video and online training to teach child abuse training (Kenny 2007; McCauley et al. 2003; Paranal et al. 2012; Walsh and Major 2011). While these approaches can be easy to implement and update, reach a large audience, and maintain a low cost, a pitfall of such approaches is the lack of opportunity for discussion among participants. As Alvarez et al. (2010) report, laws are often unclear, and professional dialogue in a training permits occasions to reflect different opinions, enhance interpretative ideas, and recall information. Feedback can also be provided about erroneous assumptions in reporting due to personal biases. Another advantage of "live trainings" is the ability to address feelings from participants. Lidchi (2007) recommends that training address feelings of impotence and occasional burnout that often arises in mandated reporters due to frustrations with the system. This may prove critical since previous research has found that mandated reporters often do not comply with their legal duty due to negative feelings toward child protective services (e.g., delays in responding, poor responses) (Kenny 2001a; Kenny and McEachern 2002). McCauley et al. (2003) also report on clinician barriers that are inherent to the discussion of sensitive topics, such as child maltreatment, and how training can assist in breaking down these barriers. Paranal et al. (2012) utilized an online format for child sexual abuse training with professionals and compared it with the same training done face-to-face. Participants who received the web-based training were more likely to report feeling discomfort while reading the training materials compared to the in-person participants who had the same materials presented to them aloud by a live trainer. In addition, participants from the web-based group reported higher mean levels of discomfort while viewing video clips, reported a lower likelihood of using steps for protecting children in their lives and a lower likelihood of discussing information from the training with a coworker or supervisor, and found the videos less helpful compared to participants in the in-person training group. Finally, the in-person group participants were more likely to report that there were enough emotional resources provided during the training compared to the web-based group participants.

Certain procedural interventions, such as the use of checklists and structured forms, can result in improved reporting behavior (Carter et al. 2006). One advantage of checklists is the ease of simplicity of design and implementation and the way in which they can be easily audited. As previously noted, the 29-item checklist developed and used by Donohue et al. (2002), along with multiple sessions of training, resulted in improved skills in the area of initiating abuse reports (from baseline to follow-up) and an improved ability to resolve upset by the caregiver to the abuse report by the participant. This checklist could be utilized with any professional who has to make a report of abuse in the context of a clinical relationship.

Effective Evaluation of Training Programs

While training may be provided, the extent to which it results in improved skills for detecting and reporting abuse is unknown. As training programs evolve, performing evaluation of them is critical to understanding their effectiveness and helping to shape future program planning. Carter et al. (2006) performed a systematic review of studies that evaluated child protection training and procedural interventions from 1994 to 2005 and concluded that on the whole, evaluation of interventions was poor. Most outcome measures were learning achievement, attitudinal change, and clinical behavior. Alvarez and colleagues (2010) report that there are currently no psychometrically validated measures specifically developed to assess skills in reporting suspected child maltreatment. Another assessment concern is the lack of control groups to which comparisons can be made or the use of follow-up to gauge maintenance of knowledge of reporting over time. To date, there has been an absence of rigorous, evidence-based approaches to evaluation.

One often used measure to ascertain the effectiveness of training is the increase in reports made to child protection following training. While researchers would like to conclude that increased levels of training lead to greater knowledge and thus more reporting, training that focuses on guidelines and reporting regulations may not be sufficient to improve reporting behavior (Kenny 2004). In New South Wales, Australia, after mandatory reporting of CSA was extended to teachers, in-service trainings were provided for school personnel. Following these trainings, the proportion of cases reported to the authorities by school personnel increased from 11 to 24 % (Lamond 1989). Similarly, Eissa and Almuneef (2010) state that the reported annual referral rate of child abuse and neglect cases in Saudi Arabia (to one particular child protection center) increased ten-fold from 6.4 cases per year in 2000–2004 to 61.5 cases per year in 2007–2008 (following the implementation of mandatory reporting in January 2008 and subsequent training). However, both of these studies provide only causal links between training and reporting. In addition, the extent to which the reports made are substantiated is unknown. Thus, potentially spurious reporting (or overreporting) is one possible effect of increased training.

Much research on professionals and child maltreatment relies on self-report (self-reported knowledge and reporting skills). Carter et al. (2006) found that some training programs showed self-reported increases in knowledge and confidence following the intervention. Cavanagh et al. (2004) found that training had a self-reported positive effect on confidence and self-perceived abilities both in asking about abuse and responding to disclosures. Ward et al. (2004) had residents self-rate their personal competency in the initial evaluation and management of abuse cases. However, self-reporting may not be a measure of actual competency. Factors associated with higher competency scores included more years of training and number of cases of suspected abuse seen during training. Surprisingly, the completion of a clinical rotation was not associated with the competency score. Thus, those who had done a rotation in child protection desired more training just as those who had not. Narayan et al. (2006) based their data on chief residents' perceptions of the performance of residents rather than assessing clinical skills of the resident themselves. Thus, it may not correlate with actual improved clinical skills. As these authors state, more direct measures of the clinical skills of residents in child abuse and neglect would be a preferred method of assessment. Another means of data collection has been to ask program directors to rate the adequacy of their training program, demonstrating a potential bias (Dubowitz 1988). Self-report is subject to social desirability and other biasing influences (Cavanagh et al. 2004), particularly when reporting on behavior that may not be consistent with one's role as a mandated reporter (Bryant 2009) or admits to not protecting children.

Some researchers have tested participant knowledge, which is an improvement in measuring outcome, although comparison control groups and follow-up are still lacking (e.g., Kenny 2007). However, gains in knowledge captured on a test may still not demonstrate actual knowledge gained or translate into clinical competence. For example, Botash et al. (2005) utilized a pre-/posttest design with 30 questions. While they found that all medical providers showed significant cognitive gains following this self-study course on sexual abuse, knowledge did not imply competence. Specifically, in an essay question, the participants misinterpreted test results and failed to make recommendations for legal advocacy.

Learner satisfaction, another common form of measurement, cannot be used to indicate learning gains (Howarth and Morrison 1999). Frequently, training programs employ course evaluations at the end of the training with the belief that if the training is rated useful, there is no need for further evaluation. While participants may be very satisfied with training (which is often the case), satisfaction does not equal learning. While learner satisfaction may be important to measure in terms of knowing what types of training are agreeable to professionals, it does not measure knowledge.

Many studies use case vignettes and alter characteristics or wording (Johnson et al. 1990) in order to gain participants' responses. Ford et al. (2001) used professionals' assessment of an artificial "as if" situation. While Donohue et al. (2002) used a multiple baseline design and empirically evaluated the results of the training, the evaluation of the participant occurred in a contrived child abuse situation with a confederate mother. When contrived or "as if" situations are used, it is not possible to determine how participants will perform in actual abuse scenarios. Transfer of skills from vignettes and case examples to real-life situations remains uncertain. Further, contrived scenarios do not allow for a full inspection of all the relevant variables that would be present in a real-life situation (Ford et al. 2001).

Researchers acknowledge the limitations of the current evaluation methods (primarily self-report) which may not accurately reflect participants' actual level of knowledge or reporting behavior. Future evaluation may want to include video vignettes as a useful alternative to written narratives. This would allow for visual cues of victims, disclosure in the victims' own words, and a more realistic case presentation. Botash et al. (2005) used videotaped case examples which they believe may have improved physicians' competence in correct identification of sexual abuse. They also recommend the use of a series of cases, where the practitioner has to make more complete assessments.

Kirkpatrick (1967) offers a multidimensional model of evaluation which has four goals and would be useful to employ in future evaluations of training programs. The first dimension, reaction, includes the participants' reaction during and after the training to gauge their sense of satisfaction with the training. Learning, the second dimension, is the extent to which the participant has acquired new knowledge, values, and skills, with an emphasis on long-term learning. The third dimension, behavior, is the impact of the training on changing or improving the participants' behavior, evaluating ways in which the participant has applied their learning to practice. Finally, the fourth dimension, ultimate goals, refers to the extent to which the training has helped the organization achieve its goal. In this case, the goal would be the extent to which the training has impacted the identification and reporting of abuse by participants.

Conclusion

One way to help protect children from child maltreatment is to adequately train those who are charged with their care in the necessary skills and knowledge to carry out their duties. Given the social and legal importance of child maltreatment, it is important that adequate training be provided to all professionals and that this training is rigorously evaluated to ensure competence and skill development. Mandated reporters need to be able to act quickly when faced with a situation of potential abuse, but their response must be founded in understanding and confidence (Baginsky and Macpherson 2005). Educators of future professionals must ensure available curriculum, and resources are developed to meet the needs of training in child maltreatment and the employment of a resident expert in child abuse or use of available multidisciplinary community resource professionals. Repeated training throughout professionals' career is necessary to ensure dissemination of the latest research findings as well as to address emerging trends in child abuse and changes to legislation. While web-based training shows promise, the ability to discuss the information, process sensitive and emotionally distressing information in person with colleagues or a facilitator, and receive necessary feedback is critical. Skill development, including through role-play, and use of checklists for abuse reporting are essential elements for any training. Although empowering individuals with knowledge and skills in detecting and reporting child abuse is important, it should not continue to be the only focus of prevention. Enhanced training for professionals is a precondition for all communities working toward more comprehensive efforts to diminish child abuse.

References

Alvarez, K., Kenny, M. C., Donohue, B., & Carpin, K. M. (2004). Why are professionals failing to initiate mandated reports of child maltreatment, and are there any empirically based training programs to assist professionals in the reporting process? *Aggression and Violent Behavior, 9*(5), 563–578.

Alvarez, K., Donohue, B., Carpenter, A., Romero, V., Allen, D., & Cross, C. (2010). Development and preliminary evaluation of a training methods to assist professionals in reporting suspected child maltreatment. *Child Maltreatment, 15*(3), 211–218.

Baginsky, M., & Macpherson, P. (2005). Training teachers to safeguard children: Developing a consistent approach. *Child Abuse Review, 14*, 317–330.

Botash, A., Galloway, A., Booth, T., Ploutz-Snyder, R., Hoffman-Rosenfield, J., & Cahill, L. (2005). Continuing medical education in child sexual abuse: cognitive gains but not experience. *Archives of Pediatrics and Adolescent Medicine, 159*(6), 561–566.

British Psychological Society. (2007). *Child protection portfolio*. Leicester: British Psychological Society Professional Practice Board.

Bryant, J. K. (2009). School counselors and child abuse reporting: A national survey. *Professional School Counseling, 12*(5), 333–342.

Buckley, H., & McGarry, K. (2011). Child protection in primary schools: A contradiction in terms or a potential opportunity? *Irish Educational Studies, 30*, 113–128.

Carter, Y., Bannon, M., Limbert, C., Docherty, A., & Barlow, J. (2006). Improving child protection: A systematic review of training and procedural interventions. *Archives of Disease in Childhood, 91*, 740–743.

Cavanagh, M., Read, J., & New, B. (2004). Sexual abuse inquiry and response: A New Zealand training programme. *New Zealand Journal of Psychology, 33*(3), 137–144.

Champion, K. M., Shipman, K., Bonner, B. L., Hensley, L., & Howe, A. C. (2003). Child maltreatment training in doctoral programs in clinical, counseling, and school psychology: Where do we go from here? *Child Maltreatment, 8*(3), 211–217.

Chen, Y., Fetzer, S., Lin, C., Huang, J., & Feng, J. (2013). Healthcare professionals' priorities for child abuse educational programming: A Delphi study. *Children and Youth Services Review, 35*, 168–173.

Christian, C. (2008). Professional education in child abuse and neglect. *Pediatrics, 122*, 13–17.

Crettenden, A., & Zerk, D. (2012). Child protection and psychology education in Australian universities. *Australian Psychologist, 47*, 77–89.

Donohue, B., Carpin, K., Alvarez, K. M., Ellwood, A., & Jones, R. W. (2002). A standardized method of diplomatically and effectively reporting child abuse to state authorities: A controlled evaluation. *Behavior Modification, 26*(5), 684–699.

Dubowitz, H. (1988). Child abuse programs and pediatric residency training. *Pediatrics, 82*(3), 477–480.

Eissa, M., & Almuneef, M. (2010). Child abuse and neglect in Saudi Arabia: Journey of recognition to implementation of national prevention strategies. *Child Abuse and Neglect, 34*, 28–33.

Ford, H. H., Schindler, C. B., & Medway, F. J. (2001). School professionals' attributions of blame for child sexual abuse. *Journal of School Psychology, 39*(1), 25–44.

Hawkins, R., & McCallum, C. (2001). Mandatory notification training for suspected child abuse and neglect in south Australian schools. *Child Abuse & Neglect, 25*(12), 1603–1625. doi:http://dx.doi.org/10.1016/S0145-2134(01)00296-4

Hicks, C., & Tite, R. (1998). Professionals' attitudes about victims of child sexual abuse: Implications for collaborative child protection teams. *Child and Family Social Work, 3*, 37–48.

Hinkelman, L., & Bruno, M. (2008). Identification and reporting of child sexual abuse: The role of elementary school professionals. *The Elementary School Journal, 108*(5), 376–391.

Howarth, J., & Morrison, T. (1999). *Effective staff training in social care: From theory to practice*. London: Routledge.

Johnson, C. F. (1993). Physicians and medical neglect: Variables that affect reporting. *Child Abuse & Neglect, 17*(5), 605–612.

Johnson, P. A., Owens, R. G., Dewey, M. E., & Eisenberg, N. E. (1990). Professionals' attributions of censure in father-daughter incest. *Child Abuse & Neglect, 14*(3), 419–428.

Kenny, M. C. (2001a). Child abuse reporting: Teachers' perceived deterrents. *Child Abuse and Neglect, 25*, 81–92.

Kenny, M. C. (2001b). Compliance with mandated child abuse reporting: Comparing physicians and teachers. *Journal of Offender Rehabilitation, 34*, 9–23.

Kenny, M. (2004). Teachers' attitudes toward and knowledge of child maltreatment. *Child Abuse and Neglect, 28*, 1311–1319.

Kenny, M. C. (2007). Web-based training in child maltreatment for future mandated reporters. *Child Abuse & Neglect, 31*(6), 671–678.

Kenny, M., & McEachern, A. (2002). Reporting suspected child abuse: A pilot comparison of middle and high school counselors and principals. *Journal of Child Sexual Abuse, 11*(2), 59–75.

Khan, A. N. G. A., Rubin, D. H., & Winnik, D. H. (2005). Evaluation of the mandatory child abuse course for physicians: Do we need to repeat it? *Journal of the Royal Institute of Public Health, 119*, 626–631.

Kirkpatrick, D. L. (1967). Evaluation of training. In R. Craig & I. Bittel (Eds.), *Training and development handbook* (pp. 87–112). New York: McGraw-Hill.

Lamond, D. (1989). The impact of mandatory reporting legislation on reporting behavior. *Child Abuse & Neglect, 13*, 471–480.

Lentsch, K. A., & Johnson, C. F. (2000). Do physicians have adequate knowledge of child sexual abuse? The results of two surveys of practicing physicians, 1986 and 1996. *Child Maltreatment, 5*, 72–78.

Lidchi, V. G. (2007). Reflections on training in child abuse and neglect prevention: Experiences in Brazil. *Child Abuse Review, 16*, 353–366.

Mathews, B. (2011). Teacher education to meet the challenges posed by child sexual abuse. *Australian Journal of Teacher Education, 36*(11), 13–32.

Mathews, B., & Kenny, M. C. (2008). Mandatory reporting legislation in the United States, Canada, and Australia: A cross-jurisdictional review of key features, differences, and issues. *Child Maltreatment, 13*, 50–63.

McCauley, J., Jenckes, M., & McNutt, L. (2003). ASSERT: The effectiveness of a continuing medical education video on knowledge and attitudes about interpersonal violence. *Academic Medicine, 78*(5), 518–524.

McKee, B. E., & Dillenburger, K. (2009). Child abuse and neglect: Training needs of student teachers. *International Journal of Educational Research, 48*(5), 320–330.

Miller-Perrin, C. L., & Malloy, L. C. (2006). *Curriculum guide for instruction in child maltreatment*. American Psychological Association, Division 37, Section on Child Maltreatment. Retrieved October 10, 2013, from http://www.apa.org/divisions/div37/child_maltreatment/Curriculum%20Guide.pdf

Narayan, A., Socolar, R., & St. Claire, K. (2006). Pediatrics residency training in child abuse and neglect in the United States. *Pediatrics, 117*(6), 2215–2221.

O'Toole, R., Webster, S., O'Toole, A., & Lucal, B. (1999). Teachers' recognition and reporting of child abuse: A factorial survey. *Child Abuse and Neglect, 23*(11), 1083–1101.

Orelove, F., Hollahan, D., & Myles, K. (2000). Maltreatment of children with disabilities: Training needs for a collaborative response. *Child Abuse and Neglect, 24*(2), 185–194.

Palusci, V. J., & McHugh, M. T. (1995). Interdisciplinary training in the evaluation of child sexual abuse. *Child Abuse and Neglect, 19*(9), 1031–1038.

Paranal, R., Thomas, K., & Derrick, C. (2012). Utilizing online training for child sexual abuse prevention: Benefits and limitations. *Journal of Child Sexual Abuse, 21*, 507–520.

Patterson, G. (2004). Evaluating the effects of child abuse training on the attitudes, knowledge, and skills of police recruits. *Research on Social Work Practice, 14*(4), 273–280.

Pope, K., & Feldman-Summers, S. (1992). National survey of psychologists' sexual and physical abuse history and their evaluation of training and competence in these areas. *American Psychological Association, 23*(5), 353–361.

Portwood, S. G., Grady, M. T., & Dutton, S. E. (2000). Enhancing law enforcement identification and investigation of child maltreatment. *Child Abuse & Neglect, 24*(2), 195–207.

Skarbek, D., Hahn, K., & Parrish, P. (2009). Stop sexual abuse in special education: An ecological model of prevention and intervention strategies for sexual abuse in special education. *Sexuality and Disability, 27*(3), 155–164.

Starling, S., Heisler, K., Paulson, J., & Youmans, E. (2009). Child abuse training and knowledge: A national survey of emergency medicine, family medicine, and pediatric residents and program directors. *Pediatrics, 123*(4), 595–602.

Swann, A. (2000). Recognition of abuse. In H. Owen & J. Pritchard (Eds.), *Good practice in child protection: A manual for professionals* (pp. 39–55). London: Jessica Kingsley.

UN General Assembly. (1989, November 20). Convention on the rights of the child, United Nations, Treaty series, vol. 1577, p. 3. Available at: http://www.refworld.org/docid/3ae6b38f0.html

UNICEF. (2010, January 6). *Child protection from violence, exploitation and abuse.* Retrieved October 10, 2013, from http://www.unicef.org/media/media_45451.html

U. S. Department of Health & Human Services. (2012). *Child maltreatment 2011: Reports from the States to the National Child Abuse and Neglect Data System.* Washington, DC: U. S. Government Printing Office.

Walsh, M., & Major, J. (2011). Child sexual abuse: A new approach to professional education. *Nursing Standard, 25*(37), 35–40.

Walsh, K., Bridgstock, R., Farrell, A., Rassafiani, M., & Schweitzer, R. (2008). Case, teacher and school characteristics influencing teachers' detection and reporting of child physical abuse and neglect: Results from an Australian survey. *Child Abuse & Neglect, 32*(10), 983–993.

Ward, M. G. K., Bennett, S., Plint, A., King, W. J., & Jabbour, M. (2004). Child protection: A neglected area of pediatric residency training. *Child Abuse and Neglect, 28*, 1113–1122.

Wurtele, S. (2012). Preventing the sexual exploitation of minors in youth-serving organization. *Children and Youth Services Review, 34*, 2442–2453.

Yehuda, B., Attar-Schwartz, S., Ziv, A., Jedwab, M., & Benbenishty, R. (2010). Child abuse and neglect: Reporting by health professionals and their need for training. *The Israel Medical Association Journal, 12*(10), 598–602.

Chapter 17
An Evidence-Supported Approach to Reporting Child Maltreatment

Brad Donohue, Krisann M. Alvarez, and Kimberly N. Schubert

Introduction

The reporting of suspected child maltreatment by professionals to appropriate authorities is a complicated process that is typically mandated by law. However, professionals seldom receive sufficient training in this area (Wright et al. 1999), including basic knowledge of appropriate state laws and rules governing the reporting of child maltreatment (Sandberg et al. 1986). Lack of training in the reporting of child maltreatment leaves professionals with insufficient knowledge of the reporting process (Abrahams et al. 1992; Bavolek 1983; Baxter and Beer 1990) and lack of comfort in complying with it (Zellman 1990a). Ultimately, lack of training in child maltreatment reporting contributes to poor decisions that negatively affect the protection of children (Bavolek 1983; Hinson and Fossey 2000). Indeed, Brosig and Kalichman (1992) determined that 40 % of mental health professionals failed to report suspected maltreatment during their professional career. Failure to report suspected cases (and failure to suspect a case when a reasonably knowledgeable reporter would do so), and reporting child maltreatment unnecessarily, cannot be eradicated but can be minimized by effective training. Therefore, it is necessary to ensure that professionals know how to identify and report child maltreatment and feel comfortable in this process.

B. Donohue (✉)
Department of Psychology, Family Research and Services, University of Nevada, Maryland Parkway, 5030, Las Vegas, NV, USA
e-mail: bradley.donohue@unlv.edu

K.M. Alvarez
Early Childhood Mental Health Services, State of Nevada Division of Child and Family Services, Las Vegas, NV, USA

K.N. Schubert
University of Nevada, Las Vegas, NV, USA

B. Mathews, D.C. Bross (eds.), *Mandatory Reporting Laws and the Identification of Severe Child Abuse and Neglect*, Child Maltreatment 4,
DOI 10.1007/978-94-017-9685-9_17

We begin this chapter by reviewing general issues in reporting child maltreatment to provide a backdrop against which to appreciate state and federal laws protecting children from maltreatment and to identify evidence-based methods of involving family members in the mandated reporting process. We then review standardized programs that have been utilized to train professionals to report child maltreatment effectively and highlight our evidence-supported training program to assist professionals in achieving requisite competencies and motivation to optimize their skill sets in reporting suspected child maltreatment to appropriate authorities.

General Procedures Involved in Reporting Child Maltreatment

Reporting Requirements and Processes

Professionals (e.g., medical or mental health providers, teachers, military) are mandated by governments in many jurisdictions to report suspected child maltreatment to appropriate child protective service (CPS) agencies or local police departments, usually through telephone correspondence and followed by written documentation (Heymann 1986). In the United States, toll-free telephone lines have been established to facilitate this process. The initial oral report assists in protecting children from imminent danger and is a first step in determining reporting requirements (Merriwether 1986). Individuals who receive these reports (local police departments; CPS) are designated to assess potential child maltreatment as consistent with state and federal laws (Koralek 1992). In rural areas, and when children are in immediate danger, mandated reporters of child maltreatment should contact the police to satisfy their legally sanctioned reporting commitments, particularly outside business hours (US Department of Health and Human Services 1992a, b). Some agencies will permit the initial report of suspected child maltreatment to be provided through fax or online, and most have standardized reporting forms that are either required or encouraged to be used.

After the report is initiated, the recipient or intake agency (i.e., CPS, local police) typically solicits information that is relevant to assessing immediate danger, such as the context in which the incident or circumstances were determined and a description of the incident or circumstances leading to child maltreatment suspicion. This information is important as it helps the recipient to assess immediate safety needs and respond to determined safety needs accordingly (i.e., send an investigative child protective service officer or police officer to the child victim within 4 h, 24 h, or 72 h depending on severity level). Mandated reporters who are legally obligated to assure confidentiality of their clients or patients should initially withhold identifying information about the suspected perpetrator and victim of child maltreatment until the recipient of the report indicates that this information is required. That is, after the initial information about the incident is provided, some intake agency officers will indicate if an official report needs to be filed by law, which includes disclosure of identifying information. Some officers will indicate it is up to the person making the report to determine if child maltreatment needs to be reported, as consistent with the law. If the latter choice is offered to the reporter, it is prudent to consider full disclosure of the suspected child maltreatment to assist in the investigatory process after consultation with other professionals. The recipient's identification number or name should be obtained and documented in the reporter's professional records after the official report is provided. After an official report is accepted, the receiving agency will determine if an investigation is warranted (i.e., Kemp 1998).

Involving Caregivers in the Reporting Process

Mandated reporters often believe reports of suspected child maltreatment should exclude caregivers of children who are suspected victims of maltreatment. However, Berliner (1993) found that 96 % of caregivers who were involved in the reporting of child maltreatment responded without threats or attempts to hurt the persons making these reports, and involving family in the reporting process enhances trust of caregivers in persons who initiate these reports (Dawes-Night et al. 2006). Therefore, there may be inherent benefits to including caregivers in the reporting of suspected child maltreatment (Stadler 1989). In doing so, it is advisable to listen to caregiver concerns about the reporting process and reiterate federal and state laws necessitating suspicion of child maltreatment (Weinstein et al. 2000).

Written Report

Written reports of child maltreatment are often required immediately but in some jurisdictions are legally mandated to occur within 72 h of an initial oral report. These reports may provide more details of suspected child maltreatment than originally provided to assist investigative officials (Heymann 1986). Forms are available from most CPS agencies to assist in reporting suspected child maltreatment (Shanel-Hogan and Jarrett 1999). Typically these forms include the vital information about the child's situation: demographics about the child (or children) who is the suspected victim of child maltreatment, demographics and other relevant details about the parents of the suspected victim, the nature and extent and timing/duration of the maltreatment suspected, relevant injuries suspected to have been caused to the child, relevant behavior of the child (including any disclosures) and her or his siblings, and demographics of the reporters (Merriwether 1986). It is imperative that information is provided objectively, without judgment or interpretation, focusing on the objective facts about the child (Berliner 1993). Reporters may provide information to ensure safety of the child victim (e.g., perpetrator's violence history) consistent with state and federal laws. However, reports about suspected perpetrators should be limited to the suspected incident of child maltreatment or protection of children.

Institutional Requirements

Schools, businesses, and other organizations often have child maltreatment reporting policies that are governed internally. For example, some school policies require that parents be informed that the report has been made (Remley and Fry 1993) or that school-appointed officials report suspected child maltreatment. In such situations, it is important that mandated reporters maintain conduct that is consistent with state and federal laws where these exist. For instance, if the institutional administration or head decides not to report an incident in which child maltreatment is suspected by a subordinate mandated reporter, the subordinate's obligation to report remains.

Established Training Programs to Assist in Reporting Child Maltreatment

Although training programs have been developed to teach professionals to report suspected child maltreatment, most of these programs were not developed utilizing controlled research methodology. Macleod et al. (2003) conducted a training program with medical doctors, but did not assess the participants' competencies in reporting child maltreatment. McCauley et al. (2003) empirically developed a training program for physicians and other staff members that involved a 35-min training video showing how to report suspected child maltreatment. The video provided definitions, epidemiology, patient presentations, and treatment options. Additionally, the program included role-plays to teach participants to respond to violence. Results of questionnaires, completed before and immediately after training, indicated that the program was effective in the identification of physical indicators of child maltreatment, but not in their knowledge of legal reporting requirements.

To assess child sexual abuse reporting, Palusci and McHugh (1995) developed a training curriculum for physicians and students working in a medical hospital setting. The program involved approximately 90 min of didactic training in interviewing, sexual development, and the psychological basis of sexual abuse evaluation. Participants also evaluated a child through a medical exam for sexual abuse and spent 1 year training in a child abuse clinic. Results indicated that there was a significant improvement for those who took the training course in female anatomy, reporting of sexually transmitted infections (STI), and case analyses of four possible child sexual abuse scenarios. Overall, it was shown that this training program increased the extent to which the participating medical doctors and students would be capable of competently reporting child sexual abuse as per case studies and increased knowledge in STIs and female anatomy.

Hawkins and McCallum (2001a, b) examined the Southern Australia Education Department Mandated Notification Training program, which is a 1-day training program designed to increase knowledge or awareness of intrapersonal variables that influence educator responses to child maltreatment, how to take the perspective of the child victim, and recognize child maltreatment, including knowing when to report and how to do so. They evaluated individuals who had previously completed the program compared to those who had not. Those who had completed the program demonstrated greater perceptions of preparation to report suspected maltreatment, had more appropriate responses to hypothetical conditions, and were more likely to recognize sexual maltreatment in vignettes.

McGrath et al. (1987) demonstrated the initial efficacy of a teacher awareness workshop to assist elementary teachers in detecting and reporting child maltreatment. In this study, a baseline of questionnaires was administered to 184 elementary teachers. Eight questions were specific to the teachers' own experience with child maltreatment and knowledge of indicators of child maltreatment, five questions assessed legislative requirements specific to reporting child abuse and neglect, and five questions assessed school board policy on abuse and neglect, and 19 statements about child abuse and neglect were answered "true," "false," or "I don't know." Teachers were randomly assigned to a workshop that targeted the aforementioned areas or a wait-list control. Two months after the workshop, 37 teachers in the workshop condition and 94 participants in the wait-list control condition were re-administered the questionnaires. Results indicated that workshop participants were more familiar with indicators of sexual and emotional abuse than control participants (but not physical or child neglect). Workshop participants were also more knowledgeable of institutional structure and legal issues and child maltreatment facts than control participants at a subsequent 3-month follow-up. Although the interpretation of study results was compromised due to high dropout in the experimental condition, this pioneering study supports utilization of standardized assessment measures in the evaluation of training programs to assist professionals in reporting child maltreatment and offers promise in the development of the examined training approach.

Reiniger et al. (1995) evaluated the Identification and Reporting of Child Abuse Maltreatment program as a prerequisite for individuals seeking social work licensure. The program delineates child maltreatment and shows when these behaviors need to be reported. The program was examined using a pre/post experimental design, with 60 % of the participants completing post assessment. Results indicated that individuals who completed the program were more knowledgeable about reporting child maltreatment.

More recently, Kenny (2007) conducted a study evaluating a web-based program to assist educating students in identifying and reporting child maltreatment. The program was self-paced, supported by research, and consistent with Florida statutes. The program was evaluated for feasibility and appropriateness by several professionals, including a pediatrician, clinical psychologist, and child forensic psychologist. Training included information about incidence and prevalence of child maltreatment, descriptions and indicators of abuse, emotional and behavioral indicators of child maltreatment, legislative mandatory reporting duties, and statistics and reporting procedures related to reporting suspected child maltreatment. There was a significant improvement in participants' knowledge of child maltreatment symptoms and child maltreatment reporting procedures and legislative mandatory reporting duties after their completion of the training program. Participants reported that they enjoyed the training program. The study supported for the first time the benefits of web-based technology in learning to report suspected child maltreatment, demonstrating feasibility and enhanced applicability of child maltreatment reporting to the professional development of future educators.

A skill acquisition program was developed by Donohue et al. (2002) that includes protocol checklists to assist professionals in reporting child maltreatment with caregivers being invited to participate in the reporting procedure to some extent. The program involved several hours of training and was evaluated in a medical student utilizing controlled multiple baseline methodology. The participant's performance in reporting suspected child maltreatment, and managing upset, during standardized role-play vignettes with a confederate caregiver (trained research assistant enacting the role of a caregiver) significantly improved, but only after the respective skills were targeted in training according to an expert who was blind to experimental design. Results were reliably maintained in role-play vignettes at 45-day follow-up. The participant reported that the program increased her knowledge and confidence in performing these skills. The study, although controlled, was limited to a medical student, and training scenarios were specific to managing the reporting process with a caregiver who was not identified to perpetrate child maltreatment. Additionally, the training program did not include information about state or federal laws.

Alvarez et al. (2010) extended the work of Donohue et al. (2002), assisting dissemination of this intervention by converting program content to slideshow format (i.e., PowerPoint), restricting training to a single 2-h group workshop, inclusion of videotape vignettes showing successful implementation of skill sets (rather than live-modeling), disseminating state and federal laws that are relevant to the reporting of suspected child maltreatment, review of child maltreatment indicators, and clarification of misconceptions that result in failure to report child maltreatment. In a controlled trial of 55 mental health professional and student practitioners, participants were randomly assigned to the aforementioned training program or an ethnic cultural sensitivity workshop. Results indicated that participants who received the child abuse reporting intervention, as compared with participants who received the control condition, demonstrated greater knowledge of child maltreatment laws, were better able to differentiate situations that required a child maltreatment report from those situations that did not require a report (situations were validated by CPS caseworkers), and demonstrated improvements in clinical skills specific to reporting suspected child maltreatment (as assessed in a questionnaire). Therefore, this program is both feasible and empirically validated utilizing controlled methodology.

This review indicates that there are several training programs that have been, to some extent, successfully evaluated in outcome studies. Only three of these studies have utilized controlled methodology (Alvarez et al. 2010; Donohue et al. 2002;

McGrath et al. 1987). Most of the child abuse reporting training programs involve review and discussion of methods to determine occurrence of child maltreatment and child protection laws, and a few teach child reporting behaviors in response to relevant case scenarios that involve suspected child maltreatment. The child maltreatment reporting intervention that was developed by Alvarez et al. (2010) includes many of these strategies and appears to be feasibly and effectively implemented in large groups. Therefore, this curriculum provides an evidence-supported training exemplar of the child maltreatment reporting process and is underscored below as an exemplary model (see Fig. 17.1 for a summary of its components).

I. Pre-workshop assessment (optional)
II. Facilitator introduction
III. Training agenda
IV. Relevant Background Information Specific to Reporting Child Maltreatment
V. Identifying Child Maltreatment
    a. Child Maltreatment Definitions
        i. Physical abuse (e.g., NRS 432b.090)
        ii. Sexual abuse (e.g., NRS 432b.100)
        iii. Sexual exploitation (e.g., NRS 432b.110)
        iv. Negligent treatment (e.g., NRS 432b.140)
        v. Mental injury (e.g., NRS 432b.070)
    b. Child Maltreatment Indicators
        i. Physical abuse
        ii. Sexual abuse
        iii. Neglect
        iv. Psychological/Emotional abuse
    c. Consultation
        i. Colleagues
        ii. CPS
VI. Reporting Requirements & Procedures
    a. Verbal report procedure (e.g., NRS 432b.200)
    b. Timetable for reporting (e.g., NRS 432b.220)
    c. Report contents (e.g., NRS 432b.230)
VII. Involving Caregivers in the Reporting Process
    a. Informed consent/Limits of confidentiality
    b. Report initiation
        i. Informing caregiver(s)of intent to report
            1. Donohue, et al. (2002) checklist
        ii. Providing caregiver with options in reporting process
    c. CPS procedures involved in the initial investigative process
        i. Screening
        ii. Investigation
        iii. Substantiation
        iv. Service Provision
            1. Voluntary
            2. Mandated
        v. Child Placement
        vi. Prosecution
VIII. Skills Training Specific to Involving Caregivers in the Reporting Process
    a. Videotape modeling of the initiation of child maltreatment report w/ caregiver
    b. Videotape modeling of management of upset in child maltreatment report w/ caregiver
    c. Participant practice of the initiation of child maltreatment report w/ caregiver
    d. Participant practice of the management of upset in child maltreatment report w/ caregiver
IX. Final discussion
X. Post-workshop assessment (optional)

Fig. 17.1 Child maltreatment reporting training: workshop format and overview of content of training curriculum

Training Workshop Curriculum to Assist in Reporting Child Maltreatment: An Exemplary Model

The remaining part of this chapter depicts the training program for child maltreatment reporting that was validated by Alvarez et al. (2010) and briefly reviewed above. This section is written much like a treatment manual and includes factors to assist in determining appropriate participants, trainers, necessary materials or methods of obtaining necessary materials (i.e., PowerPoint presentation of training curriculum, evaluation materials, videotapes of curriculum implementation), protocol required to implement assessment and training, and background support. It is our intention that this information be utilized as a general guide in reporting child maltreatment to appropriate authorities, with the assumption that some of its protocols may need to be altered to accommodate the broad international audience for which this book is targeted.

Workshop Participants

Workshop participants are typically professionals who are mandated by law, or by industry policy, to report child maltreatment (e.g., mental health providers, teachers, physicians). Their educational degrees and experience in the identification and reporting of child maltreatment may vary considerably. The ideal number of workshop participants is about 13 people per trainer. This number of participants permits sufficient oversight of role-play interactions, which is a critical training component.

Training Instructors

Training instructors should be professionals who are mandated by law to report child maltreatment (e.g., teachers, mental health providers, physicians), familiar with local/provisional and federal laws relevant to the reporting of child maltreatment, and formally trained in the curriculum. Whenever possible, it is helpful to include trainers who espouse a multidisciplinary perspective and to have co-trainers from diverse backgrounds.

Materials

PowerPoint presentation of training curriculum

- Used by instructors to review training program.
- Authors may be contacted to obtain this presentation.

Protocol checklist: Initiating Child Abuse Report with Caregiver(s)

- Behavioral instructions in reporting child maltreatment with participating caregiver.
- Used by instructors to teach reporting skills and to assess participants in these skills.
- See Appendix A.

Protocol checklist: Resolving Upset of Caregiver(s) in Reporting Process

- Behavioral instructions involved in resolving upset during reporting process.
- Used by instructors to teach these skills and to assess participants in these skills.
- See Appendix B.

Knowledge of Child Maltreatment Reporting Laws Test

- Multiple choice test.
- Used to assess participants' knowledge in reporting child maltreatment.
- See Appendix C.

Recognition of Child Maltreatment Test

- Vignettes with Likert-type response sets.
- Used to assess participants' ability to identify scenarios that warrant a report.
- See Appendix D.

Clinical Expertise in Reporting Child Maltreatment Test

- Multiple choice test.
- Used to assess participants' clinical expertise in reporting child maltreatment.
- See Appendix E.

Videotape Modeling of the Initiation of a Child Abuse Report with a Caregiver

- Videotape demonstrating behavioral steps involved in reporting child maltreatment.
- Used by trainers to demonstrate the relevant skill sets.
- Authors may be contacted to obtain this videotape.

Videotape Modeling Specific to Resolving Upset of Caregiver in Reporting Process

- Videotape demonstrating behavioral steps involved in resolving upset during reporting.
- Used by trainers to demonstrate the relevant skill sets.
- Authors may be contacted to obtain this videotape.

Workshop Format and Overview of Content of Training Curriculum

The workshop is implemented in a 2-h meeting, and its training components are summarized in Fig. 17.1. The workshop begins with a formal introduction of trainers, training agenda, and dissemination of study results and jurisdictional laws and/or policies that are conceptualized to enhance motivation of participants in the mandated reporting of child maltreatment. Instructors describe evidence-supported steps involved in reporting child maltreatment, including rationales for doing so. Two videotapes are subsequently shown to exemplify the implementation of the steps with a caregiver of a suspected victim of child maltreatment, including appropriate responses to an upset caregiver. Participants are instructed to practice the modeled skill sets, while instructors provide assistance. The workshop concludes with a discussion about child maltreatment reporting. When evaluation of participants is important, the participants may be tested before and after the workshop utilizing protocols in Appendices A and B (percentage of steps/instructions listed in the protocols that are satisfactorily demonstrated in role-play vignettes with a confederate caregiver) or multiple tests in Appendices C, D, and E.

Pre- and Postworkshop Assessment

When it is necessary to evaluate workshop performance (i.e., knowledge and skill sets specific to understanding and reporting child maltreatment), we have developed three assessment measures with good clinical utility, face validity, reliability, intervention sensitivity, and discriminative validity (Alvarez et al. 2010).

The first scale, i.e., Knowledge of Child Maltreatment Reporting Laws Test, is a 15-item multiple choice test with a four-item response set (see Appendix C). The first seven items of this scale are specific to federal law, whereas the last eight items are specific to Nevada and may need to be revised when assessing other jurisdictions.

The second measure (i.e., Recognition of Child Maltreatment Test; Appendix D) consists of four scenarios that depict child maltreatment and four scenarios that do not depict child maltreatment. Participants read each vignette and subsequently rate how likely they suspect child maltreatment and their likelihood of reporting the scenario. Responses are based on a seven-point scale from highly unlikely to highly likely, with higher scores indicating greater likelihood of suspecting and reporting child maltreatment. Better recognition of child maltreatment is indicated when scenarios that depict child maltreatment are scored high and scenarios that do not depict child maltreatment are scored low.

The third measure (i.e., Clinical Expertise in Reporting Child Maltreatment Test; Appendix E) is a 15-item multiple choice examination with a four-item response set. Items query participants about the various types of child maltreatment, child maltreatment reporting procedures, and the influence of the caregiver when reporting child maltreatment.

There is one correct answer for each item. All items and their respective response sets in each of the three measures were reliably assessed to be accurate as per professionals employed by a local child protective service agency. Answer keys are included at the end of each test. Each test requires about 5 min for completion, and these tests may be administered in group format. Therefore, they are feasible to administer.

The two protocol checklists (i.e., Initiating the Child Abuse Report with the Caregiver, Resolving Upset of Caregivers in the Reporting Process) may be utilized to assess skill sets of participants that are specific to reporting child maltreatment and managing upset in response to the reporting process. These scenarios involve a confederate (usually an instructor) portraying the role of a caregiver of a child who is suspected of child maltreatment. The participant is instructed to initiate a report of child maltreatment with the confederate (caregiver) either not utilizing the protocol checklists or utilizing the checklists to assist in guiding the report. At first the confederate is compliant (to assess skills that are specific to initiating the report) and later becomes upset (to assess skills that are specific to managing upset). Each instruction listed in each of the protocol checklists in Appendices A and B is assessed as being satisfactorily completed or not. A percentage score (# of completed items divided by total items possible multiplied by 100) may be quickly derived for each protocol (initiating the report in Appendix A, responding to upset in Appendix B) separately after the role-play interaction. Completion of 70 % of the protocol steps or more in each of the protocols is an indication of satisfactory completion for each skill set. Each role-play assessment requires approximately 5 min to administer and needs a confederate and examiner. Therefore, this measure offers the benefits of observational assessment, but may be limited to individual or research settings because this assessment strategy requires a trained confederate to portray the role of a caregiver and an independent rater to score the role-play interaction.

Implementing the Workshop

Introduction

The workshop begins with the trainer providing a personal introduction and posing the following three questions in a slide show.

1. *How many of you have previously reported child maltreatment?*
2. *What problems, if any, have you experienced in reporting child maltreatment?*
3. *What concerns do you have with the child abuse reporting process?*

These questions provide an outlet for participants to indicate both good and bad experiences with the reporting process and provide an opportunity for the instructor to empathize with participant responses prior to the presentation of training material. Participants are typically quick to engage when these questions are presented, appearing more receptive to subsequent workshop information. This is important as some participants may be compelled to attend the workshop by their employers and may lack intrinsic motivation to receive training.

Agenda for Training Workshop

The training agenda includes a summary of the 2-h workshop format and topics to be discussed (see Fig. 17.1). It is reported that a PowerPoint presentation will be utilized to review definitions of the various types of child maltreatment and legal requirements specific to reporting suspected child maltreatment in their respective state or province (including a timetable of when reports must be made, report content, and what occurs within CPS after a report is made). The agenda indicates that participants will have opportunities to practice and discuss child maltreatment reporting skill sets with their peers after viewing videotapes of a professional initiating a child maltreatment report with a caregiver who later becomes upset about the report.

Relevant Background Information Specific to Reporting Child Maltreatment

After the agenda is reviewed, instructors engage workshop participants about the impact of inaccurate reporting of child maltreatment, the intent of which is to establish their motivation for training in accurate reporting of suspected child maltreatment. Two slides are presented to address professionals' failure to report suspected child maltreatment accurately. It is indicated that approximately 40 % of mandated reporters fail to report suspected child maltreatment at some point in their careers and that 6 % consistently fail to report (Besharov 1994; Camblin and Prout 1983; Kenny and McEachern 2002; Zellman 1990a, b). Attendees are also informed that overreporting by professionals leads to a high proportion of unsubstantiated reports (Besharov 1994; Foreman and Bernet 2000; Kalichman 1999; Zellman and Coulborn-Faller 1996), some of which are clearly not warranted and can cost governments valuable resources. Instructors also provide information that is relevant to failure of professionals to report suspected child maltreatment as a result of perceived negative consequences. For instance, although it is reported by Baxter and Beer (1990) that about a quarter of professionals fear legal retaliation due to reporting suspected child maltreatment, this information is not true due to federal immunity for anyone reporting child maltreatment to officials in good faith. Relevant to concerns specific to physical retaliation by suspected perpetrators, it is pointed out that only approximately 4 % of clients respond with threats or attempts to harm professionals (Weinstein et al. 2000). Of course, trainers need to be careful to avoid negation of the potential for harm, however unlikely this may be to occur.

It is reported that Kalichman and Craig (1991) found 31 % of psychologists believed reports of child maltreatment would adversely affect relationships they had with their clients, and Kalichman et al. (1989) found 42 % of licensed psychologists believed reporting child maltreatment negatively impacted family therapy. It is therefore pointed out that some professionals may struggle between wanting to report in an attempt to improve circumstances for the child and fearing reporting efforts will result in further harm to the family unit. The instructor balances this tension in discussion, pointing out that the absence of mandated reporting may lead to continued child maltreatment, whereas reporting may lead to the provision of social and medical services to the family by CPS. It is also pointed out that Steinberg et al. (1997) determined that positive reporting of child maltreatment is significantly influenced by the presence of a positive therapeutic relationship prior to reporting, and involvement of clients in the reporting process may enhance relationships between professionals and clients throughout treatment (Levine and Doeuck 1995). For instance, Weinstein et al. (2001) determined that 40 % of reported cases of child maltreatment resulted in unchanged relationships with the professional making the report and that 32 % resulted in improved relationships. Thus, workshop participants are encouraged to utilize clinical judgment in the decision to include caregivers in the reporting process, including suspected perpetrators of child maltreatment.

Identifying Child Maltreatment

Accurate child maltreatment identification is frequently identified in the literature to be important in the reporting of child maltreatment (Foreman and Bernet 2000; Kalichman 1999). Therefore, the major types of child maltreatment are reviewed. Child maltreatment generally concerns psychological abuse, physical abuse/excessive corporal punishment, sexual abuse/exploitation, and child neglect, as governed by the state in which the workshop is conducted. However, states or local governing bodies vary as to what is specifically indicated to be child maltreatment. For instance, in Nevada "mental injury" is the concept used instead of "emotional" or "psychological" abuse. Therefore, instructors show specific definitions of child maltreatment that are governed in the state or local jurisdiction for which the workshop is conducted and subsequently attempt to solicit comments from workshop participants that demonstrate their understanding of these definitions.

To assist in further understanding how to accurately identify child maltreatment, the instructor provides a slide that specifies physical, behavioral, and emotional indications of the different types of maltreatment (see Fig. 17.2). The trainer stresses that many of the indicators of child maltreatment (e.g., difficulty sleeping) are often shared between the victim and perpetrator of child maltreatment and that victims and perpetrators of child maltreatment often experience multiple indicators of child maltreatment (e.g., low self-esteem, anxiety, depression, speech impairments). However, participants are also cautioned that specific indicators of child maltreatment may be present due to conditions or causes other than child maltreatment.

Often evidenced by victim and perpetrator	Evidenced by victim
Lack of attachment between perpetrator & victim	Unexplained or inconsistent injuries
Self-destructive or aggressive behavior	Injuries to multiple areas (bruises across arm)
Mood disorders (anxiety, depression)	Injuries w/ specific patterns (e.g., cigarette burn)
Academic difficulty or failure	Injuries in various stages of healing
Abrupt outbursts or tantrums	Child evidencing poor social skills with peers
Substance abuse	Sexually descriptive statements
Difficulty sleeping	Sexualized behavior (e.g., self-stimulation, sexual aggression & inappropriate contact
Low self-esteem	Somatic complaints
	Malnourished
	Inappropriate clothing, poor hygiene
	Lack of appropriate supervision
	Cognitive or speech impairment

Fig. 17.2 Indicators of child maltreatment in perpetrators and victims of child maltreatment

For example, academic difficulties in adolescents may be indicative of physical abuse, but may simply result from a learning disability. In addition, participants are encouraged to consider developmental appropriateness of the presented indicators. For instance, self-stimulation of genital areas may indicate sexual abuse or simply be indicative of normal developmental exploration. Although the aforementioned information suggests that apparent signs of child maltreatment may be influenced by factors that are not specific to child maltreatment, it is emphasized that, in general, professionals should attempt to validate or disconfirm their initial suspicions with other professionals after examining relevant laws governing the protection of children from maltreatment.

Reporting Requirements and Procedures

Mandated reporters' lack of knowledge regarding reporting requirements for suspected child maltreatment has been identified repeatedly in the literature and is problematic. Therefore, the federal mandate for professionals to report suspected maltreatment as required by the Child Abuse Prevention and Treatment Act (CAPTA) of 1974 for children less than 18 years of age is reviewed, including relevant laws of the state or province for which training occurs. Instructors need to adjust workshop content to accommodate local jurisdictional laws. Although child maltreatment protection laws may vary across states, instructors disclose that all states require that a report of child maltreatment has to be made when a professional believes (e.g., have reason or cause to believe, or have reasonable cause to believe) or suspects (e.g., have reason or cause to suspect, or have reasonable cause to suspect) child maltreatment has occurred or when "a reasonable person would suspect child maltreatment has occurred." Thus, attendees are strongly urged to consult with at least a couple of professionals prior to initiating the reporting process of child maltreatment with CPS and to document any discussions that influence the reporting process. It is also highlighted that the timeline for reporting child maltreatment is usually determined to be as soon as possible, but no later than 24 h after suspicion of child maltreatment. It is mentioned that some states require a formal written report to be filed within a week of the initial report of suspected child maltreatment.

The distinction between objective evidence and feelings, both of which may be acceptable in the consideration of child maltreatment depending on the local jurisdiction, is discussed. Lack of evidence has been reported as a substantial factor in the decision by professionals not to report child maltreatment (Finalyson and Koocher 1991; Kalichman et al. 1989). Therefore, concepts of suspicion and belief are discussed in light of evidence.

The workshop is best suited for professionals (usually mental health professionals). Therefore, clarification is provided that confidentiality privileges and obtaining information in the context of research do not negate the reporting mandate. Many workshop participants are surprised to learn they should only provide information about the suspected perpetrator and victim of child maltreatment that is specific to the incident or incidents of suspected child maltreatment and future protection of the child. Additional information is provided to participants regarding immunity in the United States for reporting child maltreatment in "good faith," and that failure to report may result in fines, jail time, civil liability, and/or sanctions by professional licensing boards. Workshop participants are encouraged to follow reporting practices of their employers, but are also informed that persons who suspect or believe child maltreatment has occurred are mandated to report to CPS, regardless of the beliefs or suspicions of their employers. Instructors encourage participants to consult with professional colleagues and professionals within CPS when they are unsure how to proceed and to document child maltreatment reports in clinical records as well as specific rationales leading to decisions not to report.

Workshop participants are informed that reports could be made to either local law enforcement or CPS and that these agency representatives will request specific information that is necessary to determine when official reports of child maltreatment are needed. Therefore, with few exceptions (i.e., important circumstances leading to suspected child maltreatment, information specific to the protection and whereabouts of referenced child) mandated reporters should generally not report information that is not relevant to suspected child maltreatment to assist in protecting confidentiality of clients. When children are suspected to be in immediate danger, or when suspected perpetrators are not family members or within the household of children who are suspected of child maltreatment, workshop participants are encouraged to contact the local police department rather than CPS.

Involving Caregivers in the Reporting Process

Workshop participants often do not realize that it may be advantageous to involve caregivers in the reporting of child maltreatment, including perpetrators suspected of child maltreatment when clinically determined. Similarly, they may be unfamiliar with various factors that suggest inclusion of caregivers in the reporting process is contraindicated. To assist workshop participants in gaining a better understanding of this tension, the workshop facilitators are trained to first solicit situations in which caregivers should be excluded from this process. Facilitators generally empathize or validate these scenarios and subsequently solicit situations in which the participation of caregivers in the child maltreatment reporting process may be indicated. Workshop participants are informed that clinical judgment should be emphasized in determining the appropriateness of involving caregivers in the reporting process to assist in assuring self- and other-preservation (Berliner 1993). Along these lines, it is emphasized that professionals exclude caregivers in the reporting process if they are uncomfortable doing so or suspect this process may be clinically contraindicated. Indeed, exceptions to including caregivers of child maltreatment in the reporting process are reviewed and may include their history of abrupt aggression, emotional instability or intoxication, and indications that caregivers may attempt to influence suspected victims to retract child maltreatment incidents that are valid (see Stadler 1989).

On the other hand, instructors explain that involving caregivers in the reporting process may assist in maintaining positive therapeutic relationships, particularly when limits of confidentiality are detailed during informed consent (see Weinstein et al. 2000). In doing so caregivers are less likely to become upset should a report of child maltreatment be indicated later in therapy (Steinberg 1994). Moreover, Nicolai and Scott (1994) empirically determined that professionals who routinely reviewed limits of confidentiality were more likely to report child maltreatment in case presentations, and reporting outcomes are generally more positive when caregivers are informed of the decision to report (Weinstein et al. 2001). Consistent with Taylor and Adelman (1998), instructors encourage workshop participants to explain to caregivers why reports need to be made, soliciting their input in the process of reporting and reviewing possible outcomes of reporting. Instructors also inform workshop attendees that it is generally a good idea to provide caregivers options in the reporting process. Following recommendations of Stadler (1989), instructors emphasize that caregivers should first be presented the option of initiating the report themselves. If this option is declined, professionals may offer to initiate the report in the caregiver's presence. When both of these options are declined by caregivers, professionals are encouraged to indicate that the report can be made outside the caregiver's presence. This strategy is likely to decrease anxiety while satisfying legal reporting requirements.

Workshop participants are informed about the process CPS undergoes after reports are initiated, which has been identified to be an important training strategy (Levine and Doeuck 1995; Weinstein et al. 2001). Compaan et al. (1997) found professionals are more likely to report child maltreatment when they have an understanding of the reporting process from the perspective of CPS, which helps them to guide caregivers through this process (Brosig and Kalichman 1992). The instructor indicates that there are several steps that occur after the report is made to CPS. First, the CPS agent may or may not accept the report. Reports are generally accepted when the extent of information provided is sufficient to permit an investigation to occur (e.g., identifying information provided), and the incident appears to be indicative of child maltreatment. If a report is accepted, it may or may not be recommended for investigation. If a report is accepted for investigation, most CPS organizations have a priority system to assist in determining their response time. For instance, if an incident is associated with imminent risk, the agency may need to respond immediately or at least within 24 h. In such events, the child may be removed prior to the conclusion of the investigation. In all jurisdictions, child abuse investigations must be initiated within 48–72 h of the report to determine whether maltreatment occurred and create a case plan to address potential concerns. It is explained to workshop participants that it is comforting for caregivers to learn mandated reports of suspected child maltreatment can include supportive feedback from them, such as outstanding efforts of caregivers to participate in treatment and demonstrations of affection and concern for their children. Similarly, caregivers are soothed to learn professionals can provide recommendations during their initial reports that children not be interviewed during school hours or that caregivers will be available by telephone to arrange investigative meetings that do not occur in their place of employment.

Workshop participants are informed that CPS and/or differential response agencies may provide services to families regardless of investigative outcomes and that services may be provided free of charge. Potential services may include mental health therapies, employment services, financial assistance, and parenting resources. Services are generally voluntary, although CPS agents may seek a court mandate to assure completion of services and well-being of children. Professionals and caregivers are often concerned that children will be removed or that criminal prosecution of the suspected perpetrator will occur. To reassure them, participants are informed that although this is a possible outcome of the reporting process, these consequences are unlikely unless maltreatment is severe. Indeed, separation of children from caregivers who are assessed to perpetrate child maltreatment generally occurs only when risk of harm is determined by CPS to be imminent, and in such cases separation is almost always temporary and in the homes of family members. For instance, participants are informed that prosecution rates have been reported to be 17 % for sexual abuse and approximately 2 % for other types of child maltreatment (Tjaden and Thoennes 1992). Lastly, instructors remind workshop participants that the goal of CPS is ultimately family welfare and reunification even in cases where a child needs to be removed for protective reasons.

Skills Training Specific to Involving Caregiver(s) in the Reporting Process

Two videotapes are presented to model the process of reporting child maltreatment with a caregiver, including skills that are specific to the management of an upset caregiver. The respective skill sets are consistent with the previously reviewed material. Participants are informed that the professional's modeling corresponds to the behavioral instructions specified in Appendices A and B (which are distributed to participants immediately before the workshop). To assist workshop attendees in paying attention to important details, they are asked to put checks next to each behavioral instruction that is reviewed by the professional. The instructor presents the first videotaped scenario in which the professional informs a caregiver of his intent to report child maltreatment. The caregiver reacts with delayed compliance, suggesting disbelief and concern. After all behavioral instructions in Appendix A are modeled, the caregiver demonstrates her upset with the report. This permits the professional an opportunity to model each of the behavioral instructions listed in Appendix B. At the conclusion of the videos, participants are prompted to answer two questions that are biased to solicit positive responding (i.e., What did you like about the professional's skills? If you were the professional, what would you do differently, if anything, to fit your style?). The videotapes may be obtained by the authors, or the behavioral instructions may be modeled by the instructors.

After the videotapes are briefly discussed, participants are divided into pairs and instructed to take turns role-playing the two skill sets listed in Appendices A and B, respectively. They should be told to utilize the instructions in Appendices A and B to guide their efforts. In doing so, many participants are initially hesitant to engage in role-plays and are assisted in their practice with encouragement and descriptive praise. It is also helpful to inform participants to glance at the respective checklist prior to initiating each behavioral step, rather than memorizing instructions. During role-play interactions, instructors should briefly visit with participants, pointing out their demonstration of skills and briefly answering their questions.

Concluding Discussion

The workshop concludes with a 10–15-min discussion about workshop content. Questions are solicited and the following three questions are posed to facilitate positive exchange of ideas and facilitate generalization of workshop skill sets to everyday professional situations:

- How did it feel to practice the skills presented?
- How might you be able to apply the training you've learned today?
- How might you avoid difficulties implementing this training?

Future Directions in Child Maltreatment Reporting

Research specific to the mandated reporting of child maltreatment is in its infancy. Indeed, there are literally millions of professionals mandated to report suspected child maltreatment, yet few are explicitly trained to report child maltreatment. Few training programs have been formally examined to assist professionals in the management of this mandate (see section "Established Training Programs to Assist in Reporting Child Maltreatment"), and even fewer were developed utilizing uncontrolled experimental methodology. Therefore, the controlled empirical development of training programs specific to optimizing the process of reporting child maltreatment is urgently needed, both in general, and to identify optimal components and mechanisms (such as the optimal training approach, dosage, delivery method, and teaching team composition). Along this vein, research should be focused on determining which situations warrant the inclusion of family members and suspected victims of child maltreatment in the reporting process, how best to involve these persons, and assessment of the benefits and risks of their inclusion. Indeed, there is a particular need to empirically determine the effects of training programs on family safety, cohesion, and stress during the reporting of child maltreatment. In doing so, professionals could be randomly assigned to experimental training programs in child abuse reporting or training as usual, and the effects of these training programs could be evaluated utilizing objective, *real-world* measures (e.g., cases founded for child maltreatment, days children separated from their caregivers, family cohesion). Establishing consistency in defining child maltreatment across states and provinces will assist in making it easier to develop standardized training curricula in child maltreatment reporting and facilitate dissemination of these programs. Lastly, it is important to psychometrically evaluate measures to evaluate child abuse reporting training programs, such as the ones reviewed in this chapter.

Appendices

Appendix A: Protocol Checklist: Initiating Child Abuse Report with Caregiver(s)

The following protocol checklist may be used to guide mandated reporting of suspected child maltreatment or evaluation of others in doing so. Place a check next to each instruction that is completed.

1.__ Excuse everyone but caregiver(s).
2.__ Indicate importance of talking about (description of suspected maltreatment incident).
3.__ Remind caregiver(s) that laws mandate professionals to report child maltreatment.
4.__ State why child maltreatment is suspected.
5.__ Indicate report must be submitted within 24 h to CPS.
6.__ State report may not be accepted if not enough info or incident judged not to be abusive.
7.__ State CPS may accept report but not investigate.
8.__ State if report accepted CPS may conduct investigation of child maltreatment within 72 h.
9.__ State investigation usually involves caregiver(s), caregiver's children, and relevant others.
10.__ State CPS may go wherever child is present to conduct investigation (e.g., school, home).
11.__ State you can include supportive feedback in report, including recommendations.

12.__ State prosecution estimated to occur in <3 % of abuse and neglect cases and 17 % in sex abuse.
13.__ State separation of child from caregivers almost always limited to most severe situations.
14.__ State that when separation occurs it is usually temporary and the child usually resides with family.
15.__ State report may lead to cost-free services and financial support.
16.__ Advise caregiver(s) to be cooperative and respectful with investigators.
17.__ State caregiver(s) may be present during call to CPS.
18.__ State caregiver(s) may speak privately with CPS after report is made.
19.__ State caregiver(s) may speak with CPS after report is made in your presence.
20.__ State caregiver(s) can avoid talking with CPS after report is made.
21.__ Ask how caregiver(s) would like to be involved in reporting process, if at all.
22.__ Encourage caregiver(s) to ask questions or express concerns with CPS.
23.__ Ask if additional info should be included in report.
24.__ Solicit preference of caregiver(s) regarding how report should be disclosed with others, if at all.
25.__ Assure caregiver(s) and involved parties are safe and optimally prepared for reporting process.
26.__ State you will make follow-up call to assure all is well after report is made.
27.__ Establish safety codes for follow-up call to protect privacy regarding reporting process.
28.__ Ask caregiver(s) if there is anything else that can be done.
29.__ State report will be initiated to CPS.

Answer Key for Appendix A

Protocol completion is determined by dividing the number of instructions completed by 29 and multiplying the dividend by 100 to yield the percentage of instructions completed. 70 % or higher is acceptable, 80 % or higher is good, and 90 % or higher is outstanding.

Appendix B: Protocol Checklist: Resolving Upset of Caregiver(s) in Reporting Process

The following protocol checklist may be used to guide mandated reporting of suspected child maltreatment or evaluation of others in doing so. Place a check next to each instruction that is completed.

1. Make an empathetic statement ("I can see you care about your child very deeply.").
2. State both you and caregiver(s) want to assure child and family are safe and without stress.

3. Assess concerns of caregiver (e.g., “What are you most concerned about?”).
4. Solicit potential solutions from caregiver (e.g., “What can I do to help?”).
5. Remind report may not be accepted, and if accepted, incident may not be founded.

   Note: Do not attribute blame throughout interaction.

Answer Key for Appendix B

Protocol completion is determined by dividing the number of instructions completed by 5 and multiplying the dividend by 100 to yield the percentage of instructions completed. 70 % or higher is acceptable, 80 % or higher is good, and 90 % or higher is outstanding.

Appendix C: Knowledge of Child Maltreatment Reporting Laws

Please read each of the following questions, and after each question please circle the best response. Questions 1 through 7 pertain to federal legislation, while questions 8 through 15 are specific to Nevada law. Please complete every item regardless of the certainty of your answer.

FEDERAL LAW

1. If a person makes a report of suspected child abuse in “good faith,” and the case is NOT substantiated, the reporter is:
   (a) Guilty of a misdemeanor
   (b) Guilty of a felony
   (c) Open to civil lawsuit
   (d) Immune from civil or criminal liability
2. As a mandated reporter you are to:
   (a) Report suspected child abuse and neglect.
   (b) Interpret evidence of abuse and neglect.
   (c) Investigate child abuse and neglect.
   (d) Diagnose child abuse and neglect.
3. In order to report child maltreatment, one MUST:
   (a) Observe the incident.
   (b) Suspect child maltreatment has occurred or is occurring.
   (c) Have evidence of the incident.
   (d) Have a disclosure of child maltreatment by the child.
4. Mandated reporters can be held criminally liable for reporting suspected child maltreatment only if they:
   (a) Make a report about an incident that occurred more than 5 years ago.
   (b) Make a report based only on suspicion.

(c) Make a false report that is intended to harm another.
(d) Make a report that cannot be substantiated.

5. Mandated reporters may initiate a child maltreatment report to:

    (a) Local law enforcement
    (b) Child protective services
    (c) Hospitals
    (d) Either a and b

6. Which of the following occupations are mandated to report under all circumstances?

    (a) Clergymen
    (b) Attorneys
    (c) Mental health professionals
    (d) All of the above

7. You are ONLY required to report child maltreatment inflicted on individuals:

    (a) Under the age of 5 years
    (b) Under the age of 16 years
    (c) Under the age of 18 years
    (d) Under the age of 21 years

STATE LAW SPECIFIC (The following questions pertain specifically to the Nevada Revised Statutes: Chapter 432B – Protection of Children from Abuse and Neglect and may need to be changed to accommodate recent legislation that is specific to the state to which the workshop is provided.)

8. Which of the following is NOT included in the Nevada Revised Statutes definition of "abuse or neglect of child"?

    (a) Physical or mental injury of an accidental nature
    (b) Sexual abuse
    (c) Sexual exploitation
    (d) Negligent maltreatment

9. "Reasonable cause to believe" as defined by Nevada law refers to:

    (a) When the mandated reporter suspects abuse or neglect is occurring or has occurred
    (b) When a reasonable person would believe abuse or neglect is occurring or has occurred
    (c) When a mandated reporter is told by a reasonable person that abuse or neglect is occurring or has occurred
    (d) The time a reasonable person would act if abuse or neglect is occurring or has occurred

10. According to the Nevada Revised Statutes, the filming, photographing, or recording of a child's genitals is considered which of the following:
    (a) Sexual assault
    (b) Statutory rape
    (c) Lewd acts upon a child
    (d) Sexual exploitation
11. In the state of Nevada, a mandated reporter who fails to report suspected child maltreatment is:
    (a) Guilty of a misdemeanor
    (b) Guilty of a felony
    (c) Immune from civil lawsuit
    (d) Immune from criminal liability
12. The Nevada Revised Statutes definition of "Negligent treatment" includes all of the following EXCEPT:
    (a) Improper supervision
    (b) Lack of appropriate education
    (c) Lack of caregiver employment
    (d) Failure to provide for mental health needs
13. The Nevada Revised Statutes mandate that a suspicion of child abuse or neglect must be reported no later than:
    (a) 12 hours
    (b) 24 hours
    (c) 36 hours
    (d) 72 hours
14. According to the Nevada Revised Statutes, the following must be reported:
    (a) Any instance of corporal punishment
    (b) Excessive corporal punishment resulting in physical injury
    (c) Excessive corporal punishment resulting in mental injury
    (d) Both b and c
15. Nevada law allows for a child maltreatment report to be made:
    (a) Via telephone
    (b) Via FAX
    (c) Via email
    (d) All of the above

Answer Key for Appendix C

1=d, 2=a, 3=b, 4=c, 5=d, 6=c, 7=c, 8=a, 9=b, 10=d, 11=a, 12=c, 13=b, 14=d, 15=d.

Appendix D: Recognition of Child Maltreatment

Please read each of the following vignettes, and answer each of the questions that follow as honestly as possible.

VIGNETTE #1

Six-year-old Stephanie enters your office with a long and linear bruise on her upper arm and back of her thigh. She tells you that she fell down on the sidewalk over the weekend. You recall noticing similar bruises on her upper arms on at least one other occasion. When you confront the mother about Stephanie's current injury, she tells you Stephanie fell on the sidewalk and comments on her clumsiness.

(a) From the information provided, how likely are you to suspect child maltreatment?

1	2	3	4	5	6	7
Highly Unlikely			Neutral			Highly Likely

(b) Regardless of your answer to the previous question, how likely are you to make a report?

1	2	3	4	5	6	7
Highly Unlikely			Neutral			Highly Likely

VIGNETTE #2

You are the therapist to Lisa, a 30-year-old woman struggling with her husband's relationship with his daughter. Lisa's husband, Martin, has a 10-year-old daughter, Theresa. For years, Lisa has felt that Martin and Theresa are "too close" and she is uncomfortable with their relationship. She reports that Martin is extremely protective of his daughter and does not allow her to play with other children. Lisa describes Theresa as timid and reports that she overheard Theresa say that her father shouldn't put his hand "there" one morning in her room with the door closed.

(a) From the information provided, how likely are you to suspect child maltreatment?

1	2	3	4	5	6	7
Highly Unlikely			Neutral			Highly Likely

(b) Regardless of your answer to the previous question, how likely are you to make a report?

1	2	3	4	5	6	7
Highly Unlikely			Neutral			Highly Likely

VIGNETTE # 3

Shaunte is a 13-year-old female who has been referred to you by her school counselor for treatment of test anxiety. During a session you notice multiple scratches on her shoulder. You inquire about the scratches on her arm. She reports she was having an argument with her mother, and as she turned to walk out of the room, her mother grabbed her by the shoulder and "accidentally" scratched her. Her mother apologetically recounted the same story.

(a) From the information provided, how likely are you to suspect child maltreatment?

1	2	3	4	5	6	7
Highly Unlikely			Neutral			Highly Likely

(b) Regardless of your answer to the previous question, how likely are you to make a report?

1	2	3	4	5	6	7
Highly Unlikely			Neutral			Highly Likely

VIGNETTE #4

Jason is a 9 year-old male who has been seeing you for 3 months. You notice that Jason has a burn on the inside of his hand. When asked about the injury, Jason reports that he burned himself by grabbing a hot pan when cooking his dinner last night. Upon further discussion, he reports that his mother is never home because she is either at work or gambling with her friends. Jason informs you that there is food in the house and the bills are paid, but he is almost always alone in the house.

(a) From the information provided, how likely are you to suspect child maltreatment?

1	2	3	4	5	6	7
Highly Unlikely			Neutral			Highly Likely

(b) Regardless of your answer to the previous question, how likely are you to make a report?

1	2	3	4	5	6	7
Highly Unlikely			Neutral			Highly Likely

VIGNETTE #5

You have been seeing the Parkers for family therapy for 4 months due to their recent failure in elementary school. The parents often make derogatory comments to the children during the session. They call them names (e.g., idiot, stupid) and blame them for the problems of the family. When you point out the children's positive traits, Mr. and Mrs. Parker act genuinely surprised or are highly skeptical.

(a) From the information provided, how likely are you to suspect child maltreatment?

1	2	3	4	5	6	7
Highly Unlikely			Neutral			Highly Likely

(b) Regardless of your answer to the previous question, how likely are you to make a report?

1	2	3	4	5	6	7
Highly Unlikely			Neutral			Highly Likely

VIGNETTE #6

Joan, a woman that you have been seeing for several months discloses that she is concerned about her husband's actions. She and her husband have a 2½-year-old daughter, and she is concerned that her husband will frequently shower with the child. She says that her daughter loves to shower with her father and hears the child playing in the tub as the father showers.

(a) From the information provided, how likely are you to suspect child maltreatment?

1	2	3	4	5	6	7
Highly Unlikely			Neutral			Highly Likely

(b) Regardless of your answer to the previous question, how likely are you to make a report?

1	2	3	4	5	6	7
Highly Unlikely			Neutral			Highly Likely

VIGNETTE #7

Patrick and Rhonda are attending marriage counseling. Rhonda is extremely critical of Patrick and their 16-year-old son, Charlie. Charlie is excelling in school, is the Junior Class President, and has many friends. Rhonda recently yelled at Charlie for not doing his homework and told him he'd never amount to anything if he didn't do his homework.

(a) From the information provided, how likely are you to suspect child maltreatment?

1	2	3	4	5	6	7
Highly Unlikely			Neutral			Highly Likely

(b) Regardless of your answer to the previous question, how likely are you to make a report?

1	2	3	4	5	6	7
Highly Unlikely			Neutral			Highly Likely

VIGNETTE #8

James is a 41-year-old client who you have been seeing in therapy for two sessions. He reports to you that he is worried he will not be able to pay his rent, and because this has happened before, he may get evicted. James reports if he gets evicted, he has nowhere he can go and no place that his two children can stay until he finds another place to live.

(a) From the information provided, how likely are you to suspect child maltreatment?

1	2	3	4	5	6	7
Highly Unlikely			Neutral			Highly Likely

(b) Regardless of your answer to the previous question, how likely are you to make a report?

1	2	3	4	5	6	7
Highly Unlikely			Neutral			Highly Likely

Answer Key for Appendix D

V1 = reportable, V2 = reportable, V3 = not reportable, V4 = reportable, V5 = reportable, V6 = not reportable, V7 = not reportable, V8 = not reportable.

Appendix E: Clinical Expertise in Reporting Child Maltreatment

Please read the following questions and circle the response that best answers each of the questions. Please complete every item regardless of the certainty of your answer.

1. The greatest predictor of a positive therapeutic outcome subsequent to the making of a child maltreatment report is:
   (a) The age of the client
   (b) The quality of the therapeutic relationship prior to reporting
   (c) The nature of the alleged abuse
   (d) The level of involvement of the client in the reporting process
2. Mandated reporters are always encouraged to discuss their option in making a report with:
   (a) The client
   (b) A friend
   (c) A colleague
   (d) All of the above
3. In most situations, mandated reporters should attempt to inform caregivers of a report to child protective services:
   (a) Prior to making a report
   (b) While making the report
   (c) After making the report
   (d) Subsequent to an investigation
4. In most situations, when making a report of child maltreatment, mental health providers should permit caregivers to:
   (a) Be present while making the call to CPS.
   (b) Speak with CPS after the report is made.

(c) Choose not to be involved.
(d) All of the above.

5. When a client is a suspected perpetrator of child maltreatment, the therapist should:

   (a) Never inform the suspected perpetrator of an intent to report.
   (b) Always inform the suspected perpetrator of an intent to report.
   (c) Both a and b.
   (d) Neither a nor b.

6. A child client has just disclosed a reportable instance of child abuse. You should make sure to do all of the following EXCEPT:

   (a) Remain calm and be open and honest.
   (b) Include the child in the mandated reporting process with the child's caregivers.
   (c) Stress that it is not the child's fault.
   (d) Listen carefully and remain supportive.

7. Which statement is true?

   (a) Children never tell false stories about being abused and neglect.
   (b) Some children tell false stories about being abused and neglected.
   (c) Most children tell false stories about being abused and neglected.
   (d) All children tell false stories about being abused and neglected.

8. The likelihood that a suspected perpetrator will respond to a mandated reporter's intent to report by threatening or attempting to harm the therapist is approximately:

   (a) 4 %
   (b) 8 %
   (c) 16 %
   (d) 32 %

9. Mandated reporters should thoroughly document (i.e., in progress notes):

   (a) All incidences in which a suspected child maltreatment report is made
   (b) Consultations with a supervisor regarding child maltreatment
   (c) All incidences in which a decision not to report is made
   (d) All of the above

10. Which of the following should NOT be included in a report to CPS:

   (a) The name, age, and location of the child victim
   (b) The name and location of the perpetrator
   (c) The name and location of the primary caregiver
   (d) The alleged child victim's treatment plan

11. If a decision to report suspected child neglect is made, it is usually a good idea to inform the caregiver:

    (a) What the CPS screening process involves
    (b) About the possibility of a CPS investigation
    (c) Both a and b
    (d) Neither a nor b

12. To protect mandated reporters from false and inconsistent allegations, the following information should be included when documenting the circumstances of a child maltreatment report in progress notes:

    (a) Name, age, and location of the child victim
    (b) Name of the suspected perpetrator
    (c) Name and identification number of the CPS worker contacted
    (d) All of the above

13. If a child is removed from the home due to child maltreatment, CPS will first attempt to place the child:

    (a) In a previously determined safe house
    (b) In a monitored CPS facility
    (c) With family members
    (d) Either a or b

14. When a child maltreatment report is made to CPS, the caregiver of the suspected victim may think their child will be removed from their home. This belief:

    (a) Is true
    (b) May be true depending on the findings of the investigation
    (c) Is true, but only in cases of suspected sexual abuse
    (d) Is true, but only when victims are under the age of 10 years

15. If CPS determines that child maltreatment has occurred:

    (a) CPS generally works towards reunification and treatment for the family.
    (b) CPS generally works towards foster care placement.
    (c) CPS generally works towards termination of parental rights.
    (d) CPS generally determines if the perpetrator will be sentenced.

Answer Key for Appendix E

1=b; 2=c, 3=a, 4=d, 5=d, 6=b, 7=b, 8=a, 9=d, 10=d, 11=c, 12=d, 13=c, 14=b, 15=a.

References

Abrahams, N., Casey, K., & Dora, D. (1992). Teachers' knowledge, attitudes, and beliefs about child abuse and its prevention. *Child Abuse and Neglect, 16*(2), 229–238. doi:10.1016/0145-2134(92)900030-U.

Alvarez, K. M., Donohue, B., Carpenter, A., Romero, V., Allen, D. N., & Cross, C. (2010). Development and preliminary evaluation of a training method to assist professionals in reporting suspected child maltreatment. *Child Maltreatment, 15*, 211–218. doi:10.1177/1077559510365535.

Bavolek, S. J. (1983). Why aren't school personnel reporting child abuse in Wisconsin? *Teacher Education and Special Education, 6*(1), 33–38. doi:10.1177/088840648300600106.

Baxter, G., & Beer, J. (1990). Educational needs of school personnel regarding child abuse and/or neglect. *Psychological Reports, 67*(1), 75–80. doi:10.2466/pr0.1990.67.1.75.

Berliner, L. (1993). Identifying and reporting suspected child abuse and neglect. *Topics in Language Disorders, 13*, 15–24. doi:10.1097/00011363-199308000-00006.

Besharov, D. J. (1994). Responding to child sexual abuse: The need for a balanced approach. *Future of Children, 4*, 135–155.

Brosig, C. L., & Kalichman, S. C. (1992). Clinicians' reporting of suspected child abuse: A review of empirical literature. *Clinical Psychology Review, 12*, 155–168. doi:10.1016/0272-7358(92)90112-L.

Camblin, L. D., & Prout, H. T. (1983). School counselors and the reporting of child abuse: A survey of state laws and practices. *School Counselor, 30*, 358–367.

Compaan, C., Doueck, H. J., & Levine, M. (1997). Mandated reporter satisfaction with child protection: More good news for workers. *Journal of Interpersonal Violence, 12*, 847–857.

Dawes-Night, E., Smith, J. B., Dubowitz, H., Litrownik, A. J., Kotch, J. B., English, D., &... Runyon, D. K. (2006). Reporting participants in research studies to child protective services: Limited risk to attrition. *Child Maltreatment, 11*, 257–262. doi:10.1177/1077559505285786

Donohue, B., Carpin, K., Alvarez, K., Ellwood, A., & Jones, R. W. (2002). A standardized method of diplomatically and effectively reporting child abuse to State authorities: A controlled evaluation. *Behavior Modification, 26*, 684–699. doi:10.1177/014544502236657.

Finalyson, L. M., & Koocher, G. P. (1991). Professional judgment and child abuse reporting in sexual abuse cases. *Professional Psychology: Research and Practice, 22*, 464–472.

Foreman, T., & Bernet, W. (2000). A misunderstanding regarding the duty to report suspected abuse. *Child Maltreatment, 5*, 190–196.

Hawkins, R., & McCallum, C. (2001a). Mandatory notification training for suspected child abuse and neglect in South Australian schools. *Child Abuse & Neglect, 25*, 1603–1625. doi:10.1016/SO145-2134(01)00296-4.

Hawkins, R., & McCallum, C. (2001b). Effects of mandatory notification training on the tendency to report hypothetical cases of child abuse and neglect. *Child Abuse Review, 10*, 301–322. doi:10.1002/car.699.

Heymann, G. M. (1986). Mandated child abuse reporting and the confidentiality privilege. In L. Everstine & D. S. Everstine (Eds.), *Psychopathology and the law*. Orlando: Grune & Stratton.

Hinson, J., & Fossey, R. (2000). Child abuse: What teachers in the '90s know, think, and do. *Journal of Education for Students Placed at Risk, 5*(3), 251–266. doi:10.1207/S15327671ESPR0503_4.

Kalichman, S. C. (1999). *Mandated reporting of suspected child abuse: Ethics, law, & policy* (2nd ed.). Washington, DC: American Psychological Association.

Kalichman, S. C., & Craig, M. E. (1991). Professional psychologists' decisions to report suspected abuse: Clinician and situation influences. *Professional Psychology: Research and Practice, 22*, 84–89.

Kalichman, S. C., Craig, M. E., & Follingstad, D. (1989). Factors influencing the reporting of father-child sexual abuse: Study of licensed practicing psychologists. *Professional Psychology: Research and Practice, 20*, 84–89.

Kemp, A. (1998). *Abuse in the family: An introduction*. Pacific Grove: Brooks/Cole.

Kenny, M. C. (2007). Web-based training in child maltreatment for future mandated reporters. *Child Abuse & Neglect, 31*, 671–678. doi:10.1016/j.chiabu.2006.12.008.

Kenny, M., & McEachern, A. (2002). Reporting of suspected child abuse: A pilot comparison of middle and high school counselors and principals. *Journal of Childhood Sexual Abuse, 11*, 59–76.

Koralek, D. (1992). *Caregivers of young children: Preventing and responding to child maltreatment*. Rockville, MD: US Department of Health and Human Services (User manual series).

Levine, M., & Doeuck, H. J. (1995). *The impact of mandated reporting on the therapeutic process: Picking up the pieces*. Newbury Park: Sage.

Macleod, C., Dornan, O., Livingstone, A., McCormack, L., Lees, J., & Jenkins, M. (2003). Teaching junior doctors to recognize child abuse and neglect. *Medical Education, 37*, 1165–1173. doi:10.1046/j.1365-2923.2003.01662.x.

McCauley, J., Jenckes, M. W., & McNutt, L. A. (2003). ASSERT: The effectiveness of a continuing medical education video on knowledge and attitudes about interpersonal violence. *Academic Medicine, 78*, 518–524. doi:10.1097/00001888200305000-00017.

McGrath, P., Wiseman, D., Allen, B., Khalil, A., & Cappell, M. (1987). Teacher awareness program on child abuse: A randomized controlled trial. *Child Abuse & Neglect, 11*, 125–132.

Merriwether, M. H. (1986). Child abuse reporting laws: Time for a change. *Family Law Quarterly, 20*(2), 141–171.

Nicolai, K. M., & Scott, N. A. (1994). Provision of confidentiality information and its relation to child abuse reporting. *Professional Psychology: Research and Practice, 25*, 154–160.

Palusci, V. J., & McHugh, M. T. (1995). Interdisciplinary training in the evaluation of child sexual abuse. *Child Abuse and Neglect, 19*(9), 1031–1038. doi:10.1016/0145-2134(95)00065-G.

Reiniger, A., Robison, E., & McHugh, M. (1995). Mandated training of professionals: A means for improving reporting of suspected child abuse. *Child Abuse & Neglect, 19*, 353–361. doi:10.1016/0145-2134(94)00105-4.

Remley, T. P., Jr., & Fry, L. J. (1993). Reporting suspected child abuse: Conflicting roles for the counselor. *The School Counselor, 40*, 253–259.

Sandberg, G., Petretic-Jackson, P., & Jackson, T. (1986). Physician reporting practices in child physical abuse. *Response to the Victimization of Women and Children, 9*, 6–8.

Shanel-Hogan, K. A., & Jarrett, J. A. (1999). Reporting child abuse and neglect: Responding to a cry for help. *The Journal of the California Dental Association, 27*(11), 869.

Stadler, H. A. (1989). Balancing ethical responsibilities: Reporting child abuse and neglect. *Counseling Psychologist, 17*, 102–110. doi:10.1177/0011000089171006.

Steinberg, M. (1994). *Structured clinical interview for DSM-IV dissociative disorders (SCID-D)* (Rev. ed.). Washington, DC: American Psychiatric Press.

Steinberg, K. L., Levine, M., & Doeuck, H. J. (1997). Effects of legally mandated child abuse reports on the therapeutic relationship: A survey of psychotherapists. *American Journal of Orthopsychiatry, 67*, 112–122.

Taylor, L., & Adelman, H. S. (1998). Confidentiality: Competing principles, inevitable dilemmas. *Journal of Educational and Psychological Consultation, 9*, 267–275.

Tjaden, P., & Thoennes, N. (1992). Predictors of legal intervention in child maltreatment cases. *Child Abuse and Neglect, 16*, 807–821.

U.S. Department of Health and Human Services. (1992a). *Caregivers of young children: Preventing and responding to child maltreatment*. Washington, DC: U.S. Government Printing Office.

U.S. Department of Health and Human Services. (1992b). *The role of law enforcement in the response to child abuse and neglect*. Washington, DC: U.S. Government Printing Office.

Weinstein, B., Levine, M., Kogan, N., Harkavy-Friedman, J., & Miller, J. M. (2000). Mental health professionals' experiences reporting suspected child maltreatment. *Child Abuse & Neglect, 24*, 1317–1328. doi:10.1016/S0145-2134(00)00191-5.

Weinstein, B., Levine, M., Kogan, N., Harkavy-Friedman, J. M., & Miller, J. M. (2001). Therapist reporting of suspected child abuse and maltreatment: Factors associated with outcome. *American Journal of Psychotherapy, 55*, 219–233.

Wright, R. J., Wright, R. O., Farnan, L., & Isaac, N. E. (1999). Response to child abuse pediatric emergency department: Need for continued education. *Pediatric Emergency Care, 15*, 376–382. doi:10.1097/00006565-199912000-00002.

Zellman, G. L. (1990a). Child abuse reporting and failure to report among mandated reporters. *Journal of Interpersonal Violence, 5*, 3–22. doi:10.1177/088626090005001001.

Zellman, G. L. (1990b). Report decision-making patterns among mandated child abuse reporters. *Child Abuse and Neglect, 14*, 325–336.

Zellman, G. L., & Coulborn-Faller, K. (1996). Reporting of child maltreatment. In J. Briere, L. Berliner, J. A. Bulkley, C. Jenny, & T. Reid (Eds.), *The APSAC handbook on child maltreatment* (pp. 359–381). Thousand Oaks: Sage.

Chapter 18
Mandatory Reporting of Child Abuse and Neglect by Health Professionals

Debbie Scott and Jennifer Fraser

The role of Australian health professionals in reporting child abuse and neglect, in particular medical and nursing personnel, has increased substantially during the past two decades. This chapter discusses key issues related to the recognition and reporting of child abuse and neglect by health professionals in Australia. The responsibilities of not only recognising but reporting all forms of child maltreatment by doctors and nurses are introduced. Health professionals, like teachers, police and other professional groups, are variously obligated through policy and legislation to report their knowledge or suspicion of child maltreatment. As well, health services impose policies in line with the legislation specific to their jurisdiction to assist clinical staff in responding when they know of, or have a reasonable suspicion of, harm being caused to a child. In most Australian states and territories, if doctors and nurses know or suspect that a child is, has been or is likely to suffer significant harm, then they have a legal obligation to report this to designated authorities.

The Australian Institute of Family Studies (AIFS) is committed to the creation and dissemination of research-based information on family functioning and wellbeing. Views expressed here are those of individual authors and may not reflect those of the Australian Institute of Family Studies or the Australian Government.

D. Scott (✉)
Australian Institute of Family Studies (AIFS),
485 La Trobe Street, Melbourne, VIC, Australia
e-mail: Debbie.Scott@aifs.gov.au

J. Fraser
Sydney Nursing School, The University of Sydney, Sydney, NSW, Australia

B. Mathews, D.C. Bross (eds.), *Mandatory Reporting Laws and the Identification of Severe Child Abuse and Neglect*, Child Maltreatment 4,
DOI 10.1007/978-94-017-9685-9_18

A Case Study: Sarah's Dilemma

In the case study below, we provide a scenario that is typical of the experience of health professionals working in Australian hospital emergency departments. The case study is used to illustrate the issues that they face and that are discussed throughout the chapter:

> Sarah is a Registered Nurse working a Saturday afternoon shift in the emergency department of a busy regional hospital in Australia. In the State in which she works, Sarah has a legal obligation to report knowledge or suspicion of child abuse and neglect in her professional role when she has a reasonable suspicion that a child has been, is being, or is likely to be, significantly harmed.[1] Sarah has been to all the training sessions offered by the hospital regarding reporting of child maltreatment and is aware of her responsibilities.
>
> At 5 pm, three year old Brittany presented to the hospital with her mum, Julie, and step-father, Garry for treatment of a laceration on her forehead, caused when she fell against the coffee table. This was the fifth time Brittany had been brought to the hospital for an injury. None of the previous physical injuries had been considered significant and she had never been admitted to the hospital for ongoing treatment of her injuries. Nevertheless, Sarah was concerned about a pattern emerging. She became suspicious of the previous injuries and concerned about future harm to the child. Sarah was concerned for a number of reasons. Garry, like many men in the district, had a well-paid position at the mine site within the district. He was known in the community as a heavy drinker. Each of Brittany's injuries had occurred when Garry was at home and not while he was away at work. While explaining to Sarah how Brittany sustained the injury, Julie consistently deferred to her partner Garry's version of events. While she would initiate an explanation, she seemed to be watching his reactions carefully and would be silent when he interrupted her. Brittany did not go to Garry for comfort and cried if Julie left the cubicle.
>
> Sarah was aware of her obligations to report her suspicions but was unsure if reporting would be the right thing to do for this family. Sarah's own father was an alcoholic and she grew up with him. Occasionally he was abusive to her mother and herself and she feels she has turned out well despite this. She feels she knows the family well and has a very good rapport with Julie in particular. Garry is away much of the time and Julie is a good mum to Brittany. The town they live in is small and many of the men who work on the mine drink heavily while at home. Garry behaves in much the same way socially as any of the other workers. Sarah is concerned that if she makes a notification of child abuse it might affect her relationship not just with this family but with others in the community, violating a trust that has developed. She is also concerned that it will only exacerbate the home situation and inflame Garry who will blame Julie for the situation, and may even discover that Sarah is the one who reported the abuse. She is not confident that her identity will be protected and worries about the consequences of reporting. She is not sure if she should confer with her colleagues.

---

[1] In the Queensland mandatory reporting legislation applying to nurses (the *Public Health Act 2005* (Qld)), a nurse must make a report if she or he 'becomes aware or reasonably suspects, during the practice of his or her profession, that a child has been, is being or is likely to be harmed' (s 191). 'Harm' is defined in s 158 as 'any detrimental effect on the child's physical, psychological or emotional wellbeing—(a) that is of a significant nature; and (b) that has been caused by physical, psychological or emotional abuse or neglect; or sexual abuse or exploitation'.

Health Professionals and Child Protection

Access to Families with Children, Especially in the Early Years

Health professionals play an important role in recognising and reporting child maltreatment in Australia. The health system including community and hospital services provides a first point of contact capable of intervening in child abuse and neglect. Until a child starts school or an early childhood education programme, they spend their time at home. The outside world may be largely unaware of what occurs within families. This magnifies the responsibility of the health professional in terms of identifying, documenting and reporting child maltreatment.

Few, if any, children would start formal education without having contact with a health professional at some stage prior to that time. In Australia, there is a robust Community Child Health Service in all states and territories. Community child health nurses are well trained in screening for child abuse and neglect risk indicators. Mechanisms through which child maltreatment occurs and is maintained within families generally include developmental history, personality factors, cultural expectations, familial interactions and child characteristics (Daro 1993; Zeanah et al. 1997). At the same time, it is difficult to recognise child maltreatment even for children like Brittany who present numerous times in early life for injuries. It is estimated that one in six children presented to an emergency department for physical injury and that between 1 and 10 % of these children have actually suffered physical abuse (Benger & Pearce, 2002). Children under the age of 12 months are more likely than older children to be admitted to the hospital for injuries sustained through maltreatment. Unfortunately, they are also more likely to die from their injuries (McKenzie and Scott 2011; O'Donnell et al. 2011).

Perceived Role/Reporting Practice

In Australia, reports by health professionals accounted for only 13.5 % of all reports to statutory child protection authorities. This is compared to 24.6 % from police and 15.1 % from schools (Australian Institute of Health and Welfare 2013). In Canada, other professional groups report more child abuse and neglect than health-care professionals do. In that country, school personnel, police and social workers all report more child abuse and neglect than health-care professionals (Tonmyr et al. 2009). Further research is needed to disentangle the underlying reasons for these figures. It may be that health professionals are primarily exposed to children who present with physical injury or illness. Unfortunately though, there is still the possibility that they may not view child protection as part of their role to the same extent as police, social workers and others.

A survey of the General Practitioners in Queensland, Australia, revealed that even though 97 % were aware of their legal requirement to report child maltreatment, and 69 % had done so at some stage, 26 % had decided, at least once, against reporting their knowledge or suspicion of abuse or neglect (Schweitzer et al. 2006). Unfortunately, it was beyond the scope of this particular study to be able to elicit which forms of maltreatment were less likely to have been reported. Results did reveal that if the doctor thought this was a one-off presentation of maltreatment and not likely to be repeated, then a report, they said, would not be made. Further harm to the child was thought to be very unlikely.

Similarly in their study of Queensland nurses, Fraser et al. found that of the 930 registered nurses they surveyed, 21.1 % had never reported maltreatment. Of those who had made reports in their professional role, 26.6 % had also decided not to report maltreatment on at least one occasion (Fraser et al. 2010), despite mandatory reporting requirements. These studies reveal that despite the legal obligation placed on doctors and nurses to report suspicion or knowledge of child maltreatment, sometimes they do not. The reasons are quite well known, as will be discussed in this chapter. The way forward in improving these rates is less clear.

Recognition

Diagnosis

Based on the studies reviewed above, there appears to be a number of impediments to health professionals reporting child maltreatment. The first of these that we will discuss is recognition of past, current and future abuse and neglect. Before clinical staff can respond and report, they must first make the connection that what they are seeing *is* child maltreatment. In the case of physical abuse, discerning whether a presentation such as the lacerated forehead from a fall, as in our case study, or a broken arm is due to falling down a flight of stairs or being pushed down those stairs is not easy.

There is quite a significant and well-enough understood literature about the injury type and the relationship of injury presentations and physical and sexual abuse in particular. Certain physical injury presentations are more likely to have resulted from maltreatment. Any fracture in a preambulatory child is concerning; however, fractures of the femur (Leventhal et al. 2007), rib fractures, bucket handle or corner fractures (caused by twisting forces), skull fractures or a combination of a skull and long bone fractures are immediately associated with abuse (Bandyopadhyay and Yen 2002). Head injury is the most common cause of abusive injury-related death in children (King et al. 2006), and abused children are more likely to sustain a head injury than other children, particularly in those under 2 years of age (Berkowitz 1995; DiScala et al. 2000).

Head injury in infants is commonly associated with acceleration-deceleration injuries that point to the infant having been shaken, potentially a shaken baby syndrome.

When considering the causes of injury, it is not enough to undertake a physical assessment of injury and risk alone. Shaken baby syndrome often presents with subdural or subarachnoid bleeds, cerebral oedema, long bone and/or rib fractures, retinal bleeds and little or no craniofacial trauma (Cadzow and Armstrong 2000; Kairys et al. 2001; Reece and Sege 2000). These injuries can be difficult to diagnose as patients may not exhibit any external signs of trauma, and the symptoms may mimic gastrointestinal symptoms (Jenny et al. 1999; Kairys et al. 2001; Keenan et al. 2004).

When a child presents for treatment of an injury and the parents/caregivers cannot explain how that occurred, it should be a cause of concern (Scott 2012; Scott et al. 2012). Other injuries may result as an unintended consequence of corporal punishment, for example, a child attempting to avoid being struck and falling.

In the case study presented herein, Brittany's presentation makes the diagnosis much less certain. Her parents don't seem to be telling the same story of how the injury occurred, her father appears to have been drinking, and the mother appears to be worried about saying too much.

A family approach to assessment including psychosocial risk needs to be employed. Child abuse and neglect are known to be associated with parental alcohol or drug misuse, domestic violence, mental health issues, inadequate housing, financial stress and social isolation, and all of these issues need to be considered when assessing for abuse and neglect. Understanding the context of what is occurring at home and how that impacts on the family can provide a greater understanding of a child's wellbeing within that family (Scott 2013) and inform health professionals in their decisions about reporting abuse and neglect. At the same time, it is necessary for the emergency department staff to recognise the risks of abuse and neglect and make a report of suspicion. That is, they are not making a decision to substantiate the suspicion, rather linking the risk indicators to confirm that a report is necessary based on the seriousness of the harm or the potential harm to the child.

The Impact of Training in Recognition of Abuse-Related Injury

In interviews with Australian doctors, nurses and child protection liaison officers, Scott et al. (2012) hoped to better understand factors that influence them identifying, documenting and reporting child protection issues in emergency departments. The majority of the nurses and doctors clearly understood the procedures for reporting child maltreatment. However, they reported that training in recognising maltreatment had only ever occurred during their university courses. For many, no training had ever been undertaken (Scott 2012).

Health professionals are not confident in recognising and reporting maltreatment in New South Wales (NSW) hospitals (Raman et al. 2012). There is a considerable variation across Australian jurisdictions relating to the level and types of harm that require a report to child protection authorities. At one end of the spectrum, doctors and nurses in Western Australia must only report sexual abuse. Near the other end of the spectrum, in South Australia, doctors and nurses must report situations of physical abuse, sexual abuse, emotional abuse or neglect where a child 'has suffered, or is likely to suffer, physical or psychological injury detrimental to the child's wellbeing; or the child's physical or psychological development is in jeopardy' (Mathews and Scott 2013). The complexity of the principles and the ambiguity of the terms used to describe the level of harm which activates the reporting duty – such as 'injury detrimental to the child's wellbeing' – can cause concern and confusion for some health professionals. Because of this, some doctors and nurses are inclined to report all maltreatment, regardless of the level of harm, making them liable to report cases that do not meet the threshold (Fraser et al. 2010; Scott 2012). There is a confusion around what to report, and nurses in particular may feel they are obliged to report all maltreatments as mandated reporters, while others appear to be uncertain about what level meets the reporting threshold and so report because they are concerned about the consequences for the child and for themselves professionally if they do not (Fraser et al. 2010; Scott 2012). Nurses in the Queensland study made comments like '*It's almost come to a point that we want to protect ourselves and anything that can just even come back at you … we just report, so it's almost protecting ourselves*' (Scott 2012 Page 186) and '*it's better to over report than under-report*' and '*better to be safe than sorry*' (page 191). Mathews et al. (2008) noted that this could be due to the ambiguous language in legislation that is open to personal interpretation of what constitutes an incident that meets a reportable threshold. This reporting is reliant on health professionals forming a 'reasonable' suspicion of 'significant' harm now or 'in the future'. This lack of clarity on what constitutes harm at a reportable level requires training and appears to be lacking in the training received by health professionals.

Fear of Consequences

Damage to Therapeutic Relationship

Doctors and nurses often develop strong bonds with the families they treat, and there is a fear that reporting child maltreatment may damage that relationship (Flaherty and Sege 2005; Nayda 2002, 2004; Schweitzer et al. 2003; Scott 2012; Van Haeringen et al. 1998). In the Queensland study by Scott (2012), some doctors were concerned that a record of what may end up being an unsubstantiated report of maltreatment on a medical record could prejudice the treatment of the family in the future. Indeed, they feared that if they reported the family, the family may not seek treatment for the child if there was a future injury. Nurses interviewed by Scott (2012) were reluctant to report maltreatment for families they knew well. They reported that they believed the maltreatment was not serious enough to report, sometimes not recognising the maltreatment at all. One nurse commented '*If the nurse knows the family that makes it hard. If they're family friends, especially being a small town...they don't think that they should report, you know, family friends. They don't think that it's happening*' (Page 182). In other research, this has also been noted in workers facing child neglect. As the social worker deals with the family, they are 'drawn into' the family's situation. They can be reluctant to report the maltreatment when the family is already dealing with a disadvantage and other issues, feeling it will only exacerbate the problems, or their perception changes and they become 'acclimatised' over time – failing to see the level of harm occurring to that child (Tanner and Turney 2003).

Health professionals were also concerned with damaging the relationship they had with adults in their care who were parents. If a parent's capacity is diminished by, for example, a mental illness or substance abuse disorder, the health professional may be conflicted as to whether or not to report. In the Scott (2012) study, they revealed some concern that reporting is a violation of confidentiality with the potential to exacerbate the parent's condition.

Fear of Being Identified as the Reporter

Health professionals have also mentioned a fear of retaliation from the family if the identity of the reporter is revealed and of knowing a family and therefore not wanting to 'see' the maltreatment and 'not wanting to get involved', particularly if there were issues of domestic violence in the home (Nayda 2002; Schweitzer et al. 2003; Van Haeringen et al. 1998). Scott (2012) found similar concerns, particularly in regional and remote centres. Health professionals were very concerned that there could be repercussions for them or their families. Despite laws protecting the identity of the reporter, those health professions were concerned that other health workers, who were related to the family, may note the report in the child's medical record. Comments from a child protection worker in the Queensland study included, '*I think it's very difficult ... raising reports, particularly when you live in a community and there's often retribution when Child Safety is involved and things can get pretty nasty*' and a child protection liaison officer speaking about nurses who had come back to her after a report included, '*I do have a couple of occasions where people have come back to me and said, Oh I wish I didn't put that in because the family have found out that they were the ones to initially raise the concerns; and there'd been repercussions from that*' (Page 183).

Poor Medical Documentation

The fear of being identified may go some way to explain why there is reluctance to explicitly document concerns in the medical record. Health professionals frequently rely on verbal communication rather than written documentation to relay information regarding potential maltreatment. Despite the fact that the medical record is a record of patient care and can be used as evidence in court proceedings, documentation specific to maltreatment is often lacking (McKenzie and Scott 2012; Scott 2012). One study found that fewer than 7 % of emergency department medical records complied with the recommended documentation (McKenzie and Scott 2010; Scott 2012). Emergency department nurses seldom document concerns of child abuse, instead allowing doctors and inpatient paediatric nurses, who were perceived as the experts, to take this role. When patients were transferred from the emergency department to the ward, nurses would exchange information at handover that did not use the word 'abuse' but suggested the admission was 'suspicious'. Nayda (2004, p. 194) described one nurse in South Australia saying 'We do a lot of talking and thinking and handing over…a lot of talking is going on but not documentation', and she noted that nurses were reluctant to document a thorough assessment of cases of maltreatment particularly in an emergency department, where encounters with violent patients were a commonplace. By communicating orally and not documenting the maltreatment, nurses were able to remove themselves from the immediate picture and therefore minimise their responsibility for the situation (Nayda 2004).

Medical Context: Professional Culture and Hierarchy

The medical system has traditionally included a hierarchical structure, and health professionals continue to adhere to this structure. Where differences of opinion occur between doctors about whether a child protection report should be made, the senior staff member's decision is generally adhered to, despite requirements to report all concerns to child protection authorities (Scott 2012). Nurses are reluctant to document concerns or generate a report to child protection authorities in circumstances where a doctor disagrees with the nurse's assessment of the situation. In her research, Nayda (2004) identified the subservient position of nurses as an issue in identifying and reporting maltreatment, with most nurses unwilling to speak up against a doctor who determined a patient was or was not a victim of maltreatment. Similarly, Alvarez et al. (2004) noted that where there is conflict with a supervisor about whether or not a report to child protection is necessary can result in a lack of confidence and frustration. Research in the Queensland study (Scott 2012) identified similar issues with one doctor saying '*So if the senior medical officer disagrees with the junior medical officer – the senior medical officer wins*' (Page 187). Interestingly, one of the child protection liaison officers noted that mandatory reporting was a way to deal with this medical hierarchy saying '*That's the greatest thing about mandatory reporting …if they are suspicious and the senior staff disagree, they are still obliged to report*' (Page 187).

The medical model of practice in an emergency department also plays a role in the reporting of child maltreatment. In Scott's 2012 study, clinicians noted that the processes for managing child maltreatment in an emergency department are quite different to managing other conditions. The emergency department is typically a place where the injury or disease of a patient is identified and their condition stabilised, and then the care is referred to specialists who ensure ongoing care and referral. Emergency departments are busy, high-stress environments, and the workload in a busy emergency department was considered an impediment to reporting. There is a significant time required for the completion of the reporting process, and when the department is busy, the focus has to be on the clinical wellbeing of patient care, so the paperwork required for reporting maltreatment takes a lower priority. This can occasionally lead to inadequate documentation. One doctor said that there was inadequate access to specialists and that where maltreatment was considered to be a possibility, it should not be up to the emergency department staff to gather information needed to make a report to child protection; instead, a specialist team should be called who would undertake an assessment and respond accordingly. This, he argued, would put managing child maltreatment into the same paradigm as other conditions in the emergency department. While there was an acknowledgement that there are health professionals with this expert training available in specialist paediatric hospitals and to a smaller degree during 'office hours' in regional and remote hospitals, this is not the case in smaller, less well-resourced regional and remote hospitals. Access to such expertise would contribute positively to the identification, documentation and reporting of child maltreatment in emergency departments, particularly in regional and remote hospitals (Scott 2012).

Child Protection System Responses

Practitioner Perceptions of Systemic Failure to Respond to Reports and Influence on Reporting Attitudes and Practice

For the most part, child protection system responses only occur in Australia both when there is evidence of significant harm for a child *and* where a parent is unable/unwilling to protect a child from that significant harm. Reports may be made that do not meet the threshold or are dealt with by means other than an investigation and subsequent child protection intervention. This may lead to a perception that child protection workers are failing to respond to reports by health professionals or that health professionals are reporting more cases than necessary to child protection systems (Flaherty and Sege 2005; Nayda 2002; Scott 2012). Nayda (2002) noted that some community nurses feared reporting in case the report was not substantiated, and so families might 'disappear' from the system, leaving no one able to support them and monitor the wellbeing of the children. Scott (2012) found that for some health staff, this perceived lack of action on behalf of child protection was an incentive to continue to report minor incidents or report the same incident in the hope that a multitude of reports would influence some sort of action.

As well as serving as a barrier to reporting, the lack of understanding of the different frameworks led to some professional tension, with both groups feeling undervalued by the other. Health staff felt that a perceived lack of action by child protection workers devalued their professional assessment of the need for intervention; and child protection caseworkers commented that health staff did not value their professional assessment and the fact that their investigation may reveal more than was immediately known by health staff. Child protection case workers, however, clearly valued the input from health professionals and acknowledged that in some circumstances a report from health professionals was an incentive to act more quickly than others (Scott 2012).

Perceptions of Child Protection System Responses

Scott's research (2012) highlighted the concerns of health professionals in relation to reporting child abuse and neglect. On the one hand, it is considered a tool for protecting children from harm through the implementation of family support, that is, an early intervention and protection strategy. On the other hand, it is seen as punitive with punishment for perpetrators when cases are substantiated. In the Scott (2012) study, some health professionals were reluctant to report because they feared the caseworkers would respond by removing children from their homes. Conversely, others commonly said that they didn't see a point in reporting because the child protection authorities 'never did anything anyway'; this was particularly true in cases of chronic, low-level neglect.

Sites with strong relationships that allowed for informal consultation also seemed more willing to share information. This resulted in health professionals receiving feedback on the outcomes of reports. These sites also appeared to have a better understanding of the issues the other agency faced. On the other hand, sites where the only communication was through formal documentation, health staff felt undervalued and that the child protection workers didn't respond to their concerns. At the same time, child protection workers felt that the health professionals didn't understand their priorities, and they felt undervalued by health professionals.

Interagency Alliances

The variable nature of relationships between individuals and departments in the hospital and the two agencies (health and child protection) was also a central theme that emerged in Scott's 2012 study. Clinical staff valued verbal consultation and found learning from each other's experiences. Some child protection offices noted a cooperative atmosphere whereby both agencies relied on the support and expertise of the other to make informed decisions for the wellbeing of children. In contrast, in other regions, the atmosphere was almost adversarial with all information requests having to flow through official channels and a refusal to deal one-on-one with professionals from the other agency due to years of entrenched distrust. In one site this had come about from an informal comment made by a health professional that was used in formal documentation by a child protection worker. The health professional felt she had been misrepresented and risked being identified by the family. Despite both staff members subsequently leaving their employment, this mistrust and fear of being misrepresented continued (Scott 2012).

The time they spend with children and families in their care, the intimate nature of their work, their knowledge of child health and development and the position of trust they hold places doctors and nurses in a strong position to detect child maltreatment. Skilled health professionals can identify the more subtle signs of emotional maltreatment as well as the more obvious signs of physical or sexual assault. The way in which medical and nursing staff respond to children such as Brittany, as presented in our case study at the start of this chapter, can influence how the family is supported to provide an optimal parenting environment for her and reduce the risk of further injury. Despite the potential barriers to protecting children detailed in this chapter, children like Brittany are very likely to be identified as at risk within the Australian health-care system. Where community support systems are in place, it is likely that such families will be followed up and supported. Early intervention and prevention services can be provided but only when the situation is recognised, assessed and referred to the appropriate community support networks. In the following section, we discuss the way forward in improving this potential.

What Can Be Done to Improve Culture, Education and Practice?

Identification and confidence in reporting for health may improve with better access to training for health professionals (Scott 2012). Health professionals working with children should have a comprehensive understanding of the nature and context of different types of child abuse and neglect, when to be concerned about child protection matters, how to diagnose abuse-related injury, what should be documented in the medical record, the nature of the legal reporting duty, the reporting process involved in alerting child protection authorities to a child in need of protection, what to expect after a report is made and how best to support the child and family. This training should not only occur at the pre-vocational level but needs to be maintained during the working life of the health professional. Scott (2012) identified that interdisciplinary training would be most useful. Child protection and health professionals, police, teachers and other community workers involved in protecting children and the care for their welfare could share training sessions and thereby improve their understanding of the needs and restrictions of other workers in the field and to build relationships that would facilitate future informal consultation and information sharing.

Summary

The legal obligation to report suspicion and knowledge of child abuse and neglect in Australia is well established, though perhaps not well understood. There are numerous strategies and policies in place to assist health professionals to report their concerns, and yet many children still do not benefit because their injuries are not reported and investigated. When they are reported, it is because the abuse has become so severe the child may not survive the injuries. Early identification and prevention is the goal of mandatory reporting of child abuse and neglect, and health professionals have a legal and ethical responsibility to act to protect children from all forms of harm. To do so, they need to be well supported with training in the recognition of child abuse and neglect presentations and be committed to the practice of reporting knowledge or suspicion of all forms of violence experienced by children.

References

Alvarez, K. M., Kenny, M. C., Donohue, B., & Carpin, K. M. (2004). Why are professionals failing to initiate mandated reports of child maltreatment, and are there any empirically based training programs to assist professionals in the reporting process? *Aggression and Violent Behavior, 9*(5), 563–578.

Australian Institute of Health and Welfare. (2013). Child protection Australia: 2011–2012. In *Child Welfare Series*. Canberra: AIHW.

Bandyopadhyay, S., & Yen, K. (2002). Non-accidental fractures in child maltreatment syndrome. *Clinical Pediatric Emergency Medicine, 3*(2), 145–152.

Benger, J. R., & Pearce, A. V. (2002). Simple intervention to improve detection of child abuse in emergency departments. *British Medical Journal, 324*(7340), 780–782.

Berkowitz, C. (1995). Pediatric abuse. *Emergency Medical Clinics of North America, 13*, 321–342.

Cadzow, S. P., & Armstrong, K. L. (2000). Rib fractures in infants: Red alert! The clinical features, investigations and child protection outcomes. *Journal of Paediatrics and Child Health, 36*(4), 322–326.

Daro, D., Jones, E., & McCurdy, K. (1993). *Preventing child abuse: An evaluation of services to high-risk families*. Philadelphia: William Penn Foundation.

DiScala, C., Sege, R., Li, G., & Reece, R. M. (2000). Child abuse and unintentional injuries: A 10-year retrospective. *Archives of Pediatrics & Adolescent Medicine, 154*(1), 16–22.

Flaherty, E., & Sege, R. (2005). Barriers to physician identification and reporting of child abuse. *Pediatric Annals, 34*(5), 349–356.

Fraser, J. A., Mathews, B., Walsh, K., Chen, L., & Dunne, M. (2010). Factors influencing child abuse and neglect recognition and reporting by nurses: A multivariate analysis. *International Journal of Nursing Studies, 47*(2), 146–153. doi: 10.1016/j.ijnurstu.2009.05.015. S0020-7489(09)00173-4 [pii].

Jenny, C., Hymel, K. P., Ritzen, A., Reinert, S. E., & Hay, T. C. (1999). Analysis of missed cases of abusive head trauma. *JAMA, 281*(7), 621–626.

Kairys, S., Alexander, R., Block, R., Everett, D., Hymel, K., & Jenny, C. (2001). Shaken baby syndrome: rotational cranial injuries – Technical report. *Paediatrics, 108*(1), 206–210.

Keenan, H., Runyan, D., Marshall, S., Nocera, M., & Merten, D. (2004). A population-based comparison of clinical and outcome characteristics of young children with serious inflicted and non-inflicted traumatic brain injury. *Pediatrics, 114*(3), 633–639.

King, W., Kiesel, E., & Simon, H. (2006). Child abuse fatalities – Are we missing opportunities for intervention? *Pediatric Emergency Care, 22*(4), 211–214.

Leventhal, J. M., Larson, I. A., Abdoo, D., Singaracharlu, S., Takizawa, C., Miller, C., Goodman, T. R., Schwartz, D., Grasso, S., & Ellingson, K. (2007). Are abusive fractures in young children becoming less common?: Changes over 24 years. *Child Abuse & Neglect, 31*(3), 311–322.

Mathews, B., & Scott, D. (2013, July). Mandatory reporting of child abuse and neglect. *Resource sheets*. Retrieved 20 September, 2013, from http://www.aifs.gov.au/cfca/pubs/factsheets/a141787/

Mathews, B., Fraser, J., Walsh, K., Dunne, M., Kilby, S., & Chen, L. (2008). Queensland nurses' attitudes towards and knowledge of the legislative duty to report child abuse and neglect: Results of a state-wide survey. *Journal of Law and Medicine, 16*(2), 288–304.

McKenzie, K., & Scott, D. (2011). Using routinely collected hospital data for child maltreatment surveillance: Issues, methods and patterns. *BMC Public Health, 11*, 7.

McKenzie, K., & Scott, D. (2012). Quantity of documentation of maltreatment risk factors in injury-related paediatric hospitalisations. *BMC Public Health, 12*, 563.

McKenzie, K., Scott, D., Fraser, J., & Dunne, M. (2010). *Quality of child abuse information for measurement and surveillance: Linking hospital and child welfare data.* Paper presented at the Safety 2010, London.

Nayda, R. (2002). Influences on registered nurses' decision-making in cases of suspected child abuse. *Child Abuse Review, 11*, 168–178.

Nayda, R. (2004). Registered nurses' communication about abused children: Rules, responsibilities and resistance. *Child Abuse Review, 13*(3), 188–199.

O'Donnell, M., Nassar, N., Jacoby, P., & Stanley, F. (2011). Western Australian emergency department presentations related to child maltreatment and intentional injury: Population level study utilising linked health and child protection data. Jan; 48(1), 57–65.

Raman, S., Holdgate, A., & Torrens, R. (2012). Are our frontline clinicians equipped with the ability and confidence to address child abuse and neglect? *Child Abuse Review, 21*(2), 114–130.

Reece, R. M., & Sege, R. (2000). Childhood head injuries: Accidental or inflicted? *Archives of Pediatrics & Adolescent Medicine, 154*(1), 11–15.

Schweitzer, R., Buckley, L., Harnett, P., & Loxton, N. (2003). *Suspected child abuse and neglect reporting behaviour*. Brisbane: Abused Child Trust.

Schweitzer, R., Buckley, L., Harnett, P., & Loxton, N. (2006). Predictors of failure by medical practitioners to report suspected child abuse in Queensland. *Australian Health Review, 30*(3), 298–304.

Scott, D. (2012). *Improving the measurement and surveillance of child maltreatment in Queensland Emergency Departments.* Doctor of Health Science, Queensland University of Technology, Brisbane.

Scott, D. (2013). *Meeting children's needs when the family environment isn't always 'good enough': A systems approach*. Retrieved December 20, 2013, from http://www.aifs.gov.au/cfca/pubs/papers/a144433/cfca14.pdf

Scott, D., Higgins, D., & Franklin, R. (2012). *The role of supervisory neglect in childhood injury.* Retrieved December 20, 2013, from http://www.aifs.gov.au/cfca/pubs/papers/a142582/

Tanner, K., & Turney, D. (2003). What do we know about child neglect? A critical review of the literature and its application to social work practice. *Child and Family Social Work, 8*, 25–34.

Tonmyr, L., Li, A., Williams, G., Scott, D., & Jack, S. (2009). Patterns of reporting to child protection services in Canada by healthcare and non-healthcare professionals. *Paediatrics & Child Health, 15*(8), 25–32.

Van Haeringen, A., Dadds, M., & Armstrong, K. (1998). The child abuse lottery – Will the doctor suspect and report? Physician attitudes towards and reporting of suspected child abuse and neglect. *Child Abuse & Neglect, 22*(3), 159–169.

Zeanah, C. H., Boris, N. W., & Scheeringa, M. S. (1997). Psychopathology in infancy. *Journal of Child Psychology and Psychiatry, 38*(1), 81–99.

Chapter 19
The Social Construction of Disclosure: The Case of Child Abuse in Israeli Society

Zvi Eisikovits, Jonathan Davidov, Laura Sigad, and Rachel Lev-Wiesel

Introduction

The gap between the incidence of child abuse and its disclosure is of concern for researchers and policy makers alike. The present study describes and analyzes an insider's view of the ways in which child abuse professionals perceive and understand the disclosure of child abuse in one country. A model grounded in a social and psychological constructionist perspective was developed based on qualitative data collected in 40 in-depth interviews with professionals, including law-enforcement personnel, educators, and mental health and health-care professionals. The common feature in the disclosure process is the element of social construction. In other words, the societal reaction to child abuse including disclosure or its lack thereof is a function of social processes related to the values, ideologies, ways of thinking, and interests of the various social agents involved in the process. Thus, disclosure is not an objective fact-finding process resulting in a subsequent assignment of visibility and proper societal reaction. The present paper examines these processes in action, as perceived by the members of the various professional groups involved in child abuse work. Implications for practice and policy regarding child abuse are suggested.

Z. Eisikovits
Faculty of Social Welfare and Health Sciences, the Center for the Study of Society, University of Haifa, Haifa, Israel

J. Davidov (✉) • L. Sigad, Ph.D.
The Center for the Study of Society, University of Haifa, Haifa, Israel
e-mail: jdavidov74@gmail.com

R. Lev-Wiesel
Graduate School of Creative Art Therapies/Emili Sagol Research Center for CAT, University of Haifa, Haifa, Israel

B. Mathews, D.C. Bross (eds.), *Mandatory Reporting Laws and the Identification of Severe Child Abuse and Neglect*, Child Maltreatment 4,
DOI 10.1007/978-94-017-9685-9_19

All child abuse professionals face the challenge of disclosure. This stems from the need to overcome the resistance to understanding the reality of the abuse and making it socially visible as a precondition for appropriate societal reaction. These obstructionist attempts are often described in the literature as "concealment surrounding abuse" (Katz et al. 2012). This phenomenon warrants examining the factors facilitating and impeding the disclosure of abuse.

Disclosure

Much of the disclosure literature is based on the perspective of clients (e.g., Alaggia 2004; Bal et al. 2009; Staller and Nelson-Gardell 2005). A somewhat more limited body of knowledge is based on professionals' perspectives of the disclosure processes (e.g., Ainsworth 2002; Kim et al. 2012). This literature focuses mostly on the perceived impediments to disclosure having to do with detection and reporting issues (e.g., Ashton 2004; Davidov et al. 2012; Melton 2005; Vulliamy and Sullivan 2002). Research shows that various professional groups have specialized professional tools to detect and disclose abuse, ranging from legal and punitive to therapeutic and educational, depending on their professional education, orientation, setting, and ideology. The present study addresses the detection and the reporting of child abuse from the perspective of various professional groups.

Law-enforcement officers face a unique challenge in dealing with child abuse. Ordinarily, they know a crime has been committed because of physical signs of a break in, murder, or a complaining witness. In cases of child abuse, they often are uncertain if a crime has been committed or not, and their usual investigative techniques are less effective. Suspected victims of child abuse undergo some type of mandatory forensic interview conducted by an authorized police officer or child investigator. Research has found that over one third of suspected abuse victims did not disclose physical or sexual abuse during forensic interviews, including cases in which proof-based evidence demonstrates that abuse did occur (Hershkowitz et al. 2005; Katz et al. 2012; London et al. 2005). Abused children conceal their abuse experience for a variety of reasons, including fear, shame, guilt, and the desire to protect the perpetrator (Browne and Finkelhor 1986; Farrell 1988; Goodman-Brown et al. 2003; Hershkowitz et al. 2007; Malloy et al. 2007). Furthermore, investigators have been found to impede expected abuse disclosure in cases in which suspected victims were reluctant to share information with them (Hershkowitz et al. 2006).

In educational settings, disclosure is perceived as a two-stage process: first detection and then reporting (Egu and Weiss 2003; Mathews and Walsh 2004a, b). These stages have been found to be affected by several factors, including the type of abuse (physical, sexual, emotional, or neglect) (e.g., Webster et al. 2005), teacher characteristics (years of experience, parental status, gender, amount of training) (e.g., Kenny 2001), and school characteristics (size, teacher-child ratio, climate, and socioeconomic status). The last category of school characteristics has received minimal research attention (O'Toole et al. 1999; Walsh et al. 2006). The present study helps fill this gap in the literature through an examination and analysis of the school characteristics fostered by the teachers, who are active social agents with regard to the disclosure of child abuse.

Medical personnel perceive child abuse as a problem to be handled based on the medical model. They regard the phenomenon as a type of disease (Kellog 2007). The detection of child abuse by medical personnel often begins with specific traumatic findings in children who are patients in clinics or hospitals (Narayan et al. 2006). Research shows a significant gap between the incidence of child abuse among the population of children experiencing trauma-based injuries and the reporting ratio of abuse cases by medical personnel (Stirling and Amaya-Jackson 2008). The main explanation for this detection/reporting gap is the lack of specificity of abuse signs in the diagnostic process. Thus, abuse becomes part of a long list of possible causes that can lead to the findings observed in the medical examination (Marchand et al. 2012).

Social workers and mental health professionals encounter child abuse and related disclosure issues mostly at various child protection agencies, women's shelters, and abuse prevention services that provide a safe house to those in need (Melton 2005). These professionals are responsible for identifying and responding to child abuse cases through a three-part process that includes observing, assessing parental behavior, and responding to it (Zellman 1992). The process has been found to be affected by the professionals' personal characteristics and belief systems, attitudes, and opinions (Ashton 2004). More than any other group, social workers and mental health professional ascribe relevance to their own sociodemographic characteristics that may impede or aid disclosure (Ibaneza et al. 2006; Terao et al. 2001). Such an approach attests to the underlying assumption of the professional groups that child abuse and disclosure are social and psychological constructs affected at least to some extent by the socioeconomic status and by the cultural, racial, ethnic, and personal background of the child abuse professionals. These influences are the subject of inquiry in the present study.

Child Abuse as Social Construction

The social constructionist lens enables an examination of child abuse from a broad sociocultural perspective. Social constructionists seek a heuristic model that focuses on the multiple constructions of meaning within a given social reality (Gergen 1994; Rosen 1998). Constructed realities are socially dependent and never objective because of the ever-present interaction between cultures and the self. Perceived reality is both contextual and subjective and thus co-constituted between the self and the surrounding culture and society (Lock 1981). From this perspective, the construction of social problems involves active engagement and experiencing on the part of the various protagonists (Scannapieco and Connell-Carrick 2005; Spector and Kitsuse 1977). Child abuse is therefore defined differently by the different professional groups (educators, law-enforcement agents, mental health professionals, and health-care professionals), which leads to fundamentally different attitudes, perceptions, definitions, and societal reactions to the phenomenon. Thus, we can frame child abuse as a social problem or a family issue (Ibaneza et al. 2006; Terao et al. 2001), an individual pathology (Kellog 2007), or a legal or even political concern related to children's rights (Melton 2005). Professional gatekeepers and their construction efforts are all part of the social construction process (Ibaneza et al. 2006; Fontes 2005; Melton and Anderson 2008; Haugaard 2000).

Methods

The present study attempted to capture the ways in which professionals perceive and understand the disclosure of child abuse and the obstacles to reporting. Qualitative methodology is particularly well suited for meeting this objective. Based on the social constructivist perspective that underlies our conceptual approach, we constructed a data-based theoretical model that can capture the multiple meanings participants attach to their working experience with child abuse during their everyday work (Gergen 1994). The present study is part of a larger research project that uses a mixed-methods approach and has quantitative and qualitative components.[1]

Ethics

The study, including the purposive sampling chart based on the criteria described below, was submitted for approval to the Ethics Committee at the University of Haifa. Participants received a detailed explanation of the aims of the study. To receive their informed consent and to encourage trust and security in the research process, participants were asked to sign a document explaining the aims of the research, stating their rights, and guaranteeing confidentiality (Patton 2002).

[1] The quantitative component included a national survey to determine the incidence and prevalence of child abuse and the reasons for disclosure or lack thereof. Correlates of child abuse and types of abuse were also explored. The qualitative component consisted of in-depth interviews with 130 male and female children and youths aged 12–17, victims of neglect and abuse, across various cultural groups living in Israel, including Jews and Arabs. Eighty interviews were conducted with professionals to enable the multifaceted exploration of abuse from the perspective of various participants in the process. The information will be presented to practitioners and researchers in the form of a national database, which can be used for the development of intervention models.

Sample

Participants in the present study were a purposive sample (Patton 2002) of 40 child abuse professionals, including educators (10), medical professionals (e.g., physicians and nurses) (10), law-enforcement officers (10), and social work and mental health professionals (10). Purposive sampling provides access to multiple perspectives, both within and between professions, ranging from line workers to policy makers and high-level administrators, geographically distributed throughout the country. Interviewees were between 30 and 70 years of age, and their work experience in the field of child abuse ranged from 3 to 46 years. What all groups held in common was that they were in a direct and intensive involvement in the intervention of the professionals with the child victims.

Data collection was performed using in-depth, semi-structured interviews based on an interview guide. The content categories included were identical for all participating professional groups. The content categories were definitions of abuse, belief systems regarding abuse, perceptions about disclosure and reporting, the challenges of reporting, and the overall challenges that professionals face in their daily work. The content categories of the interview guide were based on both a literature review and initial in-depth pilot interviews with key informants. The categories included in the interview guide were used for data collection and did not emerge from the data collected. The interviews lasted between one and one and a half hours. Interviews were conducted at the work place of the participants and were tape recorded and transcribed verbatim.

Analysis

Data analysis included open coding to identify the units of meaning, followed by a cross-case analysis in which segments from each interview were condensed until core themes emerged (Lincoln and Guba 2005). The analytic themes are based on a range of accounts of professionals holding various attitudes toward child abuse disclosure. For example, the theme "we are very good at closing our eyes," which focuses on the commonalities in the social constructions of disclosure and of its absence, is a collection of the different accounts that fall under a unified spectrum of responsibility for disclosure, ranging from child-centered to professional-centered accounts. The spectrum of responsibility for disclosure is the essence of the first theme.

Trustworthiness

In the present study, credibility is accomplished through the systematic presentation of quotations and their analysis, allowing the reader to evaluate the ways in which reality was constructed and themes were derived from the interviews (Henwood and

Pidgeon 1992; Maxwell 2005). In qualitative research, the emphasis shifts from validity to validation. Rather than presenting a finished product, researchers describe the process by which they arrived at the specific constructions underlying the study, enabling readers to make their own judgment and to validate or reject the interpretations suggested (Angen 2000; Patton 2002). For example, the theme "we are good at closing our eyes" is treated in the following manner: we begin by presenting the context of the information concerning the research participant; we provide the quote; we analyze the quote, including its context, structure, and relationship with the unified theme and with the subsequent quote. This detailed presentation of findings is open to scrutiny by the reader and serves to validate the researcher's systematic work. The focus in this type of research is on in-depth subjective analysis of experiences rather than on generalization. That said, the analysis provides solid exploratory ground for building a heuristic model upon which studies aimed at rigorous generalizations can be based (Babbie 2004).

Findings

As perceived by professionals working in child abuse, the processes of disclosure are loaded with obstacles and secrecy. The similarities and differences in the accounts of various professional groups are illustrated in the subsequent analysis.

Commonalities in the Social Construction of Disclosure: "We Are Very Good at Closing Our Eyes"

An examination of the impediments to disclosure common to all professionals in our study reveals a broad continuum as far as the locus of responsibility is concerned. The range extends from placing responsibility for the challenge inherent in disclosure on the victims by implying that the victims have hidden interests of their own to conceal the abuse to accepting full responsibility by acknowledging that professionals themselves have hidden reasons for concealing abuse.

Tom, a youth police investigator in a small town, accounts for the one extreme end of the continuum of placing responsibility of impeding disclosure on the victim:

> What keeps them from telling, in my opinion, that's what I think, is awareness. These children have been convinced, whether by someone in their own family, or in their close community, that it is all right, that they have nothing to fear, that this is the way things are meant to be. The abuser [leads them] to understand that they should not report: that it is OK, he gives them gifts, buys them things, and so on. When they wake up afterwards, a few years go by, and they think no one will believe them, so it's better that I keep silent. Keep the secret and not report. I don't need to tell you that these things don't get to the police, and they never will. People conquer it and 100 years later it comes up in living room conversa-

tions. And there is also fear, of the same abuser, what will he do? They don't understand that he will not hurt them. They know that if they tell their lives will be over, and more importantly is the shame. What will they say? Will they believe me? Will they not believe me? How will their parents handle the situation? What is very central is self-blame, that is to say, I am to blame for everything, I brought myself into this situation, so what do I have to complain about? It is better so keep silent, better not to report, better to not say.

Tom is exploring the state of mind of the child victim. The victim is initially unaware of the fact that he is being abused and takes abusive behavior for granted. Thus, the victim cannot be helped because there is nothing to be helped. The reality of abuse is denied by the child. When the victims "wake up" to the reality of abuse, other impediments silence them: thoughts related to their credibility as well as feelings of fear and shame that jointly and separately point in the same direction – keep silent. Although he recognizes the underlying reasons that prevent victims from telling, Tom still holds them responsible for the lack of disclosure: *they* are not talking and therefore cannot be heard. In doing so, Tom limits the responsibility of professionals like himself in the process to that of a care provider available for victims only after the children report the abuse.

Boaz, a senior pediatrician working in one of the child protection centers in Israel, accounted for his attitude concerning the source of responsibility for this situation:

Those of us who work in this field, doctors, teachers, nurses, each of us have the tendency to find it unbelievable that it is possible to harm a child. Not to believe that it happens, that it is real. This is less so today, but in the past it was clear that when the child gets up his courage and tells, in many cases nothing is done about it. The kids would say: "We told in school, but no one believed us." Why didn't they believe? They didn't believe because he is a pathological liar. They didn't believe since we cannot believe that parents can hurt their own child so we believe that someone else did this to the child; that he has a vivid imagination; that he doesn't have self-confidence; he is looking for attention. We look for all types of excuses and reasons, and actually, some of them are correct by the way: he does have a vivid imagination, he is looking for attention and reinforcement. But it may be that he is looking for attention because someone at home didn't give him the right type of attention.

Boaz offers numerous reasons why disclosure does not occur: (a) bad faith,grown-ups cannot believe that child abuse is real; (b) children are perceived to be liars; (c) social norms, "parents can't hurt their own child"; (d) children have vivid imaginations; and (e) children lack self-confidence and therefore seek our attention. As Boaz lays out the long list of excuses, he simultaneously points out the ones that hold truth in his eyes and the ones that place the responsibility on the child victim. His ambivalence becomes even more prominent in light of his awareness that perhaps professionals themselves have interests and reasons for concealing abuse, yet the responsibility is still placed on the victims and not on the professionals. Shira serves as a police officer in a domestic violence unit located in an impoverished neighborhood of a large Israeli city. She expands upon Tom's viewpoint that the victims "play a role" in silencing the abuse, but she also places the responsibility on the system and shifts it away somewhat from the victims:

The child will go on and endure beatings for five months, maybe there won't even be an investigation. And then the kid thinks to himself, wait, I told my teacher that my mother

> scratched me, or whatever she did to me, and no one approached me. Maybe this is intentional? Maybe it is better that things stay as they are? Maybe this means that people don't care about me? Or even love me? He can reach all types of conclusions and then simply not tell about the abuse that follows. And so here we lose another child who grows up with violence.

Shira's primary argument is that victims of child abuse believe that it does not help to tell others about the incidents of abuse, strengthening Tom's view. But Shira's account offers an in-depth perspective of the processes that contribute to silencing the victims. Victims are socialized or conditioned to be silent by the lack of societal reaction to their cries for help. Through a painful process, victims learn that their accounts are of no significance to others and that they may be intentionally ignored. This results in an overall experience of uncertainty and mistrust toward others, including investigators and teachers. Shira places the responsibility for the lack of disclosure not on the victims but on to the social systems that surround them, but she also voices a learned helplessness with regard to the ability of the system to effectively aid in this process. Avi, a key informant holding a high-ranking administrative position in the education system, expands on Shira's view and reveals the multiple hidden interests that professionals may have for concealing the detection and preventing the treatment of child abuse:

> It's not like, it happens [reporting abuse] and it's "off your plate." You need to remain in contact with the people that you report to, you may be called to court to testify. There is a never-ending process that does not stop at the initial discovery. There is a process here, and in the end someone needs to be blamed. How is it that in the State of Israel, where reporting abuse is mandated by law, we are only seeing the tip of the iceberg? That is why I say, it is a very complicated process. You know where you start, but you never know where and how it is going to end. It may be that this discourages people to start it from the outset.

Whereas Shiras's account describes the system failures in the detection and treatment of child abuse, Avi provides an explanation for it. The lasting effect of disclosure, the fact that it generates added work and creates conflict at the working place, makes the potential consequences of reporting unpredictable and open ended. Such loss of control over the situation created by reporting may be an important impediment in performing it. Avi's account sheds light on the conflict between the professional interests involved in helping the child and the personal interest of avoiding added work, uncertainty, and the associated discomfort. In other words, recognition involves the duty to report or the potential for guilt feelings for not having acted upon one's ascribed professional responsibility. Such feelings interfere with one's own sense of self-worth, courage, and self-image of being a "good" or a morally righteous person. They stimulate what is known as gaze aversion (Doherty-Sneddon and Phelps 2005), which is the human inclination to divert ones gaze when facing difficult social problems, in order to protect ones sense of a positive identity as a human being.

There is an ongoing process of negotiating responsibility which in turn creates double messages toward both the victims and the public at large. Professionals admit that victims are socialized to avoid reporting and disclosing abuse and that they themselves play a role in the avoidance of disclosure through their behavior and personal agenda. The following theme explores in greater depth the role of professionals who obstruct disclosure by examining the particular methods of discourse of each child abuse profession.

Avoiding Discourses by Professional Groups: "We Don't Unveil It"

Common to all professionals in our study is the perception that the concealment of abuse is the main obstacle to its treatment. But each professional group constructs the concealment using different terminologies, suitable to its own professional perspective and agenda. We examine below the professional construction of disclosure by educators, law-enforcement officials, therapists, and medical professionals.

Educators: "It's a Mafia-Like Code of Silence"

The educational system was found to be less involved with the reporting and disclosing of child abuse that occurs in the family, but more engaged with peer violence occurring within the boundaries of the schools. Rafi is a chief administrator in charge of a school system serving students from nursery school through high school. He is a representative of the typical way in which educators, principals, and individuals in the educational system account for child abuse concealment:

> I can identify a mafia-like code among the students. Mafia code means, don't tattle, don't rat on them! Never cooperate with the school administration. When is the mafia code broken? One: when there is some piece of external incriminating information. Two: when there are students who interpret whatever happened in a negative light and for their own reasons they feel that it is the right thing to rat on someone, to come and tell. Of course, right away they ask for protection so that no one will know that they told, because they'll be hurt, this is clear. That is to say, they stumble and fall in this case. In my opinion, it's the mafia code: you don't tell. In this respect they are no different from anyone else in Israeli society, not better not worse. How many people have the courage to go to the police and file a complaint about something that happened? A dangerous driver, for example. There is a real danger here, a threat; it could come back as a boomerang against you.

Rafi portrays a tribal reality in which the community takes precedence over individual existence. In a reality of this type, rules such as keeping the dirty laundry concealed within the communal circle makes perfect sense. Individuals who communicate with strangers outside this circle (teachers, counselors, etc.) are perceived as traitors, subject to social penalties and even excommunication. Even after the circle of concealment is broken, the need to maintain it continues in the form of the protection that is sought, and the main concern of the individual who broke the circle is to remain anonymous. This tribal reality is not perceived negatively, but rather it is granted positive reinforcement and is generalized to the society at large. Terms such as "traitors" and "stumble and fall" in the context of disclosure reveal Rafi's negative perception of those who break the code, even in the case of abuse. His perception of the law-enforcement system further strengthens his argument, as Rafi regards their interference in a negative manner and implies that problems should be resolved within the community without outside intrusion. In other words, Rafi upholds the social reality of the tribal code and in a subtle manner may socialize his students to follow his lead and accept this social reality. The question remains on who is responsible for the concealment of abuse.

Orna, a school counselor, reinforces Rafi's point of view by describing the active participation of the schools in the concealment of abuse:

> In terms of offenders in the school, I think there is a range of reactions from keeping a distance from the offenders for a while after the incident, to increasing their popularity in school… Just like the stereotype goes, that's the way it is in reality. The perpetrator is a Don Juan. [as for the victims] I think that the reaction of the environment is not at all simple. Well, it is not by chance that the victims are rejected. Very often these stories don't add to their popularity, just the opposite; somehow they make the victim look even more undesirable and despicable. Either he [male victim] is suspected of framing someone, or she [female victim] is suspected of acting like a whore. For the girls, it is very often hard to cope later, and this is why they prefer to remain silent. This turns into a level of fear: "Don't tell anyone, I'll get the reputation of a whore." Beyond this, we don't let these cases out [to the public outside the school]. We carefully guard them so that they will not get out and be exposed. So it's hard to know the reaction, since we don't let it out.

Orna presents a clear division of reactions customary in cases of abuse toward the perpetrators and toward the victims. Both occur only within the confines of the social circle of peers. Orna is well aware of the tribal terminology used by the youth to describe interpersonal violence. As a component of such tribal discourse, the aggressor is perceived as a dominant and desirable male, while the victims are perceived as amoral, even despicable agents deserving collective social penalties. The reaction of the outside social agents, such as school, family, and beyond, is absent from her account. Orna understands the lack of reaction but emphasizes the importance of keeping these stories unpublicized and unknown outside the school and the educational system. By actively concealing this tribal reality of the students, Orna protects the stability of this stereotype and perpetuates it. In doing so she serves as a passive collaborator, revealing that she herself is guided by the same tribal discourse that she attributes to others. In doing so, she protects her identity and membership in the "tribe" of school, culture, and teachers and thus guards against personal loss. The informant explicitly protects children's' culture, while parallelly implicitly protecting his/her own, as they share the same cultural norms and values.

Orna and Rafi's positions reflect the sensitive interrelationship between what they see among their pupils and their own perceptions of social reality. The reality of violence and abuse is co-constituted and socially constructed by students and educators alike as a regrettable interference with their community life, which poses a threat to its unity and cohesion. Therefore, the responsibility for concealing violence and abuse falls on the intersubjective and interactive relationship of the educators and their charges, the students.

Law Enforcement: "Her Story Is Full of Inconsistencies"

The predominant agenda of law-enforcement agents is the implementation of a "law and order" ideology. For these professionals, a clear and proven case is a condition for enabling the intervention and treatment of child abuse. Because of the fragmented and contradictory nature of most testimonies in abuse cases, this condition is seldom met, leaving the investigators in a state of frustration. The depth of this frustration is illustrated by Betty, a police officer investigating child abuse cases:

"It's very suspicious: why didn't you tell? Why not? It is as if she jumped around and there were all sorts of holes in her story. She told parts of it, but cut out other parts. Wait! If it was such a central and important thing, why did you choose not to tell? So we conducted a repeat investigation, and we discovered all kinds of problems with the testimony of the youth. Sometimes the youths don't help me, they cause me a lot of problems, and there are many contradictions in their testimonies: things that they didn't tell, suddenly you see that they cooperated in the incident. Then there is a problem. I need to understand from her what happened, how did he entice her? How did he convince her? Sometimes the issue of age comes up: I need to know how old she told him she was. How does she look? I need to consider this. Sometimes he didn't know that she was underage, sometimes she says, no I told him this. As difficult as it is, sometimes you need to push them [the victims]."

Betty describes her dissatisfaction and frustration with the unorganized and problematic nature of the testimony of abuse victims. The gaps, contradictions, and changing versions in the testimony set the stage for a general atmosphere of mistrust. This hampers her goal-directed approach to construct a clear and well-defined case of abuse. All means, including the use of pressuring the victim, justify the professional aim. The need to succeed overcomes the sensitivity to the plight of the victims, resulting in a conflicted interaction between her and the youths. Her suspicion is at the basis of the transformation of the victims into troublemakers and at times accused suspects.

Betty, relying strictly on clear evidence, places the responsibility for thwarting effective disclosure on the victims themselves. Shirley, a child investigator, while still engaging in the same type of discourse, also acknowledges the role of law-enforcement officers in the processes of obstructing disclosure:

> I investigated a girl once. There was suspicion that her father hit her, beat her. Nothing dramatic followed the investigation, and apparently as a result of the disclosure she got it really hard at home. After a year there was suspicion that her father was sexually abusing her. I came to her a second time. She didn't tell me "nothing happened" anymore; rather she told me, "I'm managing."

Superficially, Shirley's account is similar to Betty's in that it argues that disclosure is hindered by the victims' inconsistent testimonies. But from the subtext, we learn that the law-enforcement agents contributed to this situation both passively and actively. By handling the case in an unorganized and potentially sloppy manner, they created an unsafe environment for the victim and planted the seeds for an inconsistent testimony. In other words, after the fact, each respondent officer tacitly recognized that they were responsible for socializing the victims to denial ("nothing happened") and causing the victim to reject the help of the law-enforcement agents ("I'm managing"). Victims learn not only to conceal abuse but also that disclosing it may worsen their situation and further damage their quality of life. They surrender to a life of "coping" by themselves with abuse, at the cost of losing trust in a protective law-enforcement system and the hopes attached to it.

Shirley's account exposes the active role that law-enforcement agents assume in the construction of the victim's inconsistent and at times contradictory testimony. As in the case of educators, we witness again the ways in which professionals perceive their client-victims and socialize them to the role of the victim. Victims and social control agents co-construct the reality of abuse.

Therapists: "Nothing Will Come Out of It"

The mental health professionals in our study regarded the trust between themselves and the child victims as the key element in the process of disclosure. Such relationships, together with a supportive and pleasant context, are believed to be conducive to disclosure, as Liora, a former therapist, currently holding the position of chief administrative director, stated:

> We have a very nice center here: aesthetic, developed, pleasant, and the services here are very discrete. There is no waiting room here. There is a family waiting here now, and soon another will arrive. As each family arrives they are cared for by the staff, so that actually there is no waiting room here, and people don't see one another. The services here are extremely discrete. It doesn't look like the police or the social welfare here. We want to create the optimal conditions so that that child will speak. Not that it works for us in every case. There are children who have difficulty separating from their parents. There are children who are threatened that if they tell the abuser will hurt them and they are afraid that the moment they open up someone will kill them. So the process here is done gently and in an atmosphere of friendliness.

Liora is focusing on the description of the type of setting in which disclosure is most likely to occur. She labors to produce an environment that is aesthetic, discrete, friendly, and caring in order to allay the victim's assumed suspicions and foster a helping relationship between the victims and the professionals. Disclosure is perceived to be hampered by the established relationships of the child with meaningful others such as parents, and it is the therapist's aim to destabilize, distance, and replace these, if only temporarily, in order to achieve disclosure. The main perceived difficulty in Liora's view is the lack of trust of the victim toward the therapist and the system that the therapist represents. The responsibility for the potential impediments to disclosure is centered on the victims and their significant others.

By contrast, Shani, a social worker in the field of child abuse, although she uses the same argument of mistrust in the system, places responsibility for impeding disclosure squarely on the therapists themselves:

> There are therapists who even when they see something are afraid to report. Why are they afraid to report? Because it's not safe. What, now because of me the entire family [of the

> victim] will be investigated? Because of me, and they will know that it happened because of me. What will I do? They'll fire me; they'll subpoena me to testify at the police. I'll have to testify in court! I won't sleep at night. After all is said and done, nothing comes of it, only they will think of me as someone who is looking for trouble.

Shani suggests numerous explanations to account for the therapists' reluctance to report abuse centered around personal and professional costs. Her account reveals her internal dilemmas and the perceived serious burdens of disclosure that she and her colleagues will have to shoulder. Central to her narrative is mistrust in a malevolent system that ultimately leaves both the therapists and the victims unprotected.

As in the case of the other professional groups presented above, the "problem of disclosure" is again constructed between what the therapists identify in their patient-victims as fear and a lack of trust and their own mistrust, weariness, and avoidance of the system in which they work.

Medical Professionals: "Piecing the Puzzle Together"

Medical professionals described a tendency to experience the occurrence of abuse through the dominant medical model of strict, methodical, and rational organization of knowledge. Disclosure is constructed as a process of "experimenting" with different hypotheses and trying to narrow the possibilities down to the most likely occurrence. Yael, a pediatrician in a large municipal hospital, responsible primarily for child abuse detection, is a representative voice of the medical discourse:

> When you stand in front of a child who has no visible signs, and you start to think and put the pieces of the puzzle together, you can see the signs. They don't have horns, neither the abused, nor the abusers. You can stand in front of a child and he seems like a regular boy in every respect, but when you start to put the pieces of the puzzle together and to ask questions you understand that his aggressive, violent behavior, his verbal expressions, his sexual behaviors that don't suit his age, the signs on his skin, his fear of strangers, his failing grades in school, his hyperactivity – are all not just psychological, dyslexia, ADHD, but they can also be the signs of child abuse, physical, mental or sexual abuse. You won't always see it, it is not like there are typical signs that you can say: this differentiates it from other diseases. You need to always remember that it could be many other things…there is nothing definitive that shows if it is that or not that.

Yael reveals her methodical use of hypothesizing and calculating when diagnosing cases of child abuse. Yael uses familiar medical terminology to describe the processes of detection of child abuse. By conceptualizing it as a medical condition, she focuses primarily on to the various observable signs as pieces of information to be assembled into an intelligible perception of the phenomenon. Her problems in detecting child abuse derive from the fact that the measurable and visible signs can be interpreted in many different ways, so that a clear diagnosis is difficult to achieve. Yael works through the medical measures she knows, despite her awareness of the limitations of the process. The victim's voice is limited, and the process of identifying the "disease" occurs on scientific grounds which can't account for the complexity and multifaceted nature of the phenomena. Lack of clarity, ambiguity, and uncertainty which are part and parcel of child abuse detection can hardly be accounted for by any scientific paradigm including the medical one.

Sharply different from Yael's account, Ilan, an expert physician, reveals the ways in which ambiguity and uncertainty play a role in the physician's inner experience:

> People have all kinds of interests, and we have an interest not to discover abuse, since if I find out, then I'll need to testify in court, and will need to waste my time and write a report and an expert opinion, which in and of itself is a problem. Sometimes you can encounter a defense attorney who is not nice and may insult you, hurt you, hurt your professional respect, and waste your time. Every person in the system has its own set on interests of why not to uncover. When I evaluate a case, I need to do all sorts of tests, need to follow up. I need to notify the social services, to get reports, to record all sorts of things; this takes time, energy, and efforts. Why should I – it is much more convenient for me not to think about it, and it is emotionally and mentally challenging to deal with it, so maybe I should leave it alone and shut myself off to the idea. There are a million reasons. For physicians in the community, there are real reasons to be fearful. Fear from being physically hurt, fearful of financial hardship; if they suspect and report, very quickly that doctor will be slandered in his community and hurt financially. They may threaten to hurt him physically; many doctors sit alone in their clinics and no one can protect them from threat. There are many reasons not to report, and many interests that cause us to shut our eyes.

Ilan exposes a variety of reasons why professionals conceal and ignore child abuse, including personal, emotional, and professional ones. Unlike the scientific-rational script adopted by Yael as part of an overall rational model, Ilan describes the uncertainty and ambiguity associated with child abuse. His script is emotion governed, ridden by fear and uncertainty, and it describes a failure to detect child abuse and a "shut-eye" strategy.

The medical professionals who participated in the study revealed an identical pattern in constructing the prevention of disclosure with that of the other professionals. The most serious obstacle in the processes of properly diagnosing child abuse by physicians was the uncertainty reflected in their inner experience and their attitude toward the phenomenon.

We described the discourse used by various professionals to construct the suppression of disclosure. As shown, each professional socially constructs the impediments of disclosure, using specific professional accounts. This discourse initially places the responsibility for the challenges of disclosure on the child victims, but our analysis reveals that the professionals are aware of their own role and input in the avoidance to disclose.

Discussion

Analysis of the data indicates that professionals working in the field of child abuse understand the processes of disclosure along two interrelated dimensions: one is related to the issue of responsibility, whether it is the child victims' or the professionals'; the other is related to the discourse and accounting used to disclose or to conceal the abuse by any specific professional group.

These two interacting dimensions are illustrated in the graphic representation (Fig. 19.1) below.

As shown in the above illustration, the discourse of each professional group defines the disclosure "issue" by using slightly different terminologies, rooted in its professional orientation. In a broader sense, "passing the buck" is the key feature of avoiding responsibility in every professional group, as practitioners transfer the responsibility among themselves and between themselves and their clients. Thus, the co-creation of the avoidance of disclosure is the most viable option. The process is a constructed social reality of joint making between the clients and the professionals coming in contact with them.

How can we explain the fact that the professional groups responsible for disclosing and treating child abuse are making every effort to conceal it? To understand this, we need to turn to the cultural context of being a victim in the Israeli culture. Since the establishment of the modern State of Israel, the image of the victimized Jews was viewed as part of the humiliating past of the Diaspora (Sand 2009; Zimmerman 2002) and assumed a highly undesirable and negative connotation (Almog 2000). Therefore, the professionals in question can be seen as attempting to "normalize" victimhood by denying victims the status of abused and neglected children. This move is associated with an increased emphasis on the conscious break with the perceived Diaspora Jew seen as a timeless and placeless victim. Increased personal responsibility and empowerment have been regarded

Fig. 19.1 The professional construction of nondisclosure

as an important building block in the changed narrative of the newly emerging society (Mayer 2005).

The theme of silencing and devaluing perceived victims, and at the same time valuing strength in the face of extreme hardship, may be a primary aspect of the Israeli culture (Segev 1991; Soloman 1995; Zimmerman 2002). Cultural contexts shape the construction of nondisclosure of child abuse by professionals, so that the social construction of child abuse disclosure in Israel can be seen as a way of silencing the victims. Moreover, it may be a primary aspect of any culture, as is illustrated in the theoretical frame of theory of basic values (Schwartz 2012). In this framework, human behavior stems from a basic value structure, which is identical in all cultures, from which all normative behavior is derived. This structure is not linear but circular, and thus for each basic value there is a contradicting one. The derivative normative behavior is paradoxical. It seems that this theoretical frame is applicable to the emerging construction of disclosure, as professional norms of mandatory reporting are countered by the basic human need to exercise gaze aversion in the face of recognizing victims and thus revealing the paradox of the disclosure process.

The cultural context serves as the primary and knowledge-independent source from which society constructs itself and its different professions and services. In this respect, it is the lived communal experience by which modern society identifies social problems and constructs intervention. In the case of disclosure among child abuse professionals in Israel, these cultural lenses are also the part of the impediments for an effective intervention in the phenomenon of child abuse.

Implications

The idea that professionals working in the field of child abuse contribute to the reality of "nondisclosure" or the reality of "difficulties" surrounding disclosure is well established in research (e.g., Egu and Weiss 2003). Personal, social, or situational factors related to professionals are influential in detecting (or not) abuse (e.g., Ashton 2004; Hershkowitz et al. 2006; Kenny 2001). We argue here a more general theoretical point that conscious impeding of making child abuse visible may be part of a benevolent attempt of professionals attempting to avoid a victim status for their clients which is not highly rewarding in a society based on power and control. It may not be much different from the social policies of "don't ask, don't tell" used with gays and additional de-victimizing policies with marginal populations. The Israeli case is just one example of how specific cultural traditions, values, and preferences set the tone for what to report and make visible and what to mask and make transparent.

The immediate implication of such theorizing is that before "throwing more money" on the problem of "nondisclosure" and non-detection of child abuse, we should consider working on a more general, cultural, and attitudinal change in communities concerning the impact of being a victim of any kind of social deviance.

One way of approaching this would be to enhance the use of interdisciplinary and interprofessional teamwork (Kempe 1978). Such teams would be more competent in assessing both the cultural context and social cost of disclosure vs. the benefits of investing in such endeavors. It would further save much effort presently invested in interprofessional bickering leading to burnout (Kaminer et al. 1988; Bross et al. 2000) and masking and enable a more integral and culturally sensitive approach (Fontes 2005) to dealing with victims of child abuse through balancing their needs with their rights.

The present study encourages scholars and policy makers to examine the phenomenon of child abuse and the processes of child abuse disclosure in their respective cultural contexts. A main benefit of an in-depth analysis of the cultural background of professional work is the awareness that the workers might gain on the perceived obstacles that stem from the reported gap between the incidence of abuse and actual disclosure and recognition that whatever the obstacles they can be addressed and must be addressed to reduce child maltreatment and its effects.

References

Ainsworth, F. (2002). Mandatory reporting of child abuse and neglect: Does it really make a difference. *Child and Family Social Work, 7*, 57–63.

Alaggia, R. (2004). Many ways of telling: Expanding conceptualizations of child sexual abuse disclosure. *Child Abuse & Neglect, 28*(11), 1213–1227.

Almog, O. (2000). *The Sabra: The creation of the new Jew*. Berkeley: University of California Press.

Angen, M. J. (2000). Evaluating interpretative inquiry: Reviewing the validity debate and opening the dialogue. *Qualitative Health Research, 10*(3), 378–398.

Ashton, V. (2004). The effect of personal characteristics on reporting child maltreatment. *Child Abuse & Neglect, 28*, 985–997.

Babbie, E. (2004). *The practice of social research* (10th ed.). Belmont: Thomson/Wadsworth Learning.

Bal, S., Crombez, G., Bourdeaudhuji, I., & Van Oost, P. (2009). Symptomatology in adolescents following initial disclosure of sexual abuse: The roles of crisis support, appraisals and coping. *Child Abuse & Neglect, 33*, 717–727.

Bross, D. C., Ballo, N., & Korfmacher, J. (2000). Client evaluation of a consultation team on crimes against children. *Child Abuse & Neglect, 24*(1), 71–84.

Browne, A., & Finkelhor, D. (1986). Impact of child sexual abuse: A review of the research. *Psychological Bulletin, 99*, 66–77.

Davidov, D., Jack, S., Frost, S., & Coben, J. (2012). Mandatory reporting in the context of home visitation programs: Intimate partner violence. *Violence Against Women, 18*(5), 595–610.

Doherty-Sneddon, G., & Phelps, F. G. (2005). Gaze aversion: A response to cognitive or social difficulty? *Memory and Cognition, 33*(4), 727–733.

Egu, C. L., & Weiss, D. J. (2003). The role of race and severity of abuse in teachers' recognition or reporting of child abuse. *Journal of Child and Family Studies, 12*(4), 465–474.

Farrell, L. G. (1988). Factors that affect a victim's self-disclosure in father–daughter incest. *Child Welfare, 67*, 462–468.

Fontes, L. A. (2005). *Child abuse and culture: Working with diverse families*. New York: Guilford Press.

Gergen, K. J. (1994). *Realities and relationship*. Cambridge, MA: Harvard University Press.

Goodman-Brown, T. B., Edelstein, R. S., Goodman, G. S., Jones, D. P. H., & Gordon, D. S. (2003). Why children tell: A model of children's disclosure of sexual abuse. *Child Abuse & Neglect, 27*, 525–540.

Haugaard, J. J. (2000). The challenge of defining child sexual abuse. *American Psychologist, 55*, 1036–1039.

Henwood, K. L., & Pidgeon, N. F. (1992). Qualitative research and psychological theorizing. *British Journal of Psychology, 83*(2), 97–111.

Hershkowitz, I., Horowitz, D., & Lamb, M. E. (2005). Trends in children's disclosure of abuse in Israel: A national study. *Child Abuse & Neglect, 29*, 1203–1214.

Hershkowitz, I., Orbach, Y., Lamb, M. E., Sternberg, K. J., & Horowitz, D. (2006). Dynamics of forensic interviews with suspected abuse victims who do not disclose abuse. *Child Abuse & Neglect, 30*, 753–769.

Hershkowitz, I., Lamb, M. E., & Horowitz, D. (2007). Victimization of children with disabilities. *American Journal of Orthopsychiatry, 77*, 629–635.

Ibaneza, E., Borrego, J., Pembertona, J., & Terao, S. (2006). Cultural factors in decision-making about child physical abuse: Identifying reporter characteristics influencing reporting tendencies. *Child Abuse & Neglect, 30*, 1365–1379.

Kaminer, B. B., Crowe, A. H., & Budde-Giltner, L. (1988). The prevalence and characteristics of multidisciplinary teams for child abuse and neglect: A national survey. In D. C. Bross, R. D. Krugman, M. R. Lenherr, D. A. Rosenber, & B. D. Schmitt (Eds.), *The new child protection team handbook* (pp. 548–567). New York: Garland Publishing.

Katz, C., Hershkowitz, I., Malloy, L. C., Lamb, M. E., Atabaki, A., & Spindler, S. (2012). Nonverbal behavior of children who disclose or do not disclose child abuse in investigative interviews. *Child Abuse & Neglect, 36*, 12–20.

Kellog, N. D. (2007). The Committee on Child Abuse and Neglect. Evaluation of suspected child physical abuse. *Pediatrics, 119*, 1232–1241.

Kempe, C. H. (1978). Foreword. In B. D. Schmitt (Ed.), *The child protection team handbook: A multidisciplinary approach to managing child abuse and neglect*. New York: Garland Publishing.

Kenny, M. (2001). Child abuse reporting: Teachers' perceived deterrents. *Child Abuse & Neglect, 25*(1), 81–92.

Kim, S., Gostin, L., & Cole, T. (2012). Child abuse reporting: Rethinking child protection. *Journal of the American Medical Association, 308*, 1,37–38.

Lincoln, Y. S., & Guba, E. G. (2005). Paradigms and perspectives in contention. In N. Denzin & Y. Lincoln (Eds.), *Handbook of qualitative research* (3rd ed., pp. 183–190). Thousand Oaks: Sage.

Lock, A. (1981). Universals in human conception. In P. Heelas & J. Lock (Eds.), *Indigenous psychologies: The anthropology of the self* (pp. 19–36). London: Academic.

London, K., Bruck, M., Ceci, S. J., & Shuman, D. W. (2005). Disclosure of child sexual abuse: What does the research tell us about the ways that children tell? *Psychology, Public Policy, and Law, 11*, 194–226.

Malloy, L. C., Lyon, T. D., & Quas, J. A. (2007). Filial dependency and recantation of child sexual abuse allegations. *Journal of the American Academy of Child & Adolescent Psychiatry, 46*, 162–170.

Marchand, J., Deneyer, M., & Vandenplas, Y. (2012). Detection, diagnosis, and prevention of child abuse: The role of the pediatrician. *European Journal of Pediatrics, 171*, 17–23.

Mathews, B., & Walsh, K. (2004a). Queensland teachers' new legal obligation to report child sexual abuse. *Australia and New Zealand Journal of Law and Education, 9*(1), 25–40.

Mathews, B., & Walsh, K. (2004b). Issues in mandatory reporting of child sexual abuse by Australian teachers. *Australia and New Zealand Journal of Law and Education, 9*(2), 3–17.

Maxwell, J. A. (2005). *Qualitative research design: An interactive approach* (2nd ed.). Thousand Islands: Sage.

Mayer, T. (2005). From zero to hero: Masculinity in Jewish nationalism. In E. Fuchs (Ed.), *Israel women's studies* (pp. 97–117). New Brunswick: Rutgers University Press.

Melton, G. (2005). Mandated reporting: A policy without reason. *Child Abuse & Neglect, 29*, 9–18.

Melton, G. B., & Anderson, D. (2008). From safe sanctuaries to strong communities: The role of communities of faith in child protection. *Family & Community Health: The Journal of Health Promotion & Maintenance, 31*(2), 173–185.

Narayan, A. P., Socolar, R., & St Claire, K. (2006). Pediatric residency training in child abuse and neglect in the United States. *Pediatrics, 117*, 2215–2222.

O'Toole, R., Webster, S. W., O'Toole, A. W., & Lucal, B. (1999). Teachers' recognition and reporting of child abuse: A factorial survey. *Child Abuse & Neglect, 23*(11), 1083–1101.

Patton, M. Q. (2002). *Qualitative research and evaluation methods*. Thousand Oaks: Sage.

Rosen, H. (1998). Meaning making as a metaframework for clinical practice. In R. Dorfmam (Ed.), *Paradigms of clinical social work* (Vol. 2, pp. 257–288). New York: Brunner/Mazel Publishers.

Sand, S. (2009). *The invention of the Jewish people*. London: Verso.

Scannapieco, M., & Connell-Carrick, K. (2005). *Understanding child-maltreatment: An ecological and development perspective*. New York: Oxford University Press.

Schwartz, S. H. (2012). An overview of the Schwartz theory of basic values. *Online Readings in Psychology and Culture, 2*(1). http://dx.doi.org/10.9707/2307-0919.1116

Segev, T. (1991). *The seventh million: The Israelis and the Holocaust*. Jerusalem: Maxwell-Macmillan-Keter Publishing House/Domino Press [Hebrew].

Soloman, Z. (1995). From denial to recognition: Attitudes toward Holocaust survivors from World War II to the present. *Journal of Traumatic Stress, 8*(2), 215–228.

Spector, M., & Kitsuse, I. J. (1977). *Constructing social problems*. Menlo Park: Cummings.

Staller, K. M., & Nelson-Gardell, D. (2005). "A burden in your heart": Lessons of disclosure from female preadolescent and adolescent survivors of sexual abuse. *Child Abuse & Neglect, 29*(12), 1415–1432.

Stirling, J., Jr., & Amaya-Jackson, L. (2008). Traumatic stress understanding the behavioral and emotional consequences of child abuse. *Pediatrics, 122*(3), 667–673.

Terao, S., Borrego, J., & Urquiza, A. (2001). A reporting and response model for culture and child maltreatment. *Child Maltreatment, 6*(2), 158–168.

Vulliamy, A., & Sullivan, R. (2002). Reporting child abuse: Pediatricians' experiences with the child protection system. *Child Abuse & Neglect, 24*(11), 1461–1470.

Walsh, K., Farrell, A., Bridgstock, R., & Schweitzer, R. (2006). The contested terrain of teachers detecting and reporting child abuse and neglect: The need for empirical research in an Australian state with unique reporting laws. *Journal of Early Childhood Research, 4*(1), 65–76.

Webster, S. W., O'Toole, R., O'Toole, A. W., & Lucal, B. (2005). Overreporting and underreporting of child abuse: Teachers' use of professional discretion. *Child Abuse & Neglect, 29*(11), 1281–1296.

Zellman, G. L. (1992). The impact of case characteristics on child abuse reporting decisions. *Child Abuse & Neglect, 16*(1), 57–74.

Zimmerman, M. (2002). *Don't touch my Holocaust*. Haifa: The University of Haifa Press [Hebrew].

Part V
Relationship of Reporting with Response Systems, and Practical Issues and Challenges for Response Systems

Chapter 20
What Will Happen to This Child If I Report? Outcomes of Reporting Child Maltreatment

Theodore P. Cross, Betsy Goulet, Jesse J. Helton, Emily Lux, and Tamara Fuller

Individuals reporting suspected child abuse or neglect will naturally wonder what will happen to the child once they report. Any consideration of policy and practice on reporting should also be informed by knowledge of the outcomes of reporting. These outcomes vary enormously, from screening the referral out with no further action on one end of a continuum to placing a child outside the home against the child and family's will at the other end, with a range of possible outcomes in between. The difference in impact on children and families is substantial. For the most part, these outcomes result from decisions made by child protective services about (a) the extent and continuing risk of child maltreatment and (b) what services if any to deliver. Through a review of empirical and practice literature, this chapter discusses this range of possible outcomes. We describe each outcome and report on the factors affecting each, including differences by type of abuse and neglect. We then use US national data to estimate the proportion of reports with each outcome. Finally we discuss the implications for understanding and positively influencing the reporting situation.

We make use of two US national data sets extensively, in some circumstances citing already published results from these data sets and in other circumstances doing our own data analysis. One data set is the National Child Abuse and Neglect Data System (NCANDS), an annual federal compilation of data from state CPS client information systems. NCANDS includes both data on individual cases (e.g., on substantiation and child placement) and aggregate data in which states simply report

T.P. Cross (✉) • J.J. Helton • E. Lux • T. Fuller, Ph.D.
Children and Family Research Center, School of Social Work,
University of Illinois at Urbana-Champaign, Champaign, IL, USA
e-mail: tpcross@illinois.edu

B. Goulet, DPA
Department of Public Administration, University of Illinois at Springfield,
Springfield, IL 62703, USA

B. Mathews, D.C. Bross (eds.), *Mandatory Reporting Laws and the Identification of Severe Child Abuse and Neglect*, Child Maltreatment 4,
DOI 10.1007/978-94-017-9685-9_20

totals in a given category (e.g., number of reports, screen ins, and screen outs). States voluntarily submit NCANDS data to the federal government, which assembles them into a national data set and commissions periodic reports from it. For this chapter, we used data published in the most recent NCANDS report at the time of this writing, entitled *Child Maltreatment 2011* (US Department of Health and Human Services 2012), in some cases doing extra calculations to answer our particular questions. NCANDS' strength is its provision of timely, detailed data from the vast majority of the states. It has several limitations, including missing data from several states on numerous variables and the fact that variables such as reporting, substantiation, and service delivery are not uniformly operationalized and depend heavily on each state's policies and procedures (Finkelhor and Wells 2003). The lack of standardization in NCANDS contributes to substantial variation across states on rates of several different CPS decisions, and it is very difficult to separate meaningful state differences in child protective intervention from state differences in categorization and measurement.

The other data set is the National Survey of Child and Adolescent Well-Being (NSCAW), an in-depth longitudinal national probability study of children involved in maltreatment investigations. NSCAW utilizes interviews with caseworkers, caregivers, teachers, and children themselves as well as standardized measures of child well-being (see, e.g., Dolan et al. 2011). The first cohort of NSCAW (NSCAW I) sampled 5,501 cases from CPS investigations that were completed in 1999 and 2000, and the second cohort (NSCAW II) sampled 5,872 cases from investigations completed in 2008 and 2009. NSCAW employed two-stage random sampling in which primary sampling units (PSUs, defined as the geographic area served by a single CPS agency) were randomly sampled (over 80 in each cohort), and children involved in child maltreatment investigations were randomly sampled within PSU. Because of NSCAW's sampling methodology, percentages calculated from NSCAW can legitimately be considered to be population estimates. NSCAW included oversampling to provide a sufficient number of cases for analysis in certain categories, so statistical weights are applied and all percentages reported here represent weighted percentages. The cohorts included substantiated and unsubstantiated investigations, as well as cases that received ongoing child protective services following an investigation and cases that did not receive ongoing child protective services. Baseline data were collected by an interview on average 4 months after the investigation was closed. In this chapter, we both cite studies using NSCAW and analyze NSCAW data ourselves.

In the final section, we discuss the implications of this analysis for understanding the outcomes of reporting. A caveat is that, given the existing literature, it was impossible to focus specifically on mandatory reporting, so instead this analysis necessarily concerns reporting in general. Although, as we discuss below, the type of reporter has some impact on the beginning of the process, our findings are general and therefore should apply meaningfully to the mandatory reporting situation.

Decision Points

A report of child maltreatment triggers a series of decisions. Child protective services screen the case in or out, deciding whether the reported maltreatment falls within its purview and whether the report is legitimate and indicates potential risk. If screened in, additional decisions are made in two domains: (1) investigation and (2) service delivery. Investigative decisions concern a determination of whether a child is actually maltreated, while service delivery decisions concern what services children and family will receive to protect children's safety and well-being and include the possibility in some serious cases of placing children outside the home.

Below we discuss five key decisions: screening, substantiation, protective service delivery, child placement, and referral to differential response.

Screening

When individuals report child maltreatment, they typically contact a referral center established by the state child protective service (CPS) agency, generally through a widely distributed "hotline" number. The hotline is staffed by child protection agency workers whose job is to screen reports to determine whether they are appropriate for additional CPS response. This so-called intake stage is one of the most important decision-making points in the child protection system, since opening an investigation can have a major effect on reported families whether their case is ultimately substantiated or not, whereas screening a case out immediately ends CPS involvement with the family (DePanfilis and Salus 2003; Wells et al. 2004). Wells (1997) has described screening as a complex decision with a multitude of factors influencing it, including federal and state laws—interpreted differently by workers and agencies—differing agency policies and procedures, and individual worker decision-making processes.

At intake, the child protection agency worker assesses the allegation, determining if the alleged victim and perpetrator meet the statutory criteria for investigation. A small percentage of cases (about 9 % in Wells et al.'s 1995 study) are screened out because the case occurred outside of the agency's jurisdiction, the report does not provide the information to locate the child and alleged perpetrator, or the perpetrator is not a caregiver (which in most states place the report outside CPS' purview, at least for some types of maltreatment). The child protection agency worker must then determine the validity of the report and the seriousness of the risk (Wells et al. 1995). The priority is to determine whether a child could be at imminent risk of harm or likely to experience maltreatment sometime in the future. In most states, individual hotline workers make the screening decisions, but in many states, one or more additional workers (e.g., a supervisor) also participate in the screening decision (Tumlin and Green 2000). Cases that are screened in are referred for investigation, or if a state has a differential response system, they may be referred to that system either for assessment or investigation (see below). Cases that are screened out have no further contact with CPS unless there is another report, though the screener may refer the caller to other appropriate agencies (e.g., a family service agency or the police if the alleged perpetrator is not a caregiver).

The hotline worker needs to collect information in a wide array of areas, including material on (DePanfilis and Salus 2003, p. 30):

- Contacts for the child and family
- The alleged maltreatment (e.g., type, nature, severity, chronicity, and where it occurred)
- The child (e.g., the child's condition and behavior, which helps in evaluating whether the child is in immediate risk or danger and determining the urgency and type of the responses)
- The parent or caregiver (e.g., their emotional and physical condition, behavior, history, view of the child, child-rearing practices, and relationships outside of the family)
- The family (e.g., family characteristics such as household composition, dynamics, and supports)

This list suggests how challenging it can be to make screening decisions, since most reporters do not have in-depth information readily available when they make the report. Reporters vary considerably in the amount of information they can provide, ranging from detailed specifics of serious injuries to vague indicators of suspected maltreatment. Thus, decisions about whether to accept a case for investigation can be based on "skeletal" information, leaving some children still at risk of harm if suspected maltreatment is not investigated and other families unnecessarily involved in investigations when there is no need (Tumlin and Green 2000). CPS participants in Lee et al.'s focus groups (Lee et al. 2013) discussed the difficulties associated with missing report information, how mandated reporters are not trained to understand what information is the most critical, and how hotline intake workers often neglect to ask for vital information that CPS investigators need to locate the alleged victim(s).

State Rates of Screening In

According to the most recent NCANDS report from 2011 data, overall 60.8 % of referrals to child protective services were screened in (US Department of Health and Human Services 2012). However, states varied considerably in the proportion of cases they screened in. In 2011, the rate varied from a low of 24.4 % (Vermont) to a high of 98.6 % (Alabama). Differences in screening rates do not necessarily reflect differences in states' attention to the problem of child maltreatment—states organize their screening and assessment processes differently. Not only do states vary among themselves, but some data suggest that state screening rates vary over time in response to the number of reports and the availability of resources. Tumlin and Green (2000) cite a 1995 survey showing that almost half of child welfare administrators reported that their screening policies excluded a higher proportion of cases than they had 5 years earlier by using more stringent criteria for accepting a case.

The overall state rate can be misleading, as there can be substantial differences between counties within a state. Tumlin and Green (2000) cite a 1996 California report showing that the overall screen out rate of 32 % encompassed a wide range across counties, from a low of 19 % in Los Angeles to a high of 55 % in Contra Costa. Wells et al.'s (1995) study found that screen out rates ranged from 1 to 71 % in 12 local agencies across 4 states, although Wells and colleagues did not report variation within state.

Factors Related to Screening

Wells and colleagues examined agency, community, worker, and case factors associated with the screening decision (Wells et al. 1995, 2004). The small sample of sites and the ambiguity of the statistical analysis make results by community difficult to interpret. However, across these 12 agencies, the screen out rate was significantly higher when agencies had a larger number of reports and when communities had a larger number of families with children, suggesting that the amount of demand may have an impact on how many cases can be screened in. Lower median income and higher proportion of neglect reports (which may be a function of income) also predicted screening cases out. It is hard to know how to interpret this, but one possibility that should be explored is that with lower median income, many reports of neglect may be a function of poverty, which CPS agencies may prefer to refer to other agencies rather than handle as child maltreatment cases (Wells et al. 2004). Again, resources played a role, as screen outs were more likely when workers reported in a survey conducted for the study that resource availability was a factor in screening decisions. Wells et al. (2004) also reported that screening out cases was more likely when workers reported that they held a narrower view of CPS responsibility, although this should be interpreted cautiously, as it is not clear from the article how Wells et al. measured this and how their statistical results support this conclusion.

The initial study using this sample data (Wells et al. 1995) examined case factors that predicted whether cases would be screened in or out. Calls from mandated reporters or from others outside the family were more likely to be screened in than calls from alleged victims, alleged perpetrators, family members, or friends. Wells et al. do not suggest reasons why calls from mandated reporters and others outside the family were more likely to be screened in, but possible explanations include a greater likelihood of encountering actual child maltreatment, greater access to information about the maltreatment, greater ability to recognize it and/or report it accurately and thoroughly, and greater credibility. A call was more likely to be screened in if it reported an injury and if the allegation concerned sexual abuse. Calls were more likely to be screened out if they lacked specific information about maltreatment, if they were less complete, and if the identity of perpetrator and the household type (two parents, single parent, single parent with paramour, etc.) were unknown. Investigation was most likely when children were under age 2 and least likely for teenagers. Close examination of the cases led Wells et al. to state that "one of the most startling findings of this study was the degree to which some agencies were not investigating what appeared to be bona fide allegations of child maltreatment" (p. 542).

Investigation and Substantiation

Unless a case is diverted to a differential response pathway (see below), cases that are screened in receive a formal investigation of maltreatment by child protective services. Within a specified time period that is typically determined by statute or policy, child protective investigators need to assess the child's situation and make decisions about whether a report of child maltreatment is substantiated or not substantiated (sometimes other terminology is used to describe the same process). Many states have a third category that represents the inability to determine the truth of an allegation—this category is called *indicated* in NCANDs and NSCAW, though states use different terms such as *inconclusive*. Although the focus in investigation is mostly on evaluating the truth about suspicions of maltreatment and assessing children's safety, most states also require CPS to provide families with short-term services if needed during the investigation (Walter R. McDonald and Associates 2003).

Substantiation is important for several reasons. It is a public statement about the abuse, it leads to families being maintained in child protective service records (most states expunge records on unsubstantiated cases immediately or within 3 years), and it can be a factor in decisions to remove children from the home and involve families in court supervision (Kohl et al. 2009). Most importantly, it affects the likelihood of a family receiving ongoing child protective services. Some states limit ongoing child protective service delivery to substantiated cases, and in all states, service delivery is much more likely for substantiated than unsubstantiated cases. Overall, substantiated cases are about twice as likely to receive ongoing child protective services as unsubstantiated cases (Kohl et al. 2009; see also US Department of Health and Human Services 2007, 2012). Nevertheless, an unsubstantiated designation does not have to mean an ineffectual child protective intervention, because even an unsubstantiated investigation can lead to service delivery in some cases and can facilitate intervention during the investigation phase to increase children and families' safety and well-being.

DePanfilis and Salus (2003) describe the substantiation decision as a result of the answers to two questions which are presented by legislative definitions of child maltreatment (see Cross and Casanueva 2009):

1. Is the harm to the child severe enough to constitute child maltreatment?
2. Is there sufficient evidence that the harm is caused by child maltreatment?

Drake (1996) developed a theoretical model of substantiation related to these questions in which thresholds of both harm and evidence must be met for a case to be substantiated. Cross and Casanueva's (2009) analysis of NSCAW data found that this model predicted substantiation well for the vast majority of cases, but not all. Indeed, child age and gender were significant predictors even when harm and evidence were statistically controlled, suggesting that there are other case factors influencing the substantiation decision. The level of evidence was the strongest predictor of substantiation, and in 9 % of cases, the report was not substantiated even though case worker rated harm to the child as moderate to severe. Both theory (Drake 1996) and empirical research (e.g., Cross and Casanueva 2009; Kohl et al. 2009) suggest that one cannot necessarily conclude from an unsubstantiated designation that maltreatment did not occur or that a child was not harmed, because of the need for evidence to substantiate a case.

State Rates of Substantiation

According to the most recent NCANDS data (US Department of Health and Human Service 2012), of the 3.7 million children nationwide who were subjects of at least one report, 18.5 % cases were substantiated. However, the substantiation rate varied substantially between states, from a low of 5.83 % (Kansas) to a high of 55.96 % (Georgia). The causes of this variation have not been thoroughly studied (Wulczyn 2009). Differences in state criteria, procedures, and policies for substantiation seem to play a role (Paxson and Waldfogel 2002; Straus and Moore 1990). For example, to substantiate physical abuse, states differ in how severe an injury must be and whether or not the child must experience severe harm. On sexual abuse, states differ on defining the range of who is considered a caregiver of the child and therefore is dealt with by the child protection system in addition to the criminal justice system. States vary in the strictness of the evidence standards they apply to determining child maltreatment, from reasonable suspicion, credible evidence, or probable cause on one end to preponderance of evidence, material evidence, and clear and convincing evidence on the other end (US Department of Health and Human Services 2012). Fluke et al. (2001) found a difference in substantiation rates by the evidence standard; Levine (1998), on the other hand, found no statistically significant effect of the evidence standard, although apparently he examined a narrower range of evidence standards. States with the third indeterminate option have smaller proportions of cases in the unsubstantiated category than cases with only the two options of substantiated and unsubstantiated (Child Welfare Information Gateway 2003). One might also think there was a relationship between screening and substantiation, with states that screened in more cases substantiating fewer and vice versa, but Tumlin and Green (2000) found no such relationship in their analysis.

Factors Related to Substantiation

Agency factors play a role in substantiation (Child Welfare Information Gateway 2003). Studies of practice (see Depanfilis and Girvin 2005; English et al. 2002 for reviews) and a survey of CPS administrators (Walter R. McDonald and Associates 2003) suggest that the availability of resources affects substantiation rate, but Cross and Casanueva (2009) found no studies with case-based data that tested this hypothesis. Reports by CPS supervisors of the cohesiveness of their work units and their supportiveness to workers predict a lower substantiation rate (Child Welfare Information Gateway 2003). Stress from a high workload predicted a higher substantiation rate; possible explanations posited for this included overuse of an indeterminate category and more hurried investigations tending to lead to substantiation (Child Welfare Information Gateway 2003).

Which worker is investigating appears to make a difference, as caseworker experience, self-reported skills, supportive relationships with co-workers, and stated adherence to state policy were all related to a lower probability of substantiation (Child Welfare Information Gateway 2003). In McGee's (1989) study of substantiation decisions, worker burnout was identified as a factor in how quickly decisions might be made and whether these decisions were altered when new information suggested a possibly different outcome. More so than years in child protection or professional experience, Lamb (1979) found that workers' educational level had a stronger association with substantiation, indicating that those workers with master's degrees were likely to judge cases less severely than workers without advanced degrees.

Case factors also predict substantiation. Several studies have found that reports by professionals are more likely to be substantiated than reports by nonprofessionals (King et al. 2013), and King et al. found that reports by law enforcement, medical professionals, and workers in public agencies had the highest substantiation rates. Cases involving girls have been found to be more likely to be substantiated than cases with boys (Cross and Casanueva 2009; English et al. 2002). Findings are mixed on child age (see, e.g., Child Welfare Information Gateway 2003; Cross and Casanueva 2009; Eckenrode et al. 1988; English et al. 2002; Trocmé et al. 1995; Fluke et al. 2001; Winefield and Bradley 1992). Not surprisingly, a number of parent problems that plausibly affect risk and harm to the child are also associated with substantiation, including reduced income and employment, parental history of assaultive behavior, domestic violence, parental substance abuse, significant parental health or mental health impairment, and history of maltreating another child (Child Welfare Information Gateway 2003).

Service Delivery Following Investigation

The CPS investigation is completed within a specified period of time that varies between states, typically ranging from 14 to 30 days (Walter R. McDonald and Associates 2003). In a large majority of cases, children are not placed outside the home (see below), and CPS must then decide whether to offer families ongoing services (DePanfilis and Salus 2003). In most states, it is possible to offer services in either substantiated or unsubstantiated cases, but a 2003 study of CPS systems found that 11 states restricted child protective service delivery to cases with substantiated child maltreatment (Walter R. McDonald and Associates 2003). Which families are offered services varies by state and even sometimes by county and depends on both policy and availability of services (DePanfilis and Salus 2003). Depending on the state system, these services could be provided by ongoing public CPS workers or private child welfare or human service agencies with financial support from CPS contracts. If CPS keeps the case open, a public agency or private agency caseworker will visit the family periodically to provide support and monitoring, and CPS may also pay for a range of services such as homemaking, respite care, and mental health services. In many cases, participation is voluntary, but court orders may also be sought requiring families to participate.

State Rates of Service Delivery

The latest NCANDS report data (US Department of Health and Human Services 2012) shows such extreme variation across states in the proportion of families receiving post-CPS response services that the meaning and accuracy of these proportions are questionable. The rates ranged from 100 % of substantiated cases receiving services (3 states) to 21.5 % (District of Columbia) and from 100 % of unsubstantiated cases receiving services (Iowa) to 2.7 % (District of Columbia). We conducted further analysis of numbers from the NCANDS report (Tables 6.3 to 6.5, pp. 89–91) to exclude children placed out of home and to focus specifically on CPS service delivery in in-home cases (we discuss out-of-home placement separately below). We found that the rate of providing in-home services ranged from 100 % (3 states) to 0.21 % (District of Columbia). We have found no studies, however, comparing communities or agencies on CPS service delivery.

Factors Related to Service Delivery

Few studies have examined what variables predict whether families receive ongoing child protective services, and those that have did not separate out cases in which children were placed outside the home, making it difficult to determine which families receive services when CPS has decided that children should remain in the home. Most of the analysis that has been done has examined the relationship between substantiation and service delivery. Our understanding of the process suggests a number of reasons that substantiation may be more likely to lead to services: (1) it may indicate a higher likelihood of actual maltreatment, which could indicate greater need; (2) it may be associated with more thorough assessment; (3) caseworkers may perceive greater need in cases they have substantiated; (4) families may feel a greater need to adhere to CPS service recommendations in cases in which maltreatment has been officially sanctioned by being substantiated; and (5) substantiated cases may be more likely to have court mandates. However, service delivery is not necessary or possible in every substantiated case. Drake and Jonson-Reid (2007) list a number of such circumstances: isolated or past events, situations in which the perpetrator no longer has access to the child, and clients who decline further involvement but whose cases are not egregious enough to obtain a court order mandating services.

An analysis of the first cohort of the National Survey of Child and Adolescent Well-Being (NSCAW I) examined the relationship between substantiation and various forms of service delivery (US Department of Health and Human Services 2007). Children in substantiated and unsubstantiated cases did not differ significantly across measures of child well-being such as scales measuring behavior problems, cognitive deficits, and language delay. However, children were more likely to be provided with CPS services or to be referred for services in substantiated cases (77.4 %) than in indicated (57.7 %) or unsubstantiated cases (30.4 %). Children in substantiated cases were still significantly more likely to receive services 12 months after the investigation. Yet, when the analysis examined the specific services of formal assessments for emotional or behavioral problems, and referrals to mental health and special education services, there was no significant difference between substantiated and unsubstantiated cases. These services are typically provided by non-CPS agencies; they may result from a referral from CPS, but they may also come about from families seeking or being referred to these services in other ways. English et al. (2002) found that 86 % of substantiated (founded) cases in Washington State were recommended services, compared to 59 % in both inconclusive and unfounded cases. Looking at those cases that received service recommendations, 77 % of families in which maltreatment had been substantiated engaged with those services, compared to only 54 % in inconclusive cases and 52 % in unfounded cases.

Jud et al. (2012) examined predictors of the delivery of CPS services or referral to specialized services following Canadian child protective service investigations, which led to these services in 59 % of cases. The following variables were all substantial predictors in a multilevel statistical model, increasing the odds of receiving services by 1.79 or greater: the substantiation of a variety of types of maltreatment, including exposure to intimate partner violence, child functioning problems, lack of social supports, and financial issues. The model also revealed substantial differences between provinces in service delivery. The limitations of this study for the current chapter are the following: (a) Jud et al.'s analysis includes out-of-home placements, which we see as fundamentally different from service delivery in which children are left in the home, and (b) we do not know how well Canadian results apply to the US child protection system, which has been the focus of most of this chapter.

We conducted an analysis from the second cohort of the National Survey of Child and Adolescent Well-Being (NSCAW II) to examine the differences between US cases that received ongoing child protective services and those that did not. Because some children come into contact with CPS for reasons other than abuse and neglect (such as having a substance-abusing parent, domestic violence, child in need of services for emotional and behavioral problems, etc.) and are not representative of most mandated reporting situations, the NSCAW sample for our analysis was restricted to cases in which there was an abuse or neglect allegation. These included physical abuse, sexual abuse, emotional abuse, physical neglect, supervision neglect, abandonment, moral abuse, and educational maltreatments. For this analysis, we also excluded cases with out-of-home placements, because of our wish to focus on in-home cases.

The sample size for the analysis was 2,546. Overall, 24 % of cases received ongoing CPS services. As in studies cited above, substantiated cases were much more likely to receive ongoing CPS services (45 %) compared to unsubstantiated cases (18 %). This had the largest impact on service delivery. Not surprisingly, the caseworker judgments of harm, risk, and evidence that Cross and Casanueva (2009) found to predict substantiation also predicted service delivery. We tested 14 different measures of children's cognitive, developmental, and behavioral-emotional problems. CPS services were significantly more likely when children had language delays (31 % vs. 21 % without) or deficits in daily living skills (35 % vs. 25 % without). Paradoxically, CPS service provision was significantly *less* likely when children had cognitive difficulties with applied problem solving (28 % vs. 16 % without). Otherwise there were no significant differences by child well-being measures. There was a statistical trend ($p = .08$) for children under age 2 and youths aged 12–17 to receive CPS services compared to children in the middle and another trend ($p = .07$) toward families with prior reports being more likely to receive CPS services. The following variables that were tested were not significantly related to whether ongoing CPS services were provided: child sex, most serious type of child maltreatment, caregiver depression, caregiver alcohol abuse, caregiver substance abuse, caregiver experience of domestic violence, family income, and urbanicity. Therefore, overall, there is a strong relationship of ongoing CPS service delivery to the substantiation decision that maltreatment occurred, but there is only a modest relationship to child and family problems or other characteristics.

Child Placement

The responsibility of CPS is to try to maintain children safely in their homes. However, in some cases where this is not possible or not practicable and there is no less intrusive alternative, CPS places children outside of the home to protect their safety. Children are removed in only a fairly small minority of cases (see below), but the consequences can be profound and varied, making this perhaps the most difficult decision CPS has to make. Workers may lack training to make this decision effectively (Glisson 1996). Removing children from the home can literally save their lives if children are at substantial risk. However, it can also cause children considerable distress, disrupt their relationships with their parents, and cause havoc to family life.

Children can be removed immediately in emergency placements for brief periods during investigations. For longer placements, CPS must petition civil courts to transfer custody to the agency in order to proceed with a placement, and parents can contest this petition. Children can be placed with kin or foster parents; smaller percentages are placed in residential or group care. CPS policy is to reunify children with their families when possible. If, after a reasonable period of time, this is determined to be impossible without jeopardizing children's safety, CPS will seek a permanent home for children through adoption, guardianship, independent living, or other options.

State Rate of Child Placement

We again conducted further analysis of numbers from the NCANDS report (Tables 6.3 to 6.5, pp. 89–91) to examine the percentage of investigations that led to child placement outside the home. For every state but Hawaii, the placement rate ranged from 2 % (Delaware and New Hampshire) to 14 % (California); Hawaii was an outlier at 28 %. Differences in intervention philosophy, policy, and procedure could well affect the proportion of children placed outside the home, but we are aware of no empirical study that explains differences in state rates of foster care placement.

Factors Related to Child Placement

A number of studies have examined community, agency, and situational factors related to the likelihood of child placement. Community variables associated with higher placement rates include poverty, child care burden, residential mobility, female-headed households, lack of education, and crime (Jantz et al. 2012; Lery 2009; Wulczyn and Lery 2007). Jantz et al. (2012) found that the effect of such social disorganization variables on the likelihood of placement was greater in African American communities. Freisthler and colleagues (2007) even found a relationship between the number of liquor stores in a community and the child placement rate. It is not clear, however, to what extent community variables are related to child placement rates because of differing levels of risk, differing resources to prevent placement, or differing perceptions of communities by CPS workers (Jantz et al. 2012). Finding appropriate matches or bed space, caregivers' preferences, administrative expectations, funding constraints, time efficiency, and the child's perspective can all affect the decision where to place a child (Chor 2013; Jones 1993). Worker characteristics that might predict placement have not been adequately studied (Jones 1993).

Voluminous research has identified a number of case characteristics that predict placement (for reviews, see, e.g., Bhatti-Sinclair and Sutcliffe 2012; Jantz et al. 2012; Jones 1993; Ubbesen et al. 2013; Wulczyn et al. 2005). Placement is more likely when parents have substance abuse problems or a psychiatric history. A number of other parent background and behavior factors predict child placement:

perpetrator status of parents, parent lack of remorse, parent history of abuse, irresponsible partners, parent difficulty dealing with life stress, single parent stress, and nonuse of available support systems. Overall neglect is more likely to lead to placement than other forms of maltreatment, though it is unclear how much this applies to different age groups. Younger children are substantially more likely to be placed out of home. Wulczyn et al.'s analysis found that 18–20 % of children placed in foster care were infants under the age of one, while no other single age constituted more than 7 % of the sample (Wulczyn et al. 2007). Among infants, low birth weight and birth abnormalities predict placement (Needell and Barth 1998). Children over the age of 12 are much less likely to be placed out of home, perhaps because of workers' views that they were more likely to have a greater capacity to protect themselves; when older children were placed, it was primarily because of emotional or behavioral problems and not for protective purpose (Jones 1993). Most but not all studies have found African American children are more likely to be placed than White children (see Jantz et al. 2012). Though some literature suggests this reflects case factors correlated with race (such as the social disorganization variables discussed above), several studies have found direct effects of race even when confounding factors are controlled (Hill 2007; Jantz et al. 2012; Needell et al. 2003). Rivaux et al. (2008) found that workers were more likely to recommend placement for African Americans than for Whites at equivalent risk, suggesting that workers tolerate less risk for African American families. Some studies have found that families who are poor are at greater risk of child placement, despite the fact that it is an established principle that children should not be placed outside of the home merely because their families are poor (Eamon and Kopels 2004). Other studies, however, have not found this. Katz et al. (1986) found that poor families were more likely to experience child placement for physical abuse but less likely for neglect.

Differential Response

Until recently, the only way that most CPS systems could respond to allegations of child abuse and neglect was through an investigation. Over the past two decades, an increasing number of states are reforming their CPS systems through the implementation of differential response (DR)—as of 2011, 13 states had implemented DR statewide and 6 in pilot programs (National Quality Improvement Center for Differential Response in Child Protective Services 2011). DR has also been implemented extensively in Australia (Mathews and Bromfield 2012) and Canada (Trocme et al. 2003) and introduced in the United Kingdom (Platt 2001) and New Zealand (Waldegrave and Coy 2005). Loosely defined, DR allows CPS systems the flexibility to respond to screened-in reports of child maltreatment in more than one way, depending on the initial level of risk. In a CPS system that has implemented DR, once a case has been screened in, a second screening then occurs to determine the type of CPS response the family will receive. Moderate- to high-risk reports that include allegations of severe physical or sexual abuse, imminent risk of harm to a child, or a high likelihood of court involvement are assigned a traditional investigation and proceed through the child protection system in the same manner as any other investigations. In contrast, low- to moderate-risk reports, defined in a variety of ways (but generally more often involving neglect and emotional abuse), can receive a family assessment instead of an investigation. The focus of this assessment is on the child's and family's needs, rather than an investigation aimed at determining whether and to what extent a child has been maltreated. Families are visited by a CPS caseworker who engages them as active partners in the assessment and service planning process, which includes not only safety assessment but strengths and needs assessments. If the initial assessments change the worker's view of the level of risk present in the family, cases can be reassigned from a family assessment to an investigation. If the risk level remains low to moderate and the family has identified needs that would benefit from supportive services, services can be offered to the family following the assessment. Families may choose to accept these services, at which point an ongoing service case is opened. Alternatively, no service needs may be identified by the family or they may choose not to accept the offered services, and the case would be closed. Unlike an investigation, there is no formal substantiation decision about whether abuse or neglect occurred at the conclusion of a family assessment.

State Rates of Different Response

States vary considerably in the percentage of screened-in reports that receive a family assessment instead of an investigation. Illinois was at the lower end of the distribution with 8 % of screened-in reports in 2011 served by family assessment. This option was limited to families with no prior substantiated reports of maltreatment and current allegations of neglect or emotional maltreatment (Fuller et al. 2013). Nevada family assessment, which served 9 % of reported cases, was only open to children 6 years and older with allegations of educational neglect, environmental neglect, medical neglect, improper supervision, or inappropriate discipline with non-severe physical harm (Siegel et al. 2010). Three of the six New York counties that implemented differential response in a pilot study limited the family assessment response to reports of educational neglect (Ruppel et al. 2011), which equaled about 4–7 % of screened-in reports.

In other states, such as Minnesota and Ohio, the working assumption used by intake workers is that families will be provided with a family assessment response unless there are reasons why a traditional investigation has to be pursued. Reports that must be investigated include those that allege sexual abuse or serious harm to a child, those involving suspicions of child fatality or homicide, and those involving persons acting in place of parents (e.g., day care providers or foster parents) or child welfare workers. Because the eligibility criteria for a family assessment are more liberal in these states, a greater percentage of families receive them: over 50 % in Ohio and over 70 % in Minnesota (Loman et al. 2010; Loman and Siegel 2004). We are not aware of any studies that examine the relationship between case characteristics and referral to a differential response versus an investigation track.

The actual services provided to families in the assessment pathway can differ significantly from one county or state to the next. This is partially dependent on both the types of reports that are eligible to receive services and local service availability. Consistent with the focus on low- to moderate-risk reports, services provided through a family assessment are typically short term (60–90 days) and focus on the provision of concrete assistance, sometimes through the use of flexible funds offered to families (Fuller 2014). Other differential response programs have no extra funds available for services or cash assistance and must rely entirely on community referrals and informal supports (Siegel 2012). Some CPS agencies have combined differential response with other family-oriented approaches such as solution-based casework or family group decision making.

Estimating the Probability of Different Outcomes Following Reporting

In this section, we use results from the National Child Abuse and Neglect Data System (NCANDS) and the National Survey of Child and Adolescent Well-Being (NSCAW) to develop rough nationwide estimates of the probability of the different outcomes discussed above following reporting of child maltreatment. The percentage of cases screened out nationally was obtained directly from the latest NCANDS (US Department of Health and Human Services 2012) and was 39 %. The percentages for all other outcomes were derived by taking the percentage of cases screened in nationally from NCANDS (61 %) and multiplying that percentage by the percentage of cases in NSCAW that experienced different investigation or assessment outcomes from investigations (by design, all cases included in the NSCAW sample received either an investigation or a differential response assessment). NSCAW data used here came from caseworker interviews, except for the variable measuring whether CPS services were provided post-investigation, which, like NCANDS, came from administrative data. We recognize that these likelihoods would differ depending on the characteristics of the case and would vary across local communities and states. Nevertheless, we think that enough is known and enough is common across communities and states to permit a rough estimation that has useful implications for understanding some of the outcomes of reporting child maltreatment.

The estimated frequency of different investigation outcomes is presented in Table 20.1 and the estimated frequency of different service outcomes in Table 20.2. Table 20.1 shows that fairly small minorities of cases are either substantiated or receive a family assessment that eschews the substantiation decision. Most cases are either screened out or investigated and not substantiated. Table 20.2 shows that only a small percentage of cases feature out-of-home placement, but most cases in which children remain in the home do not receive services, either because they are

Table 20.1 Frequency of different investigation outcomes following reporting

Investigation outcome	%
Screened out	39
Differential response-assessment track	8
Investigated-unsubstantiated	42
Investigated-substantiated	11

Table 20.2 Frequency of different CPS service outcomes following reporting

Service outcome	%
Screened out	39
No services	43
In-home services	14
Out-of-home placement	4

screened out or because no CPS services are delivered following investigation or substantiation. Not receiving services may stem either from CPS not offering them or from families declining them. In an additional analysis, we found a major difference between substantiated and unsubstantiated cases in service delivery: 50 % of substantiated cases received services compared to 21 % of unsubstantiated cases.

Implications

This analysis has gone far afield, but now we bring it back to the situation of individuals reporting child maltreatment. What can they expect? Our review of outcomes of reporting suggests several conclusions we can draw that would interest reporters, child welfare professionals, and indeed the public at large.

Most Cases Receive a Modest Response

An individual contemplating reporting child maltreatment might imagine that their report might result in a vigorous child protective service response. However, in majorities of cases, the response is limited. Over half of the reports to CPS do not lead to families receiving ongoing child protective services. Most of these cases without services were screened out; but even some cases that are investigated and substantiated do not lead to services. Nor do all cases referred to the assessment track in differential response systems lead to services—contributing to this is the fact that participation is voluntary and some families decline services. The results on investigation are similarly modest—over half of the reports do not result in an investigation; the bulk of these because of screen outs and others because they are placed on an assessment track. Altogether, substantiation of child maltreatment occurs in about one quarter of reports. A caveat to our point about the modesty of the child protective response is that an intervention may have an effect even if the suspicions of maltreatment are not substantiated, as investigation can sometimes lead to service delivery even in unsubstantiated cases, and interventions undertaken during the investigation phase may in themselves have a positive effect.

We have no judgment about these results, as we cannot ascertain how often less vigorous and more vigorous responses are genuinely warranted. Our main point is that potential reporters may be surprised by the modesty of response in most cases, given that research suggests that many people who choose not to report are concerned about the negative impact of a vigorous child protective response. Sege et al. (2011) found that primary health-care providers who did not report certain cases indicated that, in addition to clinical factors, they were concerned about the impact on their relationships with the involved families and their "perceptions of expected outcomes of filing" (p. 464). In a review of the literature on mandated reporting, Alvarez and colleagues (Alvarez et al. 2004) list some of the more common reasons professionals fail to report their suspicions of maltreatment: they believe it is not in the best interest of the child to report; they fear that the report will result in further harm to the family/child; and they are concerned that the report will create further instability for a family, particularly if criminal charges result or a child is removed. Lee et al. (2013) include a direct quote from one investigator expressing her frustration with mandated reporters who fail to report: "I asked the (hospital) social worker, why didn't you guys call it in? Her exact word was, and my supervisor had me document it in my report, that the doctors do not want to call in because they don't want to testify in court" (p. 638). While it is true that the child protective response can be invasive to protect children's safety, in a large proportion of cases it is not—would those who choose to not report suspicions be more open to reporting if they knew the overall modesty of the response? Conversely, many people who do report hope that children and family receive services as an effect of their contact with CPS. They might be disappointed at the modest levels at which reported cases receive child welfare services—although mitigating this is the finding that children in investigated but unsubstantiated cases are as likely to receive formal assessments for emotional or behavioral problems—and referrals to mental health and special education services. To what extent is the modest response by CPS discouraging reporting? The modest response is not a reflection of modest need among families involved with CPS, as voluminous data point to substantial need in the entire child welfare population, in both cases that are substantiated and unsubstantiated and cases in which children are placed outside the home and remain at home (see, e.g., Casanueva et al. 2011; Ringeisen et al. 2011; US Department of Health and Human Services 2005, 2007). Perhaps the modesty of the response could be cited in calls for increasing resources for child protective services.

Information Plays an Important Role

Outcomes following reporting stem from decisions, mostly by CPS, based on information obtained through various forms of information gathering: screening, investigation (which ideally includes an assessment of children's well-being), and assessment in differential response. What decisions are made will depend on what information is available, but it can often be difficult to obtain information. The literature on screening reveals frequent challenges due to limited information. Information is similarly a key to the substantiation decision, since the amount of evidence of maltreatment is the most important predictor of whether a case is substantiated, and child protective service agencies will often complete investigations by their deadlines with insufficient information to make a judgment about whether or not maltreatment occurred. Likewise, information is central to making good child placement decisions, which depends on so many child, family, and environmental factors. It is also critical in differential response, since the decision to refer and keep families in an assessment pathway does not introduce the same level of scrutiny and social control that the investigation pathway entails. We do not know whether decreased information is likely to lead to increased or decreased rates of child placement and referral to differential response; it is likely, however, that decreased information is likely to lead to a higher rate of poor decisions.

In their examination of the decision-making process related to mandated reporting and child protection, Hughes and Rycus (2007) suggest that it is an iterative process, requiring skilled assessments throughout the life of the case. Further, it is their contention that decisions at each point can only be accurate and discerning when the information gathered is reliable and solid—clearly a concern, given the literature that indicates the numerous problems from the vantage points of reporter and intake worker. As discussed above, many reporters of child abuse and neglect provide only fragmentary or unclear information. Our attempt to examine these different outcomes of reporting underscores the need for clarification about "how much is enough" to make a report and to screen in a report for investigation. Unfortunately, quantification is an elusive concept in mandated reporting, and though no one would argue against additional training for mandated reporters, we recognize a paradox in this search for more prescriptive guidelines. To train mandated reporters to collect more detailed information may have an unintended consequence—absent their understanding of "how much is enough"; mandated reporters, already fearful that their suspicions are not enough, could fail to make reports, believing their information falls short of the threshold for reporting. Training of mandated reporters could reduce this risk by instructing reporters on which information is valuable and which is superfluous.

States and Communities Differ

Outcomes of reporting vary dramatically between states and communities. NCANDS reports significant differences between states on rates of screening in cases, substantiating allegations, providing child protective services, and placing children outside of the home. States also vary in whether they have a differential response system, and when they do, states differ dramatically in how often they use the assessment track. Even within state, agencies vary on screen in rates, substantiation, and child placement, and the New York State evaluation of differential response showed differences in the use of the assessment track by county (Ruppel et al. 2011). Several factors contribute to state and community differences, including differences in legislation, philosophy, training, and resources for information gathering and providing services. Thus it is somewhat misleading to talk about what a reporter might expect without knowing where that reporter lives.

Almost as astonishing as the variation between states on rates of these outcomes is the fact that this variation has mainly gone unstudied. Research is needed to assess the causes of this variation, as well as the variation between communities and agencies within a state, and understand the implications for policy and practice. One key question is the degree to which this variation stems from actual differences in state practice versus differences between states in measurement systems. Better standardization of measurement in NCANDS would help. In our view, it seems unlikely that the fact that Iowa reports a 100 % rate of delivering services in in-home cases and the District of Columbia a 0.21 % rate means that Iowans' hearts are full and Washingtonians' are made of stone. We are just speculating, but perhaps D. C. is effecting service delivery through outside agencies in a way that does not get recorded in NCANDS, or Iowa's service delivery includes some limited intervention that is not even counted in other states' statistics. They may also differ substantially in resource availability—see below for a discussion of resources. Better standardization of state data could help eliminate statistical anomalies and confusion.

Actual differences between states and communities on outcomes following reporting (above and beyond differences in measurement) raise questions about equity and may be of interest to advocates. The substantial variation suggests the value of communities developing their own statistical profiles of what happens following child maltreatment reports and comparing these to other communities within their state. We recommend that community children's service coalitions build such statistical profiles into their needs assessment and/or program evaluation efforts. Given a community statistical profile, our hypothetical reporter would have a better understanding of what will happen following reporting and may feel more ownership and more commitment to doing their part to maximizing the quality of the process. Moreover, local studies shared among multiple stakeholders of outcomes of reporting could inform community policy around the decision points reviewed here, helping to empower communities to achieve the outcomes of reporting that best match their values.

Outcomes Vary by Case Characteristics

Research has identified a number of case characteristics that predict outcomes following reporting. Variables such as type of maltreatment, age of child, and family's previous protective service history can have a major impact on what decisions are made in the child protective response. Thus what happens following reporting very much depends on the nature of the particular case. Differences in the probability of outcomes given reporting are magnified if a given case characteristic affects multiple decisions in the response process. Consider child age. Cases with children under the age of 2 are more likely to be screened in and also substantially more likely to be placed in out-of-home care. Thus, these children are more likely to have a more substantial child protective service response. Prior history with child protective services similarly may have a dramatic effect in increasing the magnitude of the response, because it increases the odds of screening in, substantiating, and placing children outside the home. Reporters who have a modicum of knowledge about influential case factors will be better able to anticipate what outcomes may result from reporting.

Not only do outcomes of reporting differ, but who the reporter is tends to differ depending on the characteristics of the case. Kesner (2008) compared the characteristics of cases reported by four different types of reporters: legal, medical, social service, and educational. Medical personnel report maltreatment for children who are almost 2 years younger on average than in every other group, an average of 5.2 years old. Younger age means more screening in and more child placement, so medical personnel may be more likely to encounter a more vigorous CPS response, and they accordingly may have greater concerns about family disruption from reporting. Educational personnel reported the oldest children, an average of 9.1 years, who have lower screening, service, and placement rates. These reporters' concerns may focus more on CPS inaction. Reports from legal and medical personnel were more likely than other reporters to identify neglect, while school personnel were more likely to report physical abuse than other reporter groups; again, these patterns can lead different outcomes. More work needs to be done on identifying profiles of outcomes by case characteristics and reporter types and considering whether procedures and training need to be adapted for these differences.

Resources May Affect Outcomes

This review also suggests that the resources that states and communities have for different response options are likely to affect outcomes of reporting. Although the empirical evidence is limited, several sources suggest that substantiation rates are lower for a given level of suspicion of maltreatment when resources are less available, and the likelihood of service delivery and child placement are lower for states and communities with fewer resources. Moreover, limited resources likely means less agency cohesiveness and support for workers, less compensation and training for workers, and more turnover. Agency stress, worker inexperience, and lack of education may add more unpredictability to outcomes, and the research cited above suggests it may also change outcomes by increasing substantiation rates, perhaps because substantiating an allegation is a safer call when a worker is stressed, unsupported, or uncertain. A call for more resources is a frequent cry by child advocates. The analysis of the outcomes of reporting and their relationship to resources could help provide persuasive evidence of the need for more resources.

One key resource variable is whether a state has developed a differential response system, and if so, what the capacity of this assessment track is to respond to reports. A substantial minority of states have differential response options, yet where they exist, they reduce the formal investigation rate and increase the proportion of families who receive services. There is variation in outcomes even within the subset of states that have differential response systems, since states differ dramatically in the proportion of reports they assign to the assessment and investigation tracks. Accordingly, greater resources are needed to fully implement differential response systems even when they have been initiated. Additional resources need to be devoted to supplying services to implement service plans developed in the assessment track; without these services, differential response can be a hollow offering.

Conclusion

Research and policy and practice discussions of each of the decisions explored here are usually conducted in isolation. Rarely is the discussion of reporting child maltreatment placed in the context of what comes afterward. Outcomes of reporting should not influence the mandated decision to report, but a consideration of outcomes would help shape effective policy, practice, and training around reporting. Although we have been able to assemble a substantial number of empirical results, it should be noted that the variation in outcomes of reporting is still largely unexplained, particularly differences between states and communities. More research is needed to explicate the system of response to reporting and relate it to the reporting decision. More research is also needed on the effects of the quantity, quality, and salience of information provided by reporters. Studies should also examine more thoroughly the impact of different child protective and service interventions within such understudied categories as unsubstantiated cases and substantiated cases that do not receive ongoing child protective services. Research should actually track cases from reporting to final outcome and should gather empirical evidence about prospective reporters' anticipation of the outcomes of reporting and how that affects their decision to report. Program evaluations of state and local child protective service agencies also need to gather data on these decisions and report on the entire profile of outcomes of reporting to inform the development of policy and practice.

References

Alvarez, K., Kenny, M., Donohue, B., & Carpin, K. (2004). Why are professionals failing to initiate mandated reports of child maltreatment, and are there any empirically based training programs to assist professionals in the reporting process? *Aggression and Violence Behavior, 9*(5), 563–578. doi:10.1016/j.avb.2003.07.001.

Bhatti-Sinclair, K., & Sutcliffe, C. (2012). What determines the out-of-home placement of children in the USA? *Children & Youth Services Review, 34*(9), 1749–1755. doi:10.1016/j.childyouth.2012.05.004.

Casanueva, C., Ringeisen, H., Wilson, E., Smith, K., & Dolan, M. (2011). *NSCAW II baseline report: Child well-being* (OPRE report #2011-27b). Washington, DC: Office of Planning, Research and Evaluation, Administration for Children and Families, U.S. Department of Health and Human Services. http://www.acf.hhs.gov/programs/opre/resource/nscaw-ii-baseline-report-child-well-being-final-report. Accessed 7 Jan 2015

Child Welfare Information Gateway. (2003). *Decision-making in unsubstantiated child protective services cases: Synthesis of recent research.* https://www.childwelfare.gov/pubs/focus/decisionmaking/decisionmaking.pdf. Accessed 11 Jan 2007.

Chor, K. H. B. (2013). Overview of out-of-home placements and placement decision-making in child welfare. *Journal of Public Child Welfare, 7*(3), 298–328. doi:10.1080/15548732.2013.779357.

Cross, T. P., & Casanueva, C. (2009). Caseworker judgments and substantiation. *Child Maltreatment, 14*(1), 38–52. doi:10.1177/1077559508318400.

DePanfilis, D., & Girvin, H. (2005). Investigating child maltreatment in out-of-home care: Barriers to effective decision-making. *Children and Youth Services Review, 27*(4), 353–374. doi:10.1016/j.childyouth.2004.11.010.

DePanfilis, D., & Salus, M. K. (2003). *Child protective services: A guide for caseworkers.* Washington, DC: U.S. Department of Health and Human Services. http://www.ssw.umaryland.edu/faculty_and_research/bios/depanfilis/cps.pdf. Accessed 18 Oct 2013.

Dolan, M., Smith, K., Casanueva, C., & Ringeisen, H. (2011). *NSCAW II baseline report: Introduction to NSCAW II* (OPRE report #2011-27a). Washington, DC: Office of Planning, Research and Evaluation, Administration for Children and Families, U.S. Department of Health and Human Services. http://www.acf.hhs.gov/programs/opre/resource/nscaw-ii-baseline-reportintroduction-to-nscaw-ii-final-report. Accessed 18 Oct 2013.

Drake, B. (1996). Unraveling "unsubstantiated". *Child Maltreatment, 1*(3), 261–271. doi:10.1177/1077559596001003008.

Drake, B., & Jonson-Reid, M. (2007). A response to Melton based on the best available data. *Child Abuse & Neglect, 31*(4), 343–360. doi:10.1016/j.chiabu.2006.08.009.

Eamon, M. K., & Kopels, S. (2004). 'For reasons of poverty': Court challenges to child welfare practices and mandated programs. *Children and Youth Services Review, 26*(9), 821–836. doi:10.1016/j.childyouth.2004.02.023.

Eckenrode, J., Powers, J., Doris, J., Munsch, J., & Bolger, N. (1988). Substantiation of child abuse and neglect reports. *Journal of Consulting and Clinical Psychology, 56*(1), 9–16. doi:10.1037//0022-006X.56.1.9.

English, D. J., Marshall, D. B., Coghlan, L., Brummel, S., & Orme, M. (2002). Causes and consequences of the substantiation decision in Washington State Child Protective Services. *Children and Youth Services Review, 24*, 817–851. doi:10.1016/S0190-7409(02)00241-4.

Finkelhor, D., & Wells, M. (2003). Improving data systems about juvenile victimization in the United States. *Child Abuse & Neglect, 27*(1), 77–102. doi:10.1016/S0145-2134(02)00508-2.

Fluke, J., Parry, C., Shapiro, P., Hollinshead, D., Bollenbacher, V., Baumann, D., & Davis-Brom, K. (2001). *The dynamics of unsubstantiated reports: A multi-state study*. Englewood: The American Humane Association.

Freisthler, B., Gruenewald, P. J., Remer, L. G., Lery, B., & Needell, B. (2007). Exploring the spatial dynamics of alcohol outlets and child protective services referrals, substantiations, and foster care entries. *Child Maltreatment, 12*(2), 114–124. doi:10.1177/1077559507300107.

Fuller, T. (2014). Beyond investigations: Differential response in child protective services. In J. E. Korbin & R. D. Krugman (Eds.), *Handbook of child maltreatment* (pp. 443–461). Dordrecht: Springer.

Fuller, T., Nieto, M., & Zhang, S. (2013). *Differential response in Illinois: Final evaluation report.* Urbana: Children and Family Research Center, University of Illinois at Urbana-Champaign.

Glisson, C. (1996). Judicial and service decisions for children entering state custody: The limited role of mental health. *Social Service Review, 70*(2), 257–281. doi:10.1086/604182.

Hill, R. B. (2007). *An analysis of racial/ethnic disproportionality and disparity at the national, state, and county levels*. Baltimore, MD: The Annie E. Casey Foundation.

Hughes, R. C., & Rycus, J. S. (2007). Issues in risk assessment in child protective services. *Journal of Public Child Welfare, 1*(1), 85–116. doi:10.1300/J479v01n01_05.

Jantz, I., Rolock, N., Leathers, S. J., Dettlaff, A. J., & Gleeson, J. P. (2012). Substitute care entry: The relationship between race or ethnicity and levels of county organization. *Child Abuse & Neglect, 36*(11/12), 771–781. doi:10.1016/j.chiabu.2012.08.002.

Jones, L. (1993). Decision making in child welfare: A critical review of the literature. *Child & Adolescent Social Work Journal, 10*(3), 241–262. doi:10.1007/BF00757822.

Jud, A., Fallon, B., & Trocmé, N. (2012). Who gets services and who does not? Multi-level approach to the decision for ongoing child welfare or referral to specialized services. *Children and Youth Services Review, 34*(5), 983–988. doi:10.1016/j.childyouth.2012.01.030.

Katz, M. H., Hampton, R. L., Newberger, E. H., Bowles, R. T., & Snyder, J. C. (1986). Returning children home: Clinical decision making in cases of child abuse and neglect. *American Journal of Orthopsychiatry, 56*(2), 253–262. doi:10.1111/j.1939-0025.1986.tb02725.x.

Kesner, J. (2008). Child protection in the United States: An examination of mandated reporting of child maltreatment. *Child Indicators Research, 1*(4), 397–410. doi:10.1007/s12187-008-9019-1.

King, B., Lawson, J., & Putnam-Hornstein, E. (2013). Examining the evidence: Reporter identity, allegation type, and sociodemographic characteristics as predictors of maltreatment substantiation. *Child Maltreatment, 18*, 232–244. doi:10.1177/1077559513508001.

Kohl, P., Jonson-Reid, M., & Drake, R. (2009). Time to leave substantiation behind: Findings from a national probability study. *Child Maltreatment, 14*, 17–26.

Lamb, K. L. (1979). *Outcomes of child abuse complaints: Caseworkers as predictors*. Ph.D. dissertation. University of Arizona: Tempe, AZ.

Lee, S., Sobeck, J., Djelaj, V., & Agius, E. (2013). When practice and policy collide: Child welfare workers' perceptions of investigation processes. *Children and Youth Services Review, 35*(4), 634–641. doi:10.1016/j.childyouth.2013.01.004.

Lery, B. (2009). Neighborhood structure and foster care entry risk: The role of spatial scale in defining neighborhoods. *Children and Youth Services Review, 31*(3), 331–337. doi:10.1016/j.childyouth.2008.08.001.

Levine, M. (1998). Do standards of proof affect decision making in child protection investigations? *Law and Human Behavior, 22*(3), 341–347. doi:10.1023/A:1025710707682.

Loman, L. A., & Siegel, G. L. (2004). *Minnesota alternative response evaluation: Final report*. St. Louis: Institute of Applied Research. www.iarst.org/papers/ARFinalEvalautionReport.pdf Accessed 7 Jan 2015

Loman, L. A., Filonow, C. S., & Siegel, G. (2010). *Ohio alternative response evaluation: Final report*. St. Louis: Institute of Applied Research.

Mathews, B., & Bromfield, L. (2012). Australian laws and policies on child neglect. In H. Dubowitz (Ed.), *World perspectives on child abuse* (pp. 61–66). Aurora: ISPCAN.

McGee, R. A. (1989). Burnout and professional decision making: An analogue study. *Journal of Counseling Psychology, 36*(3), 345–351. doi:10.1037/0022-0167.36.3.345.

National Quality Improvement Center for Differential Response in Child Protective Services. (2011). *Differential response in child protective services: A literature review*. Version 2. Englewood, CO: Author.
Needell, B., & Barth, R. P. (1998). Infants entering foster care compared to other infants using birth status indicators. *Child Abuse & Neglect, 22*(12), 1179–1187. doi:10.1016/S0145-2134(98)00096-9.
Needell, B., Brookhart, M. A., & Lee, S. (2003). Black children and foster care placement in California. *Children and Youth Services Review, 25*(5/6), 393–408. doi:10.1016/S0190-7409(03)00028-8.
Paxson, C., & Waldfogel, J. (2002). Work, welfare, and child maltreatment. *Journal of Labor Economics, 20*(3), 435–474. doi:10.1086/339609.
Platt, D. (2001). Refocusing children's services: Evaluation of an initial assessment process. *Child and Family Social Work, 6*, 139–148.
Ringeisen, H., Casanueva, C., Smith, K., & Dolan, M. (2011). *NSCAW II baseline report: Caregiver health and services* (OPRE report #2011-27d). Washington, DC: Office of Planning, Research and Evaluation, Administration for Children and Families, U.S. Department of Health and Human Services. http://www.acf.hhs.gov/programs/opre/resources/nscaw-ii-baseline-report-caregiver-health-and-services. Accessed 7 Jan 2015
Rivaux, S. L., James, J., Wittenstrom, K., Baumann, D., Sheets, J., Henry, J., & Jeffries, V. (2008). The intersection of race, poverty, and risk: Understanding the decision to provide services to clients and to remove children. *Child Welfare, 87*(2), 151–168.
Ruppel, J., Huang, Y., & Haulenbeek, G. (2011). *Differential response in child protective services in New York State: Implementation, initial outcomes and impacts of pilot project*. Albany: New York State Office of Children and Family Services.
Sege, R., Flaherty, E., Jones, R., Price, L. L., Harris, D., Slora, E., Abney, D., & Wasserman, R. (2011). To report or not to report: Examination of the initial primary care management of suspicious childhood injuries. *Academic Pediatrics, 11*(6), 460–466. doi:10.1016/j.acap.2011.08.005.
Seigel, G. L. (2012). *Lessons from the beginning of differential response: Why it works and when it doesn't*. St. Louis: Institute of Applied Research. www.iarstl.org. Accessed 7 Jan 2015
Siegel, G. L., Filonow, C. S., & Loman, L. A. (2010). *Differential response in Nevada final evaluation report*. St. Louis: Institute of Applied Research. www.iarstl.org. Accessed 7 Jan 2015
Straus, M. A., & Moore, D. W. (1990). Differences among states in child abuse rates and programs. In D. J. Besharov (Ed.), *Family violence: Research and public policy issues* (pp. 150–163). Washington, DC: AEI Press.
Trocmé, N., Tam, K. K., & McPhee, D. (1995). Correlates of substantiation of maltreatment in child welfare investigation. In J. Hudson & B. Galaway (Eds.), *Child welfare in Canada: Research and policy implications* (pp. 20–39). Toronto: Thompson Educational Press.
Trocmé, N., Knott, T., & Knoke, D. (2003). *An overview of differential response models*. Toronto: Centre of Excellence for Child Welfare, Faculty of Social Work, University of Toronto. www.ct.gov/dcf/lib/dcf/drs/pdf/pc-dr-overview-models.pdf. Accessed 7 Jan 2015
Tumlin, K., & Green, R. (2000). *The decision to investigate: Understanding state child welfare screening policies and practices*. Washington, DC: The Urban Institute. www.urban.org/pdf/anf_a38.pdf. Accessed 7 Jan 2015
U.S. Department of Health and Human Services, Administration for Children and Families. (2005). *National Survey of Child and Adolescent Well-Being: CPS sample component, Wave 1 data analysis report*. Washington, DC: Author.
U.S. Department of Health and Human Services, Administration on Children and Families. (2007). *No. 9: Does substantiation of child maltreatment relate to child well-being and service receipt?* (National survey of child and adolescent well-being). http://www.acf.hhs.gov/sites/default/files/opre/substan_child_0.pdf. Accessed 18 Oct 2013.
U.S. Department of Health and Human Services, Administration for Children and Families, Administration on Children, Youth and Families, Children's Bureau. (2012). *Child maltreatment 2011*. Washington, DC: Children's Bureau. Retrieved from http://www.acf.hhs.gov/programs/cb/research-data-technology/statistics-research/child-maltreatment. Accessed 8 Oct 2013

Ubbesen, M. B., Petersen, L., Mortensen, P. B., & Kristensen, O. S. (2013). Temporal stability of entries and predictors for entry into out-of-home care before the third birthday: A Danish population-based study of entries from 1981 to 2008. *Children and Youth Services Review, 35*(9), 1526–1535. doi:10.1016/j.childyouth.2013.05.020.

Waldegrave, S., & Coy, F. (2005). A differential response model for child protection in New Zealand: Supporting more timely and effective responses to notifications. *Social Policy Journal of New Zealand, 25*, 32–48.

Walter R. McDonald & Associates. (2003). *National study of child protective services systems and reform efforts*. Denver: Walter R. McDonald & Associates. Retrieved from http://aspe.hhs.gov/hsp/cps-status03/. Accessed 18 Oct 2013.

Wells, S. J. (1997). Screening for child protective services: Do we accept a report? How do we respond? In T. D. Morton & W. Holder (Eds.), *Decision making in children's protective services* (pp. 94–106). Atlanta: Child Welfare Institute.

Wells, S. J., Fluke, J., & Brown, C. H. (1995). The decision to investigate: Child protection practice in 12 local agencies. *Children and Youth Services Review, 17*(4), 523–546. doi:10.1016/0190-7409(95)00037-D.

Wells, S. J., Lyons, P., Doueck, H. J., Brown, C. H., & Thomas, J. (2004). Ecological factors and screening in child protective services. *Children and Youth Services Review, 26*, 981–997.

Winefield, H. R., & Bradley, P. W. (1992). Substantiation of reported child abuse or neglect: Predictors and implications. *Child Abuse & Neglect, 16*, 661–671.

Wulczyn, F. (2009). Epidemiological perspective on maltreatment prevention. *The Future of Children, 19*(2), 39–66. doi:10.1353/foc.0.0029.

Wulczyn, F., & Lery, B. (2007). *Racial disparity in foster care admissions*. Chicago: Chapin Hall at the University of Chicago.

Wulczyn, F., Barth, R., Yuan, Y., Jones Harden, B., & Landsverk, J. (2005). *Beyond common sense: Child welfare, child well-being, and the evidence for policy reform*. New York: Aldine Transaction.

Wulczyn, F., Chen, L., & Hislop, K. B. (2007). *Foster care dynamics 2000–2005: A report from the Multistate Foster Care Data Archive*. Chicago: Chapin Hall Center for Children at the University of Chicago.

Chapter 21
Rethinking the Functioning of Child Protective Services

John D. Fluke and Katherine Casillas

Chapter Abstract

When considering the concerns about mandatory reporting, it is helpful to consider that adequate child protection is rarely tied to a single policy concern and that it is ultimately based on the capability of the systems of interventions and the decisions about these interventions made by all involved parties including professionals, families, and children. No matter how a case comes to the attention of child protection services (CPS), decision-making at the CPS continuum points (intake, assessment, and so on) regulates the flow of families and children into or out of the CPS system. At its core, a basic purpose of the CPS system across the decision-making continuum is to protect children from harm; however, the meaning of the concept of harm is surprisingly unclear which has important implications for effective decision-making. Almost without exception, decision-making in child welfare occurs under conditions of risk and more frequently conditions of uncertainty. It is generally also acknowledged that decision-making errors are inevitable in CPS and at the worst involve situations of severe avoidable maltreatment or even fatalities. The lack of knowledge regarding our understanding of harm and the commission of errors hinders the development of feedback mechanisms that might allow for a better understanding of whether CPS is effective. In the absence of this knowledge, research has little to offer concerning the evaluation of CPS effectiveness.

J.D. Fluke (✉) • K. Casillas
Department of Pediatrics, Kempe Center for the Prevention of Child Abuse and Neglect, University of Colorado School of Medicine, Aurora, CO, USA
e-mail: info@americanhumane.org

B. Mathews, D.C. Bross (eds.), *Mandatory Reporting Laws and the Identification of Severe Child Abuse and Neglect*, Child Maltreatment 4,
DOI 10.1007/978-94-017-9685-9_21

This paper makes an argument for altering CPS decisional state space in a way that acknowledges and utilizes features of child and family functioning tied more directly to a research-based understanding of patterns of short- and long-term harm, as well as, improvements in well-being. It is premised on the very basic idea that specific groups or classes of families would benefit from a differentiated continuum of decision processes that can tie them more directly to the evidence-based services that would benefit them and their children more optimally. It assumes that the understanding of safety and well-being are grounded in a better evidence base than exists currently and that decision-making in CPS will become more risk based rather than being based in uncertainty. It also offers a long-term general research framework directed toward changing the CPS decisional state space.

Overview

When considering the concerns about mandatory reporting, it is helpful to consider that adequate child protection is rarely tied to a single policy concern and that it is ultimately based on the capability of the systems of interventions and the decisions about these interventions made by all involved parties including professionals, families, and children. Thus, a broader view of context and systems is required, and therefore mandatory reporting may have an exaggerated role if presented in a "picture" where other important concerns have yet to be addressed. The first section of this paper describes the CPS system and then goes on to address a question regarding the effective functioning of the system, a difficult prospect to address and one for which a definitive answer probably cannot be informed with the existing research base. Following this discussion regarding the gaps in our understanding, some possible approaches to improve CPS functioning are presented.

The CPS System and Decisions

CPS generally consists of an initial intake service and an investigation or assessment process. However, depending on the state, province, or county, CPS sometimes includes in-home services and may often include initial placement activities as well. Each of these service processes has beginning and ending points that are tied to a decision along a continuum. Decisions at these continuum points regulate the flow of families and children into or out of the CPS system. These decisions are illustrated in the figure (Fig. 21.1), which references the CPS decision-making continuum, that is to say, that each point along the continuum depends on the assessment and decision made at the prior point.

From the illustration above, mandatory reporting functions in the early part of the continuum in as much as the decision to report to CPS influences the CPS screening decisions. However, once the screening decision is made, children and

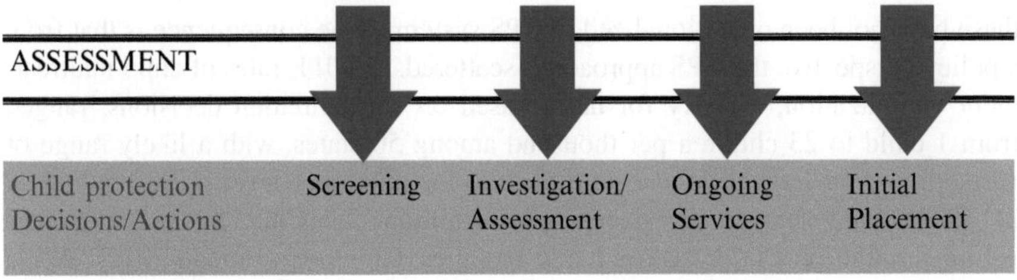

Fig. 21.1 Child protective services decision-making continuum (Baumann et al. 2011)

families must respond to an array of possible interventions with both positive and negative consequences that often have little to do with the originator of the report. The intent of this paper is to contextualize the functioning of the CPS system, what could be done to improve its functioning, and what research is needed to improve system functioning and outcomes for children and families. In addressing these concerns, the paper takes a decision-making perspective based on the theoretical framework referred to as the Decision Making Ecology/General Assessment and Decision Making Model (Baumann et al. 2011).

What Does Research Tell Us About the Current Functioning of Child Protective Services?

At its core, a basic purpose of the CPS system across the decision-making continuum is to protect children from harm or further harm and to protect children from being maltreated. However, the meaning of the concept of harm is surprisingly unclear, which as discussed here makes it difficult to assess how well the system is functioning.

A Word About Definitions, Concepts of Harm, Policy, and Role of CPS

In articulating CPS functions, it is important to consider that in the United States within the social services sector, it is far from clear what is meant by concepts of harm to children. Further, other sectors (health, judicial) that have an impact on CPS functioning have divergent perspectives about what constitutes harm due in part to differences in their experiences (samples) with children and families, the roles these sectors play in civil society, and the nature of their organizational stakeholders.

This is aside from the related issue of the difficulty of the meaning of CPS substantiation (Drake 1996). While some efforts have been made to develop standardized methods to define abuse and neglect (Heyman and Smith Slep 2006), thus far these have not been operationalized in CPS systems. One consequence is that from a policy perspective the CPS approach is scattered. In 2011, rates of child maltreatment victimization, a proxy for harm based on substantiation decisions, ranged from 1 child to 23 children per thousand among 50 states, with a likely range of variability even larger at the county or sub-jurisdictional level (US Department of Health and Human Services, Administration for Children and Families, Administration on Children, Youth and Families, Children's Bureau 2012). While the unknown level of underlying actual incidence of maltreatment may in fact vary from jurisdiction to jurisdiction, the variability in officially recognized maltreatment by CPS agencies most likely reflects heterogeneity in the implementation of decision-making policy (Baumann et al. 2011).

Among the related persistent issues for CPS is the definition of various forms of child maltreatment; generally speaking abuse, deprivation of necessities, sexual maltreatment, and psychological abuse. One thing we know is that estimates of maltreatment incidence and prevalence vary by the type of measurement we use and the source of measurement. There is a major gap in overall incidence and prevalence rates in comparing official statistics with self-report studies or NIS like studies (Sedlak et al. 2010). There are also major differences depending on the source of official data (e.g., Hospital ICD 10 vs. CPS) (Gilbert et al. 2012).

We have also not done a good job of clearly identifying relevant distinctions between key harm-related constructs including maltreatment, risk of harm, and severity of harm (Sedlak et al. 2010). A common concept is to consider risk of future reporting or future substantiation, and there appears to be some relationships between concrete indicators of severe harm with risk (Baird et al. 1993). Nevertheless, it is not clear whether the bulk of moderate to high risk cases is at all likely to experience harm or at least severe harm, and some sense that important indicators of harm, particularly for neglect, are likely to be distal (Widom et al. 2012). Except in a very broad and highly ambiguous sense as of yet, there are no consistent definitions that lend themselves to clearly informing policy and practice in addressing what is meant by harm. Perhaps, more importantly, we lack a shared understanding of harm that would lend clarity to improving outcomes for children and families, although the concept of trauma and the underlying genetic impacts may come closest (Mehta et al. 2013).

Unfortunately, when the layers are peeled back often, what CPS is left with is the responsibility for fairly rare but obviously severe harm events: fatalities, severe physical injuries, and extreme cases of neglect including confinement and starvation that afflict very young children. However clear this view is of CPS' responsibility; attention focused in this direction rarely succeeds in improving the underlying severe harm event frequency; that is, changes directed at CPS systems on this basis appear to be unable to prevent similar events in the future. For example, the reported level of fatalities known to CPS has not changed much during the past 20 years (DHHS 2012). Of course, part of the reason is that the solutions for CPS systems scrutinized for their failures to protect children against fatalities and other low-frequency events typically result in blame being placed on decision-makers, the introduction of overly prescriptive policy, commensurate with a lack of attention to conditions in the system that make errors likely (Munro 2011).

Formal Assessment Tools Such as Risk and Safety

Assessments or assessment processes are a key part of the decision-making process, and for many professionals and administrators in CPS, these are the first and last method for improving decision-making. Many formal assessments are designed to support decisions along the CPS/CW continuum. For example, the National Resource Center for Child Protective Services (NRCCPS 2010) has documented many of the risk and safety instruments currently in use in states and some of the policy. However, this line of research has languished, and in fact, compared to the 1990s, there is very little published research. Almost no innovative research in the way of new approaches to CPS assessment and decision support has been published, although some important development without peer-reviewed research has occurred (Turnell and Edwards 1999).

To the extent we know how well these tools and processes function, the evidence suggests that they are modestly effective at prediction and probably work better under controlled evaluation conditions compared to actual practice (Camasso and Jagannathan 2012; Shlonsky and Wanger 2005). Still, they are better than nothing, and the research is sufficient to suggest that they should be used. However, there are fundamental research questions about how they should be used and whether actual decision-making can be improved upon. For some time these questions have not been pursued, and one is left with the impression that we have solved the problem.

Decisions

Assessments are important but have important limitations in supporting decision-making in CPS. Mostly this is due to contextualizing issues as illustrated by the Decision Making Ecology/General Assessment and Decision Making Model (DME/GADM) concept (Baumann et al. 2011). A key concept is the action threshold embedded in the GADM, separating assessment from action. In several studies, factors other than case characteristics have been found to influence decisions. The function of context and decision-maker characteristics at each point along the decision continuum is the focal point for determining how decisions are impacted by factors other than case assessment. This has been instructive in looking at service and placement decisions, thus far. There is also fertile ground for exploring issues of disparities, but this is ultimately limited by our understanding of decision errors (see below).

Who's the Decider?

Decisions are actually made by a number of agents in CPS. While caseworkers are obvious and important decision-making agents, there are potentially many others depending on the system and the point on the decision continuum. In addition to the other agents such as supervisors and judges, an important area of decision-making work involves decisions in groups. These can be professional groups (e.g., team decision-making and red team models) or some combination of professional and family groups (e.g., family group conferences). There is some evidence that decisions involving groups are effective, but many of the same DME factors that influence individual decision-makers also operate with groups. Each decision-maker brings their own history and understanding of the system into the process and evaluates the likely perceived consequences in the context of their values (Baumann et al. 2011). Studies of how the range of decision-makers including groups affects decisions in CPS are needed in order to take these effects into account and devise better workforce and workforce development policies.

Decision Errors and Error Criteria

Decision-making errors are present in CPS decision-making and at the worst involve situations of severe avoidable maltreatment or even fatalities. Balancing these errors are service decisions that may have adverse perhaps distal (longer-term) impacts on children's outcomes, including the possibility that placements may play a role in these outcomes (Doyle 2008). Without exception, decision-making in child welfare occurs under conditions of risk and most often under conditions of uncertainty (Wakker 2010). A major conundrum for CPS administrators, and that ties into our confusion about concepts of child maltreatment related harm, is to clarify what type of error their system would least like to make and then design policy and resources accordingly to reinforce this perspective.

Unfortunately, and regardless of values perspectives, there is an absence of information that would allow us to objectively determine which type of error valuing is best. This condition is called decision-making under uncertainty. This is in part because, despite our recognition of the presence of these errors, we have no idea how often they are made or broadly speaking why. As a consequence, we have only a very limited capacity to avoid errors. It would be naïve to assume that these errors occur due solely to a specific factor like judgment, training, resources, or policy although these all play a role. Nevertheless, the lack of knowledge regarding the commission of errors and the interplay of these many factors hinders the development of feedback mechanisms that might allow for better pattern recognition and valid expertise.

James Mansell and colleagues (2011) have had some success in defining errors for CPS decision-making at intake: the decision to respond to a referral with an assessment/investigation. Their study attempts to define the problem as one of decision-making under risk, rather than uncertainty which is more typical. They found that, in the presence of a major increase in the proportion of cases investigated, some children that should have been investigated/assessed are still missed. They were able to specify a response rate balance between the likelihood that an agency will fail to act when they should have or exceed the available financial resources by responding more often than they should have. Given the ability to quantify the balance point, the agency is able to articulate the likely degree of defined error going forward. One of the findings of their study is that the agency actually did a fairly good job of distinguishing cases that required an investigation at the intake point.[1]

The difficulty and challenges in researching similar errors for decisions related to other points along the decision-making continuum, and in particular removals, are well recognized. There is no gold standard that will tell us that we should or should not remove a child.

To summarize, there is an absence of clarity around the expectations of the CPS system, and if we acknowledge that a basic role of CPS is decision-making, the lack of clarity is compounded because we have no real method to evaluate error. So, in answer to the question posed above about what research has to say about the functioning of the CPS system, it has as yet little to offer regarding whether CPS is functioning well or poorly overall.

Addressing Complex Needs in the Context of Improving CPS Functioning and Child Well-Being

Modifications to the CPS State Space

The continuum of CPS decision-making is a systems construct, and it classically defines the structure of the response pattern in the form of a decisional state space (Wakker 2010). That is, the actionable decisions are defined consistently as a series of choices: the state space. In the CPS state space for each individual family or child, an evaluation of the consequences of the decisions at each point is made. Some decisions, like intake decisions with immediately observable outcomes, appear to have a greater decisional consensus (narrower range of variability) compared to decisions where the consequences are less well understood, and it may be more straightforward to transform these to decision-making under risk, where outcome probabilities can be determined. Unfortunately, decision-making under conditions of risk in CPS is rare (Mansell et al. 2011). For the most part, conditions of decision-making under uncertainty prevail, meaning that the probability of decision outcomes is objectively difficult to specify even after the decision is made.

So perhaps another way to approach the problem of decision-making under uncertainty in CPS is to modify the state space for decisions, that is, modify the available choices in the continuum. Triage has been discussed as an important aspect of CPS systems that may permit different configurations of decisions. One approach to triage is differential response which in some jurisdictions has emerged

[1] >0.90 area under the receiver operator characteristics (ROC) curve, where 1.0, is completely accurate, and 0.5 is random.

as a formal response to maltreatment (Merkel-Holguin et al. 2006). Another approach might be to distinguish different classes of familial conditions (Casillas and Fluke 2014; Trocme, 2013, personal communication). For example, Trocmé (2013, personal communication) has suggested that maltreatment reports could be classified as acute and chronic, and maltreatment may be a secondary concern. Drake et al. (2009) have argued that the substantiation decision is superfluous and should be discarded in favor of identifying reported maltreatment cases as open or not for ongoing services. These approaches represent different formulations of child maltreatment decisional state space in as much as they focus attention on attaining information where the focus is on taking actions. To be clear, a decision to substantiate may permit or inhibit taking actions in some jurisdictions, but there is no information content from the standpoint of what action to take.

One possible advantage of orienting the system differently is that classes of families and children could be more clearly aligned with their likely proximal and distal outcomes. These outcomes would necessarily encompass both safety and well-being. Given this perspective, one way of thinking about an assessment process is to identify the possible outcomes based on classification and create a more fine grained and distally integrated view of the possible decisional consequences for taking actions or not. This idea while beyond our current base of research is described from a conceptual perspective in more detail in the following sections.

Intensity and Multidimensionality of Needs

Needs among children in the child welfare system can be defined as cognitive and socioemotional conditions relating to emotional/behavioral disturbances, speech/language impairments, and learning/developmental delays. These problems are particularly important as they occur at a much higher rate compared with children in the general population (USDHHS-ACF 2007a). Child welfare studies estimate that 23–80 % of children exhibit mental health problems, while chronic health problems range from 35 to 80 %, and educational difficulties range between 31 and 67 % (Chernoff et al. 1994; Clausen et al. 1998; Pilowsky 1995; Schor 1982; Simms 1989; Stein et al. 1996; Szilagyi 1998). Using a representative US sample, NSCAW showed that within 3 years of a child welfare investigation 22 % of children have been identified as having a learning disability (vs. 8 % of US children), 15 % with an emotional disturbance (vs. 6 %), and 13 % with a speech impairment (vs. 5–9 %; USDHHS-ACF 2007a). Similar numbers have been found in Australia, Sweden, and Canada (Bromfield et al. 2010; Hessle and Vinnerljung 1999; Trocmé et al. 2010). Compounding these problems, it appears to be the norm that children with a special need tend to have multiple needs. In fact, 42 % of children in this US National Survey of Child and Adolescent Well-Being (NSCAW) who were identified as having a special need actually had two identified needs, and another 31 % had three or more needs (USDHHS-ACF 2007a).

Likewise, caregivers exhibit a number of service needs, including substance abuse, mental health problems, and cognitive impairments. Some of these needs are especially pervasive. For example, in one study of families involved in a child welfare investigation, Burns and colleagues found that 40 % of mothers suffered from depression (Burns et al. 2009). The mental health needs of caregivers of young children (ages 1 to 4 years) in the NSCAW seem to be similar, with 46 % of caregivers experiencing major depression at some point across the 5- to 6-year wave 5 follow-up (USDHHS-ACF 2009). Furthermore, 40 % of caregivers of young children had major depression at more than one point in time. Likewise, caseworkers' reports on families with an infant or adolescent show that caregivers abuse alcohol (7–14 %) and drugs (8–30 %) and have serious mental health problems (18–23 %), cognitive impairments (7–11 %), poor parenting skills (41–43 %), and unrealistic expectations of their child (15–22 %; USDHHS-ACF 2008a, b). As with children followed in the same study, these problems tend to co-occur (USDHHS-ACF 2009). Other co-occurring needs include basic living assistance (33 %, e.g., transportation, food, housing), child care assistance (30 %), individual services (19 %, e.g., job-related, support groups, legal aid), and home assistance services (12 %, e.g., home management training; USDHHS-ACF 2008a). While these issues come from US child welfare data, similar challenges are also of concern in other nations such as Australia (Bromfield et al. 2010), Canada (Burnside 2012), England (Cleaver et al. 2007), and Scotland (Rosengard et al. 2007).

Underservicing of Needs

Unfortunately, it appears that both child and family needs are being underserviced in the current child welfare context. With respect to children, findings from the NSCAW indicate that children investigated for child maltreatment in the United States have a much greater risk of cognitive and socioemotional problems when compared with normed national samples (USDHHS-ACF 2005). However, they are not receiving needed services. Depending on the time of assessment, between 35 and 42 % of children assessed at baseline when they were 3 years of age or younger had a developmental delay or an established medical condition or will have developed one within the next 5–6 years. Yet only 10–26 % of those in need received necessary developmental or medical services, with percentages worsening the longer children were involved with the child welfare system (USDHHS-ACF 2007b). Similarly, although 31 % of preschoolers had cognitive deficits and 27 % had behavior problems, only 13 % and 12 %, respectively, of those in need received special educational services to address them (USDHHS-ACF 2005). The situation is similar for school-age children investigated for maltreatment in the United States. Depending on the measure, 5–12 % of school-age children exhibited cognitive development or academic achievement risks (intelligence, reading, math), and another 10–45 % exhibited developmental risk on one or more socioemotional measures (problem behavior, social skills, living skills, depression). Yet, only 54 % of those school-age children who exhibited risk on at least one of the measures were receiving special education services for cognitive/academic difficulties and 25 % for socioemotional functioning (USDHHS-ACF 2005).

With respect to caregivers, although 27 % had a mental health need, a minimum of 26 % of those in need received a mental health service (USDHHS-ACF 2008a). Most often the mental health service received was psychotropic medication, with few actually ever seeing a mental health practitioner. Similarly, almost no caregivers of infants received substance abuse services (though 30 % were in need). The services more often provided were basic living assistance (33 %, e.g., transportation, food, housing), child care assistance (30 %), individual services (19 %, e.g., job-related, support groups, legal aid), and home assistance services (12 %, e.g., home management training; USDHHS-ACF 2008a).

Although far fewer children and caregivers receive services than those in need, involvement with child welfare has been shown to increase service receipt. That is, similar children and families who are not involved with the child welfare system are even less likely to receive needed services. For instance, across child age groups, there is an increase in receipt of school-based or specialty mental health services for child welfare cases (Leslie et al. 2005). Thus, despite high levels of unmet need, the ability of the child welfare system to connect families to services is promising.

However, consistent with the DME framework (Baumann et al. 2011), factors other than the type of services needed appear to influence which services are received. For example, for children 3 years and under, the percentage of those with developmental or medical risks receiving services does not differ from the percentage of those without such risk receiving services. Furthermore, although children in substantiated and unsubstantiated cases have similar special needs (Drake 1996; USDHHS-ACF 2007c), service receipt is instead best predicted by substantiation and poverty, irrespective of current developmental status (at least between baseline and 12-month follow-up for children 3 years and under; USDHHS-ACF 2007b). This is important because services are being implemented similarly across clients regardless of their actual need, resulting in wasted service provision for some, and lack of service provision for others that actually need it. Such inadvertent care translates into financial waste or potential deterioration in functioning depending on which group is in question. The child welfare field must better understand these complex needs that touch multiple systems and better integrate across systems to get those needs addressed.

Absence of Integrative Assessment Protocols and Decision-Making Processes

There is an absence of integrated assessment protocols. On one hand, a variety of organizations have issued guidelines and screening tools for the assessment and treatment of children, including the array of issues faced by children and caregivers involved in the child welfare system (American Academy of Child and Adolescent Psychiatry 1997a, b, 2007; Spivak et al. 2006; Scottish Executive 2005). The set of tools as a whole cover just about every issue possibly faced by any family. Yet concrete guidance is missing on how and when to use this information, and this disconnect is crucial given the high degree of complexity in both the lives of children and families and the service system of which they are a part. In order to proceed effectively, guidance is needed with respect to organizing multiple assessments across different problem domains, coordination of care across multiple needs, and selection and timing of specific empirically supported treatments or interventions (Johnson et al. 2006; Lou et al. 2006).

We face an almost identical problem in decision-making for treatment planning and service integration, service configuration, and alignment of service resources. To date, most of the intervention and treatment research have relied on variable-centered approaches, which assume all individuals come from the same population. Perhaps as a product of this, as well as our focus on internal over external validity, most evidence-based treatments are designed for single conditions or groups of closely related conditions (e.g., a cluster of anxiety disorders with partially overlapping symptoms). However, the high degree of comorbidity of conditions calls this approach into question. Recent studies of treatment effectiveness have found decreases in effectiveness as impairment increases, if co-occurring conditions are present or if multiple concrete needs are observed (Curry et al. 2006; Hinshaw 2007; Jensen et al. 2007; Owens and Chard 2003). These findings seem to indicate that children and families with multiple needs should be identified and provided with applicable services, perhaps using collaborative, cross-system approaches. However, we would argue that treatment-as-usual is not enough nor is mere coordination (Bickman 1996). Rather than just determining which cross-systems approaches are needed, so too must we determine how to prioritize, order, integrate, and allocate multiple services.

The Role of CPS in Screening and Prioritizing Needs

Child welfare can be viewed as a surveillance and referral system that is dealing with decisions regarding a complex array of needs for both children and their caregivers. In and across systems beyond child welfare, there are certain barriers to effective care for the social, educational, and health-care needs of children and families. These systems rarely interact in the United States, and when they do, the inherent structure within each does not promote the sharing of information or the integration of services. Yet, as the gatekeepers to many needed supports and services, some barriers are contained or controlled by the child welfare system. Obstacles that could hinder a caseworker from helping children and families receive effective care include skill deficits in assessment, engagement, and referral (Burns et al. 2009). Without effectively knowing how to best screen for and prioritize needs, appropriate referrals are all but impossible.

Figuring out needs is no simple task. Assessments must be comprehensive enough to identify an array of needs while maintaining speed, accuracy, and client engagement. Once needs are ascertained, those posing the greatest risk are prioritized and balanced with the stated desires of the clients. If needs are multiple and complex, the assessment process may need to include multiple and contingent steps including consultation with mental health or other system representatives. Again, the desires and input of the client are critical along every step to obtain needs that are meaningful and to promote client engagement (Gibbs 2003; Gibbs and Gambrill 2002). Like a medical screening test, screening for multiple and complex needs should come first, followed by substantial assessment by the requisite professional. Ideally, whenever possible, families must be involved and engaged in ways that help them to define and articulate their needs. Despite the existence of statements regarding the importance of screening, there is little guidance let alone research concerning what assessments or assessment process to use and when or what professionals should conduct these processes.

The Role of Child Welfare in Service Engagement and Tracking Outcomes

Child welfare caseworkers also have a key role in getting children and families to the *right* supports and services. In part, some knowledge is needed about which evidence-based practices are best for which problems. Additionally, knowledge of the family's support network and the community service base is necessary, including which services are at least evidence informed or evidence based. Finally, referral skills are needed to be able to describe and share the nature of the problem, as well as engage and build a relationship with supports and services. Client input and engagement are again critical.

In order to address well-being, child welfare also needs to be able to monitor well-being outcomes. Completing services does not just mean showing up.

Studies in the psychotherapy literature have found that improved client outcomes can be achieved simply by providing ongoing feedback (Lambert et al. 2001), and this common factor should be considered when setting up case plans. Goals should be achievable, some in the short term, and client feedback on progress should be regularly provided. However, there may be insufficient outcome monitoring supports and structures in child welfare settings (Burns et al. 2009), hindering the delivery of effective services. Monitoring outcomes must be a part of services from the beginning stages of engagement in order to reinforce positive changes and be alerted to movement in the other direction. Practitioners of course have the flexibility to adjust the intervention to tailor it to individual client needs yet need to keep a consistent measure of change that can be shared with the child welfare system. It almost goes without saying, especially in populations with multiple needs, that transitioning back and forth between implementing an intervention and evaluating ongoing change is particularly necessary in cases where the intervention was modified to fit a client's needs (Mildon et al. 2014).

We have argued based on the research regarding co-occurring conditions among child welfare populations (Fluke et al. 2008) that one missing aspect of information obstructing the implementation of effective programs and practices is a better understanding of these conditions and how often they occur. For example, NSCAW has provided us an extensive national review of the special needs among children in the child welfare system (i.e., developmental, behavioral, and emotional, USDHHS-ACF 2007a), but we still do not have any comprehensive national-level estimates of the need for various services *which focus on more than a few critical needs at one time*. Missing to date for child welfare is a valid starting point for identifying treatment subgroups early on that, in turn, can guide integrated assessment, treatment planning, and service delivery. As opposed to variable-centered process, or a focus on maltreatment and maltreatment-centered information, a person-oriented approach asserts that human development must be understood by examining multiple factors in relation to one another (Magnusson 1995). According to this theory, development is a product of the pattern of relevant factors, and the related research requires identifying configurations of factors that distinguish different subgroups (Bergman and Magnusson 1997; Magnusson 1998). Thus far, with some exception, attention has been paid to isolating and enumerating single conditions that could be the focus of empirically supported programs and practices. For example, such conditions could be caregivers with substance abuse issues, children who experience types of maltreatment, children who experience trauma, and family poverty. Taken together, these individual enumerations constitute an overall profile of the needs of children and families (Samuels 2012; USDHHS-ACF 2007a).

Combined interventions have proven advantages and improved robustness when addressing more severe individual needs or multiple conditions (Curry et al. 2006; Hinshaw 2007; Jensen et al. 2007; Owens and Chard 2003). We would argue that it is important, also, to know how to prioritize needs in order to guide a superior matched combination and ordering of effective programs and practices, including evidenced-based practices. From a child welfare service delivery system perspective, this concept leads to other implications. For one, the information could be used for planning purposes to determine how many families would benefit from specific interventions. For another, it would be crucial in identifying gaps in the fabric of the existing array of evidence-based treatments and services. In addition, some combinations of treatment type, dose, and timing may work better than others. Further, families are typically already overwhelmed when they come to the attention of child welfare. They cannot do everything at once, and some decisions need to be made with respect to what should be addressed first. No doubt, the family should have some say. But so, too, should the evidence.

This goal is not easy to achieve but, if successful, could result in a practical model that can successfully account for the complexity of these conditions, one that both systematically organizes the cases for intervention planning and evaluation and retains the complexities of the underlying conditions. These prospects at the system level hold a great deal of promise with respect to implementing empirically supported interventions and may be vital if the expectations regarding such interventions are to be realized.

The immediate implication is that we would need to be prepared to invest resources differently in order to change the state space. It may also help to clarify very difficult decisions (deeply uncertain decision-making) such as when it is appropriate to remove a child. Underlying the revised state space is the commonly understood idea that not all families and children will benefit from the same set of services and responses. This conceptualization allows for a much more systemic approach since there would be sufficient number of families and children in each class to justify the creation of service delivery system for the class (Casillas and Fluke 2014) and the resulting quantification of the resources needed to do so.

What Areas of Research Are Crucial to Defining and Evaluating an Initiative That Would Improve CPS Functioning and Outcomes?

As a practical matter, and even if it could be well justified, a systems shift of this nature described above could not be accomplished at once. For one, the research base to understand decision-making errors is hardly developed at all in child welfare. Furthermore, the infrastructure to provide effective services to different classes of families does not exist, even though efforts to promulgate evidence-supported assessment processes and related interventions with high fidelity implementation are underway. Even so, one clear example of CPS state space modification is differential response: a policy framework that is currently being adopted by many jurisdictions. Finally, it may be that the most expeditious change in classification would be to focus CPS responses only on family conditions where proximal safety outcomes are the concern; thus, the CPS response would only be offered to a small fraction of the current reported volume of maltreatment reports.

Is state space modification for CPS a realistic strategy for improving CPS functioning? Obviously, this question would need to be reframed for different audiences, and there is no clear answer, just some beginning points for discussion, piloting, evaluation, and research.

An overall goal would be to systematically define alternative service delivery systems with different decisional state spaces for distinct classes of families. As described above, once a set of classes is defined, it would be possible to define a continuum of CPS responses that are most appropriate based on describing the demographics, behavioral conditions, and outcome probabilities (both safety and well-being).

This of course is a retrospective approach. The more difficult task would be to develop an accurate and reliable methodology to classify families at the point of intake and possibly refine the classification during an assessment phase. While risk of future harm is certainly an important ingredient, classification based solely on our current approach to risk and safety assessment is not likely to be very productive since, for many classes, risk and safety ratings would not necessarily be able to distinguish differences, that is, reporting risk is likely to be the same between classes. Other types of assessment including multi-criteria assessments of risk (rather than rereporting risk) would become more prominent, and specific assessments designed for the class would need to be developed. Ideally, any assessment utilized would have some evidence of scientific support and ideally be well supported. In the view of this author, a valid severity of harm rating and a rating for chronicity would have to be one of the assessment elements included, though perhaps, only for some classes. Furthermore, these assessments must be designed with proximal and distal outcomes of well-being in mind.

Figure 21.2 provides an illustration of a state space diagram describing how a modified CPS system might be configured. Systematically, at each node, a decision is required about what level and type of assessment is needed tied to a statistical classification system for families like the one described above. As the assessment progresses and more information are organized for each family, the classifications may shift and a family may be recategorized. Ultimately, a decision regarding the configuration of services is made. The state space framework assumes that the CPS agency will commit to services for as long as necessary, but no longer to resolve the underlying conditions. It also assumes that the configuration of possible decision pathways is complex but that it is finite based on the classes of the population of families exposed to the system. Importantly, the framework assumes that the commonly understood child welfare continuum would need to be modified in ways that are consistent with the family need-based framework classes, as described below. Finally, it is apparent that the greatest investment in analysis and decision-making occurs after a child protection matter comes to the attention of CPS, irrespective of the way in which the CPS agency is notified about a possible CPS matter.

Overview and Examples of Key Efforts to Support Development of Research-Based Models to Improve CPS Functioning and Outcomes

The development of a research-based CPS decisional state space framework along the lines described above would be an ambitious initiative, would be long-term, and no doubt would be daunting to achieve. We believe at least small steps in this direction could be productive and have potential to produce a more effective system and fulfill the promise of a child-centered and family-focused service.

There are three main ingredients that need to be assembled for this to be a possibility. First, we need to formulate classes of CPS families that share common needs around which we can begin to assemble the best array of evidence-based services and develop implementation tests to determine if outcomes are improved in the presence of these services. Second we think computer simulation is likely to be the most productive way to model the behavior of the CPS system agents in order to test different probability configurations of decisional state space and assess the amount of decisional error that can be anticipated. Third, we need to develop ways to determine decisional error, that is, contextually based ways to determine when errors in decision-making actually occur in the continuum.

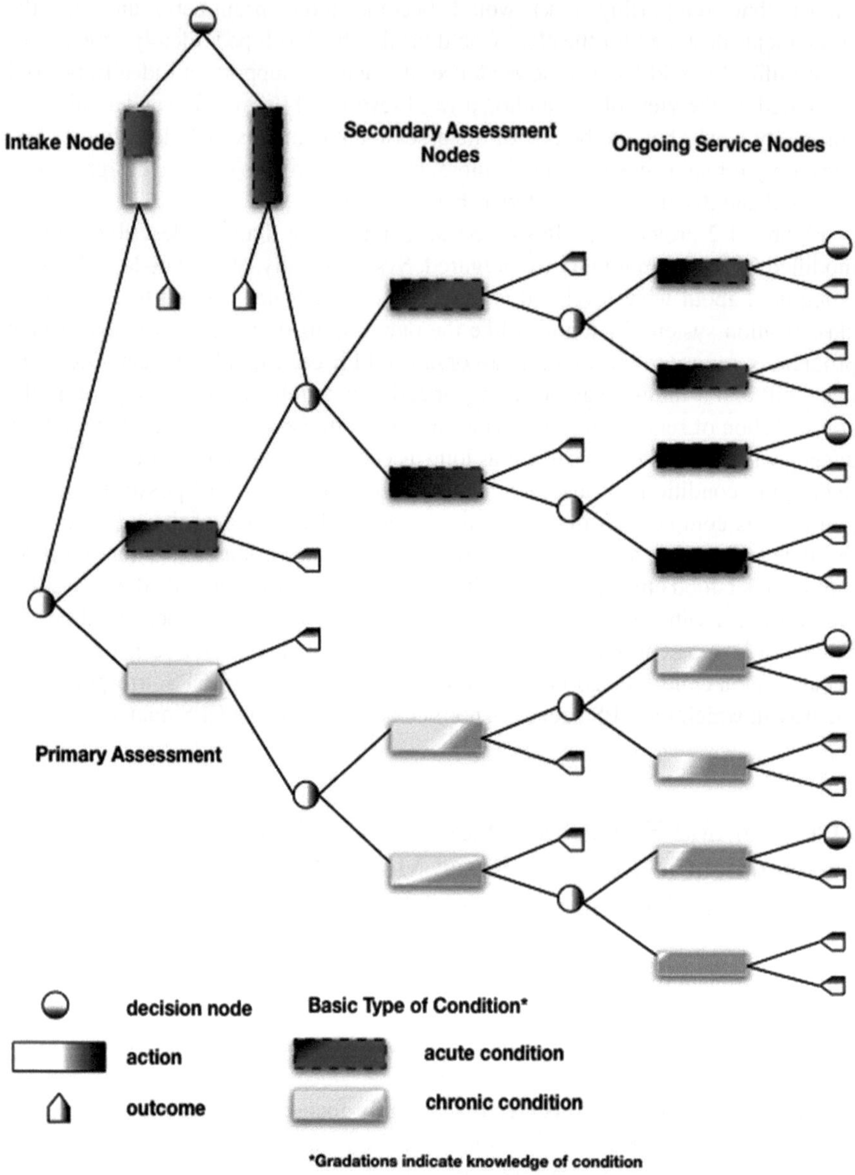

Fig. 21.2 Child protection decisional state space framework

Classes of CPS Families (Need-Based Framework Approach)

Figure 21.2 schematically depicts a multidimensional matrix of patterns of co-occurring conditions that would constitute classes of families as originally conceived by Casillas and Fluke (2014). The number of patterns that could be identified

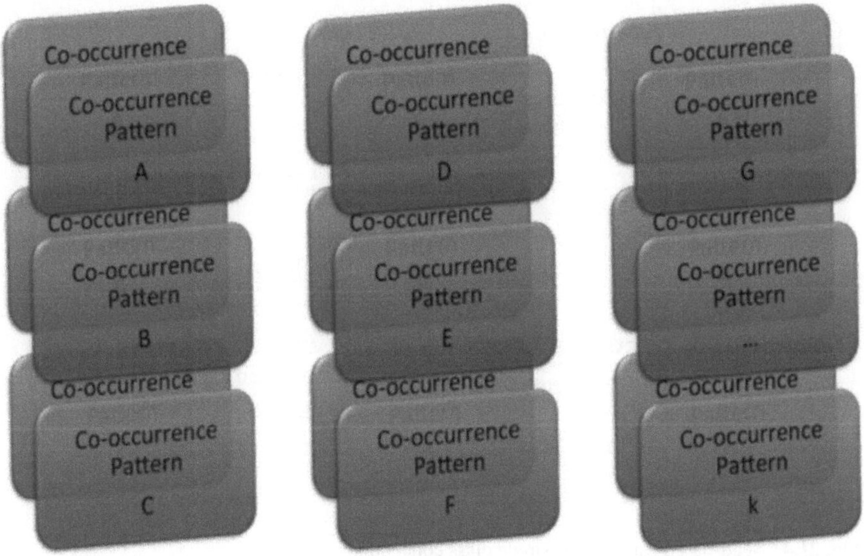

Fig. 21.3 Need-based framework: multiple co-occurrence classes

is potentially infinite, but it is much more likely that a finite set of patterns would emerge, and it is also likely that a relatively small number of classes would account for most of the cases in the child welfare system.

Each pattern contains a set of cases. Figure 21.3 shows some examples of the underlying conditions and characteristics of children and families that could be associated with the classes which we refer to as a pattern of characteristics. While each pattern would be independent in principle, it is clear that characteristics would overlap to some extent and that case members in the class would share distributions to some extent. Nevertheless, a distinct set of cases/families would be classified within each pattern, referred to as a class (Fig. 21.4).

Among the requirements for such a system is access to data from at least representative samples of child welfare cases (this could be within an administrative jurisdiction, a state, or even a nation) that include a comprehensive set of assessment data. Once identified through multivariate procedures, these classes can be deconstructed in turn for content and evaluated relative to possibilities of improving conditions through the application of empirically supported interventions. Alternatively, it may be that given the underlying conditions, no intervention would likely be effective for a given class; this represents an intervention gap.

Based on this information, several possibilities emerge:

- For classes where empirically supported interventions may be effective, further tests of these interventions could be performed with cases in the class to determine the level of expected efficacy for the class. This could also be "staged," as it seems clear that multiple simultaneous interventions may not be effective (Chaffin et al. 2011). However, sequencing these services in minimally overlapping

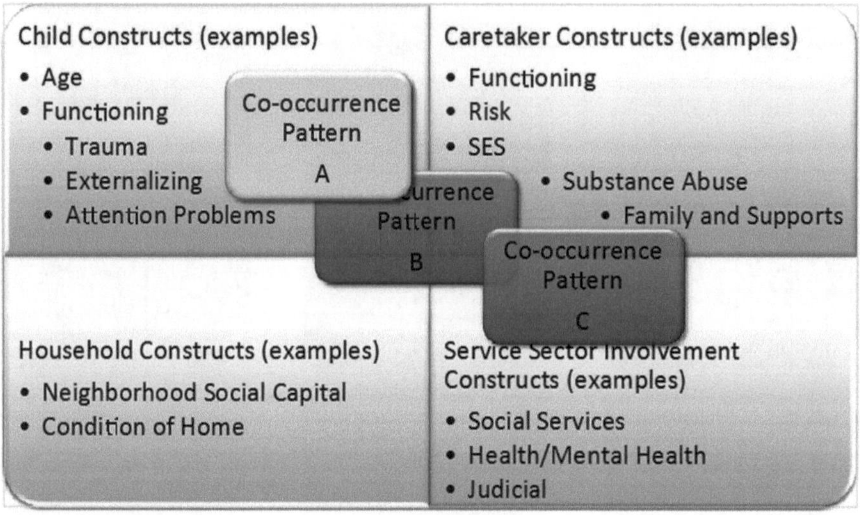

Fig. 21.4 Need-based framework: single class conceptual view

ways over a proscribed period of time may be more effective than a simultaneous or haphazard delivery of multiple services.

- The size of the class and its distribution with respect to population concentration, length of service delivery, and its estimated effect size could be used to estimate the type, scope, and dose (as in concentration across area) of specific empirically supported interventions or treatments that would be needed to achieve predetermined goals. This would have implications for determining effectiveness as well as for workforce development, workload, and costing.
- Some classes may not benefit or only minimally benefit from the existing array of empirically supported interventions. Thus, the existence of certain patterns may highlight the gaps in the available array of effective services and practices. Identification of such gaps would also be tied to a determination of the size of the class allowing for an informed evaluation of the utility of prioritizing research and evaluation efforts that could address these gaps.
- Outcomes could be monitored relative to the class of which the family is a member. This would also serve as a form of risk adjustment such that outcome expectations could be formulated relative to expected efficacy for the class.
- Finally, because class membership could shift over time, a longitudinal approach could be employed to "tune" the service array as the dynamics of the family shift.

One way to approach this would be to start with a small-scale pilot, perhaps involving a focus on a few classes of families. This could also be organized through a consortium method where different groups with key expertise would organize tests for specific classes in the framework.

Simulation of CPS Decisional State Space

To help address the incorporation of a different state space for CPS decision-making, agent-based modeling and simulation (ABMS) affords a method by which hypothetical classes of families and different CPS continuum configurations could be modeled to evaluate decision prospects leading to at least short-term outcome probabilities. ABMS are increasingly being utilized to design intervention strategies for complex systems operating under uncertainty ranging from global pandemic disease response to housing investment decisions in tourist communities (Macal and North 2006). In this context where actual errors in CPS decision-making have consequences for children, families, workers, and agencies, simulation offers a way to test configurations of continuums, assessments, and service decisions in a safe environment. In this fashion the ABMS aids in guiding eventual implementation through the identification of key leverage points and developing baseline expectations against which the actual system performance can be evaluated over time.

Defining Error Criteria in CPS

Clearly, a lot of knowledge about the decision-making context is required in order to model CPS decisions and understand errors. Ideally, we should be moving toward the evaluation decisional errors from the standpoint of decision-making under risk (e.g., Mansell et al. 2011) instead of uncertainty which is the status today. A crucial question though is whether developing a reasonable scientific understanding and capacity to enumerate such errors is beyond our reach. As described above, we currently have no way to be certain that a decision to remove a child is in error or not, the very definition of decision-making uncertainty. To some extent this lack of knowledge and criteria against which to judge decisional errors can be addressed through the simulation work described above. However, there are important limitations to simulations, the fundamental one being that, while they can offer great insights, they cannot take the full real-world context into account; we are always missing some important information.

Thus, it is important to employ scientific methods that address real families, children, workers, and other human agents to get at this question of understanding CPS decision errors. Some (Gilbert et al. 2012) have even suggested that we consider conducting random control trials for such decisions. However unlikely the use of random control trails, there have been natural comparison studies that come close and that might be good methodological models for CPS (Nelson et al. 2007). Ultimately, without some effort in this direction, major improvements in our decision-making capacity will continue to be elusive.

Acknowledgments The authors wish to thank the Annie E. Casey Foundation (AECF) for its support in the development of aspects of the content of this chapter. We especially want to acknowledge John Mattingly at AECF for his continuing commitment to improving the systems of child protection which was the impetus for the material presented here. Portions of this chapter appear in the author's publication: Casillas, K. and Fluke, J.D. (2014). The Case for a Needs-Based Model in Child Welfare: A Concept to Address Child Well-Being. In A. Shlonsky and R. Benbenishty (Eds.). From Evidence to Outcomes in Child Welfare: An International Reader (pp. 133–144). New York, NY: Oxford University Press.

References

American Academy of Child and Adolescent Psychiatry. (1997a). Practice parameters for the psychiatric assessment of children and adolescents. *Journal of the American Academy of Child and Adolescent Psychiatry, 36*(10 Suppl), 4S–20S.

American Academy of Child and Adolescent Psychiatry. (1997b). Practice parameters for the psychiatric assessment of infants and toddlers (0–36 months). *Journal of the American Academy of Child and Adolescent Psychiatry, 36*(10 Suppl), 21S–36S.

American Academy of Child and Adolescent Psychiatry. (2007). Practice parameters for the assessment of the family. *Journal of the American Academy of Child and Adolescent Psychiatry, 46*(7), 922–937.

Baird, C., Wagner, D., & Neuenfeldt, D. (1993). Actuarial risk assessment and case management in child protective services. In T. Tatara (Ed.), *Sixth national roundtable on CPS risk assessment, summary of highlights*. Washington, DC: American Public Welfare Association.

Baumann, D. J., Dalgleish, L., Fluke, J., & Kern, H. D. (2011). *The decision making ecology*. Denver: American Humane Association.

Bergman, L. R., & Magnusson, D. (1997). A person-oriented approach in research on developmental psychopathology. *Development and Psychopathology, 9*, 291–319.

Bickman, L. (1996). The evaluation of a children's mental health managed care demonstration. *Journal of Mental Health Administration, 23*(1), 7–15.

Bromfield, L., Lamont, A., Parker, R., & Horsfall, B. (2010). *Issues for the safety and wellbeing of children in families with multiple and complex problems: The co-occurrence of domestic violence, parental substance misuse, and mental health problems*. Melbourne: National Child Protection Clearinghouse.

Burns, B., Mustillo, S., Farmer, E., Kolko, D., McCrae, J., Libby, A., & Webb, M. B. (2009). Caregiver depression, mental health service use, and child outcomes. In M. B. Webb, K. Dowd, B. J. Harden, J. Landsverk, & M. Testa (Eds.), *Child welfare and child well-being: New perspectives from the National Survey of Child and Adolescent Well-Being* (pp. 351–379). New York: Oxford University Press.

Burnside, L. (2012). *Youth in care with complex needs*. Special report for the Office of the Children's Advocate, Manitoba, Canada.

Camasso, M., & Jagannathan, R. (2012). Decision making in child protection: A risky business? *Society for Risk Analysis*. doi:10.1111/j.1539-6924.2012.01931.

Casillas, K., & Fluke, J. D. (2014). The case for a needs-based model in child welfare: A concept to address child well-being. In A. Shlonsky & R. Benbenishty (Eds.), *From evidence to outcomes in child welfare: An international reader* (pp. 133–144). New York: Oxford University Press.

Chaffin, M., Bard, D., Hecht, D., & Silovsky, J. (2011). Change trajectories during home-based services with chronic child welfare cases. *Child Maltreatment, 16*(2), 114–125.

Chernoff, R., Combs-Orme, T., Risley-Curtiss, C., & Heisler, A. (1994). Assessing the health status of children entering foster care. *Pediatrics, 93*(4), 594–601.

Clausen, J. M., Landsverk, J., Ganger, W., Chadwick, D., & Litrownik, A. (1998). Mental health problems of children in foster care. *Journal of Child and Family Studies, 7*, 283–296.

Cleaver, H., Nicholson, D., Tarr, S., & Cleaver, D. (2007). *Child protection, domestic violence and parental substance misuse: Family experiences and effective practice*. London: Jessica Kingsley.

Curry, J., Rohde, P., Simons, A., Silva, S., Vitiello, B., Kratochvil, C., & March, J. (2006). Predictors and moderators of acute outcome in the Treatment for Adolescents with Depression Study (TADS). *Journal of the American Academy of Child and Adolescent Psychiatry, 45*(12), 1427–1439.

Doyle, J. (2008). Child protection and adult crime: Using investigator assignment to estimate causal effects of foster care. *Journal of Political Economy, 116*(4), 746–720.

Drake, B. (1996). Unraveling unsubstantiated. *Child Maltreatment, 1*(5), 261–271.

Drake, B., Kohl, P., & Jonson-Reid, M. (2009). Time to leave substantiation behind: Findings from a national probability study. *Child Maltreatment, 14*, 17–26.

Fluke, J. D., Shusterman, G., Hollinshead, D., & Yuan, Y. T. (2008). Longitudinal analysis of repeated child abuse reporting and victimization: Multistate analysis of associated factors. *Child Maltreatment, 13*(1), 76–88.

Gibbs, L. E. (2003). *Evidence-based practice for the helping professions: A practical guide with integrated multimedia*. Pacific Grove: Brooks/Cole–Thomson Learning.

Gibbs, L., & Gambrill, E. (2002). Evidence-based practice: Counterarguments to objections. *Research on Social Work Practice, 12*, 452–476.

Gilbert, R., Fluke, J., O'Donnell, M., Gonzalez-Izquierdo, A., Brownell, M., Gulliver, P., Janson, S., & Sidebottom, P. (2012). Trends in child maltreatment in six developed countries. *Lancet, 379*(9817), 758–72.

Hessle, S., & Vinnerljung, B. (1999). *Child welfare in Sweden: An overview*. Stockholm: Stockholm University Department of Social Work.

Heyman, R. E., & Smith Slep, A. M. (2006). Creating and field-testing diagnostic criteria for partner and child maltreatment. *Journal of Family Psychology, 20*(3), 397–408.

Hinshaw, S. P. (2007). Moderators and mediators of treatment outcome for youth with ADHD: Understanding for whom and how interventions work. *Ambulatory Pediatrics, 7*, 91–100.

Jensen, P. S., Arnold, L. E., Swanson, J., Vitiello, B., Abikoff, H. B., Greenhill, L. L., & Hur, K. (2007). Follow-up of the NIMH MTA study at 36 months after randomization. *Journal of the American Academy of Child and Adolescent Psychiatry, 46*, 988–1001.

Johnson, M. A., Stone, S., Lou, C., Vu, C., Ling, J., Mizrahi, P., & Austin, M. J. (2006). *Family assessment in child welfare services: Instrument comparisons*. Berkeley: Bay Area Social Services Consortium, University of California.

Lambert, M. J., Hansen, N. B., & Finch, A. E. (2001). Patient-focused research: Using patient outcome data to enhance treatment effects. *Journal of Consulting and Clinical Psychology, 69*(2), 159–172.

Leslie, L. K., Gordon, J. N., Lambros, K., Premji, K., Peoples, J., & Gist, K. (2005). Addressing the developmental and mental health needs of young children in foster care. *Journal of Developmental and Behavioral Pediatrics, 26*(2), 140–151.

Lou, C., Anthony, E. K., Stone, S., Vu, C., & Austin, M. J. (2006). *Assessing child and youth well-being: Implications for child welfare practice*. Berkeley: Bay Area Social Services Consortium, University of California.

Macal, C. M., & North, M. J. (2006). Tutorial on agent-based modelling and simulation. *Journal of Simulation, 4*, 151–162.

Magnusson, D. (1995). Individual development: A holistic, integrated model. In P. Moen, G. H. Elder, & K. Luscher (Eds.), *Examining lives in context: Perspective on the ecology of human development* (pp. 19–60). Washington, DC: American Psychological Association.

Magnusson, D. (1998). The logic and implications of a person approach. In R. B. Cairns, L. R. Bergman, & J. Kagan (Eds.), *Methods and models for studying the individual* (pp. 33–64). Thousand Oaks: Sage.

Mansell, J., Ota, R., Erasmus, R., & Marks, K. (2011). Reframing child protection: A response to a constant crisis of confidence in child protection. *Children and Youth Services Review, 33*(2011), 2076–2086.
Mehta, D., Klengel, T., Conneely, K. N., Smith, A. K., Altmann, A., Pace, T. W., Rex-Haffner, M., Loeschner, A., Gonik, M., Mercer, K. B., Bradley, B., Müller-Myhsok, B., Ressler, K. J., & Binder, E. B. (2013). Childhood maltreatment is associated with distinct genomic and epigenetic profiles in posttraumatic stress disorder. *Proceedings of the National Academy of Sciences, 110*(20), 8302–7.
Merkel-Holguin, L., Kaplan, C., & Kwak, A. (2006). *The national study on differential response in child welfare*. Denver: American Humane Association.
Mildon, R., Dickinson, N., & Shlonksy, A. (2014). Using implementation science to improve service and practice in child welfare: Actions and essential elements. In A. Shlonsky & R. Benbenishty (Eds.), *From evidence to outcomes in child welfare: An international reader* (pp. 83–101). New York: Oxford University Press.
Munro, E. (2011). *The Munro review of child protection: Final report a child-centred system*. London: Department for Education.
Nelson, C. A., Zeanah, C. H., Fox, N. A., Marshall, P. J., Smyke, A., & Guthrie, D. (2007). Cognitive recovery in socially deprived young children: The Bucharest early intervention project. *Science, 318*, 1937–1940.
NRCCPS (2010). http://nrccps.org/information-dissemination/1249-2/
Owens, G. P., & Chard, K. M. (2003). Comorbidity and psychiatric diagnoses among women reporting child sexual abuse. *Child Abuse & Neglect, 27*(9), 1075–1082.
Pilowsky, D. (1995). Psychopathology among children placed in foster care. *Psychiatric Services, 46*(9), 906–910.
Rosengard, A., Laing, I., Ridley, J., & Hunter, S. (2007). *A literature review on multiple and complex needs*. Edinburgh: Scottish Executive Social Research.
Samuels, B. (2012). *Trauma and treatment in child welfare policy and practice*. Presentation at the Society for Social Work Research, Washington, DC.
Schor, E. L. (1982). The foster care system and the health status of foster children. *Pediatrics, 69*(5), 521–528.
Scottish Executive. (2005). *Getting it right for every child: Proposals for action*. Edinburgh: Crown, St. Andrew's House.
Sedlak, A. J., Mettenburg, J., Basena, M., Petta, I., McPherson, K., Greene, A., & Li, S. (2010). *Fourth national incidence study of Child Abuse and Neglect (NIS–4): Report to Congress*. Washington, DC: U.S. Department of Health and Human Services, Administration for Children and Families.
Shlonsky, A., & Wanger, D. (2005). The next step: Integrating actuarial risk assessment and clinical judgment into an evidence-based practice framework in CPS case management. *Children and Youth Services Review, 27*(2005), 409–427.
Simms, M. D. (1989). The foster care clinic: A community program to identify treatment needs of children in foster care. *Journal of Developmental and Behavioral Pediatrics, 10*, 121–128.
Spivak, H., Sege, R., Flanigan, E., & Licenziato, V. (Eds.), American Academy of Pediatrics. (2006). *Connected kids: Safe, strong, secure clinical guide*. Elk Grove Village: American Academy of Pediatrics.
Stein, E., Evans, V., Mazumdar, R., & Rae-Grant, N. (1996). The mental health of children in foster care: A comparison with community and clinical samples. *Canadian Journal of Psychiatry, 41*, 385–391.
Szilagyi, M. (1998). The pediatrician and the child in foster care. *Pediatrics in Review, 19*(2), 39–50.
Trocmé, N., Fallon, B., MacLaurin, B., Sinha, V., Black, T., Fast, E., & Holroyd, J. (2010). *Characteristics of children and families. In Canadian incidence of reported child abuse and neglect—2008: Major findings*. Ottawa: Public Health Agency.
Turnell, A., & Edwards, S. (1999). *Signs of safety: A safety and solution oriented approach to child protection casework*. New York: WW Norton.

US Department of Health and Human Services, Administration for Children and Families (USDHHS-ACF). (2005). *National Survey of Child and Adolescent Well-Being, No. 3: Children's cognitive and socioemotional development and their receipt of special educational and mental health services. Research brief: Findings from the NSCAW Study*. Washington, DC: Author.

US Department of Health and Human Services, Administration for Children and Families. (2007a). *National Survey of Child and Adolescent Well-Being, No. 7: Special health care needs among children in child welfare, Research brief: Findings from the NSCAW study*. Washington, DC: Author.

US Department of Health and Human Services, Administration for Children and Families. (2007b). *National Survey of Child and Adolescent Well-Being, No. 8: Need for early intervention services among infants and toddlers in child welfare. Research brief: Findings from the NSCAW study*. Washington, DC: Author

US Department of Health and Human Services, Administration for Children and Families. (2007c). *National Survey of Child and Adolescent Well-Being, No. 9: Does substantiation of child maltreatment relate to child well-being and service receipt? Research brief: Findings from the NSCAW study*. Washington, DC: Author.

US Department of Health and Human Services, Administration for Children and Families. (2008a). *National Survey of Child and Adolescent Well-Being, No. 10: From early involvement with child welfare services to school entry: Wave 5 follow-up of infants in the national survey of child and adolescent well-being. Research brief: Findings from the NSCAW study*. Washington, DC: Author.

US Department of Health and Human Services, Administration for Children and Families. (2008b). *National Survey of Child and Adolescent Well-Being, No. 11: Adolescents involved with child welfare: A transition to adulthood. Research brief: Findings from the NSCAW study*. Washington, DC: Author.

US Department of Health and Human Services, Administration for Children and Families. (2009). *National Survey of Child and Adolescent Well-Being, No. 13: Depression among caregivers of young children reported for child maltreatment. Research brief: Findings from the NSCAW study*. Washington, DC: Author.

US Department of Health and Human Services, Administration for Children and Families, Administration on Children, Youth and Families, Children's Bureau. (2012). *Child maltreatment 2011*. Available from http://www.acf.hhs.gov/programs/cb/research-data-technology/statistics-research/child-maltreatment

Wakker, P. (2010). *Prospect theory for risk and ambiguity*. New York: Cambridge University Press.

Widom, C., Czaja, S., Bentley, T., & Johnson, M. (2012). A prospective investigation of physical health outcomes in abused and neglected children. *American Journal of Public Health, 102*(6), 1135–1144.

Chapter 22
The Role of Mandatory Reporting in Preventative Child Welfare Reforms: An Uneasy Fit?

Leah Bromfield

Child maltreatment and child protection have commanded much public attention in recent years. From persistent media scrutiny of child protection systems (e.g. Bibby and McIlwain 2013) to public outrage over the abuse of children in institutional settings and their subsequent cover-up by the institutional hierarchy (e.g. Box 2013), the protection of children is a topic that ignites popular interest like few others. It is easy to forget, then, that contemporary approaches to child protection have relatively recent origins in the 1960s (Feerick and Snow 2006; James 2000). In 1962, Kempe and colleagues published their seminal article in which they coined the term "the battered-child syndrome" to describe nonaccidental injury to children (typically under 3 years) caused by caregivers and characterised by "symptoms" such as multiple long bone fracture, subdural haematoma and parent explanations inconsistent with the medical evidence. The study findings garnered significant media attention, which Tomison (2001) argued was as important as the research findings in the impact of this research. As a consequence, contemporary child protection systems were established in the USA underpinned by a forensic-legal model; a model adopted in other developed countries including Australia. In this model, statutory child protection services were established under legislation that gave them the authority to intervene into the private realm of the family to investigate suspected child abuse and neglect and take action to protect children from harm (Lamont and Bromfield 2010). Previous laws did exist that enabled concerned individuals or groups to make application to protect a child from cruelty (e.g. NSPCC 2000); however, a critical change that accompanied the professionalisation of child protection in the 1960s was that child protection authorities were not just *able* to intervene to protect a child, they were *expected* to do so. Therefore, a central

L. Bromfield (✉)
Australian Centre for Child Protection, University of South Australia,
Adelaide, SA, Australia
e-mail: leah.bromfield@unisa.edu.au

B. Mathews, D.C. Bross (eds.), *Mandatory Reporting Laws and the Identification of Severe Child Abuse and Neglect*, Child Maltreatment 4,
DOI 10.1007/978-94-017-9685-9_22

element of the new wave of child welfare was the establishment of a mechanism by which cases of child abuse came to the attention of statutory child protection services: individuals within the community who suspected a child was experiencing abuse could report their concerns (typically over the phone) to child protection authorities for follow-up. Further laws were implemented that required or *mandated* specified categories of people (e.g. doctors, teachers) to report their suspicions (Lamont and Bromfield 2010).

Essentially, child protection services were designed as a safety net to respond to what was believed to be a problem affecting a relatively small number of children. Adopting the language of social policy, this represents a "residual" approach to protecting children. Wilensky and Lebeaux, in 1958, defined "institutional" and "residual" approaches to social welfare as reflecting different philosophies of social policy and the role of the welfare state. Under a *residual* approach, people are expected to meet their needs and the needs of their dependents through the primary institutions of the market and the family. "Welfare" is a secondary institution, which only comes into effect where these primary institutions have failed. In contrast, Wilensky and Lebeaux defined the *institutional* approach as one in which welfare is a primary institution designed to meet the needs of the whole population rather than just the disadvantaged. Under an institutional approach the role of the state is to provide universal programmes to support the well-being of the public, not just those in crisis, through provision of measures such as universal health care, free education, social security and support services (Wilensky and Lebeaux (1958) in Ife and Fiske 2003; Graycar 1979). Applied to child abuse and neglect, an institutional approach prioritises services and supports to prevent abuse and neglect at a population-wide level rather than prioritising individual responses after abuse and neglect has occurred. Theoretically, residual approaches were to be provided to a (presumably small) population of individuals for whom the market and family had failed, and it was therefore thought that they would be of low cost to the government. The residual approach to social welfare represented a "good fit" with both (a) the 1960s understanding of the scope of the problem of child abuse and the needs of children affected and (b) expectations regarding the role of mandatory reporting.

Grounded in the Australian child welfare context, this chapter charts the broadening of the scope of child protection services. It discusses both differential response as one of the primary reforms to the way in which vulnerable children and their families become known to services under a residual approach to child protection and a public health approach to child protection, which represents an institutional rather than a residual approach to social policy. The implementation of major reforms designed to (a) prevent abuse and neglect and (b) reduce reports to child protection services are discussed in the context of two Australian states. A particular focus is the extent to which the different mandatory reporting provisions in each state were aligned with the intent of the child and family welfare reforms.

The Broadened Scope of Child Protection

The circumstances for which child protection services were designed have changed. One of the critical changes to child protection services has been the long-term trend of increasing demand on these services through numbers of reports and numbers of children in care (Bromfield et al. 2014; Holzer and Bromfield 2008). Many factors have been attributed to increases in the demands on child protection services, including trends shared across anglophone countries (i.e. the UK, the USA, Canada, Ireland, New Zealand, Australia) such as the impacts of risk assessment and risk aversion on thresholds for child protection activity (Bromfield and Holzer 2008; Holzer and Bromfield 2008) and local factors such as the high-profile death of a child, an inquiry into child welfare or legislative changes within a specific jurisdictional area (Holzer and Bromfield 2008). Of specific relevance to the discussion in this chapter is the shared trend across anglophone countries to broaden the nature and scope of what constitutes child abuse and neglect, thus lowering the threshold for child protection involvement.

The 1960s and 1970s were a period of rapid social change within Australia; the progressive Whitlam government introduced a raft of provisions to reduce social inequity, including, for example, free tertiary education, welfare payments for single mothers and a national health care scheme (Graycar 1977, 1979, 1983). Changes such as the women's liberation movement and the introduction of no fault divorces saw the beginnings of a period of rapid change in the diversity and structure of Australian families (de Vaus 2004). Against this social backdrop, professional and community attitudes to children have also changed, including a broadening of where childhood starts and ends (Gough 1996), as illustrated through increased knowledge of in utero impacts on healthy birth outcomes at one end of the spectrum (Taylor et al. 2012) and increases to school leaving age at the other end of the spectrum (NSW Education and Communities 2011). Standards regarding what constitutes appropriate care have also changed since the 1960s (Gough 1996); examples include attitudes towards corporal punishment and what constitutes adequate supervision. Concurrently there has been increasing evidence about the impacts of parenting and the risks associated with abuse and neglect (CFCA 2014; Zubrick et al. 2008). The impacts of the sociolegal context on the conceptualisation of parenting and childhood have in turn impacted the remit of those organisations established to protect children from harm.

The types of behaviours that are considered to be abusive or neglectful have changed considerably over time. In the nineteenth century, laws passed to protect children were concerned with issues of extreme cruelty and neglect, abandonment and moral corruption. These laws gave society (typically in the form of charitable groups) the right to intervene to protect children (Lamont and Bromfield 2010). Earlier laws that applied to the issues of abuse or neglect did exist; however, their primary function appeared to be the protection of community rather than the protection of children (Scott and Swain 2002). The discovery of the battered-child syndrome in the 1960s saw child physical abuse elevated as the primary issue of concern and pushed the response from a charitable response to a state-based professional intervention. Child sexual abuse was not widely acknowledged or recognised until the mid-1980s, attributed to the impacts of feminism (Scott and Swain 2002). In the 1980s and 1990s, a growing body of research demonstrated the impacts of absence of adequate care on children's development, heralding the "rediscovery" and focus on child neglect (Scott and Swain 2002). In the same period researchers began to focus on the emotional and psychological impacts of abuse and neglect, ultimately culminating in the recognition of emotional maltreatment as a distinct abuse type (Lamont and Bromfield 2010). In the last two decades, there has also been increasing support for the recognition of exposure to domestic violence as an additional type of maltreatment (Humphreys 2007). These changes all broadened the range of behaviours that were considered to be abusive or neglectful. Over the same period the threshold for what is considered *significant* harm has also decreased. The overall result of these developments has been to broaden the scope of statutory child protection services established in the 1960s to respond primarily to severe physical abuse resulting in multiple fractures and brain injury (Kempe et al. 1962) to now include harms such as bruising, developmental delay and psychological harm caused by incidents of physical abuse, neglect, sexual abuse, emotional maltreatment and exposure to domestic violence. These are positive changes that align with both social values and research evidence. However, the broadening of what constitutes child maltreatment means that child maltreatment, which was originally thought to be an extreme problem affecting relatively small numbers of children, is now a highly prevalent phenomenon (Price-Robertson et al. 2010). The broadened scope of what constitutes child abuse and neglect has in turn increased real demand on statutory child protection services (Bromfield et al. 2014).

The Australian Child Welfare Context

Australia is made up of a federation of eight states and territories, with child protection being a state rather than a federal responsibility. Child protection legislation varies across each of the states and territories; however, a common framework has emerged whereby in each statute there is a provision defining what constitutes "a child in need of protection" (Bromfield and Holzer 2008); and a separate provision in the relevant statute defines the categories of mandated reporters and the circumstances in which they are required to make a report. There are varying degrees of difference across the states and territories between (a) persons within the community who are *able* to report suspicions of maltreatment and those who are *mandated* to report their suspicions, (b) the categories of maltreatment mandated persons are required to report and (c) the definition of what constitutes a child in need of protection (which in seven of the eight jurisdictions have elements additional to the mandated reporting provision) (see Table 22.1).

In some Australian jurisdictions the broadening scope of what constitutes abuse and neglect is reflected only in the legislative definition of a child in need of

Table 22.1 Comparison of maltreatment[a, b] types incorporated in definitions of children in need of protection and mandatory reporting requirements in Australian legislation

	Child in need of protection or "at risk"[c]	Mandatory reporting requirements
ACT	Physical abuse, sexual abuse, emotional abuse, neglect	Sexual abuse, nonaccidental physical injury
NSW	Physical abuse, sexual abuse, neglect, emotional maltreatment (developmentally or psychologically harmful "domestic environment")	Physical abuse, sexual abuse, emotional maltreatment, neglect, exposure to domestic violence
NT	Physical abuse, emotional abuse, neglect, sexual abuse, exposure to physical violence	Physical abuse, sexual abuse, emotional abuse, neglect, exposure to physical violence
QLD[b]	Physical abuse, emotional abuse, neglect, sexual abuse	Physical abuse, sexual abuse, emotional abuse, neglect
SA	Abuse (physical, sexual, emotional), neglect	Physical abuse, sexual abuse, emotional abuse, neglect
Tas	Abuse (physical, sexual, emotional), neglect, exposure to family violence	Abuse (physical, sexual, emotional), neglect, exposure to family violence
VIC	Physical abuse, sexual abuse, emotional maltreatment, neglect	Physical abuse, sexual abuse
WA[b, d]	Physical abuse, sexual abuse, emotional abuse, neglect	Sexual abuse

Source: CFCA (2013) and Mathews and Scott (2013)
[a]Legal definitions were categorised into the five maltreatment types: physical abuse, sexual abuse, emotional abuse/maltreatment, neglect, exposure to domestic violence.
[b]Harm experienced or likely to be experienced as a result of abuse or neglect must be significant. Noting that the significance test is not applied to child sexual abuse in five jurisdictions: ACT, NT, SA, Tas and WA.
[c]Note that in five jurisdictions (Australian Capital Territory, Northern Territory, Queensland, Victoria and Western Australia), not only must the relevant maltreatment and harm be found but also the child's parents must be found to be unable or unwilling to protect the child.
[d]Expectations were different across categories of mandated professionals, most expansive expectation included.

protection, which prescribes the conditions under which statutory child protection services are mandated to intervene to protect children from harm. For example, when Western Australia updated their very dated child protection legislation, they changed from a list of specific behaviours (e.g. is ill-treated or suffers injuries apparently resulting from ill-treatment) outlined in 11 separate articles in the Child Welfare Act 1947, s 4(1)(a)-(k) to very broad and inclusive definitions: "the child has suffered, or is likely to suffer, harm as a result of any one or more of the following: physical abuse, sexual abuse, emotional abuse, psychological abuse, neglect" (Children and Community Services Act 2004s 28(2)(c)). They did not introduce any mandatory reporting requirements into legislation at that time. Further, when the Western Australian legislation was amended in 2008[1] to include mandatory reporting

[1]Note that while the legislation was passed in 2008, the mandatory reporting provisions commenced (i.e. they came into effect) on 1 January 2009.

provisions, the mandatory reporting requirements did not mirror the definition of a child in need of protection and instead were restricted only to a reasonable belief that a child had experienced child sexual abuse (*Children and Community Services Amendment (Reporting Sexual Abuse of Children) Act 2008*, WA).

In comparison, in NSW when the definition of a child in need of protection was expanded to include exposure to domestic violence,[2] mandatory reporting requirements were also changed to correspond with this change. One can only assume this was a purposeful decision on the part of the NSW government as there was no legal requirement for mandatory reporting provisions to align with the definition of a child in need of protection. In both states, the broadening of the scope of what constituted child abuse and neglect did not alter the fundamental approach to child welfare, that is, a residual model that relied on suspected maltreatment being detected and reported to child protection services (either voluntarily or under mandatory reporting provisions). In New South Wales, the broadened scope of what constituted maltreatment increased the scope of what was reported to child protection; in Western Australia, only sexual abuse was subject to mandatory reporting laws. In neither State did the new provisions fundamentally change the way in which mandatory reporting schemes work.

The Impacts of Broadening the Scope of Child Abuse and Neglect on the Residual Child Protection System

The residual approach to social welfare originally represented a "good fit" with the understanding of the scope of the problem of child maltreatment. However, child protection systems based upon a residual approach are best suited to problems that are low in prevalence. The increased demand on child protection, particularly attributable to the fundamental change in the scope of what constituted child abuse and neglect, placed increasing demands on what was a crisis response system (Fogarty and Sargeant 1989). Child protection services became subject to increasing criticism regarding their capacity to respond to cases of severe abuse. For example, in Victoria, Australia in 1990, toddler Daniel Valerio was murdered by Paul Aiton who had partnered with Daniel's mother only 5 months prior to Daniel's death (Goddard and Liddell 1993, 1995). In the months prior to Daniel's death, many people, including five doctors, saw evidence of Daniel's physical abuse including photographs of Daniel with bruising to his face and eyes taken by a police surgeon only days prior to Daniel's death (Goddard and Liddell 1993, 1995). The heart-wrenching photographs presenting evidence that Daniel was a victim of serious physical abuse combined with the shocking inaction and failure to recognise clear signs of abuse

[2] In NSW the Children and Young Persons (Care and Protection) Act 1998 s 23(1)(d) states that a child is at risk of significant harm (and by virtue of s 71, will be "in need of protection") if the child or young person is living in a household where there have been incidents of domestic violence, and as a consequence, the child or young person is at risk of serious physical or psychological harm.

among professionals angered the community and led Justice Cummins (1993) to conclude "There is no doubt, I consider, that if the law in this state was that child abuse be mandatorily reported, this child's life would have been saved" (p. 741). A concerted community campaign calling for the introduction of mandatory on the basis of Daniel's case was credited with the introduction of mandatory reporting laws in Victoria in 1993 (Children and Young Persons (Further amendment) Act 1993 Vic). However, others have commented that it was hard to see how mandatory reporting would have changed the outcome in Daniel's case as Daniel had in fact been the subject of multiple reports to child protection services prior to his death (Goddard and Liddell 1995; Scott and Swain 2002). These commentators instead laid fault on poor decision-making in the context of an underfunded child protection service and a "dual track" system of shared police and child welfare responsibility that had the effect of child protection diverting excess cases to the police for a response (Scott and Swain 2002). It is this author's position that Daniel's tragic death was a failure of governments to adequately resource and a failure by those authorities to recognise and respond to serious abuse rather than a failure by the community to detect and report a child at risk to the authorities. While the residual approach to child protection and mandatory reporting were a good fit in terms of their intended function, the residual approach to child protection had become a poor fit for the changed nature and scope of the problem – the failure of child protection authorities to prioritise a clear case of serious physical abuse being symptomatic of an overwhelmed system.

Differential Response

One of the reasons child protection services are overwhelmed is that a large number of the reports of children perceived by members of the community or other professionals as concerning a child at risk of abuse or neglect are subsequently assessed by child protection services as not requiring a statutory child protection response. For example, within Australia, 46 % of reports are investigated and only 19 % of reports are substantiated (AIHW 2013). This leaves a large number of cases in which there are no legislative grounds for intervention, and yet some level of vulnerability, need or risk may have been identified. One of the major strategies implemented from the mid-1990s to better respond to families known to child protection services, but in which children were assessed as not requiring a coercive statutory response, is "differential response" (also referred to as a dual track, multiple track or alternative response; Merkel-Holguin 2005; Schene 2005). Implemented in some form in all Australian jurisdictions, differential response provides a pathway for less severe allegations not requiring an investigation to be referred to voluntary family support services (Bromfield and Higgins 2005a). Differential response essentially comprises the following process: reports received by child protection services are assessed to determine whether a child protection investigation or referral to voluntary family support services is warranted (Connolly 2005). This is presented in Fig. 22.1.

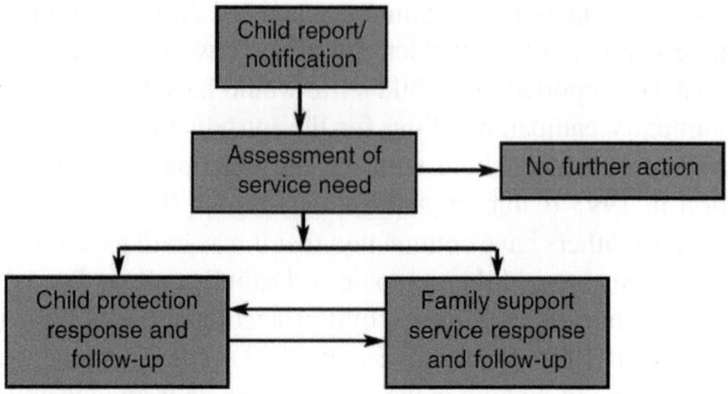

Fig. 22.1 Differential response process (Source: Connolly 2005, p. 15)

The rationale underpinning differential response: (a) responses to concerns about a child should be commensurate with the level of risk, and (b) non-accusatory assessments and responses to families are typically more effective than adversarial approaches (Merkel-Holguin 2005). In systems in which differential response has been implemented, allegations of serious physical abuse and sexual abuse will still be referred for investigation. However, many of the allegations arising from the broadening of the definition of what constitutes child maltreatment such as chronic neglect are provided an alternate pathway into family support services. Differential response does not represent a fundamental change of approach. Rather, differential response leverages the identification of vulnerable families through the existing residual child protection system with the hope that providing referrals to families not requiring an investigation will divert those families in need into services.

The implementation of a differential response at child protection intake may, therefore, decrease demand for child protection investigations by preventing the escalation of problems and the subsequent re-referral of families to statutory child protection services. However, differential response is not designed to reduce the number of reports to child protection report lines. In fact, it may serve to increase reports to child protection report lines by providing a visible pathway into services for professionals or community members who are concerned about a child. Bromfield et al. (2014) argue that differential response is a sensible reform to child protection services; however, it is still a residual approach and does not include a wider system of targeted early intervention designed to prevent abuse and neglect from occurring. If anything it is likely to increase rather than decrease the vast population of vulnerable children referred to child protection intake services. Within Australia, a groundswell has emerged of academics, child and family advocacy groups along with those government departments responsible for child protection calling for a fundamental change of approach to protecting children: an approach based on prevention and early intervention (Bromfield 2012). Alongside state-based reforms, this culminated in the Council of Australian Governments endorsement in 2009 of the *National Framework for Protection Australia's Children*, which explicitly adopted a public health approach to child protection.

The Public Health Approach to Child Protection

Public health approaches, originating from the field of preventable illness, strongly emphasise health promotion and prevention with increasingly intensive interventions targeting identified risks (Baum 1998; Garrison 2005). A public health approach is used when a preventable problem is prevalent and serious and is associated with severe long-term effects on individuals and populations. Public health approaches incorporate a range of strategies determined by the target of intervention efforts and are typically represented as a pyramid and characterised as having three levels of intervention: primary interventions universally available to the whole population, secondary interventions targeted at vulnerable populations and tertiary interventions for populations with indicated problems present. Applied to the issue of child abuse and neglect (represented visually in Fig. 22.2), a public health approach could comprise:

- Primary intervention: universal services and supports available to all children and families to enhance child well-being (e.g. parenting education, prenatal and postnatal care including home visiting, health care, education, income support)
- Secondary intervention: targeted services and supports for vulnerable children and families (e.g. teenage parents) and those with indicated problems (e.g. parental alcoholism), in which children are at risk but parents are willing to voluntarily engage with needed services and supports
- Tertiary intervention: statutory child protection services for families in which children are experiencing serious abuse and neglect (e.g. sexual abuse, severe physical abuse, criminal neglect) or in which children's needs are not being met

Fig. 22.2 Primary, secondary and tertiary interventions in a public health approach to child protection

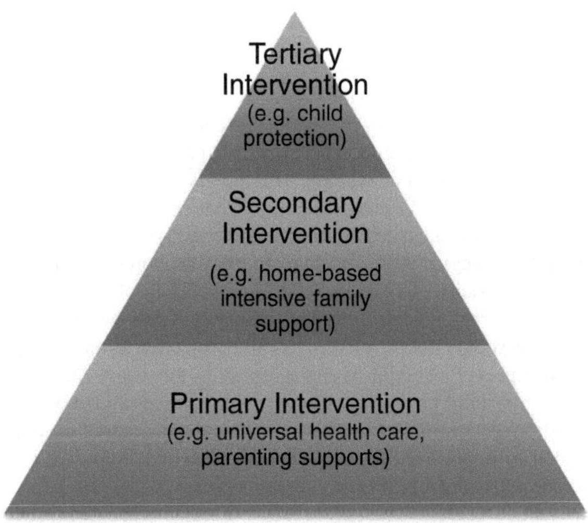

and parents are unwilling to engage with available services and supports (Arney and Bromfield 2010; Bamblett et al. 2010)[3]

Under a public health model, there should be sufficient universal interventions for all families. Further, there must be sufficient secondary services available to meet the needs of identified families. Tertiary interventions are framed as an option of last resort. The representation of primary interventions as a pyramid denotes the relative sizes of both the extent of services required to be available and the relative size of the populations to be served by each of the ascending levels of intervention.

Referral Pathways into Prevention and Early Intervention Services

The funding of primary, secondary and tertiary services so that they exist and have adequate capacity to meet demand is a necessary but not a sufficient condition to the successful implementation of a public health approach. The axiom "build it and they will come" does not necessarily translate to vulnerable children and their families. Attention needs to be given to how families can best access and enter available services and supports. A case in point is the funding of the statewide Brighter Futures intensive family support programme as an early intervention strategy in New South Wales (NSW), Australia. Brighter Futures was established in an effort to address demands on the child protection system through intervening earlier. It represented 22 % of the funding ($260 million) in a statewide reform package (Wood 2009). The majority of places in the Brighter Futures programme (80 %) were allocated for referrals from child protection services. The Brighter Futures programme was also able to accept a proportion of self-referrals and referrals from community agencies; however, eligibility for the programme had to be approved by child protection (Wood 2009).

[3] For the second category of cases – those in which the child's needs are not being met and parents are unwilling to engage – theoretical and practical issues about the scope of tertiary intervention become important. For example, if a child is moderately neglected and the parents will not engage with help, are court orders sought, to what extent and is this justifiable? At present the system is not sufficiently nuanced to ensure consistent practice in this scenario. Children who are mild/moderately neglected may end up in family support or child protection dependent on the individual worker, capacity of child protection, availability of services for referral, etc. I would argue that where a parent is neglecting their child but is able and willing to engage with relevant supports, then this should not be referred to child protection as a first response. However, if a child is facing the prospect of a childhood characterised by persistent chronic mild/moderate neglect and the parent is unwilling to engage with available services and supports, then this ought to be referred to child protection to use their coercive powers to compel engagement with services or where warranted to remove children. Where this does not occur, we knowingly condemn children to the severe detrimental effects of chronic neglect.

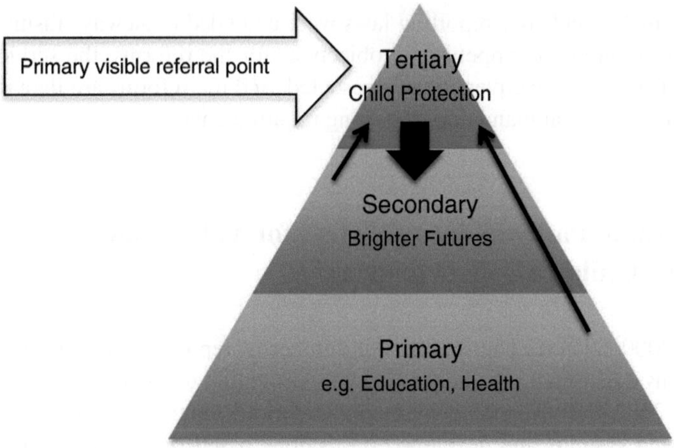

Fig. 22.3 Intended referral pathways into the Brighter Futures secondary services under a differential response approach in NSW

Brighter Futures was a key reform designed to ensure programme capacity existed to provide early intervention (initially targeted at families with young children) for families identified as low risk of child harm under differential response (see Fig. 22.3). This period of time marked unrivalled growth in reports to child protection services in NSW, from approximately 30,000 reports in 1999/2000 to a record high for the nation of 213,686 reports in 2008/2009 (AIHW 2009). A number of factors were attributed to these increases: the establishment of a centralised child protection intake centre (the Helpline) for the state, the expansion of mandatory reporting to include domestic violence, progressive implementation of a $1.2 billion reform package, internal and external scrutiny of child protection and accompanying media attention (Holzer and Bromfield 2008). In 2009, Justice Wood in his *Inquiry into Child Protection Services in New South Wales* (NSW) found that demand had outstripped capacity and, in particular, that the large volume of reports to the child protection report line had become a bottleneck into the child welfare service system. A critical finding pointing to an unintended consequence of differential response was that while reports were being closed with no action due to a lack of capacity within the statutory child protection services, there was capacity within the Brighter Futures programme to accept a greater proportion of referrals from child protection services (Wood 2009). This represents a tragedy of service system design where the service existed but was inaccessible to families in need due to the inadequacy of the referral pathway into the service.

In the following section, two case examples are presented which describe the introduction of a welfare reform designed to provide an alternate and more direct pathway into secondary services for vulnerable children and their families: one in which mandatory reporting laws were unchanged (Child FIRST, Victoria) and the other in which mandatory reporting laws were amended (Gateway, Tasmania). For each case example, the impetus and objectives for the reforms, the service model and evidence of its effectiveness are presented, and the reforms are then discussed in the context of local mandatory reporting requirements.

An Alternate Pathway into Services for Vulnerable Families: Child FIRST (Victoria)

In 1999–2000, Victoria had the highest number of reports to child protection services of any Australian jurisdiction and was struggling to meet demand (Bromfield 2012). In 2002, the Victorian government undertook extensive data mining of their internal data systems and developed projections based on the current trajectories (Victorian Government Community Care Division 2002). These data trajectories predicted that if nothing were done to reduce demand on Victorian child protection services, within 5 years one in five Victorian children would be reported to child protection services at some stage in their childhood. This statistic was incredibly powerful and was communicated to Treasury, the Premier and Cabinet and other government departments to successfully argue that the approach to child protection at that time was unsustainable (Humphreys et al. 2010). In seeking to adopt an alternative approach, it was recognised that within Victoria there was both a dearth of secondary services with capacity to respond to vulnerable families and that those services that did exist were not well positioned to be visible or accessible within the community (KPMG 2011). As a result, "child protection had inadvertently become the major pathway by which families could gain access to community based [services] and supports" (KPMG 2011, p. 16).

Following extensive planning and a successful pilot (Thomas and Naughton 2005), the Child FIRST and Integrated Family Services welfare reforms were rolled out statewide: Child FIRST being a new referral pathway established as an alternate to child protection and Integrated Family Services describing the array of local service responses. The primary objective of the Child FIRST and Integrated Family Services welfare reforms was to create a visible point of entry into the local service network that would eventually become the first point of contact for individuals concerned about a child, enabling child protection to become a system of last resort (see Fig. 22.4). For example, Child FIRST explanatory material reads:

> Knowing how and where to access the service system, or making an appropriate referral can be challenging. To make it easier to access family services, a clearly identifiable point of entry has been established. Each Child FIRST provides a central referral point to a range of community-based family services and other supports within each of the Child FIRST catchment areas (State Government of Victoria 2011).

The second objective of Child FIRST and Integrated Family Services was to provide an integrated service response that addressed the risks and needs of families that without support were likely to progress into the child protection system. Thus,

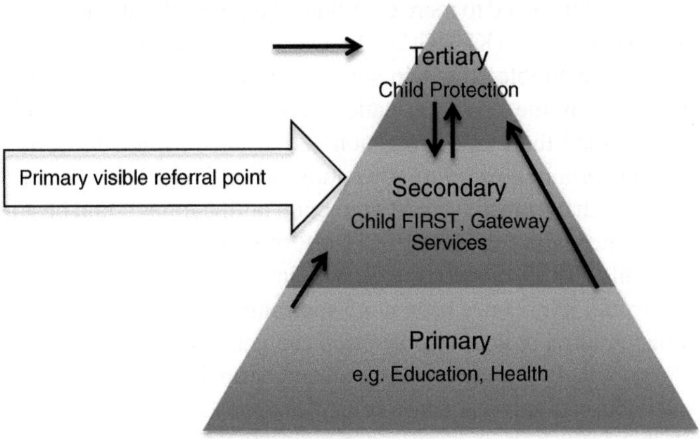

Fig. 22.4 Intended referral pathways into secondary and tertiary services under the Child FIRST (Vic) and Gateway Services (Tas) reforms

it was expected that Child FIRST would reduce demand on child protection services (i.e. notification and re-notifications) in two ways: (a) providing an alternate pathway into services for families with risk subthreshold for statutory child protection services and (b) preventing problems in those families from escalating to the point that they reached the threshold for child protection intervention.

The model comprised Child FIRST intake teams skilled in family needs assessment located in the same geographically defined regions as the local child protection district offices (24 in total) and the co-location of an experienced child protection practitioner from the local district office to promote a shared understanding of the statutory threshold for risk and to ensure that Child FIRST remained an adequate safety net referring high-risk cases to child protection when needed. Referrals could come from anywhere within the community from local schools to self-referrals from families themselves. Referrals were also made to Child FIRST from the local child protection office as a differential response option. Integrated Family Services described an alliance of community service organisations serving the needs of vulnerable children and their families in each local area required to be formed as part of the reforms as well as newly funded intensive family support and case management positions. The simultaneous implementation of Child FIRST and Integrated Family Services as a single service description ensured that the newly established Child FIRST intake teams were able to act as a single coordinated gateway into local services and supports.

An evaluation of the reforms concluded that there were good indications that secondary service visibility had improved as evidenced by increasing referrals from a range of professionals and that more families were accessing services (KPMG 2011). The pairing of Child FIRST with an alliance of community services that formed the backbone of the Integrated Family Services component of the reforms appeared to have contributed to more coordinated intake, allocation, service delivery and demand management (KPMG 2011). During the pilot project for the reform model, there was negligible growth in notifications and re-notifications (Holzer and Bromfield 2008). In the final evaluation report of the statewide roll-out, the evaluators concluded that child protection activity had "generally grown at a far lower rate in Victoria compared to other jurisdictions" (KPMG 2011, p. 2). They further concluded that growth in child protection notifications could be attributed to factors unassociated with the Child FIRST reforms and used modelling to conclude that without Child FIRST moderating growth, impacts of the broader sociopolitical environment would likely have been more substantial (KPMG 2011).

In Victoria, children *in need of protection* can generally be defined as those who have, or who are, likely to experience significant harm as a consequence of physical injury, sexual abuse, emotional abuse or neglect (see Box 1). In practice, and consistent with this definition, children experiencing incidents of low severity such as those commonly comprised in allegations of child neglect are typically not assessed as reaching the threshold for statutory child protection (Bromfield and Higgins 2005b; Frederico et al. 2006). The theoretical intent of the referral pathways established through Child FIRST was for concerns regarding children experiencing circumstances such as chronic neglect or emotional abuse to be referred for a non-adversarial family support response (Bromfield and Holzer 2008; Holzer and Bromfield 2008; Bromfield and Miller 2012). In comparison, *mandatory reporting* laws in Victoria are relatively narrow in scope, requiring that only five mandated professions (medical practitioners, nurses, teachers, principals, police officers) report a belief formed on reasonable grounds that a child has suffered, or is likely to suffer, significant harm as a result of only physical injury or sexual abuse and does not have a parent who is able to protect the child from that harm (*Children, Youth and Families Act 2005* ss 182(1)(a)–(e), 184 and 162(c)–(d)). While the definition of a child in need of protection includes neglect, emotional and psychological harm, these maltreatment types are not included in mandatory reporting requirements.

What this means is that a professional concerned that a child is experiencing neglect is *able* to refer the case to child protection services which have a legal authority to intervene if the situation is of sufficient severity and if the child does not have a parent who is able to protect the child. However, professionals are not *required* to report neglect to child protection, and other services can accept a referral and provide services to such children and their families without any legal requirement that child protection be advised or involved. Child FIRST took advantage of these legal circumstances hoping to change reporter behaviour and divert cases of child neglect (which comprise the bulk of reports and substantiations) out of child protection services into voluntarily family support services. It is worth noting that in cases combining child neglect and physical abuse consistent with inappropriate use of corporal punishment, professionals would be mandated to report their concerns to child protection rather than making a direct referral to Child FIRST (see Fig. 22.5).

Box 1: Victorian Legislative Definition of a Child in Need of Protection: Children, Youth and Families Act 2005, Section 162

1.

(a) The child has been abandoned by his or her parents and after reasonable inquiries: (1) the parents cannot be found and (2) no other suitable person can be found who is willing and able to care for the child.
(b) The child's parents are dead or incapacitated and there is no other suitable person willing and able to care for the child.
(c) The child has suffered, or is likely to suffer, significant harm as a result of physical injury and the child's parents have not protected, or are unlikely to protect, the child from harm of that type.
(d) The child has suffered, or is likely to suffer, significant harm as a result of sexual abuse and the child's parents have not protected, or are unlikely to protect, the child from harm of that type.
(e) The child has suffered, or is likely to suffer, emotional or psychological harm of such a kind that the child's emotional or intellectual development is, or is likely to be, significantly damaged and the child's parents have not protected, or are unlikely to protect, the child from harm of that type.
(f) The child's physical development or health has been, or is likely to be, significantly harmed and the child's parents have not provided, arranged or allowed the provision of, or are unlikely to provide, arrange or allow the provision of, basic care or effective medical, surgical or other remedial care.

2. For the purposes of subsections (1)(c) to (1)(f), the harm may be constituted by a single act, omission or circumstance or accumulate through a series of continuing acts, omissions or circumstances.

Mandatory reporting laws were not introduced in Victoria until the early 1990s. They were controversial, subject to extensive media coverage and were adopted reluctantly by the then government (Bromfield 2012). In this context, and despite the narrow range of professions and abuse types that fall within the scope of Victorian mandatory reporting provisions, the introduction of mandatory reporting was associated with significant increases in reports for all types of abuse and neglect. It is important to note previous research which has suggested that approximately 40 % of reports are made by non-mandated reporters and that patterns of reporting vary by reporter group and type of maltreatment (Mathews 2012). Research across Australian states and territories has suggested that mandatory reporting law alone does not dictate reporter behaviour. Media attention, professional anxiety about

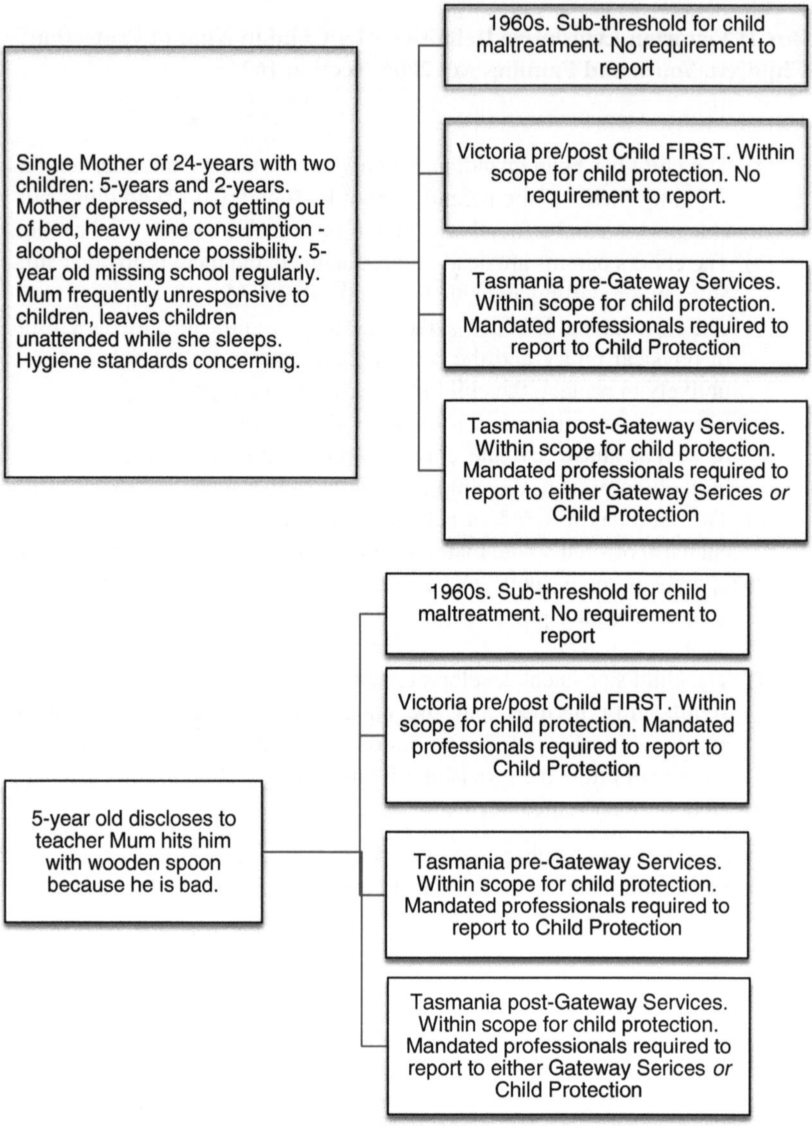

Fig. 22.5 Casting the net: changing reporting requirements for chronic neglect and corporal punishment with object

"getting it wrong" and beliefs about the role of child protection are among a variety of factors that appear to also be associated with reporting behaviour (Holzer and Bromfield 2008; Donovan et al. 2010). While Victoria's existing mandatory reporting legislation facilitated the implementation of a new referral pathway that diverted cases of child neglect out of child protection services, further research is required to determine the extent to which this has changed mandated reporters' (and non-mandated reporters) attitudes, beliefs and behaviours regarding their reporting obligations when they suspect a child is being neglected.

Aligning Alternate Referral Pathways with Revised Mandatory Reporting Laws: Gateway Services (Tasmania)

A review of child protection services in Tasmania critiqued the dearth of early intervention and prevention services within the state, concluding that there were children who had been removed into the care of the state who would likely have remained in the care of their parents if there were services and supports available for their families (Jacobs and Fanning 2006). Comparable with many other Australian states and territories, Tasmania had also experienced significant increases in reports to child protection services attributed to legislation and policy changes including the shift from a localised to a centralised intake service and changes to mandatory reporting provisions requiring that children exposed to domestic violence be reported to child protection services (Holzer and Bromfield 2008). The state took the decision to adopt the recommendation of an independent review (KPMG 2008) that Tasmania establish a community-based intake service for vulnerable children and their families that was located in each of the Department's geographical catchment areas, had a single phone number and included a co-located senior child protection practitioner (i.e. a modified Victorian Child FIRST approach), which it named Gateway Services. A memorandum of understanding between child protection services and the nongovernment agency partners who would provide the Gateway Services was executed in November of 2009. The aim of Gateway Services was "to provide a single, well publicised access point for individuals, agencies, services, and other professionals such as teachers, community agencies and general practitioners to refer clients for services and to obtain information and advise in relation to family support and specialist disability services" (Department of Health and Human Services n. d.).

In comparison to Victoria, mandatory reporting obligations in Tasmania are broad and mirror the types of maltreatment included in the definition of a child in need of protection. Specifically, the *Children, Young Persons and Their Families Act 1997* (Tas) describes a child at risk as a child who "has been, is being, or is likely to be, abused or neglected" (s 4(1)(a)) and where "the child is an affected child within the meaning of the *Family Violence Act 2004*" (s 4(1)(ba)). Noting in accordance with Section 3(1) of the Act, "abuse" or "neglect" means sexual abuse, or physical or emotional **injury** or other abuse, or neglect *to the extent that* (1) the injured, abused or neglected person has suffered, or is likely to suffer, physical or psychological **harm *detrimental to the person's well-being*** or (2) the injured, abused or neglected person's physical or psychological development is in jeopardy. Reporting requirements in Tasmania compel mandated professionals (14 categories, including employees across five government departments) to report a belief or suspicion formed on reasonable grounds that "a child has been or is being abused or neglected or is an affected child within the meaning of the Family Violence Act 2004" (*Children, Young Persons and Their Families Act 1997* ss 3, 4 and 14). Pre-Gateways, professionals were required to report their concerns to child protection services[4] regardless of what other services or supports the family might be receiving (see Fig. 22.5).

With the adoption of the KPMG report recommendations in 2008, preparations commenced for the introduction of the Gateway Services model. Existing mandatory reporting obligations clearly did not align with the intent of the Gateway Services model. Were they to remain unchanged, the implementation of an alternate referral pathway directly into secondary services for families of children at risk of neglect would have little impact on reports to child protection services, as mandated reporters would still be required to report these cases to child protection services.

Recognising the potential disabling effect of mandatory reporting provisions to the implementation of Gateway Services, the Tasmanian Government enacted new provisions within the *Children Young Persons and their Families Act 1997* (Tas) in August 2009 in readiness for the community-based intake service embedded in the Gateway Services model. These provisions stipulated that mandated reporters could report their concerns about the care of a child to Gateway Services and that such a report would fulfil their mandatory reporting obligations. Practitioners within Gateway Services were also mandated reporters, providing a safety net should children at high risk of abuse and neglect be wrongly reported to Gateway rather than child protection services. It is interesting to note that the amendments to the Tasmanian legislation mean that any form of suspected maltreatment can be reported to either child protection services or Gateway Services in fulfilment of a reporter's legislative responsibility. This means that cases of physical abuse, such as inappropriate use of corporal punishment, could be referred directly to Gateway Services (see Fig. 22.5). In this respect, the Tasmanian legislative amendments and service system reforms present a greater fit than the original Victorian model, strengthening a service and legislative environment in which child protection is a service of last resort.

Gateway Services is yet to be evaluated. When the current authors requested information from the Department of Health and Human Services regarding the effectiveness of the model, the Department's nominated officers reported that from their perspective, Gateway Services' ability to respond was positive. Four broad client groups were identified as now being reported to Gateway Services: (1) families that are reported directly to Gateway Services and have no child protection contact, (2) families referred to Gateway Services and subsequently referred by Gateway Services to child protection due to an unacceptable level of risk, (3) families referred

[4] Noting that concerns already reported to child protection were not required to be re-reported, for instance, where child protection received a notification and made a report to a family support service, the family support worker would not be required to re-report the same concerns to child protection upon completion of her initial assessment of the family.

to Gateway Services by child protection for voluntary services and (4) families referred to Gateway Services by child protection services with the caveat that if families do not consent to voluntary services they be re-reported to child protection. The Departmental officers' perception was that as a result of the implementation of Gateway Services, families in which children were not at high risk of abuse or neglect but where complex needs were present were getting a response. This conclusion is consistent with the findings of the Victorian evaluation of Child FIRST (KPMG 2011). The Departmental officers did note that while families were receiving some form of service, there is a continuing challenge (not unique to Gateway Services) to ensure that responses provided are effective in supporting families to reduce risks to children. The Department's nominated officers reported that there were some initial implementation issues where there was disagreement between child protection and Gateway Services regarding the threshold at which child protection services were required to respond. This was anticipated and perceived to have been resolved through good working relationships, and the role of the community-based child protection worker was seen as critical in this regard (a perception also supported by the findings of the Victorian evaluation of Child FIRST; KPMG 2011). In some catchment areas there was an initial spike in reports to child protection from Gateway Services with the identification of previously undetected children at high risk; this was seen as an unexpected positive outcome.

However, the expected obvious decrease in reports to child protection services had not occurred. National data show that a 4 % decrease was observed in the first year of implementation, followed by incremental increases of 7 and 9 % in the subsequent 2 years (AIHW 2013). The Department's nominated officers reported that the primary reason that the expected larger decrease in reports to child protection was not observed was that reporting practices had not changed among some groups of mandated reporters.[5] This was despite the changes to legislative provisions regarding reporting requirements and the information sessions and kits provided to support the roll-out of the legislative amendments and Gateway Services. As notifications are caller-defined under Tasmanian legislation, child protection services were obliged to accept these reports even if the child protection response was a referral to Gateway Services. The Departmental officers' perception was that some mandated reporters chose to report to child protection where they felt "this family needs a bit of a scare" rather than the noncoercive supportive response of Gateway Services. The second and more significant issue in terms of its impact on notification numbers was a decision taken by the police not to amend the standard operating procedures in relation to domestic violence incidents where a child resided in the home. The Tasmania Police continues to require its officers to report *all* incidents of domestic violence where a child resides in the house to child protection rather than Gateway Services, regardless of the individual circumstances of the case. This is clearly not required by the mandatory reporting provisions. Despite continuing implementation issues, the overall perception of the Department's nominated

[5] This is borne out by an extensive research study currently being conducted by a team involving the author of this chapter and the first editor of this volume (results forthcoming).

officers was that Gateway Services was making good assessments and having a positive impact on the accessibility of services for vulnerable children and their families. However, a key message from the Tasmanian experience is that changing legislative provisions for mandated reporters is not sufficient; attention also needs to be given to the barriers and facilitators to changing the behaviours and reporting practices of mandated notifiers where alternate referral pathways into early intervention and prevention services are being implemented.

Conclusion

In this chapter, the history of contemporary approaches to child welfare and the broadening of the scope of child protection in terms through both the expansion of maltreatment types and the lowering of the threshold for intervention were briefly discussed. The conceptualisations of the "residual" and "institutional" approaches to social welfare were described, as were the "differential response" and the "public health approach". Australian examples were used to illustrate the impacts of the broadened scope of child protection on demand for child protection services and the problems that can be encountered where differential response is the only referral pathway into secondary prevention services. The implementation of a specific programme of reform in two states was examined, where the aim of the reforms was to reduce demand on child protection services by (a) reducing the number of reports assessed by child protection intake prior to being referred to secondary services and (b) identifying and providing intervention to vulnerable families to prevent abuse and neglect; the primary target of these reform programmes being families in which children were at risk from neglect.[6] Each of these examples highlighted the alignment between legislated mandatory reporting provisions and the intended referral pathways into services for vulnerable families as central to the success of reforms aimed at changing referral pathways into services for vulnerable and at risk children and their families.

A primary objective of the *National Framework for Protecting Australia's Children* (COAG 2009, 2013) is to make "protecting children everyone's responsibility", a common goal globally in child welfare reform. Australia's National Framework sets as a high-level indicator of its success, a significant and sustained reduction in child abuse and neglect as measured through child protection services activity data (COAG 2009, 2013). As part of this agenda, the federal government has funded a suite of pilot initiatives designed to make the community and other service providers such as those in adult drug and alcohol and mental health services more "child aware" and to consider what they can do to support vulnerable families and prevent the need for child protection involvement (Department of Social Services 2013). However, the funded programmes are typically local service

[6]Neglect represents 29 % of all substantiated child protection cases in Australia and is second only to emotional abuse which constitutes 37 % of all substantiations (AIHW 2013).

initiatives or professional development packages. They are not part of a coordinated systems reform and have not been accompanied by a review of mandatory reporting requirements to examine the extent to which existing provisions are a barrier or facilitator to the pilot "Child Aware" Approaches. This chapter has demonstrated that having effective referral pathways into services is as important as the funding of the services themselves. The implementation of reforms aimed at shifting child welfare orientations from a residual to a public health approach could be compromised if the extent to which mandatory reporting laws and reporting practices can enable the intended model are not reviewed and best practice measures identified and implemented. Australia is not alone in either its experience of growing demand on child protection services or its desire to implement more preventative approaches to reduce this demand. Whether implemented in Australia or elsewhere, misalignment of mandatory reporting provisions and referral pathways may undermine the intent of both mandatory reporting and preventative approaches.

References

AIHW. (2009). *Child protection Australia 2007–2008*. Canberra: Australian Institute of Health and Welfare.

AIHW. (2013). *Child protection Australia 2011–2012*. Canberra: Australian Institute of Health and Welfare.

Arney, F., & Bromfield, L. (2010). *Frameworks for integrated strategies and services supporting vulnerable families*. Paper presented at the Effective integration of services for children and families symposium, Darwin.

Bamblett, M., Bath, H., & Roseby, R. (2010). *Growing them strong, together: Promoting the safety and wellbeing of the Northern Territory's children, Report of the Board of Inquiry into the Child Protection System in the Northern Territory*. Darwin: Northern Territory Government.

Baum, F. (1998). *The new public health: An Australian perspective*. Melbourne: Oxford University Press.

Bibby, P., & McIlwain, K. (2013, July 11). DOCS plays 'Russian roulette' with lives. *Sydney Morning Herald.* Retrieved from http://www.smh.com.au/nsw/docs-plays-russian-roulette-with-lives-20130710-2pqhm.html

Box, D. (2013, December 17). Marist Brothers leader Alexis Turton 'failed to act' over alleged abuse. *The Australian.* Retrieved from: http://www.theaustralian.com.au/national-affairs/in-depth/marist-brothers-leader-alexis-turton-failed-to-act-over-alleged-abuse/story-fngburq5-1226784962700

Bromfield, L. (2012). Child protection in Australia. In J. Nett & T. Spratt (Eds.), *Child protection systems: An international comparison of "good practice examples" of five countries (Australia, Germany, Finland, Sweden, United Kingdom) with recommendations for Switzerland.* Bern: Swiss Project Fund for Child Protection.

Bromfield, L., & Higgins, D. (2005a). Chronic and isolated maltreatment in a child protection sample. *Family Matters, 70*, 38–45.

Bromfield, L., & Higgins, D. (2005b). *National comparison of child protection systems* (Child abuse prevention issues, 22). Melbourne: Australian Institute of Family Studies.

Bromfield, L., & Holzer, P. (2008). *A national approach for child protection: Project report. A report to the Community and Disability Services Ministers' Advisory Council (CDSMAC).* Melbourne: Australian Institute of Family Studies.

Bromfield, L., & Miller, R. (2012). *Cumulative harm: Specialist practice resource*. Melbourne: Department of Human Services.

Bromfield, L., Arney, F., & Higgins, D. (2014). Contemporary issues in child protection intake, referral and family support. In A. Hayes & D. J. Higgins (Eds.), *Children and families in Australia: Selected policy, legal and practice issues* (pp. 121–129). Melbourne: Australian Institute of Family Studies.

Child, Family, Community Australia (CFCA). (2013). *Australian legal definitions: When is a child in need of protection?* Melbourne: Australian Institute of Family Studies.

Child, Family, Community Australia (CFCA). (2014). *Effects of child abuse and neglect for children and adolescents*. Melbourne: Australian Institute of Family Studies.

Connolly, M. (2005). Differential responses in child care and protection: Innovative approaches in family-centered practice. *Protecting Children, 20*(2–3), 8–21.

Council of Australian Governments. (2009). *Protecting children is everyone's business: National framework for protecting Australia's children 2009–2020*. Canberra: Commonwealth of Australia.

Council of Australian Governments. (2013). *Protecting children in everyone's business: National framework for protecting Australia's children 2009–2020* (Annual report to the Council of Australian Governments 2012–13). Canberra: Department of Families, Housing, Community Services and Indigenous Affairs.

Cummins, P. (1993, February 26). Sentence remarks in the trial R v Aiton, Paul Leslie [Daniel Valerio] [1993] VicSC. Retrieved from http://www.austlii.edu.au/cgi-bin/sinodisp/au/cases/vic/VicSC/1993/78.html?stem=0&synonyms=0&query=title%28R%20and%20Aiton%20%29

Department of Health and Human Services. (n. d.). *Gateway services*. Hobart: Department of Health and Human Services, Tasmania. Retrieved from www.dhhs.tas.gov.au/__data/assets/pdf_file/0020/36038/Gateway_Fact_Sheet_2008-11-17_2.pdf

Department of Social Services. (2013). *Child aware approaches: Successful organisations have been announced.* Retrieved from: www.dss.gov.au/families-and-children/grants-funding/child-aware-approaches-successful-organisations-have-been-announced

de Vaus, D. (2004). *Diversity and change in Australian families: Statistical profiles*. Melbourne: Australian Institute of Family Studies.

Donovan, R., Wood, L., Jalleh, G., & Ivery, P. (2010). *"Help break down the wall": Community attitudes survey summary of results*. Sydney: NAPCAN.

Feerick, M. M., & Snow, K. L. (2006). An examination of research in child abuse and neglect: Past practices and future directions. In M. M. Feerick et al. (Eds.), *Child abuse and neglect: Definitions, classification, and a framework for research*. Baltimore: Paul H. Brooks Publishing Company.

Fogarty, J., & Sargeant, D. (1989). *Protective services for children in Victoria: An interim report*. Melbourne: Community Services.

Frederico, M., Jackson, A., & Jones, S. (2006). *Child death group analysis: Effective responses to chronic neglect*. Melbourne: Office of the Child Safety Commissioner.

Garrison, M. (2005). Reforming child protection: A public health perspective. *Virginia Journal of Social Policy and the Law, 12*(3), 590–637.

Goddard, C., & Liddell, M. (1995). Child abuse fatalities and the media: Lessons from a case study. *Child Abuse Review, 4*, 356–364.

Goddard, C., & Liddell, M. (1993). Child abuse and the media: Victoria introduces mandatory reporting after an intensive media campaign. *Children Australia, 18*(3), 23–27.

Gough, D. (1996). Defining the problem. *Child Abuse and Neglect, 20*(11), 993–1102.

Graycar, A. (1977). The politics of social policy in Australia. *Social Policy & Administration, 11*(1), 3–20.

Graycar, A. (1979). *Welfare politics in Australia: A study in policy analysis*. South Melbourne: Macmillan.

Graycar, A. (1983). *Retreat from the welfare state: Australian social policy in the 1980s*. Sydney: Allen & Unwin.

Holzer, P., & Bromfield, L. (2008). *NCPASS comparability of child protection data: Project report*. Melbourne: Australian Institute of Family Studies.

Humphreys, C. (2007). *Domestic violence and child protection: Challenging directions for practice* (Issues paper 13). Sydney: Australian Domestic and Family Violence Clearinghouse.

Humphreys, C., Holzer, P., Scott, D., Arney, F., Bromfield, L., Higgins, D., & Lewig, K. (2010). The planets aligned: Is child protection policy reform good luck or good management? *Australian Social Work, 63*(2), 145–163.

Ife, J., & Fiske, L. (2003, July 1–4). *Institutional and residual conceptions of human rights*. Paper presented at the activating human rights and diversity conference, Byron Bay Community Centre, Byron Bay.

Jacobs, A., & Fanning, D. (2006). *Child protection services in Tasmania*. Hobart: Tasmania Department of Health and Human Services.

James, M. (2000). *Child abuse and neglect: Part 1 – Redefining the issues*. Canberra: Australian Institute of Criminology.

Kempe, C. H., Silverman, F. N., Steele, B. F., Droegmemueller, W., & Silver, H. K. (1962). The battered-child syndrome. *JAMA, 181*(1), 17–24.

KPMG. (2008). *New directions for child protection in Tasmania: An integrated strategic framework*. Hobart: Department of Health and Human Services Tasmania.

KPMG. (2011). *Child FIRST and integrated family services – Final report*. Melbourne: Victorian Government, Department of Human Services.

Lamont, A., & Bromfield, L. (2010). *History of child protection services* (NCPC resource sheet). Melbourne: Australian Institute of Family Studies.

Mathews, B. (2012). Exploring the contested role of mandatory reporting laws in the identification of severe child abuse and neglect. In M. Freeman (Ed.), *Current legal issues: Vol. 14. Law and childhood studies* (pp. 302–338). Oxford: Oxford University Press.

Mathews, B., & Scott, D. (2013). *Mandatory reporting of child abuse and neglect*. Melbourne: Australian Institute of Family Studies.

Merkel-Holguin, L. (2005). Differential response: A common sense reform in child welfare. *Protecting Children, 20*(2–3), 2–3.

National Society for the Prevention of Cruelty to Children (NSPCC). (2000). *A history of the NSPCC: Protecting Children from Cruelty since 1884*. London: NSPCC.

NSW Education & Communities. (2011, March 2). *The new school leaving age: A parent's guide*. NSW Education & Communities. Retrieved from www.schools.nsw.edu.au/leavingschool/schoolleaveage/faqs.php

Price-Robertson, R., Bromfield, L., & Vassallo, S. (2010). Prevalence matters: Estimating the extent of child maltreatment in Australia. *Developing Practice, 26*, 12–20.

Schene, P. (2005). The emergence of differential response. *Protecting Children, 20*(2–3), 4–7.

Scott, D., & Swain, S. (2002). *Confronting Cruelty: Historical perspectives on child protection in Australia*. Melbourne: Melbourne University Press.

State Government of Victoria. (2011). *Child and family services information, referral and support teams*. Melbourne: State Government of Victoria. Retrieved from: www.dhs.vic.gov.au/for-individuals/children,-families-and-young-people/family-and-parenting-support/family-services/child-first-child-and-family-information,-referral-and-support-teams

Taylor, L., Hutchinson, D., Rapee, R., Burns, L., Stephens, C., & Haber, P. S. (2012). Clinical features and correlates of outcomes for high-risk, marginalized mothers and newborn infants engaged with a specialist perinatal and family drug health service. *Obstetrics and Gynecology International*. doi:10.1155/2012/867265.

Thomas, S., & Naughton, M. (2005, February). *Developing innovative partnership approaches to support vulnerable children and their families: Preliminary Victorian research findings*. Paper presented at the 9th Australian Institute of Family Studies Conference, Melbourne.

Tomison, A. (2001). A history of child protection. Back to the future? *Family Matters, 60*, 46–57.
Victorian Government Community Care Division. (2002). *An integrated strategy for child protection and placement services*. Melbourne: Victorian Government Community Care Division.
Wood, J. (2009). *Report of the Special Commission of Inquiry into Child Protection Services in NSW* (Vol. 1). Sydney: Special Commission of Inquiry into Child Protection Services in NSW.
Zubrick, S., Smith, G., Nicholson, J., Sanson, A., & Jackiewicz, T. (2008). *Parenting and families in Australia* (Social Policy Research Paper 34). Canberra: FaHCSIA.

Chapter 23
Mandatory Reporting of Child Abuse and Marginalised Families

Heather Douglas and Tamara Walsh

Introduction

The introduction of laws requiring the mandatory reporting of serious child abuse and neglect, usually by professionals, has received significant attention, and many researchers have considered the advantages and disadvantages of mandatory reporting (Mathews and Bross 2008; Melton 2005). One advantage, it has been argued, is that the requirement sends a strong message that child abuse will not be tolerated (Takis 2008, p. 126). Other advantages include that it raises awareness of child abuse (Cashmore 2002, p. 9) and that it resolves conflict for some about whether or not to report incidents (Australian Law Reform Commission 1997, p. 435; Tomison 2002a, p. 17). Mandatory reporting laws can ensure that cases of child abuse are brought to the attention of child protection authorities so that further harm may be prevented and services can be provided, especially in cases where, without such laws, the family would remain hidden (Mathews and Bross 2008, p. 515; Cashmore 2002, p. 9). It has also been pointed out that reporting of child abuse by clinicians is consistent with other duties to report, for example, suicide risk and homicide risk (Wekerle 2013, p. 93).

At the same time, some disadvantages associated with mandatory reporting laws have been identified. It has been claimed that they lead to overreporting and greater numbers of unsubstantiated reports and that this puts unnecessary pressure on an already under-resourced child protection system (Takis 2008, p. 126; Jacob and Fanning 2006). Professionals have also raised concerns about loss of the family as clients if they report and many have expressed doubts about the benefits of contact with the child protection system for families under their care (Pietrantonio et al. 2013, p. 105). Another key concern raised about mandatory reporting laws is that

H. Douglas (✉) • T. Walsh
Law School, The University of Queensland, St Lucia, QLD, Australia
e-mail: h.douglas@law.uq.edu.au; t.walsh@law.uq.edu.au

B. Mathews, D.C. Bross (eds.), *Mandatory Reporting Laws and the Identification of Severe Child Abuse and Neglect*, Child Maltreatment 4,
DOI 10.1007/978-94-017-9685-9_23

they may force parents and children underground and deter them from seeking help (Adler 1995, p. 194; Australian Law Reform Commission 1997, p. 2333; Stretch 2003; Melton 2005, p. 14).

In this chapter we draw on two qualitative studies we conducted in Queensland, Australia, to consider how frontline workers (both support workers in nongovernment organisations and lawyers) who work with marginalised groups, for example, with families from culturally and linguistically diverse (CALD) groups,[1] Indigenous families and families experiencing poverty and homelessness or domestic violence, view mandatory reporting of abuse to child protection authorities. Our research has suggested that workers' experiences of the interaction between their clients and child protection services are extremely negative overall (Douglas and Walsh 2009; Walsh and Douglas 2012). As a result, some workers are very reluctant to report abuse because they perceive the response of child protection services to be poor. The kinds of abuse most often referred to by participants in this research were neglect, domestic violence, physical violence and emotional or psychological abuse. Sexual abuse was not specifically discussed by our participants. Thus, our findings are most applicable to situations in which non-sexual abuse is alleged to have occurred.

We begin with a brief outline of the Australian laws that require mandatory reporting. This is followed by a discussion of some of the issues raised in our studies of child protection and the broader literature. In the final section we draw some conclusions about the potential value and risks of mandatory reporting in the context of working with marginalised families and consider possible improvements to current approaches.

Mandatory Reporting in Australian Law

All Australian states and territories have legislated to impose mandatory reporting requirements on at least some professional groups.[2] The requirements vary widely across the jurisdictions: in some states and territories, only a few classes of professionals are required to report suspicions of child maltreatment (most often doctors, nurses, teachers, child care workers and police officers), while in the Northern Territory, every adult who suspects that a child is being harmed or likely to be harmed has a legal duty to report. In Victoria and the Australian Capital Territory,

[1]This term refers to individuals and families that have come to Australia from another country; they may speak a language other than English at home, and they may have special cultural practices and customs.

[2]*Children and Young People Act 2008* (ACT) s 356; *Children and Young Persons (Care and Protection) Act 1998* (NSW) s 27; *Care and Protection of Children Act 2007* (NT) s 26; *Child Protection Act 1999* (Qld) s 148; *Public Health Act 2005* (Qld) ss 191, 192; *Education (General Provisions) Act 2006* (Qld) ss 365, 365A, 366, 366A; *Children's Protection Act 1993* (SA) s 11; *Children, Young Persons and Their Families Act 1997* (Tas) ss 13, 14; *Children, Youth and Families Act 2005* (Vic) ss 182, 184; *Children and Community Services Act 2004* (WA) s 124B.

mandatory reporters are only required to report suspicions of physical or sexual abuse. In Western Australia, only sexual abuse must be reported. In all other states and territories, the types of reportable maltreatment are broader than this. For example, suspicions of neglect and emotional or psychological abuse must be reported by mandatory reporters in New South Wales, the Northern Territory, Queensland, South Australia and Tasmania. In New South Wales, the Northern Territory and Tasmania, mandatory reporters must also report if they are aware that a child has been exposed to family violence or is living in a household where family violence is occurring, provided the required level of harm exists or is likely to occur.[3] Most statutes stipulate financial penalties if professionals fail to report when required to (Mathews et al. 2006, p. 507). Mandatory reporting does not guarantee a particular intervention; rather it operates as a notification to child protection authorities who make a decision about what needs to happen.

Specifically in Queensland, the Australian state where our research was undertaken, section 148 *Child Protection Act 1999* (Qld) (the Act) states that a 'responsible person' who:

> …becomes aware, or reasonably suspects, that harm has been caused to a child placed in the care of an entity conducting a departmental care service or a licensee, the person must, unless the person has a reasonable excuse, report the harm, or suspected harm, to the chief executive- immediately…

The Act defines 'responsible person' for the purposes of the provision as 'an authorised officer' or 'an officer or employee of the department involved in administering' the *Child Protection Act 1999* (Qld) or 'a person employed in a departmental care service or licenced care service'.[4] 'Harm' is broadly defined as 'any detrimental effect of a significant nature on a child's physical, psychological or emotional well-being' and can be caused by physical, psychological or emotional abuse or neglect or sexual abuse or exploitation resulting from a single act or series of acts.[5] 'Significant' harm is not defined in legislation; however the Department of Communities, Child Safety and Disabilities (2013) defines significant harm as harm that is substantial or serious and more than transitory; 'it must be demonstrable in the child's presentation, functioning or behaviour'. This definition is obviously open to interpretation, and in a risk-averse environment, where child protection agencies operate in a 'better safe than sorry' culture (Carmody Inquiry 2013, pp. xvii, 205), 'significant harm' may be interpreted widely. This is a particular problem for certain types of child abuse and neglect, especially exposure to domestic violence and emotional abuse (Mathews 2012). The Queensland Civil and Administrative Tribunal (QCAT) has acknowledged that witnessing domestic violence can cause harm to children (*CT v Commissioner for Children and Young People and Child Guardian* [2012] QCAT 354 at 49–50).

---

[3] *Children and Young Persons (Care and Protection) Act 1998* (NSW) s 23 (see definition of 'at risk of significant harm'); *Care and Protection of Children Act 2007* (NT) s 15 (definition of 'harm to child'); *Children, Young Persons and Their Families Act 1997* (Tas) s 14(2)(a).

[4] See *Child Protection Act 1999* (Qld) ss 6, 148.

[5] *Child Protection Act 1999* (Qld) s 9.

Further, staff of the Commission for Children and Young People and Child Guardian,[6] and doctors or registered nurses[7] who become aware, or reasonably suspect during the practice of their profession, that a child has been, is being or is likely to be harmed also have a duty to report. Staff members of state and non-state schools are required to report sexual abuse or likely sexual abuse of students under 18 years.[8] Penalties apply as a consequence of failure to report.[9]

Marginalised Mothers and the Child Protection System in Australia

It is well established that marginalised mothers, particularly those who are poor, homeless, Indigenous or victims of domestic violence, are more likely to become known to child protection authorities (Thomson 2003; Keegan Eamon and Kopels 2004; Busch et al. 2008; Marts et al. 2008). Dettlaf and colleagues (2009) suggest that there is an important relationship between race, income and risk assessment but also that disproportionality in the child welfare system is a complex phenomenon that cannot be explained by a single factor.

Poverty has long been associated with child maltreatment but the causal effect of poverty on child maltreatment has received limited attention (Walsh and Douglas 2008). Studies undertaken in Missouri, by Drake and colleagues (2009, p. 315, 2011, p. 471), concluded that there is no evidence that visibility to mandated reporters causes higher reporting rates among the poor whatever their race. In contrast, and drawing on a number of empirical studies undertaken in the United States, Roberts (2012, p. 1478) focuses on the intersectional nature of race and poverty and argues that foster care 'is only one example of the many forms of over policing that overlap and converge in the lives of poor women of colour'. She observes that mothers involved in the child welfare system in the United States are disproportionately poor women of colour (Roberts 2007, 2008), a situation that is mirrored in Australia (Douglas and Walsh 2013). Aboriginal and Torres Strait Islander children in Australia are increasingly on child protection orders; in 2011–2012 they were almost ten times more likely than other children to be subject to a child protection order and to be in out of home care, with the most common type of abuse reported

[6] *Commission for Children and Young People and Child Guardian Act 2000* (Qld) s 20.

[7] *Public Health Act 2005* (Qld) ss 191 and 192. Pursuant to the *Family Law Act 1975* (Cth), s 67ZA, family court personnel and counsellors are also required to report.

[8] *Education (General Provisions) Act 2006* (Qld) ss 365, 365A, 366, 366A. The reporting requirements differ depending whether the report emanates from a state or non-state school.

[9] For employees of the Child safety Department, those employed in a departmental care service or licensed care service 20 penalty units: *Child Protection Act 1999* (Qld) s 148. For doctors and registered nurses 50 penalty units – *Public Health Act* (Qld) s 193. A penalty unit is currently $110; see *Penalties and Sentences Act 1992* (Qld) s 5(1)(d).

being neglect.[10] Of course, neglect is often directly associated with poverty. The conflation of harm and neglect is questionable because an inability to materially provide for a child does not mean the child lacks nurturing or protection. It would seem cruel and inhuman to punish a mother and child with removal for reasons of neglect resulting from poverty, when supports and less invasive interventions through differential response approaches could remedy the situation (Walsh and Douglas 2009; Mathews and Kenny 2008; Mathews 2012). However in Australia, few child protection statutes explicitly mandate against removal on the basis of neglect even if the neglect is the result of poverty.[11] Recent United States research has found that poverty is associated with reports of child abuse but that ensuring that mothers receive all eligible child support for their children significantly reduces the reporting of child maltreatment (Cancian et al. 2009, p. 14).

American studies have also noted the disproportionate representation of ethnic minorities in out of home care. For example, in a study in Indiana, Hispanic and black children were disproportionately encountered in out of home placements compared with white children (Busch et al. 2008, pp. 256–257). In Australia there are no reliable figures on the numbers of children from culturally and linguistically diverse (CALD) backgrounds in the child protection system (Kaur 2012, p. 17). However misunderstandings of cultural differences in child rearing practices may contribute to a finding of child abuse.[12] For example, such misunderstandings might include different approaches to physical discipline in other cultures (Brophy 2008, p. 82).

Studies in the United States have also noted that there are broader 'treatment disparities', with black and Hispanic children much slower to exit care than their white counterparts (Busch et al. 2008, p. 256; Derezotes 2009, p. 44; Church 2006). Racial bias in decision-making has been found to be an important consideration in decision-making about child protection responses (Dettlaff et al. 2009, p. 1635). The United States policies such as reducing in-home support for families, focussing increasingly on out-of-home care and emphasising adoption as a solution to the rising foster care population, reflect, according to Roberts (2012, p. 1485), an increasingly punitive approach to child welfare and that it has been a political choice to fund punitive rather than supportive programmes. These punitive approaches also feature in Australia's child protection environment. Increasingly, some child protection advocates are pushing for long-term guardianship orders and adoption, and child protection services are focussed on tertiary intervention rather than focussing on building the strengths of families (Betts 2013; Rath 2001). Roberts (2012, p. 1486) maintains that this punitive response is justified by 'stereotypes of black

[10] See Australian Institute of Health and Welfare (2013) at 16–17, 32, 34 and 41. The second most common abuse was emotional abuse.

[11] One exception is NSW where legislation prevents the Children's Court from concluding that the basic needs of a child are not likely to be met because of poverty; *Children and Young Persons (Care and Protection) Act 1998* (NSW) s 71(2)(b).

[12] Kaur (2012, p. 11) cites differences in child discipline, physical displays of affection, educational attainment expectations, respect for elders and use of natural remedies.

maternal unfitness'. She argues that in some United States communities the spatial concentration of child welfare supervision and removal creates an expectation of supervision and removal and it has become normalised. This is also occurring in some Australian communities with, in some cases, five generations of Indigenous children being placed in care (see McGlade 2012). Given the history the removal of Indigenous children from their families, many Indigenous people perceive current child protection interventions as an ongoing process of removal (Bamblett et al. 2010, p. 19). Roberts (2012, p. 1491) describes how the child welfare system in the United States operates to discipline and control poor women and poor black women. Such a claim could also be made about Australian approaches to child protection. In the Australian child protection context, there have been concerns expressed about the lack of cultural competency among child protection workers and the very limited number of Aboriginal people employed as child protection workers (Kaur 2012, p. 15; Bessarab and Crawford 2010, p. 190).

There is a risk that, in this environment, mandatory reporting requirements are likely to further entrench the disproportionate representation of poor and Indigenous or ethnic families in the child protection system.[13] Also, if professionals who work with children and families are not able to collaborate effectively with child protection authorities and there is a context of mutual distrust, there is a risk that professionals may not comply with their reporting obligations.

Empirical Research in Brisbane, Australia

Methodology

We undertook two studies in Brisbane, Australia. The aim of both studies was to investigate professionals' views on the nature of mothers' experiences within the child protection system in Queensland. In the first study, five focus groups were held at community organisations in Brisbane involving 32 workers (hereafter referred to as 'community service providers').[14] The community organisations that participated are all engaged in direct service delivery and have a client base which consists, at least in part, of mothers of children either in the care of, or 'known' to, child protection authorities. They provide services to a wide range of female clients including poor and homeless women, women experiencing domestic violence, Aboriginal women and women from CALD communities.[15] The second study involved 21 interviews with 26 lawyers with substantial experience in child protection

[13] In Australia Aboriginal and Torres Strait Islander children were almost eight times more likely than non-Indigenous children to be the subject of substantiated reports of harm/risk of harm with neglect and emotional abuse the most commonly substantiated maltreatment; see Scott (2013).

[14] The results of this research are reported in Douglas et al. (2009).

[15] See Kidd and Parshall (2000) at 294 and Kitzinger (1994) at 105 for a discussion of the pros and cons of focus group research.

law (in five of the interviews there were two participants). A snowball sampling method was employed whereby interviewed lawyers recommended other child protection lawyers for interview (Doreian and Woodard 1992). All of the lawyers we interviewed commonly represented parents or children in child protection matters, either in private practice or within a legal organisation such as Legal Aid or a community legal centre.[16] Three had previously worked within child protection departments. Both studies focused on the experiences of mothers as they are more likely to have care responsibilities for children particularly in those cases where there is child protection intervention (see Lewis and Welsh 2005). Neither study focused on mandatory reporting, but the issue of mandatory reporting was raised and discussed in the focus groups and interviews.

Based on a literature review, a semi-structured interview guide was created for each study. The guides focused on facilitating in-depth discussion and analysis of current practices and challenges associated with working in the child protection field. Ethical approval was obtained from the Ethics Committee at the University of Queensland. Each focus group and interview ran for between 60 and 90 min. Focus groups and interviews were recorded and transcribed, and the qualitative data yielded was pattern coded (Miles and Huberman 1994, pp. 69–72). The limitations of our approach are conceded. The findings reported on here are based on accounts of lawyers and community service providers who advocate for and represent mainly parents within the child protection system in Queensland. It cannot be understood as a literal description of the system as a whole or of the workings of the child protection systems in other states (Dingwall 1997, p. 54).

Results

Our research participants identified a number of concerns regarding mandatory reporting. The concern most commonly noted was that mothers might choose not to seek help and support for medical issues, housing or police intervention in response to domestic violence as examples, if they are fearful that they might be reported to child protection authorities and their children could be removed.

Some of our participants said that their clients avoid social services altogether, including family support services and homelessness services, because they fear being referred to child protection authorities. In one of our focus groups, the following comments were made:

> There are those family crisis centres, but that's where they're reporting to Child Safety … So, you're giving them that invitation to take you kids while you're trying to escape violence.

[16] We conducted interviews with lawyers instead of focus groups for practical reasons. Most of the lawyers we interviewed work alone as individuals and their demanding schedules made conducting group interviews extremely difficult. The interviews with two participants were conducted with the lawyers who worked together in the same organisation.

> And they don't want to tell anyone cause if they tell anyone then their children will be taken away and then they can't get their kids back. Cause even if they are homeless and they do get shelter, where do you get a place where you can have your kids for 3 nights a week, because with homelessness at the moment, even in a boarding house it's full of really intense issues and it's not a safe place and there's usually not any other immediate housing other than a boarding house or a refuge, where they take the kids off you anyway. And it's meant to provide safety for you and your children, but if you take them there you'll end up losing them.

In another focus group, participants said that some women avoid accessing health services because they fear being reported to Child Safety. The following exchange occurred:

> Worker: I.'ve found that. It is often that the children get taken to visit a GP and it is on that occasion that a notification results from that.
> Facilitator: What kinds of things are alerting the doctor?
> Worker: I don't know. Maybe they go in for a cold or something and then next thing they know there is a notification made against them.

This worker is not suggesting that child protection authorities have become involved simply because the child has a cold; rather the worker is emphasising the point that it is an attendance at a doctor's appointment which has triggered involvement of child protection services.

The lawyers in one of our interviews claimed that some young women even try to avoid giving birth in the hospital because of the fear that they will be reported to Child Safety and have their child removed:

> Lawyer 1: So really, in some ways, it's putting child safety – in that way putting the child's life and the mother's life at risk if they then decide to, okay, I can't go to hospital because I know they're going to take my baby so I'll have it at home …
> Lawyer 2: Oh, yeah, women do do that. You know, they will try and run away to have the baby and …
> Lawyer 1: Self-preservation sort of thing.

The two lawyers here are reporting on their clients' behaviours. Their point is that young women may avoid contact with health professionals because they believe there is a risk that they may be reported to child protection authorities.

In the context of domestic violence, some participants suggested that women may decide not to report abuse to police because they fear the removal of their children. In one focus group, the following exchange occurred:

> Facilitator: Do you think that the fear of their kids being taken away stops them calling the police about violence?
> Speaker: Yeah, because as soon as you call the police, there'll often be a juvenile aid [worker] that comes out with them

In a separate group, a similar comment was made:

> Facilitator: So do you think that women are less likely to seek help from the police [who have mandatory reporting requirements] than ringing [a crisis counsellor who does not have a mandatory reporting requirement]?

Worker: Yeah,because the police stuff, particularly. But also I think generally, because they're scared because, even with a shift in the culture people are going to be scared about what to say, and whether to give their name. Is it confidential and what does confidential really mean? A lot of the clients, even without reporting issues, they are very sceptical about whether or not to trust us. And that issue of reporting, I mean, it's something that has come up for us a number of times.

The fear of intervention may seem unreasonable, but often it arises because of some prior experience with child protection authorities, for example, where the mother was subject to a child protection order as a child or where the mother is otherwise 'known' to child protection authorities. One of the lawyers we interviewed said:

> The police have an obligation to report child abuse or domestic violence of course.[17] Clearly this information is exchanged between the various child protection units in the core service delivery areas. That needs to happen. But, sometimes, yes I have seen that because certain families do come to the attention of a particular service delivery agency they may have a perception that they are being targeted. Although I've not seen that to be vexatious or scurrilous. They are people that, unfortunately, are known because there is a particular history there.

Another lawyer stated:

> No one is going to go, after having their child in protection for a short period of time or a long period of time, are going to go to the Child Safety and say, listen, John's beating me or Sue's beating me, or whatever, for the pure fear factor that they're going to lose their kids again.

Another concern identified by our participants was that professionals might not report instances of child maltreatment, despite their mandatory reporting obligations, because they lack confidence in the child protection system. Some of the community service providers who participated in our research said they were reluctant to report instances of potential harm to children because they were not confident that the system would respond appropriately. The following exchange occurred in one of our focus groups:

Worker 1: Yeah, and we don't generally report. Our bottom line is that we wouldn't report unless we absolutely had to. But there have been these three cases where we've had to almost have a mini case to really talk about those issues.

Worker 2: And the difference I suppose it that – as opposed to [a referral agency] … I will have a bit of a luxury in that you know you're going to have continued contact, so you give the woman the opportunity to explain the situation more fully.

One community service provider said:

> This mandatory reporting thing is very… can often just lead to being that kind of quick-to-judge-and-remove before even talking to anyone, before finding out the situation or the dynamic.

[17]While current legislation in Queensland does not mandate police reporting of children living with domestic violence, Queensland Police have a blanket policy of reporting children living with domestic violence. A recent inquiry has recommended that this policy be repealed; see Carmody Inquiry (2013) at xviii.

In a separate focus group, a community service provider said that child protection workers are 'too young and inexperienced' to effectively deal with situations where children are at risk. She said they 'may be putting their organisations at risk' because 'they know they can do a better job than handing them over [to child protection services]'. The following exchange occurred in another focus group:

Speaker:	We have also made notifications with the support of women.
Facilitator:	What about where women don't want to notify but you perceive an issue. How do you deal with that?
Speaker:	We don't readily notify, we don't take it lightly and we have significant discussion with the people we work with. Most of the time if we are concerned with child safety, where there are high levels of DV, there is often a lot of information sharing in relation to the impact on children and issues in relation to safety and protection, particularly recognising the capacity for women to protect their children from violence where she is exposed to violence. So we look at providing support to women and recognising the challenges of living in a violent or abusive situation and the effect on children.

In one of our focus groups, the community service providers discussed circumstances in which they decided to report an instance of child abuse, but the child protection department did not offer any assistance. They said:

> I remember when we picked up two little girls, who had been thrown out of the house with all their belongings, and I went and picked them up from Logan and brought them here, rang child safety and they said, well she's just a naughty girl, she could go back if she behaved. You've got to solve the matter. You've got yourself in a corner because you've picked them up – it's their responsibility. So I said, 'was I supposed to leave them on the footpath with their belongings?' And she said 'well then they would have had to do the right thing'.
>
> We had a little girl who rang in a couple of weeks ago, and said, I'm at the neighbour's house because Mum's just lost it, yelling and screaming and telling me she never wants to see me again and all the rest of it. And she was in tears, sobbing, and she had been under the care of the Department previously, but they put her back with Mum and said everything was solved. I rang up the Department said you're going to have to intervene. It was a Friday night, and they asked whether she had anywhere to go, and I said 'well that's up to you to decide'. She said to me, do you think the neighbour would be happy to keep her?

Some of the lawyers we interviewed also discussed the negative impacts on mothers of notifications as another reason not to report. One said:

> … what I found is that if case workers from the hospital or what they call their outreach workers – and this is what I've discovered going through subpoenaed documents, is they'll make a note and then they'll make a notification to Child Safety. It doesn't necessarily mean that it was a life threatening situation. It's more of a situation where a mother might yell at her child and give it a whack and that then becomes a notification, that then becomes part of the history and then that notification will either be verified or not verified, you know. I think that's a statutory requirement anyway on the hospital but again I think it's also up to the individual and how they view the situation. Remote communities and small communities are quite volatile places.

One of the lawyers we interviewed questioned the child safety department's capacity to deal appropriately with such cases. She said:

> Cause the Department isn't a therapeutic body. I feel if they're going to do any constructive work with families it really should be another family or another agency doing the work.

Discussion

Mandatory Reporting and the Risk That Mothers Will Not Seek Help

Consistent with our findings, a common claim that is made in the literature about mandatory reporting requirements around child abuse is that parents may not seek help from professionals if they fear being reported to police or child protection agencies (Alvarez et al. 2004; Smith and Parsons Winokur 2004; Gielen et al. 2000).

For example, it has been suggested that mothers may avoid services that offer home visits because they fear child protection intervention. Davidov and colleagues (2012) interviewed workers and their clients involved in a home visitation programme in Virginia which involved nurses and social workers visiting disadvantaged first-time mothers. The workers were mandated to report child abuse. Some women reported to the researchers that they would limit their disclosures of abuse to visiting nurses because of the risk of being mandatorily reported for child abuse (by virtue of their children observing domestic violence). Drawing on the perspectives of both the home visitors and the mothers, the study also found that some clients cancelled visits or dropped out of the programme because of a fear of being reported (Davidov et al. 2012, pp. 600–601). The study concluded that mandated reporting issues 'transcend clinical care' and have significant consequences for women in other contexts (Davidov et al. 2012, p. 604). The study found that 'clients' fears of mandated reporting and losing their children seem to act as barriers within the home visitation program, especially with regard to establishing trust… and disclosure' (Davidov et al. 2012, p. 602).

Unfortunately there are few studies that have considered parents' views of mandatory reporting or the views of those who support them. However some studies have been undertaken in places where there are mandatory reporting requirements relating to domestic violence. These studies may give some indication of how mothers might engage with services in an environment of mandatory child abuse reporting. It is relevant to note, for example, that some studies have demonstrated that abused women may be less likely to seek medical attention in the context of mandatory reporting laws around domestic violence (Smith and Parsons Winokur 2004, p. 208). For example, a study by Smith and Winokur (2004) examined battered women's views of doctors' mandatory reporting requirements. This study related to the mandatory reporting requirements surrounding the doctors' duty to report injuries suspected to be associated with domestic violence. What is particularly interesting about this study, and important in considering the mandatory reporting of child abuse where there is also domestic violence, is that battered women who did not want police involvement in their circumstances stated they were less likely to seek medical attention as a result of the requirement of mandatory reporting (Smith and Parsons Winokur 2004, p. 219). In a study conducted by Gielen and colleagues (2000), the researchers interviewed 442 women (202 of these women were abused women) about their policy preferences concerning domestic violence screening and mandatory reporting. In the study, abused women were more likely than non-abused women to support routine screening for domestic violence, and the majority of women in both groups believed that routine screening would make it easier to get help (Gielen et al. 2000, p. 284). However, two thirds of the women interviewed thought that women would be less likely to tell their health-care provider about the abuse under a mandatory reporting policy, and many of the women expressed fear and concern about negative consequences resulting from mandatory reporting (Gielen et al. 2000, p. 282).

The problem, of course, is not mandatory reporting per se but rather the ineffectiveness of the child protection system as a whole. If the system does not support families to bring about protective outcomes for their children, and if child protection interventions are punitive in nature, then mandatory reporting and the response to it simply casts the net of affected families wider. Where child protection systems focus on working with mothers to support them to retain care of their children, the experience of mandatory reporting may be more positive. For example, one mandatory reporting programme for domestic violence, in the US state of Kentucky, has had some success, most likely because it was strongly connected to the provision of services to families (Bledsoe et al. 2004). In Kentucky reporting domestic violence is mandatory and anyone who suspects domestic violence must report it, not just professionals working with families. Notably, reports are made to a social service agency rather than a law enforcement agency. In a review of 631 adult protective service cases resulting from reports of domestic violence, Bledsoe et al. (2004) found that just under half of the referrals came from law enforcement, around 16 % came from women's shelters and some came from women experiencing violence themselves. Although this study did not ask whether women were less inclined to report violence to police or child protection agencies in the context of mandatory reporting, it was undertaken in light of concerns that had been expressed about possible unintended consequences of mandatory reporting law to victims (Bledsoe et al. 2004, p. 535). The researchers found that over half of those reported cases received social services, including safety plans and shelter (Bledsoe et al. 2004, p. 553). Arguably the Kentucky model is a more positive one as the focus is on family support rather than child removal or criminalisation.

While there is no specific requirement for mandatory reporting of domestic violence in Queensland, the emotional effects of domestic violence on the child may well result in reportable harm or in reporters making reports on this basis even where there is no harm to the child.[18] The study conducted in Kentucky suggests that systems focussed on family support may be more likely to be supported by mothers and those organisations that support them.

A recent inquiry into child protection in Queensland has recommended a 'dual reporting pathway' which would allow some concerns about child protection to be referred to a nongovernment broker, and ideally, under this model, many families would be referred quickly to the services they need (Carmody Inquiry 2013, pp.

[18] For example, under Queensland legislation, harm includes emotional and psychological harm (see *Child Protection Act 1999* (Qld) ss 9, 148).

xviii–xix). The Carmody Inquiry emphasised that child protection interventions need to be child *and* parent sensitive to ensure that services address the risk factors that give rise to child protection concerns in the first place, for example, drug addiction, domestic violence, mental illness and social exclusion (Carmody Inquiry 2013, p. 134 (emphasis added)).

Mandatory Reporting and Lack of Confidence in the Child Protection System

Many studies have found that mandatory reporting creates moral, ethical and practical dilemmas for professionals and that professionals often decide not to report suspected child abuse despite their legal obligations (Bunting et al. 2010, pp. 191, 198). For example, in their 2004 study, Alvarez and colleagues (2004) found that mandatory reporters often choose not report child abuse for various reasons including the negative impact on the therapeutic relationship, negative intrusion into the family's life and the risk of mislabelling and stigmatising families, particularly since many reports are unsubstantiated (Alvarez et al. 2004, pp. 326–327; Vulliamy and Sullivan 2000, pp. 1467–1468; Feng et al. 2012, p. 278; Wiseman 2008; cf Sege et al. 2011, p. 465).

In their survey of 26 paediatricians, Vulliamy and Sullivan (2000) found that the respondents were sometimes non-compliant with the duty to report, and many of those that did report were undecided as to whether this had resulted in a positive outcome. One of three main reasons why paediatricians in the Vulliamy and Sullivan (2000, p. 1467) study did not report was that they believed that there were problems with the child protection system.[19] Another study involving interviews with 110 primary health-care providers noted that these professionals were unlikely to report suspected child abuse, even in a mandatory reporting environment, unless they believed child protection intervention would benefit the child (Sege et al. 2011, p. 465; see also Feng et al. 2012, p. 278). Other studies have also pointed to the decision not to report being linked to perceptions that reporting would make the situation worse or to uncertainty about the child protection system's ability or willingness to deal with the case (Bunting et al. 2010, pp. 198–199; Gunn, et al. 2005, p. 99). In a qualitative study involving interviews with nurses, many of the respondents, despite mandatory reporting requirements, had delayed reporting suspected child abuse on the basis that they would be able to provide better support and intervention for the child and family given the 'overwhelmed' child protection system (Eisbach and Driessnack 2010, pp. 321–322).[20] Delaronde and colleagues (2000, p. 908)

[19] See also Jacob and Fanning (2006), where it was suggested that a number of professionals had begun to see reporting as pointless due to lack of services and follow-up from child protection authorities.

[20] Similarly in a study of doctors and nurses in Israel, nurses were more likely to consider the outcomes of reporting (as compared to doctors) before reporting; see Ben Natan et al. (2012) at 336.

emphasise that even where reporters do report suspected abuse, 'there is no evidence to suggest that these children would receive appropriate attention' from the child protection system.

Some studies suggest that the experience of women who engage with the child protection system can actually be harmful. In a Canadian study undertaken by Hughes and colleagues (2011), the researchers spoke to 64 women who had experienced domestic violence and had become involved in the child protection system. The authors found that some women had contacted child protection services seeking assistance, yet they found they were the investigated and told to leave abusive partners without being provided with appropriate support or concrete assistance (Hughes et al. 2011, p. 1088; see also Douglas and Walsh 2010). The researchers concluded that the child protection system was not an effective system for supporting women who have experienced domestic violence. In their study referred to above, Davidov and colleagues (2012, pp. 601–602) found that both mothers and the home visitors identified that mothers held strong fears of child removal if domestic violence was reported. Some of the home visitors interviewed in Davidov et al.'s (2012, pp. 601–602) study agreed this fear was legitimate. Indeed, one unintended consequence of mandatory reporting may actually be the revictimisation of abused women (Jaffe et al. 2003). Unsubstantiated reports may be held on file for many years and it can be difficult to have them removed. As one writer from the United States observes, even baseless reports can have implications for employment (Owhe 2013, p. 317).

Improving Current Approaches

It seems that mandatory reporting can have the effect of casting the net of child protection system wider for some kinds of abuse, not necessarily to the benefit of children and families. In 2002 research, Ainsworth (2002, p. 8) observed that considerably more resources were applied to unsubstantiated cases in a mandatory reporting environment (NSW) compared to a non-mandatory reporting environment (WA). The diversion of much needed resources to situations that can be dealt with more effectively outside the child protection system is undesirable, and service providers who work closely with children and their families believe that they are often in the best position to judge what kind of intervention will be appropriate in the circumstances.

In most circumstances, it will be appropriate that consultation with the mother occurs before a report is made to child protection services. In the context of reporting domestic violence, some have suggested that victims of violence should be consulted and consent to the reporting. This might encourage attendance at doctors and other service providers (Smith and Parsons Winokur 2004, p. 219).

In their research, Delaronde and colleagues (2000 p. 903) suggested that only a narrow group of matters – sexual abuse, serious physical abuse or maltreatment which places the child in imminent danger – be immediately reported by mandated reporters by telephone with a written report to follow to child protection services within 72 h.[21] In Delaronde and colleagues' (2000) study, the researchers found that for a significant number of mandated reporters, this option was preferred to traditional mandatory reporting obligations.

Some have suggested that professionals who have mandatory reporting duties should at least advise their clients of this before consulting with them. Adler (1995, p. 193), a psychiatrist, accepts that the number of fatalities stemming from child abuse has reduced since the introduction of mandatory reporting. He says there have been discussions in his field of expertise about developing a consent form for patients to sign which makes it clear that they allow doctors to disclose information that reveals the patient may be a danger to others, for example, to children (Adler 1995, p. 197).

It is also important that professionals who work with children and families have confidence in the child protection system. This will encourage reporting and ensure compliance with any mandatory reporting requirements that do exist. For participants in our research, it was important that the removal of a child only occurs as a last resort and that every effort be made to support a family to bring about protective outcomes for their child. Our participants felt that often this did not occur, and this is a common complaint by professionals about child protection systems in Australia and elsewhere (Penn and Gough 2002; McConnell and Llewellyn 2005; Tomison 2002b; Masson 2008). This is ameliorated to some extent in New South Wales and Victoria by the legislative requirement that every effort be made to assist the family to maintain care of the child before placing a child in alternative care.[22] In Queensland, no such provision exists; rather the test applied is a broad 'best interests' of the child test.[23] This means that workers can feel alienated from the system rather than working in partnership and collaborating on the kind of intervention that is best for the child and the family. In recognition of these concerns, the recent Carmody Inquiry into child protection in Queensland recommended a new statutory practice framework, 'Signs of Safety', should be introduced (2013, p. xx). Such an approach would allow child protection workers to use their casework skills and focus more on what works for the individual family. This strength-based approach would allow child protection workers to 'rebalance case-work and decision-making back in favour of professional judgment' (Carmody Inquiry 2013, p. 204). The Carmody Inquiry also recommended legislative reform to the definition of 'child in need of protection' to emphasise that a child must be 'at risk of significant harm to meet the legislative threshold' (2013, p. 504).

---

[21] Another aspect to this alternative strategy was that in less severe cases the mandated reporter may report to the child protection service or discuss with an independent reviewer.

[22] *Children and Young Persons (Care and Protection) Act 1998* (NSW) s 63; *Children, Youth and Families Act 2005* (Vic) s 276(2)(b).

[23] *Child Protection Act 1999* (Qld) s 5A.

Conclusion

Our research has suggested that mandatory reporting is problematic if the child protection system cannot be relied upon by professionals to adequately and effectively support children and families. In cases of serious abuse, particularly sexual abuse, mandatory reporting serves a useful function and is important to protect children. However in a punitive child protection environment, mandatory reporting may discourage vulnerable mothers from seeking assistance from social services. Where child protection services are unable to offer substantive assistance to families, their capacity to respond appropriately to the reports they receive may be limited, and mandatory reporters may actually choose not to comply with their reporting obligations.

References

Adler, R. (1995). To tell or not to tell: The psychiatrist and child abuse. *Australian and New Zealand Journal of Psychiatry, 29*, 190–198.

Ainsworth, F. (2002). Mandatory reporting of child abuse and neglect: Why would you want it? *Developing Practice: The Child, Youth and Family Work Journal, 4*, 5–8.

Alvarez, K., Donohue, B., Kenny, M., et al. (2004). The process and consequences of reporting child maltreatment: A brief overview for professionals in the mental health field. *Aggression and Violent Behaviour, 10*, 311–331.

Australian Institute of Health and Welfare. (2013). *Child protection in Australia 2011–2012* (Child welfare series No. 55). Canberra: Australian Institute of Health and Welfare.

Australian Law Reform Commission. (1997). *Seen and heard: Priority for children in the legal system* (Report No 84). Canberra: Australian Law Reform Commission.

Bamblett, M., Bath, H., & Roseby, R. (2010). *Growing them strong, together: Promoting the safety and well-being of the Northern Territory's Children.* Report of the Board of Inquiry into the Child Protection System in the Northern Territory, Northern Territory Government, Darwin.

Ben Natan, C., Faour, S., Naamhah, K., et al. (2012). Factors affecting medical and nursing staff reporting of child abuse. *International Nursing Review, 59*(3), 331–337.

Bessarab, D., & Crawford, F. (2010). Aboriginal practitioners speak out: Contextualising child protection interventions. *Australian Social Work, 63*(2), 179–193.

Betts, A. (2013, May 14). Indigenous adoption push prompts stolen generation fears. *ABC News*. Available from http://www.abc.net.au/news/2013-05-14/indigenous-child-adoption-proporal-and-reaction/4688232

Bledsoe, L. K., Yankeelov, P., Barbee, A., et al. (2004). Understanding the impact of intimate partner violence mandatory reporting law. *Violence Against Women, 10*, 534–560.

Brophy, J. (2008). Child maltreatment in diverse households: Challenges to law, theory and practice. *Journal of Law and Society, 35*, 75–94.

Bunting, L., Lazenbatt, A., & Wallace, I. (2010). Information sharing and reporting systems in the UK and Ireland: Professional barriers to child maltreatment concerns. *Child Abuse Review, 19*, 187–202.

Busch, M., Wall, J. R., Koch, S., et al. (2008). Addressing the disproportionate representation of children of color: A collaborative community approach. *Child Welfare, 87*, 255–278.

Cancian, M., Slack, K., & Yang, M. (2009). *The effect of poverty on risk of child maltreatment* (Discussion Paper 1385–10). Institute for Research on Poverty. Available from http://www.irp.wisc.edu/publications/dps/pdfs/dp138510.pdf

Carmody Inquiry: Queensland Child Protection Commission of Inquiry. (2013). *Taking responsibility: A roadmap for Queensland child protection*. Brisbane: Queensland Child Protection Inquiry.

Cashmore, J. (2002). Mandatory reporting: Is it the culprit? Where is the evidence? *Developing Practice: The Child, Youth and Family Work Journal, 4*, 9–12.

Church, W. T. (2006). From start to finish: The duration of Hispanic children in out of home placements. *Children and Youth Services Review, 28*, 1007–1023.

CT v Commissioner for Children and Young People and Child Guardian [2012] QCAT 354.

Davidov, D., Jack, S., Frost, S., et al. (2012). Mandatory reporting in the context of home visitation programs: Intimate partner violence and children's exposure to intimate partner violence. *Violence Against Women, 18*, 595–610.

Delaronde, S., King, G., Bendel, R., et al. (2000). Opinions among mandated reporters toward child maltreatment reporting policies. *Child Abuse and Neglect, 24*(7), 901–910.

Department of Communities, Child Safety and Disability Services. (2013). *What is child abuse?* Queensland Government. Available from http://www.communities.qld.gov.au/childsafety/protecting-children/what-is-child-abuse

Derezotes, D. (2009). *Child welfare commentary, racial and ethnic disparity and disproportionality in child welfare and juvenile justice: A compendium* (pp. 41–46). Chicago: Centre for Juvenile Justice Reform, University of Chicago.

Dettlaff, A. J., Rivaux, S. L., Baumann, D. J., et al. (2009). Disentangling substantiation: The influence of race, income, and risk on the substantiation decision in child welfare. *Children and Youth Services Review, 33*(9), 1630–1637.

Dingwall, R. (1997). Accounts, interviews and observations. In G. Miller & R. Dingwall (Eds.), *Context and method in qualitative research* (pp. 52–66). London: Sage.

Doreian, P., & Woodard, K. L. (1992). Fixed list versus snowball selection of social networks. *Social Science Research, 21*, 216–233.

Douglas, H., & Walsh, T. (2009). Mothers and the child protection system. *International Journal of Law, Policy and the Family, 23*(2), 211–229.

Douglas, H., & Walsh, T. (2010). Mothers, domestic violence and child protection (symposium centrepiece). *Violence Against Women, 16*(5), 489–508.

Douglas, H., & Walsh, T. (2013). Continuing the stolen generations: Child protection interventions and indigenous people. *The International Journal of Children's Rights, 21*(1), 59–87.

Douglas, H., Walsh, T., & Blore, K. (2009). Mothers and the child protection system (Research Report). Brisbane: The University of Queensland.

Drake, B., Moo, S., & Jonson-Reid, M. (2009). Race and child maltreatment reporting: Are blacks overrepresented? *Children and Youth Services Review, 31*, 309–316.

Drake, B., Jolley, J., Lanier, P., et al. (2011). Racial bias in child protection? A comparison of competing explanations using national data. *Pediatrics, 127*(3), 471–478.

Eisbach, S., & Driessnack, M. (2010). Am I sure I want to go down this road? Hesitations in the reporting of child maltreatment by nurses. *Journal for Specialists in Pediatric Nursing, 15*(4), 317–323.

Feng, J., Chen, Y., Fettzer, S., et al. (2012). Ethical and legal challenges of mandated child abuse reports. *Children and Youth Services Review, 34*, 276–280.

Gielen, A. C., Schollenberger, J., & Dienman, J. (2000). Women's opinions about domestic violence screening and mandatory reporting. *American Journal of Preventive Medicine, 19*(4), 279–285.

Gunn, V., Hickson, G., & Cooper, W. (2005). Factors effecting paediatricians' reporting of suspected child maltreatment. *Ambulatory Pediatrics, 5*, 96–101.

Hughes, J., Chau, S., & Poff, D. (2011). "They're not my favourite people": What mothers who have experienced intimate partner violence say about involvement in the child protection system. *Children and Youth Services Review, 33*, 1084–1089.

Jacob, A., & Fanning, D. (2006). *Report on child protection services in Tasmania*. Hobart: Department of Health and Human Services.

Jaffe, P., Crooks, C., & Wolfe, D. (2003). Legal and policy responses to children exposed to domestic violence: The need to evaluate intended and unintended consequences. *Clinical Child and Family Psychological Review, 6*(3), 205–213.
Kaur, J. (2012). *Cultural diversity and child protection: Australian research review on the needs of culturally and linguistically diverse (CALD) and refugee children and families*. Cleveland: JK Diversity Consultants.
Keegan Eamon, M., & Kopels, S. (2004). 'For reasons of poverty': Court challenges to child welfare practices and mandated programs. *Children and Youth Services Review, 26*, 821–836.
Kidd, P. S., & Parshall, M. B. (2000). Getting the focus and the group: Enhancing analytical rigor in focus group research. *Qualitative Health Research, 10*, 293–308.
Kitzinger, J. (1994). The methodology of focus groups: The importance of interaction between research participants. *Sociology of Health and Illness, 16*, 103–121.
Lewis, J., & Welsh, E. (2005). Fathering practices in twenty-six intact families and the implications for child contact. *International Journal of Law in Context, 1*, 81–99.
Marts, E., Eun-Kyoung, O. L., McRoy, R., et al. (2008). Point of engagement: Reducing disproportionality and improving child and family arguments. *Child Welfare, 87*(2), 335–358.
Masson, J. (2008). The state as parent: The reluctant parent? The problems of parents of last resort. *Journal of Law and Society, 35*(1), 52–74.
Mathews, B. (2012). Exploring the contested role of mandatory reporting laws in the identification of severe child abuse and neglect. In M. Freeman (Ed.), *Current legal issues: Vol. 14. Law and childhood studies* (pp. 302–338). Oxford: Oxford University Press.
Mathews, B., & Bross, D. C. (2008). Mandated reporting is still a policy with reason: Empirical evidence and philosophical grounds. *Child Abuse and Neglect, 32*, 511–516.
Mathews, B., & Kenny, M. (2008). Mandatory reporting legislation in the USA, Canada and Australia: A cross-jurisdictional review of key features, differences and issues. *Child Maltreatment, 13*, 50–63.
Mathews, B., Walsh, K., & Fraser, J. A. (2006). Mandatory reporting by nurses of child abuse and neglect. *Journal of Law and Medicine, 13*, 505–517.
McConnell, D., & Llewellyn, G. (2005). Social inequality, the "deviant parent" and child protection practice. *Australian Journal of Social Issues, 40*(4), 553–566.
McGlade, H. (2012). *Our greatest challenge: Aboriginal children and human rights*. Canberra: Aboriginal Studies Press.
Melton, G. (2005). Mandated reporting: A policy without reason. *Child Abuse and Neglect, 29*, 9–18.
Miles, M. B., & Huberman, A. M. (1994). *Qualitative data analysis: An expanded sourcebook* (2nd ed.). Thousand Oaks: Sage.
Owhe, J. (2013). Indicated reports of child abuse or maltreatment: When suspects become victims. *Family Court Review, 51*(2), 316–329.
Penn, H., & Gough, D. (2002). The price of a loaf of bread: Some conceptions of family support. *Children and Society, 16*(1), 17–32.
Pietrantonio, A. M., Wright, E., Gibson, K., et al. (2013). Mandatory reporting of child abuse and neglect: Crafting a positive process for health professionals and caregivers. *Child Abuse and Neglect, 37*, 102–109.
Rath, A. (2001) *Permanency planning and adoption* (Briefing Paper No. 2/2001). Sydney: NSW Parliamentary Library Research Service.
Roberts, D. (2007). Child welfare's paradox. *William and Mary Law Review, 49*, 881–901.
Roberts, D. (2008). The racial geography of child welfare: Toward a new research paradigm. *Child Welfare, 87*(2), 125–150.
Roberts, D. (2012). Prison, and foster care: The systemic punishment of black mothers. *UCLA Law Review, 59*, 1474–1500.
Scott, D. (2013). *Child protection statistics for aboriginal and Torres Strait Islander children.* Australian Institute of family Studies. Available from http://www.aifs.gov.au/cfca/pubs/factsheets/a142117/index.html

Sege, R., Flaherty, E., Jones, R., et al. (2011). To report or not to report: Examination of the initial primary care management of suspicious childhood injuries. *Academic Pediatrics, 11*(6), 460–466.

Smith, A., & Parsons Winokur, K. (2004). What doctors and policymakers should know: Battered women's views about mandatory reporting laws. *Journal of Criminal Justice, 32*, 207–221.

Stretch, R. (2003). The duty to report child abuse in France, lessons for England? *Child and Family Law Quarterly, 15*, 139–154.

Takis, A. (2008). The mandatory reporting debate. *Macquarie Law Journal, 8*, 125–152.

Thomson, J. (2003). This is nothing new: Child protection concerns and poverty. *Children Australia, 28*(1), 4–10.

Tomison, A. (2002a). Mandatory reporting: A question of theory versus practice. *Developing Practice, 4*, 13–17.

Tomison, A. (2002b). Preventing child abuse: Changes to family support in the 21st century. *National Child Protection Clearinghouse, 17*, 1–24.

Vulliamy, A., & Sullivan, R. (2000). Reporting child abuse: Pediatricians' experiences with child protection system reporting. *Child Abuse and Neglect, 24*(11), 1461–1470.

Walsh, T., & Douglas, H. (2008). Homelessness and legal needs: A South Australia and Western Australia case study. *Adelaide Law Review, 29*(2), 359–380.

Walsh, T., & Douglas, H. (2009). Legal responses to child protection, Poverty and Homelessness. *Journal of Social Welfare and Family Law, 31*(2), 133–146.

Walsh, T., & Douglas, H. (2012). Lawyers' views of decision-making in child protection matters: The tension between adversarialism and collaborative approaches. *Monash University Law Review, 38*(2), 181–211.

Wekerle, C. (2013). Resilience in the context of child maltreatment: Connection to the practice of child maltreatment. *Child Abuse and Neglect, 37*, 93–101.

Wiseman, H. (2008). Failed by the system. *Australian Doctor, 22*, 13–14.

Part VI
International Variations/Challenges

(the potential of socio-legal measures such as MR, or variants of it, to respond to particular phenomena)

Chapter 24
The Identification and Reporting of Severe Violence Against Children: International Standards and Practices

Jaap E. Doek

Introduction

The UN Study on Violence Against Children (Pinheiro 2006) documented and confirmed that various forms of violence against children, such as physical, emotional and sexual abuse, exploitation and neglect, take place not only in the family and care settings but also in other settings like the school, the work place and in the community.[1] The study contains specific recommendations for action for prevention and intervention for each of the settings in which violence against children occurs. The international legal framework for the study was the UN Convention on the Rights of the Child (CRC), its Optional Protocols,[2] the ILO Conventions 138 and 182 and other international legal documents.[3] Most of these documents are ratified

[1] The study was undertaken at the request of the UN Committee on the rights of the child after it had conducted Days of General Discussion in 2000 and 2001; see for the result of these Discussion days www2.ohchr.org/english/bodies/crc/discussion2013.htm

[2] The CRC was adopted on 20 November 1989 by the UN General Assembly (Resolution 44/25) and entered into force on 2 September 1990. Two Optional Protocols, one on the involvement of children in armed conflict (OPAC) and the one on the sale of child prostitution and child pornography (OPSC), were adopted on 25 May 2000 (Resolution A/RES/54/263) and entered into force on 12 February 2002 and on 18 January 2002, respectively. The OPAC has been ratified by 152 States and OPSC by 166 States. The USA is not a State party to the CRC but has ratified both Optional Protocols. A third Optional Protocol on a Communication Procedure was adopted on 27 January 2012 (Resolution A/RES/66/138); it has entered into force on 14 March 2014.

[3] ILO Convention 138 on the Minimum Age for Admission to Employment (adopted on 26 June 1973 by the General Conference of the International Labour Organisation and entered into force on 19 June 1976 and ratified by 166 countries) and ILO Convention 182 concerning the Prohibition and Immediate Action for the Elimination of the Worst Forms of Child Labour (adopted on 17 June 1999

J.E. Doek (✉)
Family and Juvenile Law, VU University of Amsterdam, Amsterdam, Netherlands
e-mail: jaap@jaapdoek.nl

B. Mathews, D.C. Bross (eds.), *Mandatory Reporting Laws and the Identification of Severe Child Abuse and Neglect*, Child Maltreatment 4,
DOI 10.1007/978-94-017-9685-9_24

by a vast majority of States (see footnote 2 and 3) and their provisions constitute a body on international customary law.

The CRC is the most ratified international human rights treaty. By their ratification, 194 countries have committed themselves to undertake all appropriate legislative, administrative and other measures for the implementation of the rights recognised in the CRC (art. 4).

Many articles of the CRC provide the child with the right to protection from all forms of physical and mental violence, including abuse and neglect and sexual abuse (art. 19), from all forms of economic exploitation (art. 32), from involvement in armed conflicts (art. 38 and OPAC), from sexual and other forms of exploitation (art 34+OPSC and 36), and signatories agree that no child shall be subjected to torture or other cruel, inhuman or degrading treatment or punishment (art. 37).

These articles are not explicitly addressing the matter of identification and reporting of children who have been or are at risk of becoming victims of these forms of violence or exploitation with one exception: article 19. This article deals with the prevention and protection from all forms of violence in the family and other care settings. In addition to targeted efforts to prevent child abuse and neglect, the 194 States parties to the CRC are obliged to take protective measures which should include identification, reporting, referral, investigation, treatment and follow-up and as appropriate, judicial involvement.

For all other forms of violence and exploitation mentioned before, it is left to the States parties whether and how they will develop and implement measures for the identification of children who have been or are at risk of becoming victims of economic, sexual and other forms of exploitation. For the field of commercial sexual exploitation and economic exploitation, this results in an international picture of varied rules and practices.

The right of the child to protection from all forms of violence, as enshrined in international human rights treaties, requires a comprehensive policy which includes both various measures of prevention and effective intervention in cases in which children are victims of violence. Such interventions are only possible if professionals working with and for children, as well as others who have the knowledge and skills for a timely identification of these children, report to the relevant authorities, when necessary, such instances of violence. But identification and reporting are not goals in themselves but tools for providing the child victim with all necessary protection and support for a full recovery. The focus in this chapter will be on timely identification and reporting whilst keeping in mind that these acts are only the beginning of efforts to provide the child with the protection he or she is entitled to. Under the CRC and the Optional Protocols, it is the obligation of States parties to make this right to protection a reality.

In line with the UN Study on Violence Against Children, this chapter will present and discuss international standards and practices of identification and reporting of child abuse, neglect and other forms of violence in the family and other care settings,

---

by the General Conference of the ILO and entered into force on 19 November 2000 and ratified by 177 countries).

the work place (taking into account ILO Conventions 138 and 182) and the community, in particular various forms of sexual exploitation of children. Given the different rules and practices across national boundaries, a distinction is made between child abuse and neglect in the family and other care settings (hereafter para. 2) and economic and sexual exploitation (para. 3). The focus will be on the implementation of the relevant provisions in the CRC and the Optional Protocols by the States parties at the national level.

But States parties are held accountable (to some extent?) for their performances in implementing children's right to protection. Most importantly, they have agreed that they are obliged to report regularly on their activities to international monitoring bodies, in particular the CRC Committee. In a separate paragraph, some attention will be paid to this accountability and monitoring process.

The final paragraph contains conclusions and some recommendations.

Identification and Reporting of Child Abuse and Neglect in the Family

Article 19 CRC and General Comment No. 13 of the CRC Committee, not only recognises the right of the child to be free from all forms of abuse and neglect in the family and other care settings but also spells out in a rather specific manner the obligations of States parties to respect and fulfil this right (Doek 1994):

> *1. States Parties shall take all appropriate legislative, administrative, social and educational measures to protect the child from all forms of physical or mental violence, injury or abuse, neglect and negligent treatment, maltreatment or exploitation, including sexual abuse, while in the care of parent(s), legal guardian(s) or any other person who has the care of the child.*
>
> *2. Such protective measures should, as appropriate, include effective procedures for the establishment of social programmes to provide necessary support for the child and for those who have the care of the child, as well as for other forms of prevention and for identification, reporting, referral, investigation, treatment and follow-up of instances of child maltreatment described heretofore, and, as appropriate, for judicial involvement.*

Compared to the other articles of the CRC dealing with protection of children from sexual exploitation, sale and trafficking, this article is very detailed. The drafting history does not explain the detailed attention expressed in the article (Detrick 1992). My assumption is that this attention during the drafting of the CRC in the 1980s can be explained by the growing international attention for child abuse and neglect promoted by activities of the International Society for Prevention of Child Abuse and Neglect (ISPCAN) (Donelly 2002). Representatives of this International Society and of the International Institute for Child Rights and Development (IICRD, Victoria University, Canada) were actively involved in the drafting of General Comment No. 13 on Article 19 (Hart et al. 2011).

In 2011 the CRC Committee issued a General Comment in which it provides the States parties with guidance in the interpretation of this article and recommendations for actions which should be undertaken for the implementation of this article (GC 13).[4] In this document, the CRC Committee provides, amongst others, elaborate examples of acts which fall under mental or physical violence, as well as a specification of the legislative, administrative and educational measures States parties should take with a strong emphasis on prevention. Much more could be said about the rich content of GC 13 (see, e.g. Hart et al. 2011; Svevo-Cianci et al. 2011), but in the context of this chapter, we will focus on the Committee's views on identification and reporting (para. 44 and 45 of GC 13).

Identification. This should not be limited to identifying signs of actual maltreatment (in order to trigger appropriate interventions as early as possible) but also include the identification of risk factors for particular individuals or groups of children and caregivers in order to trigger targeted prevention initiatives. Identification requires that all persons who come in contact with children are aware of risk factors and indicators of all forms of violence and have received guidance on how to interpret such indicators and have the necessary knowledge, willingness and ability to take appropriate actions. Children must be provided with as many opportunities as possible to signal emerging problems before they reach the state of a crisis.

Reporting. This requires, according to the CRC Committee, that States parties develop safe, well-publicised, confidential and accessible support mechanism for children, their representatives and others to report violence against children, including through the use 24-h toll-free hotlines and other information and communication technologies. Reporting mechanism must be coupled with and should present themselves as help-oriented services offering public health and social support rather than triggering responses which are primarily punitive.

In every country, reporting of actual incidents, suspicions or risks of violence should, as a minimum, be required by professionals working directly with children. When reports are made in good faith, processes must be in place to ensure protection of the professional making the report.

Some comments to the implementation of the views of the Committee.

The Committee does not elaborate on *identification*, but it is obvious that it requires that in particular professionals and volunteers working with children be trained in identifying children who are or at the risk of becoming victims of violence in the family or other care settings such as foster care and institutional care. Many States parties to the CRC Committee report that they carry out awareness raising and training on the various aspects of child abuse prevention and intervention. But in too many countries, little or no attention is paid to these matters.

[4]The CRC Committee (like other human rights treaty bodies) issues regularly the so-called General Comments. They are authoritative documents in which the Committee provides States parties with guidance for the implementation of a specific article, e.g. General Comment No. 1 deals with article 29 CRC (aims of education), GC No. 14 on article 3 (the best interest of the child), GC No. 17 on article 31 CRC (the right to play, leisure and cultural activities) or for the implementation of the CRC for a specific vulnerable group of children such as children with disabilities (GC No. 9) and indigenous children (GC No 11). For the full list of General Comments issued so far, see www.ohchr.org/english/bodies/crc/comments.htm

A lot still needs to be done to ensure the timely identification of children who are (possible) victims of violence. Without such identification, the child's right to protection is void.

Reporting: Mandatory or non-mandatory? The Committee is, without specific arguments, in favour of mandated reporting at least for professionals working directly with children such as social workers, psychologists, family doctors and paediatricians. Some countries do have laws requiring professionals and others to report instances or suspicion of child abuse and neglect, i.e. to designated authorities or services. These reporting laws have been discussed extensively in the previous chapters, including inter alia the advantages/benefits and the disadvantages of mandatory reporting. To balance this, I will deal here with an example of a non-mandatory reporting system developed and implemented in the Netherlands in the 1970s.

An Example of a System That Emphasises Voluntary Reporting: The Netherlands

In 1972, four Bureaus of Confidential Doctors were established. The primary purpose of these bureaus was to provide medical professionals with the possibility of contacting the bureau for advice on how to deal with a concrete case of (suspected) child abuse whilst maintaining the confidentiality they are bound to maintain. They could also refer the case to the bureau requesting it to investigate the case and initiate the necessary actions for the protection of the child. Also, in addition, other professionals and the public at large could contact the bureau for advice or referral of a (suspected) child abuse cases. The focus was first on cases of physical abuse,[5] but the mandate of the bureaus was broadened to all forms of child abuse, including physical and emotional neglect and sexual abuse. In 1972, 430 cases were reported to the bureaus, and this number rapidly increased to approximately 13,000 in 1993 (Doek 1978, 1986). The development of this system has been described in detail (van Montfoort 1994), inspired Belgium to establish similar services (Marneffe and Lampo 1989) and was compared with the reporting practice in the UK (Christopherson 1981). It goes beyond the scope of this chapter to present detailed information on the developments since 1972. However, the following information fills in some of the details:

- Following extensive negotiations (van Montfoort 1994), the bureaus were replaced by centres for advice and reporting of child abuse (AMK, Advies en meldpunt kindermishandeling) and made subject to rules contained in the Law on Youth Care. Currently there are 12 regional AMK's covering the whole country.

[5] In the first years of their activities, the bureaus and the reportable cases were defined in accordance with Henry Kempe's definition: Any child who receive nonaccidental injury (or injuries) as a result of acts (or omissions) on the part of his parents or guardians.

First contacts on cases of child abuse with the centres increased from 34,000 in 2004 to almost 66,000 in 2011, and the increase continues. In 70 % of all the cases, the person contacting the Centre needed an advice. The remaining 30 % were referred to the Centre for further investigation and action as necessary. These percentages are virtually the same over the years. Parents and children rarely contacted the Centre (less than 1 %). For 2011, professionals who knew the child contacted the Centre for advice were 56.4 % of all the contacts for advice, and 43.5 % of the contacts were made by nonprofessional persons who knew the child and/or parents (e.g. family members, friends, neighbours). Also from the 2011 data set,[6] more than 47 % of the cases for which the Centre was contacted were cases of physical, emotional or pedagogical neglect, 17 % were cases of physical abuse or violence and in 22 % of the cases the child was a witness of violence in the family. Only 2.2 % were cases of sexual abuse. To continue, in 7 % of the cases referred for further investigation, there was no child abuse, in 11.7 % child abuse could not be corroborated and child abuse was stopped in 7.8 % of the cases. After investigation, 60 % of the contacts were referred to existing social or children's care services, along with 12.5 % referred to the Council for child protection for an assessment of the need to file a petition for a measure of child protection required of the family by a juvenile court/judge.[7]

From these data, the following can be concluded. As has been found in countries other than the Netherlands, most cases reported are not about abuse, but various forms of neglect. The "system" is not exclusively meant for reporting cases for further investigation by a Centre staff. Around 70 % of all the contacts were for the purpose of advice, whereas only 30 % of cases resulted in investigations. This is a significant difference compared to the traditional reporting practices under the reporting laws of some countries. Recent estimates are that around 118,000 children annually are victims of abuse and neglect in the Netherlands. The Dutch reporting system covers almost 60 % of these cases. More needs to be done to provide all these victims with the necessary protection. This brings us to the question whether the Netherlands needs to introduce mandatory reporting of child abuse and neglect by everyone.

This question has been repeatedly discussed, but recently the government decided not to introduce a mandatory reporting by law. Instead of a reporting law for everyone the government decided to make it mandatory for professionals working in indicated services and institutions and for individual professionals to establish a Reporting Protocol covering both domestic violence and child abuse and to act in

[6] The figures mentioned here are from the annual report of the Centres for advice and reporting of child abuse (Jaarrapport 2011).

[7] The Council for child protection is an agency under the Ministry of Security and Justice and mandated by law to file a petition for a measure of child protection. Although others can file such petition, more than 90 % is submitted to courts by this Council.

accordance with this protocol.[8] The protocol is not meant to make reporting as such mandatory. It sets rules for handling cases of (suspected) child abuse in a step-by-step process (see hereafter) in which reporting can be the last step depending on the seriousness of the abuse and possibilities to provide the necessary support.

This decision was based on a survey of the literature on mandatory reporting from which the government concluded[9]:

- That the implementation of mandatory reporting passes over the autonomy of the victim. The professional cannot make an assessment but has to report immediately without consultation with the victim or her/his parents. It deprives the victim, who has approached the professional for help and empowerment, of the possibility to make choices.
- That the pressure of the law to report leaves the professional with the feeling that he loses the possibility to carefully assess which steps are necessary in the interest and for the protection of the victim.
- That the introduction of mandatory reporting has negative consequences, such as overburdening of the system and unnecessary and stigmatising investigations without clear benefits with a view to the help and protection of the child and the family.

In addition, the government felt that the protocol should be mandatory because, despite various efforts to encourage the introduction of reporting protocols for all professionals, in 2010 only 40 % of the professionals working in inter alia education, health care, welfare and sports and in youth care were using a reporting protocol.[10] The overall goal of the introduction of the obligation to have and act in accordance with the reporting protocol (meldcode) is not primarily to increase the number of reported cases but to provide more quickly and more adequate help in cases where there is a reason to believe that domestic violence or child abuse takes place.

In order to support the relevant services and institutions in developing their reporting protocol, the government shall issue a regulation containing the minimum elements of such protocol. The following steps have to be included in the protocol:

1. Mapping all the information which indicates that child abuse or domestic violence may take place, including information which may contradict the suspicion that violence or abuse occurred.
2. Consultation with colleagues and the centre for domestic violence and the Centre for advice and reporting child abuse for an interpretation of the available information.

[8] Law of 14 March 2013, Official Journal (Staatsblad), 2013, 142 on Mandatory Reporting Protocol, domestic violence and child abuse (verplichte meldcode huiselijk geweld en kindermishandeling).

[9] Meldplicht bij huiselijk geweld, literatuurverkenning naar ervaringen met meldplicht in het buitenland (mandatory reporting in cases of domestic violence a survey of literature about experiences in other countries) Den hag: Ministerie van Justitie mei 2008.

[10] The Netherlands Medical Association was one of the few organisation that issued for their members a reporting protocol.

3. A meeting with the client (can be an adult victim of violence or the child victim and her/his parents) to discuss the available information (facts and observations) with the invitation for the client to react to this information. In cases of child abuse, the professional should talk with the child, except when that is not possible, e.g. in case of very young children. Also a meeting with the parent(s) should take place, regardless whether they are the possible perpetrator(s).

   All this will be followed by an interpretation of all the information, including the client's reactions and conclusion: if the suspicion is unfounded, the case will be closed; if the suspicion is confirmed, the next steps should be taken.
4. Assess the nature and the seriousness of the abuse or violence (using risk-taxation instruments if appropriate). Consult with experts and/or the centres for domestic violence and the Centre for advice and reporting of child abuse. On the basis of this assessment, the professional must then? take step 5.
5. The professional has to decide whether he can organise the necessary support and protection for the victim and her/his family. This would include monitoring the effects of the victim's activities and leading to a referral of the case to one of the centres if the violence or abuse does not stop. Alternatively, he must refer the case to one of the centres mentioned before, again depending on the nature of the case. Based on all the information provided by the professional, the Centre will undertake measures for organising the most appropriate support, services and protection.

From the steps to be included in the reporting protocol, it can be concluded that the focus is not on reporting as such but shows that in the best consultation possible with colleagues and experts and after meeting with the victim and her/his parents in case of child abuse, the professional's first choice should be to provide and/or organise adequate support and protection and that the reporting to one of the designated centres is the last option. It will be critical to evaluate (after 2 or 3 years) whether this system of reporting protocols does indeed provide the child victim more speedily and with more adequate and effective support and protection.

Finally from a conceptual point of view, it is interesting that the system of reporting protocols covers both domestic violence and child abuse.[11] Required reporting of domestic violence has rarely been pursued in other countries.

Summing up the identification and reporting of the (worst) forms of child abuse and neglect in the family setting and in other care settings like foster care, residential care and schools can be based on relatively clear international rules of children's rights. But there does not have to be one fixed model. States parties to the CRC have considerable freedom to organise good quality identification and reporting practices. Although the CRC Committee is in favour of mandatory reporting, at least for professionals working directly with children, there are States parties which developed a system of non-mandatory reporting. One approach is not necessarily better

[11] The need for a comprehensive approach of both family violence and child abuse was recognised by Alan Davis when he established the National Council on Child Abuse and Family Violence in 1984 (see www.nccafv.org).

than another because the critical indicator is the existence of safe, well-publicised, confidential and accessible support mechanisms for children, their representatives and others to *report violence against children* (GC No. 13, para 45 and Pinheiro 2006, Overarching Recommendation 8). As explained above with regard to the Dutch approach, such reporting is possible thanks to the existence of the Centres for advice and reporting of child abuse but is not the first and immediate reaction. Such reaction is not required by the Dutch law.

Identification and Reporting of Economic and Sexual Exploitation of Children Outside the Family

Economic, sexual and other forms of exploitation of children are recognised, amongst others, by the Special Representative of the UN Secretary General on Violence against Children as serious violations of the right of the child to protection.[12] The seriousness of these violations is confirmed by specific international and regional human rights instruments, such as the ILO conventions 138 and 182,[13] the Optional Protocol to the CRC on the sale of children, child prostitution and child pornography, the African Charter on the rights and welfare of the child[14] and the European on the protection of children against sexual exploitation and sexual abuse, also known as the Lanzarote Convention.[15]

This chapter focuses on the identification of victims. But to avoid misunderstanding, the protection of children from these forms of exploitation starts with the implementation of an intensive and effective prevention policy that addresses the root causes of this violation of the rights of the child. Within international documents, one can find specific provisions requiring measures of prevention from economic exploitation (see, e.g. art. 7 ILO 182 and para. 2 ILO R146 and para. 2 ILO R190) and from sexual exploitation (see, e.g. art. 9 OPSC and art. 4–9 of the Lanzarote Convention). Actions aiming at prevention of exploitation of children include awareness raising campaigns, and programmes to reduce poverty and to promote education.[16]

[12] See the most recent report of this special representative: Annual Report to the Human Rights Council 2014. UN Doc. A/HRC/25/47, 3 January 2014 (www.srsg.violenceagainstchildren.org).

[13] http://www.ilo.org/ilolex/english/convdisp1.htm

[14] http://www.africa-union.org/official_documents/Treaties_%20Conventions_%20Protocols/a.%20C.%20ON520The%20RIGHT%20AND%20WELF%20CHILD.pdf

[15] http://conventions.coe.int/Treaty/EN/treaties/html/201.htm

[16] It goes beyond the scope of this chapter to elaborate on prevention. But it should be noted that the key measures of prevention coincide with two of the Millennium Development Goals (MDGs): reduction by half of poverty and completion of a full course of schooling by all children by 2015. The MDGs were adopted by the UN in September 2000 UN Doc. A/RES/55/2.

In the following paragraphs, the focus will be on the international human rights instruments.[17] These instruments do not contain specific provisions on the identification of children who are potential victims of economic or sexual exploitation.

It means that with regard to the protection of children against these forms of exploitation, one will not find extensive discussions on mandatory or non-mandatory reporting. There are other and different ways to identify these children, either in the context of a monitoring system and/or through activities of non-governmental organisations.

Identification and Reporting of Economic Exploitation of Children

The right of the child to protection from economic exploitation can be found in article 32 CRC and in the ILO Convention 138 concerning Minimum Age for Admission to Employment (Minimum Age Convention 1973) and the ILO Convention 182 concerning the Prohibition and Immediate Action for the Elimination of the Worst forms of Child Labour (Worst forms of Child Labour Convention 1999). The key provisions in these documents for the protection of the child to be implemented by States parties are the following:

- Set a minimum age for admission to employment or work (art. 32 CRC) which shall not be less than the age of completion of compulsory schooling and in any case not less than 15 years (ILO 138, art. 2).[18]
- Take, as a matter of urgency, immediate and effective measures to secure the prohibition and elimination of the worst forms of child labour. In this context, a child is a person under the age of 18. More specifically, States shall take effective and time-bound measures to, inter alia (ILO 182, art. 7):
- Prevent the engagement of children in the worst forms of child labour.
- Provide direct assistance for the removal of children from the worst forms of child labour and for the rehabilitation and social integration.
- Ensure access to free basic education or vocational training for all children removed from the worst forms of child labour.
- Identify and reach out to children at special risk and take account of the special situation of girls.
- The worst forms of child labour are defined in article 3 ILO 182 and include amongst others all forms of slavery or practices similar to slavery such as the sale and trafficking of children, debt bondage, serfdom and forced or compulsory

[17] Regional instruments such as the African Charter and the Lanzarote Convention are important, but it goes beyond the desired length of this chapter to give them adequate attention.

[18] There are exceptions to this rule, e.g. States whose economy and educational facilities are insufficiently developed can set the minimum age at 14 years and light work, defined in art. 7 ILO 138, can be allowed by national laws for children age 13–15 (or 12–14).

labour and recruitment of children for the use in armed conflict, the use, procuring or offering of a child for prostitution, for the production of pornography and for the production and trafficking of drugs and other forms of work likely to harm the health, safety and morals of children.

Linked to each of these ILO Conventions are recommendations for their implementation.[19] They include inter alia measures for enforcement, e.g. the strengthening of labour inspection and related services, for instance, by special training of inspectors to detect abuses in the employment or work of children and young persons and to correct such abuses (R146, art. 14) and regarding the elimination of the worst forms of child labour to cooperate with international efforts, for example, by detecting and prosecuting those involved in the sale and trafficking of children or in the use, procuring and offering children for prostitution and pornography (R190, art. 10).

There are more and other recommendations, but from both Conventions and the related recommendations, it has to be concluded that the attention for identification, reporting and referral is very limited.

The most important international body for the implementation of these standards is the ILO Programme on the Elimination of Child Labour (ILO-IPEC). It was established in 1991 thanks to a grant of the German government of 50 million Deutsch marks. It operates in 88 countries and is carrying out many projects in close collaboration with governments, trade unions, employers association and other civil society organisations.[20]

Child Work, Child Labour: Debates and Figures

Child labour is not a social problem limited to the present. Attention to child labour emerged in the nineteenth century and was closely linked to the introduction of compulsory education as an instrument in reducing the number of economically exploited children (Heywood 2009; Hendrick 2009; Stearns 2009; Fyfe 2009). It goes beyond the purpose of this chapter to present the history of the fight against child labour. But it should be noted that also today education is still seen as an important instrument in reducing child labour. In 2008 the ILO International Programme for the Elimination of Child Labour (hereafter: ILO-IPEC) launched a major new project aimed at tackling child labour through education (TACKLE). The overall objective of this project is to contribute to poverty reduction by

[19] R146 Minimum Age Recommendation (Recommendation concerning the Minimum Age for Admission to Employment 1973) and R190 Worst Forms of Child Labour Recommendation (Recommendation concerning the prohibition and immediate action for elimination of the worst forms of child labour 1999).

[20] See for more information: The International Programme on the Elimination of Child Labour (IPEC). What it is and what it does. Geneva: ILO 2010.

providing equitable access to basic education and skills development of children in or at risk of being involved in child labour.[21]

In the debates regarding the elimination of child labour, one group of experts questions the ILO approach of eliminating child labour and emphasises the importance of work in the daily life of children and their families. In their view, it is better to regulate existing child work than to invest only in the elimination of child labour (Bourdillon et al. 2011). Others argue that these views deal with child work that is not hazardous or otherwise harmful for the child's development or is not interfering with the child's education (art. 32 CRC). In other words, the labour referred to by the first group is not the type of work that the ILO Conventions 138 and 182 want to eliminate (Lieten 2011, ch. 1.). It is beyond the scope of this chapter to elaborate more on the differences between the so-called regulators (or "regulacionistas") and the eradicators (or "erradicacionistas"). But it should be kept in mind that figures on child labour do not include data on permitted forms of child work and that not all child work even for children below the age of 15 is prohibited. Children age 15 and above who have the right to work can be engaged in the worst forms of child labour.

Children do a variety of work under very different circumstances and conditions. It is a continuum with at the one hand work that can be considered as beneficial, promoting capacities and a sense of responsibility without interfering with schooling and leisure. On the other hand, there exists work done by children that is or becomes harmful, hazardous and exploitative (Lieten 2011, p. 6). The ILO observes that: "Child labour does not include activities such as helping out, after school is over and school work has been done, with light household or garden chores, child care or other light work. To claim otherwise only trivializes the genuine deprivation of childhood faced by the millions of children involved in child labour that must be effectively abolished" (ILO 2002, p. 9).

One of the challenges in combating child labour is to produce reliable figures on the magnitude of the problem. For the collection of data, the ILO-IPEC has developed and implements the Statistical Information and Monitoring Programme on Child Labour (SIMPOC).[22] It assists countries in the collection, documentation, processing and analysis of child labour relevant data.

Since the beginning of this century, ILO-IPEC has been publishing Global Child Labour Reports every 4 years. These reports contain detailed data on child labour in general and about the worst forms of child labour, disaggregated by gender, types of work, regions and trends.[23] The most recent report was published in 2013.[24]

---

[21] See for more information: good practices in tackling child labour through education. Selected examples from the IPEC TACKLE Project. Geneva: ILO –IPEC 2013.

[22] For further information, see www.ilo.org/ipec/childlabourstatisticsSIMPOC/lanDOUBLEHYPHENn/index.htm

[23] The first report was published in 2002 with data of 2000 (and before), the second in 2006 (with data and trends between 2000 and 2004) and the third in 2010 (data and trends between 2004 and 2008); see report in the next footnote, p. vii–ix.

[24] Marking progress against child labour. Global estimates and trends. Geneva: ILO 2013.

According to this report, there were 168 million children in child labour and hazardous work in 2012 (The figure in 2008 was 215 million). Amongst these children, 85 million were involved in hazardous work in comparison to 115 million in 2008. The number of children age 5–14 in child labour came down from 152 million in 2008 to 120 million in 2012, and 37 million of them were involved in hazardous work (2008: 52 million). In the age group 5–11, 73 million were involved in child labour accounting for 44 % of the total child labour population.[25] In the age group 15–17, 47 million were involved in hazardous work, a decrease from 62 million in 2008.[26] The number of girls in child labour went down significantly from 87 million in 2008 to 68 million in 2012; this applies also for the girls involved in hazardous work, down from 41 million in 2008 to 30 million in 2012.

It is evident that child labour, including the worst forms, is affecting the healthy development of millions of children. Identifying and reporting children victims of economic exploitation remain a matter of high priority. The ILO, meaning its participating governments, trade unions and employers associations, has committed itself to the eradication of all of the worst forms of child labour by 2016.[27] If the current pace of decrease continues, the world will still have 65 million children involved in the worst forms of child labour in 2016 and 50 million in 2020.[28] In other words, the world has to take extra efforts to eliminate at least the worst forms of child labour by 2020. This requires a reduction of 7 million per year in the next 7 years.

Identification, Reporting and Referral

The traditional means for monitoring the compliance with national and international labour laws are the national labour inspectorates. The ILO adopted a number of Conventions[29] which establish the basis for developing a labour inspection system that is flexible enough to take account of different national circumstances.[30] These Conventions provide inter alia that labour inspectors should have the power to enter

[25] For the first time, the ILO made a distinction within the age group 5–14, between the age group 5 11 and the age group 12 14. The first group is the most vulnerable, and a total of 73 million of them were in child labour and 18 million of them in hazardous work.

[26] From 2004 to 2008, this number increased from 52 to 62 million. The significant decrease since 2008 may be one of the effects of the efforts to implement the Hague Roadmap.

[27] See The End of Child Labour: Within Reach. Geneva: ILO 2006 and the Global Child Labour Conference (The Hague 2010) producing The Hague Roadmap to end worst forms of child labour by 2016.

[28] See Global report 2013: Marking the progress against child labour, p. 13.

[29] The Labour Convention and Recommendation 1947 (No. 81) and a protocol of 1995 to this Convention. Labour Inspection (Agriculture) Convention (No. 129) and Recommendation (no. 133) 1969. Labour Inspection (Seafarers) Convention 1966 (No. 178).

[30] See the ILO document GB.309/ESP/3 (Nov. 2010) on Labour administration and inspection: Challenges and perspectives.

freely and without previous notice at any hour of the day or night and any workplace liable to inspection to interrogate employers and employees (alone or in the presence of witnesses) and to take steps with a view to remedy the defects and shortcomings (art. 12, 13 ILO 81 and art. 16 and 18 ILO 129).

However, in the enforcement of child labour laws, the role of labour inspectorates seems to be rather limited or even non-existent. In the literature, there are hardly any article on the role of labour inspectorates in the identification and reporting of instances of (worst forms of) child labour.[31] The limited role of the inspectorates might be the result of the fact that they lack resources and expertise in the field of child labour. As the ILO observed in 2010: "Labour inspectorates, particularly in developing countries, face numerous challenges. (….). These challenges include inadequate financial resources to invest in inspection personnel and equipment, insufficient training for new recruits and existing staff (….) and the absence of appropriate regulatory framework".[32] But over the last decade, the labour inspectorates are increasingly active in monitoring the compliance with national and international standards and provisions regarding child labour. The ILO-IPEC played an important role in this development by the publication of the IPEC Manual on Labour Inspection and the establishment by the ILO-IPEC of a Child Labour Monitoring System (CLMS).[33]

In 2005 the ILO-IPEC defined child labour monitoring as an active, regular and ongoing process of identifying and referring child labourers to appropriate services.[34] In the mid-1990s, labour projects began to build child labour monitoring in their activities, and the ILO-IPEC designed the Child Labour Monitoring System (CLMS) which promotes and supports the introduction of this system at the national level.[35] In 2013 monitoring mechanisms were introduced in around 115 countries.[36]

The CLMS addresses the identification, referral, protection and prevention of child labourers through the development of a coordinated multi-sector monitoring and referral process that aims to cover all children living in a given geographical region. Its principal activities include regularly repeated direct observations to identify child labourers and to determine the risk to which they are exposed, referral of these children to services and verification that they have been removed and tracking them afterwards to ensure that they have satisfactory alternatives. The system provides

[31] See for instance the huge volume by Hugh D. Hindman (ed.), The World of Child Labour. An historical and regional survey. Armonk, London: M.E. Sharpe 2009. It does not contain any article specifically dealing with the role of labour inspectorates.

[32] ILO Document GB.309/ESP/3, para. 36.

[33] See www.ilo.org/ipec/action/childlabourmonitoring/lanDOUBLEHYPHENn/index.htm

[34] Overview of Child Labour Monitoring and Guidelines for Developing Child Labour Monitoring Process. Geneva: ILO 2005. And Child labour Monitoring and Referral Options for Malawi. Paper for the National Conference in Eliminating Child Labour in Agriculture by Archangel Bakolo, National Program Coordinator ILO-IPEC Malawi.

[35] The establishment of a CLMS requires various steps described in the overview mentioned in the previous footnote.

[36] Global report 2013, p. 9.

information for the stakeholders on the location and magnitude of the problem, the environmental and workplace conditions and the children's lifestyle and living conditions. This information facilitates the withdrawal of children from child labour as well as the enforcement of laws and regulations aimed at protecting children from being subjected to them in the first place. It furthermore generates reliable data which can be used to effectively raise awareness with key actors and community involvement in the elimination of child labour.

One of the cornerstones of the CLMS is the involvement of labour inspectorates (and school or health inspectors), which carry an official mandate to ensure that children are not working in violation of the law. The CLMS is a complementary mechanism to labour inspection as it provides an opportunity to increase the emphasis of labour inspection on child labour. It is linked to labour inspection in order to provide it with legitimization, input of critical information to competent authorities and improve coordination and action needed. Some examples of this involvement include labour inspectors who regularly participate in child labour units and planning committees in Ecuador, El Salvador, Moldova and Turkey. Labour inspectors provided training in youth employment programmes for 20,000 youth from the informal sector for jobs in the formal economy as plumbers, electricians and auto repair workers in the Dominican Republic. In Turkey they expanded, in collaborations with other institutions, their supervisory activities to include referral and monitoring services such as placing young children in primary schools and older children in vocational training centres and following up with the children's families. In Morocco, labour inspectors have been appointed as focal points responsible for coordinating efforts to combat child labour at the local level in 47 districts.[37]

Monitoring systems can be school based, industrial/sector based, workplace/labour based or community based. None of these models is absolute and can be used in isolation or at the same time with linkages to each other.

The *school-based model* is based on the use of school teachers and school inspection system to conduct surveillance and identification of working children. It wants to guarantee that identified child labourers have adequate alternative services such as schooling and vocational training. ILO-IPEC has developed the programme Supporting Children's Rights through Education, the Arts and the Media (SCREAM). It helps child labourers make themselves visible to society and gives them a voice. This approach started in 2002 and is used in over 65 countries.

The *industry/sector-based model* works from the concept that monitoring of the industry will be undertaken by independent monitoring associations and based on the assumption that it is in the interest of, as examples, tobacco, tea and cocoa plantations and mining to show that they are free from child labour. The model thrives on the commitment of stakeholders in the industry to completely eliminate child labour. One of the problems of the model is that it often does not go beyond the

[37] See Towards elimination of hazardous child labour.... Practices with good potential. Geneva: ILO 2012.

targeted industry and that whilst the cocoa plantations are free from child labour, we don't know how many children are attracted by other industries or sectors.[38]

The *workplace/labour-based model* focuses on a (limited) number of workplaces like automobile repair centres. There is an active involvement of employers and workers' organisations in the concerned sector. It is a relative simple and less costly model than, e.g. the industry-based model. But a key problem is the same as in the industry-based model: it does not control child labour mobility and job displacement, and it is therefore not clear how many children continue to work in other workplaces.

The *community-based model* uses the community-based structures that exist at the local or district level in the country. For instance, one can think of village or areas development committees (VDC and ADC). The model is cost-effective, thriving on locally available resources, whilst engendering community ownership. With a view to empowering and motivating communities, community infrastructure programmes (CIPs) can be developed. Private companies should support the community infrastructure programmes either as directly useful to the business or as part of their corporate social responsibility. As an example, in Cambodia, the establishment of child labour monitoring committees (CLMCs) is promoted at the community level. These consist of volunteers, meaning community members, such as the village chief, youth and parents' representatives, teachers and police.[39]

Summing up, from the information available, it can be concluded that many and different measures are being taken to identify, report and refer children victims of economic exploitation. The ILO-IPEC plays a critical role in this development. It is active in 88 countries supporting governments including their labour inspectorates, civil society organisations, employers and workers organisation and other stake holders, in particular at the community level, in their efforts to eliminate child labour with special attention for the worst forms.

Identification is followed by referral to relevant services and in particular to primary education and vocational training centres. This can include the use of mobile schools to ease the transition from working on the street to education.[40]

The experiences so far show that identification and referral of children victims require coordinated actions of many stakeholders at various levels via child labour monitoring. An infrastructure has to be in place to establish a monitoring system that effectively protects children who are the victims of economic exploitation or are at the risk of becoming victims. It is a slow and often cumbersome process, but we will get there. First there must be the elimination as soon as possible of all of the worst forms of child labour and finally of all child labour.

---

[38] See, for example, Part II of the publication mentioned in the previous foot note. And also, e.g. Lynn Losert, Good Practices and Lessons Learned for ILO-IPEC's Partnership of Combating Hazardous Work of Child labour in Salt Production, Rubber Plantation and Fishing sectors in Cambodia. Phnom Penh, April 2004.

[39] See Lynn Losert mentioned in the previous footnote.

[40] See as an example the project in Romania. ILO 2012, pp. 39–40.

Identification and Reporting of Sexual Exploitation of Children

International standards for the protection of children from sexual exploitation have developed primarily in the past two decades. In the beginning of the 1990s, the only provision of international human rights law that dealt explicitly with sexual exploitation of children was article 34 CRC. It established the obligation for States parties to protect the child from all forms of sexual exploitation and sexual abuse. International attention on sexual exploitation was raised as an issue via reports on the practice of sexual exploitation of children by paedophiles in well-known tourist centres like Sri Lanka, Thailand and the Philippines.[41] The attention raised resulted, along with other developments, in the establishment of the international non-governmental organisation for the prevention and fight against commercial sexual exploitation of children ECPAT[42] and the organisation of the first World Congress on commercial sexual exploitation of children in Stockholm in 1996.[43] This Congress created the momentum inter alia for the drafting and adoption by the General Assembly of the UN in 2000 (May 25) of the Optional Protocol to the CRC on the Sale of Children, Child Prostitution and Child Pornography (OPSC).

Today, article 34 CRC is no longer the only international human rights provision on the protection of children from sexual exploitation. The OPSC still contains specific standards for that protection.[44] Provisions regarding this protection can also be found in regional human rights instruments such as the African Charter on the Rights and Welfare of the Child (art. 27) and the European Convention on the Protection of Children Against Sexual Exploitation and Sexual Abuse (the Lanzarote Convention). It should be noted that this European Convention contains the most elaborated provisions regarding the definitions of child prostitution and child pornography (with attention for the role of new technologies), the measures which should be taken to prevent and to criminalise sexual exploitation and abuse, the protection of child witnesses and victims and the recovery and social integration of child victims. The Lanzarote Convention can be ratified by States which are not a member of the Council of Europe. Another important regional instrument is the directive of the European Union on combating the sexual abuse and sexual exploitation of children and child pornography.[45] It obliges member states of the EU inter

[41] See e.g. Child Sex Tourism Action Survey 2008; www.ecpat.net.

[42] ECPAT was initially the abbreviation for End Child Prostitution in Asian Tourism, but the activities of the organisation became less regional and was covering more aspects of sexual exploitation of children. The abbreviations ECPAT now stands for End Child Prostitution, Child Pornography and Trafficking of Children for Sexual purposes. See for more information www.ecpat.net.

[43] The second international congress took place in Yokohama in 2002 and the third in Rio de Janeiro in 2008.

[44] See for more information on this Optional Protocol the Handbook on the Optional Protocol on the sale of children, child prostitution and child pornography. Florence: UNICEF Innocenti Research Centre 2009.

[45] Directive 2011/92/EU of the European Parliament and the Council.

alia to amend their rules on jurisdiction to ensure that sexual abusers or sexual exploiters of children from the European Union face prosecution even if they commit their crimes outside the Union, in particular via so-called sex tourism.

To summarise the core standards which emerged from these instruments:

- Prevention must be a matter of high priority.[46]
- Acts and activities of sexual exploitation of children as defined in article 3 OPSC must be covered by the criminal or penal law of States parties whether such offences are committed domestically or transnationally or on an individual or organized basis.[47]
- States parties should establish jurisdiction which would allow investigation and prosecution of sexual exploitation if committed by a national or resident of the State or if committed against a child who is a national of the State (extraterritorial jurisdiction).[48]
- The offences mentioned in art. 3 CRC should be included as extraditable offences in any existing extradition treaty or a state party may consider the OPSC as a legal basis for extradition (art. 5 OPSC).
- The rights and interests of child victims of sexual exploitation must be protected at all stages of the criminal justice process, such as the right to information, the right to express views, the right to supportive services and the right to protection of the child's privacy and the specific identity of the child (art.8 OPSC).[49]
- The child victim shall be provided with all appropriate assistance for her/his full physical and psychological recovery and social reintegration and have access to adequate procedures to seek compensation for the damages from those legally responsible (art. 9 OPSC).

The instruments mentioned before, besides some attention for prevention, have a strong focus on the criminalization of all acts of sexual exploitation. The investigation and prosecution of these acts include special attention to the protection of the child victim involved as a witness in these criminal law proceedings. This may explain that the interest for the legal responses to combat sexual exploitation and the enforcement of laws (e.g. via extraterritorial jurisdiction) is quite high and that enhancement of legal responses is recommended (Johnson 2011; Baines 2008).

---

[46] See inter alia Art. 34 CRC requiring States parties to take all appropriate national, bilateral and multilateral measures to prevent sexual exploitation of children (idem art. 27 ACRWC), further specified in art. 9 and 10 OPSC. Chapter II of the Lanzarote Convention is devoted to prevention and requires that each State party shall take measures for training, awareness raising, education for children and the participation of children and the private sector (e.g. the tourism and travel industry) in the development and implementation of policies to prevent sexual exploitation.

[47] See also Chapter VI of the Lanzarote Convention which specifies the activities of sexual abuse, child prostitution and child pornography which should be criminalised and also contains the sanctions and measures that should be imposed.

[48] Article 4 OPSC and art. 25 Lanzarote Convention.

[49] See also about the protection of the child victim Resolution 2005/20 of the Economic and Social Council of the UN on Guidelines on Justice in matters involving Child Victims and Witnesses of Crime.

The right of the child victim to full recovery and social reintegration is mentioned, but there is no specification of measures to be taken to achieve them, e.g. the provision of shelters, medical care and education and family reunification where appropriate. But in practice there are a variety of examples of NGO activities to provide assistance for child victims of sexual exploitation and of trafficking for sexual purposes.[50]

Finally it should be noted that in the context of the prevention of sexual exploitation of children, rather extensive attention is devoted to the trafficking of children. For instance, ECPAT conducted a global campaign Stop Sex Trafficking of Children and Young People. The petition to end this form of trafficking was signed by 7,044,278 persons and organisations and presented on 29 September 2011 to the president of the UN Human Rights Council. It was the largest human rights petition on a single issue ever presented to the United Nations.

Sexual Exploitation: Some Developments and Figures

Since the adoption of the CRC in 1989, many developments and activities took place in the field of sexual exploitation of children. It goes well beyond the scope of this chapter to describe them all. But for an understanding of the identification and reporting of child victims of sexual exploitation, it may be helpful to mention some of them.

The establishment of ECPAT in 1991 is one example of the growing civil society attention to the plight of these children and was followed by increased attention to sexual exploitation of children by other international NGOs like Terre des Hommes, Save the Children and World Vision and their respective national sections or branches. Furthermore other organisations and agencies were established to combat (inter alia) the use of the Internet for sexual exploitation of children including the Internet Watch Foundation, the European Financial Coalition and including financial institutions, credit card companies and ISPs. These steps have the objective of eroding the profitability of child pornography. Also part of the overall effort is the Virtual Global Taskforce, which includes amongst others, INTERPOL and Australian and USA law enforcement agencies. This taskforce has the objective of identifying child victims, determining their location and assisting children at risk, and identifying predators with a view to holding them accountable.[51]

The prevention and fight against sexual exploitation of children became a permanent item on the international and regional political agenda reflected in the adoption of the treaties mentioned in the previous paragraph and in the appointment in 1992

[50] See for more information, e.g. the handbook mentioned in footnote 42, the Reports of the Special representative of the UN Secretary General on the sale of children, child prostitution and child pornography and the Country monitoring reports of ECPAT.

[51] See www.europeanfinancialcoalition.eu and the report: Commercial Sexual exploitation of Children Online. A Strategic Assessment 2013 and (www.virtualglobaltaskforce.com).

by the UN Human Rights Commission (now the UN Human Rights Council) of a Special Rapporteur on the sale of children, child prostitution and child pornography. This Rapporteur submits annually a report on her/his activities to the UN Human Rights Council; these reports provide information on developments in combating sexual exploitation of children.[52]

In the domain of sexual exploitation, child sex tourism is a phenomenon not explicitly covered in the OPSC nor in the Lanzarote Convention. But over the past two decades, it received increasing attention not only from governments and NGOs but also from the travel and tourism industry. This resulted, in 1998, in the Code of Conduct for the Protection of Children from Sexual Exploitation in Travel and Tourism. It is currently endorsed by 1,266 travel agents, tour operators, hotels and restaurants. They commit themselves, inter alia, to train the personnel in the countries of travel origin and travel destination, to introduce clauses in contracts with suppliers stating a common repudiation of sexual exploitation of children and providing information to travellers and to local key persons at destination via such means as brochures, in-flight films, ticket slips and websites.[53]

The UN World Tourism Organisation established a Network on Child[54] Protection, a global platform bringing together governments, tourist industry, international organisations, NGOs and media associates, for the purpose of sharing information, experiences and best practices for the protection of children affected by tourism.

Another new rather phenomenon being addressed is "grooming". This term refers to the preparation of a child for sexual abuse, motivated by the desire to use the child for sexual gratification. It may involve the befriending of a child, often through the adult pretending to be another young person, drawing the child into discussing intimate matters and gradually exposing the child to sexually explicit materials in order to reduce resistance to or inhibition about sex. The child may also be drawn into producing pornography by sending compromising photos using a digital camera, webcam or phonecam, which provide the groomer a means for controlling the child through threats. Once a physical meeting is arranged the child can be sexually abused or otherwise harmed.[55]

Article 23 of the Lanzarote Convention requires States parties to take the necessary legislative or other measures to criminalise grooming via "the intentional proposal". When information and communication technologies are used by an adult to meet a child below the age of sexual consent for the purpose of committing sexual activities with the child or to produce child pornography, the setting up of the

---

[52] See, e.g. the 2009 report, UN Doc. A/HRC/12/23. 13 July 2009 and the report 2013 UN Doc. A/HRC/25/48, 23 December 2013.

[53] The implementation of this code is financed by contributions from the European Commission, European ECPAT partners and supported logistically by the UN World Tourism Organisation and the tourism industry. The secretariat is based in new York at ECPAT USA.; see for more information: www.thecode.org

[54] See http://www2.unwto.org/en/protect-children

[55] See the Explanatory Note to the Lanzarote Convention, para. 155–160 (http://conventins.coe.int/Treaty/EN/Reports/Html/201.htm).

meeting might not be, in and of itself, a crime. However, when the proposal is followed by material acts leading to such meeting, it can become a separate crime. In other words, the proposal as such is not a crime but the resulting meeting is.

The increasing role of new technologies such as Internet chat rooms and game sites also raises the question whether and to what extent virtual child pornography, which is sexual abusive images of a non-existent child, should be treated as a crime. The Lanzarote Convention (art. 20) and the Cybercrime Convention (art. 9)[56] indicate that virtual child pornography should be criminalised, although both treaties make that optional for the States parties. But EU Directive 2011/92 requires all 28 member states to make various acts such as acquisition, possession and distribution of child pornography punishable (art. 5), and the definition of child pornography includes "any material that visually depicts any person appearing to be a child engaged in real or simulated sexually explicit conduct or any depiction of the sexual organs of any person appearing to be a child for primarily sexual purposes". In other words, the 28 member states of the EU shall make the production, possession and distribution, etc. of virtual child pornography a crime.

The Dutch criminal code provides for the criminalisation of virtual child pornography (art. 240b). In 2013, the Dutch Hoge Raad (Cassation Court) had to answer the question of how the phrase "a person appearing to be a child" should be interpreted. The Court argued as follows: sexually abusive images of a person appearing to be a child (in other words not a real child) is defined as child pornography if the picture of the child is so realistic that it cannot be distinguished from a real child. It means that if it is immediately clear for the average viewer and also for children that the person is manipulated to look like a child but is not a real child, the abusive images are not punishable child pornography. The commentator of this decision, Prof. Schalken, raised the question whether pornographic pictures of a non-existent child should be qualified as punishable (virtual) child pornography if children cannot see the difference between these pictures and similar pictures of a real child.[57]

These developments also had an impact on the terminology in the world of sexual exploitation. Due to the new communication technologies, the term "child abusive images" is used more and more, replacing the traditional term "child pornography". The term "prostitution of children" is preferred over "child prostitution" in light of the fact that in some countries prostitution is a crime, meaning that children may be treated as offenders instead of as victims of prostitution.

There is no system of data collection in the field of sexual exploitation comparable to the SIMPOC programme of the ILO-IPEC. Global estimates published by ECPAT are based on information from countries that produce such figures. ECPAT estimates that about 1.8 million children are the victim of sexual exploitation annually. There are other organisations with their own estimates or figures. For instance, the National Centre on Missing and Exploited Children in the USA reported in April 2009 that it had since 1998 identified 592,044 pornographic websites.

---

[56] This Convention was adopted and opened for signature in Budapest on 23 November 2001. It entered into force on 1 July 2004 (www.conventions.coe.int/Treaty/en/Treaties/Html/185.htm).

[57] Hoge Raad 12 March 2013, ECCLI:NL:2013:BY7919.

The Internet Watch Foundation received in 2008 33,497 report, including 1,563 domains depicting sexual abuse of children (74 % for commercial purposes). The estimate of the number of children victims of sexual abuse on the Internet ranges from 10,000 to 100,000, and the number of predators connected to the Internet at any one time is estimated at 750,000. The production and distribution of child pornography has an estimated value between US$3 and 20 billion.[58] The Internet Hotlines received 29,908 reports on child abusive materials on the Internet in 2011, jumping to 37,404 in 2012. In 2013 INTERPOL identified 3,000 child victims of sexual exploitation and 1,500 offenders in 40 countries.

Further Discussion of the Identification and Reporting of Child Victims of Sexual Exploitation

In the field of sexual exploitation of children, there is not an internationally adopted and implemented system of identification and reporting of child victims like the ILO-IPEC Child labour Monitoring System (CLMS). The international treaties mentioned before do not contain specific provisions regarding the identification and reporting of victims of child sexual exploitation with one exception, the EU Directive 2011/92. Article 16 states that all 28 member states of the EU "shall take the necessary measures to encourage any person who knows about or suspects in good faith that any of the offences referred to in article 3 to 7 (all forms of sexual exploitation) have been committed to report this to the competent services". It is the responsibility of each member state to determine the competent authorities to which report can be made. Those competent authorities should not be limited to child protection services or relevant social services. In order to facilitate the reporting, article 16 also states (para. 1) that member states shall take all necessary measures to ensure that the confidentiality rules imposed by national law on certain professionals whose main duty is to work with children do not constitute an obstacle to the possibility for those professionals of their reporting to the services responsible for child protection in any situation where they have reasonable grounds to believe that a child is the victim of sexual exploitation.

It is too early to report on the measures member states have taken to comply with this obligation. But, as can be concluded from the previous paragraph, the lack of an explicit international provision does not mean that child victims of sexual exploitation are not identified and reported. There are quite a number of examples not only at the international level (INTERPOL, EUROPOL and the Virtual Global Task Force) but also at the national level, for instance in the USA (NCMEC) and via hotlines and child helplines.

INTERPOL has the International Child Sexual Exploitation images database (ICSE DB) which allows specialised investigators around the world to share data with

[58] See for these and other figures the 2009 Report of the Special Rapporteur on the sale of children, child prostitution and child pornography; UN Doc. A/HRC/12/23, 13 July 2009.

colleagues with a view to identifying the victims and perpetrators. The database uses sophisticated image comparison software to make connections between victims and locations. Forty countries are connected to this database.[59] EUROPOL is a regional body of cooperation and support for member states in actions to prevent and combat serious and organised crime. In 2001 the organisation opened a special Analysis Work File, AWF Twins, to support member states in preventing and combating the activities of criminal networks involved in the production, sale and distribution of child sexual abuse materials. In 2011 the operation rescue and with the leading support of EUROPOL and which focused on an online forum of paedophiles succeeded in identifying 705 suspects around the world, 250 arrests were made and 252 children safeguarded.[60] When child pornographic images are found, the identification of the child and/or the perpetrators requires often meticulous investigations, an eye for details like the band on the wrist of the child with some letters on it and intense cooperation between specialised police units in different countries and involvement of NGO agencies (Sher 2007).

There is not (yet) an international guideline on how to identify children victims of sexual exploitation or at the risk of becoming one. But the American Professional Society on the Abuse of Children (APSAC), in 2013, published as part of a series, Practice Guidelines on The Commercial Sexual Exploitation of Children: The Medical Provider's Role in Identification, Assessment and Treatment. These guidelines provide a list of indicators and questions for identifying children victims of commercial sexual exploitation (or at risk of becoming one). These indicators include inter alia the following:

- There are signs that the child is controlled by domineering accompanying person (pimp/ trafficker?).
- The child shows signs of physical abuse and/or substance abuse.
- The child has a history of running away from home and/or of involvement with child protective services and/or multiple sexual partners in a short period or of multiple sexual transmitted infections.
- The child has unexplained shopping trips or large amounts of cash or expensive items (jewelry, clothing, electronics).

The guidelines also provide information and recommendations on how to interview children victims of sexual exploitation, on how to do physical examinations, etc.

It is evident that these guidelines can be very useful for the identification of particular children involved in prostitution and sex tourism. The tourist industry trained 10,000 of their workers in 2013 to improve their skills in identifying (potential) victims of sex tourism. In the coming years, the APSAC Guidelines could be a helpful in this and other trainings of workers in the tourism industry.

It goes without saying and is emphasised in the APSAC Guidelines that identification has to be followed by assessment of the problems and needs of the child, along with a referral to adequate medical, psychological and social services to

[59] INTERPOL fact sheet crimes against children.

[60] EUROPOL Child Sexual Exploitation Fact Sheet 2012.

assure her/his recovery and social reintegration. The identification of sexual abusive images of children on the Internet is important given the fact that there are so many of them and that they are so relatively accessible. Much more difficult is to identify the particular child involved. It takes a lot of police research and analytical work. INTERPOL and EUROPOL have expert police officers for this job. Given the images they are watching, it is an activity which can cause strong emotional stress. There are also examples of such experts in the national police forces. For example, the Dutch police have special units for researching the Internet and identifying not only victims but also perpetrators. Discussion takes place about the permissibility of police officers presenting themselves as adolescents in an effort to entice adults in sexual exploitative activities (decoy). It can be a tool for identifying groomers with a view of preventing that children become a victim of these predators.[61]

Summing up this subsection, the identification and reporting of child victims of sexual exploitation are a matter of using different approaches depending on the type of exploitation. Indicators have been developed which can be used for the identification of (potential) victims of the prostitution of children and of child victims of sexual exploitation in the tourism industry. The role of the police in this regard is evident, but the travel and tourist industry also should play an active role in prevention and in identification of victims of this form of sexual exploitation. Furthermore, there are hotlines or helplines for reporting instances of sexual exploitation in particular of sexual abusive images on the Internet.

Some Concluding Observations

Identification and reporting are the very important steps necessary to provide the child victim of severe violence with the protection, recovery and social reintegration he or she is entitled to under the CRC.

From the survey in this chapter, the following conclusions are possible:

- The right of the child to be protected from all forms of violence, and economic and sexual exploitation is well founded in quite a number of international and regional human rights instruments. But specific rules for identification and reporting in these instruments are limited.
- Identification and reporting of (suspicion of) child abuse and neglect are well developed in many countries. The UN CRC Committee has provided the 194 States parties to the CRC on the basis of article 19 CRC with rather specific recommendations particularly for identification and reporting of all forms of violence in the family and other care settings. It recommends inter alia that States parties make reporting an obligation, as a minimum, for professionals working directly with children. Examples of this obligation already exist in countries with so-called Reporting Laws (USA, Australia, Canada and others). The Netherlands

[61] Document of Parliament year 2012–2013, 28 638, Nr. 104, The Hague 24 oktober 2013.

is an example of a well-elaborated (since 1972) system of voluntary reporting. There is yet no evidence/ based conclusion that a system of mandatory reporting is as such more effective than a system of voluntary reporting. Much seems to depend on the quality of the professionals working with and within the system and the political commitment expressed in the allocation of adequate human and financial resources. A matter of concern is the identification and reporting of instances of abuse of children in care and other institutions.

– Identification and reporting of children victim of economic exploitation is not systematically developed. The emphasis seems to be on the identification of these children in particular through the Child Labour Monitoring System developed by the ILO International Programme for the Elimination of Child Labour (ILO-IPEC) and introduced in more than 100 countries. In that regard, different models (school-based/ workplace based and community based) have been developed and are implemented. NGOs are involved in these activities, and labour inspectorates play an increasing role in the identification of children victim of economic exploitation.
– Identification and reporting of sexual exploitation is not the result of a well-developed system. This serious form of violence against children is identified in different ways by different organisations. The development over the past two decades shows that there is a significant growth in the capability to identify children, in particular those sexually abused online. INTERPOL, EUROPOL and other agencies such as the Virtual Global Task Force with the involvement of international non-governmental organisations such as ECPAT, Terre des Homme, Save the Children and World Vision and the corporate world of travel and tourism. But till now the reporting of instances of sexual exploitation has not been made mandatory by law.

In conclusion many measures are taken to identify children victims of violence and economic and sexual exploitation. Mandatory or voluntary reporting is limited to cases of (suspicion of) violence against children in the family and in other care settings. Information about the effectiveness of identification and reporting in terms of providing the child victims with adequate assistance for their physical and psychological recovery and social reintegration is very limited. But it is clear that child victims are high on the national and international agenda. The society does not shy away from the problems of these children but wants to provide protection and recovery through identification and reporting whilst at the same time efforts are made to end impunity and bring the perpetrators to justice.

But we are still far away from ensuring that all children are free from all forms of violence and economic and sexual exploitation.

The 25th anniversary of the CRC is an opportunity to assess where we are and to identify measures for further strengthening our efforts to protect children against violence and exploitation. In that regard it seems crucial to me that all countries develop a well-organised practice of identifying child victims of violence and exploitation with the involvement of all relevant stakeholders (governments, NGOs, the corporate world and UN specialised agencies) and with the inclusion of a set of services accessible and affordable for children and their parents to assist them in the recovery and social reintegration.

From a human rights perspective, it is imperative that we move as quickly as possible to a world free from violence against and exploitation of children.

References

Baines. (2008, November). *Online Child sexual abuse: The law enforcement response*. Paper prepared by Victoria Baines for the Third World Congress on Sexual Exploitation of Children and adolescents, Rio de Janeiro. www.ecpat.net/WorldCongressIII/PDF/Publications/ICTLaw/Thematic_Paper_ICTLAW_ENG.pdf

Bourdillon, M., Levison, D., Myers, W., & White, B. (2011). *Rights and wrongs of children's work*. New Brunswick/London: Rutgers University Press.

Christopherson, R. J. (1981). Two approaches of handling child abuse: A comparison of the English and the Dutch systems. *Child Abuse and Neglect, 5*, 369–373.

Detrick, S. (Ed.). (1992). *The UN Convention on the Rights of the child. A guide to the "Travaux Préparatoires"*. Dordrecht/Boston/London: Martinus Nijhoff Publishers.

Doek, J. E. (1978). Child abuse in the Netherlands: The medical referee. *Chicago – Kent Law Review, 54*(3), 785–828.

Doek, J. E. (1986). Child abuse and neglect: Alternative approaches. In Z. Brankowski & M. Carballo (Eds.), *Battered children and child abuse, Proceedings of the XIXth CIOMS Round table Conference, Bern, Switzerland, Dec. 4–6 1985* (pp. 130–145). Geneva: Council of International Organizations of Medical Sciences CIOMS.

Doek, J. E. (1994). Child abuse and neglect: Article 19 CRC. *The International Journal of Children's Rights, 2*(1), 88–95.

Donelly, A. C. (Ed.). (2002). *An international movement to end child abuse. The story of ISPCAN*. Carol Stream: International Society for Prevention of Child Abuse and Neglect (ISPCAN).

Fyfe, A. (2009). Coming to terms with child labor: The historical role of education. In H. D. Hindman (Ed.), *The world of child labor. An historical and regional survey* (pp. 49–53). Armonk/London: M.E. Sharpe.

Hart, S. N., Lee, Y., & Wernham, M. (2011). A new age for child protection – General comment 13: Why it is important, how it was constructed, and what it intends. *Child Abuse & Neglect, 35*(12), 970–978.

Hendrick, H. (2009). Periods of history: Childhood and child work, c. 1800 – Present. In H. D. Hindman (Ed.) (see above) (pp. 33–38).

Heywood, C. (2009). A brief historiography of child labor. In H. D. Hindman (Ed.) (see above) (pp. 18–26).

ILO. (2002). *A future without child labour. Global report under the follow – Up to the ILO declaration on fundamental principles and rights at work*. Geneva: ILO.

Johnson, A. K. (2011). International child sex tourism: Enhancing the legal response in South East Asia. *The International Journal of Children's Rights, 19*(1), 55–79.

Lieten, G. K. (Ed.). (2011). *Hazardous child labour in Latin America*. Dordrecht/Heidelberg: Springer.

Marneffe. C., & Lampo, A. (Eds.). (1989). *De ontbrekende schakel. Kindermishandeling en kinderbescherming*. Brussel: VUB Press.

Pinheiro, P. S. (2006). *World report on violence against children*. Geneva: UN Publishing Services. Can be downloaded on www.ohchr.org, www.unicef.org, and www.who.int

Sher, J. (2007). *Caught in the Web. Inside the police hunt to rescue children from online predators*. New York: Carroll & Graf Publishers.

Stearns, P. N. (2009). Child labor in the industrial revolution. In H. D. Hindman (Ed.) (see above) (pp. 38–45).

Svevo-Cianci, K. A., Herczog, M., Krappmann, L., & Cook, P. (2011). The new UN CRC General Comment 13 "The right of the child to freedom from all forms of violence" – Changing how the world conceptualizes child protection. *Child Abuse & Neglect, 35*(12), 979–989.

Van Montfoort, A. (1994). *Het topje van de ijsberg. Kinderbescherming en de bestrijding van kindermishandeling in social juridisch perspectief.* Utrecht: Uitgeverij SWP.

Chapter 25
Legislation Concerning Reporting of Child Sexual Abuse and Child Trafficking in India: A Closer Look

Sibnath Deb

Introduction

The increasing rate of child sexual abuse and child trafficking has become a serious concern for national and international policy makers. Because these acts are criminal and result in serious harms to the child, and occur in closed scenarios where the situation is concealed, it is very important for people who become aware of the acts to report the incidences to the appropriate authority. Reporting of incidences could help to render justice and health rehabilitation to the victim and penalize the perpetrators. In addition, it would help to understand the nature and magnitude of the problem. The objective of this chapter is first to review the Indian legislation concerning mandatory reporting of child abuse and neglect and, second, to consider the potential for mandatory reporting of two categories of child maltreatment in particular in the Indian context: sexual abuse and child trafficking.

The Indian Constitution (adopted on Nov. 26, 1949, enforced on Jan. 26, 1950) guarantees four fundamental rights to all citizens: justice, liberty, equality, and fraternity. If any citizen experiences any form of violence, abuse, or maltreatment, they have every right to seek justice. Violence, especially interpersonal, social, and community, has existed in society since time immemorial. The nature, forms, and extents of violence vary from time to time. Recently, the active role of the media has now brought the severity of specific problems, including child sexual abuse and trafficking to the surface in India. Violence is a natural phenomenon since the inherent nature of human beings is to dominate others in different forms to gain power and resources. However, legislative and social measures taken up by the appropriate authorities

S. Deb, Ph.D., D.Sc. (✉)
Department of Applied Psychology, Pondicherry University (A Central University), Silver Jubilee Campus, R.V. Nagar, Kalapet, Puducherry 605 014, India
e-mail: sibnath23@gmail.com

B. Mathews, D.C. Bross (eds.), *Mandatory Reporting Laws and the Identification of Severe Child Abuse and Neglect*, Child Maltreatment 4,
DOI 10.1007/978-94-017-9685-9_25

of a society from time to time for combating the problem have brought some changes. Review and/or amendment of legislation is also necessary for addressing emerging challenges.

Although children have always experienced various forms of violence, this issue has been recognized by the international community in the recent past through adoption of the UN Convention on Rights of the Child (CRC) (1989) to which most nations are signatory. The Government of India is also a signatory to the CRC (1989). In addition, the Government of India has passed various pieces of legislation addressing the problems of children and promoting their rights.

The Government of India has adopted a range of legislation for the protection of child rights in addition to a number of articles for child protection in the Indian Constitution (1949). Yet, none of the legislation prescribed anything about reporting of offenses against children except two, which have only done so in a partial way: the Indian Penal Code (IPC 1860) and the Protection of Children from Sexual Offences Act, 2012 (POCSO Act 2012). Even the Immoral Traffic (Prevention) Act (ITPA), 1956, did not mention anything about reporting. In the IPC, sections like 176 (Omission to give notice or information to public servant by person legally bound to give it), 177 (Furnishing false information), 197 (Issuing or signing false certificate), and 201 (Causing disappearance of evidence of offence or giving false information to screen offender) talked about reporting of any offenses without specifying the category of professionals and/or social agents. The POCSO Act (2012) mandated all persons to report any sexual offence against a child (s 19) and the media, studio, and persons in the photographic profession to report sexual exploitation of the child (s 20).

Despite so many new measures, a major problem persists because children continue to experience violence in different forms owing to poor reporting. There is an urgent need for India to review other countries' legislation pertaining to mandatory reporting of child sexual abuse, especially the USA and Australia, and child trafficking, such as the Human Trafficking Act of Ghana (2005), to consider the potential for these approaches in the Indian context and to formulate appropriate legislation or amend existing child rights-related legislation in India, taking into account local cultural beliefs and practices and economic conditions of the people. In turn, it will help the Ministry of Women and Child Development, Government of India, and the National Commission for Child Protection and State Commissions for taking corrective measures for child protection.

Magnitude of the Problem

The Global Context

It is very difficult to measure the nature and extent of violence against children since most of such incidences occur in the privacy of family and are never reported or investigated (UNICEF 2009). The hard reality is that in some nations, data collection mechanisms do not exist (UNICEF 2009; Pinheiro 2006). However, one of the recent global meta-analytic reviews of population-based studies of childhood sexual abuse has estimated cumulative prevalence rates for sexual abuse prior to age 18 as 18.0 % for girls and 7.6 % for boys (Stoltenborgh et al. 2011). A recent discussion paper on child protection and child welfare in the Asia-Pacific region (Pouwels et al. 2010) summarized primary studies reporting the pervasiveness of physical, psychological, and sexual violence in the preceding 12 months for children in China (10 %, 13 %, and 2 %, respectively), Malaysia (19.0 %, 20.4 %, and 22.2 %, respectively), and Vietnam (47.5 %, 39.5 %, and 19.7 %, respectively). A study of childhood maltreatment in 7 low- and middle-income countries (Dunne et al. 2009) revealed rates of physical, psychological, and sexual violence ever experienced during childhood for children in India were 33.1 %, 46.8 %, and 20.2 %, respectively. The results of these studies suggest that children in different countries experience different types of victimization at different rates. Even within countries, there may be regional differences.

There are various global estimations about trafficking of women and children every year. According to the US Department of State Trafficking in Persons Report (2007), about 600,000–800,000 men, women, and children are trafficked across international borders each year. Approximately 80 % are women and girls and up to 50 % are minors. Another estimation says that approximately 80 % of trafficking involves sexual exploitation and 19 % involves labor exploitation (Source: Eleven Facts about Human Trafficking; http://www.dosomething.org/tipsandtools/11-facts-about-human-trafficking).

The Indian Context

India, with its more than one billion population, has achieved a literacy rate of 74.04 %. About 70 % of the people in India live in rural areas, while 30 % live in the urban areas (Census of India 2011). Poverty in India is widespread. Various agencies reported almost similar estimation about poverty in India. For example, according to the World Bank Report (2010), 32.7 % of all people in India fall below the international poverty line of US$1.25 per day (PPP), while 68.72 % live on less than US$2 per day (Junofy 2013). The United Nations Development Programme (2010) estimated that 29.8 % of Indians live below the country's national poverty line (Mandal 2010). The children from these families become more vulnerable to trafficking and/or sexual abuse (Census of India 2011). Of the total population, about 44.4 % of them are children, irrespective of socioeconomic background, and one in every two children is deprived in respect of not receiving primary education, adequate nutrition, and medical care (International Institute for Population Sciences 2007). Girls in India, especially in the rural areas, are discriminated against in terms of education, nutrition, and medical care and are also treated as burden for the family (India Country Report on Violence against Children 2005; Deb 2006).

Child Abuse Generally

A national level study on child abuse revealed widespread abuse of girls and boys in India. Both boys and girls are equally at risk of abuse. The persons in trust and authority are major abusers. Five- to twelve-year-old children are in the high-risk category. About 70 % of the children have not reported the abuse to anyone. Two out of every three children have been physically abused, while two out of every three school-going children are victims of corporal punishment – half of these incidents occur in government-run schools. More than half of the child respondents (53.22 %) reported facing one or more forms of sexual abuse, while 21.90 % child respondents reported facing severe forms of sexual abuse that included sexual assault, making the child fondle private parts, making the child exhibit private body parts, and being photographed in the nude, while 50.76 % faced other forms of sexual abuse such as forcible kissing, sexual advances made during travel and marriages, and exposure to pornographic materials. Every second child reported facing emotional abuse, and in more than 80.0 % of the cases, parents were the abusers (Report on Child Abuse and Neglect. New Delhi: Min Women Child Dev 2007). In another study covering students from grades 8 and 9 of eight schools in Agartala, Tripura, Deb and Walsh (2012) found that 21.9 %, 20.9 %, and 18.1 % students experienced physical, psychological, and sexual violence at home. Girls were more often victims of sexual violence (25.0 % compared with 11.3 %).

Child Sexual Abuse and Trafficking

Child sexual abuse has been an age-old and deep-rooted social and cultural problem in India. India is also witnessing an increase in child trafficking, with West Bengal a focal point of activity (*Indian Express, 16 Aug.*1999, p. 8; Sanlaap 2003; Sen 2005). As a result, child trafficking for commercial sexual exploitation has become a serious issue for policy makers (Deb 2002). Child trafficking involves the recruitment, transport, and transfer of children, through abduction, deception, or force, for exploitative purposes. Trafficking of children for commercial sexual purposes has become transnational and highly lucrative (International Labour Organization 2005; UNICEF 2005). As there is no reliable data concerning the worldwide prevalence and incidence of child trafficking for sexual exploitation, research is urgently needed to fill up the knowledge gap (United Nations Office on Drugs and Crime 2009). Although child exploitation in the form of forced economic labor is a much discussed issue, the booming industry of child sexual exploitation after trafficking is yet to receive adequate attention from researchers, academics, and social activists. In India, every year about 10.0–15.0 % of children, especially girls, become victims of child trafficking for a number of reasons like poverty, demand for girls as sexual commodities, and lack of adequate parental supervision (Indian Express, 16 August 1999). There have been many cases where children just disappear overnight, as many as 1 every 8 min, according to the National Crime Records Bureau, Ministry of Home Affairs, Govt. of India.

Social Factors Behind Trafficking and Sexual Exploitation of Children

Child trafficking and sexual exploitation of children, especially girls, is the product of a number of forces in Indian society and families. Socially, there is a lack of compulsory education until 2009, with about half of all primary school-aged children not attending school (Government of West Bengal 2008). Other statistics indicate that 73 % of children attend school to the end of primary school (UNICEF 2008), but even if accurate, this still means that more than one quarter of all primary school-aged children do not complete primary school. Because of the vast population of India, this means that tens of millions of young children are denied an opportunity to gain an education and skills, thus vastly limiting life chances and social mobility. It is relevant to mention here that the Government of India has enacted the Rights of Children to Free and Compulsory Education Act, 2009, which ensures free education for children between 6 and 14 years. Undoubtedly, this legislation will save a large number of children from trafficking although this law is yet to be implemented effectively in the truest sense.

Further, the traditional class system in India aggravates the problem as children from lower classes are denied rights and are habitually maltreated. This is exacerbated by a lack of functional child protection services. At a social and familial level, there is extreme poverty (Deb et al. 2005; Government of India, Press Information Bureau 2007), which compounds these societal factors. Indicating the widespread economic deprivation, 28 % of all children are born with low birth weight (UNICEF 2008), and the India National Family Health Survey-III found that more than 56.0 % of teenage girls in India are anemic, with a hemoglobin count of less than 12 g/dl, the world standard; this is especially serious in rural areas. In a study of 40 trafficked girls, Deb and Sen (2005a) found indications of these factors: the majority (82.9 %) were aged between 18 and 20 years; respondents were largely illiterate (57.1 %) or semiliterate (42.9 %); nearly all (91.4 %) had more than two siblings; and parents, who were mostly illiterate and very poor, were involved in agriculture as laborers or vegetable traders.

In another study, Deb et al. (2011) observed that a large number of trafficked were illiterate, with only 29.2 % and 26.6 % having attended primary school and secondary education, respectively. With regard to their parents' education, about 38.3 % of the respondents' fathers and 70.8 % of their mothers were illiterate. About 33.3 % of the fathers and 19.2 % of the mothers studied up to primary level of education. Only a few (19.2 % of the fathers and 8.4 % of the mothers) had studied at secondary level. The majority of the respondents lived in rural areas, while 33.3 % lived in urban areas and about 20.8 % of the girls lived in semi-urban areas. The monthly income of 45.8 % of the families was below Rs. 1,000 (US$24), 27.5 % of the families' incomes ranged between Rs. 1,001 and Rs. 2,000 (US$24–US$48), and 13.3 % had an income above Rs. 2,001. Therefore, it may be stated that more than half of the families were living below the poverty line, according to the definition of poverty stated by the Indian Government's Planning Commission

(Government of India, Press Information Bureau 2007). Further, the authors revealed that about one third of the girls were sexually abused before being trafficked, and all of the girls were sexually abused after being trafficked. Nearly 45.8 % of the respondents indicated that they were sexually abused between 14 and 17 years of age, while 37.5 % were sexually abused between 10 and 13 years. The other 16.7 % were sexually victimized while very young, aged between 6 and 9 years. Regarding the perpetrators of the abuse, nearly 55.8 % were strangers, while 29.2 % were relatives. The remaining 15.0 % belonged to the "other" category, which mostly constituted known local acquaintances. About 73.3 % of the respondents stated that they were abused after being drugged and sold to brothels in major cities like Mumbai, Delhi, Pune, and Kolkata. Others stated that they left home after being lured by better job prospects in big cities and then became trapped in a cycle of abuse.

Finally, there are factors associated with perpetrators: In India, the male gender is dominant, making girls even more vulnerable. And there is a common misconception among the rural folk that people infected by sexually transmitted diseases including HIV/AIDS can get rid of the problem if they have sexual intercourse with a minor girl. Thus, a high risk for child trafficking and sexual exploitation is created by the proclivity of many adults to exploit children financially and sexually, within this atmosphere of overpopulation, poverty, lowly paid employment, illiteracy, lack of educational opportunities, general lack of promotion of children's rights, and the limits on children's life chances through poor education (Deb et al. 2011).

Dynamics of Trafficking

Offers of false marriages and jobs are the main two methods adopted by the traffickers in addition to abduction and sale for child trafficking (Deb et al. 2005; Deb and Mukherjee 2011). Many of those seeking marriage, enhanced employment prospects, and a higher standard of living are particularly susceptible to traffickers (Kempadoo et al. 2005). In cases of sale, parents sell their children, mostly daughters, for meager sums of money, who are then trafficked to cities or across borders. There is some evidence that relative poverty is more relevant to trafficking than the general socioeconomic status of the individual (Kempadoo et al. 2005). Deb et al. (2005) found that trafficking and commercial exploitation of children is overlooked in spite of border security and patrol. Typically separated from their family's domestic servants or in other commercial roles in industries including agriculture, mining, and manufacturing, fishing, and begging, many victims end up in prostitution. Even in the apparently more regulated forms of commercial work, the trafficked children are susceptible to exploitation, including low wages, physical and psychological abuse, and overwork. These children are extremely vulnerable to abuse and exploitation, due to their low status and their traumatic experiences of parental abandonment, sexual abuse, transplantation into unfamiliar surroundings, and accumulation of denied rights, all without resources to assist (Mukherjee 2006).

Impact of Child Sexual Abuse and Trafficking

Like sexual abuse, trafficking causes numerous adverse consequences including psychological trauma (Pinheiro 2006; WHO 2002). In a study of 40 children, Deb and Sen (2005a) found that after their initiation into prostitution, about 80.0 % of the trafficked children became dependent on illegal substances and 20.0 % became pregnant unintentionally. Four children (11.4 %) were also HIV positive (Deb and Sen 2005a). Chatterjee et al. (2006) identified three categories of consequences: mental, physical, and social. Unsurprisingly, among the mental consequences, nearly every child suffered depression, loneliness, and loss of interest. Physically, nearly one in seven (6/41) was HIV positive. Socially, trafficked children were severely discriminated against in social and family life, by being disowned and exiled from their home village and family and excluded from marriage.

High-Profile Cases and Media Reports

In the last decade, the media has reported a number of cases related to violence against children. One such incident in the village of Nithari, Noida, Uttar Pradesh, revealed a horrifying picture of death of many children mostly girls after they had been sexually abused. Perhaps, the media coverage brought such practices to the attention of the public and policy makers that might have alerted them to the possibility of such a horrible crime taking place in their own backyard (The Times of India, Delhi, Feb. 14, 2009). Thereafter, the Ministry of Women and Child Development, Govt. of India felt the necessity to carry out a national level investigation to find out the nature and extent of child abuse and neglect in India.

Another recent case which shook the morale of most of the people in India is the gang rape of a 23-year-old physiotherapy student on a public bus, on 16 December 2012 in Delhi, the capital of India. This incident raised the issue of security for women and children in India. If incident like this could happen in the capital of India, what will happen in case of security of women and children of the rest of the country? This incident sparked large protests across the capital Delhi (Telegraph, Dec. 19, 2012). She was with a male friend who was severely beaten with an iron rod during the incident (NDTV, Dec. 21, 2012). This same rod was used to penetrate her so severely that the victim's intestines had to be surgically removed, before her death 13 days after the attack (Hindustan Times, Dec. 21, 2012). In the 24-h period after the gang rape of the victim, at least two girls under the age of 18 were gang raped and one of them was murdered (CBS News, Dec. 21, 2012). The following day, there was uproar in the Indian Parliament over the incident. Members of Parliaments in both houses had set aside their regular business to discuss the gruesome rape case and demanded strict punishment for those who carried out the attack. Leader of the opposition in the Lok Sabha demanded that "the rapists should be hanged" (BBC News, Dec. 18, 2012). Thousands of people, mostly young, participated in a massive demonstration in 22 December in protest (ITV News, Dec. 23, 2012).

Signing International Protocols

This worsening situation has occurred despite India acceding to the United Nations Convention on the Rights of the Child (on 11 December 1992), which contains a number of articles requiring States parties to take measures to prevent abduction, sale, and trafficking of children (e.g., art 35) and sexual exploitation of children (e.g., art 34). On 15 November 2004, India signed the Optional Protocol to the United Nations Convention on the Rights of the Child (UNCRC) on the Sale of Children, Child Prostitution, and Child Pornography (2000), and India ratified this on 16 August 2005. This Optional Protocol contains a range of provisions about child trafficking and prostitution. States parties are required to prohibit the sale of children and child prostitution (art. 1), to ensure such acts are covered by criminal laws (art. 3), and to take measures to prevent sale and prostitution of children (art. 9). In addition, India has signed (on 12 December 2002), but not ratified, the Protocol to Prevent, Suppress and Punish Trafficking in Persons, Especially Women and Children (2000), which is a protocol to the United Nations Convention against Transnational Organized Crime. Article 9 of the Protocol requires States parties to establish policies and programs to prevent trafficking, to protect victims of trafficking (especially women and children) from revictimization, to reduce the vulnerability of women and children to trafficking, and to reduce the demand for trafficking. Article 6 requires parties to provide assistance to victims of trafficking so that they may recover physically, psychologically, and socially. This article also requires that domestic legal systems offer victims the capacity to obtain compensation for their suffering. In reality, much of the response in India to trafficking and child labor is undertaken by nongovernment organizations (NGOs), which provide services to the community such as rehabilitation shelters and homes, socio-legal services to victimized children, providing counseling to victimized children, and promoting awareness about children's rights.

Reported Cases of Child Rape, Kidnapping, and Abduction in India

A large number of children across the world experience various forms of criminal offenses which include murder, rape, trafficking, kidnapping, and infanticide. There is no separate classification of offenses against children in India. Generally, the offenses committed against children or the crimes in which children are the victims are considered as crimes against children. Indian penal code and the various protective and preventive "Special and Local Laws" specifically mention the offenses wherein children are victims. The age of child varies as per the definition given in the concerned acts and sections, but age of child has been defined to be below 18 years as per Juvenile Justice Act, 2000.

The cases in which the children are victimized and abused can be categorized under two broad sections:

- Crimes committed against children which are punishable under Indian Penal Code, 1860 (IPC)
- Crimes committed against children which are punishable under Special and Local Laws (SLL)

A total of 5,484 cases of child rape were reported in the country during 2010 as compared to 5,368 in 2009 accounting for an increase of 2.2 % during the year, while a total of 10,670 cases of kidnapping and abduction of children were reported during the year as compared to 8,945 cases in the previous year accounting for a significant increase of 19.3 %. It can clearly be seen that there is an astonishingly low level of reporting of child sexual abuse and trafficking, given the real incidence.

Disposal of Crimes Against Children by Police and Courts

The average rate of charge sheet (a formal document of accusation prepared by the law enforcement agency after preliminary investigation) for all the crimes against children (IPC & SLL) was 83.9 % in 2010, which was the same in 2009 as well. The highest charge-sheeting rate was observed in cases under "Buying of Girls for Prostitution" (97.9 %) followed by "Rape" (97.5 %) in comparison to the national level charge-sheeting rate of 79.1 % for IPC crimes and 94.7 % for SLL crimes (National Crime Record Bureau, Crime in India, MHA, Govt. of India 2010).

State-Wise Conviction Rate in India (National Crime Records Bureau 2010, Ministry of Home Affairs, Government of India)

In general, reporting is very low in India because of delayed justice system and perceived harassment and threats. However, high conviction rate in some of the small and backward states in India is a good example before rest of the country. Although it is believed that community pressure on the Criminal Justice System helped to take rape cases seriously results into higher conviction rate, there is a need to carry out a study to find out the facilitating factors behind high conviction rate. In turn, this learning lesson will help other states to improve the situation.

States with high conviction rate:

- Mizoram – 96.9 %
- Nagaland – 73.7 %
- Arunachal Pradesh – 66.7 %
- Sikkim – 66.7 %
- Meghalaya – 44.4 %

The question arises why conviction rate in the major cities and states with reasonably better infrastructure and personnel is low. Perhaps, poor investigation and delayed justice system are mainly responsible for poor conviction rate. In the given situation, it is important to think what needs to be done for higher conviction rate based on evidence.

States with low conviction rate:

- Maharashtra – 13.9 %
- Andhra Pradesh – 13.7 %
- West Bengal – 13.7 %
- Karnataka – 15.4 %
- Jammu and Kashmir – 2.6 %

Amendments to the Indian Penal Code (1860) Following Delhi Gang Rape and Other Similar Incidents in India

In April 2013, the Indian Parliament introduced amendments to the Indian Penal Code making various changes to the antirape laws in India [Criminal Law (Amendment) Act, 2013]. The offense of rape under section 375 has made both penile and non-penile insertion into bodily orifices of a woman by a man an offense. The definition is broadly defined in some aspect, with acts like penetration by penis, or any object or any part of body to any extent, into the vagina, mouth, urethra, or anus of a woman or making her to do so with another person or applying of mouth to sexual organs without the consent or will of the woman constituting the offense of rape.

The section has also clarified that penetration means "penetration to any extent," and lack of physical resistance is immaterial for constituting an offense. Except in certain aggravated situation, the punishment will be imprisonment not less than 7 years but which may extend to imprisonment for life, and shall also be liable to fine. In aggravated situations, punishment will be rigorous imprisonment for a term which shall not be less than 10 years but which may extend to imprisonment for life and shall also be liable to fine. A new section 376A has been added which states that if a person committing the offense of sexual assault "inflicts an injury which causes the death of the person or causes the person to be in a persistent vegetative state, shall be punished with rigorous imprisonment for a term which shall not be less than twenty years, but which may extend to imprisonment for life, which shall mean the remainder of that person's natural life, or with death" (Section, 376, Criminal Law (Amendment) Act, 2013). In the case of "gang rape," persons involved regardless of their gender shall be punished with rigorous imprisonment for a term which shall not be less than 20 years, but which may extend to life and shall pay compensation to the victim who shall be reasonable to meet the medical expenses and rehabilitation of the victim.

Certain changes have been introduced to promote victims' rights in the Criminal Procedure Code, 1973, and Indian Evidence Act. The recording of statements of the victim has been made more friendly and easy, the character of the victim is irrelevant, and there is a presumption of no consent where sexual intercourse is proved and the victim states that there has been no consent. Controversially, the age of consent in India has been increased to 18 years, which means any sexual activity irrespective of presence of consent with a woman below the age of 18 will constitute statutory rape. Marital rape is still not accepted as a criminal offense within Indian legal framework, except during the period of judicial separation of the partners.

Mandatory Reporting: Global Scenario

The World Perspectives on Child Abuse (7th ed.), a document of the International Society for Prevention of Child Abuse and Neglect (ISPCAN), indicated that out of 72 responding countries to ISPCAN survey, 49 indicated the presence of policy-based reporting duties of child abuse in law or policy, and 12 respondents indicated the presence of voluntary reporting by professionals (Daro 2007). For countries who are considering adopting legislation, it is worth referring to legislation of the USA, Australia, and Canada for demonstration of the issues to be faced and different models (Mathews and Kenny 2008).

Publication of the article titled "Battered Child Syndrome" by Kempe et al. in 1962 prompted the US administration to bring legislation for mandatory reporting. Available evidence indicates that the first mandatory reporting laws were enacted in the USA between 1963 and 1967 (Besharov 1985; Nelson 1984). The Child Abuse Prevention and Treatment Act (CAPTA, 1974) which was adopted and enacted in the USA on 31 January 1974 allocated funds to states based on the parameters of their laws. First, state laws were amended to require members of additional professional groups to report suspicions of abuse. Second, the types of reportable abuse were expanded to include not only physical abuse but sexual abuse, emotional or psychological abuse, and neglect (Kalichman 1999).

India

Although reporting and recognition of various forms of child abuse and neglect have increased significantly in some of the industrial countries such as the USA and Australia (Leventhal 1990), in India, reporting is still very low, as indicated by two recent local studies (Mukherjee 2006; Modak 2009). Csorba et al. (2006) remarked that reporting of cases of sexual abuse is always very low across the geographical boundaries because of a number of factors. Reporting of CAN cases in Indian society is very low owing to a number of factors like social stigma, perceived harassment, unwillingness of parents, disbelief of parents, and threat by perpetrators. For example, in a study in Kolkata, India, only 1.7 % of sexually abused cases were reported to the police (Deb and Mukherjee 2009), while in case of another study carried out in Agartala, Tripura (India), 15.5 % of the sexually abused cases were reported to the police (Modak 2009). The causes behind non-reporting are similar as stated above.

Although the Government of India has produced a number of child protection policies and there are a number of laws for protecting children's rights, child protection services are yet to be introduced in most of the states in India. Security of the victim's family is compromised when they report the incident to the police. In a number of cases in the recent past, when a victim's family members reported the incident to the police, they were further victimized by the perpetrators for reporting the incident. At the same time, social stigma always discourages a victim's family member from reporting the incident of sexual abuse to the police (Mukherjee 2006). In addition, there are an inadequate number of professionals to deliver psychosocial and medical services to sexually abused children. Therefore, the majority of sexually abused children live with the psychological trauma of the abuse life long, affecting their interpersonal relationships, personality, and career development (Deb and Sen 2005b).

Reporting of Abuse: What the Evidence Indicates

A number of studies have been carried out in different parts of the world on reporting of sexual abuse to police; the development of instrument for measuring attitudes toward reporting of child sexual abuse; review of merits of US, Australia, and Canada legislation; medical assessment of suspected child sexual abuse; and so on. Some of the relevant study findings regarding reporting have been presented in the following section.

From a retrospective and descriptive study based on a review of medical records of child sexual abuse (CSA) cases from 2000 to 2009 at Sulmaniya Medical Complex, the main secondary and tertiary medical care facility in Bahrain, Al-Mahroos and Al-Amer (2011) diagnosed 440 children with CSA. Out of them, 222 were males (50.5 %) and 218 were females (49.5 %). There was a steady increase in cases from 31 per year in 2000 to 77 cases in 2009. Children disclosed abuse in 26 % of cases, while health sector professionals recognized 53 % of the cases. Genital touching and fondling (62.5 %) were the most common form of CSA, followed by sodomy in 39 %. Gonorrhea was documented in 2 % of the cases and pregnancy in 4 % of the females. There was referral to police in 56 %, public prosecution in 31 % of the cases, but only 8 % reached the court. In fine, it may be stated that during 10 years, there has been a 2.5 % increase in reported cases of CSA in Bahrain. Improving the skill of professionals in identifying CSA indicators and a mandatory reporting law might be needed to improve the rate of recognition and referral of CSA cases. Walsh et al. (2012) did an evaluation of an instrument for measuring teachers' attitudes toward reporting child sexual abuse and discussed the instrument's merit for research into reporting practice. The findings provide insights into the complexity of studying teachers' attitudes toward reporting of child sexual abuse and have implications for future research. Mathews and Kenny (2008) carried out a secondary research on mandatory reporting related legislation in the USA, Canada, and Australia and found that all three countries adopted legislation in this regard. But the terms of these laws differed in significant ways, both within and between these nations, with the differences tending to broaden or narrow the scope of cases required to be reported, and by whom. The recommendations of the secondary study will be beneficial for other countries which are yet to adopt legislation in this regard.

In a study following Factorial Survey Design, González Ortega et al. (2012) attempted to study the criteria professionals use to identify and report child sexual abuse cases. Findings disclosed that the factors or criteria that most impact assessments are age asymmetry and use of coercion. Specifically, professionals are significantly more likely to perceive abuse and intend to report it if the other person involved in the interaction is much older than the minor and/or uses a coercive strategy, especially force, drugs, or blackmail. Another relevant criterion is the type of sexual act, since acts involving intercourse, digital penetration, and oral sex are significantly more likely to be deemed as abuse and reported. Jenny and Crawford-Jakubiak (2013) stated that the medical assessment of suspected child sexual abuse should include obtaining a history, performing a physical examination, and obtaining appropriate laboratory tests. The role of the physician includes determining the need to report suspected sexual abuse; assessing the physical, emotional, and behavioral consequences of sexual abuse; providing information to parents about how to support their child; and coordinating with other professionals to provide comprehensive treatment and follow-up of children exposed to child sexual abuse. So far as forensic procedures for interview physical exam and evidence collection in children and young people victims of physical and/or sexual abuse are concerned, Magalhães et al. (2011) stated some technical orientations to be followed. These orientations should aim at ruling the reporting of the occurrence in good time, guarantee an appropriate collection of evidence, guarantee good medical procedures in medical exams and evidence collection, and avoid repetition of exams of the victims, preventing secondary victimization and cross-contamination of child report.

Legislation Concerning Reporting of Human Trafficking in Ghana

For reporting of trafficking, Ghana has passed the Human Trafficking Act (2005) for the prevention, reduction, and punishment of human trafficking, for the rehabilitation and reintegration of trafficked persons, and for related matters. As per section 6 of the Act, it is the duty of a person with information about trafficking to inform the police or other concerned authorities like (1) the Commission of Human Rights and Administrative Justice, (2) the Department of Social Welfare, (3) the Legal Aid Board, or (4) a reputable Civil Society Organization.

The legislation defines that if a person fails to inform the police, he or she commits an offense and is liable on summary conviction to a fine of not less than 250 penalty units or a term of imprisonment not less than 12 months or to both. The legislation also clearly defines that a complaint about trafficking shall be filed by a social welfare officer, probation officer, health-care provider, teacher, district labor officer, or any other person if the victim is unable to complaint personally. According to section 9(1), a victim of trafficking or a person with information about trafficking may file a complaint with the police or other security services at the place where (a) the offender resides, (b) the victim resides, (c) the trafficking occurred or is occurring, or (d) the victim is residing temporarily, if the victim has left his or her normal place of abode.

Section 10(1) mandates the police officer to respond to any complaint immediately and arrange safe shelter for the person even before becoming the victim of the trafficking, while section 10(2) states the disciplinary measures for the police officers if they fail to respond to a complaint immediately.

Legislation Concerning Protection of Child Rights, Reporting of Sexual Abuse, and Child Trafficking in India

General Measures

In order to address any social and health issue effectively, multiple strategies are to be adopted. Among all strategies, legal measures are the first step as a yardstick accompanied by need-based social and health measures.

As stated earlier, rights of the children have been violated grossly in Indian Society despite many legal measures being introduced. The Indian Constitution (Nov. 26, 1949, and enacted in Jan. 26, 1950) has a number of provisions for protection of child rights. In addition, there are a number of other policies adopted for protection of child rights, and they include the National Policy for Children, 1974; the Integrated Child Protection Scheme, 2012; and others. The National Charter for Children (2003) states (article 9) that all children have a right to be protected against neglect, maltreatment, injury, trafficking, sexual and physical abuse of all kinds, corporal punishment, torture, violence, and degrading treatment. The Commissions for the Protection of Child Rights Act, 2005 (implemented in 2006), is an act to provide for the constitution of a National Commission and State Commissions for the Protection of Child Rights and Children's Courts for providing speedy trial of offenses against children or of violation of child rights and for matters connected therewith or incidental thereto (Commissions for The Protection of the Child Rights Act 2005). This law was passed when the Nithari serial killing incidents after sexual abuse of children in Noida District, Uttar Pradesh (India), was disclosed.

Indian Penal Code

The Indian Penal Code (IPC), 1860, provides for criminal liability and prosecution of offenders for simple and grievous hurt (sections 319 to 329), wrongful restraint and wrongful confinement (sections 339, 340–346), criminal force and criminal assault (sections 350 and 351), and dealings such as buying and selling of any person as a slave (section 370).

Section 372 and 373 of the IPC set punishment for selling and buying of minors for purposes of prostitution, while section 376-2C spells out the punishment for rape. There are standard provisions (e.g., section 201) which prohibit the active destruction of evidence to protect an offender and to guard against situations – common in India – where crimes against children are suppressed because of pressure from powerful people. Other provisions prohibit the active giving of false evidence (section 177); and others (e.g., section 197) prohibit issuing or signing false certificate. However, there are no provisions which require named persons to report known or suspected cases of abuse or trafficking.

Offenses and Provisions Related to Trafficking

In India, women and girls are mostly trafficked from the rural areas within the country for the purposes of commercial sexual exploitation and forced marriage especially in those areas where the sex ratio is highly skewed in favor of men. In order to address this issue, the Immoral Traffic (Prevention) Act (ITPA), 1956, was passed by the Indian Parliament. The ITPA is a special statute dealing with offenses of trafficking for commercial sexual exploitation. This act specified the punishment for various acts against children and women which include:

- Section 3: Punishment for keeping a brothel or allowing premises to be used as a brothel
- Section 4: Punishment for living on earnings of prostitution
- Section 5: Procuring, inducing, or taking person for the sake of prostitution
- Section 6: Detaining person in premises where prostitution is carried on
- Section 7: Prostitution in or in the vicinity of public places

However, ITPA did not mandate any specific category of professional or social agent to report the incident of child trafficking to the police or any appropriate authority or any person with information about trafficking to inform the issue to the police.

The Juvenile Justice (Care and Protection of Children) Act, 2000 (amended in 2006), helps ensure care and protection for trafficked children and their restoration and reintegration with their families and the community. The law also recognizes certain offenses against children as special offenses and provides for punishment. However, there is no provision for mandatory of reporting of sexual abuse and child trafficking in this law.

The Child Marriage Restraint Act, 1929, prohibits marriage of a male child below 21 years of age and that of a female child who is yet to reach 18 years of age. Further, the Prohibition of Child Marriage Act, 2006 s 9, prohibits a male adult above 18 years from contracting a child marriage. Section 10 says that whoever performs, conducts, directs, or abets any child marriage shall be punishable with rigorous imprisonment which may extend to 2 years and shall be liable to fine which may extend to one lakh rupees. At the same time, section 11 of the same act punishes a person for promoting or permitting solemnization of child marriages.

Protection of Children from Sexual Offenses Act, 2012

Given the increasing rate of sexual offenses against children across the country in the last decade and to combat this problem, the Protection of Children from Sexual Offenses Act, 2012 (POCSO Act 2012), was passed by the Indian Parliament mandated reporting of offenses against children without specifying the category of person or profession. For example, section 19 of POCSO Act, 2012, defines reporting of offenses:

> Any person (including the child), who has apprehension that an offence under this Act is likely to be committed or has knowledge that such an offence has been committed, he shall provide such information to(a) the Special Juvenile Police Unit; or(b) the local police.

Section 19 has given sufficient importance on proper recording of complaint and gets it checked by the informant to avoid any discrepancy. The section clearly states that

> (2) Every report given under sub-section (1) shall be
>
> (a) ascribed an entry number and recorded in writing;
> (b) be read over to the informant;
> (c) shall be entered in a book to be kept by the Police Unit.
>
> (3) Where the report under sub-section (1) is given by a child, the same shall be recorded under sub-section (2) in a simple language so that the child understands contents being recorded.
> (4) In case contents are being recorded in the language not understood by the child or wherever it is deemed necessary, a translator or an interpreter, having such qualifications, experience and on payment of such fees as may be prescribed, shall be provided to the child if he fails to understand the same.

Further, section 19 has mandated the Special Juvenile Police Unit or local police to make immediate arrangements for care and protection of the child informant into safe shelter within 24 h and report the matter to the Child Welfare Committee and/or the Special Court within 24 h.

The POCSO Act, 2012, also mandated the media, studio, and photographic profession-related persons to report sexual exploitation of the child to the police. For example, section 20 of POCSO Act, 2012, states the obligation of media, studio, and photographic facilities to report cases.

> Any personnel of the media or hotel or lodge or hospital or club or studio or photographic facilities, by whatever name called, irrespective of the number of persons employed therein, shall, on coming across any material or object which is sexually exploitative of the child (including pornographic, sexually-related or making obscene representation of a child or children) through the use of any medium, shall provide such information to the Special Juvenile Police Unit, or to the local police, as the case may be.

Section 21 of POCSO Act, 2012, clearly states the punishment for failure to report or record a case. As per subsection (2) of section 19, a person shall be punished with imprisonment of either description which may extend to 6 months or with fine or with both.

It is too early to comment about efficacy of the POCSO Act, 2012. There is a need to carry out a study to explore its efficacy and make necessary changes in the Act.

The Potential for Mandatory Reporting of Two Categories of Child Maltreatment in Particular in the Indian Context: Sexual Abuse and Child Trafficking

Regarding child trafficking, mandatory reporting is necessary. It is relevant to mention here that child trafficking is more of a rural phenomenon in India. Girl children from the rural areas with poor economic background and low social network are more vulnerable to child trafficking. Therefore, for reporting of child trafficking, Gram Panchayat Members (elected by the villagers) and health workers at the village level in addition to parents are the potential for reporting the incident to local police, child protection officer, and/or child welfare committee members since they have close contact with the village people.

Sexual violence against children is a worldwide problem generating serious short- and long-term effects on children's health and development and severe consequences for the well-being of families, communities, and nations (Pinheiro 2006; WHO 2002). Reporting of sexual abuse should be mandatory in any nation like India where social disparity and inequality is very high.

Sexual violence toward children is defined as a crime involving a child in sexual activity with an adult or older person (generally 5 or more years older). It may involve contact or noncontact sexual acts. Contact acts include unwanted touching, masturbation, oral-genital contact, digital penetration, and vaginal and anal rape. Noncontact acts include voyeurism, exposure, making sexual comments, and showing children pornography (Gilbert et al. 2009; Putnam 2003; WHO 2002). While bringing the legislation for mandatory reporting of sexual violence against children, these issues should be taken care of.

There are some provisions for reporting of any offense in the IPC (1860) and POCSO Act, 2012. There is an urgent need for the amendment of child welfare-related legislation and incorporation of provision for mandatory reporting of child sexual abuse and child trafficking since these two types of abuse badly affect the future of the children and their mental health.

For sexual abuse, people/professionals like parents, doctors, nurses, teachers, and personnel from NGOs should be mandated for reporting. It is also necessary to state very clearly about the range of activities which should be considered as sexual abuse as defined by the international legislation and/or WHO. Normally, in Indian society, sexual intercourse with a minor is considered as sexual abuse, and other forms like stimulation, showing pornographic picture, touching private parts of a child, and so on are not generally recognized as sexual abuse and ignored.

Training for Reporters and Professionals

Professionals Who Are Required to Report Abuse

There is a need for organizing orientation training for other reporters so that they gain knowledge of the indicators of sexual abuse, know how to deal appropriately with a situation of disclosure or suspicion, know the situations when a report is and is not required, and know how to make a report that both satisfies the legislative reporting requirements and provides useful assistance to child protective services intake. Of course, while legislation and training are two important components of the child protection system, they interact with others, principally the systems of assessment, response, and case management. The content of the law therefore must be sensitive and adapted to the entire child protection apparatus in any given jurisdiction, and the most successful approach requires coordinated efforts by the whole of government (Mathews and Kenny 2008).

Interviewing of Children by Police

Reporting of sexual abuse will be higher if female juvenile/police officers are posted in all the police stations. Although it was mentioned in the JJ Act, 2000, in reality it has not been implemented across India. Therefore, a victim of sexual abuse does not feel comfortable to report the incident to a male police officer.

Leander (2010) investigated 27 sexually abused children's reports about abuse given in the context of police interviews. All abuse cases had been verified (with, e.g., photographs or video films), proving that abuse had occurred. The interviews with the children were analyzed regarding the amount and type of information reported and the frequency of denial and avoidance. Furthermore, children's reporting on different interview occasions was investigated. Children reported significantly more neutral information from the abusive acts per se than sexual information. The children were also highly avoidant and, on several occasions, denied that (documented) sexual acts had occurred. Furthermore, the second and third interviews generated twice as many (new) sexual details as the first interview. The children also produced more denials and avoidances at the first interview compared to subsequent interviews. The present study indicates that sexually abused children may be highly resistant to reporting about the abuse in police interviews and that two or three interviews may be needed to enable children to give complete and informative reports.

It is of vital importance that professionals within the legal system be aware of this problem when conducting child interviews and when evaluating the reliability of child sexual abuse reports.

Medical Examinations

There is no standard method for medical examination of sexual abuse cases in India. In the same medical institution, two doctors follow two different procedures for medical examination and come out with two different types of reports. In order to avoid this sort of confusion, there is an urgent need to bring uniform and/or standard procedure for medical examination of sexual abuse cases in accordance with guidelines developed by the World Health Organization. It is important to ensure that physicians and other medical staff respond to cases of sexual abuse in a sensitive manner that minimizes invasive examination and provides access to continued reproductive, sexual, and mental health services. Organizing training for the doctors in all public health facilities to adopt and use this protocol will be immensely beneficial. In addition, there is an urgent need to incorporate this issue in the medical curricula.

Prosecutors

There is also a need to organize periodic training program for the public prosecutors to sensitize them about sensitivity issue involved in child sexual abuse incidents, victim's mental state, and how to probe the issues and proceed further. It is relevant to mention here that case load of the public prosecutors is a challenge to pay proper attention to each case. Therefore, there is a need to appoint more number of government lawyers.

Conclusion and Recommendations

Child sexual abuse and child trafficking for commercial exploitation has become a serious problem in India, influenced by poverty, low education and denial of life chances and social mobility, overpopulation, class and gender disparities, historic denial of children's rights, ineffective child protection policies, and high demand for sexual contact with girls (Bennett 1999; Deb 2006, 2009; Deb and Sen 2005a; Deb et al. 2011).

Review of existing Indian legislation concerning reporting of child sexual abuse demonstrates a sorry state (Deb and Bernadette 2014). Although there are some general provisions for reporting of any offense in the IPC (1860) and POCSO Act (2012), no legislation specifically states which professionals must make reports except media and related professionals for sexual exploitation offences (POCSO Act 2012). The review of legislation clearly indicates the necessity for amendment of Indian legislation for incorporation of provisions for mandatory reporting of child sexual abuse and trafficking of children as demonstrated in legislation in the USA, Australia, and Ghana. Mandatory reporting of child sexual abuse and child trafficking for commercial sexual abuse is a very fundamental issue which the Government of India has ignored since independence. Now, every day reporting of sexual abuse by the media has sensitized the policy makers about the seriousness of the issue. Children's rights to safety and security are fundamental human rights mentioned in all the national and international laws. The Government of India has to take steps to ensure the same in truest possible sense. Introducing mandatory reporting of child sexual abuse and trafficking will not cost much especially compared with the benefits which can flow. This should be introduced in the existing system and with other strategies it will help to bring positive changes in society.

However, important consideration should be given to the categories of people who are to be named as mandatory reporters of child sexual abuse and child trafficking, the types of sexual abuse, nature of evidence or proof for reporting, time limit for reporting, and agency to be reported to other than local police and bodies under Juvenile Justice System. In addition, accountability on the part of executing agency, time frame for investigation, and needful measures and safety of the victim and reporting person must be considered.

There is a challenge for family members when a child experience sexual abuse in the hand of biological father especially when the family belongs to lower socioeconomic strata. The issue of economic security and possibility of social isolation become a big threat for the family. Therefore, family members have a tendency not to report the incident to police. This type of critical situation should be taken into account when new legislation is framed or amends the existing laws.

In addition, there is an urgent need for providing psychological support to the victim and her family. This is missing in India and this issue should be mentioned in the legislation. One-time counseling may not be adequate in every case. Therefore, ongoing supportive psychological services should be available. In this regard, coordination with local NGOs and hospitals is essential for ensuring psychological support to the victim and the family. Some sections of the media and activist groups demanding *One Stop Abuse/Rape Crisis Center* for addressing all related issues like reporting, medical care and examination, investigation, and justice and a case should be dealt with in a satisfactory time period.

It is also necessary to review the amendments of the Protection of Children from Sexual Offenses Act's effectiveness within a reasonable period of time in consultation with women's, children, and civil rights activist groups. Prioritizing effective implementation of the Integrated Child Protection Scheme and ensuring that states properly and promptly utilize the resources allocated to them to create effective child welfare committees will improve the situation. Facilitating training of all child welfare committee members on India's juvenile justice and child protection systems is essential. Ensuring effective implementation of the Juvenile Justice (Care and Protection) Act, 2000, will in turn ensure safety for most of the children.

Since a major factor in both decreasing and facilitating reporting of child abuse and sexual abuse in particular is linked with knowledge and attitudes toward children, it would be helpful if the National Commission for Protection of Child Rights and the national Ministry of Women and Child Development would take the initiative to educate or sensitize the broader society through both electronic (during peak hours) and print media about children's rights to security which will in turn increase their knowledge about the issue and might change their attitudes toward children. In addition, education of children in schools about their own rights and the rights of others would help to change attitudes and shape behavior.

In India, the value of psychological support services in cases of any crisis in different life situations has not received proper attention from policy makers, resulting in an absence of posts for psychologist in the educational institutions and health centers. People realize the importance of a psychologist when they undergo a serious crisis in life and do not find a psychologist. Therefore, like other professions, posts for psychologists should be created in all relevant institutions especially in child protection systems, law enforcement agencies, educational institutions, health institutions, child-related industries, and NGOs working with families and children.

References

Al-Mahroos, F., & Al-Amer, E. (2011). Reported child sexual abuse in Bahrain: 2000–2009. *Annals of Saudi Medicine, 31*(4), 376–382.

BBC News. (2012, December 18). Delhi bus gang rape: Uproar in Indian parliament. *BBC News*. Retrieved 19 Dec 2012.

Bennett, T. (1999). Preventing trafficking in women and children in Asia: Issues and options. *Impact on HIV, 1*(2), 9–13.

Besharov, D. (1985). "Doing something" about child abuse: The need to narrow the grounds for state intervention. *Harvard Journal of Law and Public Policy, 8*(3), 539–589.

CBS News. (2012, December 19). Brutal India gang rape triggers outrage. *CBS News*. Retrieved 21 Dec 2012.

Chatterjee, P., Chakraborty, T., Srivastava, N., & Deb, S. (2006). Short and long-term problems faced by the trafficked children: A qualitative study. *Social Science International, 22*, 167–182.

Criminal Law (Amendment) Act, 2013. Government of India. Retrieved 16 Apr 2013.

Csorba, R., Lampe, L., Borsos, A., Balla, L., Poka, R., & Olah, E. (2006). Female child sexual abuse within the family in a Hungarian county. *Gynecologic and Obstetric Investigation, 61*(4), 188–193.

Daro, D. (Ed.). (2007). *World perspectives on child abuse* (7th ed.). Chicago: International Society for Prevention of Child Abuse and Neglect.

Deb, S. (2002). Child sexual abuse: An overview with special reference to role of Police. *Social Defense, 53*(154), 44–58.

Deb, S. (2006). *Children in Agony*. New Delhi: Concept Publishing Company.

Deb, S. (2009). Child protection: Scenario in India. *International Journal of Child Health and Human Development, 2*, 339–348.

Deb, S., & Bernadette, M. (2014). Burden of child abuse and neglect with special reference to socio-legal measures: A comparative picture of India, Philippines and Japan. In J. Conte (Ed.), *Child abuse and neglect worldwide* (pp. 77–106). Santa Barbara: PRAEGER.

Deb, S., & Mukherjee, A. (2009). *Impact of sexual abuse on mental health of children*. New Delhi: Concept Publishing Company.
Deb, S., & Sen, P. (2005a, September 11–13). *A study on socio-economic profile of young trafficked women, their substance abuse and HIV status*. Presented in the European Conference on Child Abuse and Neglect, Germany.
Deb, S., & Sen, P. (2005b, November 16–18). A study on psychological trauma of young trafficked women. In *6th Asian conference on child abuse and neglect*, Singapore.
Deb, S., & Walsh, K. (2012). Impact of physical, psychological, and sexual violence on social adjustment of school children in India. *School Psychology International, 33*(4), 391–415.
Deb, S., Srivastava, N., Chatterjee, P., & Chakraborty, T. (2005). Processes of child trafficking in West Bengal: A qualitative study. *Social Change, 35*(2), 112–123.
Deb, S., & Mukherjee, A. (2011). Background and adjustment capacity of sexually abused girls and their perceptions of intervention. *Child Abuse Review, 20*, 213–230.
Deb, S., Mukherjee, A., & Mathews, B. (2011). Aggression in sexually abused trafficked girls and efficacy of intervention. *Journal of Interpersonal Violence, 26*(4), 745–768.
Dunne, M. P., Zolotor, A. J., Runyan, D. K., Andreva-Miller, I., Choo, Y. W., Gerbaka, B., Isaeva, O., Jain, D., Kasim, M. S., McFarlane, B., Mamyrova, N., Ramirez, C., Volkova, E., & Youssef, R. (2009). ISPCAN Child Abuse Screening Tools Retrospective version (ICAST-R): Delphi study and field testing in seven countries. *Child Abuse & Neglect, 33*(11), 815–825.
Eleven Facts about Human Trafficking. http://www.dosomething.org/tipsandtools/11-facts-about-human-trafficking
Gilbert, R., Widom, C. S., Browne, K., Fergusson, D., Webb, E., & Janson, S. (2009). Child maltreatment 1: Burden and consequences of child maltreatment in high-income countries. *The Lancet, 373*, 68–81.
González Ortega, E., OrgazBaz, B., & López, S. F. (2012). Professionals' criteria for detecting and reporting child sexual abuse. *Spanish Journal of Psychology, 15*(3), 1325–1338.
Government of India, Press Information Bureau. (2007). *Poverty estimates for 2004–2005 in India*. New Delhi: Author.
Government of West Bengal. (2008). *District census handbook*. West Bengal: Author.
Hindustan Times. (2012, December 21). No option, victim's intestines removed. *Hindustan Times*. Retrieved 21 Dec 2012.
Human Trafficking Act, 2005 (Ghana).
India Country Report on Violence Against Children. (2005). Ministry of Women and Child Development, Government of India.
Indian Express. (1999, August 16). Child prostitution is increasing in India. *Indian Express*. New Delhi.
International Institute for Population Sciences. (2007). *National family health survey 2005–06: India*. Mumbai: Author.
International Labour Organization. (2005). *A global alliance against forced labour*. Geneva: Author. Retrieved March 8, 2010, from http://www.ilo.org/wcmsp5/groups/public/---ed_norm/---declaration/documents/publication/wcms_081882.pdf
ITV News. (2012, December 23). Thousands protest in Indian capital after gang-rape. *ITV News*.
Jenny, C., Crawford-Jakubiak, J. E., Committee on child abuse and neglect, & American Academy of Pediatrics. (2013). The evaluation of children in the primary care setting when sexual abuse is suspected. *Pediatrics, 132*(2), e558–e567.
Junofy, A. R. N. (2013). A study on poverty and hunger in India. *Mediterranean Journal of Social Sciences, 4*(12), 147.
Kalichman, S. (1999). *Mandated reporting of suspected child abuse: Ethics, law and policy* (2nd ed.). Washington, DC: American Psychological Association.
Kempadoo, K., Sanghera, J., & Pattanaik, B. (Eds.). (2005). *Trafficking and prostitution reconsidered: New perspectives on migration, sex work, and human rights*. Boulder: Paradigm.
Kempe, C. H., Silverman, F., Steele, B., Droegemueller, W., & Silver, H. (1962). The battered child syndrome. *Journal of the American Medical Association, 181*, 17–24.

Leander, L. (2010). Police interviews with child sexual abuse victims: Patterns of reporting, avoidance and denial. *Child Abuse & Neglect, 34*(3), 192–205.
Leventhal, J. M. (1990). Epidemiology of child sexual abuse. In R. K. Oates (Ed.), *Understanding and managing child sexual abuse*. Sydney: Harcourt Brace Jovanovich.
Magalhães, T., Ribeiro, C. S., Jardim, P., Vieira, D. N., & Instituto Nacional de Medicina Legal. (2011). Forensic procedures for interview physical exam and evidence collection in children and young people victims of physical and/or sexual abuse. *Acta Médica Portuguesa, 24*(2), 339–348.
Mandal, J. (2010). Poverty Reduction, the United Nations Development Programme (2010). http://www.undp.org.in/whatwedo/poverty_reduction
Mathews, B. P., & Kenny, M. (2008). Mandatory reporting legislation in the USA, Canada and Australia: A cross-jurisdictional review of key features, differences and issues. *Child Maltreatment, 13*(1), 50–63.
Modak, S. (2009).*Violence against children in Tripura and its impact*. Unpublished doctoral dissertation, Calcutta University, India.
Mukherjee, A. (2006). *A study on impact of sexual abuse on mental health of children*. Unpublished doctoral dissertation, Calcutta University, India.
NDTV.com. (2012, December 21). Delhi gang-rape: Victim's friend, also on bus, gives statement in court. *NDTV.com*. Retrieved 21 Dec 2012.
Nelson, B. (1984). *Making an issue of child abuse*. Chicago: University of Chicago Press.
Office of the Registrar General, Government of India. (2011).*Census of India*. New Delhi: Government of India. Retrieved March 8, 2010, from http://www.censusindia.gov.in/Census_Data_2001/India_at_glance/popu1.aspx
Optional Protocol to the United Nations Convention on the Rights of the Child on the Sale of Children, Child Prostitution and Child Pornography. (2000). Retrieved March 8, 2010, from http://www1.umn.edu/humanrts/instree/childprotsale.html
Pinheiro, P. S. (2006). *World report on violence against children*. Geneva: United Nations Secretary-General's Study on Violence against Children.
Pouwels, R., Swales, D., Mccoy, A., & Peddle, N. (2010, November 4–6). *Child protection and child welfare in the Asia Pacific region: Discussion paper*. High-Level meeting on Cooperation for Child Rights in the Asia-Pacific Region. Beijing, China.
Protocol to Prevent, Suppress and Punish Trafficking in Persons, Especially Women and Children. (2000). Retrieved March 7, 2010, from http://treaties.un.org/doc/source/RecentTexts/18-12-a.E.htm
Putnam, F. W. (2003). Ten-year research update review: Child sexual abuse. *Journal of the American Academy of Child and Adolescent Psychiatry, 42*(3), 269–278.
Report on Child Abuse and Neglect. New Delhi: Min Women Child Dev, 2007.
Sanlaap. (2003). *Red alert: Combat commercial sexual exploitation of children*. Kolkata: Author.
Sen, S. (2005). *Trafficking in women and children in India*. New Delhi: National Human Rights Commission.
Stoltenborgh, M., van Ijzendoorn, M. H., Euser, E. M., & Bakermans-Kranenburg, M. J. (2011). Global perspective on child sexual abuse: Meta-analysis of prevalence around the world. *Child Maltreatment, 16*(2), 70–101.
Telegraph. (2012, December 19). Video: Protests grow over gang rape of Indian woman. Telegraph. Retrieved 21 Dec 2012.
The Child Abuse Prevention and Treatment Act, CAPTA (US), 1974.
The Child Marriage Restraint Act, 1929.
The Commissions for The Protection of the Child Rights Act, 2005.
The Immoral Traffic (Prevention) Act, 1956.
The Indian Constitution, Nov. 26, 1949 (enforced on Jan. 26, 1950).
The Indian Penal Code, 1860.
The Juvenile Justice (Care and Protection of Children) Act, 2000 (amended in 2006, India).
The National Charter for Children. (2003).

The National Crime Records Bureau 2010, Ministry of Home Affairs, Government of India.
The Prohibition of Child Marriage Act, 2006.
The Protection of Children from Sexual Offences Act, 2012.
The Rights of Children to Free and Compulsory Education Act, 2009.
The Times of India, Delhi. (2009, February 14). *AbhinavGarg 'Death for Pandher, Koli in Nithari case'*. http://timesofindia.indiatimes.com/Death-for-Pandher-Koliin-Nithari-case/articleshow/4121835.cms. 25 Feb 2011.
UNICEF. (2005). *Combating child trafficking*. Retrieved March 8, 2010, from http://www.unicef.org/publications/files/IPU_combattingchildtrafficking_GB(1).pdf
UNICEF. (2008). *India: Maternal, newborn and child survival*. Retrieved March 8, 2010, from http://www.childinfo.org/profiles.html
UNICEF. (2009). *Progress for children: A report card on child protection: Innocenti report card number 8*. New York: UNICEF Division of Communication.
United Nations Convention on the Rights of the Child. (1989). Retrieved March 8, 2010, from http://treaties.un.org/Pages/ViewDetails.aspx?src=UNTSONLINE&tabid=2&mtdsg_no=IV-11&chapter=4&lang=en
United Nations Office on Drugs and Crime. (2009). *Global report on trafficking in persons*. Retrieved March 8, 2010, from http://www.unodc.org/documents/human-trafficking/Global_Report_on_TIP.pdf
Walsh, K., Rassafiani, M., Mathews, B., Farrell, A., & Butler, D. (2012). Exploratory factor analysis and psychometric evaluation of the teacher reporting attitude scale for child sexual abuse. *Journal of Child Sexual Abuse, 21*(5), 489–506.
World Bank Report. (2010). *India – New Global Poverty Estimates*.
World Health Organisation. (2002). *World report on violence and health*. Geneva: Office of Publications, World Health Organisation.

MIX
Papier aus verantwortungsvollen Quellen
Paper from responsible sources
FSC® C105338

If you have any concerns about our products,
you can contact us on
ProductSafety@springernature.com

In case Publisher is established outside the EU,
the EU authorized representative is:
Springer Nature Customer Service Center GmbH
Europaplatz 3, 69115 Heidelberg, Germany

Printed by Libri Plureos GmbH
in Hamburg, Germany